Classical Political Economics and Modern Capitalism

Lefteris Tsoulfidis • Persefoni Tsaliki

Classical Political Economics and Modern Capitalism

Theories of Value, Competition, Trade and Long Cycles

 Springer

Lefteris Tsoulfidis
Department of Economics
University of Macedonia
Thessaloniki, Greece

Persefoni Tsaliki
Department of Economics
Aristotle University of Thessaloniki
Thessaloniki, Greece

ISBN 978-3-030-17966-3   ISBN 978-3-030-17967-0   (eBook)
https://doi.org/10.1007/978-3-030-17967-0

This Springer imprint is published by the registered company Springer Nature Switzerland AG.
The registered company address is: Gewerbestrasse 11, 6330 Cham, Switzerland

Preface

This book deals with the economics of capitalism, that is, the economic system, the salient feature of which is 'generalized' commodity production. The characterization 'generalized' refers to the systematic presence of labour markets specific to capitalism. The analysis is based on 'classical political economy', a term coined by Karl Marx in *Capital* I (p. 81), to describe 'that economy which, since the time of W. Petty, has investigated the real relations of production in bourgeois society in contradistinction to vulgar economy, which deals with appearances only'. The classical political economy or rather economics approach originates with the old classical economists of the nineteenth century (Adam Smith and David Ricardo, in the main), although Marx was critical and made his distance from this tradition clear; nevertheless, his economics belongs to the same tradition, which reached its apogee in his own mature work, namely, the three volumes of *Capital*. This tradition of economic theory was 'submerged and forgotten' since the advent of neoclassical economics in the last quarter of the nineteenth century. The classical political economics (CPE) approach re-emerged mainly through Sraffa's works and, in particular, his influential book (1960) that sparked the famous Cambridge Capital Theory Controversies, among others. Alongside these developments, the CPE approach has been enriched by new theoretical advancements, which have been substantiated by respective empirical research; this combination gave rise to new questions that can be further pursued lending support to the view that the CPE is a 'progressive research programme'.

Theoretical developments in the CPE approach became possible for a number of reasons, which include the advancement in mathematics and, in particular, the discovery of a number of theorems in linear algebra that have been fruitfully integrated and strengthened with Leontief's input-output analysis and economics. It goes without saying that the availability of consistent and detailed data concerning both national income accounts and input-output tables contributed, on the one hand, to the empirical content of the CPE approach and, on the other, to its further development by the new questions that could be raised. It is important to point out that in the not very distant past, there were heated debates among economists of the classical tradition, for example, the so-called neo-Ricardians versus the Marxists of various strands, especially in the late 1970s, post-Keynesians (with or without the hyphen) among themselves and others, etc.; nevertheless, in recent years, it has become increasingly accepted that these various strands, despite their individual and sometimes significant differences, converge in the pursuit of a long-period method of analysis based on the same set of data, namely: (a) the level of output produced and its distribution, (b) the real wage (or the rate of profit or even the wage share) and (c) the technology described by the input-output structure of the economy.

By using the above set of data, the equilibrium (or long-run) prices can be estimated which are absolutely necessary in an economy characterized by 'generalized commodity production'. A superficial look at the actual or market prices that commodities exchange would suggest that they are arbitrary; however, a more thorough examination would reveal that underneath the persistent fluctuations of market prices there are some other more fundamental prices, which Francois Quesnay first pointed out as being governed by forces 'independent of men's will'. Consequently, these objectively operating forces can be studied independently of subjective evaluations, which is equivalent to say that these more fundamental or natural prices in Quesnay, Smith and Ricardo or prices of production in Marx are amenable to abstract theorization. In other words, the permanent (rather than the ephemeral and the transitory) factors that determine natural prices become the object of CPE analysis and, through the study of natural prices and other independent of 'people's will' economic variables, the CPE approach obtains scientific status.

In our effort to explain the market phenomena, the first thing to explicitly acknowledge is the kind of economic system within which such phenomena emerge. The economic system is capitalism defined as 'generalized commodity production', in the sense that the workers' labour services themselves have become a commodity to be traded. Therefore, this book refers to the economics of capitalism and attempts to reveal the mechanisms governing the operation of the system at both the microeconomic level (relative price theory) and at the macroeconomic level (theory of output determination and its fluctuations in the long run). This observation is by no means original. However, surprisingly enough, in standard textbooks of economic theory and analysis, the word 'capitalism', i.e. the subject of such books, is regrettably missing! For example, Joseph Stiglitz (2001 Nobel Laureate in Economics), not exactly a mainstream economist, in his introductory book on economic theory uses the word 'capitalism' only once (p. 473) and this by coincidence, because of his reference to Schumpeter's book *Capitalism, Socialism and Democracy* (1942). In his *Economics* (2006), co-authored with Carl Walsh, the word capitalism occurs three times (pp. 14, 809, 811): the first is a quotation from Allan Greenspan (the former chairperson of the Fed), the second is about the failures of communism and the third about the Russian economy and the effects of a 'shock therapy' to establish capitalism, whatever this might be, because nowhere in the book is there any discussion of the nature of the system. Paul Krugman's *Economics* (2009), co-authored with Robin Wells, is not better in this respect: the word 'capitalism' appears only twice (both on p. 890). It is interesting to stress, at this point, that economics makes its first appearance as an independent scientific discipline in the eighteenth century, but, unlike neoclassical economists (old and new), classical political economists did not seek to universalize their economic mechanisms looking backwards in time to cover the entire human history, but, rather, looking at the present economic system and its future evolution. In effect, the economic mechanisms are expected to work in greater precision with the further development of capitalism.

The Great Recession that broke out in 2007 took many of the (neoclassical) economists by surprise, as they have adopted the idea of a fundamentally sound and also self-equilibrating economic system, growing steadily since the early 1980s. Some of them, sometimes with disarming honesty, admit that they did not know how to handle the situation, while others have advanced interpretations that are anything but convincing. For example, a real business cycle economist, Edward Prescott (2004 Nobel Laureate in Economics) in a 2000 radio interview (see Tsoulfidis 2017) interpreted the crisis as a wave of inexplicable fears that captivated people and governments, discouraged consumption and investment expenditures and drove the economy into a crisis; interestingly, for such 'a voodoo approach', it is particularly odd to look for ways to cure the problem! Paul Krugman (2008 Nobel Laureate in Economics), not exactly a heterodox economist, rightly, in our opinion, described the current phase of macroeconomic theory as a 'dark age of macroeconomics'. The idea is that, as in the Middle Ages, contact with the ancient Greek tradition, that is, the reason ($\lambda \acute{o} \gamma o \varsigma$) where the proof was the quintessence of theory, was lost, similarly, the recent neoclassical macroeconomic theory lost, to a great extent, its contact with reality and also with the Keynesian tradition, namely the tradition that theorizes and seeks political intervention to guide the economy in directions that favour the society at large and strengthen social cohesion.

This book aims at contributing mainly to the understanding of the mechanisms governing the operation of the capitalist economy in light of the CPE approach. The remainder of the book is structured as follows: Chapter 1 starts with the theory of value and distribution in which the ideas of Smith, Ricardo and Marx are presented and critically assessed so that they may become operational and, therefore, useful. The idea is that capitalism is a system of 'generalized commodity production', which means that, since this system is dominated by monetary exchanges, it follows that a consistent theory of value and distribution is absolutely necessary for the understanding of its surface economic categories and their underlying mechanisms. With this in mind, Smith's labour theory of value is introduced as an intermediate step to a more advanced Ricardo's labour theory of value or, rather, relative prices. Ricardo's successes and failures are explained by referring to his numerical examples, from which is extracted the core of a realistic approach to the estimation of natural prices as the centres of gravitation for market prices. The analysis shows that Ricardo's theory of value is intertemporal in character, and this is an issue the empirical details of which are pursued further in Chap. 4. Marx's labour theory of value follows immediately after and in which both the object of analysis and the data remain the same as those of other classical economists; however, Marx's notions of abstract labour time, the two senses of socially necessary labour time as well as the introduction of the concept of labour power enabled Marx to demonstrate the exploitative nature of the system and the production of value and surplus-value, all discovered through and evaluated by labour time. The difficulty to identify the exploitative nature of the capitalist system lies in the mediation of monetary relations, which give the impression of equivalent exchanges and conceal the exploitative nature of the system. The centrality of surplus in the growth and stagnation of capitalist economy is a common feature in the analysis of Quesnay, Smith, Ricardo and Marx.

Chapter 2 deals with the conditions of reproduction of the capitalist system. Classical analysis explicates that the system is not only capable of reproducing itself on the same scale as shown in Quesnay's *Tableau Économique* and Marx's schemes of simple reproduction, but also endowed with a relentless drive for expansion and steady growth, as shown in Marx's schemes of expanded reproduction. Both conditions are hypothetical because economic growth is periodically punctuated by long-lasting crises. Therefore, economic growth and crises represent inherent salient features of the modus operandi of the capitalist system. In this chapter, the schemes of reproduction are cast in terms of input-output tables with the aid of which estimates of both the labour values and their monetary expression (direct prices), alongside with prices of production, are provided.

Chapter 3 concerns itself with two central issues of economic theory: the first is the famous 'transformation problem', which essentially refers to the logical consistency of the classical theory of value and, in particular, to Marx's labour theory of value. The chapter continues by detailing the various approaches and solutions to the transformation problem starting from Marx's one, which, despite its semifinished character, was in the right direction and that could not be further advanced because of the lack of necessary mathematical theorems, which were discovered much later. The second issue that this chapter deals with is what came to be known as 'capital theory controversy'. Hence, the two competing theories of value: the labour theory of value and the marginal theory of value are brought together in an effort to show their internal consistency. To be specific, if the classical theory of value makes the labour time expressed in terms of technological requirements of production the principal determinant of equilibrium prices, then the neoclassical theory makes preferences and endowments, along with technology, the key determinants of equilibrium prices. In the neoclassical theory of value, prices reflect relative scarcities, and the capital theory controversies refer precisely to whether or not this holds true when evaluating capital goods as produced means of production, and according to those involved in the debate, the answer was negative.

Chapter 4, in a preparatory step, starts off with the explanatory power and significance of the classical theory of value and argues that market prices are, in fact, attracted to labour values and to prices of production as more concrete centres of gravitation. For this, detailed data are utilized starting from the US economy and include a number of countries and studies; the empirical results confirm that the classical theory of value contains explanatory power that cannot be ignored. The chapter also analyses related to the theory of value issues of technological change, as this is reflected in the rising capital intensity of industries and long-run falling labour content of commodities and questions related to the effect of distribution changes on relative prices. These findings are particularly useful in the discussions of the law of the tendential fall in the rate of profit and lend support to Marx's view that technological change is capital using-labour saving in the long run. Furthermore, the results from detailed input-output tables of the US economy ascertain the Ricardian and Marxian views, that is, the movement of prices, induced by changes in distribution, is monotonic. There may be exceptions, but these are very few and hold for unrealistically low or high values in the distributive variables. In effect, using input-output data, the results show that prices move monotonically in both directions and the estimated wage rate of profit curves rules out the case of reswitching. Nevertheless, the lack of reswitching is not proof that the neoclassical scarcity theory of relative prices really holds; the reason for this is that the scarcity theory of relative prices faces a more fundamental problem, namely, measurement of capital in a way that is consistent with its initial premises.

In Chap. 5, the discussion is on the classical theory of competition as a dynamic process of rivalry in the struggle of units of capital (or firms) to gain the largest possible market share for themselves at the expense of their rivals. The CPE dynamic theory of competition is characteristically different from the neoclassical static conception of competition as an end-state, where actual prices and quantities produced are compared to those that would have been established had perfect competition prevailed. In fact, the neoclassical analysis of competition is quantitative in nature for its focus is on the number (manyness or fewness) and also the size of contestants. After a comparison of the two characteristically different conceptualizations of competition, the analysis continues with deriving the laws of classical or real competition between and within industries and their integration with the mediation of regulating capital.

Chapter 6 deals with empirical aspects of the classical theory of competition and examines the extent to which a central proposition or economic law of the CPE theory of competition, that is, the inter-industry equalization of profit rates, is confirmed. Among the other important aspects of the CPE approach include issues such as whether there is monopoly and whether or not phenomena usually attributed to the presence of monopoly power may have an alternative explanation based on the classical theory of competition. The empirical research refers to the Greek economy, continues with the Japanese one and ends with the US economy. The empirical results corroborate the classical theory of competition and rule out the case of monopoly and its power over market forces.

Chapter 7 extends the discussion of classical competition from the domestic to international markets and the formation of international prices. The old debates on unequal exchange and transfer of values are reintroduced in an effort to shed further light on issues related to international trade and economic development. At first sight, such a discussion may appear as a 'relic' of the past, but in the last decades, there has been a revival of interest. The empirical analysis uses input-output data available from the WIOD (2013, 2016) and provides approximate estimates of the transfer of value between three pairs of countries, Greece-Germany, China-USA and Germany-USA. Starting with the bilateral trade between Germany and USA, the results indicate not so different unit labour values as to give rise to significant inter-country transfers of value. However, when the comparison is between Germany and

Greece, the differences in unit labour values are large and in favour of Germany. As a consequence, when the exchange takes place, it follows that there are significant transfers of labour values from Greece to Germany. Similar were the initial findings in the USA-China bilateral trade. In particular, productivity in the USA is several times higher than that of China and the wage rate in China is considerably lower than that of the USA; however, both productivity and wage differentials in the last years of the analysis tend to get narrower. Hence, the USA appears to possess an absolute advantage when the comparison between the two countries is in terms of unit labour values at the official exchange rate; on further examination and by taking into account the purchasing power parity, the results reveal China the country with the absolute cost advantage throughout the investigated period.

Chapter 8 opens with a discussion of the cyclical movement of capitalist economy. The idea is that besides the more or less expected short-term (inventory and investment) cycles, there are other longer-term cycles. The time series data on a number of variables lend support to the view of long cycles, also known as Kondratiev waves, lasting around 50 years. Five such long cycles are identified, from the industrial revolution to our times. A number of phenomena appear regularly with the long cycles and an effort is being made to go beyond the surface and identify the causes of the phenomena. The chapter concludes with the idea that the evolution of profitability is responsible for the 'ebbs and flows' of economic activity and the phenomena associated with it. More specifically, the chapter presents the views of major economists on the tendential fall in the rate of profit and the attainment of the 'stationary state' of the economy. Marx also argued that a secularly falling rate of profit leads to the point of 'absolute overaccumulation' of capital. Unlike the other economists, according to Marx 'absolute overaccumulation' is not necessarily the end-state and collapse of capitalism, but rather a long gestation period of major institutional changes which promote new profitability-restoring innovations.

Chapter 9 focuses on the national income accounts (NIA) and the difference between the official NIA based on neoclassical economics from those of the CPE. The difference is the result of the dichotomy of economic activities in production and non-production, which exists in both the CPE and the neoclassical economics. Neoclassical economics considers all paid labour as productive regardless of where it is employed. By contrast, the CPE distinction is like that followed in good business practices and accounting of (industrial) corporations. In these practices, there is a clear demarcation line drawn between workers engaged in production and those engaged in activities assisting production (superintendents, accountants, guards, CEOs, etc.). The distinction is significant in businesses but not in neoclassical economics and the official NIA. As a consequence, the CPE distinction of production and non-production labour gives rise to markedly different estimates of strategic economic variables from those of the neoclassical NIA.

Chapter 10 is about the long-run movement of the rate of profit in the postwar US economy. The rate of profit follows a downward trend as a result of the rising capital-output ratio measured in both nominal and real terms and of the rising value composition of capital. The falling rate of profit is intrinsically connected to the economy's growth rate, which also follows a downward trend. The econometric analysis confirms this interconnection and bidirectional causality. This chapter also tests the extent to which unproductive expenditures are subject to limitations that restrict their 'ratchet expansion' as was once thought and concludes with the idea that the falling rate of profit past a point should lead to a stagnating mass of real net profits. The testing terrain is, once again, the US economy, and the hypothesis is to what extent and in which time period the evolution of real net profits follows an S-shaped pattern. The empirical analysis uses quarterly data on corporate profits of the US economy in two long postwar periods, the first during 1947:1–1982:4 and the second during 1983:1–2018:2. The characteristics of these two long cycles are discussed, and an attempt is made to predict the end of the recessionary period of the second long cycle and the beginning of a new, the sixth, long cycle.

Thessaloniki, Greece   Lefteris Tsoulfidis
March 2019   Persefoni Tsaliki

Acknowledgements

This book was in progress for many years and parts of it were presented at conferences, where we had the opportunity to discuss issues with many colleagues and friends. We are indebted to our teachers at the New School for Social Research and, we would like to thank, in particular, without implicating, Anwar Shaikh, whose works have been an inspiration for us, and Willi Semmler, with whom we discussed crucial aspects of the book. We also thank Dimitris Paitaridis for his invaluable help in the estimation and updating of variables, particularly those in Chap. 10, and Achilleas Tsimis for his help with econometrics in Chaps. 4 and 10. Finally, we thank our students at the University of Macedonia and Aristotle University of Thessaloniki, who actively participated in our lectures and helped us improve the book with their questions and comments.

Lefteris Tsoulfidis
Persefoni Tsaliki

Contents

Part I
Theories of Value and Empirical Evidence

Chapter 1
The Classical Theory of Value and Distribution

The study of the 'surplus product' is the true object of economic analysis.

Piero Sraffa (D3/12/7:161.1) [The Piero Sraffa Papers are kept at the Wren Library, Trinity College, Cambridge (catalogue and access to documents at https://janus.lib.cam.ac.uk/db/node.xsp?id=EAD%2FGBR%2F0016%2FSRAFFA). Also, in Carter S. (2018)]

Every child knows that a nation which ceased to work, I will not say for a year, but even for a few weeks, would perish. Every child knows, too, that the masses of products corresponding to the different needs require different and quantitatively determined masses of the total labor of society. That this necessity of the distribution of social labor in definite proportions cannot possibly be done away with by a particular form of social production but can only change the form in which it appears, is self-evident. No natural laws can be done away with. What can change, in historically different circumstances, is only the form in which these laws operate. And the form in which this proportional distribution of labor operates, in a state of society where the interconnection of social labor is manifested in the private exchange of the individual products of labor, is precisely the exchange value of these products.

Karl Marx (*Letter to Kugelmann*, July 11, 1868)

Abstract The theories of value and distribution of Smith, Ricardo and Marx are presented and critically assessed so that they may become operational and, therefore, useful. We explain Ricardo's successes and failures by referring to his numerical examples, from which we try to extract the core of a realistic approach to the estimation of natural prices as the centre of gravitation for market prices. We argue that Ricardo's theory of value is intertemporal in character and its fundamental premise can be tested empirically. The discussion of Marx's labour theory of value follows immediately after, and we explain his notions of abstract labour time, the two senses of socially necessary labour time as well as the concept of labour power.

© Springer Nature Switzerland AG 2019
L. Tsoulfidis, P. Tsaliki, *Classical Political Economics and Modern Capitalism*,
https://doi.org/10.1007/978-3-030-17967-0_1

The latter enabled Marx to show the exploitative nature of the capitalist system and the production of value and surplus-value, all discovered through and evaluated by labour time. We further argue that the economic theories advanced by the old classical economists and Marx along with more recent theoretical developments following Sraffa's (*Production of commodities by means of commodities: A prelude to economic theory*. Cambridge, UK: Cambridge University Press, 1960) book share the same set of data and may be fruitfully integrated into the classical political economics (CPE).

Keywords Market and natural price · Elasticity of relative prices · Labour theory of value · Law of value · Surplus value

1.1 Introduction

This book deals with the economics of modern capitalism, that is, the mode of production whose major characteristic is the 'generalized' commodity production, 'generalized' in the sense that the services of labour are purchased and sold in the labour market; in fact, the presence of labour market is the salient feature of capitalism distinguishing it from past modes of production. Furthermore, commodities are produced in order to be exchanged for profit, and production for profit-making becomes a purpose in itself. In such an economic system, the role of the market, where exchanges take place, is central as opposed to the previous modes of production, where the role of the market was only peripheral and the exchange was more accidental and, by far, less regular. The exchange of commodities takes place at market prices which are characterized by high volatility. A superficial examination of the movement in market prices might lead to the conclusion that they are purely stochastic, and their behaviour resembles more of a random walk and less of an ordering principle. A more thorough study of the movement of market prices, however, would reveal that their fluctuations may be subjected to abstract theorization, which is another way to say that beneath the 'ebbs and flows' of the market and the actual movement of prices, there is another set of more fundamental prices which function as centres of gravitation of the seemingly stochastically behaving market prices.

    The purpose of this chapter is to show to what extent, if any, the classical theory of value and distribution—based on the writings of the old classical economists (mainly Smith and Ricardo) and Marx and in the more recent classical literature, especially after Sraffa's seminal contribution—is logically consistent and contains the required explanatory content with respect to the determinants of the observed market prices. In this book, all of the above contributions are integrated into a single one which came to be known as the classical political economics (CPE) approach, whose salient feature is the long-period method of analysis and the object of study is the determination of a set of more fundamental economic categories underneath the observed and ephemeral ones, namely, the market prices.

The classical approach (in its old and modern version) shares a set of common data which is the starting point for the assessment of equilibrium prices. This set of data includes:

- The level and composition of output
- The real wage
- The state of technology

The old classical approach since the last quarter of the nineteenth century has been marginalized by an alternative which, although shares the long-run perspective, uses a quite different set of data to explain the exact same object of analysis, that is, the equilibrium prices. This alternative is the neoclassical approach, which is based on the following set of data for the derivation of equilibrium prices:

- The preferences of individuals, as these are expressed by the ordinal or cardinal utility functions
- The size and distribution of the initially given endowment of goods as well as the services of factors of production
- The array of cost minimizing technological alternatives

In what follows, we pursue the CPE strand of economic thought which in the last decades made significant progress. In fact, this book is an effort to show the areas of progress made by the CPE perspective on theoretical and empirical issues of importance to economic theory in general and to point out questions that can be further pursued in future studies. Naturally, in the next section, we introduce Smith's achievements in the theory of value and continue with Ricardo's contributions, and subsequently we deal with important aspects of Marx's theory of value.

1.2   The Object of Economic Analysis

Adam Smith (1723–1790) was the first economist, who defined in a clear and analytically sound way the distinction between the market prices of commodities and a more fundamental set of prices, that is, the natural prices. The latter are characterized by relative stability and function as the centres of gravitation for the continually fluctuating market prices. According to Smith (1776), the natural (or equilibrium) price gathers all the systematic and therefore long-lasting characteristics of the commodity, whereas its market price congregates all the ephemeral ones. Hence, the natural price is the one that can be subjected to abstract theorization, while the market price is not amenable to such theorization. Smith, by making this fundamental distinction between natural and market price, essentially determined the object of economic analysis which is the identification of the determinants of natural prices of commodities. The distinction between these two kinds of prices is of supreme importance and led to the genesis of economic theory or political economy. As a matter of fact, for this conceptualization, Smith is rightly regarded as the *father of political economy*.

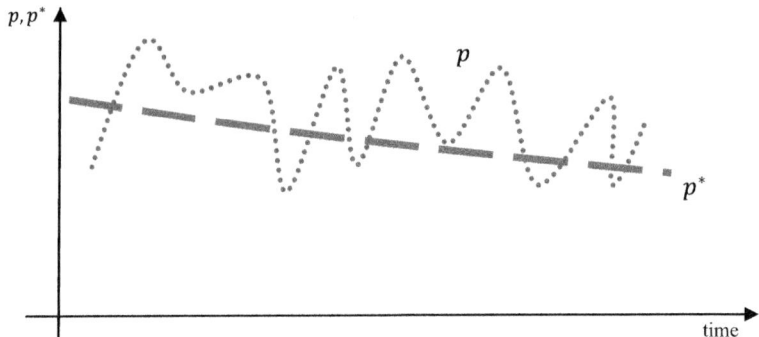

Fig. 1.1 Market and natural price over time

This 'discovery' of natural prices by Smith constituted the object of analysis in economic theory, and since then economic approaches share the same object of analysis although they use different sets of data to explain it. For example, the natural price in Marx's analysis is called 'price of production', and the famous 'transformation problem' (whose details we discuss in Chap. 3) refers to the complex mediations between the natural and market prices. This same distinction can also be found in neoclassical economics; for example, in the works of Alfred Marshall, the 'long-run price' is another name for the natural price. Consequently, both the classical and neoclassical schools of economic thought share a common object of analysis which is the determination of long-run equilibrium (natural) prices of commodities.[1]

In what follows, we take a closer look at the elemental distinction between natural and market prices starting from Smith's definitions according to which:

> [t]he actual price at which any commodity is commonly sold is called its market price. It may either be above, or below, or exactly the same with its natural price.
>
> (*Wealth of Nations*, p. 56)

Figure 1.1 above illustrates Smith's view on the relation between the natural price, p^*, of a commodity and its respective market price, p, over time.

In Smith's analysis, market prices are merely a descriptive category and as such may fluctuate for a number of reasons (i.e. the presence of shocks of various kinds) which by their very nature are not characterized by any systematic feature and, therefore, cannot be theoretically analysed. By contrast, natural prices are the result of permanent and long-lasting economic forces that are in place over time, and therefore they can be theoretically derived. Simply put, the natural prices are the centre of gravitation for market prices which, at times, may significantly deviate but

---

[1]Since the 1960s, the object of analysis of a strand in neoclassical economics—known as the intertemporal equilibrium approach—is no longer the natural and therefore the long-run but rather the short-run prices (Milgate 1979; Dixit and Norman 1980).

from a point onwards revert towards the natural ones. In Smith's words, commodities are sold at their natural price, that is, the price at which:

> is neither more nor less than what is sufficient to pay the rent of land, the wages of labour and profits of the capital employed to create, prepare and bring it to market, according to their natural payments.
>
> (*Wealth of Nations*, p. 55)

One could argue that the movements in the market price of a commodity are determined by the combination of forces of supply and demand. But in this case, if supply equals demand, then how is the value of a commodity determined? And what determines supply and demand? Marx characterized the economists that explained the equilibrium prices by the ephemeral forces of supply and demand as 'vulgar economists'.[2] The reason for this characterization is that the so-called forces of demand and supply must be explained with something more fundamental. In this sense, one cannot characterize as 'vulgar' the neoclassical economics because underneath the demand curves are the preferences or utility of individuals and behind the supply curves are the disutility of individuals when they decide to offer or sacrifice their endowments. One may criticize the neoclassical approach for subjectivity for it relies on preferences, but not on the grounds that it does not recognize the difference between surface economic variables and their respective more fundamental ones. Similarly, the classical approach cannot be characterized as 'vulgar' since the given technology and real wage which are both amenable to quantification and when combined together may determine the natural (or equilibrium) prices.

As Rubin (1972, p. 174) notes, the term 'natural' in Smith has two dimensions:

- 'Spontaneity' according to which the natural price is imposed by the operation of the market and free competition (more on this in Chaps. 5 and 6) and not by law, ethics or morality as used to be during the period of feudalism, where the 'just price' (*justum pretium*) or 'fair' or 'legally determined price' dominated the formation of actual prices
- 'Law-determined regularity' according to which the natural price is regulated by the operation of economic laws or market mechanisms which are independent of 'man's will'

Therefore, the natural price is neither arbitrary nor random, which means that all prices are not natural ones. Thus, only a single price can be thought of as the centre of gravitation around which market prices turbulently fluctuate. Only at that price is demand equal to supply, and only this central price is equal to the sum of natural wages for labour, natural profits for capital and natural rent for land. According to Smith the natural remunerations of the factors of production (labour, capital and land) are also set by the market mechanism. More specifically, individuals motivated by their self-interest inescapably are brought to conflict with other similarly

---

[2]"The vulgar economists [. . .] assume the value of one commodity [. . .] in order in turn to use it to determine the values of other commodities" (*Capital* I, p. 174).

motivated individuals, and from these competitions of self-interests, the formation of natural prices for goods and natural rewards for factors of production are formulated.

In order to illustrate the way in which the natural prices of commodities and natural payments of factors of production are attained, let us hypothesize a producer who naturally would like to sell his commodity at the highest possible price but cannot do so because of competition from similarly motivated and therefore rival producers; as a result, the producers of the same commodity tend to sell at approximately the same price, which is another way to say that we have the operation of the 'law of one price'. In a similar fashion, the profits of the invested capital tend to equalize; hence, we have the 'law of equal profitability'. More specifically, if producers in an industry make excessive profits, competition (other things equal) will increase their supply relative to demand (due to acceleration of investment) in this particular industry; hence, the price will be reduced to the point ensuring that the industry in question will be making the economy-wide average rate of profit. The converse will be true, if an industry's profit rate falls short of the economy's average one.[3]

Turning now to the definition of natural wage, this is assumed equal to the money wage which ensures the reproduction of workers, in effect, the reproduction of the supply of labour services. A higher money wage, according to Smith, leads to the growth in population through a higher birth rate (and, at the same time, lower child mortality rate) which eventually increases the labour supply, reduces wages and brings down the wage to its socially determined level, that is, back to its natural level; the converse will be true if the money wage falls short the socially determined natural one. The natural rent is defined in similar fashion, that is, the rent which is paid on lands of similar quality.

At this point of analysis, it is of interest to mention Smith's view on the interplay between natural price and demand or supply according to which:

> [t]he market price of every particular commodity is regulated by the proportion between the quantity which is actually brought to market, and the demand of those who are willing to pay the natural price of the commodity, or the whole value of the rent, labour, and profit, which must be paid in order to bring it thither. Such people may be called the effectual demanders, and their demand the effectual demand; since it may be sufficient to effectuate the bringing of the commodity to market. It is different from the absolute demand. A very poor man may be said in some sense to have a demand for a coach and six; he might like to have it; but his demand is not an effectual demand, as the commodity can never be brought to market in order to satisfy it.
>
> (*Wealth of Nations*, p. 56)

Figure 1.2 below encapsulates the above discussion about the classical long-run approach of analysis, and, at the same time, it reveals the characteristic difference to the determination of equilibrium price between the classical and neoclassical approaches (Garegnani 1983).[4] If a commodity is sold at its natural price, this is because a specific amount of it is being demanded. Therefore, in Smith and in the

---

[3]The details of this competitive process are discussed in Chaps. 5 and 6.
[4]See also Eatwell (1977), Eatwell and Milgate (1983 and 2011) and Eatwell et.al. (1987).

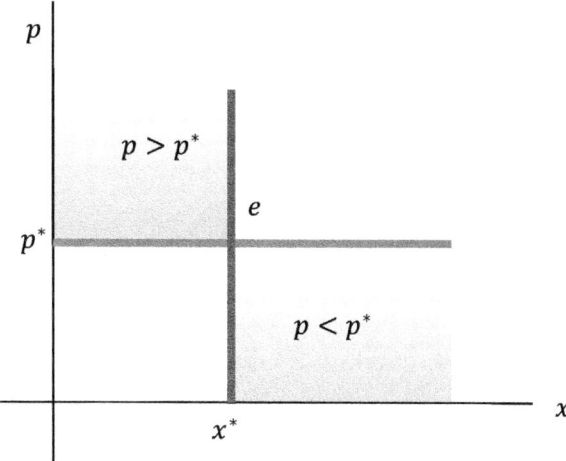

Fig. 1.2 Natural and market price, effectual demand and supply

classical approach in general, the natural price is a prerequisite for the determination of both the demand and supply and not the other way around as in the neoclassical approach! In Fig. 1.2, the vertical axis depicts the market price, p, of a commodity, whereas the horizontal axis its quantity produced, x.

According to Smith, the effectual demand is defined at point x^* on the horizontal axis corresponding to the natural price, p^*, on the vertical axis. For example, if the quantity supplied falls short of that demanded, the market price p will be higher than the natural price p^* giving rise to excess profits. This is not an equilibrium situation, and it is restored through an increase in investment and output produced; as a consequence, in due course, the market price will fall to its natural price. Should production exceed the effectual demand x^*, the converse is expected; that is, the withdrawn of investment and the corresponding reduction in supply will raise the market price up until it is equated to natural price. Hence, in Fig. 1.2 only the shaded areas are of economic interest since it is not logical to assume cases where the actual demand to be lower (higher) than the effectual demand and prices to be lower (higher) than the natural price as the non-shaded areas indicate. That is, the south-west and the northeast areas of Fig. 1.2 lack economic interest.

The above analysis often gives the impression that Smith refers to the usual demand and supply curves which, however, he did not draw simply because it was not customary in his time (Blaug 1997; Ekelund and Hébert 2007, inter alia). In Smith as well as in the classical economic analysis, however, there are no demand curves as they are found in the usual economic textbooks. The reason is that each point on an ordinary (neoclassical) demand curve indicates a possible equilibrium situation; the latter implies that each point on a demand curve corresponds to a possible natural price arising from the intersection of demand and supply curves. By contrast, in the classical analysis, the natural price is a single equilibrium point, and the market prices arise either in the northwest or southeast quadrant, as shown by the shaded areas in Fig. 1.2. Furthermore, market prices are not related to any equilibrium conditions, and instead they reflect the 'noise' and turbulence of reality, where profits, wages and rents are away from their natural magnitudes! Hence, in CPE market prices display, on the one hand, high volatility over time which is attributed to any number of factors and, on the other hand, erratic behaviour for which there is no theory that can explain it. Among these seemingly nonsystemic factors that affect market price are uncertainty, preferences, natural phenomena in general, conflicts of any kind, etc.

From the above, it becomes abundantly clear that the Smithian conceptualization of natural price and its connection to free competition is what elevated the discipline of economics and rightfully gave it a scientific status. Smith argued that the competitive process tends to integrate the regular and systematic relationship between the various types of prices. He described this relationship as the law of supply and demand,[5] which is characteristically different from the theory of supply and demand of the neoclassical economics. In fact, the law of supply and demand does not refer to the determination of the natural (normal) price but only to the proposition that market prices will orbit continuously around their normal (natural) ones. In Smith's analysis, the market prices reflect the distorted reality, that is, they are disequilibrium prices, whereas the neoclassical supply and demand schedules represent sets of market prices that are viewed as the locus of potentially equilibrium points. In particular, the typical demand schedule in microeconomic framework shows how much of a commodity individuals would be willing and able to pay for at each potential natural price from the list of alternatives; the usual supply curve indicates how much (and at what natural price) a certain quantity of a commodity should be produced, if the costs (payments for the services of the factors of production) are estimated at their natural price. Hence, any point of intersection between the demand and supply schedules, as already mentioned, is a potential equilibrium point that might be the equilibrium price. Thus, in the neoclassical tradition, there is an array of potential natural prices defined by the forces of demand and supply, whereas in the classical analysis, given the state of technology and the real wage, the natural price is uniquely defined. Eatwell (1977, pp. 61–68) points out that according to Smith market prices are determined by the law of demand and supply but not by the neoclassical theory of demand and supply which is based on the intersection of demand and supply curves or schedules.

Both classical and neoclassical approaches, despite their paradigmatic difference, attempt to determine the natural prices of commodities. This is the reason why they are 'antagonistic' to each other's approaches because they share the exact same object of analysis. In this chapter, we present and examine the CPE price theory based on the writings of the old classical economists (mainly Smith and Ricardo) and Marx.

---

[5]The truth is that Smith never used this expression (see also Löwe 1975, p. 417).

1.3 The Old Classical Economists and the Labour Theory of Value

The classical economists—hence we will discuss the essentials of the contributions of Smith and Ricardo—classified commodities into two broad categories: those that are not reproducible, such as rare books and coins, works of art, and the like, and those that are produced. The non-reproducible commodities constitute a negligible proportion of total production, and their price determination is not possible since it depends on ephemeral and therefore nonsystematic factors. By contrast, for the reproducible commodities making up the totality of production and constituting the main bulk of commodities, Smith, initially, and Ricardo, subsequently, argued that their relative prices are determined by the respective quantities of labour time required for their production.

1.3.1 Adam Smith's Theories of Value

We begin by presenting Smith's analysis in which the production and exchange processes take place in a hypothetical primitive society ("the rude and early stage of society") of hunters who are engaged in the hunting of two species, namely, deer (D) and beavers (B). Assuming that the hunting of a deer needs 4 h, while that of a beaver requires twice as long (8 h), the price of deer relative to beaver would be

$$\frac{P_D}{P_B} = \frac{L_D}{L_B} = \frac{4\,\text{h}}{8\,\text{h}} = \frac{1}{2} \tag{1.1}$$

where P_D and P_B are the prices for deer and beaver, respectively, and L_D and L_B correspond to the labour times needed to catch the two species; hence, we can say that in this society two deer will be exchanged against one beaver. In Smith's example (Eq. 1.1), the exchange ratio $2D = 1B$ is the only one that can last, that is, to provide an equilibrium set of relative prices, where the hunter spends 8 h to catch either two deer or one beaver. Any other exchange (or relative price) ratio (other things equal) would be out of equilibrium and, therefore, could not last.

By way of an example, let us suppose an exchange ratio $1D = 1B$. In such a case, very few hunters would continue hunting beavers simply because 4 h of hunting deer could be exchanged with one beaver. Hunters alternatively could spend 8 h and capture two deer, one of which they will gladly exchange it against a beaver whose hunting time requires 8 h. It is certain that the ratio of one-to-one could not last since the oversupply of deer would reduce their price while the shortage of beavers would increase their price. Thus, other things constant, it would not take long for the restoration of the equilibrium exchange ratio at $2D = 1B$, that is, the rate at which hunters would not have any particular interest or concern to revert exclusively to hunting deer or beavers.

Smith, parallel to the labour theory of value (LTV), however, developed the labour-commanded theory of value, whereby the value of a commodity is determined by the amount of labour that it can purchase or command. In Smith's words:

> The value of any commodity, therefore, to the person who possesses it, and who means not to use or consume it himself, but to exchange it for other commodities, is equal to the quantity of labour which it enables him to purchase or command. Labour, therefore, is the real measure of the exchangeable value of all commodities.
>
> (*Wealth of Nations*, p. 30)

Following Smith's argument and assuming away the land input, the natural price of a commodity will be

$$p^* = w^*L + r^*K \tag{1.2}$$

where starred variables indicate the natural payments. In particular, p^* is the natural price of commodities, w^* is the natural wage of labour, L, r^* is the natural rate of profit and K is the value of the invested capital. We may write Eq. (1.2) as follows:

$$p^*/w^* = L + (r^*/w^*)K \tag{1.3}$$

In a hypothetical society like the one with hunters, there is no capital ($K = 0$); hence we hypothesize a society of self-employed, where we will have

$$p^*/w^* = L \tag{1.4}$$

that is, the natural price of each commodity commands a respective amount of labour required for its production.

Smith argued that in a primitive society and economy, the hypothesis of determining relative prices according to relative labour times needed for their production is absolutely correct; the same holds true for the labour-commanded theory of value. But when Smith's analysis was extended to modern society, he found that the presence of capital and wage labour invalidated the initial hypothesis of the determination of natural relative prices according to the relevant quantities of labour. In other words, he found that the natural price of a commodity is no longer equal but exceeds the cost of labour (the product of the quantity of labour, L, times its normal remuneration, w^*), because its price includes now also the profits on invested capital (and/or the rent in the case of agricultural products). In such a society, where production takes place with the employment of both labour and capital, the natural price of a commodity will be greater than its labour value. Alternatively, the labour commanded, that is, the ratio of the price of a commodity to the wage exceeds the amount of labour spent on its production.

$$p^*/w^* > L \tag{1.5}$$

Figuratively speaking, the case of labour-commanded theory of value of a commodity can be portrayed in the following way.

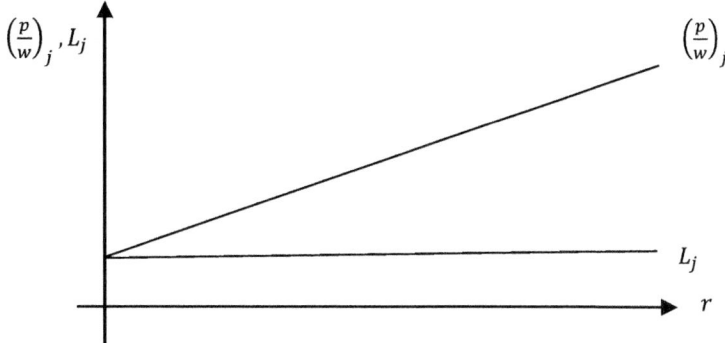

Fig. 1.3 Labour-commanded theory of value

From Fig. 1.3 below, we observe that $(p/w)_j = L_j$ when $r = 0$ and deviations start for a rate of profit $r > 0$; that is, the deviations are directly related to the rate of profit. Hence, the question is how large are these deviations and at what rate of profit? These are questions that we grapple with in Chap. 4.

Problems of this kind led Smith to abandon the LTV in conditions of capitalism and instead to focus on different theories of value, such as the so-called adding-up theory of value [a term attributed to Dobb (1973)], according to which the natural price of a commodity is determined by the sum of the three (natural) incomes, i.e. wages, profit and rent times the quantities of labour, capital and land, respectively. Formally,

$$
\begin{aligned}
\text{Natural price } (p^*) = {} & \text{Natural wage } (w^*) \times \text{Labour } (L) \\
& + \text{Natural rate of profit } (r^*) \times \text{Capital } (K) \\
& + \text{Natural rent rate } (\rho^*) \times \text{Land } (T)
\end{aligned}
\tag{1.6}
$$

Nevertheless, two problems arise in this last theory of value: First, the problem of circularity, since natural prices require natural payments and natural payments require natural prices; in other words, we enter into a vicious circle from which there is no way out. Second, Smith's definition and the subsequent use of this definition to real world conditions entails that changes in natural payments lead to changes in the price level; thereby, questioning the fundamental classical assumption, that is, the antagonistic relationship between wages and profits.

1.3.2   *Ricardo and the '93% Labour Theory of Value'*

Ricardo (1819) in the introduction of his book *Principles of Political Economy and Taxation (Works* I) boldly states that the supreme problem of political economy is to identify the laws that determine income distribution and the prerequisite to study these laws is a theory of relative prices (a theory of value) of commodities (*Works* I, pp. xiv–xv). Ricardo advanced the theory of value more than any other economist of his time; it was, however, impossible to supersede a series of hurdles that continue even today to occupy the economists' attention.

The first chapter of the *Principles* titled 'On Value' begins with a discussion about Smith's distinction between use value and exchangeable value. Ricardo argues that the use value of a commodity is a prerequisite for exchange, yet the exchangeable value of a commodity cannot be assessed in terms of its usefulness (*Works* I, p. 6). Furthermore, he argues that the issue of scarcity is important only in the case of non-reproducible goods whose relative prices are determined entirely by subjective and therefore not amenable to theorization factors. The vast majority of goods are reproducible, and, with regard to them, Ricardo accepts Smith's LTV according to which the relative prices of commodities are approximately proportional to the relative quantities of labour that were spent on their production. In Ricardo's words:

> [t]he value of a commodity, or the quantity of any other commodity for which it will exchange, depends on the relative quantity of labour which is necessary for its production, and not on the greater or less compensation which is paid for that labour.
>
> (*Works* I, p. 11)

Ricardo, being more insightful in his analysis, argued that Smith did not notice that although the LTV does not apply fully to capitalism, nevertheless it applies to a quite satisfactory extent. After all, even laws of physics do not fully hold, but they are modified by the presence of external factors, for example, the 'law of gravity' and the atmospheric frictions.

Ricardo's contribution to the theory of value is that he studied further the relation between relative prices and the labour time required to produce commodities, and he insisted on the idea that labour time is the central determining factor of the movement of natural prices. For example, notes Ricardo:

> The main cause of change in relative values of commodities is the increase or decrease in the amount of labour required to produce them.
>
> (*Works* I, p. 36)

Ricardo understood fully well that market prices are, prima facie, determined by the forces of supply and demand. Furthermore, he pointed out that the continual fluctuations in market prices are regulated by something more fundamental and persistent than the ephemeral forces of supply and demand. Ricardo identified this more fundamental and persistent force with the 'principle of equal profitability' whose operation entails the establishment of 'natural prices' across industries.

Furthermore, Ricardo introduced to his analysis the dimension of time. More specifically, if we hypothesize two commodities A and B and their respective prices P_A and P_B whereas the associated with these prices labour times are L_A and L_B, the relative prices of the two commodities are not equal to relative labour times, that is, $P_A/P_B \neq L_A/L_B$, as in Smith's LTV, but rather the change in relative prices depends on the change in the relative labour times.

$$\Delta(P_A/P_B) = f[\Delta(L_A/L_B)] \tag{1.7}$$

That is, the intertemporal changes in relative prices of commodities depend on the changes in relative labour times. Hence, if for some reason the ratio P_A/P_B changes, then it is not enough to know that this is due to a change in the ratio of L_A/L_B, because such a change can come from a number of causes. For example, supposing that the ratio P_A/P_B rises, this might be due to a rise in L_A while L_B remained constant or due to a fall in L_B while L_A remained constant or because L_A increased at a faster rate higher than that of L_B or L_B fell by more than the fall in L_A.

According to Ricardo, a way out of these riddles would be a commodity whose production would always require the same quantity of labour and whose price would not change with changes in the income distribution. Furthermore, by using such a commodity as a numéraire, one could identify the source of variation in relative prices in the face of changes in the quantity of labour contained in the production of the other commodities. Ricardo called a commodity with these two qualifications an 'invariable measure of value' (IMV)[6] and searched, in fact, devoted the rest of his intellectual life to the discovery of either an actual or analytical such a commodity, without success.[7] It is important to note that in Ricardo's time the right-hand side of the relationship (1.7) was unknown, and, therefore, Ricardo was searching for an IMV in order to determine the cause of change in the visible part of the relation (1.7), that is, the relative prices. Nowadays, the need for a Ricardian IMV is less imperative because we now have the required data for both sides of the above relation.

Ricardo argued that the value of the product is determined not only by the direct labour expended on its production but also by the indirect labour expended on its means of production. He notes:

> Not only the labour applied immediately to commodities affects their value, but also the labour which is bestowed on the implements, tools, and buildings, with such labour is assisted.
>
> (*Works* I, p. 23)

In other words, the exchange ratios of commodities are determined by their respective labour times with fixed capital only transferring its exchange value gradually through its depreciation. However, in the numerical examples that he used, which today might be called economic models, for simplicity reasons, Ricardo assumed that the fixed capital does not depreciate at all.

For Ricardo, the LTV applies fully to primitive (or pre-capitalist) societies and to a great extent to the modern capitalist society, where production of commodities takes place with the combination of capital and wage labour. Ricardo was keen to notice that in capitalism the accuracy and, therefore, the one hundred percent validity

---

[6]The IMV could also be used as an index for the intertemporal estimation and comparisons of the wealth and therefore the well-being of a society.

[7]Marx called these efforts 'blind alleys' precisely because they could not reach any satisfactory answer to the question.

Table 1.1 Determination of relative prices in Ricardo with the presence of fixed capital

	K	$W = wL$	K/L	$\Pi = r(K + wL)$	$P = wL + \Pi$
Commodity A	£5500	£5000	£55	£1050	£6050
Commodity B	£1500	£5000	£15	£650	£5650

of the LTV is somewhat reduced by three factors, namely, the presence of fixed capital, the changes in income distribution and the difference in turnover times in the production processes. It is worth noting that Ricardo is the first economist, who systematically constructed economic models on the basis of which he derived theoretical propositions with sufficient generality. These models are typically cast in terms of super-simple numerical examples with the aid of which Ricardo revived and, at the same time, strengthened the validity of the LTV by showing the limited effects of the above three factors on the relative prices of goods. The resulting deviations of estimated relative natural prices from their respective relative labour times in his numerical examples were usually minimal, typically less than 7%, and in the subsequent literature (e.g. Stigler 1956), this came to be known as the '93% labour theory of value'.

1.3.3   Deviations from the Labour Theory of Value Induced by the Presence of Fixed Capital

According to Ricardo, the relative price of the industries that employ more capital than labour will be greater than their relative amounts of labour and vice versa. Based on Ricardo's numerical example which we modify somewhat but always remain within his spirit, let us suppose two industries producing commodities, A and B, by employing labour and capital. In particular, the two industries employ 100 workers (L) with an annual wage $w = £50$; hence, the amount of labour is the same in both industries. However, the industry producing commodity A (cotton in Ricardo's example) employs a capital good (machine) worth £5500, while the industry producing commodity B (corn in Ricardo's original example) uses another capital good with much less value, only £1500. Hence, it is important to note that commodity B in Ricardo's example is supposed to be produced with no fixed capital. In our view, this is a super extreme example, and we opted to modify it only with respect to the commodity B by assuming that employs some fixed capital, however, far less than that of industry's A. The purpose of this modification is to derive some interesting generalizations while at the same time maintaining the extreme character of Ricardo's numerical example. Let us further assume (with Ricardo) that the rate of profit (r) is the same in both industries and equal to 10%. With this information in mind, we construct Table 1.1.[8] where K denotes the value of the machine, W denotes the wage bill, w stands for the annual wage per worker, L stands for the number of

---

[8] For reasons of simplicity and clarity of presentation, Ricardo assumes that capital lasts forever which is another way to say that there is no depreciation.

workers, Π stands for total profits, r is the uniform profit rate equal 10% and P is the price of the commodity. The above numerical example shows that the relative prices of commodities are no longer proportional to the amount of labour employed, a result displayed in the last column of Table 1.1.

$$\frac{P_A}{P_B} = \frac{6050}{5650} = 1.07 > \frac{L_A}{L_B} = \frac{100}{100} = 1 \qquad (1.8)$$

The differences between the relative prices and the relative quantities of labour spent on the production of both commodities is what made Smith to abandon the LTV. Ricardo, however, noticed that such deviations are relatively small and can be theorized for they depend on the different capital-wage ratios (K/W) or, in Marxian terms, the different value compositions of capital, a concept whose details are discussed in the next chapters. Because the wage rate is supposed to be given and uniform across industries, the relative prices depend essentially on the differences between the capital-labour ratios of the two goods. If the capital-labour ratios were the same, there would be no deviation between relative prices, P_A/P_B, and the respective labour quantities, L_A/L_B. These results become more transparent, if we formulate the relative prices from the data displayed in Table 1.1. Thus, we may write

$$\frac{P_A}{P_B} = \frac{wL_A + r(wL_A + K_A)}{wL_B + r(wL_B + K_B)} \qquad (1.9)$$

By factoring out in the numerator the term wL_A and in the denominator the term wL_B, we get

$$\frac{P_A}{P_B} = \left[\frac{wL_A}{wL_B}\right] \frac{\left[1 + r\left(1 + \frac{K_A}{wL_A}\right)\right]}{\left[1 + r\left(1 + \frac{K_B}{wL_B}\right)\right]} \qquad (1.10)$$

The subtraction of relative labour times from both sides of Eq. (1.10) gives

$$\frac{P_A}{P_B} - \frac{L_A}{L_B} = \left[\frac{L_A}{L_B}\right] \frac{\left[1 + r\left(1 + \frac{K_A}{wL_A}\right)\right]}{\left[1 + r\left(1 + \frac{K_B}{wL_B}\right)\right]} - \frac{L_A}{L_B}$$

$$= \left[\frac{L_A}{L_B}\right] \underbrace{\left[\underbrace{\frac{r}{w + r\left(w + \frac{K_B}{L_B}\right)}} \underbrace{\left(\frac{K_A}{L_A} - \frac{K_B}{L_B}\right)}_{\text{sign of deviation}}\right]}_{\text{size of deviation}} \qquad (1.11)$$

The relation (1.11) shows that the relative prices of the two commodities are affected by the presence of capital and the rate of profit but only in a strictly defined and therefore predictable way. Clearly, both the sign and size of the difference between relative prices and labour times depend 'almost exclusively' on the capital-labour ratios of the two commodities since all the above variables are strictly positive and assumed given. In effect, by entering the numbers from Table 1.1, we derive the percentage deviation which will be

$$100\frac{\left(\frac{P_A}{P_B} - \frac{L_A}{L_B}\right)}{\left(\frac{L_A}{L_B}\right)} \approx 7\% \qquad (1.12)$$

The numerical example is extreme for it accepts the presence of very large differences in capital-labour ratios in the production of the two commodities. Nevertheless, even in such an extreme case, the difference between relative prices and relative quantities of labour is only 7%. Furthermore, this difference is predictable since it depends on the capital-intensities measured by the capital-labour ratio.

The profit rate also affects relative prices but in a limited and predictable way, and its effect gradually fades away due to its long-term downward trend, a common contention of classical economists and in effect of all major economists as we discuss in Chap. 8. If, for example, the rate of profit falls to 5%, then the deviation between relative prices from relative quantities of labour (which are not affected by changes in distribution) is reduced to about 3.7% (see Table 1.2 and Fig. 1.4, below).

Table 1.2 Relative prices and their elasticities with respect to selective profit rates

r	0%	5%	10%	20%	40%	62.5%	70%	80%	90%	100%
$\frac{P_A}{P_B}$	1.00	1.037	1.070	1.127	1.210	1.275	1.293	1.310	1.332	1.347
e_r		0.026	0.053	0.086	0.114	0.119	0.118	0.117	0.115	0.112

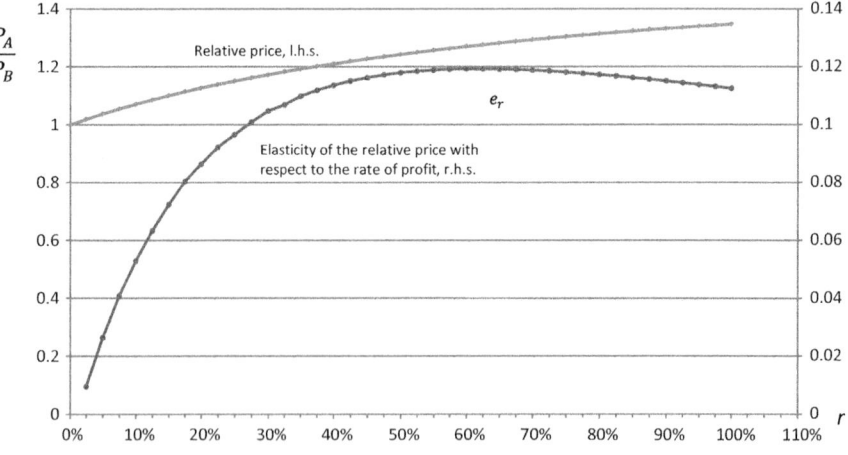

Fig. 1.4 Relative prices, elasticity and rates of profit

In the extreme and, therefore, entirely hypothetical case where the rate of profit is zero, the percentage difference of the relative prices from the relevant quantities of labour is also zero, regardless of the differences in the capital-labour ratio which is another way to say that the LTV fully holds. It is important to stress that the resulting size of the deviation of relative prices from the respective relative labour times not only is expected to be small but also predictable for it depends on the difference between the capital-labour ratios of the two industries provided that the wage rate is uniform and remains constant in the face of hypothetical changes in the rate of profit. Nevertheless, these assumptions are only made for illustrative purposes, and in the next subsections, we bring into the analysis Ricardo's 'fundamental law of distribution', according to which there is an inverse relationship between the wage rate and the rate of profit (Kurz 2018).

With the above in mind, we derive the dependence of the direction or the sign of the relative prices on the changes in the rate of profit by differentiating Eq. 1.9 with respect to r. Thus, we may write

$$\frac{d\left(\frac{P_A}{P_B}\right)}{dr} = \frac{d}{dr}\left[\frac{wL_A + r(wL_A + K_A)}{wL_B + r(wL_B + K_B)}\right] = \frac{w(K_A L_B - K_B L_A)}{(wL_B + rwL_B + rK_B)^2} \tag{1.13}$$

Since, the denominator of the above fraction is always positive, it follows that the sign of the above derivative depends exclusively on the sign of the numerator. In particular,

$$K_A L_B - K_B L_A = \left(\frac{K_A}{L_A} - \frac{K_B}{L_B}\right) L_A L_B \tag{1.14}$$

and

$$\text{sign}\left[\frac{d\left(\frac{P_A}{P_B}\right)}{dr}\right] = \text{sign}\left(\frac{K_A}{L_A} - \frac{K_B}{L_B}\right) L_A L_B \tag{1.15}$$

Table 1.2 below presents selected results of our experiments with different rates of profit starting from zero until we reach the 100% taken as a kind of a maximum possible rate of profit. It is important to stress that at the time that Ricardo was writing both the assumptions of 10% and 100% rate of profit were rather extreme and the actual economy's rate of profit should lie somewhere between these two percentages. Ricardo selected a rate of profit of 10% for the shake of simplicity and convenience although it was not too unrealistic if we think that he was writing during the first major downturn of the long wave after the industrial revolution (see Chap. 8).

For reasons of visual inspection and clarity of presentation, the pairs of rates of profit—relative prices—from Table 1.2 are plotted in Fig. 1.4. The relative prices are estimated on the left-hand side (l.h.s.) axis and the rate of profit (which increases by increments of 2.5% at a time) on the horizontal axis whereas the elasticity of the relative price with respect to the rate of profit on the right hand side vertical axis (r.h.s.), such an experiment although in slight deviation, nevertheless, is in full compliance with Ricardo's spirit and logic.

Table 1.2 as well as Fig. 1.4 show that when $r = 0$, the relative prices of the two commodities will be equal to relative labour times and also equal to one

$$P_A/P_B = L_A/L_B = 1 \qquad (1.16)$$

We observe that the deviations between relative labour values and relative prices are directly related to the rate of profit shown on the horizontal axis; the deviations start from zero when $r = 0\%$ and $P_A/P_B = 1$, and, as the rate of profit increases, the deviations also increase but at a decreasing rate. For example, when the rate of profit doubles (say from 10% increases to 20%), the deviation between relative prices and relative labour times increases from 7% to 12.7%. From the results displayed in Table 1.2 and Fig. 1.4, it becomes abundantly clear that past a point the relative price becomes increasingly less sensitive to changes in the rate of profit. In effect, the second derivative of relative price with respect to the rate of profit (Eq. 1.13) gives

$$\frac{\mathrm{d}^2(P_A/P_B)}{\mathrm{d}r^2} = -\frac{2w(wL_B + K_B)(K_A L_B - K_B L_A)}{(wL_B + rwL_B + rK_B)^3} \qquad (1.17)$$

Clearly, if the capital-labour ratio in the production of commodity A is higher than that of commodity B as in the numerical example, it follows that the second derivative will be negative, which is another way to say that the relative price path will be concave.

Although Ricardo did not use calculus and elasticities, nevertheless by presenting his views in modern terms, we make easier for nowadays economist to appreciate better Ricardo's contribution to theory of value by casting it in terms of modern microeconomics. Thus, it comes as no surprise that the elasticity of relative price with respect to the rate of profit, e_r, displayed in the third row of Table 1.2, is smaller, in fact, much smaller than one.[9] In particular, we have

$$
\begin{aligned}
e_r &= \frac{\mathrm{d}(P_A/P_B)}{\mathrm{d}r} \frac{r}{(P_A/P_B)} \\
&= \frac{w(K_A L_B - K_B L_A)}{(wL_B + rwL_B + rK_B)^2} \frac{r}{\dfrac{wL_A + r(wL_A + K_A)}{wL_B + r(wL_B + K_B)}} \\
&= \frac{w(K_A L_B - K_B L_A)}{(wL_B + rwL_B + rK_B)} \frac{r}{(wL_A + rwL_A + rK_A)} < 1
\end{aligned}
\qquad (1.18)
$$

---

[9]The estimation of elasticities is based on the application of midpoint formula.

In the above numerical example, where the rate of profit increases from 10% to 20%, the respective elasticity is $e_r = 0.086$, which is another way to say that the realistic percentage changes in relative prices brought about by a percentage change in the rate of profit are relatively small and get smaller as the rate of profit increases even more; for example, if the rate of profit rises from 20% to 40%, the relative price elasticity becomes 0.114; in other words the elasticity increases by a decreasing rate. These results and discussion lend support to Ricardo's view that the relative labour times are the decisive regulators of the variation in relative prices (though not the exclusive ones).

The inclusion of fixed capital by Ricardo and the resulting changes in relative prices lend support to the labour theory of relative prices. More specifically, if the capital-labour ratio does not differ between the two sectors of the economy, then the LTV holds 100%. On the other hand, if the capital-labour ratio differs between the sectors, then this difference as multiplied by the rate of profit, which is typically relatively small, tends to have a relatively minor influence over the relative prices.[10] The above numerical example, with no doubt, presents extreme conditions,[11] since we examine only two industries with rather super-high differences in capital-labour ratios (in our case, 55 vs. 15); yet, the differences that arise between relative prices and relative labour quantities are only of the order of 7% which amounts to a convergence by 93%! Generally, we find that for realistic numerical examples derived from real economies (see Chap. 4), the differences between relative prices and relative labour quantities are very small and Ricardo's analysis and intuition were to the right direction.

1.3.4   Deviations from the Labour Theory of Value Induced by Changes in Income Distribution

According to Ricardo, another important source of deviations between relative prices and relative labour times is the change in income distribution; however, as he argued, the effect of this factor is on the one hand limited, especially in the face of increase in the wage rate and respective fall in the rate of profit, and on the other hand predictable, and thus it can be explained theoretically. It is important to note, once again, that for Ricardo (but also for the classical economists) wages and profits are two antagonistic variables, i.e. the increase of one implies the fall in the other. This is the 'fundamental law of distribution' in the classical political economy tradition.

---

[10]Empirically, we find that the economy-wide net rate of profit for a number of countries is not far from 10% (see Chaps. 4, 6 and 10). In addition, by taking into account that Ricardo was writing during a recessionary period, this assumption is not only convenient in estimations but also not out of touch from reality.

[11]Ricardo presents his arguments under situations that are unfavourable to the propositions he seeks to prove. This is a very wise methodological approach. The idea is that if an argument holds under the unfavourable circumstances then, *a fortiori*, it will hold under normal ones.

Presenting now Ricardo's argument, let us assume that wages, for some reason, increase. Hence, we distinguish the following cases: first, if the capital-labour ratio is the same across industries, then no deviation is expected between relative prices and relative labour times because the profit losses will be proportional between industries and there is no reason whatsoever for any change in the relative price of goods. Second, in the general case of differences in the capital-labour ratios between the two industries, an increase in the wage will lead to a fall in the rate of profit in both industries. But this fall will not be uniform, because of the different capital-labour ratios. The capital-intensive industry will suffer a proportionately smaller loss in its profits and in its rate of profit than the labour-intensive industry. However, the resulting inequality in the rates of profit indicates disequilibrium, and as such, it can only be temporary because the acceleration of accumulation in the capital-intensive industry will increase its supply; the deceleration of capital accumulation will be true in the labour-intensive industry whose supply will decrease. As a result, the price of the labour-intensive industry will rise somewhat, while the price of the capital-intensive industry will fall, so that both industries in the end will earn the same, but a lower, average rate of profit. It is interesting to note that Ricardo's conclusions hold true to the extent that we refer to two industries. If the number of industries increases, the degree of complexity increases, and Ricardo's conclusions do not necessarily hold with the same accuracy because of the development of complex feedback effects which may give rise to quite unexpected results, as Sraffa (1960) so eloquently has shown. These issues are important in their own right, and we grapple with them both analytically and empirically, mainly in Chaps. 3 and 4, respectively.

In Ricardo's original example (*Works* I, p. 36) as well as in the amended one presented in Table 1.1, where we assume the presence of fixed capital in industry B equal to £1500 instead of Ricardo's assumption of zero fixed capital, we find that an increase in wage implies a fall in the rate of profit and brings the resulting relative prices even closer to relative labour quantities. In effect, when the rate of profit falls from say 10% to 5%, the relative price falls from 1.07 to 1.037. Hence, we arrive at two important conclusions: first, a fall in the rate of profit by 5% led the relative prices to come even closer to their respective labour times, and second, a significant percentage reduction in the rate of profit (by 50%) impacted on relative prices by only 3%. Ricardo, after a kind of sensitivity analysis, notes:

> The greater effects which could be produced on the relative prices of these goods from a rise of wages, could not exceed 6 or 7%; for profits could not, probably, under any circumstances, admit of a greater general and permanent depression than to that amount.
>
> (*Works* I, p. 36)

The effect of changes in relative prices because of changes in income distribution in the case of the two industries can be estimated straightforwardly starting from the formalization of the previous section, with the difference that now we have more variables and we partially differentiate with respect to wage. For this reason, let us consider Ricardo's 'fundamental principle of distribution' of $r = f(w)$ and $dr/dw < 0$ while we assume away the probable negligible changes in the value of capital of each industry resulting from changes in income distribution, that is, $dK/dw = 0$. By partially differentiating the relative prices with respect to the wage rate, we get

$$\frac{d(P_A/P_B)}{dw} = \frac{d}{dw}\left[\frac{wL_A + r(wL_A + K_A)}{wL_B + r(wL_B + K_B)}\right]$$

$$= \frac{\overbrace{\left[\dfrac{dr}{dw}w - (r+1)r\right]}^{-}}{\underbrace{(wL_B + rwL_B + rK_B)^2}_{+}}\left(\frac{K_A}{L_A} - \frac{K_B}{L_B}\right)\underbrace{L_A L_B}_{+} \qquad (1.19)$$

The bracketed term in the numerator of Eq. (1.19) will always be negative, while the denominator will always be positive together with the quantities of labour; therefore, it follows that the sign of the above partial derivative will depend exclusively on the term $(K_A/L_A - K_B/L_B)$. Consequently, we will have

$$\text{sign}\left[\frac{d}{dw}\left(\frac{P_A}{P_B}\right)\right] \text{ depend on sign}\left(\frac{K_A}{L_A} - \frac{K_B}{L_B}\right) \qquad (1.20)$$

Finally, the elasticity of the relative price with respect to the change in wage rate, e_w, will be

$$
\begin{aligned}
e_w &= \frac{d(P_A/P_B)}{dw}\cdot\frac{w}{(P_A/P_B)}\\[2mm]
&= \frac{\left[\dfrac{dr}{dw}w - (r+1)r\right](K_A L_B - K_B L_A)}{(wL_B + rwL_B + rK_B)^2}\cdot\frac{w}{\dfrac{wL_A + rwL_A + rK_A}{wL_B + rwL_B + rK_B}} \qquad (1.21)\\[2mm]
&= \frac{\left[\dfrac{dr}{dw}w - (r+1)r\right](K_A L_B - K_B L_A)}{(wL_B + rwL_B + rK_B)}\cdot\frac{w}{(wL_A + rwL_A + rK_A)} < 1
\end{aligned}
$$

The above formalizations lend support to Ricardo's intuition and numerical example according to which the change in relative prices of commodities, resulting from changes in the distributive variables, will depend on the differences between the capital-labour ratios. As we already mentioned, in the case of three or more industries, the analysis becomes much more complicated, and we deal with these complications, mainly, in Chaps. 3 and 4.

1.3.5 Deviations from the Labour Theory of Value Induced by Differences in Turnover Times

According to Ricardo, the different turnover times, n, in production (other things equal) may also give rise to deviations between relative prices and relative labour times. Let us hypothesize with Ricardo two industries investing the exact same amount of money and employing the same number of people; the only difference is that in the first industry all investment takes place in two equal installments allocated into two equal sub-periods while in the second industry the same amount is invested once in the beginning. Under these circumstances, Ricardo argued that the relative price of the first industry will be somewhat higher than the second one. The idea is that in the first industry the 'interest' (profit) that is forgone at the end of the first period is also estimated in the price at the end of the year.

In order to illustrate the effects of different turnover times or what is the same thing different time periods for the completion of the production process, let us hypothesize two producers, A and B, who earn a given profit rate of 10%. Producer A invests £2000 (40 workers × £50 annual wage) in total, £1000 in the first year and the rest in the second. At the end of the second year, the price of the commodity will be £2310 which results from the following calculations:

$$£1000 \times (1 + 0.10)_{\text{first year}} + £1000 \times (1 + 0.10)^2_{\text{second year}} = £2310 \qquad (1.22)$$

The calculations of the second year are based on the idea that the producer treats the non-invested capital in the production of the first year as a kind of opportunity cost that must be compensated for by 10% on the second year plus another 10% when this capital is actually invested in the second year.

By contrast, producer B invests all his capital of £2000 (40 workers × £50 annual wage) in the first year, and so the price for his product at the end of the production process (end of the second year) will be

$$£2000 \times (1 + 0.10) = £2200 \qquad (1.23)$$

We observe that the same quantities of labour paid the same wage correspond to different values. Hence, the assumptions of a uniform rate of profit and differential turnover times of capital lead to deviations of relative prices from labour quantities employed in the production of commodities. It is obvious that this example used by Ricardo shows that the labour theory of (exchange) value or relative prices is still valid albeit somewhat modified. In the above example, we observe that despite the large differences in the turnover times of the production process, the deviation of relative prices from labour quantities (whose ratio is equal to one) is only 5% (£2310/£2200 = 1.05). Alternatively, the proximity of relative prices to relative labour quantities is 95%! If we formalize Ricardo's example and replace $n = 2$ and $r = 10\%$, we may write

$$\frac{P_A}{P_B} = \frac{wL(1+r) + wL(1+r)^n}{2wL(1+r)} = \frac{wL(1+r)\left[1 + (1+r)^{n-1}\right]}{2wL(1+r)}$$
$$= \frac{1 + (1+r)^{n-1}}{2} = 1.05 \tag{1.24}$$

and the size and the direction of change in relative price with respect to turnover time will be

$$\frac{\mathrm{d}(P_A/P_B)}{\mathrm{d}n} = 0.5 \ln{(1+r)}(1+r)^{n-1} \approx 0.05 > 0 \tag{1.25}$$

while the change in the rate of change [second derivative of Eq. (1.25)] will be negative

$$\frac{\mathrm{d}^2(P_A/P_B)}{\mathrm{d}n^2} = 0.5 \ln^2(1+r)(1+r)^{n-1} \approx -1.3 < 0 \tag{1.26}$$

that is, the relative price of the good with the (higher) turnover rate, other things equal, will be higher than its relative labour time; however, as the turnover time increases, the increase in relative price will be diminishing since the second derivative of relation (1.26) is negative, assuming of course that the rate of profit does not take exorbitant values. Finally, the elasticity with respect to turnover time n and by assuming that $n = 2$ following Ricardo's numerical example will be

$$e_n = \frac{\mathrm{d}(P_A/P_B)}{\mathrm{d}n} \frac{n}{(P_A/P_B)} = \frac{\ln{(1+r)}\left[(1+r)^{n-1} + 1\right](1+r)^{n-1}}{4n} \approx 0.03 \tag{1.27}$$

Of course, we may build more complex cases, but for realistic examples the deviations of relative prices from relative values are expected to be small, since there cannot be wild differences in turnover times as in this particular Ricardo's example, whereas the elasticity of the relative prices w.r.t. turnover time is nearly zero. If we suppose that the turnover time, other things equal, increases (doubles) say from $n = 2$ to $n = 4$, then it follows that although the elasticity w.r.t. turnover time experiences a tenfold increase, $e_n = 0.3$, nevertheless, the good in question remains highly inelastic; as a consequence, the relative prices will differ from relative labour values only by 16.55%. These results lend further support to Ricardo's thesis about the inelastic nature of relative prices also w.r.t. turnover time. In particular, the results that we derive are pretty robust, as this can be judged by the fact that the unrealistically high percentage increase in the turnover time entails a by far smaller change in relative prices.

Summing up, Ricardo's numerical examples that we examined are extreme in that the approximate determination of relative prices of goods by their relative quantities of labour times is conducted under very unfavourable circumstances. Ricardo shows that the observed deviations between relative labour times and relative prices are not only small, but also the sign and size of these deviations can be theorized. Thus, by stipulating realistic capital-intensities and turnover times of capital, the deviations of relative prices from relative labour times might be even smaller. The formalization of Ricardo's examples and the use of calculus give more precise meaning in Ricardo's numerical models and pave the way for the empirical investigation of the LTV, since no theory operates 100% under actual conditions. The issue with Ricardo is that he considered natural prices, i.e. the prices that embody the average rate profit of the economy, as deviations from labour values at which normally the commodities should be exchanged and not that natural prices are more specific price expressions of the LTV and as such a more accurate centre of gravitation for market prices. It is important to stress that Ricardo's analysis concerns the long run, and in the long run one may expect natural prices to be equal to the average (equilibrium) prices. This is an issue that we grapple with in Chaps. 3 and 4.

1.4   Marx's Labour Theory of Value

Marx accepts the importance of labour time in determining commodity prices in capitalism. Contrary to both Smith and Ricardo who considered the LTV to hold in pre-capitalist societies whereas under capitalism either it does not hold (Smith) or it holds but with some modifications of minor quantitative significance (Ricardo), Marx argued that the law of relative prices is expected to fully operate in conditions of fully fledged capitalism and not in pre-capitalist societies. The reason is that the LTV becomes effective in the presence of commodity exchange and the more widespread and developed is this exchange, the more effective becomes the operation of the law. Notes Marx:

> The economic concept of value does not occur in antiquity [...]. The concept of value is entirely peculiar to the most modern economy, since it is the most abstract expression of capital itself and the production resting on it. In the concept of value, its secret is betrayed.
>
> (*Grundrisse*, p. 776)

Thus, according to Marx, the validity of the LTV will increase (and not decrease) with the expansion of the commodification of economic life. This is equivalent to saying that as the capitalist mode of production advances, the LTV becomes more effective in explaining the surface economic categories of prices and incomes.

1.4.1   Commodity Production and Value

The purpose of Marx's economic studies was 'to *lay bare* the economic *law* of *motion* of *modern society*' (*Capital* I, p. 10), that is to say, to discover social regularities described mainly as economic mechanisms and long-run tendencies. Marx observes that capitalism is a historically specific system characterized by 'generalized' commodity exchange whose understanding requires an in-depth knowledge of its most important and essential component, the commodity. He notes:

> the commodity-form of the product of labour—or value-form of the commodity—is the economic cell-form.
>
> (*Capital* I, p. 90)

The commodity appears to be the only logical starting point for the analysis of capitalism (i.e. the anatomy of the system); in fact, through a 'trial and error' process, any other possible starting point leads back to the notion of the commodity. For example, starting the analysis with either production or national income or population, soon we discover that one way or another, we essentially deal with the exchange of commodities; thus, the commodity becomes the logical starting point for the study of the 'laws of motion' of capitalism.

The commodity according to Marx has a dual role: on the one hand, it is to be used to satisfy the manifold human needs regardless where they come from, and, on the other hand, it is to be exchanged. An individual purchases a commodity in order to meet his diverse needs, real or fictitious. The seller exchanges the commodity for the purpose of profit-making. Consequently, a commodity is at the same time use value and (exchange) value. The prerequisite for the understanding of the notion of value is the relationship between use value and exchange value, the two 'opposite poles' of a commodity. We say 'opposite poles' since the seller of the commodity is interested in its exchange value while the buyer in its use value. According to Marx:

> Use value is anything necessary, useful or pleasant. The use of its properties allows us to meet some of our needs or desires.
>
> (*Capital* I, p. 35)

As use value, a specific commodity is socially useful and therefore is exchangeable with any other commodity, a feature applicable to nearly all societies. The hallmark of a capitalist society compared to earlier ones is that in the pre-capitalist societies the production and the exchange of commodities were primarily intended to satisfy human needs; while profit, if it existed, had a subsidiary role and not in a few cases, it was considered to be a result of immoral behaviour and activity.[12] Production for the purpose of exchange in order to yield profit became systematic and widespread only in conditions of capitalism during the last three centuries essentially after the industrial revolution of the last quarter of the eighteenth century. In capitalism what matters is not the use value of the object but the amount of money received by the commodity seller when the exchange is completed. In other words, only in capitalism does it hold that the main purpose of the produced use values is not to satisfy a social need but to be sold for a profit.

Turning now to the exchange value aspect of commodities, we observe that when they are exchanged, in effect, a mutual comparison takes place. For example, when

---

[12]For example, merchants in feudalistic societies were thought as stingy, greedy and arrogant people who lived at the margins of the social hierarchy.

we say that a commodity contains value, this is equivalent to saying that x quantity of commodity A is equal to y quantity of commodity B or z quantity of commodity gold and so forth. These comparisons between commodities indicate that they are endowed with a common property rendering reciprocal comparisons possible. It is important to stress at this point that the property that gives to commodities exchange value and thus makes them comparable must be distinguished from the measurement of their value. If, for example, we measure commodity A in terms of commodity B, we will get a different result from what we would receive had we measured commodity A in terms of commodity C or of commodity G (gold = money) and so forth. The measurement of values of commodities bears a resemblance to the weighting of goods with weight units (kilos) according to which a definite quantity of metal is taken as a standard for the measurement of the goods' weight. It is not the weight units that cause goods to have weight but their mass. Similarly, it is not gold (or whatever might possibly be the money commodity) that gives worthiness to the commodities but the fact that they are products of labour. Consequently, when we refer to the exchange value (or price) of a commodity, we are essentially asking for:

- First: the common property of commodities that renders them exchangeable
- Second: the measurement of worthiness of commodities during the exchange

1.4.2   Concrete and Abstract Labour

The recurrent reproduction of any society, along with the social relations that govern it, requires the production of large quantities of use values to cover the diverse social needs. In every society, the production of use values necessitates a definite distribution of total social labour. Each specific type of labour (concrete labour) is what gives the features characterizing any single commodity, for example, the labour of a shoemaker in the case of a pair of shoes, of a tailor in the case of a suit, etc. Hence, the reproduction of the society's material base requires the appropriate diversity and quantities of use values which cover the manifold social needs.

Having discussed the notion of a commodity, the questions that come to the fore are: first, what is the cause that gives commodities their use value aspect? And second, what is the cause that gives commodities their (exchange) value aspect? The usefulness or use value and value aspects of a commodity stem from the dual nature of labour which in its concrete form (i.e. the labour of the carpenter, painter, designer and the like) gives rise to the useful properties of a commodity to satisfy human needs (real or imaginary) and in its abstract form, that is, labour in general, gives rise to the (exchange) value aspect of the commodity. In fact, Marx, by experimenting with different properties of commodities, concludes with the idea that the only economically meaningful property characterizing all commodities is that they are all products of human labour. This common property makes possible the comparison of commodities according to the quantity of labour that they contain.

However, as in the case of different commodities which when they are expressed in a common denominator become comparable to each other, it is that the quantity of labour which is embodied must be quantitatively comparable since different types of labour may differ with respect to the quantity of value that they create. The kind of labour that furnishes commodities with a quantitatively measurable value is called 'abstract labour' by Marx and is defined as the labour from which all specific and concrete characteristics have been removed in the actual process of production of commodities and not in a notional process of exchange.[13] All specific and therefore secondary concrete differences of commodities are subsumed by their common feature, that is, the amount of abstract labour time that has been expended on their production. Labour time becomes abstract and is at the same time objectified in value already in the sphere of production. In other words, the concept of abstract labour is not a mental generalization that we somehow choose to make but rather the reflection in thought of a real social process; this, in turn, means that abstract labour and hence value are also real and therefore quantifiable (Shaikh 1981, p. 273).

In fact, when commodities are exchanged, different kinds of labour are equalized to each other, thereby necessitating the presence of a common property or denominator for all commodities. The common economically meaningful feature of all commodities is that they are products of human labour;[14] this property of commodities makes them comparable to each other on the basis of the amount of abstract labour time spent on their production. The individual specificities of each particular commodity are removed reducing them to their common social status which endows them with the property of exchangeability. In other words, a use value becomes a commodity only when an additional feature is added to it, that is, exchange value. This abstraction from the specific characteristics of labour makes inter-commodity comparisons possible and therefore allows the realization of exchange. In effect, exchange in itself confirms the presence of abstract labour which is equivalent to saying that a certain amount of labour of one producer is worth a certain amount of labour of another.

It is important to emphasize that only the labour of a capitalist society can be abstract and that only this kind of labour regulates the exchange value of commodities; the reason is that only in capitalism, the market mechanism is dominant in nearly all aspects of economic life. Moreover, we should note that the total abstract

---

[13]Sweezy (1942), among many others, considers abstract labour to be the result of a mental and, therefore, notional abstraction according to which the specific characteristics of labour are removed and what is left is just spending of human effort. This view is different from the one we describe in the main text. Under capitalist production, which is production for exchange, labour time from the start is conceived without its specific characteristics, and it is, in this sense, 'abstract labour'; labour becomes 'abstract' already in the production process. Hence, 'abstract labour' is neither notional as Sweezy had opined nor does it acquire its 'abstract' quality during the exchange process as many Marxists have argued, continuing a tradition that claims its roots in Rubin (1928).

[14]Another common feature of commodities is their utility, that is, the intensity of satisfaction that consumers derive from the consumption of goods. However, utility is beyond the confines of Marx's analysis because of its subjective as opposed to the objective and, therefore, quantifiable character of labour time.

labour time for the production of each commodity consists of the direct or living labour engaged in its production and the indirect labour, that is, the labour time which is materialized into the production inputs. According to Marx, the total amount of abstract labour time incorporated in a commodity is its 'immanent measure of value' (*Capital* I, p. 403).

1.4.3   Socially Necessary Labour Time

The value of a commodity is equal to the quantity of socially necessary abstract labour time required for its production. Hence, particular attention must be paid in order to comprehend the exact meaning of Marx's concept of socially necessary abstract labour time, which differs from the undifferentiated amount of labour used by the classical economists. According to Marx, socially necessary labour time is defined as:

> [...] The labour time required to produce any value with the existing social normal conditions of production and with the social average degree of skills and labour-intensity.
>
> (*Capital* I, p. 53)

This means that the unit value of a commodity is directly proportional to the amount of the socially necessary labour time required for its production, and it is therefore inversely proportional to labour productivity. We should note that the socially necessary labour time required in the production of a commodity may change because of technological innovations that reduce the abstract labour time requirements per unit of output; in this sense, the notion of the socially necessary labour time is independent of any particular concrete labour. A related often-cited historical example that Marx mentions is that of England during the period in which the mechanical loom began to displace the hand operating one, resulting in a reduction by 50% in the socially necessary labour time needed to produce a given quantity of fabric. The hand loom weavers soon realized that the value of their commodity was halved not because in the reduction of their own labour time but because of the introduction of the mechanical loom which doubled the labour productivity and reduced in half the socially necessary labour time needed to produce a given quantity of fabric.

In Marx's *Capital*, the term socially necessary labour time (SNLT) is used in two senses.

- SNLT in the first sense presupposes equilibrium conditions in the market (supply equal to demand). According to this first meaning, the SNLT is equal to the total labour time spent on the production of all commodities of an industry over the number of commodities produced (*Capital* I, p. 39). Hence, there is no difference between total demand and supply for the produced commodity.
- The second sense of the SNLT is related to demand and does not require the equality between supply and demand. If the amount of labour spent on the production of a commodity falls short of that actually demanded in the market. In other words, the total labour time spent on the production of the commodity in

question falls short of what is deemed socially necessary by the consumers, and so its market price is expected to rise. The converse will be true, if the amount of labour time spent on a commodity is in excess of that demanded (*Capital* III, p. 635).[15] It should be stressed that the value (equilibrium price) of a commodity is determined by the SNLT in the first sense while the SNLT in the second sense refers to the relation between market prices and the normal (equilibrium) price.

Although the notion of average SNLT (in the first sense) is an extremely good first approximation of the value of a commodity, nevertheless at a lower level of abstraction, as in *Capital* III, the notion of SNLT is expanded to account for the specific conditions prevailing in each particular industry. For example, in agriculture or mining, the value of the commodities is determined not by the average but rather by the marginal conditions, that is, the type of land that production will be expanded or contracted, which is usually the least fertile one because the more fertile lands are already cultivated. The converse might be true in industries which use advanced techniques or capitals as is the case, for instance, in the capitals activated in the information or high-technology industries. The relation of the SNLT with the marginal conditions of production is presented in Chaps. 5 and 6 where we discuss and empirically test the Marxian theory of competition and we grapple with the concepts of regulating capital and the associated with it dominant technique.

Finally, the magnitude of a commodity's value depends not only on the quantity but also on the quality of labour. On this basis, we must distinguish between simple and complex labour. Simple labour does not require any special training or particular skills; in contrast, complex or specialized labour requires a preparatory training phase during which the worker acquires the required skills and knowledge. Consequently, 1 hour of skilled labour should create a multiple value compared to the value created by 1 hour of unskilled labour. This is an old issue that Ricardo was from the first in the classical political economy that dealt with in an effective and in our view lasting until our days way:

> In speaking [...], however, of labour, as being the foundation of all value, and the relative quantity of labour as almost exclusively determining the relative value of commodities, I must not be supposed to be inattentive to the different qualities of labour, and the difficulty of comparing an hour's or a day's labour, in one employment, with the same duration of labour in another. The estimation in which different qualities of labour are held, comes soon to be adjusted in the market with sufficient precision for all practical purposes, and depends much on the comparative skill of the labourer, and intensity of the labour performed. The scale, when once formed, is liable to little variation. If a day's labour of a working jeweller be more valuable than a day's labour of a common labourer, it has long ago been adjusted, and placed in its proper position in the scale of value.
>
> (*Works I*, pp. 20–21)

---

[15]These two concepts of socially necessary labour time have been extensively analysed by Shaikh (1982, 1984 and 1998) and also by Mandel (1984) and Catephores (1989, pp. 44–45).

Wage differentials in classical political economy are taken as evidence of differences in skills which persist over long time, and it is argued that higher wages correspond to higher productivity of labour and vice versa. A prerequisite of this is that the labour market functions without impediments; Botwinick (1993), based on his theoretical and empirical analysis for the US economy, argues that market forces are dominant and overcome in the long run any obstacles that prohibit the proper operation of the labour market.

1.5   The Law of Value in Marx

The discussion thus far brings to the fore the most fundamental contradiction in the operation of capitalism, a contradiction that has to do with the anarchy of the production process, where huge numbers of participants each acting independently and in isolation of the others having the same purpose, namely, the extraction of the maximum possible profits. In this system there is no any central authority to dictate to each one of the participants how to organize the labour and the production process in general. Every one of the participants anticipates the market outcome and finds the results of such anticipation in the market. The market in other words is the coordinating mechanism whose results are almost never correctly anticipated by the participants, and all the outcomes are likely to occur, sometimes for some producers surprisingly favourable and other times disappointingly unfavourable.

The market system is an entire network of production and exchange processes where each and every individual production process presupposes that the other similarly motivated production processes will simultaneously take place. Moreover, individual supplies and demands will precisely match to each other, and such extremely subtle and difficult to organize coordination will take place not only once but time and again; furthermore, the system will be, in the long run, at least growing. Such a coordination of privately assumed production processes takes place in the sphere of exchange, where individual producers first recognize through the signals of prices and profit the extent to which their production efforts are sufficiently rewarded or not and accordingly adjust their future plans and behaviour.

However, on further consideration, we discover that the fluctuations in prices and profits are not random but are determined by their 'centres of gravitation'. These 'centres' at a high level of abstraction, that is, in the analysis of *Capital* I, are the values of commodities, which in turn are determined by the socially necessary labour time. In short, Marx argued that:

- The socially necessary abstract labour time, directly and indirectly embodied in a commodity, is the regulator of the movement of its market price.
- Prices are the means through which capitalists realize their profits or losses and regulate their actions accordingly.

These two relations constitute 'the law of value' according to which:

- Prices and profits are the direct regulators of the reproduction process.

- The socially necessary labour time is the regulator of prices and profits and therefore of the social reproduction.

In Marx, the law of value is very similar to Smith's 'invisible hand' since it explains how a capitalist society is reproduced and on what scales of reproduction, namely, increasing, stationary or even declining. Smith's 'invisible hand' is Marx's 'law of value', which is relevant only for an economy characterized by a 'generalized' commodity production, that is, a capitalist economy, where the commodities form the material basis of social reproduction and the production takes place without being linked to social needs in any direct way.[16]

It follows that both abstract labour and value are not notional or metaphysical but real in that both are quantifiable. In capitalist production, the use values are produced as commodities, and the whole production process is characterized by the fact that the exchange value of a commodity constitutes the dominant side of the entire production process. Consequently, use values are considered commodities from the time of production (conception), and the labour is, at the same time, concrete and abstract from the outset of the production process.

It is important to stress at this point that the labour which is employed in the production of commodities creates value, while the labour employed in the exchange simply realizes this value in money form (see Chap. 9). This point is worth reiterating because it has been the source of much discussion and confusion in the post-Marxian literature where it has been claimed that the exchange process is what validates the labour expended in production and renders its abstract character; so the value is validated in the process of exchange. This argument has been advanced by many Marxist economists inspired by Rubin's (1928) work and continues to more recent authors (Mohun 1984). The careful reader of Rubin's book (1928, p. 148 and 155), however, would also find that the abstract labour is already determined in production and is modified in exchange.

1.6 Money and Price

The 'law of value' has special meaning in Marx's analysis according to which commodities in the exchange process reflect the presence of the abstract labour time expended on their production. The abstract socially necessary labour time becomes the regulator of the prices of commodities. In other words, the price of a commodity reflects the quantity of the socially necessary abstract labour time required for its production.[17] The price of a commodity is the monetary expression

---

[16]The resemblance of Marx's law of value with Smith's invisible hand is discussed in Shaikh (1984) but also in Mandel (1984) and Catephores (1989).

[17]It is worth noting that in Marx's analysis the magnitude of the value of a commodity is defined by its current reproduction cost in terms of abstract labour and not by its historical reproduction cost (*Capital* I, p. 39).

of its labour value in the sphere of exchange as Marx's analysis of the various forms of value shows in *Capital* I. In fact, the analysis in *Capital* I is conducted at a high level of abstraction, and it does not even require the mediation of money except in its role as the general equivalent (or universal commodity) through which the process of exchange becomes transparent in as much as the individual characteristics of each labour are removed, thereby reducing it into labour activity in general, that is, abstract labour. Barter, so often mentioned in orthodox economic analyses as if it were a historical stage of exchange without money proper, has actually never existed in any systematic and generalized form a historical mode of exchange, because there has always been a universal commodity (money) that served as a facilitator or mediator of exchange. When Marx refers to price as a form of value, he in effect means that the value of a commodity is reflected in its money price and not in its relative value, as it happens in neoclassical economics whose focus is on relative prices; therefore in neoclassical approach any commodity may play the role of the numéraire commodity, and the passage from relative prices to absolute prices is without much meaning.

At first glance, it is obvious that there are as many ways to express the exchange value of a commodity as the number of all the other commodities. Yet such a comparison procedure is complex on the one hand and presents difficulties in the operation of exchange on the other. Consequently, it becomes necessary for a commodity to be excluded from the rest and to become the money commodity that is the commodity in terms of which all the other commodities will express their value. This particular commodity is called the 'general equivalent' or the 'universal commodity'. Historically, the precious metals such as gold and silver have played this role. Gold can function as the 'universal commodity', since it contains value and, therefore, exchange value along with other unique properties which we grapple with in the Appendix of Chap. 7. Consequently, the money price of a commodity constitutes the external measure of its exchange value, that is, the form that value takes in exchange.

1.7 Surplus-Value and Profit

For Marx, labour activity is fundamental for the production of use values which constitute the material wealth of any society. Without labour activity, no society can be sustained, let alone be reproduced on an expanded scale. The reason is that labour activity on the one hand produces the social wealth and on the other hand determines and reproduces the existing social relations of production.

In all past societies, prerequisite for the reproduction of the dominant social class (or classes) was the withholding of the surplus generated by the work of the dominated classes. This means that for the ruling classes the only way possible for the maintenance of their *status quo* was to force the subordinate classes to produce use values in excess of those actually required for their own reproduction. Indeed, the subordinate classes were forced to work harder and for a longer time than that which was necessary for their own reproduction, and the surplus use values produced were appropriated by the ruling classes; hence, the exploitative relationships of the past were quite transparent and therefore easily understood. By way of example, in slavery, the slave class was creating the surplus, and the masters were the legitimate, so to speak, recipients of this; in addition, the whole process seemed quite plausible for both the dominant and dominated classes. The dominant class morally justified this exploitative relationship by arguing that the slaves were worthy of their position because instead of dying fighting in the battlefield, they preferred their captivity, and therefore their enslavement was their best option. A similar justification can be made for the feudalistic society, where the serfs, in the usual description, were working certain days of the week for their own needs and the rest in the estate of the landlord. The serfs were involved in this exploitative relationship and exchanged their surplus (or overtime) for protection by the feudal lord either from possible external raids or from natural disasters by getting protection they needed within the castle of their lord. Everything seemed fairly normal as each in this society was born to serve the others, that is, the serfs served the feudal lord, the feudal lord served the pope and the pope served the God. Turning now to capitalism, the exploitative relations continue to be present, Marx argued, albeit are much more complex for they are 'hidden' under the veil of equivalent exchange taking place through the mediation of money.

In order to show the exploitative nature of capitalism where the surplus is called surplus-value and it is distributed (mainly as profits and rents) to the exploitive classes, Marx made the novel and very crucial distinction between labour and labour power. According to him, labour power is defined as:

> all the intellectual and physical capabilities available to a human being, who carries them when producing use values of any kind.
>
> (*Capital* I, p. 186)

Labour is defined as the use of the labour-power, i.e. the amount of useful labour performed by a labourer in a given period (e.g. a working day). As already discussed, according to the LTV, the amount of labour contained in the production of a commodity determines its value; hence, the value of the labour power—like the value of any other good bought by the entrepreneur—equals to the SNLT required to produce the commodities purchased by the worker in order to reproduce himself and his family or, what amounts to the same thing, to guarantee the normal supply of labour services. According to Marx, the labour time required to produce the workers' means of subsistence during a working day is less than the labour time a labourer provides to entrepreneur during a workday. Hence, workers produce more value than the equivalent of their wage paid by the entrepreneur for the use of their labour power. Marx calls this difference 'unpaid-labour' and 'surplus-labour' and considers it as the source of the social surplus forming the salient feature of capitalism and its exploitative nature.

In order to prove the existence of surplus labour and therefore exploitation in capitalism, Marx initially assumes that the monetary value of each commodity is proportional to the total socially necessary abstract labour needed for its production.

For the production of any commodity, two forms of abstract labour are required: dead labour (c) and living labour (l).

- Dead labour refers to non- (directly at least) labour inputs (i.e. raw materials and intermediate input flows, in general, as well as capital assets) used in the production process. The raw materials transfer their value entirely to the new product during the production process, while capital assets transfer their value only fractionally through depreciation. Marx calls the above two costs (raw materials and depreciation) constant capital.
- Living labour refers to labour flows, for example, 8 h a day times the number of workers. Workers sell their labour power, i.e. their ability to work, and wages are proportionate to the number of labour hours that workers must put forward in order to produce the necessary means of their survival. Marx calls variable capital (v) the portion of the total capital set to pay for the wages.

The division of total capital into constant and variable capital purposefully adopted by Marx in order to indicate that the term 'variable capital' signifies that in the production process labour power creates more value than the value needed for its own reproduction; in other words, it changes (increases) the value of the utilized inputs. The term 'constant capital' on the other hand signifies that in the formation of the value of the new product, the means of production merely transfer their own value and create no new value. It is worth noting that the division of total capital into constant and variable capital is in sharp contrast with the classical division of total capital into fixed and circulating capital where the circulating (or 'variable' in neoclassical analysis) capital includes the costs of labour along with other inputs. The classical economists (see, e.g. Ricardo) as well as neoclassical economists assume that the circulating capital changes with the amount of output produced, while the fixed capital is what is being installed and remains the same.

If the value of a commodity is proportional to the overall labour (dead and living) required for its production, then the total value of the new commodity will be

$$\lambda = c + l \tag{1.28}$$

where λ denotes the value of a commodity and the other symbols as above. The cash value equivalent to production cost is proportional to the sum of constant and variable capital. From the above analysis, it can be shown that profits may exist, if and when the following holds true:

$$\underbrace{c+l}_{\text{value}} > \underbrace{c+v}_{\text{cost}} \tag{1.29}$$

From relation (1.29) it follows that $l > v$, that is, the labour time spent on production is higher than that required for the production and reproduction of the labour power. This is the reason why, the excess or surplus labour time, $l - v > 0$, we call it surplus-labour or surplus-value, s. It is worth noting that in the above description all commodities (including the commodity labour power) are supposed to be sold at their values. Thus, exploitation is shown not only in the obvious and easy case in which the worker is paid a wage lower than the normal one but rather in the difficult and not obvious case in which the worker is paid the normal wage.[18]

The process of creation of new value and surplus-value can be represented symbolically by the circuit of productive capital, according to which the capitalists advance money (M) to buy commodities as inputs (C). These commodities are divided into two categories: means of production, such as raw materials and machinery, and labour power; in other words, the capitalists invest in constant (c) and variable (v) capital. As already mentioned, constant capital consists of circulating and fixed capital; in the production process, the value of circulating capital (raw materials) is wholly transferred into the value of produced commodities, while the value of fixed capital is transferred into the value of commodities piecemeal through depreciation. In addition, the variable capital is invested in the purchase of labour power. The production process (P) is completed with the production of new commodities (C') which not only are different than those in the beginning of the production process (C) but also they are of higher value ($C' > C$) for they include the surplus-value which, when sold, can raise an amount of money (M') greater than that originally invested (M), that is, $M' > M$. The above circuit of (productive) capital can be written

$$M - C <^c_v \cdots P \cdots C' - M' \tag{1.30}$$

The surplus or profit is the difference between the two ends of this circuit, i.e. $\Delta M = M' - M$. We observe that money capital is used to produce more money capital. In other words, money is a self-expanding value, and the acquisition of more money or profit becomes the 'determining purpose' of the capitalist process of production. It is worth pointing out that there is no guarantee that the above circuit will be necessarily successful; it can be interrupted at any stage. In addition, the production process takes place in real time something that is indicated in the above circuit by the dots before and after P.

It is worth noting that the means of production in of themselves are not regarded capital, unless they are combined with labour power engaged for the production of new commodities which, in order to be meaningful, the value produced must be greater than that initially brought into the circuit of production. It is obvious that in Marx's analysis, capital is a social relation of production that appears in a historically determined society; on the contrary for the classical (Smith and Ricardo) and neoclassical economists, the produced means of production are considered capital irrespective of the prevailing production relations. Indeed, in Marx, capital is not necessarily an object, such as a machine or a tool, but a social relation between the holders (owners) of the means of production and the possessors of labour power. In

---

[18]Methodologically, Marx (like Ricardo) always attempts to prove the consistency of his theory under the least favourable for his theory circumstances. This does not necessarily mean that the assumptions should or can be unrealistic; to the contrary, the assumptions on which a theory is based must be realistic for the phenomenon under study.

fact, capital is a value or rather a set of values (commodities), and it is only under a particular organization of the society that these specific commodities (machinery, tools and means of production in general) become capital (see Mandel 1991; Shaikh 1990; Tsaliki 2006).

1.8 Summary and Conclusions

In this chapter, we showed that the aim of a theory of value is to determine the centres of gravitation for the ever-fluctuating market prices. For the identification of these centres of gravitation, classical economists and Marx consider, as givens (data) of their analysis the level of output, the real wage and the production technique whose exact meaning and use we discuss further in Chap. 2 dealing with physio-crats' *Tableau Économique* and subsequently with Marx's schemes of reproduction. These same givens are utilized in Chap. 3, focusing on Marx's derivation of prices of production (or natural prices); and in Chap. 4 testing empirically the explanatory power of the classical approach with respect to the economy's actual prices. More-over, we argued that in the tradition of the classical political economy, a theory of value is absolutely necessary to identify and meaningfully assess the social surplus (or surplus-value) produced which takes on mainly the forms of profit, rent, interest and taxes.

We showed that Smith and Ricardo begin their analysis by considering labour as the source of the wealth (and of the surplus) of a society and attempted to determine prices through the quantity of labour. But as we have seen, Smith abandoned this effort, as he observed that going from primitive to modern economies, the relative prices of commodities are no longer equal to relative quantities of labour because of the presence of capital and wage labour. Ricardo, in contrast, argued that the LTV holds also in the modern capitalist economy, although in a modified form which, however, does not deviate significantly (hence the famous 7% deviation or 93% convergence) from what the pure LTV postulates. More importantly, Ricardo understood that the factors that modify the fundamental principle of relative prices being determined by relative quantities of labour times can be identified and therefore can be subjected to abstract theorization.

Marx, contrary to Smith and Ricardo, considers that only in capitalism, i.e. in a 'generalized' commodity production system, the LTV fully applies; furthermore, he argues that the fluctuations in the market price of commodities are around their values which are determined by the abstract labour time needed for their production. According to Marx, the notion of abstract labour cannot exist in the pre-capitalist societies because market forces had not been developed or operated in any system-atic way; thus, any attempt to discover laws of motion of market phenomena in these primitive societies makes no sense. Only in the capitalist mode of production does the market mechanism shapes the laws of motion behind the economic phenomena and assigns meaning to the efforts to unfold the systematic forces that operate behind the surface economic categories of prices and the forms in which surplus comes into sight, namely, profit, rent on land, interest, taxes and royalties in general.

Furthermore, we may argue that in the classical analysis in general there are solid foundations on which to build a microeconomic theory (in modern terms). As we shall see in the following chapters, based on data from input-output tables, employment and invested capital, we can determine the equilibrium prices which are consistent with Ricardo's intuition and of course Marx's analysis.

Chapter 2
Circular Flow of Capital and Social Reproduction

I agree with Morishima (and I think, with Joan Robinson and Nicholas Kaldor) that Marx's volume II models of simple and extended reproduction have in them the important germ of general equilibrium, static and dynamic. If Schumpeter reckoned Quesnay, by virtue of his Tableau Économique, *among the four greatest economists of all time, Marx's advance on Quesnay's Tableau should win him a place inside the Pantheon.*

Paul Samuelson (1974, Vol. 4)

Abstract Starting with Quesnay's *Tableau Économique* and Marx's schemes of simple reproduction, CPE analysis shows that the system is not only capable of reproducing itself on the same scale but also is endowed with a relentless drive for expansion and steady growth, according to Marx's schemes of expanded reproduction. Both simple and (steady) expanded reproduction are only hypothetical because, in reality, economic growth is periodically punctuated by long-lasting slowdowns in economic activity. Therefore, economic growth and crises are inherent salient features of the *modus operandi* of the capitalist system. In this chapter, the schemes of reproduction are cast in terms of input-output tables, and estimates of labour values and their monetary expression (direct prices), alongside prices of production, are obtained. These estimates are preparatory before we proceed to those derived using input-output data from a number of actual economies.

Keywords Tableau Économique · Schemes of reproduction · Direct prices · Prices of production · Input-output · Eigenvalues

© Springer Nature Switzerland AG 2019
L. Tsoulfidis, P. Tsaliki, *Classical Political Economics and Modern Capitalism*,
https://doi.org/10.1007/978-3-030-17967-0_2

2.1   Introduction

Social reproduction, on simple or expanded scale, is one of the key issues of the classical political economy. The physiocratic school of economic thought that emerged in the pre-revolutionary France dealt for the first time systematically with the question of creation of surplus and social reproduction in their famous *Tableau Économique*. Although a distinct school of economic thought, nevertheless physiocrats' approach is in the classical political economics (CPE) tradition because of the use of the same set of data, namely:

- The level and composition of output
- The real wage
- The state of technology

In the physiocratic analysis, the social surplus (*s*) is defined as the difference between the output (*x*) produced and the labour (*l*) and non-labour (*nl*) inputs used in production. Formally

$$s = x - (l + nl) \tag{2.1}$$

Naturally, the above residually determined surplus is disposed of by society in order to reproduce itself on any possible scale. The particular scale of reproduction, however, depends on the way in which the surplus is allocated between production and consumption. The more (less) the surplus is allocated to production, the higher (lower) the scale of reproduction; this is equivalent to saying that the way in which surplus is spent determines whether the economy will expand, contract or remain stationary.

The key issue here is the measurement of surplus which appears in its physical form, that is, in a vector whose particular elements are quantities of heterogeneous goods and productive services that have to be evaluated. Evaluations, however, presuppose the homogenization of the heterogeneous elements of the vectors expressing them in common units of measurement and in so doing enable proper interpretations, reliable estimations and therefore meaningful comparisons. Physiocrats dealt with this problem by assuming that corn is both an input and output at the same time; as a consequence, the amount of surplus and its ratio over total inputs, that is, the rate of profit, could be estimated. The use of corn as the measurement unit of both inputs and output produced, according to Sraffa's interpretation, was intially adopted by Ricardo (*Works* I, p. xxxii, *inter alia*) in his famous (*aka* 1814) but hotly debated 'corn model' (see Eatwell 1980; Gehrke and Kurz 1995, p. 74 and the literature cited). The super-simplyfying assumption of expressing both inputs and output in terms of a single commodity, i.e., corn, was abandoned later by Ricardo as we know from his correspondence to Malthus and soon became imperative to reduce the vector of outputs in terms of prices (values), making thus possible the meaningful assessment of surplus and its forms of appearance, that is, profits, rents, interest and taxes.[1]

---

[1]Details on the estimations of equilibrium prices and rate of profit can be found in the sections below as well as in Chap. 3.

Physiocrats were the first that presented a comprehensive discussion of the importance of surplus and the way that it should be allocated to different activities so as society to attain at least a state of reproduction on the same scale. However, physiocrats attributed the creation of surplus to nature; namely, surplus was viewed as 'a gift of nature' simply because it was much more transparent in agricultural production, whereby a given invested quantity of corn could, on the one hand, sustain the workers, and, on the other hand, it could be used as input with the output being a multiple of the original investment. Hence, surplus, that is, the difference between total corn output and labour and non-labour corn inputs, was seen by physiocrats as the result of nature's surplus-generating capacity. This view of surplus creation is the salient difference between the physiocrats and economists in the classical tradition, mainly Smith, Ricardo and Marx, who regarded labour instead of nature as the source of surplus.

There is no doubt that physiocrats' greatest contribution to economic thought is the *Tableau Économique* (Quesnay 1758), with the aid of which, they placed surplus creation in the centre of the discussion of social reproduction. This great contribution of the physiocrats was not fully understood, and therefore its scientific value could not be fully appreciated by the first classical economists. This is certainly true for Smith who, although spent two years in France and had discussions with the major physiocrats and held Quesnay in high esteem recognizing in him "the very ingenious and profound author of this system" while the importance of the *Tableau Économique* was rather downplayed to mere "arithmetical formularies" (*Wealth*, p.637). The same is true with Ricardo who does not deal with reproduction or the *Tableau Économique* in any formal way. In contrast, Marx understood in depth the physiocratic theory of reproduction which became the source of inspiration for the development of his own theory of the schemes of social reproduction. The reproduction theory revived in the early twentieth century in the writings of a number of authors starting with Vladimir Dmitriev (1868–1913) and continued with Ladislaus Bortkiewicz (1868–1931) and Georg Charasoff (1877–1931) as well as with the so-called material balance accounts utilized in the former Soviet Union. These developments were further concretized in Leontief's input-output analysis and in Sraffa's linear models of production and models of modern economic growth theory.[2]

In the remainder of the chapter, we deal with Quesnay's *Tableau Économique* and explore the relevant issues connected to Marx's schemes of simple and expanded reproduction. The latter are critically evaluated, and they are contrasted to modern growth models developed by Harrod (1948) and Domar (1946). A short description of input-output tables and economic analysis follows, which enable us to cast both the *Tableau Économique* and the schemes of reproduction in input-output form. We show that this formalization may be fruitfully generalized and may inspire the development of alternative and more effective macroeconomic and growth theories.

---

[2]For the relation between Sraffa and Leontief, see Kurz and Salvadori (2000, p. 169) and Baumol (2000).

2.2 The *Tableau Économique*

Physiocrats used their *Tableau Économique* to address the following question: how does the distribution of social product among the three social classes (landlords, industrialists and farmers) take place in order for society to reproduce itself at least on the same scale? In order to follow their argument, we use Quesnay's numerical example and monetary units, and we hypothesize that at the beginning of the production process (autumn), farmers have already collected their output, the value of which is estimated at 5 milliards.[3] Farmers for the production of this output employed:

- Circulating capital (wages, raw materials, etc.) worth of 2 milliards
- Advanced capital (tools, animals, etc.) whose depreciation equals to 1 milliard (10% out of 10 milliards of invested capital)

In other words, farmers invested 3 milliards as inputs and produced output worth 5 milliards. The additional 2 milliards worth of output is the surplus that is taken by landlords as rent in order to grant farmers the right of cultivating their land. Subsequently, landlords spend the 2 milliards of their rent income on agricultural and industrial products. Finally, industrialists or the 'sterile' class begin the new production period with a stock of industrial goods of 2 milliards from last year's production.

As a consequence, in the beginning of production period, the three social classes (or rather sectors) under investigation possess (either in money or commodity form) the following:

- Farmers: Agricultural goods worth 5 milliards denoted by a.
- Landlords: Rents of 2 milliards in money form, denoted by m, which they have received from farmers to grant them the right to cultivate the land
- Industrialists: Industrial products, denoted by i, of 2 milliards

This initial position and subsequent transactions are presented in Fig. 2.1.

The dashed arrows represent money flows of 1 milliard, while the flows of goods are presented by solid arrows. The distribution of social product is made in the following five transactions:

- Landlords exchange with farmers 1 milliard (m), in order to buy agricultural products of equal value (a).
- Landlords exchange 1 milliard (m) with industrialists in order to buy luxury goods of equal value (i).
- Industrialist exchange 1 milliards (m) with farmers for raw material of equal value (a).
- Farmers exchange 1 milliard (m) with industrialists for industrial goods (raw materials) of equal value (i).

---

[3]Milliard is the physiocratic monetary unit.

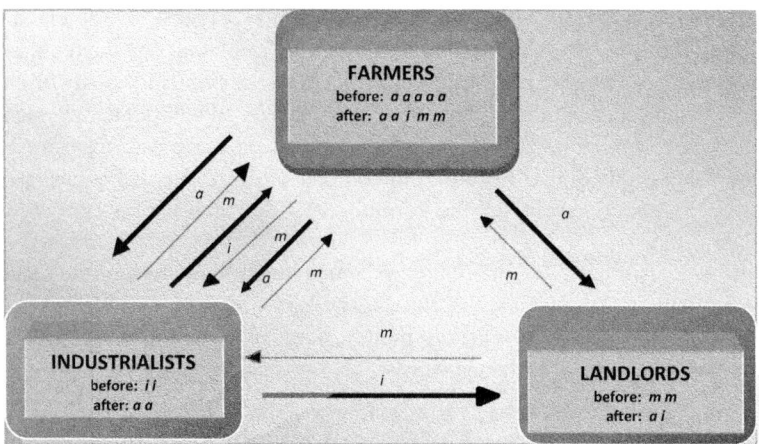

Fig. 2.1 The distribution of social product among social classes

- Industrialists with 1 milliard (m) in their disposal buy from farmers goods of equal value (a).

After the above allocations, farmers have at their disposal agricultural products worth 2 milliards to be utilized for both their productive consumption (i.e., corn consumed by workers) and investment requirements (corn as an input, i.e., seed) and industrial products worth 1 milliard, while the remainder 2 milliards are the rent requirement of the landlords to grant cultivation rights to the farmers for the new production period. The industrialists possess agricultural products which are to be transformed into industrial ones in the new production period. Finally, landowners have agricultural and industrial goods worth 1 milliard each, for their necessary consumption and luxury needs, meanwhile they expect to receive their rents from the farmers in order to grant them cultivation rights. Consequently, everything is set for the new production period to begin.

The physiocratic analysis of social reproduction relates to simple reproduction in which there is neither increase nor decrease in total output produced, and this is because the generated surplus is spent entirely on consumption (luxury) purposes by the landlords. There is nothing left for investment besides for replacement of raw materials and depreciation; hence, the net investment is zero. However, the analysis can be easily extended to include the case of expanded reproduction, that is, reproduction with economic growth. For example, if landowners invest their surplus instead of consuming it, or if farmers somehow succeed to decrease their rents and thus have more to invest, they will end up with even more output, higher surplus and so forth.

It is worth pointing out that in the physiocratic analysis, society is divided into social classes with distinct roles and interests. In addition, there is a clear distinction of the money flows from those goods; money and goods are moving in opposite directions, and in that movement, goods circulate the money rather than the other way around. Money simply facilitates the circulation of goods; in other words,

money mediates in order to carry out the transactions between social classes
(or sectors). Furthermore, the quantity of money required for conducting the required
transactions is much smaller than the value of goods in circulation since many of the
transactions may cancel each other out and may take place even without the physical
presence of money; that is, money functions in its ideal presence as a measure of
value! These conclusions drawn from the functioning of the *Tableau Économique*
can be proved extremely useful in the formulation of a theory of money (see
Appendix 1 in Chap. 7).

Hence, the monetary needs of circulation are much lower than those of the value
of goods in circulation; the reason is that goods are either consumed or invested and
thus disappear from circulation, whereas money remains in circulation ready to
mediate in new transactions. In Marx's words:

> But in fact it was an attempt to portray the whole production process of capital as a *process of
> reproduction*, with circulation merely as the form of this reproductive process; and the
> circulation of money only as a phase in the circulation of capital; at the same time to include
> in this reproductive process the origin of revenue, the exchange between capital and revenue,
> the relation between reproductive consumption and final consumption; and to include in the
> circulation of capital the circulation between consumers and producers (in fact between
> capital and revenue).
>
> (*TSV* I, pp. 343–344)

Marx held in high esteem the physiocrats, and he especially appreciated their
Tableau Économique, for which he wrote admiringly:

> [...] and finally to present the circulation between the two great divisions of productive
> labour—raw material production and manufacture—as phases of this reproductive process;
> and all this depicted in a *Tableau* which in fact consists of no more than five lines which link
> together six points of departure or return—[and this was] in the second third of the
> eighteenth century, the period when political economy was in its infancy—this was an
> extremely brilliant conception, incontestably the most brilliant for which political economy
> had up to then been responsible.
>
> (*TSV* I, p. 344)

Clearly Marx, unlike Smith and Ricardo, not only fully realized the significance
of the physiocratic conceptualization of the *Tableau Économique* but also expanded
on their contribution in his analysis of the schemes of reproduction that we
discuss next.

2.3 Marx's Schemes of Reproduction

In his effort to develop his own *Tableau Économique*, Marx borrowed some
important elements whose details are analysed mainly in the second volume of
Capital under the generic name of schemes of reproduction. Like physiocrats,
Marx starts his presentation with the schemes of simple reproduction, and then he
advances his analysis to deal with economic growth in the schemes of expanded
reproduction. We note that in Marx the simple reproduction appears as a working
hypothesis (*Capital* II, pp. 398–399) and not as a description of how capitalism

actually operates; it only shows that the economy's reproduction is theoretically possible, and it may actually exist in the rare situation when the net investment is zero. Simple reproduction also serves to enhance our understanding of the way in which the more realistic expanded reproduction may take place.

Marx, like the physiocrats, assumes that the production time for all commodities is the year, and his analysis is performed simultaneously in labour units (or values), commodities (or use values) and direct prices (or money). The analysis in terms of values and use values refers to developments taking place in the sphere of production, while the analysis in terms of use values and direct prices refers to developments taking place in the sphere of circulation. Marx further assumes that society's total capital is divided into two departments classified into I and II according to the character of the use values produced. More specifically, Department I produce means of production (MOP) or investment goods, whereby a unit of MOP (e.g. a machine) is worth 500 €. Department II produce means of consumption (MOC), where a unit of MOC (e.g. food) is worth 500 €, while a unit of labour power (LP) employed in both departments is also worth 500 €; finally, for convenience purposes 1 labour hour is valued at 1 €.

Given the above assumptions, the total output produced in both departments will be

$$\text{Department I}: C_1 + V_1 + S_1 = X_1 \qquad (2.2)$$

$$\text{Department II}: C_2 + V_2 + S_2 = X_2 \qquad (2.3)$$

where C_i is constant capital consumed in the production of use value i (where $i = 1$, 2), V_i is variable capital employed in the production of use value i, S_i is surplus-value created during the production of use value i and X_i is the value of output in Department i. Following Marx's numerical example (*Capital* II, p. 397), the reproduction in terms of values (i.e. in terms of socially necessary labour time) will be

$$\text{Department I}: 4000C_1 + 1000V_1 + 1000S_1 = 6000X_1$$

$$\text{Department II}: 2000C_2 + 500V_2 + 500S_2 = 3000X_2$$

The same numerical example can also be written in terms of use values as follows:

$$\text{Department I}: 8MP + 2LP \rightarrow 12MP$$

$$\text{Department II}: 4MP + 1LP \rightarrow 6MC$$

Finally, the schemes of reproduction expressed in terms of direct prices will be

$$\text{Department I}: €4000C_1 + €1000V_1 + €1000S_1 = €6000X_1$$

$$\text{Department II}: €2000C_2 + €500V_2 + €500S_2 = €3000X_2$$

The schemes of reproduction pose and seek to answer the following question: how should the total output of the first year be allocated between the two departments such that production to continue uninterrupted in the next years? Clearly, the newly produced output must be sold and the money received must be invested in certain proportions between the two departments. Hence, the classical assumption of given technology defines the exact way in which the allocation of the surplus-value between departments will take place at certain proportions so as for reproduction to take place.

2.4   Schemes of Simple Reproduction

The analysis that follows is based on the following set of assumptions:

- Capitalists consume all the surplus-value produced.
- Workers spend all their wages on consumption goods.
- The rate of surplus-value is 100% and remains constant and the same in both departments.
- The value composition of capital ($C/V = 400\%$) is also constant and the same in both departments.

2.4.1   Equilibrium Between the Two Departments

In order for capitalists to be able to repeat their production on the same scale, their current output should acquire a physical form which makes possible the renewal of the means of production and the workforce employed in the current period. Therefore, the output (supply) of Department I, producing MOP, should be equal to demand for MOP from both departments; thus, for the attainment of economy's reproduction, the following equality must hold in Department I:

$$\text{Department I} : \underbrace{C_1 + V_1 + S_1}_{\text{supply}} = \underbrace{C_1 + C_2}_{\text{demand}} \qquad (2.4)$$

In other words, the total output of Department I should be equal to the economy's total demand for MOP from both departments.[4] Similarly, the economy's supply of MOC should be equal to the sum of workers' and capitalists' demand for MOC. Hence, the reproduction of the total economy on the same scale requires the following condition to hold true in Department II:

$$\text{Department II} : \underbrace{C_2 + V_2 + S_2}_{\text{supply}} = \underbrace{V_1 + V_2 + S_1 + S_2}_{\text{demand}} \qquad (2.5)$$

---

[4]Hence, we assume that the analysis is carried out in terms of direct prices.

Consequently, and after simple mathematical manipulation of Eqs. (2.4) and (2.5), for each of the two departments, we will have

$$\text{Department I} : \underbrace{V_1 + S_1}_{\text{supply}} = \underbrace{C_2}_{\text{demand}} \tag{2.6}$$

$$\text{Department II} : \underbrace{C_2}_{\text{supply}} = \underbrace{V_1 + S_1}_{\text{demand}} \tag{2.7}$$

If the above conditions hold, then the total output produced is realized in the circulation sphere in a way such that the production process can be repeated uninterrupted year after year. If, however, there is no balance, i.e. $C_2 \neq V_1 + S_1$, different implications follow on the two conditions of equilibrium [Eqs. (2.6) and (2.7)]. For example, in the case that $C_2 > V_1 + S_1$ then

- For Department I it implies that the supply of MOP falls short to the economy's demand for MOP.
- For Department II it implies that the supply of MOC exceeds the economy's demand for MOC.

The above different implications of the inequalities emerge because the analysis is carried out in terms of values or money and not in terms of use values. This is the reason why the same inequality bears different implications to each department, while this inconsistency can be resolved by casting the exchanges in terms of use values.

Although Marx's analysis is conducted mainly on the basis of two departments, it can be easily extended to three or more departments (e.g. Department III producing luxury goods) and each of the departments to industries and so forth; for instance, Department I can become more detailed by including all industries (in any available level of detail) producing MOP. The same applies to Department II, which can be divided into all possible industries comprising the respective department.

2.4.2 Exchange Between Departments

In what follows, we present the paths of money and commodities so as the conditions of social simple reproduction are fulfilled.

2.4.2.1 The Circuit of Money Capital Beginning from Department I

Let us assume following the standard presentation that capitalists of Department I initiate the exchange between departments. It is important to emphasize that similar results could have been obtained should capitalists of Department II have taken the

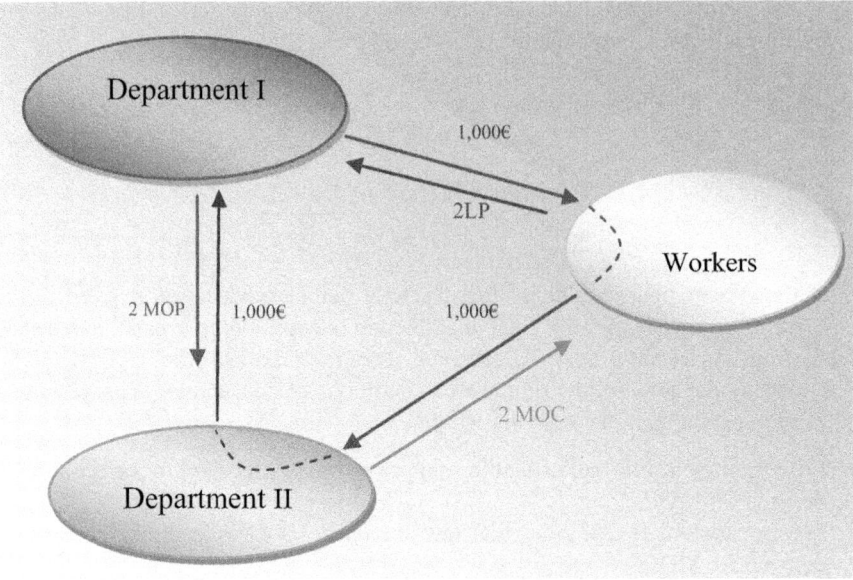

Fig. 2.2   The circuit of money capital of Department I

first step initiating the sequence of exchanges.[5] In Fig. 2.2 below, we describe the
flows of money and commodities that take place starting with Department I.

- Capitalists of Department I pay 1000 € in variable capital (wages) in order to buy
  two units of labour power (LP).
- Workers in Department I spend their wage of 1000 € to buy two units of means of
  consumption (MOC) from Department II.
- Capitalists in Department II with their 1000 € buy two units of MOP (to be used
  as constant capital) from Department I. Hence, money returns back to
  Department I, that is, to its starting point.

It is clear that money completed a full circle mediating three times in order to
exchange six units of goods (2LP, 2MOP and 2MOC). In this sequence of exchanges,
money acted as variable capital in its first mediation while in its second as workers'
income and in its third as constant capital. In addition, the velocity of money is 3, since
commodities worth of 3000 € 'changed hands' with the mediation of only 1000 €.

---

[5]The starting point of analysis in the schemes of reproduction is not relevant to the final outcome;
nevertheless, the priority to a specific department of production has tremendous social implications
as it happened in the former Soviet Union and other Eastern European countries. Even the Marshall
Plan in 1947, in one way or another, was influenced by developments taking place in the Eastern
European countries. We may speculate that the priority of the Marshall Plan to the industrialization
of the Western European economies was inspired, to some extent, by the idea that Department I
(investment goods) is more decisive for the rapid economic development than Department II
(agriculture and consumer goods sectors). Similarly, in a Kaldorian framework, manufacturing, especially the investment goods producing industries (identified with Department I) is considered the 'engine' of economic growth.

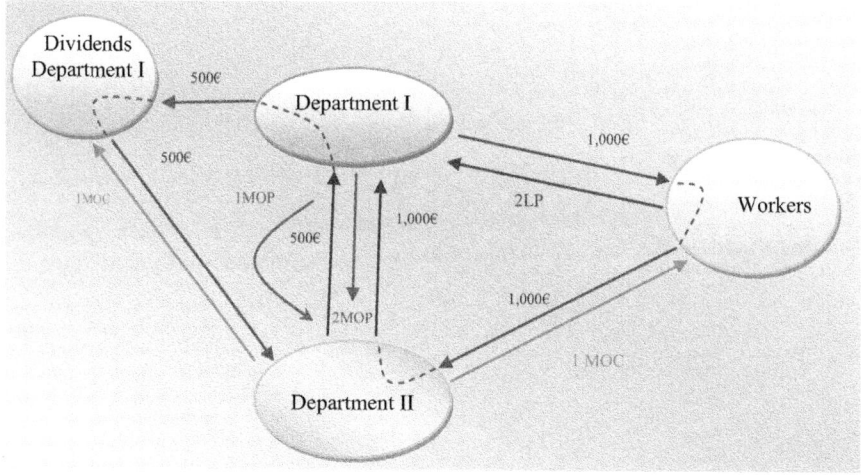

Fig. 2.3 The circuit of money capital of Department II

2.4.2.2   The Circuit of Money Capital Beginning from Department II

Our focus now is on capitalists of Department II, who in order to 'set on' the production of articles of consumption take the following actions shown in Fig. 2.3.

- The capitalists in Department II pay 500 € to capitalists in Department I in order to acquire one unit of constant capital (MOP). This amount of money now is placed in the disposal of capitalists in Department I.
- The 500 € that are now in Department I are distributed as dividends to the capitalists of the same department. Money now is out of the circuit of production and is placed in the private accounts of capitalists of Department I.
- The capitalists in Department I consume this 500 € of dividend income in order to buy MOC from Department II.

We observe that money performed, once again, a full circle to return back to its starting point, namely, the Department II. In this circle, the 500 € set in circulation two units of goods, namely, 1MOP as constant capital invested in the Department II and 1MOC which was purchased by the capitalists of Department I with their dividend income. The velocity of money, in this particular case, is equal to 2. It is also of interest to note that money, which left the circuit of capital to enter the circuit of revenue as dividends, returns back to the initial circuit.

2.4.2.3   The Circuit Beginning from Dividends of Capitalists in Department I

The next step is to keep track of the income flows (dividends) emanating from capitalists of both departments, starting from Department I (see Fig. 2.4).

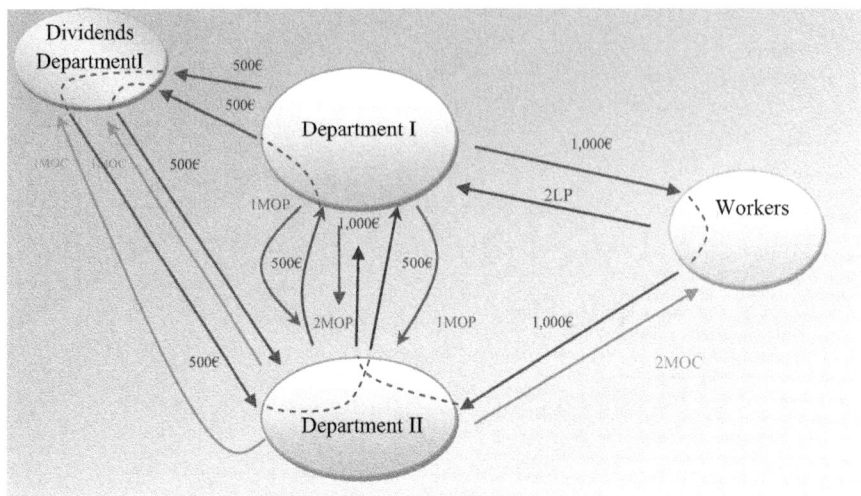

Fig. 2.4 Dividends of capitalist in Department I

- Department I distribute an additional amount of 500 € from its total capital as dividend income (which is part of the surplus-value produced) to its capitalists. Money, once again, flows out of the circuit of capital and is placed in the personal accounts of capitalists.
- Capitalists of Department I consume this additional 500 € received as dividends to buy means of consumption (1MOC) from Department II.
- In turn, the 500 € received by Department II are invested to acquire an additional unit of MOP and use it as constant capital. Hence, the additional 500 € return back to Department I, which is the starting point of the circuit.

Like in the previous case, we observe that money (500 €) set in motion two units of goods (1MOP, 1MOC) worth of total value of 1000 €. The MOP are used as constant capital in Department II, whereas the MOC are used by capitalists of Department I. The velocity of money in circulation is once again equal to 2.

2.4.3   Transactions Within Departments

2.4.3.1   Transactions Within Department I

In Fig. 2.5 we depict the following:

- The capitalists of Department I invest 4000 € in MOP (constant capital); hence, 4000 € are exchanged against 8MOP in the beginning of the production process.
- Department I uses these inputs (constant capital equal to eight units of MOP and variable capital equal to two units of LP) to set in motion the production process.

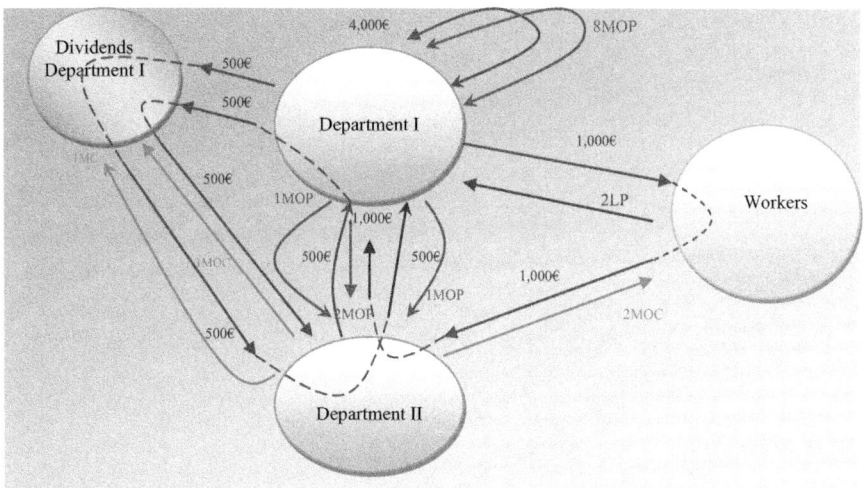

Fig. 2.5 Intra-departmental transactions in Department I

In Fig. 2.5, the flows of money make a circle within Department I, since in the present case, we are dealing with intra-departmental transactions. The same is true with the MOP. The velocity of money is now equal to 1, and money circulates as capital since it is used to buy MOP.

2.4.3.2 Transactions Within Department II

The following transactions take place in Department II:

- Capitalists in Department II invest 500 € in variable capital (1LP). Workers of Department II spend their income to buy 1MOC from Department II. Hence, money stays within the department and completes the circuit.
- Capitalists within Department II receive from themselves 500 € as dividends which they spend on consumption goods (MOC) worth of 500 €; hence, money, once again, remains within the department and completes the circuit.

In short, capitalists of Department II have in their disposal 4MOP and 1LP; hence, they are in a position to continue their production activity on the same scale. The last transactions are depicted in Fig. 2.6 together with all the previous ones.

It is important to reiterate that the transactions in the schemes of simple reproduction take place in three forms, value, money and use values, and in this way one can discern the equilibrium condition of supply and demand in each department; otherwise, as we showed in Sect. 2.4.1, an inequality, such as, $C_2 > V_1 + S_1$, might imply excess demand for Department I and excess supply for Department II. Such an inconsistency, as we explained, is resolved by referring to use values produced in each department. Furthermore, simple reproduction is absolutely consistent with the extraction of any amount of surplus-value which, however, is not invested

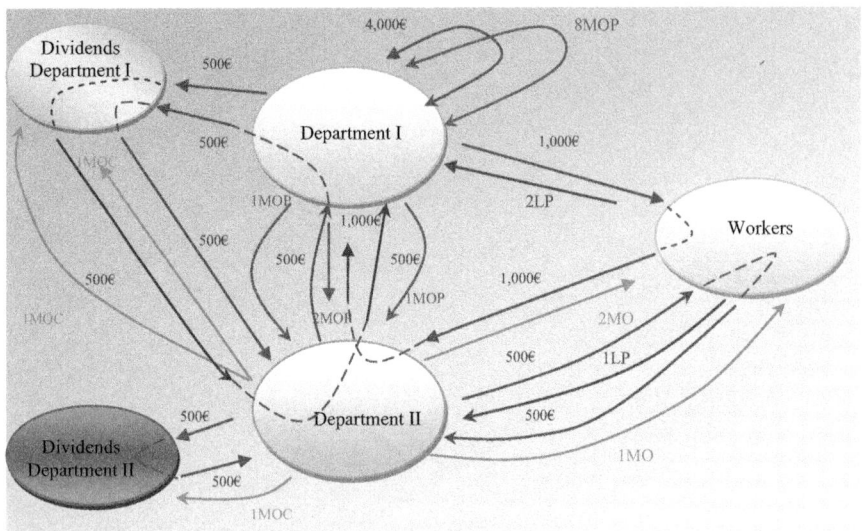

Fig. 2.6 Intra-departmental transactions in Department II

productively, but it is partly used for the replacement of means of production and partly for the unproductive consumption of capitalists. As a consequence, there is nothing left for net investment; in short, net investment is zero, a situation that rarely is met in real economies.

2.5 Schemes of Expanded Reproduction

Simple reproduction appears more as a working hypothesis and less as a realistic description of the way in which capitalism actually operates. The salient feature of capitalism, as we have pointed out time and again, is its uncontainable propensity for expansion, an expansion which is periodically interrupted by economic crises. In what follows, we describe the productive activity as a never-ending circular flow of capital activated to produce use values for the purpose of profit-making on an expanded scale. In Chaps. 8 and 10 of the book, we grapple with the discussion on possible and actual disruptions of such a process.

The transition from simple to expanded reproduction is made possible by assuming that capitalists, unlike workers, do not consume all but save part of their income, which in Marx as well as in the classical political economy approach, in general, implies that what is saved is also invested. Marx used a battery of aphorisms:

> Accumulate, accumulate! That is Moses and the prophets! [...] Therefore, save, save, i.e., reconvert the greatest possible portion of surplus-value, or surplus-product into capital! Accumulation for accumulation's sake, production for production's sake: by this formula

classical economy expressed the historical mission of the bourgeoisie and did not for a single instant deceive itself over the birth-throes of wealth.

(*Capital* I, p. 449)

The idea is that the very purpose of capitalist savings is to invest and in so doing the simple reproduction is converted to reproduction on expanded scale. It is worth noting that if we assume that capitalists save or, what is the same thing, invest all of their income, we end up with the case of maximum expanded reproduction, a complete opposite case to simple reproduction, which although hypothetical nevertheless no less useful for analytical purposes.[6]

For reasons of simplicity and clarity of presentation (the diagrams in the schemes of simple reproduction are already pretty complicated), we limit ourselves to the algebraic formalization of money or value transactions, keeping in mind that transactions in use values could also be made explicit, as in the case of simple reproduction.[7] The analysis is also limited to the usual case of schemes of expanded reproduction in which savings or net investment is greater than zero but less than their maximum. We further assume that there is no labour shortage, which is another way to say that labour supply adapts easily and rapidly to labour demand due to the ever-present reserve army of unemployed (*Capital* II, p. 505).[8]

Marx, in his numerical examples, assumes a given rate of surplus-value equal to 100% which is the same in both departments. The value composition of capital (hence, the ratio of fixed to variable capital, C/V) is equal to 4 in Department I, while in Department II it is equal to 2. This is equivalent to saying that Department I is twice more capital-intensive than Department II and also that the direct prices will be different from the respective prices of production indicating the possibility of transfers of values from the less capital-intensive to the more capital-intensive department.[9] Such a possibility, however, is excluded at the present time since the analysis is assumed to take place exclusively in direct prices. The case of prices of production is left for a more concrete level of analysis when competition of 'many capitals' takes place, giving rise to a general rate of profit.[10] Marx further assumed that half of the surplus-value produced in Department I is reinvested (accumulated) as capital and the rest is spent on consumer goods. This means that the role of Department II is passive and merely reacts in a specific way to the investment decisions of Department I, i.e. Department II adapts to developments taking place in Department I.[11]

---

[6]The Von Neumann's (1945) growth model is based on this assumption.

[7]Tsuru (1942) describes diagrammatically the conditions of expanded reproduction.

[8]See Tsaliki (2009).

[9]For further details on issues related to transfers of value, see Appendix 1 in Chap. 5 and the discussion in Chap. 7.

[10]The case of expanded reproduction in the face of prices of production (prices which incorporate a general rate of profit) is more complex but possible, as we show at the end of this chapter.

[11]As we have pointed out in the presentation of simple reproduction, the fact that the analysis begins with Department I does not imply its superiority compared to Department II. Marx begins his analysis from Department I mainly for formal reasons and not that Department I is more important than Department II.

Table 2.1 Initial scheme of year 1, ex ante

Departments	Production			
	C_i	V_i	S_i	X_i
Department I	4000	1000	1000	6000
Department II	1500	750	750	3000
Total	5500	1750	1750	9000

We start with the first numerical example given by Marx in *Capital* II (pp. 509–514) and presented in Table 2.1.

In Table 2.1 the rate of surplus-value is the same in both departments:

$$e = S/V = 100\%$$

and the value composition of capital is different between the two departments:[12]

$$\text{Department I} : g_I = [C/(C + V)]_I = 4000/(4000 + 1000) = 4/5$$
$$\text{Department II} : g_{II} = [C/(C + V)]_{II} = 1500/(1500 + 750) = 2/3$$

The production (supply) in Department I is worth 6000, whereas its demand is worth only 5500 monetary units. In Department II the production (supply) is worth of 3000, whereas its demand is 3500. It is obvious from Table 2.1 that neither the conditions of simple reproduction nor equilibrium exist. Capitalists do not consume all their surplus-value, as they did in the case of simple reproduction, but part of it is saved and by extent invested as follows:

- Capitalist of Department I invest 50% ($q_1 = 0.5$) of produced surplus-value as capital, and by assuming constant technology, it follows that part of it, that is, $4/5 = g_I = C_1/(C_1 + V_1)$ is invested as constant capital and the remaining 1/5 as variable capital $(1 - g_I) = V_1/(C_1 + V_1) = 1000/(4000 + 1000) = 1/5$. Hence, from a surplus-value of 1000, the resulting new investment amounts to 500, from which 400 is constant capital and 100 is variable capital; the remaining 500 are distributed as dividends to capitalists of Department I, who in turn buy consumer goods from Department II.
- Given the developments taking place in Department I, Department II closes the circuit so long as both the rate of surplus-value ($e = 100\%$) and its value composition of capital ($g_{II} = 2/3$) remain constant.

---

[12]The value composition of capital is written as $C/(C + V)$ instead of C/V in order to follow the usual presentation. A more detailed discussion of the various (value, materialized, technical and organic) compositions of capital is postponed until Chap. 8. It is interesting to note that although the rate of surplus-value is the same between the departments, their rates of profit are quite different. In particular Department I's rate of profit is 20%, while Department II's rate of profit is 33%, clearly a case of disequilibrium inducing adjustments which, however, can be dealt with the introduction of competition between capitals.

Starting with the data displayed in Table 2.1, the question that comes to the fore is the determination of the right share of surplus-value in Department II that should be invested in order to restore the conditions of simple reproduction. Hence, the following equilibrium condition must hold

$$\underbrace{C_1 + V_1 + S_1}_{\text{supply}} = \underbrace{C_1 + \Delta C_1 + C_2 + \Delta C_2}_{\text{demand}} \tag{2.8}$$

Replacing in Eq. (2.8) the actual figures displayed in Table 2.1 and the stipulated assumptions, we estimate the proportion of surplus-value q_2 that the Department II must invest in order to restore the conditions of simple reproduction as follows:

$$\underbrace{4000}_{C_1} + \underbrace{1000}_{V_1} + \underbrace{1000}_{S_1} = \underbrace{4000}_{C_1} + \underbrace{0.5}_{q_1} \, \overbrace{1000}^{S_1} \cdot \underbrace{1000 \cdot \left(\overbrace{\dfrac{C_1/(C_1+V_1)=4/5}{g_1}} \right)}_{\Delta C_1} + \underbrace{1500}_{C_2} + \underbrace{q_2 \cdot \overbrace{750}^{S_2} \, \overbrace{g_{II}}^{2/3}}_{\Delta C_2}$$

$$6000 = 4000 + 400 + 1500 + (q_2)(500)$$

$$q_2 = 0.20$$

Hence, 20%from a surplus-value of 750 must be invested ($0.20 \times 750 = 150$), from which 2/3 as constant capital ($\Delta C_2 = 100$) and the rest as variable capital ($\Delta V_2 = 50$). The results at the end of the year 1 are presented in Table 2.2.

Since the rate of surplus-value remains at 100% and is the same in both departments, it follows that in the beginning of the second year, we will have Table 2.3.

If capitalists of Department I continue to invest 50% of their surplus-value in a similar way as in the first year, we could re-estimate, once again, the new q_2[13] from the following:

Table 2.2 Final scheme of year 1, ex post

	C_i	V_i	S_i	X_i
Department I	4400	1100	500	6000
Department II	1600	800	600	3000
Total	6000	1900	1100	9000

Table 2.3 Initial scheme of year 2, ex ante

	C_i	V_i	S_i	X_i
Department I	4400	1100	1100	6600
Department II	1600	800	800	3200
Total	6000	1900	1900	9800

---

[13]Hence, we follow the procedure described by Marx in *Capital* II, p. 510, scheme B.

$$\underbrace{4400}_{C_1} + \underbrace{1100}_{V_1} + \underbrace{1100}_{S_1} = \underbrace{4400}_{C_1} + \underbrace{\overset{q_1}{\overset{\frown}{0.5}} \cdot \overset{S_1}{\overset{\frown}{1100}} \cdot \overset{4/5}{\overset{\frown}{g_1}}}_{\Delta C_1} + \underbrace{1600}_{C_2} + \underbrace{q_2 \cdot \overset{S_2}{\overset{\frown}{800}} \overset{2/3}{\overset{\frown}{g_{II}}}}_{\Delta C_2}$$

$$q_2 = 0.30$$

The results at the end of second year are presented in Table 2.4.

For the third year, we have Table 2.5.

The results at the end of the third year are presented in Table 2.6.

The schemes can be extended to infinity with a growth rate endogenously determined which becomes uniform and equal to 10% the second year onwards. Table 2.7 presents the evolution of the relevant figures up to the sixth year.

Table 2.4 Final scheme of year 2, ex post

	C_i	V_i	S_i	X_i
Department I	4840	1210	550	6600
Department II	1760	880	560	3200
Total	6600	2090	1110	9800

Table 2.5 Initial scheme of year 3, ex ante

	C_i	V_i	S_i	X_i
Department I	4840	1210	1210	7260
Department II	1760	880	880	3520
Total	6600	2090	2090	10,780

Table 2.6 Final scheme of year 3, ex post

	C_i	V_i	S_i	X_i
Department I	5324	1331	605	7260
Department II	1936	968	616	3520
Total	7260	2299	1221	10,780

Table 2.7 Summary results with annual growth rate of 10%

	Value of output Department I	Growth rate Department I	Value of output Department II	Growth rate Department II	Total value	Growth rate of total output	Average value profit rate $r = S/(C+V)\%$
1	6000		3000		9000		
2	6600	0.10	3200	0.07	9800	0.09	$1750/7250 = 24$
3	7260	0.10	3520	0.10	10,780	0.10	$1900/7900 = 24$
4	7986	0.10	3872	0.10	11,858	0.10	$2090/8689 = 24$
5	8784	0.10	4259	0.10	13,043	0.10	$2299/9559 = 24$
6	9662	0.10	4686	0.10	14,348	0.10	$2529/10,514 = 24$

The above discussion and numerical example of expanded reproduction leads to the following conclusions:

- The expanded reproduction is possible, and from the specific example, we conclude that it can continue to infinity.
- The growth rate of total output is endogenously determined, and it becomes uniform equal to 10% from the second year onwards.
- Only in the first year, the growth rate of total output is about 9%, as a result of the low growth rate equal to about 7% of Department II, whereas Department I grow steadily by 10%.
- From the second year foreward, both departments expand at an annual growth rate of 10%.
- The average profit rate in terms of value remains constant and equal to 24%. The same is true with the rate of surplus-value which remains constant and equal to 100% in both departments.
- Finally, the value composition of capital differs between departments, but it remains the same for all years.

These conclusions strengthen the view that Marx, following the tradition of the classical political economy, assumes the same set of givens, that is, the real wage as this is expressed in the rate of surplus-value which remains the same throughout the analysis and the technology as this is expressed in the value composition of capital which also remains the same. The level of output is always known once the rate of surplus-value and the value composition of capital are given. This does not mean that the value composition of capital does not change with the passage of time; on the contrary, both the rate of surplus-value and the value composition of capital are expected to increase. Hence, we argue that the schemes of expanded reproduction do not lack realism but rather that the study of the change in both technological change and income distribution requires the introduction of competition and a new set of prices, the prices of production, that is prices that incorporate a uniform rate of profit.

2.5.1   Critiques of the Schemes of Reproduction

From the time of their publication in 1885, the schemes of simple and extended reproduction attracted the attention of many researchers. The critiques either were levelled at the realism of the assumptions or were directed at the narrow scope of the schemes of reproduction to show the possibility, not necessarily actuality, of balanced growth and in doing so ended up to attributing to the schemes of reproduction more than there is in them. More specifically, the usual critiques referring to the seeming weaknesses or drawbacks of the schemes of reproduction and the possible responses are:

- The presence of different profit rates between the two departments without their tendential equalization is another way to say that the schemes of reproduction do not consider competition between capitals. This criticism is valid, but the differences in profitability are only due to Marx's analytical method in volumes I and II of *Capital* according to which the analysis begins by hypothesizing the case of 'capital in general', that is, the absence of competition. The implicit idea is to 'lay bare' the general 'laws of motion of capitalism' at a very abstract level, and only in the third volume of *Capital*, the analysis extends to deal with 'many capitals', that is, the case of real competition. This means that in this last more concrete level of analysis, the schemes of reproduction can be modified to account for the equalization of rates of profit between departments; however, in this case, the analysis should be carried out not in terms of labour values but in terms of prices of production. It is true that the transformation of labour values into prices of production is not without its complexities and issues of consistency (see Chap. 3), but this does not mean that such an analysis cannot be carried out (e.g. Morishima 1973; Desai 1991; Trigg 2006, inter alia). Furthermore, Marx sought to establish the basic relationships without introducing the complications arising from the distribution of surplus-value in the form of profits between the two departments.[14]

- Another often-cited, and related to the above, critique is that there is no investment activity between departments; in other words, investment takes place only within and not between departments. Furthermore, the critique continues and finds unrealistic the hypothesis that investment is only self-financed and depends exclusively on internally generated savings. As a consequence, there are neither interdepartmental flows of capital nor any credit flows. It is true that the question of various forms of money capitals (hoarding) and depreciation is not introduced into the analysis until the end of *Capital* II (Chap. XXI). Hence, we may say that in the analysis, the investment has priority over the saving and that the very purpose of capitalist savings is to finance investment activity. Hence, Marx keeps company with Keynes and Schumpeter to the extent that investment has priority over savings. After all, the circuit of capital in Marx [Eq. (1.30)] starts off with M (money), continues with investment in C (means of production and labour power), follows with production P and ends up with the production of new commodities, C', whose value is higher than the initially invested, $C' > C$, which when realized give money M' more than the initially advanced, $M' > M$. However, Marx (also Schumpeter) parts company with Keynes when it comes to the role of capitalist savings, whose very purpose is investment for the sake of profit (Kurz 2008). By contrast, Keynes argues that there is never a 'shortage of savings' which is always created as a result of the investment activity.
- The reproduction schemes have been interpreted to mean that Department I has priority over Department II, which is assumed to merely passively adjust to developments initiated in Department I. However, it can be shown that

---

[14]For instance, Marx notes that his analysis is conducted in value terms (direct price) pointing out that "the fact that prices [production] diverge from values cannot display any influence on the movements of social capital" (*Capital* II, p. 393).

investment activity could have had as its starting point the Department II with $q = 0.20$ leading to the exact same results.
- Morishima (1973) formalized the schemes of reproduction in a system of difference equations. The study of the properties of the resulting matrix of coefficients led to the conclusion that if the value composition of capital of Department I is greater than that of Department II and by assuming a given propensity to save, the resulting growth becomes explosive. Increasing oscillatory behaviour cum growth is obtained if the value composition of capital of Department II is greater than that of Department I. Given these findings, Morishima concluded that state intervention can stabilize the economy by changing the propensity to save and also by modulating the investment activity in such a way to attain the desired level of growth with minimal fluctuations.
- Capitalists are hypothesized to reinvest their profits in their department according to their value composition of capital. In other words, there is no technological change, and investment in both departments takes place on the basis of the following relation:

$$\frac{q_2}{q_1} = \frac{1 + C_2/V_2}{1 + C_1/V_1} = \frac{3}{5} = 0.6$$

A number of authors concluded that if capitalism managed to grow according to proportions specified by the schemes of expanded reproduction, the system could expand continuously (Otto Bauer 1881–1938), while any disturbance of these proportions could cause imbalances resulting in economic crises (Tugan-Baranovsky 1865–1919). This is not exactly correct, because, as we pointed out, the schemes of expanded reproduction are mainly designed to show the potentiality of capitalism to grow steadily and not that this is or could be the actual path of the system. In fact, capitalism is characterized by endemic economic growth which is interrupted by periodic crises as we show in Chaps. 8 and 10.

In the debates of the schemes of reproduction, Luxemburg (1913) criticized those who argued that capitalism can expand in a smooth and uninterrupted way. In fact, she argued that this is not possible as a result of deficiency in demand. More specifically, Luxemburg raised a number of criticisms from which in our view two stand out:

- The first criticism refers to whether and to what extent there is such a market mechanism that directs capitalists in both departments to display the very specific investment behaviour described in the schemes of reproduction. Luxemburg was the first to raise the question of system's stability, a question that was to resurface many years later by Domar's (1946) and subsequently by Harrod's (1948) analyses of warranted growth rate, which laid the foundations of the modern theory of economic growth. In the following section, we show the remarkable similarities between Domar's growth model and Marx's schemes of expanded reproduction.

- The second criticism, which is the most popular of all, relates to the deficiency in demand leading to radical conclusions. In particular, Luxemburg argued that, if we assume that capitalists invest according to the specific proportions required in the schemes of expanded reproduction, the productive capacity of the economy will expand; hence, the question she raised was: does the system find the additional consumers purchasing power to absorb the extra output produced? The counter-argument would be that the extra output could be reinvested in a way such that the demand gap could be filled. Luxemburg's response to this way out would be that the problem maybe 'contained' only temporarily, because from the next year onwards even more will be produced and so the lack of demand looms even more formidable. The effective way to deal with this problem, according to Luxemburg, is in the demand of noncapitalist sectors inside or outside of the capitalist economy, giving rise to the colonization wave in the late nineteenth and early twentieth centuries. But as she argued, eventually, both internal and external noncapitalist markets 'dry out', and society enters into a period of 'barbarism' underscoring the fact that the system reached its limits.[15]

Clearly, Luxemburg's second objection reveals that her economic analysis was based on the idea that in the capitalist mode of production, the very purpose of production is to satisfy consumption (i.e. use values) and not to exchange for money (i.e. exchange value) in order to maximize profit as a purpose in itself. Nevertheless, Marx in his schemes of expanded reproduction shows that effective demand can be sufficient to buy the available supply; that is, productive capacity and effective demand can grow at roughly the same rate with the output produced. The reason is that demand in an economy is directed to both consumer and investment goods; thus, the riddle of demand gap can find a solution in the extra demand coming from capitalists in Departments I and II who purchase both means of production and means of consumption for themselves and for the newly hired workers.

In short, Marx's purpose in the schemes of expanded reproduction was to show, among other things, the potentiality of unregulated balanced growth in a capitalist economy. In other words, Marx's purpose was not to show that the reality of capitalism might be that of balanced growth as some Marxists have argued (Tugan-Baranovsky, Otto Bauer, among others).[16] Nevertheless, regarding Luxemburg's first objection about the very specific investment behaviour of capitalists, we should point out that it still remains an open question in economic theory. Finally, it should be stressed that the reproduction schemes in *Capital* II are set to show potentialities and not to describe the exact way in which capitalist economies evolve. The reproduction schemes neither predict nor argue for the unhindered expansion of the capitalist system.

---

[15]Moreover, Luxemburg underlined that the operation of economies should not be left to the blind forces of supply and demand; but society should display the necessary political will to intervene in order to change fundamentally the system at its early stage, that is, well before the system enters the 'stage of barbarism'.

[16]These authors argued that since the reality of capitalism is the balanced growth, then only a disproportionality crisis is possible. Hence, a well-planned capitalist economy may overcome the problems resulted and attain the right proportions for a smooth and uninterrupted growth.

2.5.2 Domar's Growth Model and Marx's Schemes of Reproduction

The so-called Keynesian revolution and the associated with it macroeconomics as a distinct discipline in economic theory together with the explicit incorporation of time into the analysis brought to the fore the question of economic growth which starts with the pioneering works of Harrod (1948) and Domar (1946). Specifically, Harrod's contribution was an attempt to deal with the stability properties of capitalist growth, whereas Domar's was to determine the rate at which investment must grow to ensure the equality between aggregate demand and supply over time. Despite their differences, their growth models are aggregate formations that attempt to determine the economy's uniform equilibrium growth rate (warranted growth rate), and, as it will be shown, they share surprisingly many similarities with Marx's schemes of expanded reproduction (Lianos 1979, p. 405).

In order to reveal the similarities between Domar's growth model and Marx's schemes of expanded reproduction, we start with the standard textbook presentation of Domar's growth model. We denote income by Y, investment by I and capital stock by K; furthermore, we assume that investment equals saving and that investment (or saving) can be presented as a fraction of generated income. That is

$$I = sY \tag{2.9}$$

where s denotes the economy's constant propensity to save. By taking differences in the above relation and dividing through by the change in capital stock ($\Delta K = I$), we arrive at the familiar Keynesian multiplier. Thus, we have

$$\frac{\Delta I}{\Delta K} = s \frac{\Delta Y}{\Delta K} \text{ or } \frac{\Delta I}{I} = sa \tag{2.10}$$

The ratio $\Delta Y/I$ stands for the marginal productivity of capital or the average productivity of investment denoted by α. Thus, new investment not only leads to a multiple increase in income but also expands the economy's productive capacity according to the average productivity of investment, α. Thus, we may write

$$\Delta Y = \alpha I \tag{2.11}$$

Placing together the two alternative expressions for ΔY [Eqs. (2.10) and (2.11)], that is,

$$\Delta Y = \alpha I = \Delta I/s \tag{2.12}$$

the growth rate of investment will be

$$\Delta I/I = sa \tag{2.13}$$

and the growth rate of output from $\Delta Y = aI = a(sY)$ relation [Eqs. (2.9) and (2.12)] is

$$\Delta Y/Y = sa \tag{2.14}$$

Hence, the growth rate at equilibrium (g_w warranted growth rate) is defined as

$$g_w = \Delta Y/Y = sa = \Delta I/I \tag{2.15}$$

Equation 2.15 signifies that the requirement for the attainment of steady growth is that income and investment should grow at a specific rate determined by the product of the average (marginal) saving rate times the marginal productivity of investment. As we have already pointed out, Domar (1946) was interested in determining the rate at which investment must grow in order for the economy to attain its equilibrium growth path. Harrod (1948) arrives at the exact same condition for the attainment of steady growth but using the acceleration principle. Harrod showed that the equilibrium is not stable, that is, if for any reason the economy deviates from its warranted growth rate, it does not return to it and deviations increase, that is, the economy drifts further and further away from its steady growth path with the passage of time.

Let us now turn to Marx's schemes of expanded reproduction which are presented in Tables 2.1–2.7. The construction of Table 2.8, which refers to the developments in Department I, is straightforward, if we recall that the rate of surplus-value ($e = S/V$) is 100% and that the accumulation takes the form of additions to constant (ΔC) and variable capital (ΔV) in a way directed by the value composition of capital which for Department I is $g_I = 4/5$ and for Department II is $g_{II} = 2/3$.[17]

From Table 2.8, we observe that in the schemes of expanded reproduction, both income and investment grow at the same constant rate (10%) which is a condition found in Domar's (1946) analysis:

$$\Delta Y/Y = \Delta I/I = sa = 10\%$$

Table 2.8 Expanded reproduction in Department I

Years	Net income $Y = V + S$	Growth rate $\Delta Y/Y$	Constant capital C	Variable capital V	Surplus-value S	Net investment I	Growth rate $\Delta I/I$
1	2000	–	4000	1000	1000	–	–
2	2200	0.10	4400	1100	1100	500	–
3	2420	0.10	4540	1210	1210	550	0.10
4	2662	0.10	5324	1331	1331	605	0.10
5	2928.2	0.10	5856.4	1464.1	1464.1	665.5	0.10

---

[17]The same analysis can be applied to Department II.

In the numerical presentation of expanded reproduction of the previous section, it was assumed that half of the surplus-value produced is saved and thus invested ($S = I = 500$), resulting to an average rate to save [average propensity to save, Eq. (2.9)] equal to

$$s = I/Y = 500/2000 = 1/4$$

In addition, the average productivity of investment [a in Eq. (2.11)] is given by the change in income (200) divided by the change in constant and variable capital ($\Delta K = I = 400 + 100 = 500$) and is equal to

$$a = \Delta Y/\Delta K = \Delta Y/I = 200/500 = 2/5$$

As a consequence, from Eqs. (2.13) and (2.14), the product of the average savings rate (s) times the average productivity of investment (a) is

$$sa = (1/4) \cdot (2/5) = 0.10 = 10\% = \Delta Y/Y = \Delta I/I$$

which is equal to the growth rates of income $\Delta Y/Y$ and investment $\Delta I/I$. In other words, for a continuous expanded reproduction, the growth rate of investment should be equal to growth rate of income and equal to the product of the average saving rate times the average productivity of investment. This condition for the uninterrupted expansion of a capitalist economy is identical to the one found in Domar's growth model.

The above exposition is not affected by the numerical example used in the analysis since we can generalize it as follows: making use of the rate of surplus-value, $e = S/V$ and the distribution of net income between surplus-value and variable capital

$$Y = S + V \tag{2.16}$$

The surplus-value, after simple mathematical manipulations, can be rewritten as

$$S = [e/(1 + e)]Y \tag{2.17}$$

If a portion s is saved and thus accumulated,[18] then

$$\text{Accumulation} = \Delta K = I = sS = s[e/(1 + e)]Y \tag{2.18}$$

---

[18]In Marx's analysis workers consume all of their income, while capitalists consume part of the surplus-value they receive and save or, what is the same thing, invest the remaining according to their propensity to save.

The above equation describes capitalists' savings; moreover, the term $s[e/(1 + e)]$ corresponds to Keynes marginal (and in this case also average) propensity to save. From the definition of the value composition of capital, $\kappa = C/(C + V)$, the relationship between constant and variable capital can be derived:

$$C = \left(\frac{\kappa}{1 - \kappa}\right) V \tag{2.19}$$

and

$$\Delta C = \left(\frac{\kappa}{1 - \kappa}\right) \Delta V \tag{2.20}$$

However, $\Delta C + \Delta V = I$ and substituting for ΔC

$$I = \Delta C + \Delta V = \left(\frac{\kappa}{1 - k}\right) \Delta V + \Delta V = \frac{\Delta V}{1 - \kappa} \tag{2.21}$$

Net income, being distributed to surplus-value and variable capital [Eqs. (2.16) and (2.17)] and by some further manipulation of the equations, we arrive at

$$Y = V + S = V + eV = (1 + e)V$$

or

$$V = Y/(1 + e)$$

and

$$\Delta V = \Delta Y/(1 + e) \tag{2.22}$$

By substituting ΔV in the investment Eq. (2.21) and after simple mathematical operations, we get

$$\Delta Y/I = (1 + e) \cdot (1 - \kappa) \tag{2.23}$$

which is the average productivity of investment. It is interesting to note that the productivity of investment depends on a technological element (captured by the value composition of capital, κ) and on a distributional variable (captured by the rate of surplus-value, e). From the relation (2.23), we derive that the rate of surplus-value exerts a positive effect on the productivity of investment, whereas the value composition of capital exerts a negative one. These findings are particularly important in our discussion of economic crisis theory that we present in Chap. 8, where we show both theoretically and support empirically that the rate of profit is influenced more by the negative effect of the value composition of capital and less by the positive effect of the rate of surplus-value. Consequently, the rate of profit falls and gradually leads to a stagnant mass of profits which discourage net investment activity leading to economic crisis.

For the presence of the condition of expanded reproduction, it required a portion (s) of the surplus-value produced [Eq. (2.17)] to be accumulated, that is, to be transformed into additional capital ($\Delta K = I = \Delta V + \Delta C$). Hence it is necessary that

$$sS = s\left[\frac{e}{1+e}\right]Y = \Delta K = I = \Delta V + \Delta C \tag{2.24}$$

It is already shown from Eqs. (2.21) and (2.24) that

$$I = \Delta V/(1-\kappa) = s\left[\frac{e}{1+e}\right]Y \tag{2.25}$$

or

$$Y = I\left[\frac{1+e}{se}\right] = [\Delta V/(1-\kappa)][(1+e)/se] \tag{2.26}$$

Combining Eqs. (2.22) and (2.23), we have

$$\Delta Y = \Delta V(1+e) = I(1-\kappa)(1+e) \tag{2.27}$$

Hence, after few simple mathematical manipulations in Eqs. (2.26) and (2.27), we get

$$\frac{\Delta Y}{Y} = \underbrace{s\left[\frac{e}{1+e}\right]}_{\substack{\text{average} \\ \text{propensity} \\ \text{to save}}} \cdot \underbrace{[(1-\kappa)(1+e)]}_{\substack{\text{average} \\ \text{productivity} \\ \text{of investment}}} = se(1-\kappa) \tag{2.28}$$

which shows that an economy's growth rate depends on the proportion of surplus-value which is accumulated, the rate of surplus-value and the value composition of capital. If we now translate the above into Keynesian language, uninterrupted expanded reproduction requires that economy's growth rate to be equal to the product of the marginal (=average) propensity to save times the average productivity of investment; the same conditions are brought together in Domar's growth model [Eq. (2.15)].

From the above analysis, we conclude that Domar's analysis shares surprisingly similarities with Marx's schemes of expanded reproduction. Domar arrives at Marx's conclusion, that is, the higher the savings, the higher the investment without prioritizing the one over the other, but rather they are addressing the issue of the amount of the required investment to attain a process of balanced growth. The latter only implies the potentiality of balanced growth and not that such growth is easily reached and maintained, since an internally or externally generated interruption (shock) may lead the economy out of equilibrium.

2.6 *Tableau Économique* and Reproduction Schemes Cast in Input-Output Analysis

The classical theory of value and distribution as well as its theory of social reproduction can be casted in terms of input-output tables and analysis. Historically, Quesnay's *Tableau Économique* and Marx's schemes of reproduction are the prototypes of modern input-output tables.[19] In what follows, we start off with a short description of input-output analysis, and then we cast both the *Tableau Économique* and the schemes of reproduction in terms of input-output tables whose construction is based on the following assumptions:

- Single product industries
- Given technology
- Constant returns to scale

These assumptions, at first sight, appear restrictive; however, they are dictated by the difficulties in collecting appropriate data and information and not necessarily by the rigid theoretical framework of input-output models. More specifically:

- The first assumption is made for the sake of simplicity, since nowadays the input-output tables are published in their make form, according to which an industry produces an array of by-products along its main product.
- The second hypothesis is less restrictive than is usually thought. True, modern economies are characterized by technological progress; however, major technological advances that change dramatically the structure of an economy are not that frequent, and when they take place, their relative importance is too small relative to the totality of the economy, and so the input-output coefficients are not affected, in the beginning at least, in any significant way. It takes years for these changes to make their difference visible in the average input-output coefficients. Furthermore, and inspired by Ricardo's numerical examples, we may recall that the changes in relative prices are minimal in the face of technological change, a result which we will ascertain in our empirical analysis in Chap. 4. As a consequence, if benchmark input-output tables are constructed say every 3–5 years, they are expected to reflect the technological change that has taken place. In addition, the theoretical framework of input-output analysis includes the case of joint production as well as cases of multiple production techniques, where the choice of technique is made

---

[19]Today, it is recognized that Wassily Leontief (1906–1999) is the main representative of this field of economic analysis.

according to well-known methods of cost minimization, thereby ruling out the neoclassical theory, according to which only a slight change in the distributive variables is enough to lead to the choice of a different technique from the available blueprint of techniques.

- Finally, the assumption of constant returns to scale is realistic and can be found in empirical studies of industrial organization (Moudud 2010, Chap. 2).

An input-output table (see Table 2.9) has its number of columns equal to that of rows. In such a symmetric table, the columns refer to the value of inputs of each industry needed to produce the value of output j. The sum of elements of a column provides the total cost of production (i.e. wages, materials and depreciation, net taxes, etc.) of the respective industry. The total value-added of each industry is equal to the GDP of the industry. The rows of an input-output table present the sales of each industry to the rest of the industries and also to itself. A part of produced output goes to final demand, i.e. consumption, investment, government spending and net exports.

Given the assumptions of constant returns to scale and given technology if, for some reason, the output of industry j, x_j, increases, it follows that its inputs from the other industries, x_{ij}, increase proportionally. The technological coefficients, $a_{ij} = x_{ij}/x_j$, are assumed to remain constant in the face of a change in demand, which is another way to say that if the value of output doubles, the value of inputs should also double; that is, coefficients a_{ij} measure the fixed proportions between the output of an industry j and the required inputs i. Hence, a sustained condition of reproduction for an economy requires that $0 \leq \sum a_{ij} \leq 1$, which means that the value of produced output must exceed the value of inputs used to produce it.

The above input-output table can be converted from a descriptive devise to a useful analytical tool with the help of linear algebra. To facilitate the presentation, we limit the dimensions of the input-output table to only two industries. So, we may write

$$x_1 = a_{11}x_1 + a_{12}x_2 + y_1$$
$$x_2 = a_{21}x_1 + a_{22}x_2 + y_2$$

Table 2.9 Input-output table

| | Outputs | | | | | |
| | Intermediate demand | | | | | |
Inputs	Industry 1	Industry 2	...	Industry n	Final demand	Total output
Industry 1	x_{11}	x_{12}	...	x_{1n}	y_1	x_1
Industry 2	x_{21}	x_{22}	...	x_{2n}	y_2	x_2
...	...	....	...	...	...	...
Industry n	x_{1n}	x_{2n}	...	x_{nn}	y_n	x_n
Value-added	v_1	v_2	...	v_n		
Total	x_1	x_2	...	x_n		

where y_1 and y_2 stand for the final demand (consumption, investment, government expenditures and net exports) of industries 1 and 2, respectively. We observe that this is a system of equations which in terms of linear algebra can be written as follows:

$$\begin{bmatrix} x_1 \\ x_2 \end{bmatrix} = \begin{bmatrix} a_{11} & a_{12} \\ a_{21} & a_{22} \end{bmatrix} \begin{bmatrix} x_1 \\ x_2 \end{bmatrix} + \begin{bmatrix} y_1 \\ y_2 \end{bmatrix}$$

or in matrix form

$$\mathbf{x} = \mathbf{A}\mathbf{x} + \mathbf{y}$$

where matrices and vectors are indicated in bold face capital and lower-case letters, respectively. The vector of total output is estimated from

$$\mathbf{x} = [\mathbf{I} - \mathbf{A}]^{-1}\mathbf{y} \tag{2.29}$$

The matrix $[\mathbf{I} - \mathbf{A}]^{-1}$ is known as the Leontief's inverse matrix. The economic meaning of this matrix is that each of its elements indicates how much the production of sector j should increase if the demand for its output increases by one unit. Hence, the Leontief's inverse matrix corresponds to the Keynesian investment multiplier with the difference that instead of having a single number, that is, a scalar, as in the Keynesian multiplier, we have an entire matrix. The usefulness of the Leontief's inverse matrix will be shown in the next sections.

2.6.1 *The* Tableau Économique *as an Input-Output Table*

A modern way to present physiocrats' *Tableau Économique* is with the use of an input-output table as shown in Table 2.10 (Tsoulfidis 1989). It is true that modern input-output analysis heavily relies on the ideas of the *Tableau Économique* (Leontief 1939) which, as such, is an accounting table with double bookkeeping entries. Specifically, the transactions between the three sectors that we encounter in physiocrats can be presented in the input-output form as follows:

Table 2.10 The *Tableau Économique* as an input-output table

	Outputs			
Inputs	Agriculture	Manufacture	Final demand	Total outputs
Agriculture	2	2	1	5
Manufacture	1	0	1	2
Rent (net product)	2	0		[2]
Total inputs	5	2	[2]	7

The advantage of this presentation over others (e.g. Phillips 1975; Blaug 1997) is in the treatment of the agricultural sector, the only one that produces a value of output over and above the cost of its inputs by 2 milliards.[20] By contrast, in manufacturing, the value of total inputs equals that of total output, and so there is no surplus creation in this particular sector. Landowners, who are not supposed to comprise a separate sector, are merely the receivers of rents identified with net product or surplus that they simply consume. The landlords' consumption defines the final demand in the economy.

The matrix of technological coefficients $\mathbf{A}$ is derived by dividing each sector's value of output by the corresponding value of inputs

$$\mathbf{A} = \begin{bmatrix} 2/5 = 0.4 & 2/2 = 1 \\ 1/5 = 0.2 & 0/2 = 0 \end{bmatrix}$$

which in matrix form can be written as

$$\mathbf{x} = \mathbf{Ax} + \mathbf{y}$$

where $\mathbf{x}$ is the vector of output produced, $\mathbf{A}$ is the matrix of technological coefficients and $\mathbf{y}$ is the vector of final demand. Solving for $\mathbf{x}$, we have

$$\mathbf{x} - \mathbf{Ax} = \mathbf{y}$$

and

$$\mathbf{x} = [\mathbf{I} - \mathbf{A}]^{-1}\mathbf{y}$$

As we have mentioned, Leontief's inverse matrix corresponds to the Keynesian investment multiplier which in physiocrats' analysis is a matrix rather than a simple scalar. Furthermore, the input-output matrix representation of the *Tableau Économique* enables the determination of prices and outputs, the incidence of various taxes on prices as well as the scale of social reproduction. For example, let us introduce a diagonal matrix, and along the main diagonal, we put the rent rates to be estimated for each of the sectors of the economy.[21] The prices and the single rent rate can be estimated from the following:

$$\mathbf{p} = \mathbf{pA} + \mathbf{pA} < \rho > \quad \text{or} \quad \mathbf{p} = \mathbf{pA} < \rho > [\mathbf{I} - \mathbf{A}]^{-1}$$

and

---

[20]For a detailed presentation, see Tsoulfidis (1989), Giacomin (1995) and Steenge (2000).

[21]We recall that the rent in physiocrats has the same status as the surplus-value in Marx. The constituent components of rent are the profit and interest exactly as in Marx's concept of surplus-value which is broader for it also contains rents.

$$[p_a \ p_m] = [p_a \ p_m] \begin{bmatrix} 0.4 & 1 \\ 0.2 & 0 \end{bmatrix} \begin{bmatrix} \rho_a & 0 \\ 0 & \rho_m \end{bmatrix} \begin{bmatrix} 2.5 & 2.5 \\ 0.5 & 1.5 \end{bmatrix}^{-1}$$

where p_a and p_m are the prices of agricultural and manufacturing goods, respectively, while ρ_a and ρ_m are the corresponding rent rates. By assuming, as the physiocrats did, that $\rho_m = 0$, the above system of two equations and three unknowns gives a unique set of relative prices along with the rent rate, ρ_a. In particular, we get

$$p_a = p_m = 2.5[0.4p_a + 2p_m]\rho_a$$

and finally solve for

$$p_a = p_m = 1 \quad \text{and} \quad \rho_a = 0.66$$

Various kinds of taxes can be applied to this system and surprisingly enough give results like those anticipated by the physiocrats, that is, all taxes finally fall on rent incomes.

2.6.2   The Schemes of Reproduction and Input-Output Tables

Marx's analysis of the schemes of reproduction can also be presented in terms of input-output tables. At this point, we should emphasize that there is an extensive literature on this issue whose presentation goes beyond the scope of the book at hand (Morishima 1973; Samuelson 1974; Okishio 1988; Nikaido 1996; Trigg 2006 among others). In the present analysis, we will stand in a simplified description of the schemes of expanded reproduction, and we will assume that the analysis is carried on in terms of values, where 1 € equals say 1 h of labour time. In an effort to avoid complications, we present a simplified version based on Trigg (2006).

Table 2.11 casts the numbers of Tables 2.1 and 2.2 in terms of an input-output representation. ΔC represents the change in investment or capital accumulation, ΔV stands for the change in variable capital, F stands for capitalist consumption or final demand, X is total value produced, S is produced surplus-value, $p_1 = p_2$ are direct prices $= 1 \text{ €} = 1$ labour hour, x is total output produced, $l_j = L_j/x_j$ is labour coefficient per unit of output and $b_i = B_i/L$ is labourers' coefficient of consumption, that is, total consumption of goods over total labour employed.

Since $p_1 = p_2 =$ direct prices $= 1 \text{ €} = 1$ labour hour, from Table 2.11, we may write

$$x_1 = a_{11}x_1 + a_{12}x_2 + \Delta C$$

$$x_2 = b_2 l_1 x_1 + b_2 l_2 x_2 + \Delta V + \Delta F$$

or in matrix form

Table 2.11 Schemes of reproduction and Leontief's input-output table

	Department I	Department II	ΔC	ΔV	F	X
Marx						
Department I	4000	1500	500			6000
Department II	1000	750		150	1100	3000
S	1000	750				
X	6000	3000				9000
Leontief						
Sector I	$p_1 a_{11} x_1$	$p_1 a_{12} x_2$	$p_1 \Delta C$			$p_1 x_1$
Sector II	$p_2 b_2 l_1 x_1$	$p_2 b_2\ l_2 x_2$		$p_2 b l$	$p_2 F$	$p_2 x_2$
	S_1	S_2				
	$p_1 x_1$	$p_2 x_2$				

$$
\underbrace{\begin{bmatrix} x_1 \\ x_2 \end{bmatrix}}_{\mathbf{x}} = \underbrace{\begin{bmatrix} a_{11} & a_{12} \\ 0 & 0 \end{bmatrix}}_{\mathbf{A}} \underbrace{\begin{bmatrix} x_1 \\ x_2 \end{bmatrix}}_{\mathbf{x}} + \underbrace{\begin{bmatrix} 0 \\ b_2 \end{bmatrix}}_{\mathbf{b}} \underbrace{\begin{bmatrix} l_1 & l_2 \end{bmatrix}}_{\mathbf{l}} \underbrace{\begin{bmatrix} x_1 \\ x_2 \end{bmatrix}}_{\mathbf{x}} + \underbrace{\begin{bmatrix} \Delta C \\ \Delta V + \Delta F \end{bmatrix}}_{\mathbf{f}}
$$

The last vector in the above expression presents final demand, $\mathbf{f}$, which, unlike the physiocrats, is not restricted to non-productive consumption of landlords but is general enough to include the additional investment in constant (ΔC) and variable (ΔV) capitals, as well as the non-productive capitalists' consumption F. The above expression in its compact matrix form can be written as

$$
\mathbf{x} = \mathbf{Ax} + \mathbf{blx} + \mathbf{f} \quad \text{or} \quad \mathbf{x} - \mathbf{Ax} = \mathbf{blx} + \mathbf{f}
$$

and

$$
\mathbf{x} = [\mathbf{I} - \mathbf{A}]^{-1}\mathbf{blx} + [\mathbf{I} - \mathbf{A}]^{-1}\mathbf{f} \tag{2.30}
$$

where $\mathbf{I}$ is the identity matrix. In turn, we set the net product $\mathbf{y}$ as the difference between output $\mathbf{x}$ and intermediate inputs $\mathbf{Ax}$. Thus, we have

$$
\mathbf{y} = [\mathbf{I} - \mathbf{A}]\mathbf{x} \quad \text{and} \quad \mathbf{x} = [\mathbf{I} - \mathbf{A}]^{-1}\mathbf{y}
$$

After some manipulation, the net product described by $\mathbf{y} = [\mathbf{I} - \mathbf{A}]\mathbf{x}$ can be rewritten as

$$
\mathbf{y} = [\mathbf{I} - \mathbf{A}]\left([\mathbf{I} - \mathbf{A}]^{-1}\mathbf{bl}[\mathbf{I} - \mathbf{A}]^{-1}\mathbf{y} + [\mathbf{I} - \mathbf{A}]^{-1}\mathbf{f} \right)
$$

and

$$
\mathbf{y} = \mathbf{bl}[\mathbf{I} - \mathbf{A}]^{-1}\mathbf{y} + \mathbf{f} \tag{2.31}
$$

Finally, the labour values are defined as

$$\mathbf{v} = \mathbf{l} + \mathbf{lA}$$

or

$$\mathbf{v} = \mathbf{l}[\mathbf{I} - \mathbf{A}]^{-1} \tag{2.32}$$

where $\mathbf{v}$ is the row vector of labour values which is the sum of direct labour requirements per unit of output presented by the row vector, $\mathbf{l}$, and indirect labour requirements, $\mathbf{lA}$, that is, 'dead' or materialized labour incorporated in inputs used in current production. In other words, the vector $\mathbf{v}$ represents the quantity of homogeneous labour which is directly and indirectly incorporated into the output produced in each department.

Replacing the labour values in the equation of net output $\mathbf{y}$ (Eq. 2.31) and by premultiplying by the vector of labour values, we get

$$\mathbf{vy} = \mathbf{vbvy} + \mathbf{vf}$$

which solves for

$$\mathbf{vy} = \frac{1}{1 - \mathbf{vb}} \mathbf{vf} \tag{2.33}$$

Here, everything is expressed in terms of labour values. That is, the term $\mathbf{vy}$ represents labour time incorporated in net output, and $\mathbf{vb}$ represents labour time incorporated in workers consumption, that is, the marginal (average) propensity to consume. Finally, the term $\mathbf{vf}$ is total labour time incorporated in commodities that constitute the final consumption. Apparently, the term

$$\frac{1}{1 - \mathbf{vb}}$$

is the multiplier in terms of labourers' consumption and not of total consumption as in the Keynesian analysis.

2.6.3 Labour Values and Prices of Production Using Input-Output Analysis

In Sect. 3.2 of the next Chap. 3, we discuss in detail how direct prices and prices of production can be estimated, whereas in Chap. 4, by utilizing actual input-output data from a number of economies, we estimate these theoretical prices and evaluate their difference from the observed or market prices. Here, we attempt to make a simple introduction on the estimation of various kinds of prices with the aid of matrix algebra and input-output analysis paving the way for what is to follow in Chap. 4.

2.6.3.1   Estimation of Labour Values

For the sake of simplicity, let us hypothesize an economy with only two industries utilizing inputs from each other and employing labour in order to produce their respective outputs. As we have already discussed in Chap. 1, the concept of value in Marx is a monetary magnitude, and it is called direct price. For its estimation, and its comparison with market price, we assume that market price per unit of output will be equal to 1 (i.e. 1 million €) since we refer to sales. Thus, labour values in Marx's schemes of (simple or expanded) reproduction are equal to direct prices, and both are equal to one unit of money. The same is true with the prices in Quesnay's *Tableau Économique* as well as in Leontief's input-output tables, where prices are equal to one monetary unit, whatever this happens to be. Table 2.12 presents input-output information for a hypothetical economy.

The last row of Table 2.12 displays the vector of labour requirements per unit of output which, as we pointed out, is estimated as the ratio of sectoral employment over the respective output (=value-added). Using Marx's example, the employment coefficients for the two departments will be, respectively,

$$l_1 = \frac{L_1}{x_1} = \frac{2000}{6000} \approx 0.33 \quad \text{and} \quad l_2 = \frac{L_2}{x_2} = \frac{1500}{3000} = 0.50$$

and the vector of employment coefficients will be

$$\mathbf{l} = \begin{bmatrix} 0.33 & 0.50 \end{bmatrix}$$

In similar fashion, $b_i = B_i/L$ is labourers' consumption coefficient, that is, total consumption over total labour employed or value-added. The idea is that since 1 labour hour is equal to 1 €, it follows that total labour hours (or working time) will be equal to total value-added, that is, the sum of variable capital and surplus-value denoted by $L = y = 3500$. As a consequence

Table 2.12 Input-output table of a hypothetical economy

Input	Output		
	Sector I	Sector II	Total output
Sector I	a_{11}	a_{12}	x_1
Sector II	a_{21}	a_{22}	x_2
Initial inputs	$l_1 = L_1/x_1$	$l_2 = L_2/x_2$	

$$b_2 = \frac{v_1 + v_2}{y} = \frac{1000 + 750}{3500} = 0.50$$

and the vector of real wage or basket of wage goods consumed by workers will be

$$\mathbf{b} = \begin{bmatrix} 0 \\ 0.5 \end{bmatrix}$$

The matrix of technological coefficients is estimated as follows:

$$\mathbf{A} = \begin{bmatrix} \frac{4000}{6000} \approx 0.67 = a_{11} & \frac{1500}{3000} = 0.50 = a_{12} \\ 0 & 0 \end{bmatrix}$$

By replacing in the equation of total output [Eq. (2.30)] and employing Marx's numerical example, we get

$$\underbrace{\begin{bmatrix} 6000 \\ 4000 \end{bmatrix}}_{\mathbf{x}} = \underbrace{\begin{bmatrix} 0.67 & 0.50 \\ 0 & 0 \end{bmatrix}}_{\mathbf{A}} \underbrace{\begin{bmatrix} 6000 \\ 4000 \end{bmatrix}}_{\mathbf{x}} + \underbrace{\begin{bmatrix} 0 \\ 0.5 \end{bmatrix}}_{\mathbf{b}} \underbrace{[0.33 \quad 0.5]}_{\mathbf{l}} \underbrace{\begin{bmatrix} 6000 \\ 4000 \end{bmatrix}}_{\mathbf{x}} + \underbrace{\begin{bmatrix} 500 \\ 150 + 1100 \end{bmatrix}}_{\mathbf{f}}$$

If for the sake of simplicity, we assume that there is no depreciation, labour values are estimated [Eq. (2.32)] as follows:

$$\mathbf{v} = \mathbf{l}[\mathbf{I} - \mathbf{A}]^{-1} = [0.33 \quad 0.5] \begin{bmatrix} 3 & 1.5 \\ 0 & 1 \end{bmatrix} = [1 \quad 1]$$

where $\mathbf{v}$ is the row vector of labour values, that is, the quantity of homogenous labour which directly or indirectly is incorporated in the production for each department. Replacing labour values in the equation of net output $\mathbf{y}$ [Eq. (2.31)] and by premultiplying the resulting relation by the vector of labour values, we get

$$\mathbf{vy} = \mathbf{vbvy} + \mathbf{vf}$$

By invoking the formula for the implicit multiplier of the schemes of expanded reproduction [Eq. (2.33)], we get

$$\mathbf{vy} = 3500$$

which represents the labour time incorporated in net output. The term $\mathbf{vb} = 0.5$ represents labour time incorporated in workers consumption, that is, the marginal (average) propensity to consume. Finally, the term $\mathbf{vf} = 1750$ is the total labour time incorporated in commodities that constitute the final consumption. Apparently, the term $1/(1 - \mathbf{vb}) = 2$ is the multiplier in terms of labourers' consumption and not of total consumption as in the Keynesian analysis.

2.6.3.2 Estimation of Prices of Production

The detailed study of prices of production is presented in Chap. 3. Here, we attempt a simple definition in terms of the above input-output data. Generally, the prices of production are a sort of prices in which the cost of output includes the average rate of profit, and in this sense, they are equilibrium prices; hence, prices p_1 and p_2 correspond to commodities produced by Departments I and II, respectively. In the sake of simplicity, we temporarily assume that profits are zero. Consequently, total departmental sales will be

$$\text{Sales of Department I} : p_1 x_1$$

$$\text{Sales of Department II} : p_2 x_2$$

The departmental total cost will be

$$\text{Cost of Department I} : (p_1 a_{11} + p_2 a_{21}) x_1$$

$$\text{Cost of Department II} : (p_1 a_{12} + p_2 a_{22}) x_2$$

If we now introduce a uniform rate of profit, r, then the price of production of each department will be

$$p_1 = p_1 a_{11} + p_2 a_{21} + r(p_1 a_{11} + p_2 a_{21}) = (1 + r)(p_1 a_{11} + p_2 a_{21})$$

$$p_2 = p_1 a_{12} + p_2 a_{22} + r(p_1 a_{12} + p_2 a_{22}) = (1 + r)(p_1 a_{12} + p_2 a_{22})$$

and in matrix form

$$\begin{bmatrix} p_1 \\ p_2 \end{bmatrix} = (1 + r) \begin{bmatrix} a_{11} & a_{21} \\ a_{12} & a_{22} \end{bmatrix} \begin{bmatrix} p_1 \\ p_2 \end{bmatrix}$$

Hence, we should estimate the uniform rate of profit and the associated with it vector of positive prices. The answer to this estimation is the famous Perron-Frobenius theorem in linear algebra according to which in a positive matrix, such as the above, whose column sums are less than one, its maximal eigenvalue is associated with a unique eigenvector whose elements are all positive defined up to a multiplication by a scalar. The economic significance of the maximal eigenvalue is its correspondence to the economy's uniform rate of profit, and the associated with it unique positive eigenvector represents the vector of relative prices which must be scaled appropriately so as to become comparable to the vector of actually observed prices. It is apparent that the rate of profit will correspond to the eigenvalue of the matrix of technological coefficients, a_{ij}, where $i = 1, 2$ and $j = 1, 2$, while equilibrium prices will correspond to its eigenvector. If we express the above system in a matrix compact form, we get

$$\mathbf{P}^{\mathrm{T}}(1 + r)^{-1} = \mathbf{A}^{\mathrm{T}} \mathbf{P}^{\mathrm{T}} \quad \text{or} \quad \mathbf{P}\lambda = \mathbf{P}\mathbf{A} \tag{2.34}$$

where the eigenvalue $\lambda = 1/(1 + r)$ corresponds to the profit rate and the associated with it row eigenvector **P** corresponds to the vector of positive relative prices. As in the case of labour values, for the estimated prices of production, which are only relative prices, one must fix their scale so as to make them comparable to market prices, in our case with vector **e**. In particular

$$\mathbf{p} = \mathbf{P}\frac{\mathbf{e}\mathbf{x}}{\mathbf{P}\mathbf{x}} \tag{2.35}$$

where **p** is the normalized vector of prices of production and **e** the row unit vector. It becomes apparent that this normalization equates the sum of prices of production with that of market prices. In effect, if we post-multiply the above expression with the vector **x**, we end up with $\mathbf{p}\mathbf{x} = \mathbf{e}\mathbf{x}$. Similarly, by applying the same normalization, we end up with $\mathbf{v}\mathbf{x} = \mathbf{e}\mathbf{x}$, which implies that $\mathbf{p}\mathbf{x} = \mathbf{v}\mathbf{x} = \mathbf{e}\mathbf{x}$.

In terms of our schemes of extended reproduction, we have all the matrices and vectors we need to estimate the prices of production. Thus, we have the matrices **A** and **bl** which we add them to obtain the augmented with workers consumption circulating capital matrix

$$\mathbf{A+bl}= \begin{bmatrix} 0.667 & 0.500 \\ 0.167 & 0.250 \end{bmatrix}$$

The system of prices of production will be

$$\mathbf{P}=(1 + r)(\mathbf{A+bl}) \tag{2.36}$$

The eigenvalues of the above matrix are 0.81433349 and 0.10233318, and the respective eigenvectors are [0.45715043, 0.40503571] and [−0.25602326, 0.86689502]. We select the positive eigenvector, the only meaningful economically, which shows relative prices. The rate of profit of the economy is

$$\lambda = 1/(1 + r) \quad \text{and} \quad r = (1/\lambda) - 1 \tag{2.37}$$

After substitution we get

$$r = \frac{1}{0.814} - 1 = 23.457\%$$

We observe that the rate of profit in terms of prices of production is extremely close to that estimated in terms of values of the schemes of expanded reproduction which is equal to 24%. However, it is important to point out that the gap between the maximal and the second eigenvalue is too large and their ratio, which is equal to 7.95, indicates that the system is pretty stable and once perturbed it soon returns to its equilibrium path. Furthermore, as we will discuss in Chaps. 3 and 4, prices of production and direct prices (values) are not expected to differ by much from each other.

In effect, the vector of prices of production after their normalization with the output vector becomes

$$\mathbf{p} = \mathbf{P}\left[\frac{\mathbf{ex}}{\mathbf{Px}}\right] = [0.457 \quad 0.405]\left[\frac{9000}{3958.01}\right] = [1.040 \quad 0.921]$$

These findings derived from the numerical example of the schemes of extended reproduction prompt us to think that the difference between the rate of profit estimated in value terms and the rate of profit estimated in terms of prices of production displays negligible differences, and the same is true with the direct prices and prices of production. Naturally, the question is how different are these variables when we get data from actual economies? We grapple with this question in Chap. 4.

2.6.4 Growth Implications of Reproduction Schemes in Input-Output Form

Brody (1970) described the schemes of simple and extended reproduction using both linear algebra and developments in input-output analysis. With the aid of Brody's analysis, it is easy to show that modern growth theory and, in particular, Domar's growth model have its implicit, at least, theoretical underpinning in the schemes of reproduction. Following Brody's notation, the schemes of simple reproduction can be written as

$$\mathbf{A}^c = \begin{bmatrix} \mathbf{A} & \mathbf{b} \\ \mathbf{l} & 0 \end{bmatrix}$$

where $\mathbf{A}$ stands for economy's matrix of technological coefficients, $\mathbf{l}$ stands for employment coefficients and $\mathbf{b}$ for workers' consumption coefficients. In simple reproduction, the output produced $\mathbf{x}$ is enough to satisfy the demand for intermediate inputs, $\mathbf{Ax}$, and workers' needs for wage goods, $\mathbf{bx}$. Hence, we have the following equality:

$$\mathbf{A}^c\mathbf{x} = \mathbf{x}$$

The above condition is equivalent to saying that the maximum eigenvalue λ of matrix $\mathbf{A}^C$ is equal to 1, that is,

$$\mathbf{A}^c\mathbf{x} = \lambda\mathbf{x}$$

or

$$\lambda\mathbf{x} - \mathbf{A}^c\mathbf{x} = (\lambda\mathbf{I} - \mathbf{A}^c)\mathbf{x} = \mathbf{0}$$

Hence, the eigenvalues are those λs that make the above relation equal to zero or what amounts to the same thing the λs that make the determinant of the matrix $(\lambda \mathbf{I} - \mathbf{A}^c)$ singular. Furthermore, only the maximal eigenvalue will be associated with a positive eigenvector defined up to a multiplication by a scalar. In the case of simple reproduction, this positive eigenvector $\mathbf{x}$ corresponds to the vector of output proportions. In order to fix the scale of output proportions (or relative outputs) by an appropriate scalar, we choose the ratio of actual vector of outputs multiplied by the vector of market prices over the actual output vector multiplied by the estimated vector of output proportions.[22] The above analysis is valid in the case of zero net investment, that is, in the schemes of simple reproduction ($\mathbf{A}^c\mathbf{x} = \mathbf{x}$).

Continuing now to the schemes of expanded reproduction, the following inequality holds

$$\mathbf{A}^c\mathbf{x} < \mathbf{x} \quad \text{and} \quad (\mathbf{I} - \mathbf{A}^c)\mathbf{x} > 0$$

Hence, each and every sector in the economy produces more output than that required for its non-labour and labour inputs requirements. In addition, the growth in output depends on the portion of invested surplus (value); in the hypothetical case that all surplus is invested and therefore the economy's propensity to save is equal to 1, the economy is on its maximum expanded reproduction, or, what is the same thing, the economy expands along the von Neumann ray, that is, the economy's growth rate is always equal to the profit rate.[23]

In order to explore the conditions of expanded reproduction and balanced growth, the matrix of capital stock coefficients ($\mathbf{K}$) is introduced. Formally

$$(\mathbf{I} - \mathbf{A}^c)\mathbf{x} = r\mathbf{K}\mathbf{x}$$

The left-hand side of the above relation represents the surplus produced in the economy, whereas the right-hand side depicts the investment activity; the scalar r stands for the uniform rate of profit which, if equilibrium is to be established, shows the warranted growth rate of the economy. The above relation can be rewritten as

$$\mathbf{x} = \mathbf{A}^c\mathbf{x} + r\mathbf{K}\mathbf{x}$$

Hence, sectoral output produced is allocated to the consumption needs of a society, namely, on intermediate inputs $\mathbf{A}\mathbf{x}$, workers needs for wage goods $\mathbf{b}\mathbf{x}$ and investment requirements $\mathbf{K}\mathbf{x}$ associated with the economy-wide growth rate of output r.

Brody (1970, p. 100) showed that the schemes of expanded reproduction bear remarkable similarities to Harrod's and Domar's growth models. These similarities

---

[22]More on possibilities of fixing the scale of relative prices or output proportions are detailed in Chap. 4.

[23]More on the implications of such a hypothetical case can be found in Chap. 3.

can be shown starting with the determination of prices of production, that is, the dual of output proportions equation

$$\mathbf{p} = \mathbf{p}\mathbf{A}^c + r\mathbf{p}\mathbf{K}$$

where $\mathbf{p}\mathbf{A}^c$ stands for the value of non-labour and labour input requirements per unit of output, $\mathbf{p}\mathbf{K}$ stands for the value of the invested capital per unit of output and r is the rate of profit equal to the growth rate. The above relation can be rewritten in the form of the following eigenequation:

$$\mathbf{p}r^{-1} = \mathbf{p}\mathbf{K}(\mathbf{I} - \mathbf{A}^c)^{-1}$$

By premultiplying the equation of balanced expanded reproduction, that is, $(\mathbf{I} - \mathbf{A}^C)\mathbf{x} = r\mathbf{K}\mathbf{x}$, by the vector of normalized equilibrium prices, we get

$$\mathbf{p}\mathbf{x} = \mathbf{p}\mathbf{A}^c\mathbf{x} + r\mathbf{p}\mathbf{K}\mathbf{x}$$

or

$$\mathbf{p}(\mathbf{I} - \mathbf{A}^c)\mathbf{x} = r\mathbf{p}\mathbf{K}\mathbf{x}$$

and

$$r = \frac{\mathbf{p}(\mathbf{I} - \mathbf{A}^c)\mathbf{x}}{\mathbf{p}\mathbf{K}\mathbf{x}}$$

which can be rewritten as follows:

$$r = \frac{\mathbf{p}(\mathbf{I} - \mathbf{A}^c)\mathbf{x}}{\mathbf{p}\mathbf{x}} \frac{\mathbf{p}\mathbf{x}}{\mathbf{p}\mathbf{K}\mathbf{x}}$$

Hence, the growth rate of the economy which under conditions of expanded reproduction is identical to the rate of profit is the product of the share of savings or the average propensity to save

$$\frac{\mathbf{p}(\mathbf{I} - \mathbf{A}^c)\mathbf{x}}{\mathbf{p}\mathbf{x}}$$

times the productivity of capital, or the reciprocal of capital-output ratio

$$\frac{\mathbf{p}\mathbf{x}}{\mathbf{p}\mathbf{K}\mathbf{x}}$$

In other words, the above relation is no different than that of Domar's model presented in Sect. 2.5.2.

2.7 Summary and Conclusions

In this chapter, we dealt with social reproduction and economic growth as it has been discussed mainly in the classical approach and resurfaced in the macroeconomic analysis and economic growth of Keynesian economists. We showed that there are remarkable similarities and also significant differences between the two approaches which could be also interfaced with the aid of input-output modelling.

We started the analysis with the insights of the physiocrats and their 'greatest intellectual achievement' of the circular flow of goods and money portrayed in their famous *Tableau Économique*. The old classical economists, mainly Smith, Ricardo and J.S. Mill, accepted the notion of surplus and other insights of the physiocratic approach; nevertheless, they were repelled by the physiocrats' narrow conceptualization of production restricted to agriculture. In so doing, they did not pay sufficient attention to their *Tableau Économique* as a useful analytical tool for the understanding of the principles governing social reproduction.

By contrast Marx not only understood in depth the importance of the *Tableau Économique* which he considered

> incontestably the most brilliant idea of which political economy had hitherto been guilty.
>
> (*TSV* I, Chap. 6)

but also extended the analysis to theorize the way in which society reproduces itself. His analysis of the schemes of reproduction was not limited to money flows, or commodity flows or values, but it was carried out in all these three forms and potentially in terms of prices of production.

Simple reproduction, as we pointed out, has more theoretical importance and less empirical relevance, and this is because the capitalist economy presents a compelling propensity for expansion, an expansion that often is punctuated by periodic economic crises. We showed that under Marx's assumptions expanded reproduction is possible. Subsequently, we discuss the various critiques levelled against the schemes of expanded reproduction and in particular the attempts to relax some of their underlying assumptions. We argued that the purpose of the schemes of expanded reproduction was mainly to show the possibility of balanced growth and not that balance growth is the normal state for capitalism.

Furthermore, we argued that the schemes of reproduction when cast in input-output framework can address major issues related to both microeconomics such as the determination of equilibrium (production) prices and macroeconomics having to do with effective demand and the ivestment multiplier bearing important similarities but significant differences from the respective Keynesian multiplier. Finally, the balanced growth potentiality of the schemes of expanded reproduction is also rediscovered in the Keynesian growth theory. Both approaches show the possibility of balanced or steady growth and the insurmountable difficulties to maintain it in the long run.

Chapter 3
Controversial Issues in the Theories of Value and Distribution: The 'Transformation Problem' and the 'Capital Theory Critique'

Pathology illuminates healthy physiology. Pasinetti, Morishima, Bruno-Burmeister-Sheshinski, Garegnani merit our gratitude for demonstrating that reswitching is a logical possibility in any technology, indecomposable or decomposable. Reswitching, whatever its empirical likelihood, does alert us to several vital possibilities. . . . If all this causes headaches for those nostalgic for the old-time parables of neoclassical writing, we must remind ourselves that scholars are not born to live an easy existence. We must respect, and appraise, the facts of life.

Paul Samuelson (1966)

Abstract Two central issues of economic theory are dealt with in some detail: the first is the famous 'transformation problem', which essentially refers to the logical consistency of the classical theory of value and, in particular, to Marx's labour theory of value. We explicate the various approaches and solutions to the transformation problem starting from Marx's one, which, despite its semifinished character, was, as we argue, in the right direction that could not be further advanced because of the lack of necessary mathematical theorems, which were discovered much later. The second issue that this chapter deals with is what came to be known as 'capital theory controversy'. Hence, we bring together and compare the two distinct theories of value: the classical political economics (CPE) labour theory of value (LTV) and the neoclassical (or marginal) theory of value. We show that if the CPE theory of value makes the labour time expressed in terms of technological requirements of production, the principal determinant of equilibrium prices, then the neoclassical theory makes preferences and endowments, along with technology, the data of its theory of value. In the neoclassical theory, however, prices reflect relative scarcities, and the capital theory controversies refer precisely to whether or not this holds true when evaluating capital goods as produced means of production, and according to those involved in the debate, the answer was negative.

Keywords Transformation problem · Labour theory of value · Capital theory controversies · Scarcity prices · Capital goods

© Springer Nature Switzerland AG 2019
L. Tsoulfidis, P. Tsaliki, *Classical Political Economics and Modern Capitalism*,
https://doi.org/10.1007/978-3-030-17967-0_3

83

3.1 Introduction

This chapter takes stock on the theoretical consistency of both the classical theory of value and distribution, as it appears in the famous 'transformation problem', and the neoclassical theory of value and its critique that attracted attention, through the 'capital theory controversies'.

- The transformation problem which orthodox and heterodox economists grappled with since the publication of volume III of *Capital* (1894) relates to the conversion of labour values into the form of prices of production, or natural prices, that is to say, into a kind of theoretical prices which incorporate the economy's average rate of profit.
- The capital theory critique of the neoclassical theory, which attracted most of the attention during the 1960s and early 1970s, deals with the problem of determining the prices of reproducible means of production, that is, of capital goods in a way which is consistent with the requirements of the neoclassical theory of value and distribution.

Hence, in this chapter, the analysis refers mainly to the theoretical issues on the 'transformation problem' and the neoclassical 'theory of capital', while their empirical dimensions as well as some of their recent theoretical developments are discussed in Chap. 4.

In fact, both classical and neoclassical approaches using a set of different data (see Chap. 1) seek to determine equilibrium prices, namely, long-run prices which are the result of systematic factors that operate as centripetal forces in the market. In so doing, both approaches seek to isolate all the random and, therefore, ephemeral market forces which act in centrifugal ways imparting on market prices a continuous disorder; but by no means, the market prices escape from their attraction to their centre of gravitation, that is, the long-run equilibrium prices. In particular, classical economists argue that turbulent swings in market prices cancel each other out and lead in the long run to elimination of deviations from their centre of gravitation; in other words, classical dynamic analysis argues for a tendential equalization of market prices to equilibrium ones (i.e. prices of production), whereas in the neoclassical approach, the usual view stresses the convergence aspect of market to their long-run equilibrium prices. Furthermore, the critique levelled against the Marxian strand of the classical approach is the so-called disconnect between labour values and prices of production. On the other hand, heterodox economists criticize the neoclassical approach for lack of consistency in its theoretical requirements in dealing with the measurement of capital as a factor of production.

3.2   The Transformation Problem

It is already known from Chap. 1 that prices of production comprise a centre of gravitation for market prices, i.e. the prices at which the actual transactions take place. Market prices are, by definition, disequilibrium prices, as they reflect an array of ephemeral and therefore non-subjected to theorization variables. By contrast, prices of production (or natural prices, according to Smith and Ricardo) are determined by the operation of systematic factors and so they can be theorized. Prices of production are equilibrium prices, and their determination, in one way or another, is common to both classical and neoclassical approaches to economic analysis. In fact, since the time of Smith, the determination of the centre of gravitation of market prices is the fundamental issue for all great economists and schools of economic thought.

In Smith's and Ricardo's theories of value, the labour time is the prime determinant of equilibrium or natural prices. As we discussed in Chap. 1, Smith abandoned the LTV for he found it irreconcilable with the presence of capital and wage labour; by contrast, Ricardo argued that in effect, the LTV applies to capitalism but with minor modifications whose quantitative significance not only is limited but, to a great extent, predicted. Thus, Ricardo concluded that market prices of commodities are determined by natural prices which in turn depend on the quantity of labour required for their production, and he proceeded with the estimation of equilibrium prices directly from labour values by assuming an arbitrarily determined uniform rate of profit. He could have cast the problem in terms of a system of equations, as presented in Chap. 1 and simultaneously to determine both the rate of profit and the associated set of equilibrium prices; but such a method of analysis would be unprecedented, in as much as economists in Ricardo's time presented their arguments verbally and Ricardo's numeric economic modelling was already a departure from the usual practice of his time.

Ricardo and classical economists argued that relative prices of commodities are determined by the relative quantities of labour. However, the lack of data on labour time led classical economist and in particular Ricardo in search of a certain commodity whose production would require, everywhere and always, the exact same quantity of labour time, and it would be invariable to changes in income distribution. In fact, until the end of his life, Ricardo in vain tried to define either theoretically or practically a commodity with these two properties. At the end, he admitted that such an invariable measure of value (IMV) does not exist and that the value of gold commodity is the 'nearest approximation to the truth'.[1]

Marx, by contrast, devoted the first two volumes of *Capital* preparing methodologically the analytical ground of the third volume, in which for the first time the

---

[1] The same question was pursued by Sraffa (1960) whose device of the 'standard commodity', defined as the right and unique (semi) positive eigenvector of the matrix of technological coefficients, provides a partial fulfillment of the requirements of the IVM; that is, the 'standard commodity' remains invariable to changes in income distribution.

prices of production are reported. His analytical transition from labour values into prices of production was not free of challenges, and the analysis of the third volume of *Capital* did not leave indifferent the academic economists immediately after its publication in 1894. Thus, while the first two volumes of *Capital* did not receive attention from academics, the third volume of *Capital* attracted immediately wide interest for it dealt, among other things, with the central problem of economic theory, that is, the determination of equilibrium prices, and it relates to the logical coherence and practical significance of Marx's theory of value.

We know from the discussion in Chaps. 1 and 2 that underneath the visible market prices, there are other more fundamental prices acting as their centres of gravitation. In Marx's analysis in *Capital* I and II, the 'centre of gravity' is the direct price, that is, the money form of value which in the sphere of circulation and in the presence of competition between capitals is transformed into price of production. The movement from one type of price to a more complex one, that is, the expression of one form of value (labour values) and its monetary expression (direct price) to a more complex form of value (price of production), is known in the economic literature as the 'transformation problem'. In other words, in the famous 'transformation problem', the issue at stake is the expression of a simple form of value to a more complex form of value; as a consequence, we are dealing with a formal rather than a substantive change. In what follows, we present Marx's efforts for a satisfactory solution taking care of all possible inconsistencies which, as we will argue (with the aid of mathematics, not known to Marx and to his contemporaries), was in the right direction. We would like to clarify at the outset that our main concern in the subsequent analysis is to identify the theoretical consistency of the proposed Marx's approach towards a complete solution and its practical significance to the classical theory in general and not to present the saga of the many 'solutions' and their critiques over the years.

We start with the definition of labour value which formally is written as

$$\lambda = c + l = c + v + s \tag{3.1}$$

where λ is the unit labour value of a commodity, c is the constant capital, l is the value added, v is the variable capital and s is the surplus-value; for the sake of simplicity and clarity of presentation, we assume an economy only with constant capital, that is, an economy utilizing only flow and not stock variables. Moreover, in order to proceed with the analysis, the following key macroeconomic variables are needed to be (re)introduced

- The ratio of constant to variable capital (c/v) and the organic composition of capital $(OCC)^2$ which expresses the ratio of dead to living labour (or of constant capital to the creative power of variable capital).

---

[2]We study the exact relationship between the different compositions of capital (organic, value, materialized and technical) in Chap. 8 which refers to the law of the falling tendency of the average economy-wide rate of profit.

- The ratio of surplus-value to variable capital (s/v), that is, the rate of surplus-value denoted by e. Recall from Chap. 1 that the variable capital during the production process not only reproduces its own value but also creates additional value, i.e. surplus-value.
- The ratio of total surplus-value to the sum of constant and variable capital, $[r = s/(c + v)]$ known as the rate of profit, r. Hence, we stipulate an elementary definition of the rate of profit, based on an economy whose constant capital lasts for one period (or year). If capital lasts for more than one period, that is, we have fixed capital, then the rate of profit should be calculated as the ratio of total surplus-value over invested (fixed and variable) capital.[3]

Marx, when published the first volume of *Capital* in 1867, expected to attract the interest of academics and scholars of his time; and for that he was fully prepared to face any possible critiques because he had already completed the study of all past economists.[4] But things did not evolve as planned because academic economists of the time were occupied with the development of their own (emerging then) neoclassical theory and they would not pay attention to figure out the theoretical inquiry of a radical economist, who anyway belonged to a tradition (classical) that was under question and were taking distance from. Thus, the first volume of *Capital* was hardly read by academic economists. We cannot say the same for the second and especially the third volume of *Capital*, published posthumously. In particular, his close friend and collaborator Friedrich Engels undertook the difficult task, not always successfully, both to 'decipher' Marx's hardly read handwritten notes and to place them in a logical order so that to constitute the second volume (1885) and later the third volume of *Capital* (1894).

Böhm-Bawerk (1898), from the founders of neoclassical economics and the Austrian approach, was the first orthodox economists that read Marx's work and launched a critique to his price system. It goes without saying that the purpose of this critique was not the discovery of the truth but rather the rejection of the Marxian approach which was popular in Austria and the powerful social democratic party. Böhm-Bawerk argued that there is a logical inconsistency between the first two volumes of *Capital* where the analysis is conducted in value terms (direct prices) and the third volume of *Capital* where Marx introduces the prices of production, i.e. prices sufficient to pay for inputs and to ensure a normal (average) rate of profit on invested capital. Böhm-Bawerk claimed that he found a 'great antithesis' between the first and third volumes of *Capital*, since in the same market there cannot coexist two different systems of commodities' evaluation, one expressed in labour values or direct prices and the other expressed in prices of production, an inconsistency which, according to Böhm-Bawerk, Marx was not alert to or at least did not explain and went directly and silently to prices of production. However, this is not exactly true; Marx as we will argue was fully aware of the issues associated with the different

---

[3]The detailed discussion of these terms in their flow and stock versions is postponed to Chaps. 4 and 8.
[4]This is documented in his famous 'notebooks', which were written between 1862–1863 and published posthumously in three volumes as *Theories of Surplus Value* (1969).

kinds of prices and did not conflate them as Böhm-Bawerk chided him. The following quotation is quite revealing of Marx's awareness of both, the different kinds of prices and the possible feedback effects on prices that occupied the attention of economists since the publication of *Capital* III

> We had originally assumed that the cost-price of a commodity equalled the *value* of the commodities consumed in its production. But for the buyer the price of production of a commodity is its cost-price, and may thus pass as cost-price into the prices of other commodities. Since the price of production of a commodity may differ from the value of a commodity, it follows that the cost-price of a commodity containing the price of production of another commodity may also stand above or below that portion of its total value derived from the value of the means of production consumed by it. It is necessary to bear in mind that there is always the possibility of an error if the cost-price of a commodity is identified with the value of the means of production consumed by it.
>
> (*Capital* III, pp. 164–165)

Marxists of that time were alarmed and worried about the possible extension of such critique to the whole Marxian economic analysis. Hilferding (1910) made an effort to downplay the importance of Böhm-Bawerk's criticism and argued, among other things, that Marx was not so much interested in quantitative relations of commodities, as Ricardo was; in contrast, Marx's focus was on qualitative relations in an attempt to reveal workers' exploitation as the source of surplus-value.[5] These arguments however were rather evasive; the reason is that the LTV, without its quantitative dimension, is deprived of any economic explanatory contend.

The analysis in volume 3 of *Capital* is a continuation and further advancement of the analysis of the first two volumes, and in this advancement, key issue is the concretization of the centre of gravitation of market prices. For this purpose, Marx starts with the simplest possible monetary expression of value, that is, the direct prices assuming away competition between capitals and advances his analysis to a new lower level of abstraction where prices of production are the new more concrete centres of gravitation of market prices when taking into account the operation of competition between capitals. Prices of production are in fact those prices that incorporate the economy-wide average rate of profit whose establishment is the direct result of the competition between capitals.

Thus, starting with the simplest regulator of market price for commodity x, that is, its direct price, we may write

$$p_x^0 = \frac{\lambda_x}{\lambda_g} = \frac{\text{labour value of commodity } x}{\text{labour value of commodity gold}}$$

Even in this simple price expression, the analysis is already quite complex. For example, the direct price may rise if the commodity's x labour value increases

---

[5]Paul Sweezy, in a collective volume published in 1975, presents the works by Böhm-Bawerk, Hilferding, and Borkiewicz on the transformation problem. Regarding Hilferding, we could add that his view delineated a kind of a historical transformation problem, according to which labour values were suitable to petty commodity production which belongs to a less developed capitalism and the prices of production to a fully developed capitalism.

holding constant the labour value of gold, or if the commodity's value decreases, but gold's value decreases even more, and so on. We observe that the estimation of a commodity's direct price is already a much more complicated task than the estimation of its labour value. In other words, price as a monetary expression is always a more complex form of appearance of the value of a commodity.

As we argued above, the direct price (p^0) of a commodity regulates its market price (p^m); the two prices in general are almost never equal $(p^0 \neq p^m)$ because of the continuous imbalances between supply and demand. For example, if in an industry the demand is higher than the supply of a commodity, then it follows that $p^m > p^0$ and the presence of excess profits, other things equal, are expected to increase the supply and the market price to fall; the converse will be true if $p^m < p^0$. We note that the logic behind these adjustments is the same as in Smith's example of deer and beaver that we discussed in Chap. 1.

Marx's approach to price determination in the first two volumes of *Capital* is conducted in terms of direct prices, that is to say, in the absence of competition between capitals and, therefore, the interindustry equalization of profit rates to the economy-wide average rate of profit. All prices are proportional to labour quantities, and under such simplifying assumptions, the surplus-value produced in each industry is equal to the realized profits. Formally, we may write

$$\frac{\lambda_x}{\lambda_g} = p_x^0 \rightarrow p_x^m$$

In this simple transformation, a commodity's value, λ_x, when weighed against the value of gold, λ_g, is transformed into direct price p_x^0, which in turn functions as a centre of gravitation for its market price p_x^m. Hence, if the exchange rate of money in circulation relative to gold is taken into account in a convertible into gold monetary system, then we derive the direct price in terms of monetary units in circulation. We observe that even in this first elemental transformation, the analysis is already quite complex.

In the third volume of *Capital*, Marx develops an even more complex price relation; between direct and market prices, he introduced a third type of theoretical prices that of prices of production, p_x^*

$$\frac{\lambda_x}{\lambda_g} = p_x^0 \rightarrow p_x^* \rightarrow p_x^m$$

This more complex process refers to direct prices and their transformation into prices of production which are more concrete regulators of market prices (p_x^m). In fact, in *Capital* III, Marx introduced capital competition, and in so doing, he hypothesized the equalization of the rates of profit across industries and the formation of prices of production.

Therefore, the famous transformation problem, which so much ink has been spilled over for its solution, is essentially about the transformation of an already complex form of value (the direct price) into another even more complex form of value (the price of production). Therefore, the transformation problem refers to two kinds of prices of a commodity x: the direct price (p_x^0) and the price of production (p_x^*). The difference between the two types of prices lies in the way in which the surplus-value is distributed among industries. The so-derived new set of prices, the prices of production, in general differ from labour values. More specifically,

- In direct prices, surplus-value is distributed proportionally to variable capital, and therefore total surplus-value and total profits are the same in each particular industry.
- In prices of production, surplus-value is distributed proportionally to total capital invested, and thus surplus-value produced and realized profits will differ, in general, between industries although their sums will be equal.

In Fig. 3.1, we display the three types of prices and their evolution over time.

We observe in Fig. 3.1 that commodity's x market price (p_m^x) is subject to continuous fluctuations; also, there are two interdependent, closely related, centres of gravity: direct price (p_0^x) and price of production (p_x^*). The difference is that the price of production is a more concrete, relative to direct, price and therefore, a more accurate centre of gravitation for the market prices. Moreover, the prices of production and direct prices are expected to move not far from each other over time. In Fig. 3.1, we took the case that the price of production is below the direct price; this case, as we will argue, arises when the capital-intensity of the particular industry falls short of the economy-wide average capital-intensity. Of course, the price of production will be above the direct price if the capital-intensity of the industry in question is higher than the economy's average. It goes without saying that we expect a few cases of switching between direct prices and prices of production if the ordering between the capital-intensities and economy's wide average alters in the face of changes in

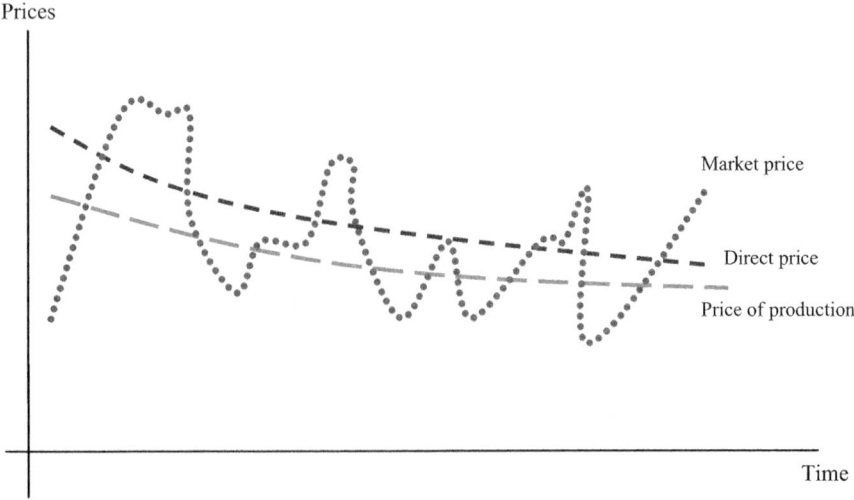

Fig. 3.1 Direct price, price of production and market price

income distribution. This might be the case when industries' capital-intensity is near the economy-wide average, and so redistribution might change their intensity from capital- to labour-intensive and vice versa. This is a rare but absolutely expected phenomenon in the classical theory of value and distribution, and we grapple with these issues in Chap. 4.

3.3 Marx's Solution

In what follows, we hypothesize that production takes place with homogenous labour paid the same real wage for a given length of working day. If exchange takes place in terms of values (or direct prices), there will be equal rates of surplus-value ($e = s/v$) across industries, that is, $e_i = e_j = e$. Hence

$$\left(\frac{s}{v}\right)_i = \left(\frac{s}{v}\right)_j = \overline{\left(\frac{s}{v}\right)} = e \tag{3.2}$$

and the distribution of surplus (profits) between industries will take place according to their variable capital. But if this is the case, capital-intensive industries would receive less surplus-value than the labour-intensive ones, for they employ less living labour. Under these circumstances, the motivation for the introduction of new technologies and general investment spending on fixed capital will evaporate since it will reduce (or at least not increase) the variable capital and by extend the surplus-value produced. From the above, we may argue that the allocation of surplus-value in the form of profit according to variable capital is not in the logic of capitalism, a system characterized by a relentless pressure for growth and expansion over time. The reason is that capitalists invest and in so doing increase their capital-labour ratio in an attempt to increase labour productivity and reduce the production cost per unit of output aiming at the attainment of the largest possible share of surplus-value generated in the sphere of production and takes on the form of profit in the sphere of circulation. Hence, although the creation of surplus-value is derived from variable capital, its distribution should be allocated (proportionally) to capital (fixed) invested. The latter is the outcome of the tendential equalization of the rates of profit across industries and the establishment of different rates of surplus-value. In other words, if the rate of profit for industry j is

$$r_j = \frac{s_j}{c_j + v_j} = \frac{(s/v)_j}{(c/v)_j + 1}$$

and if we further suppose equalization of profit rates across industries, that is, $r_i = r_j = \bar{r}$, then we will have

$$\left(\frac{s}{v}\right)_i = \bar{r}\left[\left(\frac{c}{v}\right)_i + 1\right] \text{ and } \left(\frac{s}{v}\right)_j = \bar{r}\left[\left(\frac{c}{v}\right)_j + 1\right]$$

The above indicates that the equalization of profit rates between industries characterized by different value compositions of capital $(c/v)_i \neq (c/v)_j$ dictates that each industry's rate of surplus-value is proportional to its value composition of capital. As a consequence, the prices of production of industries will deviate from their labour values (or direct prices), because sectoral profits will differ in general from their respective surplus-value. This deviation of relative prices of production from labour values was the reason that made Smith to abandon the LTV while Ricardo considered the quantitative significance of the deviations relatively small with a determinable size and direction, as we discussed in detail in Chap. 1. Marx, unlike Smith and Ricardo, argued that the presence of such deviations does not constitute distortions of the LTV; on the contrary, the prices of production are simply a more concrete form of value and more suitable to explain the observed market phenomena in the presence of competition between capitals.

In order to facilitate the presentation while following the entire theoretical tradition of classical analysis, let us hypothesize a simple economic system with three departments of production: Department I produces means of production, Department II produces means of consumption (commodities consumed by workers) and Department III produces luxury commodities consumed by capitalists. The economy is reproduced on the same scale[6] and for that the following are the required conditions

$$\text{Department I} : c_1 + v_1 + s_1 = c_1 + c_2 + c_3$$

$$\text{Department II} : c_2 + v_2 + s_2 = v_1 + v_2 + v_3$$

$$\text{Department III} : \underbrace{c_3 + v_3 + s_3}_{\text{supply}} = \underbrace{s_1 + s_2 + s_3}_{\text{demand}}$$

The left-hand side of the above equations, for simplicity reasons, represents departmental supply, while the right-hand side represents their respective demand. Department I produces means of production and demands for its own needs c_1, while c_2 is the demand from Department II, and c_3 is the demand from Department III. Similarly, the output of Department II (consumer goods) is demanded (v_1, v_2 and v_3) by workers of each department, while the output of Department III producing luxury goods is demanded by the capitalists of the three departments (s_1, s_2 and s_3). Hence, it is important to emphasize that the consumption of luxury goods has no effect in the production conditions of the economy for they are not used as inputs for further production.

---

[6]The conditions of simple reproduction have been discussed analytically in Chap. 2. Here we merely point out what is necessary for the presentation of the relevant literature on the transformation problem.

Marx's analysis of transformation of labour values into prices of production presents a crucial difference from Ricardo's and Smith's theories of labour value; instead of assuming an arbitrary uniform rate of profit, Marx derives it from the system of labour values by estimating it as the ratio of total surplus-value over total invested capital (the sum of constant and variable capital). Formally, we have

$$r = \frac{\sum s_i}{\sum (c_i + v_i)} \tag{3.3}$$

Based on this, prices of production for each department are equal to invested capital augmented by the product of rate of profit times the invested capital. Hence, for each department we get

Department I : $p_1 = c_1 + v_1 + r(c_1 + v_1) = (1 + r)(c_1 + v_1)$

Department II : $p_2 = c_2 + v_2 + r(c_2 + v_2) = (1 + r)(c_2 + v_2)$

Department III : $p_3 = c_3 + v_3 + r(c_3 + v_3) = (1 + r)(c_3 + v_3)$

Marx argued that the above system of prices of production must, generally, differ from their respective labour values ($p_i \neq \lambda_i$). It is important to note that such transfers of labour values are expected, and they are not necessarily harmful since if they remain within the domestic economy, the gains of one industry will be the losses of another, and overall the net gain for the domestic economy will be zero. However, transfers of value also take place in international trade whereby the gains of one economy are the losses of the other. The details of this crucial issue and its ramifications to economic growth are discussed in Chap. 7.

The size and sign of the deviations of prices of production from direct prices can be fully determined; if, for example, a department i (=I, II, III) has a value composition of capital $(c/v)_i$ higher than the economy-wide average one $\overline{(c/v)}$, then its price of production will be greater than its labour value and vice versa. In the special case, in which the departmental organic composition of capital is equal to the average one, then the department's production price will be equal to its labour value (or direct price). In short, we get

$$p_i \underset{<}{\overset{>}{=}} \lambda_i \text{ if } \left(\frac{c}{v}\right)_i \underset{<}{\overset{>}{=}} \frac{1}{n} \sum_i^n \left(\frac{c}{v}\right)_i \tag{3.4}$$

Hence, in Marx's analysis the deviation of prices of production from their labour values is expected and as we will show does not contradict the LTV; instead, they are inevitable in the specific mode of production, in which the economy's reproduction takes place with the mediation of, the relatively autonomous from production, sphere of circulation.

The transformation of direct prices into prices of production results in the redistribution of surplus-value in the form of profits between the different departments. But since we simply deal with a change in the form of value, the total sum of value created in the sphere of production must remain unchanged in the sphere of circulation. Therefore, the following two equalities, which Morishima (1973) calls 'invariance conditions', should apply:

The sum of direct prices should be equal to the sum of prices of production:

$$\sum_{i=1}^{n} \lambda_i = \sum_{i=1}^{n} p_i \qquad (3.5)$$

The total surplus-value produced should be equal to total profits allocated across industries according to their value composition of capital relative to the economy's average:

$$\sum_{i=1}^{n} s_i = \sum_{i=1}^{n} \pi_i \qquad (3.6)$$

Both equalities are crucial in Marx's LTV, since labour values and surplus-value are created in the sphere of production and their different forms, prices of production and profits, respectively, appear in the sphere of circulation. Consequently, one does not expect a change in their initial total figures, unless some of the produced surplus-value leaks out of the system. This case is more likely to appear in simple reproduction, where the produced luxuries, as not being inputs for further production, when consumed leak out of the system. Therefore, the deviation between surplus-value and profit is at its maximum in simple reproduction, and it is at its minimum equal to zero as expanded reproduction approaches its maximum.

3.3.1 Bortkiewicz's Critique and Proposed Solution

Bortkiewicz (1907) argued that in *Capital* III there are two logical flaws which although Marx was aware of, nevertheless he did not deal with them in any effective way. These can be shown, according to Bortkiewicz, starting off with the prices of production:

$$p_i = (1 + r)(c_i + v_i)$$

where he observed that what is actually transformed is the value of commodity's i output while the required inputs for its production, that is, c_i and v_i as well as the profit rate, r, still remain expressed in terms of labour values (direct prices). Such a transformation, however, is not only semi-finished but also is inconsistent with the reality of a capitalist economy. The idea is that capitalists and workers are hypothesized to purchase their inputs in both direct prices and prices of production; but two different evaluation systems for the same commodity cannot coexist in the same market. In addition, Bortkiewicz argued that in Marx's transformation procedure, the two equality conditions (Eqs. 3.5 and 3.6), which hold in simple reproduction on the assumption that exchange takes place in terms of direct prices, do not necessarily hold in the fully transformed prices of production. However, a consistent solution to the transformation procedure would require that moving from one evaluating system of prices to another, both conditions should simultaneously hold.

Bortkiewicz (1907) in his effort to correct Marx restated the system of simple reproduction in the following way:

$$\text{Department I} : (1 + r')(c_1 p_1 + v_1 p_2) = (c_1 + c_2 + c_3) p_1 \qquad (3.7)$$

$$\text{Department II} : (1 + r')(c_2 p_1 + v_2 p_2) = (v_1 + v_2 + v_3) p_2 \qquad (3.8)$$

$$\text{Department III} : (1 + r')(c_3 p_1 + v_3 p_2) = (s_1 + s_2 + s_3) p_3 \qquad (3.9)$$

where p_1, p_2 and p_3 are the prices of production along with the new average rate of profit r' which must be estimated. In the above statement of the problem, we observe that both inputs and outputs are expressed in the same price system along with the new rate of profit. In so doing, Bortkiewicz argued that the inconsistency in Marx's formulation may be removed, and, at the same time, the system of simultaneous equations can give an economically meaningful solution, whereby the two equalities hold and the conditions of simple reproduction are maintained, albeit under strong assumptions.

In fact, in his system of simultaneous equations, there are three equations and four unknowns (the three prices of production and the new average rate of profit); hence, there are more unknowns than equations, and the system does not solve. Under these circumstances, we fix one of the unknowns and solve for relative prices. The solution, if conditions of simple reproduction hold, can be found by stipulating the following simplifications

$$\text{Department I} : c_1 + c_2 + c_3 = c_1 + v_1 + s_1 = a_1$$

$$\text{Department II} : v_1 + v_2 + v_3 = c_2 + v_2 + s_2 = a_2$$

$$\text{Department III} : s_1 + s_2 + s_3 = c_3 + v_3 + s_3 = a_3$$

where a_i $(i = 1, 2, 3)$ symbolizes departmental output in terms of labour values. We then have

$$\text{Department I} : (1 + r')(c_1 p_1 + v_1 p_2) = a_1 p_1$$

$$\text{Department II} : (1 + r')(c_2 p_1 + v_2 p_2) = a_2 p_2$$

$$\text{Department III} : (1 + r')(c_3 p_1 + v_3 p_2) = a_3 p_3$$

We further simplify the above system by setting $m = 1 + r'$, $f_i = v_i/c_i$ and $g_i = a_i/c_i$. Hence, Bortkiewicz's system of equations can be written as

$$\text{Department I} : m(p_1 + f_1 p_2) - g_1 p_1 = 0 \tag{3.10}$$

$$\text{Department II} : m(p_1 + f_2 p_2) - g_2 p_2 = 0 \tag{3.11}$$

$$\text{Department III} : m(p_1 + f_3 p_2) - g_3 p_3 = 0 \tag{3.12}$$

which is a homogeneous system consisting of three equations and four unknowns (m, p_1, p_2 and p_3). The first two equations make up a subsystem in the sense that the price of Department III does not enter into the production conditions neither of Departments I nor of Department II. From the homogeneous subsystem of the first two equations, we can initially solve for m. Thus we have

$$(m - g_1)p_1 + mf_1 p_2 = 0$$
$$mp_1 + (mf_2 - g_2)p_2 = 0$$

or in matrix form

$$\begin{bmatrix} (m - g_1) & mf_1 \\ m & (mf_2 - g_2) \end{bmatrix} \begin{bmatrix} p_1 \\ p_2 \end{bmatrix} = \begin{bmatrix} 0 \\ 0 \end{bmatrix}$$

An economically meaningful solution requires the determinant of the above system of equations to be equal to zero

$$m^2(f_2 - f_1) - m(f_2 g_1 + g_2) + g_1 g_2 = 0$$

which solves for

$$m = \frac{(f_2 g_1 + g_2) \pm \sqrt{f_2^2 g_1^2 - 2f_2 g_1 g_2 + g_2^2 + 4f_1 g_1 g_2}}{2(f_2 - f_1)} \tag{3.13}$$

From the two estimates of m, we use the economically meaningful one.[7] In particular, we invoke the relation $m = 1 + r'$, and we estimate the new r'; we say 'new' because the estimated r' is expressed in terms of prices of production and it will be, in general, different (although not by much) from that estimated in terms of labour values.

If we now assume the familiar from Chap. 2 system of simple reproduction, we get

$$450c_1 + 180v_1 + 120s_1 = 750 a_1 f_1 = 180/450 = 0.4 g_1 = 750/450 = 1.7$$

---

[7]The structure of the system of equations always allows for a meaningful solution for m, while the negative solution is discarded.

$$200c_2 + 240v_2 + 160s_2 = 600a_2f_2 = 240/200 = 1.2g_2 = 600/200 = 3$$
$$100c_3 + 180v_3 + 120s_3 = 400a_3f_3 = 180/100 = 1.8g_3 = 400/100 = 4$$

Substituting the values of f_i and g_i in Eq. (3.13), we get $m \approx 1.27$ and thus $r' = 26.7\%$. It is worth noting that r', which is expressed in prices of production, is extremely close to the rate of profit expressed in terms of labour values. More specifically, the value rate of profit is equal to $r = 400/1350 = 29.6\%$; that is, the deviation of the two rates of profit is nearly -9.8% or, what amounts to the same thing, the proximity of the estimated rates of profit is 90.2%. Prices of production can be obtained by replacing the estimates of m in the above subsystem. Thus from the first Eq. (3.10) we get

$$p_1 = \left(\frac{mf_1}{g_1 - m} \right) p_2$$

From second and third Eqs. [(3.11) and (3.12), respectively] solving for p_2, we get

$$p_2 = \frac{g_3}{g_2 + (f_3 - f_2)m} p_3$$

By combining the three equations together, we arrive at

$$(1 + r)(p_1a_1 + p_2a_2) = p_1a_1 + p_2a_2 + p_3a_3$$

Bortkiewicz, by setting $p_3 = 1$, derived that the total profits are equal to total surplus-value in Department III [Eq. (3.6)]

$$r(p_1a_1 + p_2a_2) = a_3$$

From the above, we derive that the first equality condition [Eq. (3.5)], according to which the total sum of prices of production is equal to the total sum of direct prices, that is,

$$p_1a_1 + p_2a_2 + a_3 = a_1 + a_2 + a_3$$

does not hold in the general case for which we may write

$$p_1a_1 + p_2a_2 \neq a_1 + a_2$$

unless the following condition holds true

$$\frac{a_1}{a_2} = \frac{1 - p_2}{p_1 - 1}$$

From the above it follows that in estimating the economy's equilibrium prices, we cannot simply stipulate any rate of profit and arrive at an economically meaningful solution. Hence, if an exogenously determined profit rate is hypothesized, as, for example, Ricardo did, extreme caution should be applied, since the estimated prices may be away from those derived endogenously from the system of equations. In this light, one cannot ignore the fact that Marx's approach is vindicated, since even by carrying out his estimations in terms of direct prices, his value rate of profit, r, is not far from the equilibrium one, r'. The results of the numerical example prompt the research into the empirical front where one wonders about the proximity of value magnitudes to the estimated Marx's prices of production, the fully transformed prices of production, the actual market prices, as well as to other related economic categories, that is, rate of profit, value composition of capital and the like.

We show that in Bortkiewicz's homogenous system of equations, by setting the determinant formed by the first two equations equal to zero, we can solve in terms of relative prices p_1/p_2; and by setting $p_3 = 1$, we arrive at the equilibrium rate of profit, r'. In doing so, we attain the complete transformation of labour values into relative prices of production. Bortkiewicz by setting $p_3 = 1$, he essentially assumes that the third department produces the 'money' good, in this case produces gold used as the universal commodity. Furthermore, a price $p_3 = 1$ implies that in Department III, there is no deviation between the price of production and direct price, which are both equal to unity. If we assume that the organic composition of capital of Department III is equal to the economy's average, it follows that there is no transfer of values between the first two departments and the third one. Any transfers of values will take place exclusively between the first two departments; the gains of the one will be the losses of the other; in such a zero-sum game, the two equality conditions [Eqs. (3.5) and (3.6)] hold true for the economy as a whole.

If the value composition of capital of the third department is greater (less) than the average one, then the sum of prices of production of the other two departments will be lower (higher) than the sum of their direct prices. The idea is that for $p_3 = 1$, if Department III is capital (labour) intensive, then its price of production is higher (lower) than its direct price; so the sum of other prices of production, expressed in terms of p_3, will be lower (higher) than their respective direct prices. Hence, Bortkiewicz's solution is not problem-free, since only the second of the two equality conditions holds [Eq. (3.6)], that is, the sum of profits is equal to the sum of surplus-values.[8] The first condition, namely, the sum of values equal to sum of production

---

[8]In effect, by adding up all three equations of Bortkiewicz system, we get

$$(1 + r)(p_1 \Sigma c_i + p_2 \Sigma v_i) = p_1 \Sigma c_i + p_2 \Sigma v_i + p_3 \Sigma s_i$$

Since $p_3 = 1$, after some manipulation we get

$$r(p_1 \Sigma c_i + p_2 \Sigma v_i) = \Sigma s_i,$$

or total profits equal to total surplus-value produced

$$\Sigma s_i = \Sigma \pi_i$$

prices [Eq. (3.5)], does not hold, unless the third department's value composition of capital equals to the economy's average or in the trivial case of a uniform value composition of capital across industries.

An interesting consequence in Bortkiewicz's solution is that the rate of profit depends solely on the production conditions in the first two departments. Changes in the third department's production conditions do not affect the economy's rate of profit! An intuitive proof of the above proposal is as follows: suppose that for some reason (e.g. introduction of a new tax on production, increase in wages or in the price of a major input) the price of Department I changes and because its output is used as input in other departments, it is expected to affect the production conditions and the economy's average rate of profit. The same applies to Department II whose output is an input to other departments. But if, for some reason, the price of Department III changes, because its output is not an input to other departments, nothing really is expected to occur in the prices of Departments I and II and the economy's average rate of profit. All changes in Department III remain within the department and do not impact on the rest of the economy.[9]

3.3.2   Shaikh's Solution to the 'Transformation Problem'

The transformation problem found a satisfactory solution in Shaikh's work (1977 and 1984),[10] where he showed that Marx's formulation is merely the first step in an iterative process which leads to the complete solution of the problem. Once again, we note that Marx's transformation procedure refers to the change in the form of value, that is, from direct prices into prices of production; therefore, the transformation problem is mainly a conceptual problem that has to do with the logical consistency of the derived solution. The idea is that the essential given of the problem, that is, the required labour time, remains always the same throughout the transformation procedure. Nevertheless, Marx's analysis is incomplete in the sense that only outputs are expressed in terms of prices of production, while inputs still remain in terms of direct prices. Shaikh (1977) sought to complete the transformation process based on the usual numerical example that we find in Bortkiewicz, among others. In what follows, we simply show that the re-evaluation of inputs in terms of production prices is done in a step-by-step procedure. The steps are as follows:

---

[9]Hence if, for example, a tax is imposed onto the third department producing luxury goods, the rich consumers will suffer the consequences of such a tax without any further effect on prices and the economy's average rate of profit.

[10]Shaikh presented a solution of the transformation problem initially in his doctoral thesis in 1973. Similar solutions were presented, independently from each other, by Morishima (1973) and Okishio (1974). In evaluating the three solutions, we find that Shaikh's (1973 and 1977) is conceptually by far richer than the other two, while the solutions by Morishima (1973) and Okishio (1974) are restricted mainly to the mathematical statements of the problem and the conditions required for the fulfillment of the two equalities.

- We start off with labour time measured say in hours and assumed to remain the same throughout the transformation procedure

$$c_i + v_i + s_i = \lambda_i$$

- We assume that 1 labour hour $= 1$ €; thus, we get the direct prices

$$c_i^0 + v_i^0 + s_i^0 = p_i^0$$

- We then calculate the rate of profit in terms of direct prices

$$r^0 = \frac{\sum s_i^0}{\sum \left(c_i^0 + v_i^0\right)}$$

- With the aid of the above defined rate of profit, we calculate the prices of production of the first step

$$\left(c_i^0 + v_i^0\right)\left(1 + r^0\right) = p_i^1$$

These are the prices of production estimated by Marx, which essentially constitute the first step of an iterative process that Marx began, but left unfinished. There are parts in volume III of *Capital* that allow us to 'speculate' that Marx was aware of the incomplete nature of his solution to the transformation problem. He did not proceed to a full solution, not only because any effort to this direction required many mathematical calculations and even the application of mathematical theorems which were discovered decades later,[11] but more importantly he probably foresaw that the final results will not differ qualitatively and will display minimal quantitative significance from those arising in the first step estimated prices of production as this can be judged in his numerical examples.[12] There is no doubt that Marx was aware of the problem at hand, the difficulties associated with its solution but at the same time its minimal quantitative significance, and thus he made the following remark:

---

[11]We refer to an era that all estimations were done on paper, not at all an easy task when a solution required estimations beyond simple calculations. More importantly, they had to be done by a man who could easily criticize Newtonian calculus but felt uncomfortable when he did simple arithmetic. Perron-Frobenius theorems through which the transformation problem could be easily solved were discovered in 1907 and took many years until their application.

[12]It is interesting that classical economists, in particular Ricardo, were also aware of the feedback effects of an initial change in equilibrium prices; however, they considered that the first (or the direct) effect as the most important while those that follow, by and large, do not alter the qualitative characteristics of their conclusions (see Ricardo's treatment of taxation on profits where he explains in a letter to his friend Trower the limited significance of the probable feedback effect of taxation on the final equilibrium price) (*Works* VIII, p.154; Tsoulfidis 2005 and 2010).

Our present analysis does not necessitate a closer examination of this point.[13]

(Capital III, p. 165)

If we continue Marx's procedure, the prices of inputs must be also transformed. For this purpose, Shaikh forms a multiplier-like ratio of the first step prices of production over direct prices (or prices of the previous step). We have

$$\psi_i = p_i^1 / p_i^0$$

In re-evaluating the inputs by multiplying each of them with the corresponding multiplier, we get

$$\left(\psi_1 c_i^0 + \psi_2 v_i^0\right) = \left(c_i^1 + v_i^1\right)$$

From the above, we observe that the multiplier of Department III does not enter the estimation of prices of production, since the price of Department III is not used in the revaluation of neither the inputs of capital goods nor of consumer goods. Moreover, the departmental rates of profit differ, and therefore the estimated prices are disequilibrium ones. To continue this iterative process for the estimation of the next step prices of production for each department, we need to compute the new uniform rate of profit, that is,

$$r^1 = \frac{\Sigma p_i^1 - \Sigma\left(c_i^1 + v_i^1\right)}{\Sigma\left(c_i^1 + v_i^1\right)}$$

and use it to estimate the second step prices of production

$$\left(c_i^1 + v_i^1\right)\left(1 + r^1\right) = p_i^2$$

The multipliers of the second step prices of production with respect to the first step prices of production will be

$$\psi_i = p_i^2 / p_i^1$$

This time, the deviations from one should be less than those of the previous step, a result derived from the properties of the linear system of equations. We continue the process of redefining inputs and the new rate of profit based on prices of production of third step and so on. The process ends when the multipliers become equal to one, so it makes no sense to re-evaluate inputs. The properties of Marx's price system guarantee the following limiting relations:

---

[13]See also the previous quotation on page 6.

$$\lim_{n\to\infty} \psi_i = 1$$

$$\lim_{n\to\infty} r^n = r^*$$

$$\lim_{n\to\infty} \left(c_i^n + v_i^n\right) = c_i^* + v_i^*$$

$$\lim_{n\to\infty} p_i^n = p_i^*$$

Thus, we finally arrive at the fully transformed inputs and outputs:

$$\left(c_i^* + v_i^*\right)(1 + r^*) = p_i^*$$

where p_i^* is the fully transformed price of production. For a better understanding of the mechanics of the above-described transformation procedure, we display in Table 3.1 the usual numerical example utilized in the relevant literature (Sweezy 1942; Shaikh 1977, inter alia).

We observe that the direct prices (the monetary expression of labour value) of first step (1A) in Table 3.1 display different profit rates (19.1%, 36.4% and 42.9%) in the three departments. Following Marx's procedure, we estimate a uniform (weighted) profit rate in terms of direct prices as follows:

$$r^0 = \frac{\left[\sum p_i^0 - \sum \left(c_i^0 + v_i^0\right)\right]}{\sum \left(c_i^0 + v_i^0\right)} = 29.6\%$$

We use the above value rate of profit to estimate the first step prices of production (1B) which are in effect Marx's prices of production. We observe that both conditions of equality (Eqs. 3.5 and 3.6) are fully satisfied, in particular

- The sum of values of 1750 € equals to the sum of prices of production which is also 1750 €.
- At the same time, the sum of surplus-values (400 €) equals the sum of profits (400 €).

Hence, we may note that Böhm-Bawerk's critique was not unfounded, in as much as the new prices only transform departmental outputs while inputs continue to be expressed in terms of direct prices. In effect, inputs and outputs in step 1B are estimated at two different types of prices, a result that contradicts the logic of capitalist competition. On further examination, however, we speculate that Marx's prices of production were only a first step prices in an iterative process that, while he had the intuition, he did not pursue further the laborious calculations for reasons relating to the idea that the fully transformed equilibrium prices, whatever they might be, are not expected to be too different from the direct prices. In other words, we have two centres of gravitation of market prices that cannot be too far from each other: the first, the direct prices being defined at the highest level of abstraction and,

Table 3.1 Transformation of values into prices of production

		$€c$	$€v$	$€c+€v$	c	v	s	λ	$€p$	$€\pi$	$r\%$	$\psi\%$
1A	I	450	180	630	225	90	60	375	750	120	19.1	-----
	II	200	240	440	100	120	80	300	600	160	36.4	-----
	III	100	180	280	50	90	60	200	400	120	42.9	-----
Total		750	600	1350	375	300	200	875	1750	400		
1B	I	450	180	630	225	90	60	375	817	187	29.6	1.09
	II	200	240	440	100	120	80	300	570	130	29.6	0.951
	III	100	180	280	50	90	60	200	363	83	29.6	0.907
Total		750	600	1350	375	300	200	875	1750	400		
2A	I	490	171	661	...	...	...	...	817	156	23.5	...
	II	218	228	446	...	...	...	...	570	124	27.9	...
	III	109	171	280	...	...	...	...	363	83	29.6	...
Total		817	570	1387	...	...	...	...	1750	363		
2B	I	490	171	661	...	...	...	...	834	173	26.2	1.02
	II	218	228	445	...	...	...	...	563	117	26.2	0.983
	III	109	171	280	...	...	...	...	353	73	26.2	0.973
Total		817	570	1387	...	...	...	...	1750	363		
...	...	...	...	...					...	...	...	...
...		...	...	...					...	...	...	...
...		...	...	...					...	...	...	...
	I	504	168	672	...	...	...	...	840	168	25	1
	II	224	224	448	...	...	...	...	560	112	25	1
	III	112	168	280	...	...	...	...	350	70	25	1
Total		840	560	1400	...	...	...	...	1750	350		

the second, the prices of production which are estimated in conditions of capital competition and therefore being at lower, more concrete, level of abstraction.

The ratio of prices of step 1B over prices of step 1A gives the following departmental multipliers:

$$\psi_1 = \frac{p_1^1}{p_1^0} = 1.09 \quad \psi_2 = \frac{p_2^1}{p_2^0} = 0.951 \quad \psi_3 = \frac{p_3^1}{p_3^0} = 0.907$$

Subsequently, we re-estimate the inputs using their respective multipliers, that is,

$$\left(\psi_1 c_i^0 + \psi_2 v_i^0\right) = \left(c_i^1 + v_i^1\right)$$

In so doing, we receive the results of step 2A. Meanwhile, labour values (shown in the shaded area of Table 3.1) remain unchanged, and only the form of their expression changes until they are all transformed in terms of prices incorporating a uniform rate of profit. We observe that in this process, the multiplier of Department III plays no role whatsoever. Upon completion of Step 2A, departmental profit rates differ, signalling imbalances which cannot be maintained; they are restored by re-estimating the average rate of profit, as follows:

$$r^1 = \frac{\left[\sum p_i^1 - \sum \left(c_i^1 + v_i^1\right)\right]}{\sum \left(c_i^1 + v_i^1\right)} = 26.2\%$$

With the help of the new average rate of profit, the new prices of departmental outputs are re-estimated. The prices of production obtained in step 2B differ from those of step 1B; therefore, a new set of multipliers is calculated which this time will be

$$\psi_1 = \frac{p_1^2}{p_1^1} = 1.02 \quad \psi_2 = \frac{p_2^2}{p_2^1} = 0.983 \quad \psi_3 = \frac{p_3^2}{p_3^1} = 0.973$$

As in the previous step, these new multipliers are used to re-evaluate departmental inputs in terms of new prices, which lead us to a new uniform rate of profit; once again, differences arise between prices which include the new profit rate from those of the previous step. We may note that this set of multipliers is much closer to one than the previous step multipliers, and with the help of the so-derived new mutlipliers, we re-evaluate the inputs and so on until the differences between the new prices and the prices of previous step vanish. We can set the desired accuracy of the approximation to any desired percentage. The mathematical properties of the matrix used in the typical example guarantee the convergence of prices since the ultimate limit of each of our multipliers is one. The numerical example of the system of equations is realistic enough, in the sense that the capital intensities are not out of touch between departments and its properties guarantee both the existence and the stability of the system of prices of production.

In Table 3.1, we observe that in every single step of the iterative process, from Marx's two equality conditions [Eqs. (3.5) and (3.6)], only the sum of values equals to the sum of prices of production; the sum of surplus-values is not equal to the sum of profits. According to Shaikh (1977, 1984 and 2016), this inequality is expected and can be interpreted based on the difference between the circuit of capital and the circuit of capitalists' revenue that we discussed in Chap. 2. In the circuit of capital, deviations of prices of production from direct prices remain within the same circuit and give rise to profits or losses within the departments; hence, transfers of value between departments take place ascertaining Marx's equality conditions. However, when the analysis involves the production of luxury goods (Department III), the circuit of capitalists' revenues must be accounted for. In the circuit of revenue, the deviation of direct prices from prices of production and by extent the capitalists' profits or losses of Department III do not appear in the circuit of productive capital, and thus they are not counted for leak out of the system. That is, the differences are ascribed as gains or losses in the individual accounts of capitalists and not in business' accounts; moreover, the size of price-value deviations is related (among others) to the size of Department III; the larger this department, the greater the deviation between total surplus-value and profits. It is apparent that the greatest difference occurs in the case of simple reproduction, where capitalists spend all their profits on luxury goods. In contrast, this difference would be minimal if conditions of maximum expanded reproduction apply, where total surplus-value is productively invested. Under conditions of maximum expanded reproduction, the economy grows at its maximum possible rate; hence, the economy's growth rate equals to the rate of profit, and Marx's both equality conditions hold (Morishima 1973; Okishio 1974; Shaikh 1977 and 1984) as we show in Sect. 3.4.

3.3.3 The 'New Solution' or the 'New Interpretation'

The transformation problem continues to attract attention as researchers try to find flaws in the past treatments of the issue at hand or even propose new solutions. In doing so, a group of researchers has arrived at what they characterize as 'new interpretation' (NI) rather than another 'new solution' by arguing that in effect, there is no 'transformation problem' to find its solution, and thus the past efforts to address the issue at hand are viewed either as exercises in futility or 'much ado about nothing'. The common characteristic of different strands within this approach is first to utilize the net instead of the gross value of output in order to avoid double counting. Second, the money and not the real (basket of goods forming the necessary consumption) wage determines the allocation of new value into variable capital and surplus-value. The direct role attributed to the money wage[14] in the distribution of surplus-value is perhaps the most significant contribution to the transformation problem by the literature on the new solution.

---

[14]Rather than the hard-to-define workers' bundles of consumption goods forming the real wage.

In the interest of brevity and clarity of presentation, we deal with the fundamentals of this 'new interpretation' that appeared in the early 1980s and continue in different versions to our days. In particular, our focus will be on a very similar approach that was proposed independently and approximately at the same time period by Lipietz (1982), Foley (1982) and Duménil (1983 and 1984) and subsequently by a number of other researchers who worked in different aspects of this approach (Mohun 2004; Moseley 2000; Rieu 2008).[15] The great advantage (for others, disadvantage) of the NI is that it needs not refer to any particular equation for price determination, be it direct price, uniform rate of profit price or even monopoly price, with only two exceptions, namely, the equation determining the labour power and the equation for money which are discussed below.

More specifically, in this approach profits, Π, are defined as the difference between net revenues, R, minus total wages, that is, the product of average money wage, w, times the living labour, L, thus, we may write:

$$\Pi = R - wL$$

Surplus-value, S, is defined as the difference between living labour, L, minus the product of total wages, wL, over the value of money, $\mu = \frac{R}{L}$:

$$S = L - wL/\mu$$

The value of money, μ, or what has been established in the more recent literature as the monetary expression of labour time (MELT) is tautologically defined

$$\underbrace{R/\mu}_{\text{total (net) value}} \equiv \underbrace{L}_{\text{total price}}$$

which is another way to say that the total (net) value equals to total price. An equality which according to the NI addresses the first of Marx's 'invariance postulates' holds in terms of prices and values of net (and not necessarily gross) output.

By dividing profits by the MELT, we derive

$$\Pi/\mu = R/\mu - wL/\mu = L - wL/\mu$$

and finally

---

[15]There is another approach related to the NI of the transformation problem called 'temporal single system interpretation' (TSSI) which introduces explicitly the time element in the analysis and criticizes past solutions of a system of equations for their simultaneity and timelessness (Kliman 2007). For a critical presentation and empirical evaluation of the TSSI, see Tsoulfidis and Paitaridis (2009 and 2017).

$$S \atop \underbrace{}_{\substack{\text{total surplus-} \\ \text{value}}} \quad = \quad \Pi/\mu \atop \underbrace{}_{\text{total profits}}$$

that is, total profits is the money form of the total surplus-value. Thus, according to the NI, both of Marx's equality conditions (Eqs. 3.5 and 3.6), which are absolutely necessary for the consistency of his LTV, not only hold but in addition are made to apply to the macroeconomic framework of analysis. This is another way to say that they may be consistent with any set of prices provided that the above first three equalities hold true.

The trouble with the NI, however, is that, on the one hand, there is scant supporting textual evidence in *Capital* for the particular MELT in terms of value-added and on the other hand it is open to criticism in the sense that although the aggregate data expressed in terms of value of net output may be equal to each other, this does not, though, imply that the individual components of the aggregate data are equal to each other. Furthermore, the NI is indifferent as to what prices go into the aggregate magnitudes; it therefore excludes the possibility of transfers of values, the very essence of the transformation problem and as we saw a very central issue in Ricardo's and later in Sraffa's analyses. The transfers of values are central in our analysis of the movement of prices and international transactions. In short, the NI by introducing the concept of the MELT in terms of net value-added (not gross output) ends up with the national account identities which when multiplied by μ are expressed in terms of labour time; this identity aspect leaves the approach open to criticisms about its internal structure, let alone its explanatory content.

3.4   The Transformation Problem in Matrix Form

The complications of the transformation problem and the further advancement of the old classical and Marxian theories of value necessitate the use of linear algebra. The advantage of linear algebra is that it allows for generalizations; more importantly using linear algebra in combination with data from actual input-output tables, we may give empirical content to the LTV. The analysis begins with the definition of labour values in terms of linear algebra as follows:

$$\lambda = l + \lambda A$$

where λ is a row vector of values, l is a row vector of labour inputs per unit of output, A is the squared matrix of technological coefficients and λA is the vector of indirect labour requirements per unit of output. Thus, the vector of labour values is determined by solving the above equation for λ, that is,

$$\boldsymbol{\lambda} = \mathbf{l}[\mathbf{I} - \mathbf{A}]^{-1} \tag{3.14}$$

where $\mathbf{I}$ is the identity matrix and should not be confused with the vector of labour inputs $\mathbf{l}$. Let us now suppose the real wage, $\mathbf{b}$, a column vector whose elements are the commodities normally purchased by workers with their money wage. Hence, we further suppose that workers spend their whole money wage, w, to buy the basket of consumer goods; thus the money wage equals to the value of these goods $w = \boldsymbol{\lambda}\mathbf{b}$. The real wage, $\mathbf{b}$, multiplied by the vector of labour input coefficients $\mathbf{l}$ gives the matrix of commodities consumed by workers ($\mathbf{bl}$) per unit of output produced, while $\boldsymbol{\lambda}\mathbf{bl}$ is the variable capital per unit of output (the value of labour power times the employment coefficients). From the above we derive the scalar of the rate of surplus-value as follows:

$$e = (1 - \boldsymbol{\lambda}\mathbf{b})/\boldsymbol{\lambda}\mathbf{b} \tag{3.15}$$

With the aid of Eq. (3.15), we rewrite the value of a commodity as[16]

$$\boldsymbol{\lambda} = \boldsymbol{\lambda}\mathbf{A} + \boldsymbol{\lambda}\mathbf{bl} + e\boldsymbol{\lambda}\mathbf{bl} = \boldsymbol{\lambda}\mathbf{A} + \mathbf{l} \tag{3.16}$$

The notation is as above, while e stands for the uniform rate of surplus-value. We multiply from the right the relation (3.16) by the column vector of total output $\mathbf{x}$, and we get

$$\boldsymbol{\lambda}\mathbf{x} = \boldsymbol{\lambda}\mathbf{A}\mathbf{x} + \boldsymbol{\lambda}\mathbf{blx} + e\boldsymbol{\lambda}\mathbf{blx} \tag{3.17}$$

where $\boldsymbol{\lambda}\mathbf{x}$ is the value of gross production (sales); $\boldsymbol{\lambda}\mathbf{A}\mathbf{x}$ is the value of indirect input requirements which also include the depreciation of fixed capital; $\boldsymbol{\lambda}\mathbf{blx}$ is the value of wages; and $e\boldsymbol{\lambda}\mathbf{blx}$ is the total surplus-value (or profits).

According to Marx's definition, prices of production (or first step prices) are defined as

$$\mathbf{P} = \left(1 + r^0\right)(\boldsymbol{\lambda}\mathbf{A} + \boldsymbol{\lambda}\mathbf{bl}) \tag{3.18}$$

where the profit rate, r^0, is estimated also in value terms from

$$r^0 = (e\boldsymbol{\lambda}\mathbf{blx})/(\boldsymbol{\lambda}\mathbf{A}\mathbf{x} + \boldsymbol{\lambda}\mathbf{blx}) \tag{3.19}$$

---

[16]By replacing the rate of surplus value e by its equal, we get

$$\boldsymbol{\lambda} = \boldsymbol{\lambda}\mathbf{A} + \boldsymbol{\lambda}\mathbf{bl} + \left(\frac{1 - \boldsymbol{\lambda}\mathbf{b}}{\boldsymbol{\lambda}\mathbf{b}}\right)\boldsymbol{\lambda}\mathbf{bl} = \boldsymbol{\lambda}\mathbf{A} + \boldsymbol{\lambda}\mathbf{bl} + \mathbf{l} - \boldsymbol{\lambda}\mathbf{bl} = \boldsymbol{\lambda}\mathbf{A} + \mathbf{l}$$

We observe that inputs remain in terms of values so is the rate of profit r^0. In addition, the equality conditions [Eqs. (3.5) and (3.6)] hold, that is,

- The sum of prices of production is equal to the sum of labour values:

$$\mathbf{px} = \lambda\mathbf{Ax} + \lambda\mathbf{blx} + r^0(\lambda\mathbf{A} + \lambda\mathbf{bl})\mathbf{x} = \lambda\mathbf{Ax} + \lambda\mathbf{blx} + e\lambda\mathbf{blx} = \lambda\mathbf{x}$$

- The sum of profits is equal to the sum of surplus-values:

$$r^0(\lambda\mathbf{A} + \lambda\mathbf{bl})\mathbf{x} = \frac{e\lambda\mathbf{blx}}{\lambda\mathbf{Ax} + \lambda\mathbf{blx}}(\lambda\mathbf{A} + \lambda\mathbf{bl})\mathbf{x} = e\lambda\mathbf{blx}$$

These conditions hold only for the aggregate economy and not for the individual departments or industries. For the complete transformation of prices of production and the rate of profit (r), we have

$$\mathbf{p} = (1 + r)\mathbf{p}(\mathbf{A} + \mathbf{bl}) \tag{3.20}$$

and the total profits will be

$$r\mathbf{p}(\mathbf{A} + \mathbf{bl})\mathbf{x} = \mathbf{p}(\mathbf{I} - \mathbf{A} - \mathbf{bl})\mathbf{x} \tag{3.21}$$

Hence, the equality condition according to which the sum of prices of production equal to the sum of labour values ($\mathbf{px} = \lambda\mathbf{x}$) does not necessarily imply that the sum of profits in terms of prices of production will be in general equal to sum of surplus-values [or profits in terms of labour values, Eq. (3.6)], that is,

$$\mathbf{p}(\mathbf{I} - \mathbf{A} - \mathbf{bl})\mathbf{x} \neq \lambda(\mathbf{I} - \mathbf{A} - \mathbf{bl})\mathbf{x}$$

Henceforth, even if we assume the equality $\mathbf{px} = \lambda\mathbf{x}$, this by no means implies the following two equalities $\mathbf{pAx} = \lambda\mathbf{Ax}$ and $\mathbf{pblx} = \lambda\mathbf{blx}$ will hold, since the individual prices of production and labour values will be in general different.

3.4.1   Sraffa's Standard Commodity and the Transformation Problem

Sraffa's standard commodity is a partial answer to Ricardo's futile search effort for the discovery of an actual or the construction of a hypothetical analytical invariable measure of value (IMV). We say 'partial' answer because Ricardo's IMV requires the price of such a hypothetical and therefore analytical or actual commodity to remain the same in the face of changes in technology and distribution, whereas Sraffa's standard commodity satisfies only the invariability with respect to changes in distribution assuming the same technology. The Sraffian standard commodity consists not of a single industry but rather from the totality of industries producing basic commodities, that is, commodities which become inputs and therefore enter into the production of other commodities. And from these industries producing basic commodities, we form a kind of composite industry producing an output vector with an appropriately weighted mixture of commodities whose price remains the same regardless of changes in distribution. This 'standard industry' is growing at a pace equal to the maximum rate of profit, R, which practically is not very different from the reciprocal of the economy-wide average capital-output ratio.

Using matrix algebra and the familiar from the previous section notation, Sraffa's standard system (SSS) may be expressed by the following equations:

$$\mathbf{x_s} = (1 + R)(\mathbf{A} + \mathbf{bl})\mathbf{x_s} \qquad (3.22)$$

$$\mathbf{lx_s} = 1 \qquad (3.23)$$

where R can be also thought of as the physical rate of surplus for each of the n basic commodities produced and $\mathbf{x_s}$ the associated with R $n \times 1$ vector of physical output (proportions) of the system. Equation (3.22) defines the standard system whose dual is the system of prices of production:

$$\mathbf{p} = (1 + r)\mathbf{p}(\mathbf{A} + \mathbf{bl})$$

$$\mathbf{pb} = 1$$

In the SSS, the transformation of labour values into prices of production leaves the value of output in both price systems unchanged, including the surplus-value and profits. In addition, the rate of profit in terms of prices of production is equal to the rate of profit expressed in labour values. Thus, the labour values with a uniform rate of surplus-value $e = (1 - \lambda \mathbf{b})/\lambda \mathbf{b}$ across industries is given by Eq. (3.17) which is postmultiplied by the standard commodity

$$\lambda \mathbf{x_s} = \lambda \mathbf{A x_s} + \lambda \mathbf{blx_s} + e\lambda \mathbf{blx_s}$$
$$= \lambda(\mathbf{A} + \mathbf{bl})\mathbf{x_s} + e\lambda \mathbf{blx_s}$$
$$= (1 + R)\lambda(\mathbf{A} + \mathbf{bl})\mathbf{x_s}$$

or

$$\lambda \mathbf{x_s} = \lambda(\mathbf{A} + \mathbf{bl})\mathbf{x_s} + e\lambda \mathbf{blx_s}$$
$$= \lambda(\mathbf{A} + \mathbf{bl})\mathbf{x_s} + R\lambda(\mathbf{A} + \mathbf{bl})\mathbf{x_s}$$

and

$$e\lambda \mathbf{blx_s} = R\lambda(\mathbf{A} + \mathbf{bl})\mathbf{x_s} = \lambda \mathbf{s} \qquad (3.24)$$

where $\mathbf{s}$ is the column vector of surplus products which when multiplied by labour values gives the total surplus-value. Hence, the equality condition of Eq. (3.6) holds.

As for the other equality condition [Eq. (3.5)], that is, the sum of values equal to the sum of prices of production, in the SSS we write Eq. (3.22) as follows:

$$\mathbf{px_s} = (1 + R)\mathbf{p}(\mathbf{A} + \mathbf{bl})\mathbf{x_s} = (1 + r)\mathbf{p}(\mathbf{A} + \mathbf{bl})\mathbf{x_s}$$

so that

$$R\mathbf{p}(\mathbf{A} + \mathbf{bl})\mathbf{x_s} = r\mathbf{p}(\mathbf{A} + \mathbf{bl})\mathbf{x_s} = \mathbf{ps}$$

which means that

$$r = R = \frac{e\lambda\mathbf{blx_s}}{\lambda(\mathbf{A} + \mathbf{bl})\mathbf{x_s}} \tag{3.25}$$

where the numerator of Eq. (3.25) stands for the surplus-value of the standard system, whereas the denominator represents the value of invested capital in terms of the standard system. In accepting the condition that the transformation of labour values into prices of production should not change the value of the surplus-product in the SSS, it follows that

$$e\lambda\mathbf{blx_s} = r\mathbf{p}(\mathbf{A} + \mathbf{bl})\mathbf{x_s} = \mathbf{ps}$$

and therefore,

$$R\lambda(\mathbf{A} + \mathbf{bl})\mathbf{x_s} = R\mathbf{p}(\mathbf{A} + \mathbf{bl})\mathbf{x_s}$$

as well as

$$\lambda(\mathbf{A}+\mathbf{bl})\mathbf{x_s}=\mathbf{p}(\mathbf{A}+\mathbf{bl})\mathbf{x_s}$$

and

$$\lambda\mathbf{x_s} = \lambda(\mathbf{A} + \mathbf{bl})\mathbf{x_s} + e\mathbf{pblx_s} = \mathbf{p}(\mathbf{A} + \mathbf{bl})\mathbf{x_s} + R\mathbf{p}(\mathbf{A} + \mathbf{bl})\mathbf{x_s} = \mathbf{px_s}$$

Hence, the equality condition of Eq. (3.5) holds, as well.

From the analysis, it follows that the SSS allows the transformation of labour values (direct prices) to prices of production respecting the two invariance conditions; moreover, the SSS is a generalization of Marx's conception of the average composition of capital. The difference is that Marx's average sector is more of an 'ideal average' and not an average identified in a particular sector of the economy, whereas the SSS and composition of capital is a kind weighted average derived from the pragmatic characteristics of the economy. Empirically, we know and we will find in the next chapter that the estimated SS industry does not differ in any significant way from the economy-wide average.

3.4.2   The Iterative Procedure Once Again

It is important to note that the iterative procedure which we discussed in Sect. 3.3.2 utilizes conceptual and not calendar time; we can show that when certain conditions are fulfilled, and the time dimension is introduced, we may obtain the two equality conditions [Eqs. (3.5) and (3.6)]. Thus, by introducing the time variable in the system of prices of production, we get the following difference equation

$$\mathbf{p}_{t+1} = (1 + r_t)\mathbf{p}_t(\mathbf{A} + \mathbf{bl}) \tag{3.26}$$

For $t = 0$ we get Marx's solution, that is $\mathbf{p}_0 = \lambda$. Hence, we assume that the matrix $(\mathbf{A} + \mathbf{bl})$ is indecomposable and primitive. From the Perron-Frobenius theorem, we know that the maximum eigenvalue of the specific matrix is related to a uniquely defined positive eigenvector which corresponds to sectoral relative prices.[17] This maximum eigenvalue is taken as the limit of a sequence starting from $t = 0$ and by extent $\mathbf{p}_0 = \lambda$ and tending to infinity, $t \to \infty$ which at the limit gives $\mathbf{p}_{t+1} = \mathbf{p}_t$; the latter guarantees the full transformation of values or direct prices into prices of production.

Let us now suppose that the economy grows along the von Neumann growth path, that is, all surplus is being invested which is equivalent to saying that the economy experiences the conditions of maximum expanding reproduction. Hence, the economy's growth rate is equal to the rate of profit, and there is no capitalist consumption. In this case, both equality conditions hold; hence the sum of values is equal to the sum of prices of production [Eq. (3.5)], and the sum of surplus-value is equal to the sum of profits [Eq. (3.6)]. In order to prove the first condition, we multiply from the right the price equation by the gross output vector $\mathbf{x}$ and we get

$$\mathbf{p}_{t+1}\mathbf{x} = (1 + r_t)\mathbf{p}_t(\mathbf{A} + \mathbf{bl})\mathbf{x}$$

The output vector, which is the right vector corresponding to matrix $(\mathbf{A} + \mathbf{bl})$, can be obtained from

$$\mathbf{x} = (1 + g)(\mathbf{A} + \mathbf{bl})\mathbf{x}$$

where $g = r$ or the growth rate is equal to the economy-wide average rate of profit. We start with the normalization process, according to which the sum of prices of production should be equal to the sum of values, that is,

---

[17]Indecomposable is the (square) matrix which has at least one nonzero element outside its main diagonal in each row and column, while primitive is a square matrix with non-negative elements, which when rose to some power has only positive (nonzero) elements. The sufficient conditions for a matrix to be primitive are (a) the matrix has no negative elements, (b) is indecomposable and (c) has at least one positive element along its main diagonal. Several interesting properties of these matrices have applications to economic analysis (see Meyer 2001).

$$\mathbf{p}_{t+1}\mathbf{x} = \mathbf{p}_t\mathbf{x}$$

At the start time ($t = 0$), we have $\mathbf{p}_1\mathbf{x} = \lambda\mathbf{x}$, while for $t \to \infty$ we get $\mathbf{px} = \lambda\mathbf{x}$. The second equality condition is also fulfilled, because starting with prices of the first step, we have

$$\mathbf{p}_{t+1}\mathbf{x} = (1+\rho)\lambda(\mathbf{A} + \mathbf{bl})\mathbf{x}$$

and for $t \to \infty$ we get

$$\mathbf{px} = (1+r)\mathbf{p}(\mathbf{A} + \mathbf{bl})\mathbf{x}$$

From $\mathbf{p}_{t+1}\mathbf{x} = \mathbf{px}$, it follows

$$\lambda(\mathbf{A} + \mathbf{bl})\mathbf{x} = \mathbf{p}(\mathbf{A} + \mathbf{bl})\mathbf{x}$$

Finally, because $\mathbf{px} = \lambda\mathbf{x}$, we end up with

$$\lambda(\mathbf{I} - \mathbf{A} - \mathbf{bl})\mathbf{x} = \mathbf{p}(\mathbf{I} - \mathbf{A} - \mathbf{bl})\mathbf{x}$$

Hence, in the case when economy's growth rate is equal to the rate of profit that is in the case of maximum expanded reproduction, both equality conditions hold.

3.5   Capital Theory Controversies

The neoclassical theory of value is based on the marginal productivity theory according to which the incomes of the factors of production are determined according to their marginal contribution to production. In particular, the marginal physical product of labour is equal to the wage rate, the marginal physical product of capital is equal to the rate of profit (or interest rate) and the marginal physical product of land is equal to the rent. It is important to emphasize that in all of the above cases, the marginal products of the factors of production are estimated in physical terms. This is quite plausible in the case of labour input which can be homogenized and measured in terms of labour time. The homogenization even of this factor of production, however, is by no means an easy task if we think of the differences in skills. In the classical approach, the skilled labour is reduced to simple or unskilled labour according to the labour time required for the acquisition of the necessary skills; for all practical purposes and assuming everything else is equal, skilled labour is viewed as a multiple of the unskilled, and so the marginal productivity of each kind of labour, skilled or unskilled, is expected to be captured in wage differentials. Similarly, the land input can be homogenized and measured in hectares of the same quality of land and fertility. Hence, for both labour and land, we can stipulate economically meaningful units of measurement in the sense that they are amenable to cost minimization.

By contrast, the measurement of capital goods in terms of marginal productivity theory of income distribution displays insurmountable difficulties. The reason is that capital as a factor of production is by no means homogenous as it consists of a multitude of heterogeneous use values, whose aggregation to a single entity is fraught with problems of consistency. In fact, the problem is that capital—unlike labour or land—is an ensemble of heterogeneously produced goods, which must be added in a way such that to enable a cost-minimizing choice of technique. In other words, there is a need to devise a yardstick with the aid of which the aggregation of the different components of capital (an array of tools, machines and structures) to an economically meaningful entity becomes possible. Furthermore, the meaningful measurement of capital goods requires them to become amenable to cost minimization or, what is the same thing, to profit maximization choice of technique.

From the various available alternatives (e.g. labour values, market prices), neo-classical theory opts to measure capital goods in terms of values, in particular the capital goods in terms of physical units (buildings, machines, etc.) times their respective equilibrium prices. Hence, the neoclassical theory is in the logic and spirit of business people who evaluate every component of their entire endowment of capital stock by assigning a market price and arrive at a single value by summing them up, thereby expressing their capital stock in market value terms. The difference being that the evaluation of capital goods in neoclassical theory is carried out in terms of equilibrium prices, while the evaluation of business people is based on market prices. A cursory consideration of the problem at hand would declare it solved. However, the valuation of capital in terms of equilibrium prices is not really an option to the neoclassical theory of income distribution whose consistency to its own premises requires the quantification of the endowment of capital goods without resorting to any price measure. This is equivalent to saying that we need firstly to measure capital goods in physical terms such that to derive their marginal productivity and the associated with it prices and secondly, by assigning these prices to each and every one of the components of the entire capital stock, to arrive finally at an estimate of its total value. This problem was pointed out from the first major neoclassical economists (Jevons, Walras, Böhm-Bawerk, Marshall, Wicksell, inter alia) who tried to offer plausible solutions to this conundrum.

The logical inconsistency dimension in the measurement of capital by the neoclassical theory of value and distribution was emphasized by Piero Sraffa in his lecture notes and teaching already in the 1950s and in his book (1960). In particular, Sraffa argued that within the neoclassical theory, it is not possible to obtain a relationship between wage and profit rate (or interest), described as wage-profit rate frontier, with negative and simultaneously monotonic slope, as required by the neoclassical production function; hence, it is not possible to classify the different techniques according to their capital-intensity. Sraffa notes:

> [...] One could measure capital in pounds or dollars and introduce this into a production function. The definition in this case must be absolutely water-tight, for with a given quantity of capital one had a certain rate of interest [...]. The work of J. B. Clark, Böhm-Bawerk and

others was intended to produce pure definitions of capital, as required by their theories, not as a guide to actual measurement. If we found contradictions, then these pointed to defects in the theory, and an inability to define measures of capital accurately. It was on this—the chief failing of capital theory—that we should concentrate rather than on problems of measurement.

(Piero Sraffa, Interventions in the debate at the Corfu Conference on the 'Theory of Capital', 1958)

Joan Robinson, inspired by Sraffa's insights and teaching, raised a number of objections as to whether and to what extent it is possible to employ capital as a pure physical magnitude in a production function and in particular to be used in a theory of value and income distribution. Robinson notes:

> [T]he production function has been a powerful instrument of miseducation. The student of economic theory is taught to write $Q = f(L, C)$ where L is a quantity of labour, C a quantity of capital and Q a rate of output of commodities. He is instructed to assume all workers alike, and to measure L in man-hours of labour; he is told something about the index number problem involved in choosing a unit of output; and then he is hurried on to the next question, in the hope that he will forget to ask in what units C is measured. Before ever he does ask, he has become a professor, and so sloppy habits of thought are handed on from one generation to the next.
>
> (Robinson 1953, p. 81)

The problem of consistent evaluation of capital goods does not appear in the classical approach because equilibrium prices and rate of profit are derived on the assumptions that the size and composition of output as well as the real wage and the state of technology are given. In other words, the classical analysis assumes one of the distributive variables, usually the real wage, as given and, in turn, determines the other distributive variable, the rate profit. Alternatively, we could hold as given the rate of profit or interest rate (Sraffa 1960; Leontief 1986) and determine the other variables. Thus, the evaluation of capital goods (assuming them in physical terms in an input-output setting) can be made without the consistency problems of the neoclassical theory.[18] By contrast, in the neoclassical approach, determining the profit rate and equilibrium prices through the forces of demand and supply raises issues about the logical consistency of such determination. The reason is the heterogeneity of the endowment of capital goods and the lack of a single homogeneous or near homogeneous physical measure; the latter rules out the logical consistency of the marginal physical productivity of capital and the associated rate of profit as a scarcity reward (price). In addition to the theoretical, there are also empirical concerns about the precise form of the profit-wage curve and the price-profit rate curve of the empirical details of which we deal with in the next chapter. In effect, by utilizing data from actual economies, we subject to empirical testing the major theoretical propositions of the two competing approaches, the classical and the neoclassical using data for a number of countries and time periods.

Sraffa's work and insights were adopted by economists of the Cambridge University in England. Among his many students in the 1960s, we distinguish Joan

---

[18]For a fuller discussion of this and other related issues, see Chap. 4.

Robinson, Piero Garegnani, Geoffrey Harcourt and Luigi Pasinetti. On the other side of the Atlantic Ocean, in Cambridge Massachusetts, top neoclassical economists, of the lucks of Paul Samuelson, Robert Solow along with many others, defended the neoclassical theory, and as we shall see, without success. The exchange of views on this issue has been established in the literature as the famous *Capital Theory Controversy* between the Cambridge University in England and the MIT in the Cambridge region of Massachusetts. And once again, what the capital theory controversies of the 1960s brought about is that the concept of capital cannot be measured in a way which is consistent with equilibrium prices as determined by the neoclassical theory of value and distribution.

3.5.1 Production with Produced Means of Production

The neoclassical theory of value and distribution (at least in the Walrasian method-ological approach) has been advanced in three stages: in the first stage, the discussion is limited to a pure exchange economy, where the individuals (or households) are endowed with various commodities and their differences in preferences induce them to exchange in their effort to maximize their utility. Walras's contribution was that he managed, better than any of his contemporaries, to incorporate the (new) utility theory into an explicit model of a pure exchange economy. In his simple exchange model, the price of a commodity is determined by the forces of demand and supply, and given the preferences of individuals and their initial endowment of goods, the demand of each and every individual can be formed; by aggregating the demand curves of all individuals, the total social demand curve is obtained.[19]

The next stage is to generalize the pure exchange model to one with production. The transition was not simple and straightforward, and along the way, there were asymmetries and obstacles that had to be overcome. By assuming that individuals, besides the goods that they possess, were also endowed with factors of production, the analysis is extended but also restricted to non-capitalist production, that is, to a model with non-produced means of production (i.e. land and labour). In such a model of exchange and production, following the requirements of the marginal productivity theory of value and distribution, the equilibrium prices of commodities are determined by their cost of production (Tsoulfidis 2010, Chap. 7). The difference of this model with the one of pure exchange economy is that the endowments of households include the productive services of the non-produced means of production, land and labour.

---

[19]The model of pure exchange economy is used only for instructive purposes, and it is restricted to showing the attainment of general equilibrium, since a more realistic analysis besides exchange should include production. This analysis follows Walras's methodology and stages of the neoclassical analysis.

In fact, the analysis of an economy with non-produced means of production is an extension of the analysis of pure exchange with some asymmetries which, however, can be easily resolved. For example, the goods that individuals demand in the market are not exactly comparable to the services of the factors of production offered by them; hence, the individuals do not consume the services of the factors of production they own in any direct way. The services of the factors of production that individuals are endowed with must be transformed into supply of goods which will match the respective demand; hence there is the need of connecting the demand for final goods to the supply of services of the factors of production. This is made possible by adding in the data of the neoclassical model the technology that describes the way in which the demand for factors of production is used in the production of goods and services. In other words, the demand for factors of production is a 'derived demand' in the sense that consumers through their demand for specific final goods essentially activate the demand for the particular factors of production utilized in the production of these goods. In effect, the analysis of production with non-produced means of production is simply a generalization of the pure exchange economy and does not really present insuperable problems.

The third and final stage of development of the neoclassical theory of value and distribution, according to the Walrasian methodological approach, is the introduction of reproducible goods (i.e. capital goods) in the analysis. As we have already mentioned, the price of capital like any other factor of production is determined by its marginal physical productivity, that is, by its cost of production. But in order to define the cost of production of capital goods, we need to know their value which requires the prior knowledge of the cost of production, thereby falling to the characterization of what came to be known after Joan Robinson as 'impregnate circularity'. Naturally, one would have expected that the analysis of production with non-produced means of production could be straightforwardly generalized to include produced means of production; however, this is not the case, as the first neoclassical economists have already pointed out. The reason is that the unit of measurement of a factor of production must fulfil two basic requirements:

- The measurement unit of a factor of production must be suitable for cost minimization, which is another way to say that it must be economically meaningful.
- The measurement unit of a factor of production must be independent of equilibrium prices, since it must be used for their determination.

Clearly, in the case of non-producible means of production, their measurement units fulfil the above two requirements; for example, measuring arable land in terms of acres of uniform fertility and labour in terms of hours of work posit no, insoluble at least, problems regarding their aggregation and determination of equilibrium prices. Turning to capital, we realize that the two requirements are hard to be fulfilled because capital goods are heterogeneous, and, in order to aggregate them, one needs a common unit of measurement independent of (equilibrium) prices, which we need to estimate in the first place.

We could argue that as with Marx's theory of value the issue of inconsistency was brought about through the 'transformation problem'; a similar critique was levelled against the neoclassical theory of value through the 'capital theory critique'. However, in regard to the transformation problem, we showed that the issue of inconsistency can be addressed in a logically consistent way; as it will be shown next, we cannot say the same with the neoclassical theory of value and its associated capital theory critique. Moreover, and paradoxically how, although the neoclassical theory of value and distribution was developed mainly from the dissatisfaction about the various aspects of the LTV, nevertheless in their solutions of the problem at hand, neoclassical economists theorized and evaluated capital goods in terms of labour time.

It is important to stress, at this point, that the measurement issue has created a (usual) misconception according to which capital cannot be measured at all. This is not true, since in actual economies, capital is expressed and may be measured in market prices; in fact, there are various ways to deal with the problems of its evaluation; one way is to measure it in labour values. In the capital theory controversy, the real issue with the measurement of capital that surfaces time and again is that the capital goods cannot be evaluated in equilibrium prices that are consistent with the requirements of the neoclassical theory of value and distribution; hence, this is a problem specific to the neoclassical theory of value. Such a problem does not arise in the classical theory of value because capital can be measured in a consistent way in terms of labour values and also in terms of prices of production. Thus, the problem is not the measurement of capital per se but the logical consistency of its measurement within the requirements of the utilized theory. Moreover, if it were true that capital cannot be measured at all, then there would not be possible to theorize in any credible way any aspect of the operation of the capitalist system. It is true that capitalists always evaluate their capital goods, and it would be a mistake to say that capital cannot be measured at all.

3.5.2   Factors of Production and the Neoclassical Theory of Value and Distribution

Samuelson, in his effort to defend the neoclassical theory of value and distribution, argued that the concept of capital does not require the aggregation of homogeneous goods as suggested by the pioneering neoclassical economists Jevons, Böhm-Bawerk and Wicksell. Samuelson (1962a) essentially made valliant efforts to address the issues raised by Joan Robinson (1953) in her article of capital theory; in doing so, he created the basis for a bitter debate on both sides of the Atlantic. The essence of this debate revolved around the fundamental principles that should govern the theories of value and distribution as well as economic growth which depend on an aggregate production function whose inputs (mainly capital and labour) enter production prior to the determination of the rate of profit and wage, respectively.

According to the neoclassical theory of value and distribution, the value of each factor of production is determined by its marginal contribution to production, and the presence of substitutability between inputs leads to diminishing returns to scale. Hence, the price of a factor of production reflects its relative scarcity; so, does the rate of profit (or interest) as being the price of capital input. More specifically, the relative abundance of capital in conjunction with the law of diminishing returns[20] leads to a lower rate of profit; the converse applies to the case of its relative scarcity. Finally, the capital income is the product of the profit rate times the employed capital.

A central issue in capital theory controversies is how does one measure the quantity of capital input entering the production function? The measurement of any input entering into a production function should be in accordance to the requirements of the neoclassical theory; at the same time, the units of measurement of each of the utilized inputs must be economically meaningful such that to allow for the selection of a cost minimizing production technique. More specifically, it would be absurd to measure labour according to the weight or height of workers and capital according to some of its physical or chemical characteristics. Furthermore, the measurement of each of the factors of production should be carried out independently of prices since the purpose of the analysis is the determination of equilibrium prices.

Within the neoclassical analytical framework, the shape of isoquants depicts the various combinations of two inputs used to produce a given amount of output. The usual and consistent with the neoclassical theory shape of isoquants is convex for they are governed by the law of diminishing returns of the factors of production and the idea of nearly perfect substitutability between them and, therefore, the presence of any number of possible techniques. It is worth pointing out that this idea of substitutability is specific to the neoclassical theory; by contrast, the classical theory does not recognize substitutability of any degree other than zero which is equivalent to saying that the isoquant curves are L-shaped, thereby stressing the use of a single optimizing combination of factors of production in the production of a specific amount of output. In addition, the isocost curve depicts the price ratio of the utilized (two) inputs. Figure 3.2 presents a set of convex isoquant curves combined with the isocost curve for the simple case in which the only factors of production are the non-reproducible inputs of labour and land. The vertical axis depicts the quantity of land measured in acres of the same quality, while on the horizontal axis, we place the quantity of the labour input measured in hours of homogenous labour.

We note that both units of measurement for the two non-reproducible factors of production are independent of prices. When we refer to an amount of land expressed in hectares of the same quality (productivity) and to a quantity of labour expressed in hours of homogenous labour, it means that both variables can be expressed in an appropriate economically meaningful way to form quantity indices that minimize the

---

[20]According to the law of diminishing returns, the more extensive use of an input implies lower marginal physical product, holding constant all the other factors of production involved.

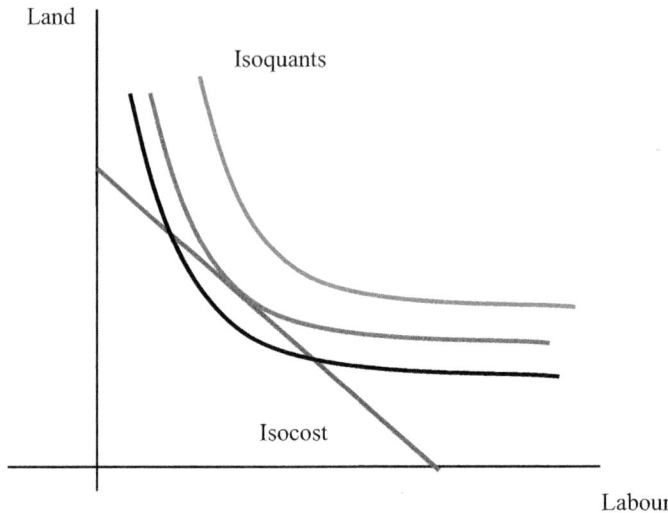

Fig. 3.2 Isocost and isoquant curves, non-reproducible inputs labour and land

production cost of a specific good. In other words, the measurement units of the two variables are amenable to the selection of their optimal economical combination which is the point of tangency of isocost curves with the highest possible isoquant curve; this point determines the optimal combination of the two inputs for a given level of output.

Although the analysis of production with non-reproducible inputs presents no particular problems, when capital goods (produced means of production) enter into the production function, we should pay particular attention to the following:

- Capital is a reproducible input, and, in this sense, it differs from both land and labour.
- Capital goods depreciate.
- Capital goods' prices are defined by their cost of production exactly as with the prices of all other goods.

While the first two characteristics of capital goods are expected and pose no analytical problems, when we come to third, certain issues arise which deserve further analysis. First of all, the price of capital goods is determined as follows:

$$P_K = \frac{X_K}{r} \tag{3.27}$$

where P_K is the price of capital good, X_K is its net (from depreciation) annual revenues and r is the rate of profit.[21] At equilibrium, the demand price of capital

---

[21]Here, capital is treated like a bond with infinite lifetime, that is, an asset whose net income, for simplicity reasons, remains the same year after year forever.

goods should be equal to its production cost. Because this condition should apply to all capital goods, it follows that the rate of profit on the cost of production for each capital asset must be equal to the economy's average rate of profit:

$$r = \frac{X_K}{C_K} \tag{3.28}$$

where C_K is the production cost of a capital good. Therefore, the presence of a uniform rate of profit dictates that the demand price for capital goods is identical to their production cost

$$P_K = C_K \tag{3.29}$$

which is a condition that should be met by all reproducible goods.

However, capital goods besides being reproducible possess another important feature: they are an endowment owned by individuals. According to this second feature, the price for its services, P_K, should be established in the capital market. But, while labour's and land's prices are specified in the relevant markets by their respective forces of supply and demand and the prices of consumer goods are determined by their production costs, the prices of capital goods are determined by two conditions at the same time:

- Firstly, by the conditions of supply and demand in the capital market, hence capital goods are treated as a component of the endowment of the individuals
- Secondly, by their production costs in the relevant market, since capital goods are also produced as means of production (Eatwell 1990; Eatwell et al. 1990, p. xii).

In other words, within the neoclassical theory of value, there is a peculiarity about the capital goods, since there are two conditions which identify the same set of values. Put in mathematical terms, the system is overdetermined and as such has an infinite number of solutions.

3.5.2.1 Samuelson's Parable Production Function

In dealing with the above challenges, Samuelson (1962a) proposed a parable economy producing only two goods (a consumer and a capital good) by employing the exact same technique to produce both goods, that is, by having the same capital-labour ratio. At equilibrium, the price of the consumer good should be equal to its production cost:

$$P_C = wL_C + rP_K K_C \tag{3.30}$$

where P_C is the consumer good's price, w is the wage rate, and L_C and K_C stand for the labour employed and capital invested in the production of the consumer good, respectively. The equilibrium price of the capital good, P_K, is equal to

$$P_K = wL_K + rP_KK_K \tag{3.31}$$

given that the subscript K refers to capital goods and the rest of the symbols of the above equation bear the exact same meaning as in Eq. (3.30).[22]

Thus, we can form a system of two simultaneous equations with three unknowns, P_C, P_K and r. For a unique and therefore economically meaningful solution, the price of the consumer good is selected as the numéraire, and the system can be written as

$$1 = wL_C + rP_KK_K$$

$$P_K = wL_K + rP_KK_K$$

Solving the second equation of the above system for the price of capital good P_K, we get

$$P_K = \frac{wL_K}{1 - rK_K}$$

Substituting P_K in the first equation of the above system, we get

$$1 = wL_C + rK_C \left[\frac{wL_K}{1 - rK_K} \right]$$

or

$$1 - rK_C = wL_C(1 - rK_K) + rK_CwL_K$$

Solving for w, we arrive at the following quadratic equation which is the wage rate of profit curve (WRPC):

$$w = \frac{1 - rK_K}{L_C(1 - rK_K) + rK_CL_K} = \frac{1 - rK_K}{L_C + r(K_CL_K - K_KL_C)}$$

$$= \frac{1 - rK_K}{L_C + r\left(\frac{K_C}{L_C} - \frac{K_K}{L_K}\right)L_KL_C} \tag{3.32}$$

Positing the constraint that the capital-labour ratio is the same in both sectors, in effect, the term in the parenthesis in Eq. (3.32) can be rewritten as

---

[22] An analytical more precise way is to state the prise equation as $P_i = wL_i + K_iP_K + (r + d)K_iP_K$, where $i = C, K$. For reasons of simplicity and clarity of presentation, we assume away the cost of circulating capital as well as depreciation expenses (where d is the depreciation rate); so, what is left includes the wage cost (wL_i) of each sector and its profits (rK_iP_K). Such a simplification does not affect our theoretical results in any qualitative way.

$$K_C/L_C - K_K/L_K = K_C L_K - K_K L_C = 0 \qquad (3.33)$$

and the following linear equation is derived

$$w = \frac{1 - rK_K}{L_C} \qquad (3.34)$$

which is displayed in Fig. 3.3a; hence, the maximum wage, w_{max} (when $r = 0$), is equal to $1/L_C$, and the maximum rate of profit, r_{max} (when $w = 0$), is $1/K_K$.

This relation can be generalized for a variety of techniques, each and every one of which is characterized by different capital-labour ratios. Theoretically, there are many possible techniques which can be expressed through the following relation:

$$w = f(r) = \frac{1 - rK}{L} \qquad (3.35)$$

from which we have removed the subscripts indicating the characterization of goods, since we assume the same capital-labour ratio for the production of both (consumer and capital) goods. These many techniques are displayed in Fig. 3.3b by the different WRPCs. The intersection points A, B, C, D and E form an outer envelope of the WRPCs which is called the wage rate of profit frontier (WRPF).

The WRPF shows the locus of points for choosing optimal techniques for it is formed by the outer segments of the WRPCs. The slope of each and every WRPC is derived by differentiating the wage rate with respect to the rate of profit,

$$f'(r) = \frac{dw}{dr} = -\frac{K}{L} = \text{constant} \qquad (3.36)$$

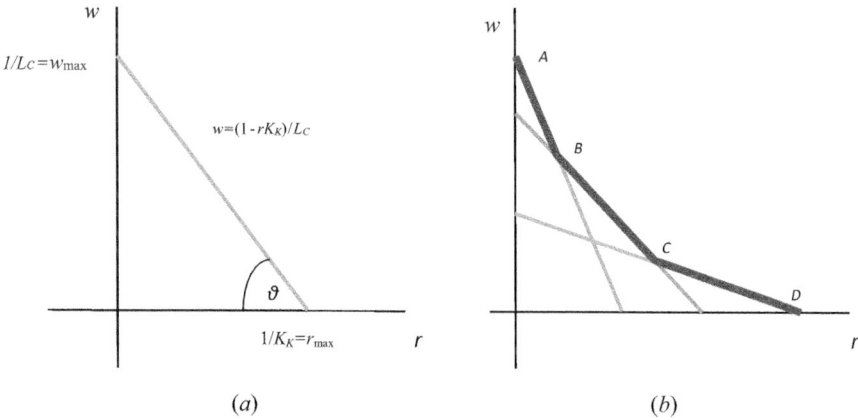

(a)   (b)

Fig. 3.3 WRPCs and their WRPF

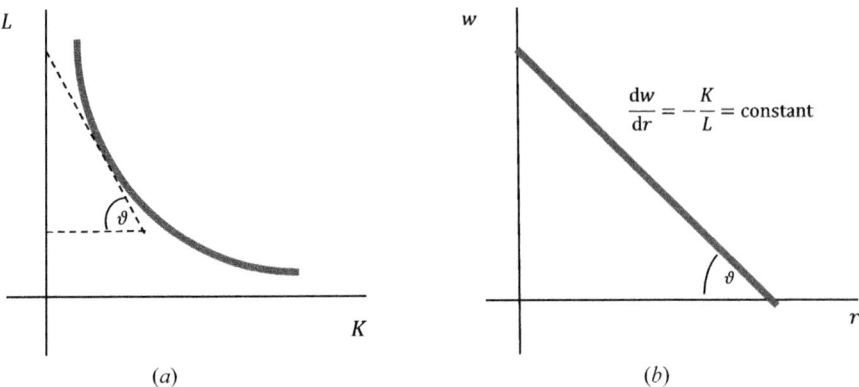

Fig. 3.4 The isoquant and the wage-profit rate curves

which implies that the WRPC is linear and its slope is negative and equals to the capital-labour ratio. By assuming a uniform capital-labour ratio across industries, the relation between the rate of profit and the wage rate becomes linear and negative.

This relation gives rise to the dual presentation of the familiar from the standard microeconomics textbooks of isoquant curve as shown in Fig. 3.4. On the left-hand side panel of Fig. 3.4a, labour is displayed on the vertical axis and capital on the horizontal axis. The isoquant curve of the figure represents the locus of points of different combinations of capital and labour producing a given quantity of output. The tangents to this curve represent the price ratios of the two factors of production, which in the case of labour and capital are the wage and profit rates, respectively. The tangent of the angle ϑ of the WRPC displayed on the right-hand side panel of Fig. 3.4b represents also the capital-labour ratio.

The above relations are further clarified by the introduction of a third technique which is all depicted in the top panel of Fig. 3.5a; the lower panel of the same figure represents the price of capital for each and every one of the three techniques. Technique A shown on the upper part of the left-hand side panel of Fig. 3.5 has the highest capital-labour ratio and thus the lower rate of profit as it is indicated in the lower panel. Continuing with technique B, we observe that the tangent of its WRPC is lower than A's and the associated rate of profit is higher. The relations are repeated in the shape of technique C characterized by an even lower capital-labour ratio and therefore a higher rate of profit. These results are consistent with the requirements of the neoclassical theory of scarcity prices.

Producers due to competition choose the technique that minimizes their cost of production or alternatively maximizes their profits. Hence, for a given wage, producers choose a technique with the highest profit rate, or, alternatively, for a given rate of profit, they choose a technique with the maximum wage. In other words, producers select points on the envelope formed by the outer segments of each WRPC, representing the three techniques; hence, entrepreneurs choose points on the envelope (the WRPF) which represents the optimal technological capabilities. Because by construction the various techniques are represented by straight lines,

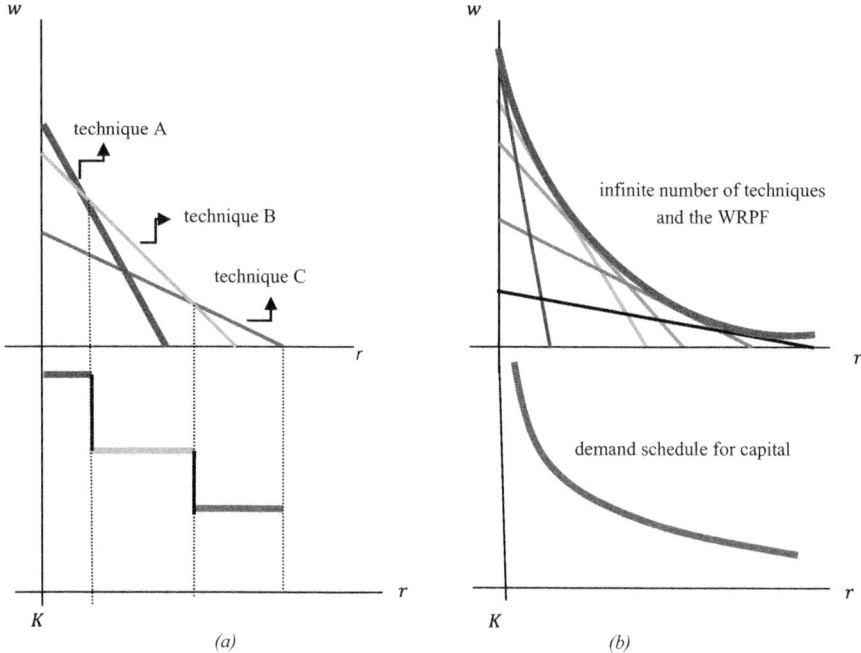

Fig. 3.5   Different techniques and the demand schedule for capital

there exists only one intersection point per pair of lines. Consequently, we derive the
negative relationship between the value of capital (or its scarcity) and the rate of
profit as theorized by the neoclassical theory shown on the lower left panel of
Fig. 3.5a with the steplike demand schedule for capital. If the number of techniques
increases indefinitely, as is represented in Fig. 3.5b, the relationship between capital
and the rate of profit becomes the usual continuous demand for capital schedule
commonly displayed in macroeconomic textbooks.

These were the relationships that led Paul Samuelson to the conclusion that if the
capital-labour ratio is uniform across sectors, or what amounts to the same thing in
the one-commodity world, the profit rate is determined by the relationship between
the cost of production and the demand for this single capital good. Moreover, the rate
of profit and the value of capital are inversely related, a result which is fully
consistent with the neoclassical theory, where the payments for the services of the
factors of production reflect their respective relative scarcities.

3.5.3   From the One to Many Commodities World

Samuelson claimed that the conclusions drawn from the analysis of the
one-commodity world can be generalized to represent the operation of real economies which produce a large variety of commodities. It is ironic and worth noting that

Samuelson criticized Marx's theory of value for its logical inconsistency, because labour values are equal to prices of production, if and only if the capital-labour ratio (or the value composition of capital) is the same across sectors (see Chap. 2 for details). However, in defending the neoclassical theory of value, Samuelson did not hesitate, although he was warned against,[23] to utilize in his analysis a uniform capital-labour ratio, a patently unrealistic assumption in the effort to rescue the logical consistency of the neoclassical theory of value. The idea is that if two commodities have the exact same capital-labour ratio (K/L), then they are similar to each other, and the analysis in effect takes place in a one-commodity economy. More importantly, Marx's theory of value (as we have already showed) need not make such a counterfactual assumption to establish the consistency between the labour values and prices of production.

But what led neoclassical economists to this unrealistic representation of the economy? The quintessence of the problem is to determine the relationship between the output price of a commodity and its cost of production which includes the factor payments in a way consistent with the requirements of the neoclassical theory of value. Starting with the super simple case of the price in a one-commodity world, we write

$$P = wL + rP_K K \qquad (3.37)$$

If $w = 1$, then for each $P > 0$ corresponds a positive profit rate, $r > 0$; hence, in the case of a one-good economy, the price of the good is determined by market forces, and r is determined indirectly in the factor markets through the associated with-it derived demand schedule. If we have two commodities, their price ratio should be derived on the condition of a uniform rate of profit as a result of competition. If more commodities are introduced, more price ratios must be determined, all of which should be consistent with a uniform rate of profit. From the above, the question is to what extent, if any, the analysis can be generalized to an economy with the production of many commodities and the employment of heterogeneous capital goods.

The complications that may arise from the production of two or more commodities are examined starting first with the introduction of a second commodity and then continuing with further generalizations. The case of two commodities which for their production require different capital-labour ratios may be described by invoking the quadratic Eq. (3.32) of the WPRC which may be either convex or concave depending on the sign of the second derivative. The curve is convex, that is, looking upward with respect to the origin, if the second derivative of the relation is positive while it is concave, that is, looking downwards the origin, if the second derivative is negative.

---

[23]Garegnani participating in the seminar at MIT taught by Samuelson had pointed out the problem and the consequences of the assumption of a one-commodity world. Samuelson (1962a), although acknowledged that he received comments by Garegnani, nevertheless he did not account for them in the article.

As a consequence, we estimate the sign of the derivatives which are necessary to state the conditions which must be fulfilled for the different shapes of the WRPCs. The first derivative of the relation (3.32) with respect to the rate of profit will be

$$
\begin{aligned}
\frac{dw}{dr} &= \frac{(1 - rK_K)'(L_C + rZ) - (L_C + rZ)'(1 - rK_K)}{(L_C + rZ)^2} \\
&= \frac{-K_K((L_C + rZ)) - Z(1 - rK_K)}{(L_C + rZ)^2} = \frac{-K_K L_K}{(L_C + rZ)^2}
\end{aligned}
\tag{3.38}
$$

where $Z = K_C L_K - K_K L_C = (K_C/L_C - K_K/L_K)L_C L_K$. The second derivative of the above will be

$$
\frac{d^2 w}{dr^2} = \frac{\left[(L_C + rZ)^2\right]' K_K L_K}{(L_C + rZ)^4} = \frac{2(L_C + rZ)Z K_K L_K}{(L_C + rZ)^4} = \frac{2Z K_K L_K}{(L_C + rZ)^3}
\tag{3.39}
$$

Since all the coefficients of Eq. (3.39) are positive, it follows that the shape of the WRPC depends completely on the sign of the factor Z. In particular

$$
\text{If } Z > 0, \text{ that is, } \frac{K_C}{L_C} > \frac{K_K}{L_K} \text{ and } \frac{d^2 w}{dr^2} > 0, \text{ the WRPC is convex}
\tag{3.40}
$$

$$
\text{If } Z < 0, \text{ that is, } \frac{K_C}{L_C} < \frac{K_K}{L_K} \text{ and } \frac{d^2 w}{dr^2} < 0, \text{ the WRPC is concave}
\tag{3.41}
$$

$$
\text{If } Z = 0, \text{ that is, } \frac{K_C}{L_C} = \frac{K_K}{L_K} \text{ and } \frac{d^2 w}{dr^2} = 0, \text{ the WRPC is linear}
\tag{3.42}
$$

The third case refers to the one-commodity world or of an economy with uniform capital-labour ratio which we examined in the previous section. All three cases are summarized in Fig. 3.6.

Our attention now focuses on an economy with two sectors, and we compare the results with those derived from the one-commodity economy. Figure 3.7 presents the WRPCs of a two-commodity economy.

More specifically, in Fig. 3.7 we have the case of a concave curve, whose area below measures the per capita physical output. If $r = 0$, then all output goes to labour and $w = w_{\max}$. If $w = 0$, then all output goes to capital and $r = r_{\max}$. The profit rate is estimated from

$$
r = \frac{\text{profits}}{\text{capital stock}} = \frac{\Pi}{K} = \frac{\Pi/L}{K/L} = \frac{\pi}{K/L}
$$

where π stands for the profits per capita or unit labour. Hence, the capital-labour ratio can be rewritten as

Fig. 3.6 Wage rates of profit curves of different shapes

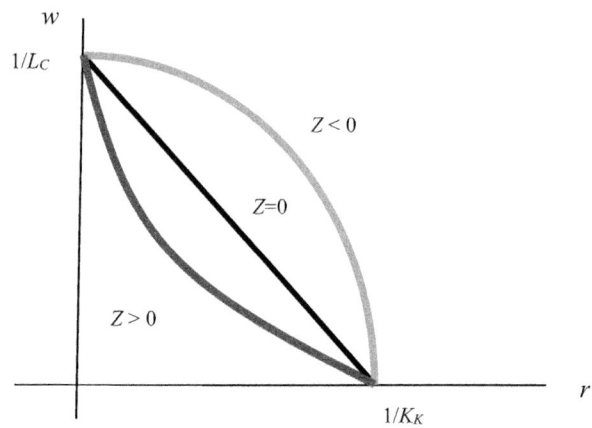

$$\frac{K}{L} = \frac{\pi}{r} \tag{3.43}$$

which is equal to the tangent of angle ϑ or

$$-\frac{K}{L} = \tan \vartheta \tag{3.44}$$

However, in the case of a two-commodity world, we observe that the tangent of angle ϑ changes as we move along the curve. This is equivalent to saying that the capital-labour ratio changes whenever the distribution between wages and the rate of profit changes.

In Fig. 3.7 we can see that in the case of a concave WRPC ($Z < 0$), if the rate of profit increases, so does the capital-labour ratio, or what amounts to the same thing, the tangent of angle ϑ increases, result of which *prima facie* contradicts the

Fig. 3.7 The wage rate of profit curve with two goods

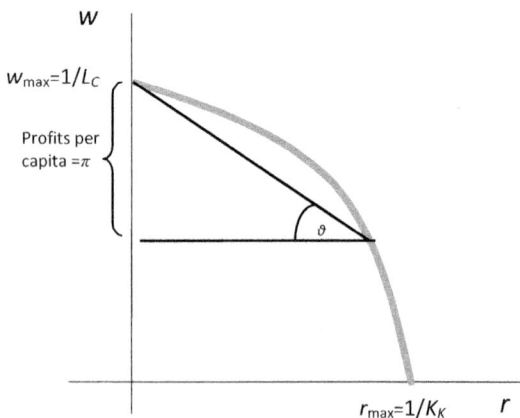

neoclassical theory according to which an inverse relation between the two variables is expected. The idea is that prices in neoclassical economics are indexes of relative scarcity; so as the rate of profit increases, one expects a pari passu falling capital-labour ratio indicating the scarcity of capital and the abundance of labour. Hence, the so-called Wicksell effect is 'perverse', because the capital-labour ratio increases following the increase in the rate of profit.[24] If now the WRPC is convex ($Z > 0$), the value of capital falls as the rate of profit rises and the Wicksell's price effect is positive or 'normal'; in that way it enhances Wicksell's actual effect. Therefore, a convex WRPC agrees with the neoclassical results, provided that we deal with a single technique. Finally, if the wage rate of profit curve is linear, the price effect completely vanishes, and the rate of profit becomes equal to the marginal physical product of capital.

We showed that in the one-commodity world, the two or more techniques are depicted with straight lines which intersect each other only once. By taking the outer segments of the curves that they form, we construct the WRPF shown in Fig. 3.3b. However, in moving from the economy of one to the multi-commodity world, the many available techniques may be represented by WRPC as shown, for example, in Fig. 3.8.

The shapes of these WRPC depend on the number of sectors. Mathematically speaking, a single sector entails a WRPC which is a straight line; a two-sector model entails one extreme, while the inclusion of a third sector may give rise to two extremes and one inflection point. Extending the analysis to four sectors, we expect three extreme and two inflection points and so forth. The maximum number of curvatures in WRPCs will depend on the number of sectors. Because of such shapes, moving from one technique to another, the value of capital and the rate of profit may display any possible relationship, and not necessarily the inverse as expected in the neoclassical theory. If the number of available techniques increases and there are many produced goods, then the argument about the uncertain and complex relationship between the relative scarcity of capital and the rate of profit is strengthened rather than weakened.

In what follows, we discuss the details of the consequences of changes in distribution on the neoclassical and classical theories of value and distribution in the effort to derive more definitive conclusions about the two competing theories. In Fig. 3.9, we represent an economy producing two goods whose techniques are displayed in the shape of their capital-labour ratios. Furthermore, let us suppose that one of these two techniques (technique A) displays concave WRPC which makes it a candidate for the appearance of 'perverse' Wicksell's effects. Let us further suppose that the technique B is a straight or a convex line. Putting together these two WRPCs in Fig. 3.9, we observe two switching points which of course

---

[24]Capital controversies often refer to Wicksell's price and real effects. The price effect refers to changes in the value of capital induced by changes in distribution (between wages and profits) with a given technique. The real effect refers to changes in the value of capital brought about by changes in distribution and by changes in the technique.

Fig. 3.8 WRPC with many goods

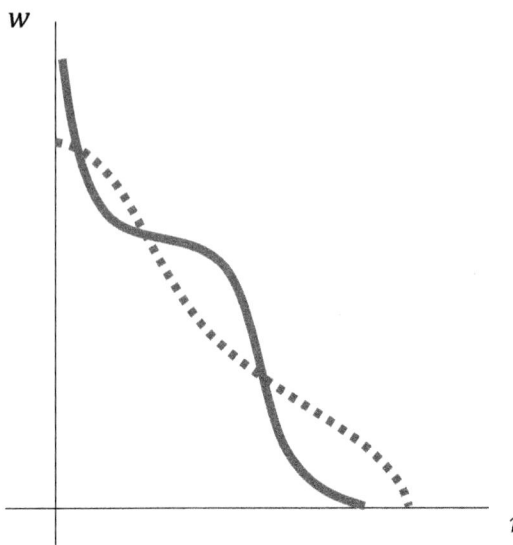

could not exist in the case of straight WRPCs of a one-commodity world. In addition, having to deal with a single or a multi-commodity world and in the presence of many alternative techniques of production, the cost minimizing technique dictates the choice of points on the WPRF. Hence, for a given rate of profit, we select the technique with the highest wage rate, or, alternatively, for a given wage rate, we choose the technique with the highest rate of profit.

Let us now assume that the rate of profit is very low which entails the choice of technique B since it is characterized by a capital-labour ratio higher than that of technique A. As the rate of profit increases and reaches the first intersection of the two techniques (first switching point), the two techniques become equally profitable; therefore, we are indifferent as to which technique to choose. However, if the rate of profit increases furthermore, the technique A becomes more profitable and, therefore, the preferred one; but this technique is characterized by a higher capital-labour ratio (or the tangent of angle ϑ is higher for technique A rather than B). In other words, as the rate of profit increases instead of selecting the technique with the lower capital-labour ratio (as required by neoclassical theory), we select a technique with higher capital-labour ratio! Until we reach the next intersection of switching point, and once again, we become indifferent whether the technique A or the technique B will be selected. As the rate of profit increases even more, we no longer become indifferent and switch, this time, to technique B, that is, a technique with lower capital-labour ratio than that of technique A. That is, from the technique with the higher capital-labour ratio, we choose the technique with the lower capital-labour ratio, which this time is consistent with the neoclassical theory. Theoretically speaking, one cannot rule out the case of many switching points as shown in Fig. 3.8.

The importance of this result (reswitching of techniques) is that Samuelson's (1962a) parable of the one-commodity world is not generalized to the real world of

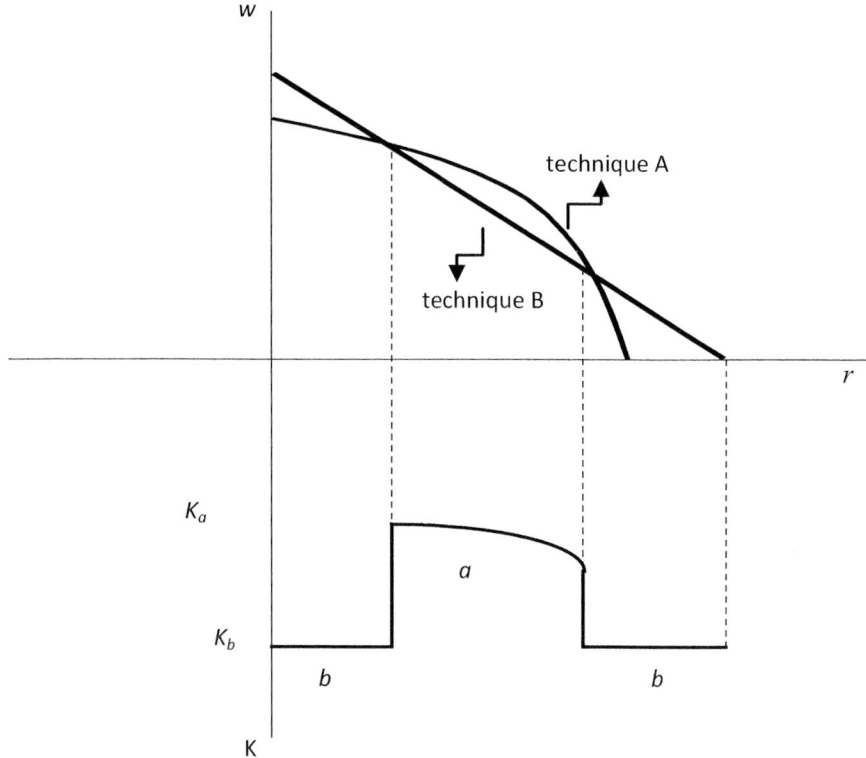

Fig. 3.9 Switching points and the demand schedule for capital

many commodities. Practically, this means that one cannot simply estimate, for example, the capital-labour ratios in constant or current prices and based on these estimates to derive some form of demand function for the overall economy. The reason is that, if the rate of profit is not equal to the marginal physical product of capital, we cannot derive a consistent schedule of the marginal efficiency of capital which is another way to say that we cannot define the demand schedule for capital goods and thus the schedule of macroeconomic analysis, that is, the IS curve. Furthermore, it is futile to estimate the scarcity of capital via another variable, such as savings, and assume that savings is a well-behaved function of the rate of profit. Finally, if we cannot formulate the demand schedule for capital goods, we cannot define the demand for labour or almost every other schedule. In effect the hypothesis of substitutability between the factors of production precludes the consistent construction of the demand curve of any factor of production. Hence, if the demand for capital so central in the neoclassical economic analysis behaves 'abnormally', it imparts its abnormal behaviour to the other schedules, and the results of the analysis may be completely out of touch with the real economy.

3.6   Summary and Conclusions

This chapter at the beginning focused on the famous problem of transformation of labour values into prices of production. We noted that this is not a problem of merely requiring computations of labour values and prices of production but chiefly a conceptual problem concerning the structure and consistency of the classical theory of value. The debate has been fierce, and many eminent economists of both the classical and neoclassical camps have been engaged. We argued that labour values (direct and indirect labour requirements contained in a commodity) are transformed into direct prices (simple form of value) and subsequently into prices of production (a more complex form of value), a more concrete centre of gravitation of the ever-fluctuating market prices. As we will discuss in Chaps. 5 and 6, there is a third kind of centre of gravitation, the regulating conditions of production of each industry and the association with these regulating prices of production whose details and consequences, theoretically and empirically, become the subject of our analysis in Chaps. 5 and 6.

The neoclassical transformation problem, that is, the determination of the value of capital in a logically consistent way, was discussed intensively mainly in the 1960s in the famous capital theory controversies. We showed that theoretically speaking, all the questions that were raised within this debate remain open issues in neoclassical theory. We have stressed, time and again, that the problem at hand is not the measurement of capital per se but its definition and measurement in a way which is consistent with the requirements of the neoclassical theory of value and income distribution.

The same issue does not appear in the classical approach, as one of the distributive variables, the real wage (or the rate of profit), is taken among the givens of their theoretical model. Finally, one wonders by how much does the capital-labour ratio or rather the capital-intensity differ across sectors and whether the resulting differences are large enough as to create more than two switch points? This is an empirical question in the main, and, as we will see in Chap. 4, there are significant differences in the capital-intensities across industries; nevertheless, these differences, whatever they might be, do not generate effects akin to those described in the capital theory debates, namely, the WRPCs are not far from straight or convex lines and, at the same time, rarely display the curvatures described by the Cambridge UK-side economists. However, the empirical results in and of themselves do not lend support to the one-commodity description of the economic world, and the consistency problems within the theory remain unresolved. On the empirical front, there are cases, not too many, that we get reswitching of the WRPCs, and the trajectories of equilibrium relative prices do not move monotonically with changes in the distribution of income between wages and profits. We grapple with this as well as with a number of related theoretical and empirical issues in the next chapter.

Chapter 4
Labour Values, Prices of Production and Wage Rate of Profit Curves in Actual Economies

The labour theory of value was devised by Ricardo as a stick to beat landlords (rent does not enter into cost of production). But later, having been adopted by Marx to beat the capitalists, it was necessary for defenders if the present system to devise a new theory. The utility theory of value.
Piero Sraffa (D3/12/3:14–15) {The Piero Sraffa Papers are kept at the Wren Library, Trinity College, Cambridge [catalogue and access to documents at https://janus.lib.cam.ac.uk/db/node.xsp?id=EAD%2FGBR%2F0016%2FSRAFFA and also in Carter S. (2018)]}.

The phenomenon of switching back at a very low interest rate to a set of techniques that had seemed viable only at a very high interest rate involves more than esoteric difficulties. It shows that the simple tale told by Jevons, Böhm-Bawerk, Wicksell and other neoclassical writers—alleging that, as the interest rate falls in consequence of abstention from present consumption in favor of future, technology must become in some sense more 'roundabout,' more 'mechanized' and 'more productive'—cannot be universally valid.
Paul Samuelson (1966, p. 568)

Abstract In a preparatory step, we start off with the explanatory power and significance of the classical theory of value, and we argue that market prices are in fact attracted to labour values and to prices of production as more concrete centres of gravitation. For this, we utilize detailed data starting from the US economy and include a number of countries and studies; we show that the classical theory of value contains explanatory power that cannot be ignored. We further discuss related issues of technological change, as this is reflected in the rising capital-intensity of industries and falling unit labour values and questions related to the effect of distribution changes on relative prices. This finding is particularly useful in the discussions of the law of the tendential fall in the rate of profit and lends support to Marx's view that technological change is capital using-labour saving in the long run. Furthermore, the results from detailed input-output tables of the US economy ascertain the Ricardian

© Springer Nature Switzerland AG 2019
L. Tsoulfidis, P. Tsaliki, *Classical Political Economics and Modern Capitalism*,
https://doi.org/10.1007/978-3-030-17967-0_4

and Marxian views expounded in Chaps. 1 and 3, that is, the movement of prices as a consequence of changes in distribution is monotonic.

Keywords Price-value deviations · Technological change · Unit labour values · Wage-rate of profit curves · US economy

4.1 Introduction

The transformation problem continues to attract the attention of many researchers, and new 'solutions' or interpretations have been suggested adding significant elements and dimensions to a long-lasting debate; however, the discussions and analyses have been theoretical in the main. The question we attempt to answer in this chapter is to what extent, if any, the classical approach in general contains satisfactory explanatory content with respect to the movement of prices in actual economies. This is a challenging issue, from our point of view, because the classical theory of value, without much consideration, has been either neglected by many economists as too sociological focusing mainly on social relations of production without any measurable substance or simply weak and even redundant compared to the contemporary neoclassical microeconomic theory. For this purpose, in this chapter, we assess empirically the scientific status of the classical theory of value and distribution using data either from an array of diverse economies for selected years, or for economies whose available data allow estimates over long stretches of time or, finally, for selected years but at various levels of aggregations.

In the late 1970s and early 1980s, there have been two major strands within the classical political economy tradition having to do mainly with whether and to what extent, if any, labour values and their monetary expressions, that is, the direct prices, are of any utility. The idea is that because prices of production, as a more concrete centre of gravitation of market prices, can be determined by the givens (technology and the real wage) of the classical system, thereby rendering the estimation of labour values redundant. Even worse, it has been argued that in the case of joint production, it is possible to derive systematically negative labour values! This is another way to say that not only the labour values are redundant but inconsistent and misleading.[1] These debates contributed to further theoretical and empirical investigations of both labour values and prices of production, their relation to each other and to the actually observed market prices. In addition, the specific controversy has also contributed to a better understanding of the mechanism underneath the estimated changes in prices of

---

[1]We do not share this view, and the reasons why are derived from our analysis and our very concrete estimates in which labour values by definition are positive. Negative labour values are the result of the initial assumptions. For further readings on joint production and related issues, see Semmler (1983, Chap. 6), Chilcote (1997, Chap. 3) and Flaschel (2010, Chaps. 2 and 4 and the literature cited there).

production induced by changes in income distribution. In this underlying mechanism, both labour values and the standard commodity are crucial in the theorization of the movement of relative prices; in particular, labour values, a constituent component of prices of production, remain constant in the face of changes in income distribution, and the invariable standard commodity is used as the descriptive to the path of relative prices numéraire. Furthermore, the movement of relative prices of production is mainly determined by the difference of the estimated capital-intensity relative to the standard capital-output ratio as an approximation of the economy-wide average capital-intensity.[2]

Empirical research, at least so far, has shown that Marx's and, in general, the modern classical theory of value and distribution explain pretty well the surface phenomena of market prices of actual economies. In effect, it has been repeatedly shown for several economies that:

- Direct prices and prices of production are extremely good approximations to market prices as this can be judged by the various statistical measures of deviation.
- Direct prices as well as Marx's first step prices of production display in general surprising small deviations from the fully transformed prices of production; thus, the complete transformation of Marx's prices of production contains more theoretical rather than practical significance. As Marx (*Capital* II, p. 393) notes in the schemes of reproduction, the analysis is conducted in value terms (direct prices) pointing out that 'the fact that prices [of production] diverge from values cannot display any influence on the movements of social capital'. The idea is that the aggregate magnitudes are pretty much the same regardless of the prices used for their estimation.

Therefore, for all practical purposes, the approach based on labour values is a satisfactory first approximation to assess the movement of market prices. Prices of production, in principle, are theoretically preferable, but practically their precise estimation is quite challenging mainly because of the lack of adequate data for variables such as the matrices of depreciation, fixed capital stock, circulating capital advanced and capacity utilization.

In effect, Marx's but also the old classical economists' labour theory of value has displayed an extremely good explanatory content and thus approximation to actual (market) prices. Moreover, if we consider that in the nineteenth century neither the necessary statistical data (on technology, real wages and output produced) nor the mathematical techniques and computer languages (that are currently widely available) were at their disposal, one cannot but admire the analytical insights and intuition of these economists. Nowadays, both mathematical techniques and required data are at researchers' disposal to subject to empirical testing the classical theory of

---

[2]It is important to note that the standard capital-output ratio is also a kind of an average capital-intensity, and this is the reason why it is not very different from the economy's average capital-intensity.

value and distribution and in so doing to lay the groundwork for an alternative microeconomic theory which will be based on an objective set of data (labour time, technology, etc.) as opposed to a subjective one (preferences, utility, etc.) of the neoclassical approach.

On further examination, we discover that even today, the data requirements are hard to come by for the implementation of an all-inclusive empirical test that starts with the monetary expression of labour values and continues to their full transformation into prices of production. In most cases, the required data for the estimation of labour values (direct prices) are available to the researcher apart from depreciation matrices. The estimation of prices of production, on the other hand, is usually conducted using data on circulating capital, while a complete empirical analysis requires data on the matrices of capital stock or rather of capital advanced; the latter includes, besides fixed capital stock, the money capital put aside for the purchase of materials, that is, the circulating capital advanced augmented by the advances of wages to start off the production process prior to the sale of output. To the extent we know the literature, official publications of investment matrices, with the help of which the construction of matrices of capital stock and depreciation is possible, exist only for a few countries (e.g. USA, Greece, UK, Japan and Korea) and for specific years. From the available studies, those by Ochoa (1984), Chilcote (1997), Shaikh (1998 and 2016) and Tsoulfidis and Paitaridis (2017) make use nearly of all the required data including the matrices of capital stock, depreciation, taxation and circulating capital advanced, while in other studies, there is always something missing, whose influence on the final result, however, is usually very limited. Chilcote (1997, p. 122) argues, and in effect empirically ascertains in his study of the US economy, that the inclusion of depreciation matrices improves the accuracy of approximations of direct prices as well as of prices of production to market prices, but only slightly. It, therefore, follows that by not including the matrices of depreciation, it becomes more difficult to show the accuracy of approximations, that is, the proximity of estimated prices and variables in general to the observed ones; this is equivalent to saying that the testing of the classical theory of value takes place under unfavourable for the theory circumstances.

In the remainder of the chapter, we bring to the fore empirical estimates of labour values and prices of production using data from a number of countries, and we show that the two types of prices are too close to each other, as this can be judged by the various metrics of deviation. Furthermore, we show that the prices of production when normalized by the standard commodity and expressed relative to labour values induced by changes in income distribution display, more often than not, monotonic movements in the upward or downward direction depending on each industry's composition of capital relative to the Sraffian standard ratio (see Chap. 3). Under these conditions, the feedback of prices on the utilized inputs along with the capital stock is, by and large, of minimal empirical significance; in the less likely to appear cases of non-monotonic movements in prices, we may encounter inflection and extreme (maxima or minima) points, and prices of production may even switch ranking with their labour values, which is equivalent to saying that the capital-intensity of these industries may switch from capital- to labour-intensive relative to the standard ratio which, as already pointed out, is not too different from the average capital-output ratio of the economy.

4.2   Labour Values and Prices of Production

We start off with the details of the estimation of labour values and prices of production in actual economies. We symbolize vectors and matrices with bold letters (lowercase and capital, respectively) and scalars with lowercase letters in italics. Thus, labour values are defined as

$$\boldsymbol{\lambda} = \mathbf{l} + \boldsymbol{\lambda}\mathbf{A} + \boldsymbol{\lambda}\mathbf{D}$$

where $\boldsymbol{\lambda}$ is the row vector of values; $\mathbf{l}$ is the row vector of labour inputs per unit of output; $\mathbf{A}$ is the square matrix of technological coefficients, which multiplied from the left by the vector of labour values $\boldsymbol{\lambda}$ gives the vector of indirect labour requirements per unit of output; and $\mathbf{D}$ is the matrix of depreciation coefficients which premultiplied by $\boldsymbol{\lambda}$ gives us the value of fixed capital stock transferred to the final output. Thus, the vector of labour values is determined by solving the above equation for $\boldsymbol{\lambda}$, that is,

$$\boldsymbol{\lambda} = \mathbf{l}[\mathbf{I}{-}\mathbf{A} - \mathbf{D}]^{-1} \tag{4.1}$$

Hence, labour values are defined in terms of vertically integrated labour coefficients.

Turning now to the evaluation of prices of production in terms of circulating capital,[3] the rate of profit is also estimated on the circulating capital. Thus, we have

$$\mathbf{P} = (1 + r)(w\mathbf{l} + \mathbf{PA}) + \mathbf{PD} \tag{4.2}$$

where $\mathbf{P}$ is the vector of prices of production, r is the rate of profit, w is the money wage rate and $\mathbf{l}$, $\mathbf{D}$ and $\mathbf{A}$ are as above. By rearranging terms, the relation of prices of production becomes

$$\mathbf{P} = (1 + r)w\mathbf{l} + \mathbf{PA} + \mathbf{PD} + r\mathbf{PA}$$

By collecting terms together, we get

$$\mathbf{P}[\mathbf{I} - \mathbf{A} - \mathbf{D}] = (1 + r)\, w\mathbf{l} + r\mathbf{PA}$$

or

---

[3]Hence, for simplicity reasons in the estimation of prices of production, we assume away the matrices of capital stock, circulating capital advanced and various indirect taxes.

$$\mathbf{P} = (1 + r)\ w\ \underbrace{\mathbf{l}[\mathbf{I} - \mathrm{A} - \mathbf{D}]^{-1}}_{\lambda} + r\mathbf{P}\ \underbrace{\mathrm{A}[\mathbf{I} - \mathrm{A} - \mathbf{D}]^{-1}}_{\mathbf{H}}$$

Hence, we express the prices of production in terms of vertically integrated labour coefficients or labour values, $\lambda = \mathbf{l}[\mathbf{I} - \mathbf{A} - \mathbf{D}]^{-1}$, and in terms of vertically integrated capital coefficients, $\mathbf{H} = \mathbf{A}[\mathbf{I} - \mathbf{A} - \mathbf{D}]^{-1}$. Thus the prices of production can be rewritten as

$$\mathbf{P} = (1 + r)w\lambda + r\mathbf{PH} \tag{4.3}$$

In the case that we include the matrix of capital stock, the prices of production are estimated as follows:

$$\mathbf{P} = \mathbf{Pbl} + \mathbf{PA} + \mathbf{PD} + r\mathbf{PK}$$

or

$$\mathbf{P}[\mathbf{I} - \mathbf{A} - \mathbf{bl} - \mathbf{D}] = r\mathbf{PK}$$

which is transformed to the following eigenequation

$$\mathbf{P}r^{-1} = \mathbf{PK}[\mathbf{I} - \mathbf{A} - \mathbf{bl} - \mathbf{D}]^{-1} \tag{4.4}$$

whose maximal eigenvalue $\lambda = r^{-1}$ is associated with a unique positively defined eigenvector, which needs to be fixed for its scale as explained below.

Having estimated the labour values and the relative prices of production which are both expressed in terms of labour time, we need to give them a proper monetary expression so as to bring them to the same dimension with the observed monetary phenomena of market prices. The monetary expression of labour values, that is, the direct prices, $\mathbf{v}$, is defined as

$$\mathbf{v} = \lambda\left(\frac{\mathbf{ex}}{\lambda\mathbf{x}}\right) \tag{4.5}$$

where $\mathbf{e}$ is the unit (or additive) row vector whose elements are equal to one representing the market prices and $\mathbf{x}$ is the column vector of sectoral outputs (or sales). It is important to stress that in input-output tables and analysis, the market prices, by definition, are equal to one. Since in input-output tables each industry produces similar although not identical products, the measurement units of output are hypothetical, and they are considered unchanged; in fact, we say that an industry produces an output of value equal to one million monetary units (i.e. dollars, euros, whatever these might be). Therefore, all market prices are set equal to one (million monetary units). Hence, $\mathbf{ex}$ is equal to the economy's total sales in terms of market prices, while $\lambda\mathbf{x}$ stands for the total sales in terms of labour values and their ratio stands for the value of money or the monetary expression of the labour time (MELT). The equation of prices of production may be rewritten as follows:

$$\mathbf{p} = (1 + r)w\mathbf{v} + r\mathbf{pH} \tag{4.6}$$

while

$$\mathbf{p} = \mathbf{P}\left(\frac{\mathbf{ex}}{\mathbf{Px}}\right) \tag{4.7}$$

It is important to emphasize that the normalization condition that we use in the next section is based on the economy's gross output vector (or sales) and the reason for this selection is to facilitate comparisons with similarly contacted past studies and, at the same time, to scale up the labour values, which are estimated in terms of abstract labour times to the level of market prices. Similarly, the prices of production, which are in effect relative prices defined up to a multiplication by a scalar. The scalar in this particular case is defined as the ratio of total economy's sales, **ex**, over the product of relative prices times the output (or sales) vector, **Px**, as shown in the term in parenthesis of the relation 4.7. The evidence so far has repeatedly shown that the use of a numéraire (gross output or total sales, net output or the Sraffian standard commodity) does not really impart any statistically significant bias to the actual deviations of various prices between themselves as this has been beard out by the various numéraire free statistics measures of deviation (see Mariolis and Tsoulfidis 2010). In Sect. 4.4 in which we bring into the analysis the effects of income redistribution, we use the Sraffian standard commodity as our descriptive numéraire for it is helpful and suitable to the problem at hand properties.

4.3 Estimates of Price-Value Deviation

In what follows, we utilize input-output data from the US economy for the period 1995–2009 for which we can construct matrices of capital stock utilizing the data available in world input-output database (WIOD).[4] We opted to present first our findings for the US economy not only because it is a major economy in which capitalist competition is widespread and intense as, perhaps, in no other economy and, therefore, the classical theory of value and distribution finds an ideal testing ground but, moreover, because there are many studies that were contacted using data of the US economy for a number of years and also different levels of aggregation. Thus, our findings for the US economy complement other similarly contacted studies

---

[4]For the detailed input-output description of the US economy with larger input-output tables at the 71-industry detail with matrices of depreciation and capital stock, see Shaikh (2016) and the literature cited there.

and in so doing lend further support to the classical theory of value and distribution rendering it a credible microeconomic approach.

In the panel of graphs portrayed in Fig. 4.1, we plot for reasons of simplicity and visual clarity the direct prices (denoted by DP) and prices of production (denoted by PP) of 34 industries over the period of 15 years; all data are expressed in constant 1995 prices. It is important to note that in the estimation of the prices of production, we used also the matrix of capital stock; the latter was derived from vectors of relative weights based on investment expenditure times the vector of capital stock per unit of output, also available in the socioeconomic data of the WIOD (see Appendix 1). The prices of production are estimated from relation (4.4) which solves for

$$\mathbf{p} = r\mathbf{P}\mathbf{K}[\mathbf{I} - \mathbf{A} - \mathbf{D} - \mathbf{b}\mathbf{l}]^{-1} \qquad (4.8)$$

where $\mathbf{p}$ is normalized by the gross output vector price of production.

An inspection of the paths of direct prices (DP) and prices of production (PP) of each of our 34 industries in Fig. 4.1 reveals that both types of prices for every individual industry move, more or less, to the same direction maintaining their ranking throughout the period of our investigation. If, however, the initial deviation between the two types of prices in an industry is relatively small, it follows that, although DP and PP move pretty much to the same direction, there are occasions that their paths cross each other indicating that the capital-intensity of this particular industry is not far from the economy-wide average one. Thus, it comes as no surprise for such industries to display non-monotonic movements of PP as well as wage rate of profit curves (WRPC) of different curvatures. We grapple with such issues in Sect. 4.4, where we examine the redistribution effects on the movement of prices and the actual shapes of the WRPC.

Similar are the results in the case that the estimations are carried out in terms of the circulating capital and in current rather than constant prices that we utilized for the US economy. The testing ground of this exercise is 19 industries for the Greek economy spanning the period 1988–1997 (Tsoulfidis and Mariolis 2007) and each of the five benchmark input-output tables available for every 5 years of the Japanese economy during the period 1970–1990 (Tsoulfidis 2008). It is important to stress that the studies of the Greek and Japanese economies were based on national sources and the analysis was carried out in current prices and circulating capital model, because the lack of reliable data or sources for depreciation and indirect business taxes did not allow the construction of these vectors and the related matrices. In addition, a fixed capital model was used in the studies of Germany and Greece for the period 1995–2011, whose details are presented in Chap. 7 on international trade (Tsoulfidis and Paitaridis 2017; Tsaliki et al. 2018).

In Fig. 4.2, we present the DP and PP of the 19 industries of the Greek economy for the decade 1988–1997. It is important to reiterate that there is no way of knowing the exact market prices because we simply cannot know the units of measurement of

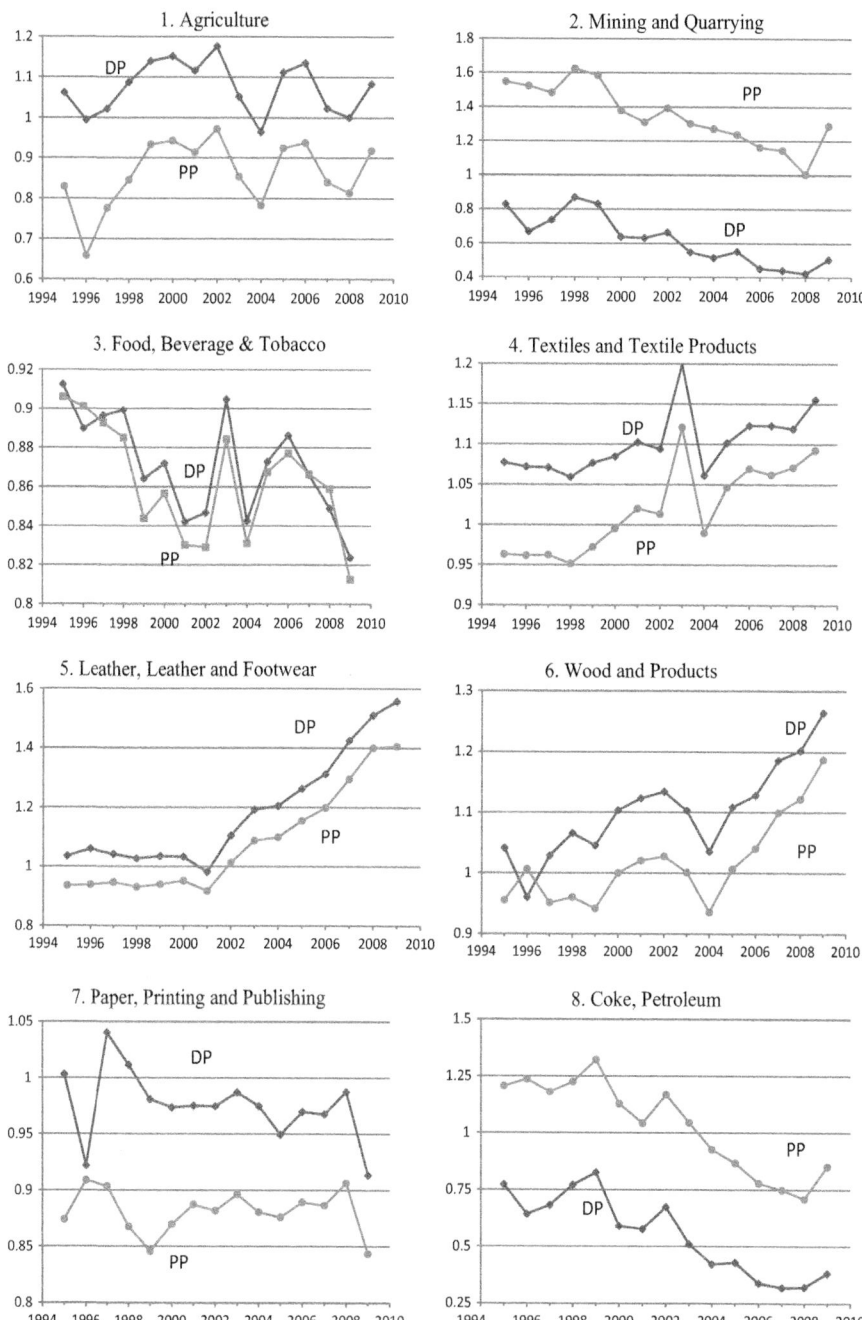

Fig. 4.1 Direct prices and prices of production for selective US industries, 1995–2009

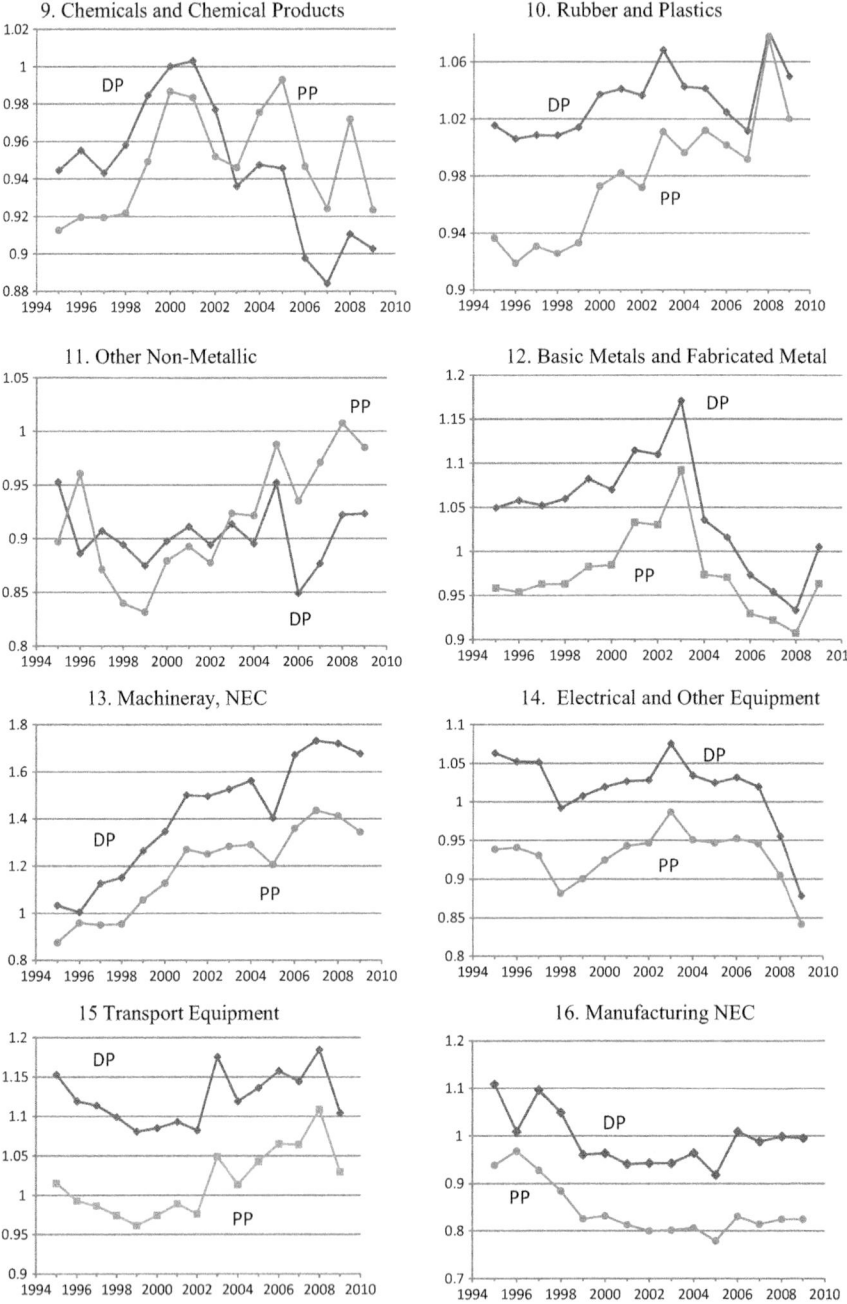

Fig. 4.1 (continued)

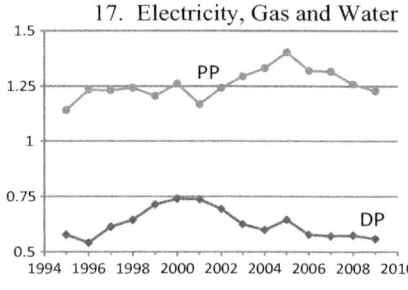

17. Electricity, Gas and Water

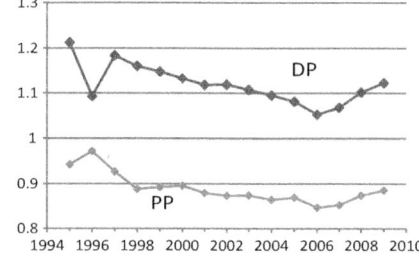

18. Construction

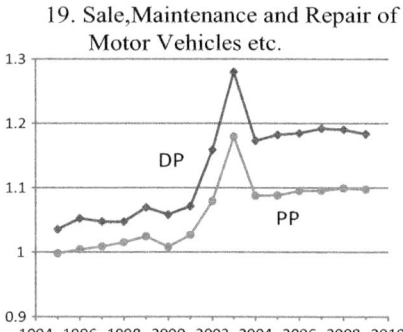

19. Sale,Maintenance and Repair of Motor Vehicles etc.

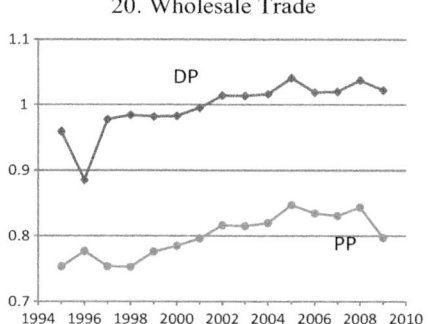

20. Wholesale Trade

21. Retail Trade *etc.*

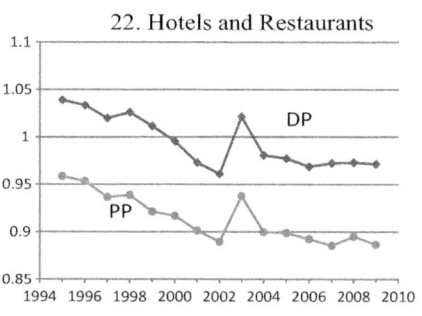

22. Hotels and Restaurants

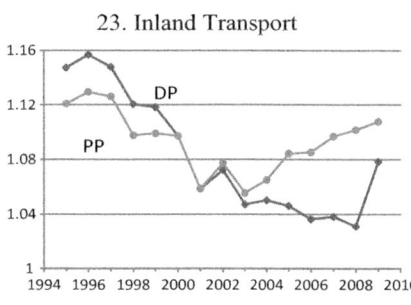

23. Inland Transport

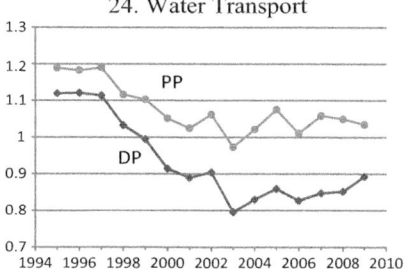

24. Water Transport

Fig. 4.1 (continued)

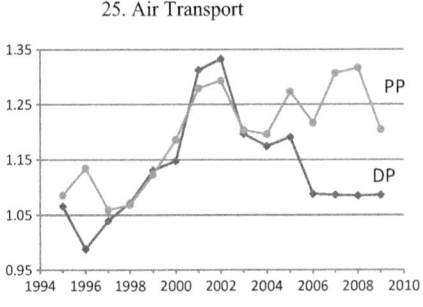

25. Air Transport

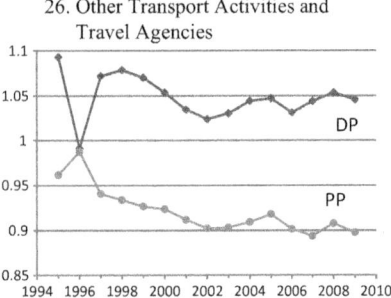

26. Other Transport Activities and Travel Agencies

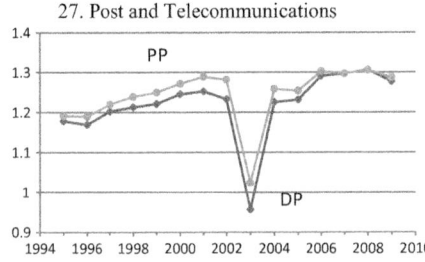

27. Post and Telecommunications

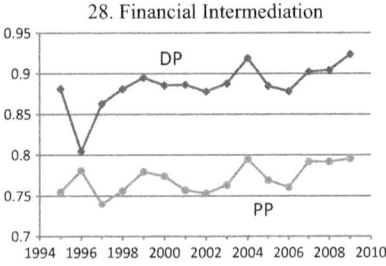

28. Financial Intermediation

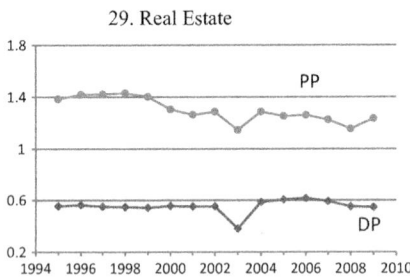

29. Real Estate

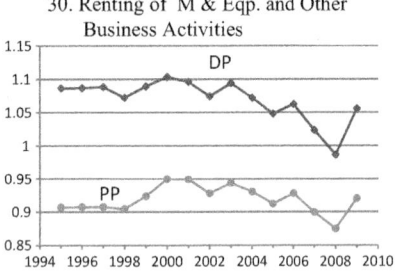

30. Renting of M & Eqp. and Other Business Activities

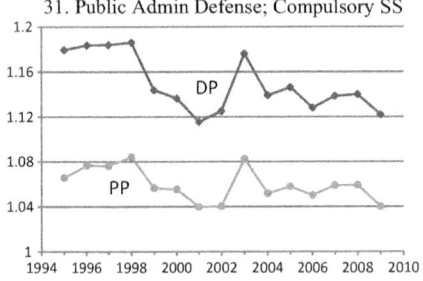

31. Public Admin Defense; Compulsory SS

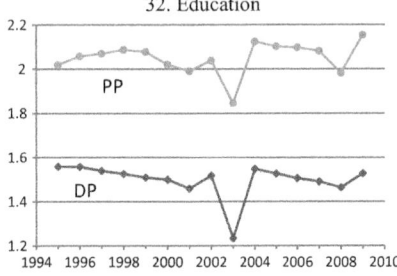

32. Education

Fig. 4.1 (continued)

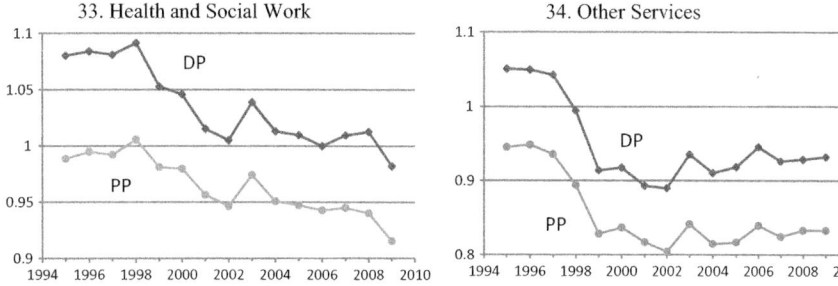

Fig. 4.1 (continued)

output produced (or sales) in any single industry of input-output tables.[5] Thus, in constructing input-output tables, researchers are bound to assume as the unit of measurement for each industry's output the value of one million monetary units, whatever these might be worth, holding constant the physical units of measurement. In this way, sectoral market prices are equated to one million monetary units (dollars, yens, euro or whatever happens to be). It should be noted that if we knew the exact physical units of measurement and the exact market prices, the estimated prices and their deviation from the market prices would not be different (see Miller and Blair 2009, Chap. 2).

A visual inspection of the trajectories of PP with respect to DP reveals that their relative position remains approximately the same over time. That is, if the DP of an industry is greater than its PP, this ranking persists, in most cases, throughout the investigated period. The deviations between these two sets of prices change over time; however, their movement is by and large to the same direction. Crossings between DP and PP are, of course, possible; however, such crossings are observed in those industries with a relatively small initial difference as, for example, the case with industries 6, 8, 14 and 18 in the above graphs of Fig. 4.2. Finally, we observe fluctuations in the PP and DP over time, which almost in every single year they point to the same direction; so, the trend in both types of prices remains the same (either in the upward or the downward direction). The crossings in the case of the Greek economy are relatively more frequent than those in the US economy precisely because the initial differences in capital-intensities are much smaller due to the use of a circulating capital model; by contrast, in the case of the US economy, where the estimates are based on a fixed capital model, the initial capital-output differences are pretty large, and the movement of relative prices is much more difficult to change the initial ranking of capital-intensities.

---

[5]By way of an example, in the food industry, whereby there is a whole array of different goods, it becomes exceedingly difficult to devise a single unit of measurement of the output produced. In Sect. 4.3.3, where we have intertemporal comparisons, we propose a new solution to the problem of approximation of market prices.

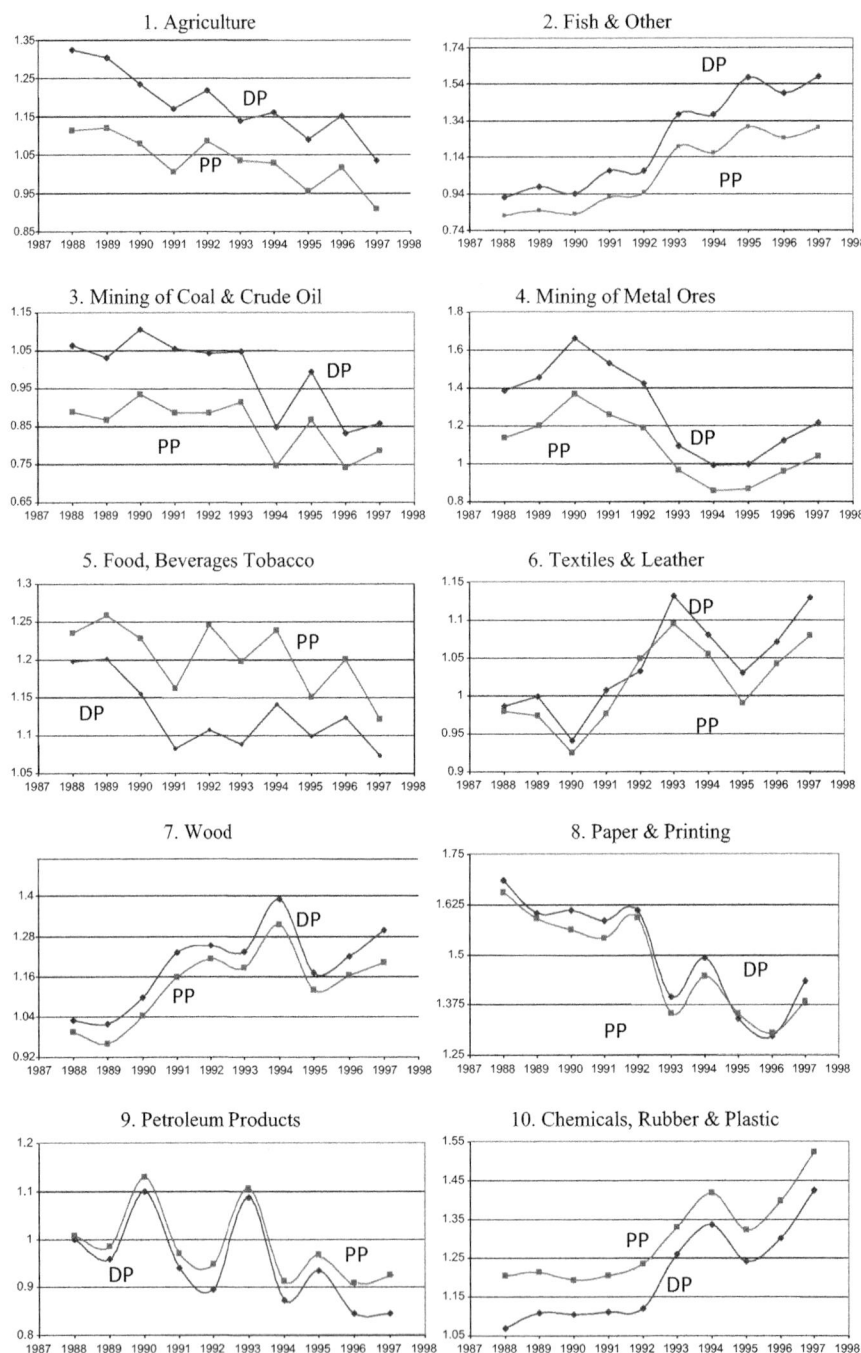

Fig. 4.2 Direct prices and prices of production, Greece, 1988–1997

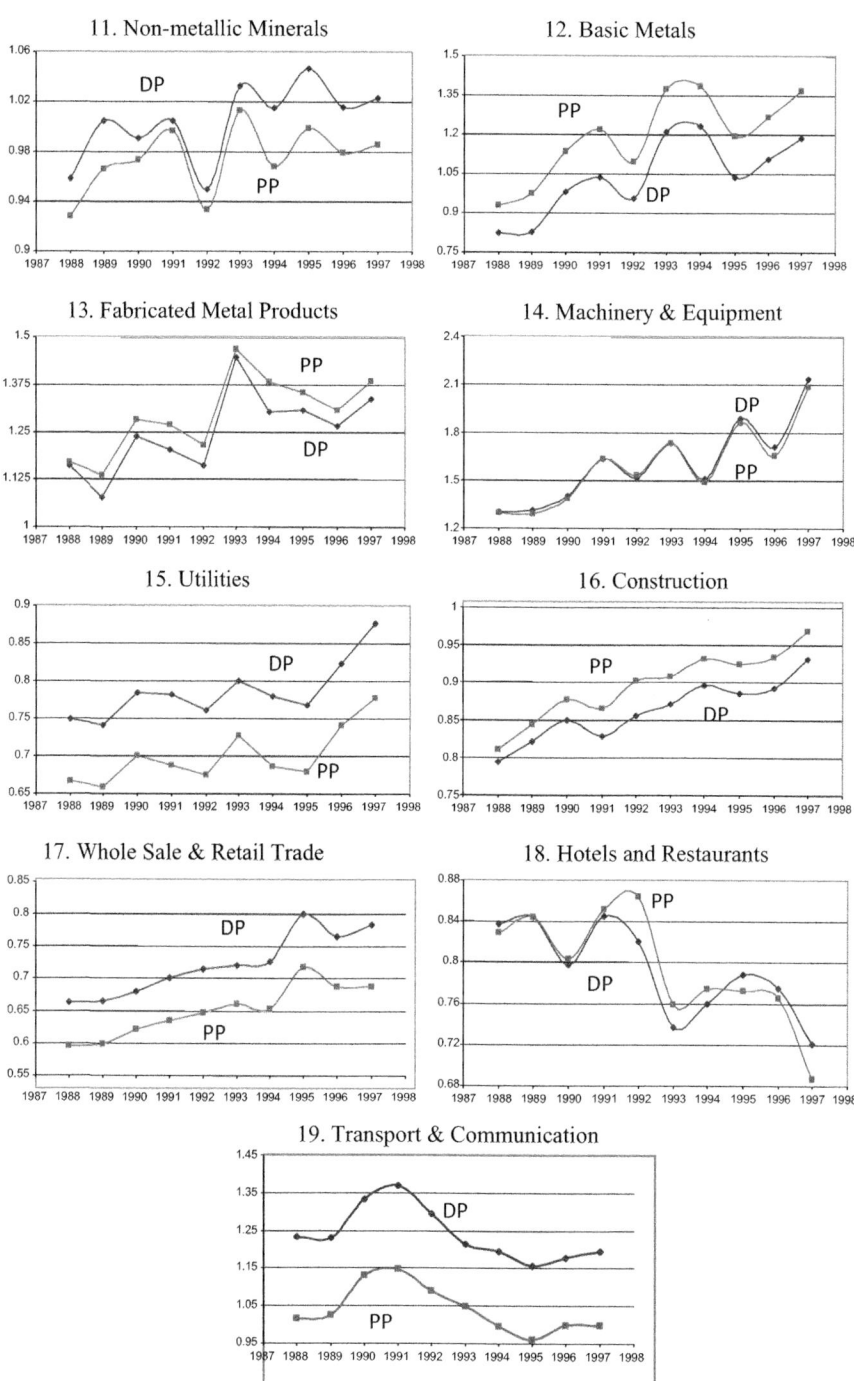

Fig. 4.2 (continued)

4.3.1   Technological Change, Capital-Intensity and Labour Values

The results from an array of different and quite diverse economies and over long enough stretches of time reveal that technological change is a slow-moving process requiring the passage of sufficiently long time to observe significant changes. Furthermore, technological change diffuses quite evenly across industries and in so doing does not usually change the ranking of industries in terms of capital-intensities. The prices of production and direct prices attest to this hypothesis and indicate that once an industry is characterized as capital- or labour-intensive, it maintains this characterization over long stretches of time, as this can be judged by the movement and ranking of direct prices and prices of production. As is usually the case, there are exceptions that have mainly to do with the initial differences of prices of production from direct prices or what is the same of an industry's capital-intensity from the economy's average. Furthermore, our empirical findings from the USA and other economies corroborate Leontief's description of technology as a 'cooking (we dare say bakery) recipe' according to which there is no or, at most, limited substitutability of factor inputs; this conclusion is in sharp contrast to what is usually assumed by the standard neoclassical microeconomic theory.

We may, therefore, conclude that technological change is slow for it takes years to observe sizeable changes in the vertically integrated productivities, that is, in the direct and indirect labour requirements per unit of output or, what is the same thing, in the unit value of produced output. The classical theory of value and distribution argues that over relatively long periods of time, the unit value or what amounts to the same thing the labour content of commodities tends to fall because of the technological change which is mainly associated with the introduction of fixed capital. In effect, the unit values fall as a result of rising fixed capital per unit of labour (capital-intensity) as we further explain in Chaps. 7 and 8. In Table 4.1, we display the direct and indirect labour requirements per unit of output for the US economy over the period 1995–2009. In these estimates, we also account for the depreciation of fixed capital.

From Table 4.1, our findings of the overall decreasing direct and indirect labour content of output produced lend overwhelming support to the view that technological progress reduces the unit cost of production and that this becomes possible through the higher capital-intensity (for more on this issues, see Chaps. 6, 7 and 8). It is important to stress at this point that the reductions in the unit labour values and associated with it unit costs are strictly related to the vertically integrated value compositions of capital of each industry. In order to show the inverse relationship between unit labour values and capital-intensity, we estimate the vertically integrated value composition of capital for each sector as follows:

$$\left(\mathbf{vK}[\mathbf{I} - \mathbf{A} - \mathbf{D}]^{-1}\right)./\left(\mathbf{vbl}[\mathbf{I} - \mathbf{A} - \mathbf{D}]^{-1}\right) \tag{4.9}$$

Table 4.1 Direct and indirect labour requirements per unit of output, USA 1995–2009

Sectors	1995	1996	1997	1998	1999	2000	2001	2002	2003	2004	2005	2006	2007	2008	2009
1	0.0169	0.0148	0.0152	0.0157	0.0169	0.0175	0.0168	0.0162	0.0135	0.0125	0.0143	0.0120	0.0133	0.0131	0.0129
2	0.0197	0.0173	0.0166	0.0188	0.0176	0.0138	0.0139	0.0140	0.0087	0.0105	0.0096	0.0078	0.0095	0.0087	0.0079
3	0.0167	0.0162	0.0157	0.0150	0.0141	0.0146	0.0139	0.0128	0.0133	0.0122	0.0126	0.0102	0.0123	0.0124	0.0105
4	0.0198	0.0196	0.0187	0.0177	0.0175	0.0181	0.0182	0.0165	0.0176	0.0153	0.0159	0.0129	0.0159	0.0164	0.0149
5	0.0190	0.0193	0.0182	0.0171	0.0169	0.0173	0.0162	0.0167	0.0175	0.0174	0.0183	0.0151	0.0202	0.0221	0.0210
6	0.0219	0.0221	0.0206	0.0202	0.0192	0.0208	0.0210	0.0192	0.0167	0.0166	0.0170	0.0142	0.0186	0.0203	0.0187
7	0.0173	0.0173	0.0171	0.0159	0.0149	0.0153	0.0152	0.0138	0.0149	0.0133	0.0131	0.0105	0.0129	0.0134	0.0112
8	0.0175	0.0160	0.0149	0.0163	0.0168	0.0125	0.0123	0.0132	0.0090	0.0083	0.0071	0.0055	0.0064	0.0061	0.0057
9	0.0173	0.0174	0.0165	0.0160	0.0160	0.0167	0.0166	0.0147	0.0137	0.0137	0.0137	0.0103	0.0125	0.0133	0.0109
10	0.0186	0.0184	0.0176	0.0168	0.0165	0.0174	0.0172	0.0156	0.0157	0.0150	0.0151	0.0118	0.0144	0.0158	0.0133
11	0.0177	0.0180	0.0161	0.0151	0.0144	0.0152	0.0153	0.0138	0.0139	0.0133	0.0133	0.0102	0.0131	0.0146	0.0122
12	0.0193	0.0193	0.0184	0.0177	0.0176	0.0179	0.0184	0.0167	0.0172	0.0149	0.0147	0.0112	0.0135	0.0137	0.0129
13	0.0195	0.0192	0.0184	0.0165	0.0164	0.0171	0.0170	0.0155	0.0158	0.0149	0.0148	0.0118	0.0145	0.0140	0.0113
14	0.0200	0.0210	0.0205	0.0200	0.0214	0.0233	0.0260	0.0239	0.0225	0.0235	0.0239	0.0196	0.0253	0.0267	0.0261
15	0.0212	0.0204	0.0195	0.0183	0.0176	0.0182	0.0181	0.0163	0.0172	0.0162	0.0164	0.0133	0.0162	0.0174	0.0144
16	0.0202	0.0203	0.0198	0.0166	0.0181	0.0168	0.0171	0.0165	0.0159	0.0148	0.0140	0.0114	0.0138	0.0143	0.0119
17	0.0137	0.0140	0.0139	0.0138	0.0142	0.0149	0.0142	0.0130	0.0099	0.0114	0.0120	0.0089	0.0111	0.0118	0.0086
18	0.0208	0.0205	0.0194	0.0181	0.0175	0.0176	0.0171	0.0156	0.0160	0.0146	0.0142	0.0112	0.0140	0.0148	0.0135
19	0.0190	0.0192	0.0183	0.0175	0.0174	0.0177	0.0177	0.0175	0.0188	0.0169	0.0171	0.0136	0.0169	0.0174	0.0158
20	0.0166	0.0167	0.0161	0.0155	0.0152	0.0155	0.0155	0.0144	0.0145	0.0139	0.0139	0.0110	0.0136	0.0142	0.0128
21	0.0175	0.0176	0.0169	0.0159	0.0155	0.0160	0.0160	0.0146	0.0147	0.0142	0.0142	0.0112	0.0140	0.0149	0.0136
22	0.0191	0.0189	0.0178	0.0171	0.0165	0.0167	0.0161	0.0145	0.0150	0.0142	0.0142	0.0111	0.0138	0.0143	0.0127
23	0.0211	0.0211	0.0201	0.0187	0.0182	0.0184	0.0175	0.0162	0.0153	0.0152	0.0151	0.0119	0.0147	0.0151	0.0136
24	0.0205	0.0204	0.0195	0.0172	0.0162	0.0153	0.0147	0.0137	0.0117	0.0120	0.0125	0.0095	0.0120	0.0125	0.0109
25	0.0207	0.0209	0.0192	0.0187	0.0192	0.0202	0.0227	0.0211	0.0175	0.0177	0.0173	0.0133	0.0167	0.0170	0.0144

(continued)

Table 4.1 (continued)

Sectors	1995	1996	1997	1998	1999	2000	2001	2002	2003	2004	2005	2006	2007	2008	2009
26	0.0211	0.0210	0.0200	0.0197	0.0185	0.0185	0.0180	0.0164	0.0160	0.0158	0.0157	0.0115	0.0145	0.0152	0.0146
27	0.0216	0.0213	0.0210	0.0202	0.0199	0.0208	0.0207	0.0186	0.0140	0.0177	0.0178	0.0148	0.0184	0.0191	0.0169
28	0.0148	0.0147	0.0138	0.0135	0.0134	0.0136	0.0133	0.0121	0.0131	0.0122	0.0124	0.0092	0.0117	0.0119	0.0111
29	0.0102	0.0103	0.0097	0.0092	0.0089	0.0093	0.0091	0.0084	0.0056	0.0085	0.0088	0.0071	0.0084	0.0081	0.0060
30	0.0199	0.0198	0.0190	0.0179	0.0177	0.0185	0.0181	0.0162	0.0160	0.0155	0.0152	0.0122	0.0145	0.0144	0.0139
31	0.0216	0.0216	0.0207	0.0198	0.0186	0.0190	0.0184	0.0170	0.0172	0.0164	0.0166	0.0129	0.0162	0.0167	0.0147
32	0.0286	0.0284	0.0269	0.0254	0.0246	0.0251	0.0241	0.0229	0.0181	0.0223	0.0221	0.0173	0.0212	0.0214	0.0181
33	0.0198	0.0198	0.0189	0.0182	0.0172	0.0175	0.0168	0.0152	0.0152	0.0146	0.0146	0.0115	0.0143	0.0148	0.0129
34	0.0193	0.0191	0.0182	0.0166	0.0149	0.0153	0.0148	0.0134	0.0137	0.0131	0.0133	0.0108	0.0131	0.0136	0.0121
Weighted average	**0.0191**	**0.0189**	**0.0180**	**0.0173**	**0.0169**	**0.0171**	**0.0170**	**0.0158**	**0.0149**	**0.0147**	**0.0147**	**0.0117**	**0.0145**	**0.0150**	**0.0133**

The estimates of labour values were carried according to Eq. (4.1), and as a way to reduce complex to simple labour, we used the industry-wide average wage. For the nomenclature of the industries, see Table 4.9

where the numerator of relation 4.9 is the matrix of vertically integrated capital coefficients which is premultiplied by the vector of direct prices and in the denominator the money wage expressed in terms of direct prices, **vb**, is multiplied by the vertically integrated employment coefficients; in so doing, we essentially derive the sectoral value compositions of capital. It goes without saying that in the presence of two vectors, the 'division' is only possible in an element by element basis, as indicated by the symbol ./. Furthermore, by multiplying the numerator and denominator of relation 4.9 by the vector of gross output **x** in constant prices, we derive a ratio of two scalars, which is the weighted by the output economy-wide value composition of capital. These estimates for each of the 34 sectors of the US economy and for each of the 15 years are displayed in Table 4.2, while their weighted average value composition of capital is given in the last row of the table.

An inspection of the figures in Table 4.2 shows that the capital-intensity during the 15 years of our investigation rises with an average annual growth rate of 1.97%; meanwhile, the average unit labour values are falling by an annual average rate of -2.57% (as shown in the last row of Table 4.1). Clearly, there has been technical change as this can be judged by the rising average capital-intensity (or value composition of capital) and the falling average unit labour values. In Fig. 4.3, we plot all the pairs of capital-intensity and unit labour values of the 34 industries pooling the cross-sectional data spanning the period 1995–2009.

We ran a linear regression using our data in a panel setting including both cross-section and time effects in the econometric specification. Thus, we estimate a twofold fixed effects model, where the inclusion of time effects is necessary to better capture the influence of the business cycles. The estimated coefficients of the regression are displayed in Eq. 4.10:

$$\text{Unit values} = 0.019808 - 0.000575 \text{ capital intensity} \qquad (4.10)$$

The estimated coefficients are statistically significant at p-value $= 0$ and the coefficient of determination quite high $R^2 = 90.57\%$. The merit of the above specification with a constant term is that it allows the testing for both the time period and fixed effects. For this purpose our panel of 510 observations of unit labour values and respective capital-intensities of the 34 industries observed over a 15-year-long time period forms an ideal testing ground for the hypothesis that rising capital-intensities reduce unit labour values. The econometric results showed that the fixed effects are statistically significant, as this can be judged by the estimated coefficients (a constant equal to 0.019 and a slope coefficient approximately equal to -0.0006 with high t-ratios). The great advantage of fixed effects estimators in panel data is that they remove the cross-sectional variation related to unobserved heterogeneity caused by disturbances of various kinds that are unaccounted for in the data forming the panel. Also, the two-way fixed effects model allows us to include both cross-section and period effects, which contain variables that are constant over time and cross-sections for every unit and at every point in time, respectively. Hence, the chief advantage of the above model is to capture both time and cross-sectional variation.

Table 4.2 Vertically integrated capital-labour ratios, USA 1995–2009

Sectors	1995	1996	1997	1998	1999	2000	2001	2002	2003	2004	2005	2006	2007	2008	2009
1	6.78	7.26	6.92	6.40	6.12	6.27	6.44	6.22	7.12	6.80	6.73	6.47	6.81	6.86	8.22
2	10.85	12.04	11.40	10.20	10.99	12.67	12.23	11.95	17.23	14.42	14.62	14.19	14.86	13.57	23.35
3	4.23	4.40	4.25	3.95	3.94	4.09	4.24	4.11	4.41	4.45	4.55	4.49	4.84	4.91	5.77
4	2.67	2.81	2.77	2.67	2.78	2.96	3.12	3.15	3.54	3.39	3.64	3.68	3.72	3.77	4.83
5	2.83	2.94	2.94	2.79	2.87	3.07	3.34	3.05	3.27	3.05	3.08	2.99	2.87	2.96	3.88
6	3.40	3.52	3.43	3.17	3.22	3.29	3.36	3.35	3.64	3.59	3.67	3.72	3.88	3.92	5.11
7	3.03	3.07	2.94	2.83	2.86	3.25	3.51	3.43	3.69	3.62	3.81	3.84	3.99	3.98	5.04
8	8.70	9.84	9.37	8.20	8.78	10.88	10.35	9.71	13.35	12.83	13.31	12.89	13.56	12.69	20.36
9	3.81	4.03	3.89	3.61	3.70	4.00	4.01	3.93	4.67	4.77	4.98	5.10	5.22	5.37	6.73
10	3.11	3.24	3.12	2.94	3.01	3.24	3.39	3.31	3.69	3.69	3.91	4.01	4.21	4.30	5.44
11	3.72	3.93	3.78	3.61	3.75	3.99	4.11	4.13	4.59	4.62	4.87	5.17	5.40	5.29	6.92
12	2.97	3.08	2.99	2.80	2.81	2.94	3.08	3.12	3.42	3.44	3.65	3.70	4.00	3.98	5.13
13	2.50	2.60	2.57	2.53	2.63	2.80	3.02	3.07	3.31	3.24	3.33	3.31	3.51	3.72	5.11
14	2.76	2.77	2.67	2.53	2.52	2.51	2.64	2.54	2.68	2.51	2.44	2.28	2.48	2.41	3.50
15	2.46	2.59	2.58	2.48	2.56	2.64	2.78	2.74	2.85	2.96	3.11	3.13	3.40	3.36	4.52
16	2.75	2.70	2.59	2.74	2.49	2.88	2.96	2.82	3.14	3.26	3.55	3.45	3.73	3.87	4.96
17	11.72	12.04	11.82	10.72	9.86	10.12	9.45	10.85	15.57	14.40	14.32	14.81	15.35	14.35	19.66
18	2.00	2.13	2.05	1.94	1.97	2.08	2.11	2.09	2.36	2.32	2.47	2.52	2.57	2.55	3.06
19	3.76	3.76	3.75	3.68	3.56	3.57	3.73	3.22	3.41	3.44	3.42	3.45	3.46	3.50	4.42
20	2.09	2.02	1.90	1.82	1.99	2.10	2.13	2.19	2.37	2.38	2.50	2.59	2.63	2.62	2.98
21	2.66	2.63	2.52	2.46	2.59	2.64	2.60	2.58	2.81	2.90	2.91	3.01	3.05	3.11	3.75
22	3.12	3.16	3.10	2.92	2.92	3.09	3.22	3.22	3.43	3.35	3.47	3.49	3.44	3.50	4.09
23	3.97	4.12	4.02	3.87	4.00	4.31	4.47	4.51	4.90	4.85	5.11	5.28	5.58	5.60	6.73
24	5.32	5.49	5.37	5.29	5.78	6.56	6.86	7.03	8.16	8.13	8.31	8.06	8.70	8.25	9.96
25	4.43	4.44	4.45	4.08	4.13	4.52	4.09	4.03	4.73	4.59	5.09	5.30	6.03	6.04	7.47
26	3.16	3.23	3.19	2.99	3.45	3.73	4.02	3.98	4.26	3.88	3.92	4.37	4.53	4.37	5.20

27	6.20	5.21	5.28	5.18	5.31	5.39	6.29	5.19	5.09	4.82	4.66	4.52	4.58	4.62	4.51
28	4.13	3.80	3.81	3.50	3.29	3.34	3.26	2.95	2.91	3.09	2.96	2.84	2.93	2.92	2.87
29	39.77	28.28	26.72	24.65	24.26	25.95	39.23	26.30	26.95	26.86	28.17	27.54	28.42	27.60	27.78
30	3.18	2.89	2.87	2.66	2.65	2.51	2.49	2.17	2.18	2.11	1.95	1.87	1.82	1.80	1.74
31	4.41	3.71	3.83	3.70	3.57	3.49	3.51	3.23	3.34	3.23	3.12	2.91	2.96	2.93	2.82
32	16.32	12.78	13.31	12.58	12.00	11.63	13.75	10.29	10.94	10.24	9.99	9.56	9.61	9.28	8.98
33	4.53	3.86	4.06	4.01	3.93	3.80	3.83	3.50	3.52	3.37	3.22	3.01	3.09	3.06	3.00
34	3.66	3.28	3.25	3.08	3.14	3.11	3.25	2.94	3.15	3.06	2.94	2.78	2.79	2.81	2.76
Weighted average	**5.72**	**5.16**	**5.24**	**5.09**	**4.88**	**4.81**	**4.88**	**4.46**	**4.52**	**4.40**	**4.79**	**4.67**	**4.81**	**4.37**	**4.34**

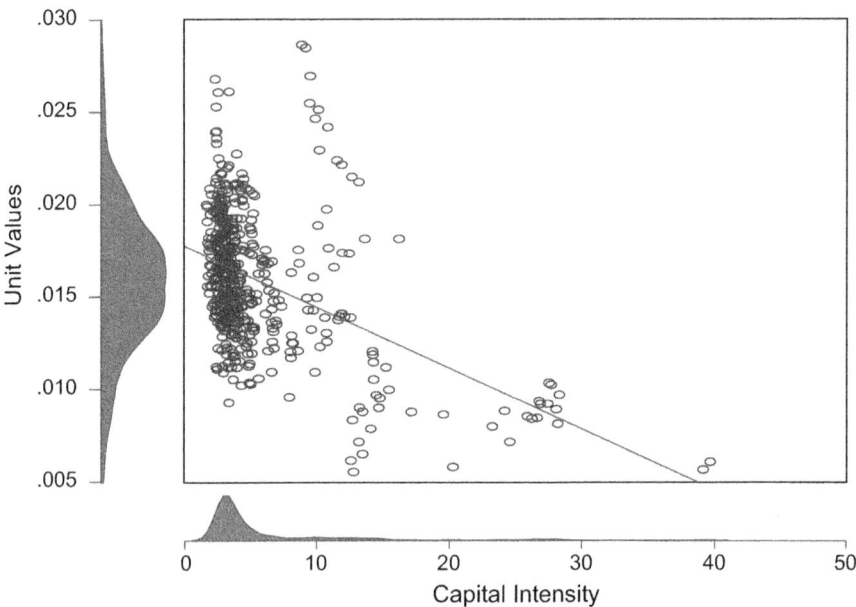

Fig. 4.3 The relationship between unit labour values and capital-intensity, USA, 1995–2009

Table 4.3 Redundant fixed effects test

Effects test	Stat.	p-value
Cross-section F	66.8458	0.0000
Period F	65.9711	0.0000
Cross-section/period F	71.9975	0.0000

The remaining variation indicates the expected causal relationship between capital-intensity and unit labour values.

Furthermore, we conducted a redundant fixed effects test in order to investigate their usefulness over the investigated period and time effects. The results displayed in Table 4.3 suggest that the two F-statistics (65.845 and 65.971) and their associated p-values (0.000) strongly reject the null hypothesis that the cross-section and time effects are redundant. Also, it is evident that the inclusion of both cross-section and time effects are jointly statistically significant as this can be judged by the value of the F-statistic (71.997) and its p-value (0.000). In other words, we can say that all the fixed effects and time coefficients are highly statistically significant at 1%, suggesting that the pooled OLS results hide the heterogeneity among cross-sectional data.

Because in Fig. 4.3 there are too many observations from a considerable large number of industries, the use of weighted averages of both capital-intensities and unit labour values of this 15-year period under study might give us a quite good idea of the way in which they move on average over the years. In Fig. 4.4 we display these two averages (last rows of Tables 4.1 and 4.2) along with their linear trend

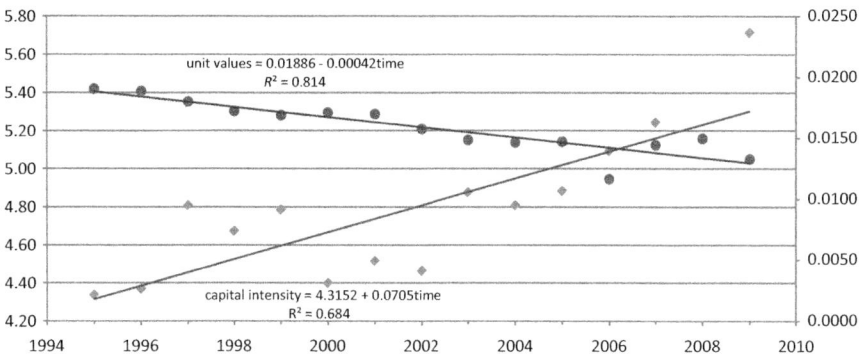

Fig. 4.4 Average capital-intensities and unit labour values, USA, 1995–2009

lines, all of which are statistically significant and the coefficient of determination is high enough once again.

As expected, the economy-wide average unit labour values follow a downward path, while the converse is true for the capital-intensity, lending support to the view that investment in structures and equipment are undertaken in the effort to undercut unit values or, what amounts to the same thing, to reduce (other things equal) the unit cost of production; thus for the same price, the lower unit values secure higher surplus-value and, by extent, more profits.

4.3.2 The Proximity of Direct Prices, Prices of Production and Market Prices

In Table 4.4, we display the estimated deviations between direct prices (DP), prices of production (PP) and market prices (MP) for the US economy over the period 1995–2009. In the last rows of the same table, we also display the average rate of profit estimated in terms of direct prices, r_{DP}; the economy-wide average rate of profit, r; the maximum rate of profit, R, the maximal eigenvalue of the matrix **H**, which is no different than the Sraffian standard ratio; and finally the relative rate of profit $\rho = rR^{-1}$.[6] The latter will become the key variable in our discussion of the effect of changes in distribution on relative prices. Furthermore, a low relative rate of profit is an indicator of relatively small deviations between the estimated prices, as these are measured by the various metrics of deviation.[7]

---

[6]See Sect. 3.4.1 of Chap. 3 for the details of the estimation of the standard commodity and ratio.

[7]A low relative rate of profit (less than 50%) indicates that direct prices are near prices of production and thus the latter can be approximated by the former by using only few terms (Tsoulfidis and Mariolis 2007; Mariolis and Tsoulfidis 2010).

Table 4.4 Measures of price deviations, USA, 1995–2009

Deviations	Years 1995	1996	1997	1998	1999	2000	2001	2002	2003	2004	2005	2006	2007	2008	2009
DP vs. MP															
MAD	0.122	0.127	0.124	0.112	0.117	0.127	0.138	0.142	0.158	0.152	0.151	0.160	0.169	0.181	0.177
MAWD	0.138	0.140	0.139	0.132	0.135	0.142	0.151	0.147	0.160	0.147	0.143	0.154	0.157	0.167	0.164
d	0.155	0.160	0.157	0.151	0.153	0.169	0.189	0.186	0.211	0.209	0.213	0.226	0.240	0.256	0.240
PP vs. MP															
MAD	0.141	0.140	0.142	0.161	0.167	0.145	0.146	0.164	0.112	0.146	0.158	0.164	0.171	0.178	0.184
MAWD	0.131	0.135	0.138	0.149	0.153	0.141	0.146	0.156	0.111	0.148	0.154	0.161	0164	0.164	0.163
d	0.218	0.222	0.221	0.238	0.236	0.213	0.216	0.225	0.172	0.229	0.229	0.234	0.240	0.240	0.248
DP vs. PP															
MAD	0.142	0.152	0.147	0.149	0.149	0.131	0.124	0.137	0.133	0.136	0.137	0.133	0.133	0.121	0.137
MAWD	0.174	0.182	0.178	0.176	0.170	0.155	0.150	0.155	0.167	0.155	0.152	0.147	0.143	0.136	0.154
d	0.165	0.175	0.174	0.168	0.166	0.166	0.158	0.161	0.200	0.176	0.177	0.172	0.173	0.165	0.170
r_{DP}	0.103	0.106	0.108	0.110	0.106	0.098	0.092	0.098	0.098	0.098	0.101	0.096	0.092	0.091	0.087
r	0.106	0.109	0.110	0.114	0.109	0.096	0.090	0.094	0.091	0.088	0.0857	0.082	0.082	0.074	0.078
R	0.540	0.538	0.532	0.563	0.550	0.497	0.477	0.474	0.420	0.402	0.363	0.356	0.339	0.350	0.355
$\rho = rR^{-1}$	0.196	0.203	0.204	0.202	0.199	0.193	0.188	0.199	0.217	0.220	0.236	0.231	0.242	0.212	0.221

From the many available metrics of deviation, we opted for the following three: the mean absolute deviation (MAD) defined as the sum of absolute deviations between direct and market prices divided by the number of industries. The mean absolute weighted deviation (MAWD) in which the weights in use are the share of each industry's sales to total sales. Along with MAD and MAWD which are both affected by the normalization condition or the numéraire chosen, we present estimates of the proposed by Steedman and Tomkins (1998) d-statistic of deviation. The main advantage of the d-statistic compared to other relevant deviation statistics is that it does not depend on the employed normalization condition (Mariolis and Tsoulfidis 2009, 2010 and 2016). Therefore, by including the d-statistic, we provide an unbiased regarding the utilized numéraire estimate of deviations for each year of the analysis, and, at the same time, we get an idea of the size of the expected bias from using other deviation statistics.

From the findings displayed in Table 4.4, we ascertain what has been, time and again, found in the relevant empirical literature that the deviations of PP from their respective DP are moderately small, as this can be judged by the three metrics of deviation that we use, the MAD, the MAWD and the numéraire bias-free d-statistic. In effect, estimated over the 1995–2009 period, these deviations on average usually range in the vicinity of 20%, which is another way to say that the proximity of DP and PP to MP often exceeds the 80%.[8] These findings encouraged us to calculate the economy-wide average rate of profit in terms of both DP and PP; the results suggest that the two rates of profit are extremely close to each other, which practically means that they can be used interchangeably. Such proximity of the two rates of profit suggests that 'too much ink' has been spilled over a theoretical issue without a matching empirical and, therefore, practical significance counterpart.

In the case of the Greek economy, the respective estimates based on a model of circulating capital for the period 1988–1997 are displayed in Table 4.5.

We observe that in terms of our three metrics of deviation, the deviations of DP and PP from MP and from themselves do not vary widely over the years. In particular, the deviation of DP from MP measured by the d-statistic varies from 0.212 to 0.273, while the deviation of PP from market prices varies from 0.208 to 0.287. Finally, the deviations of DP from PP lie between 0.079 and 0.098. In the last three rows of Table 4.5, we display the three rates of profit, average, maximum and relative which, as expected, do not display much variability. The relative rate of profit varies from 0.230 to 0.270 which is far less than 50% indicating, thus, the fast attainment of equilibrium prices. Hence, once we start with DP or an arbitrary vector of prices, soon we converge to prices of production; we deal with this and other similarly related issues in the present and next chapters of the book.

The results for the economy of Japan show that the capitalist economies, pretty much, share the same features (Tsoulfidis 2008). More specifically, we utilize the

---

[8]On closer examination, the results reveal that the deviations would be much smaller had we taken out of our estimates the oil and gas and especially the real estate industries, which in most studies are the usual obvious outliers, the oil industry because of issues of differential rent and the real estate for reasons of imputed income among others.

Table 4.5 Measures of price deviations and profit rates, Greece, 1988–1997

Deviations	Years									
	1988	1989	1990	1991	1992	1993	1994	1995	1996	1997
DP vs. MP										
MAD	0.195	0.184	0.214	0.209	0.204	0.229	0.228	0.200	0.216	0.265
MAWD	0.221	0.215	0.212	0.196	0.200	0.210	0.206	0.168	0.189	0.191
d	0.227	0.219	0.229	0.226	0.216	0.212	0.216	0.236	0.217	0.273
PP vs. MP										
MAD	0.178	0.174	0.205	0.200	0.196	0.220	0.231	0.208	0.204	0.250
MAWD	0.198	0.196	0.205	0.186	0.198	0.208	0.201	0.178	0.183	0.191
d	0.228	0.219	0.235	0.227	0.219	0.208	0.242	0.251	0.228	0.287
PP vs. DP										
MAD	0.075	0.082	0.076	0.084	0.083	0.064	0.080	0.075	0.074	0.093
MAWD	0.081	0.081	0.060	0.078	0.087	0.079	0.077	0.077	0.089	0.085
d	0.093	0.098	0.090	0.100	0.097	0.079	0.089	0.090	0.089	0.094
r	0.211	0.220	0.218	0.243	0.275	0.236	0.254	0.230	0.247	0.238
R	0.817	0.851	0.874	0.917	1.076	1.026	1.006	0.903	0.977	0.882
$\rho = rR^{-1}$	0.258	0.259	0.249	0.265	0.255	0.230	0.252	0.254	0.252	0.270

Table 4.6 Measures of price deviations and profit rates, Japan, 1970–1990

Deviations	Years				
	1970	1975	1980	1985	1990
DP vs. MP					
MAD	0.271	0.171	0.172	0.147	0.127
MAWD	0.286	0.202	0.197	0.178	0.154
d	0.371	0.233	0.226	0.185	0.171
PP vs. MP					
MAD	0.268	0.160	0.153	0.130	0.113
MAWD	0.266	0.173	0.155	0.141	0.122
d	0.323	0.216	0.212	0.181	0.161
PP vs. DP					
MAD	0.112	0.089	0.107	0.117	0.115
MAWD	0.138	0.118	0.142	0.149	0.149
d	0.125	0.110	0.135	0.156	0.141
r	0.240	0.230	0.278	0.294	0.279
R	0.788	0.770	0.788	0.795	0.842
$\rho = rR^{-1}$	0.305	0.298	0.344	0.371	0.331

33 industry detail input-output data of the Japanese economy spanning the decades of 1970s and 1980s which include the five benchmark years of 1970, 1975, 1980, 1985 and 1990. The estimates using a circulating capital model with no depreciation and current prices are displayed in Table 4.6.

The deviations of DP and PP from MP and from themselves are too small as suggested by the numéraire bias-free *d*-statistic. Thus, the deviation of DP from market prices varies from 0.171 to 0.371; the deviation of PP from market prices varies from 0.161 to 0.323; and finally the deviation of PP from DP varies from 0.110 to 0.156. In the last three rows of Table 4.5, the three rates of profit, average, maximum and relative are displayed which indicate, as expected, a low relative rate of profit in the order of much lower than 50%.

The estimates of the metrics of deviation as well as the rates of profit for a number and quite diverse economies—such as Canada for the year 1997 and 34 industries (Tsoulfidis and Paitaridis 2017); China for the year 1997 (circulating capital model) and 2009 (circulating and fixed capital models) and 38 and 33 industries, respectively (Mariolis and Tsoulfidis 2009; Tsoulfidis and Paitaridis 2017); the UK for the year 1990 and 33 industries using both circulating and fixed capital models (Mariolis and Tsoulfidis 2016); the Republic of Korea for the years 1995 and 2000 with 27 industries and in 2009 with 34 industries using both circulating and fixed capital stock models (Tsoulfidis and Rieu 2006; Tsoulfidis and Paitaridis 2017); Japan for the year 2009 (Tsoulfidis and Paitaridis 2017); and, finally, the USA for the year 1990 with 32 industry detail using both circulating and fixed capital stock models (Mariolis and Tsoulfidis 2016)—are displayed in Table 4.7.

The above findings suggest that although we are dealing with an array of quite dissimilar economies and periods of time, nevertheless these same economies display quite common features. Of course, the similarities do not cover the differences characterizing each of these economies, and their study requires much more detailed analysis and research efforts.

4.3.3 Intertemporal Price-Value Deviations

A corollary of the findings so far is that the classical theory of value and distribution contains great explanatory power not only in cross-sectional data of so diverse economies but also maintains, if not strengthens its explanatory content, when it comes to intertemporal comparisons. In effect, the salient feature of the classical political economics perspective is its intertemporal dimension precisely as it has been suggested by the old classical economists. Ricardo, for example, argued that changes in relative prices of commodities over time are explained not by changes in wages, as for example, a neoclassical or a cost of production theory of distribution would claim, but rather by changes mainly in their labour requirements. More specifically, Ricardo, after an analysis of the limited effects of changes in wages on the relative prices stated categorically:

> In estimating, then, the causes of the variations in the value of commodities, although it would be wrong wholly to omit the consideration of the effect produced by a rise or fall of labour [i.e., wages] it would be equally incorrect to attach much importance to it; and consequently, in the subsequent part of this work, though I shall occasionally refer to this cause of variation, I shall consider all the great variations which take place in the relative value of commodities to be produced by the greater or less quantity of labour which may be required from time to time to produce them.
>
> (*Works* I, p. 34)

Table 4.7 Measures of price deviations and profit rates: China, Canada, the UK, Korea and the USA

Statistics of deviation	Countries-years								
	Canada-1997	China-1997	China-2009	UK-1990	Korea-1995	Korea-2000	Korea-2009	USA-1990	Japan-2009
DP vs. MP									
MAD	0.133	0.183	0.188	0.222	0.128	0.130	0.154	0.125	0.152
MAWD	0.149	0.160	0.196	0.186	0.131	0.143	0.164	0.094	0.167
d	0.180	0.196	0.251	0.285	0.182	0.167	0.212	0.163	0.201
PP vs. MP									
MAD	0.126	0.170	0.181	0.199	0.151	0.152	0.147	0.126	0.214
MAWD	0.125	0.112	0.158	0.168	0.152	0.164	0.147	0.108	0.216
d	0.199	0.154	0.238	0.249	0.176	0.176	0.193	0.157	0.238
	Fixed capital	Fixed capital	Fixed capital	Fixed capital	Fixed capital	Fixed capital	Fixed capital	Fixed capital	Fixed capital
MAD	NA	NA	0.158	0.169	0.156	0.174	0.155	0.139	0.139
MAWD	NA	NA	0.154	0.179	0.152	0.181	0.155	0.137	0.122
d	NA	NA	0.261	0.214	0.190	0.207	0.188	0.187	0.194
PP vs. DP									
MAD	0.100	0.112	0.155	0.041	0.148	0.148	0.129	0.046	0.186
MAWD	0.098	0.109	0.194	0.045	0.161	0.173	0.156	0.061	0.182
d	0.140	0.114	0.213	0.055	0.179	0.177	0.149	0.059	0.210
	Fixed capital	Fixed capital	Fixed capital	Fixed capital	Fixed capital	Fixed capital	Fixed capital	Fixed capital	Fixed capital
MAD	NA	NA	0.144	0.135	0.146	0.151	0.101	0.097	0.095
MAWD	NA	NA	0.125	0.176	0.151	0.154	0.093	0.129	0.113
d	NA	NA	0.208	0.210	0.174	0.174	0.145	0.127	0.130

r	0.250	0.220	0.247	0.168	0.268	0.253	0.198	0.167	0.327
	Fixed capital	Fixed capital	Fixed capital	Fixed capital	Fixed capital	Fixed capital	Fixed capital	Fixed capital	Fixed capital
	NA	NA	0.307	0.092	0.123	0.133	0.056	0.085	0.068
R	0.737	0.568	0.476	0.870	0.594	0.556	0.529	0.814	0.721
	Fixed capital	Fixed capital	Fixed capital	Fixed capital	Fixed capital	Fixed capital	Fixed capital	Fixed capital	Fixed capital
	NA	NA	0.650	0.326	0.257	0.278	0.213	0.343	0.275
$\rho = rR^{-1}$	0.339	0.387	0.520	0.193	0.452	0.456	0.374	0.205	0.453
	Fixed capital	Fixed capital	Fixed capital	Fixed capital	Fixed capital	Fixed capital	Fixed capital	Fixed capital	Fixed capital
	NA	NA	0.472	0.281	0.480	0.481	0.263	0.249	0.275

It is interesting to note that in Ricardo the term price is often used in a dual sense, that is, price incorporating the average rate of profit or price of production in the Marxian use of the term and also market price. The rationale for this treatment might be that intertemporally the fluctuations in market prices on average conform to equilibrium prices (prices of production). The results of deviations displayed in Tables 4.4–4.7 show that the various measures of price-value deviations are not too different and also point to the same conclusion. For example, if the MAWD is relatively small, the much celebrated by Steedman and Tomkins (1998) bias-free of numéraire d-statistic of deviation does not show anything quite different (Mariolis and Tsoulfidis 2009, 2016). Furthermore, if the relative prices and relative labour times are close to each other in cross-sectional data, this proximity will hold, to a great extent, intertemporally. In short, the classical theory of value and distribution holds not only statically but mainly dynamically. The rationale is that the size and direction of deviations between DP, PP and market prices are expected to remain pretty much steady in a reasonably long period of time.

It seems that Ricardo's intuition was in the right direction because for him cost price is in effect the natural price of a commodity and the natural price in the long run is treated as if it were the same with the actual market price. The possible deviations of the two kinds of prices, in the long run, are expected to dissipate and so they are treated as if they were the same. Notes Ricardo,

> It is the cost of production [=natural price] which must ultimately regulate the [market] price of commodities, and not, as has been so often said, the proportion between the supply and demand: the proportion between the supply and demand may, indeed, for a time, affect the market value of a commodity, until it is supplied in a greater or less abundance, according as the demand may have increased or diminished; but this effect will be only of temporary duration.
>
> (*Works* I, p. 232)

In what follows, we report our empirical results lending overwhelming support to Ricardo's views and to the classical political economy perspective in general through the following simple econometric specification:

$$\ln \left(\mathbf{P}_{t+n} \cdot \hat{\mathbf{P}}_t^{-1} \right)_j = \alpha + \beta \, \ln \left(\mathbf{V}_t \cdot \hat{\mathbf{V}}_{t+n}^{-1} \right)_j + \gamma \, \ln \left(\mathbf{K}_{t+n} \cdot \hat{\mathbf{K}}_t^{-1} \right)_j + u_j \qquad (4.11)$$

where $\mathbf{P}$ denotes the vector of price indexes of industries j at year t and n stands for the number of years ahead of the year t. $\mathbf{V}$ denotes the vector of unit (labour) values while a is the constant of the regression and β the elasticity coefficient of the unit labour values. $\mathbf{K}$ symbolizes the vector of capital intensities derived through relation (4.9) and γ is its estimated elasticity while u is the stochastic term. Finally, ln is the natural logarithm and a caret, ^ , over a variable indicates the formation of a diagonal matrix from a respective vector. Relation (4.11) indicates that the changes in the price index, which over time are not expected to be too different from the respective changes in market prices are determined by the relative labour times and capital intensities (*Works* I, p. 36).

Hence, it is important to note that what is actually tested is the extent to which the change in the relative vertically integrated labour productivities of industries, as captured in the unit labour values, are consistent with the changes in the price indexes. The changes in the latter in effect reflect the respective changes in market prices, which may also be approximated by the respective changes in prices of production. The dimension of unit labour values are labour times per million of constant (2010) USD worth of commodities. As a consequence, the best available way to obtain estimates of the movement of market prices is through the growth rates of the respective price indexes.[9] We also test the extent to which the growth rates in prices of production or Ricardo's natural prices are close to the growth rates of the price indexes. For this purpose, we utilize input–output data of the USA and China, two major economies with many similarities but also marked differences.

We utilized the latest input–output and socioeconomic data of WIOD (2016) with 54 industry details although seven of China's industries had zero entries. All estimates are carried in terms of constant 2010 prices. For details of estimations of various matrices and vectors see Tsaliki et al. (2018) and Tsoulfidis and Paitaridis (2017).

In Fig. 4.5, we plot the growth rates in price indexes against those of the unit labour values of each of the 54 industries of the US economy displayed in the first three in the panel of six graphs. The regression lines and the kernel density functions indicate the similarities in distribution of both price changes and unit labour values. The symbolism is as follows: P_07_00 on the vertical axis stands for the growth rate of the price index of each industry between the years 2007 and 2000. For the same time period and reasons of visual clarity and convenience of presentation, we display the growth rate of unit labour values as V_00_07, the idea is that unlike prices which typically increase over time, unit labour values decline over time as a result of technological change. Similarly, with the other variables and pairs of years, where PP_14_07 stands for the growth in prices of production over the period 2007–2014 while PP_14_00 indicates the growth rates of prices of production during the entire 2014–2000 period and so forth (see the last three graphs in Fig. 4.2). Finally, K_07_00 (not shown in Figs. 4.5 or 4.6) indicates the growth rate of the vertically integrated value composition of capital between the years 2007 and 2000. Ditto for the other periods and variables. The same test is conducted for the case of the Chinese economy and the results displayed in the panel of six graphs in Fig. 4.6 strengthen the Ricardian and Marxian thesis that the intertemporal variations in market prices depend, to a large extent, on the respective variations in labour values and that the growth in prices of production are not far from those in market prices.

---

[9]This approximation market prices is inspired, in part, by an exchange we had back in 2013 with professor Takeshi Nakatani who opined (in his book published in Japanese) that we cannot get direct estimates of market prices using input–output data casting doubt to the usually found high proximity of estimated values and prices of production to market prices. And for this reason, he estimated the correlation coefficient of the ratio of unit labour values of industries over their prices in one time period against the same ratio over another time period. The results for the 83 industry structure of Japan showed that for the period 1975–1980 the correlation coefficient was 0.804, increased to 0.858 for the period 1980–1985, and finally to 0.916 for the entire 1975–1985 period.

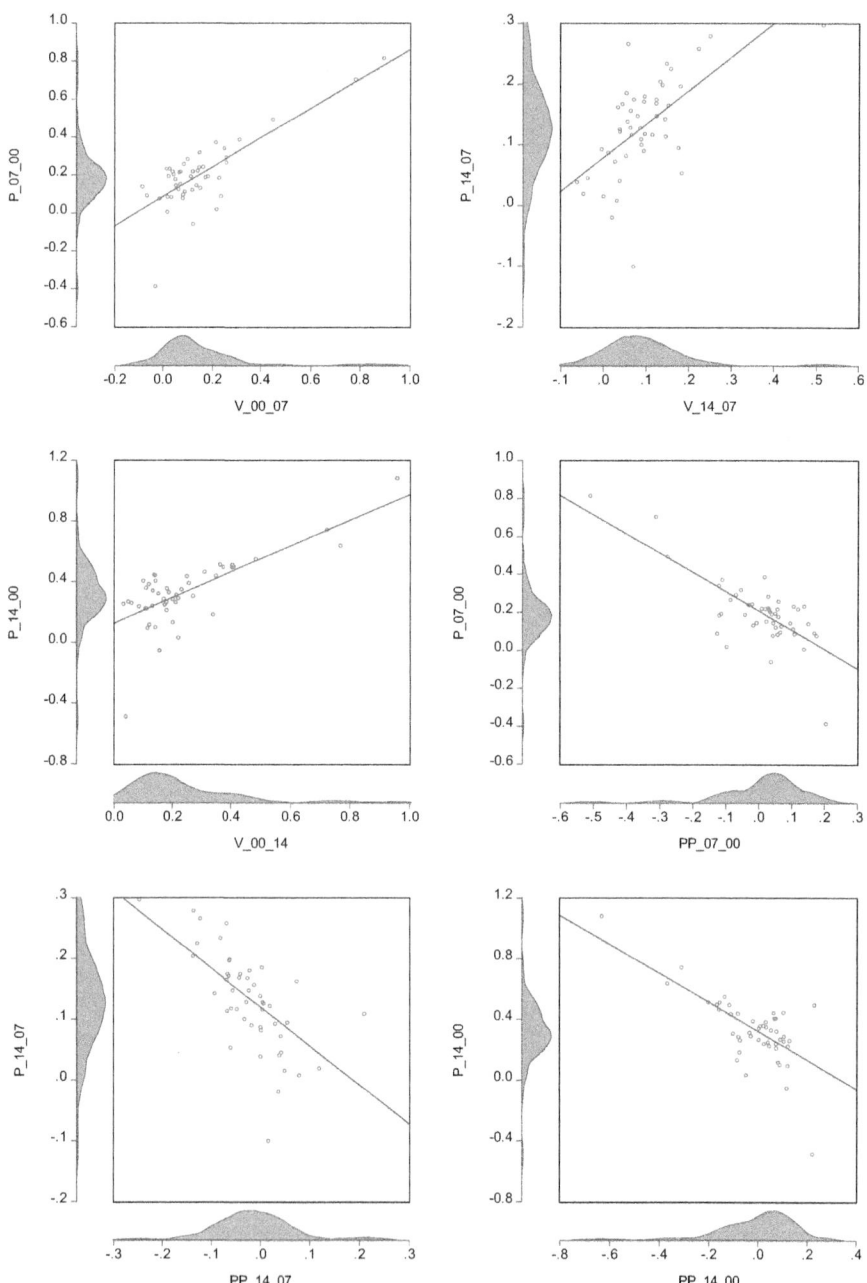

Fig. 4.5 Labour values, prices of production vs. market prices, USA, 2000–2014

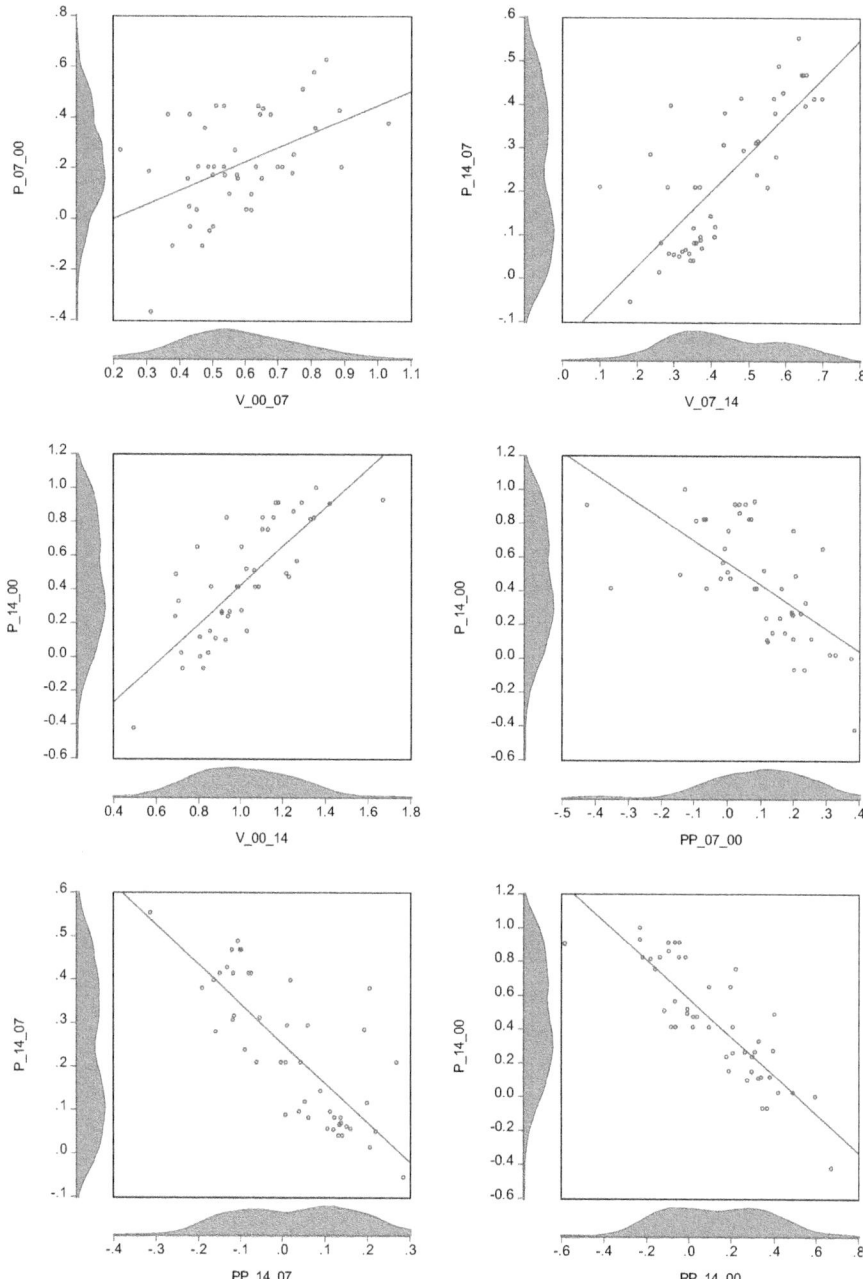

Fig. 4.6 Labor values, prices of production and market prices, China, 2000–2014

The relative effects of unit labour values on market prices is obtained through the OLS regressions, whose results are displayed in Table 4.8 for each time period and set of variables for the two countries. Clearly, the distribution of the deviations in the three pairs of years under study are quite similar, indicating that the changes in unit labour values and prices keep close to each other over long stretches of time and are nearly of the same magnitude and direction. Furthermore, the independent variables are statistically significant as this can be judged by the absolute values of the respective *t*-ratios in the parentheses and, also the adjusted R-squares are particularly high for cross-sectional regressions. Clearly, the variations in the unit labour values are always statistically significant in explaining the movement of market prices and the estimated elasticities are not far from unity lending support to the labour theory of value according to Ricardo.[10] It is important to stress that the capital-intensity as captured in the variable **K** is also statistically significant but with an elasticity coefficient much lower than that of labour values. The capital-intensity was not found statistically significant in the case of China in the last two periods and the adjusted R-square suggests the elimination of this variable. Finally, the OLS regressions revealed the close proximity of prices of production to market prices precisely as expected by Ricardo and Marx.

Other important findings are that the Great Recession (2007–2009) impacted on the US economy as this can be judged by the low elasticity of prices of production, in effect the elasticity coefficient of the PP_14_07, is the lowest and the overall performance is inferior to that of the other subperiods in both the countries. However, when we examine the entire 2000–2014 period for the US economy, the elasticity coefficient of prices of production returns to nearly unitary lending support to the view that in the long run the natural prices (or prices of production) tend to conformity with market prices. The results for China are also extremely good especially in the last two periods (2007–2014 and 2000–2014) and certainly the Great Recession did not affect the Chinese economy at least with respect to distortions of Ricardo's labour theory of value.

Not very different were the results with respect to changes in price-value deviations in Shaikh (1984 and 2016) and also in Schwartz (1961) eloquently summarized and made known by Shaikh (2016, Chap. 4). These results along with many others that one may find in the extant literature will certainly trigger and occupy the research efforts of modern economists. For the construction of the vectors and matrices of capital stock as well as the deflation of the data and other relevant information see Appendices (1 and 2).

---

[10]Ricardo for instance notes: "No law can be laid down respecting quantity, but a tolerably correct one can be laid down respecting proportions. Every day, I am more satisfied that the former enquiry is vain and delusive, and the latter only the true objects of the science" (*Works*, VIII, pp. 278–279).

Table 4.8 Unit labour values, capital intensity, prices of production vs. market prices, USA and China 2000–2014

Periods	Constant	Unit labour values	Capital intensity	Prices of production	Adjusted R-squared
USA					
2000–2007	0.086 (4.74)	0.773 (9.44)			0.624
2000–2007	0.145 (7.31)	0.797 (11.5)	−0.493 (4.69)		0.732
2000–2007	0.208 (13.4)			−1.014 (8.16)	0.553
2007–2014	0.078 (6.69)	0.551 (6.05)			0.402
2007–2014	0.074 (6.99)	0.781 (7.48)	−0.311 (3.58)		0.512
2007–2014	0.120 (14.4)			−0.641 (5.99)	0.397
2000–2014	0.127 (4.02)	0.847 (7.00)			0.543
2000–2014	0.205 (6.27)	0.857 (9.37)	−0.445 (4.33)		0.659
2000–2014	0.322 (14.9)			−0.955 (6.60)	0.445
China					
2000–2007	−0.111 (1.20)	0.559 (3.67)			0.213
2000–2007	−0.259 (3.50)	0.851 (6.84)	−0.512 (5.99)		0.557
2000–2007	0.295 (12.4)			−0.839 (6.62)	0.482
2007–2014	−0.146 (3.00)	0.866 (8.13)			0.586
2007–2014	−0.130 (2.21)	0.891 (7.42)	−0.026 (0.458)		0.576
2007–2014	0.253 (16.7)			−0.912 (8.41)	0.601
2000–2014	−0.729 (5.19)	1.152 (8.58)			0.612
2000–2014	−0.611 (3.37)	1.160 (8.63)	−0.122 (1.02)		0.613
2000–2014	0.582 (19.8)			−1.139 (10.7)	0.712

4.3.4 Further Issues on Price-Value Deviations

In order to show analytically the proximity of direct prices to prices of production on the one hand and the limited and predictable, in general, effects of changes in income distribution on prices of production, on the other hand, we invoke Sraffa's analysis of the standard commodity. To this end we hypothesize that $w = 0$, and in so doing, we get the maximum rate of profit $r = R$; the associated with it price vector will be

$$\mathbf{p} = R\mathbf{p}\mathbf{H} \qquad (4.12)$$

The right eigenvector of matrix $\mathbf{H}$ is the standard commodity $\mathbf{q}$, in the sense that the proportions of inputs multiplied by R give us the output proportions, that is, the standard ratios (the exact same vector is used for both inputs and outputs).

$$\mathbf{q}R^{-1} = \mathbf{H}\mathbf{q} \qquad (4.13)$$

Since the standard commodity $\mathbf{q}$ is in proportions, we need to fix its scale and in so doing to connect it to the economy's gross output vector, $\mathbf{x}$ as follows

$$\mathbf{s} = \mathbf{q}\left(\frac{\mathbf{v}\mathbf{x}}{\mathbf{v}\mathbf{q}}\right) \qquad (4.14)$$

where $\mathbf{s}$ is the normalized standard commodity, which in the analysis is used as numéraire.[11] For $r = 0$, we get $w = W$, that is, the maximum wage; in this case, the prices of production are proportional to direct prices

$$\mathbf{p} = W\mathbf{v} \qquad (4.15)$$

If in turn, we normalize the prices of production with the help of the standard commodity, we get

$$\mathbf{p}\mathbf{s} = \mathbf{v}\mathbf{s} = \mathbf{v}\mathbf{x} = \mathbf{e}\mathbf{x} \qquad (4.16)$$

and for $r = 0$, we get $\mathbf{p}\mathbf{s} = W\mathbf{v}\mathbf{s}$ and $w = W = 1$. However, for a positive rate of profit, prices of production will generally differ from the monetary expression of labour values; these differences are expected to be higher as r increases approaching to maximum profit rate, $r = R$. The converse will be true, that is, prices of production get closer to direct prices so long as the rate of profit decreases towards zero; and

---

[11]The selection of standard commodity as numéraire is made for its desired property, that is, its independence to changes in the distributive variables. In the first empirical studies, the gross output was mainly used as the numéraire and in far fewer studies the net output with very similar results with respect to the numéraire bias-free d-statistic of deviation. The standard commodity as the numéraire has been introduced in the empirical studies by Shaikh (1998).

when $r = 0$, direct prices and prices of production become indistinguishable from each other.

For the calculation of prices of production, we assume a circulating capital model without depreciation; so we may write

$$\mathbf{p} = (w\mathbf{l} + \mathbf{pA})(1 + r) \tag{4.17}$$

If we replace for nominal wage, $w = \mathbf{pb}$, we get the equation of the prices of production:

$$\mathbf{p} = (1 + r)w\mathbf{l} + r\mathbf{pA} + \mathbf{pA} \tag{4.18}$$

or

$$\mathbf{p}[\mathbf{I} - \mathbf{A}] = (1 + r)w\mathbf{l} + r\mathbf{pA}$$

and

$$\mathbf{p} = (1 + r)w\,\underbrace{\mathbf{l}[\mathbf{I} - \mathbf{A}]^{-1}}_{\mathbf{v}} + r\mathbf{p}\,\underbrace{\mathbf{A}[\mathbf{I} - \mathbf{A}]^{-1}}_{\mathbf{H}}$$

or

$$\mathbf{p} = (1 + r)w\mathbf{v} + r\mathbf{pH} \tag{4.19}$$

We postmultiply (see Shaikh 1998) Eq. (4.19) by the standard commodity, $\mathbf{s}$, and so we get

$$\mathbf{ps} = (1 + r)w\mathbf{vs} + r\mathbf{pHs}$$

or

$$\mathbf{vs} = (1 + r)w\mathbf{vs} + rR^{-1}\mathbf{vs}$$

We divide through by $\mathbf{vs}$ and we end up with

$$1 = w + rw + rR^{-1} \tag{4.20}$$

which solves for

$$w = \frac{R - r}{(1 + r)R} \tag{4.21}$$

The last relation describes the curvilinear shape of the wage rate of profit curve (WRPC) (Pasinetti 1977).

Steedman (1999) suggested an interesting approximation to prices of production through labour values or direct prices in case where wages are paid ex post. It can be shown that the exact same relation holds true in case where wages are paid ex ante according to the above derivation. For this purpose, let us recall Eq. (4.19) of prices of production:

$$\mathbf{p} = (1 + r)w\mathbf{v} + r\mathbf{p}\mathbf{H}$$

This can be further rewritten as

$$\mathbf{p} = (1 + r)w\mathbf{v}[\mathbf{I} - r\mathbf{H}]^{-1}$$

If we define the relative profit rate as $\rho \equiv rR^{-1}$, where $0 \leq \rho < 1$, and by taking into account the relation (4.20), we have

$$(1 + r)w = 1 - \rho$$

Therefore, the prices of production can be expressed in terms of the relative rate of profit as follows:

$$\mathbf{p} = (1 - \rho)\mathbf{v}[\mathbf{I} - \rho R\mathbf{H}]^{-1} \qquad (4.22)$$

The above bracketed expression can be rewritten as follows:

$$\mathbf{p} = (1 - \rho)\mathbf{v}\left[\mathbf{I} + \mathbf{H}R\rho + (\mathbf{H}R\rho)^2 + (\mathbf{H}R\rho)^3 + \ldots\right] \qquad (4.23)$$

The latter expression essentially is Krylov's method (Meyer 2001) of approximating the eigenvector to any degree of accuracy provided that the matrix $\mathbf{H}R\rho$ has an eigenvalue of less than one. Vector $\mathbf{v}$ stands for DP, and ρ and R (relative and maximum rates of profit) are scalars that make the estimated $\mathbf{H}R\rho$ matrix to have its maximum eigenvalue usually (much) smaller than one; hence, there is a need for few iterations to derive a reasonably good approximation of PP. In fact, the above polynomial expression in terms of $(1 - \rho)\rho^n$ shows that the PP may result from DP times the bracketed terms $\mathbf{H}R\rho$. Where $n = 0, 1, 2, \ldots$ the relation $(1 - \rho)\rho^n$ is derived from Eq. (3.23). In particular, the PP equal to direct ones multiplied by a fully determined markup. Depending on the number of bracketed terms, the PP are approximated by DP to any desired degree of accuracy simply by adding up more terms in the equation. It is important to emphasize that for a relatively good approximation, only a few terms are adequate enough provided that the value of ρ is less than 1/2 (Steedman 1999, pp. 315–316). Therefore, it presents particular interest to examine empirically the performance of Steedman's method to approximate the prices of production through direct prices.

We have already shown that for very good theoretical reasons related mainly with the low relative rate of profit, ρ, the deviations between different kinds of prices (DP, PP and MP) for an array of countries were found to be particularly small, as this can be judged by the low values of statistics of deviation, usually ranging between 10 and 20%, while the relative rates of profit are always by far lower than 50% (see Tables 4.4–4.7). We now proceed by testing the strength of the above polynomial expression of PP estimated through DP and, at the same time, showing the diminishing significance of the bracketed terms provided that the relative rate of profit is well below the 50% border line. Table 4.9 presents the results of Steedman's polynomial approximation for the US economy and the year 2009, the last year that we have all the required data at the 34 input-output industry detail.

The first two columns show the DP and the estimated PP in the case of a circulating capital model augmented by the matrix of depreciation coefficients all expressed in constant 1995 prices while the last row display the MAD of DP and PP from the market prices; the remaining MADs in the last row present the deviations of the approximated prices of production from the PP.[12] It is important to note at this point that we were bound to opt for the case of circulating capital model because the fixed capital model case did not display converging behaviour; a result which relates with the fact that the vertically integrated capital stock coefficients matrix $\mathbf{H} = \mathbf{K}$ $[\mathbf{I} - \mathbf{A} - \mathbf{D}]^{-1}$ when multiplied by the term $R\rho$ gives a maximal eigenvalue not suitable to the above approximation.[13] Having accounting for all these cautionary and at the same time crucial matters, we applied Steedman's polynomial approximation [Eq. (4.23)] to the US data for the year 2009, and the results are presented in Table 4.9. When the first term of the above polynomial expression, $(1 - \rho)\mathbf{v}$, is taken into account, the deviation, as expected, is substantial (MAD is 37%); however, by adding $(1 - \rho)\mathbf{v}[\mathbf{I} + \mathbf{H}R\rho]$, the second polynomial term, we observe that the approximation improves appreciably as the MAD drops to 13.6%; the addition of the third term improves further the approximation as the MAD drops now to 12.5%. The improvements by including the fourth and higher-order terms are only marginal, and so we do not miss much in terms of a tolerable good approximation by truncated them.

We observe that the accuracy of approximation of PP through DP increases already with the inclusion of the second term and stabilizes with the third term whereas the improvement with the inclusion of the fourth term is only marginal. Clearly, the approximation is quite accurate and depends crucially on the relatively low value of $\rho = r/R = 0.331/0.918 = 0.360$ which is lower than the 50% of

---

[12]Since we refer to the same type of price, the estimates of deviation are not affected by the normalization condition.

[13]This should not come as a surprise, as in Steedman and the extant literature, in general, the analysis is carried out mainly in circulating capital models and fixed capital models appear in systems of joint production.

Table 4.9 Direct prices, prices of production and their approximation, USA, 2009

	Sectors	DP	PP	1st term	2nd term	3rd term	4th term
1	Agriculture, hunting, forestry and fishing	1.024	1.227	0.655	0.999	1.142	1.143
2	Mining and quarrying	0.810	0.766	0.518	0.677	0.734	0.734
3	Food, beverages and tobacco	0.824	1.061	0.527	0.844	0.979	0.980
4	Textiles and textile products	1.155	1.252	0.739	1.052	1.177	1.179
5	Leather, leather and footwear	1.558	1.842	0.997	1.490	1.707	1.712
6	Wood and products of wood and cork	1.449	1.724	0.927	1.415	1.609	1.611
7	Pulp, paper, paper, printing and publishing	0.857	0.920	0.548	0.788	0.872	0.873
8	Coke, refined petroleum and nuclear fuel	0.565	0.682	0.362	0.571	0.642	0.646
9	Chemicals and chemical products	0.903	1.091	0.577	0.893	1.018	1.020
10	Rubber and plastics	1.050	1.266	0.672	1.031	1.179	1.183
11	Other non-metallic mineral	0.981	1.044	0.628	0.895	0.990	0.990
12	Basic metals and fabricated metal	1.005	1.152	0.643	0.959	1.081	1.085
13	Machinery, nec	0.878	1.006	0.562	0.836	0.944	0.945
14	Electrical and optical equipment	1.754	1.871	1.122	1.600	1.773	1.778
15	Transport equipment	1.104	1.408	0.706	1.128	1.303	1.306
16	Manufacturing, nec; recycling	0.938	1.027	0.600	0.865	0.968	0.968
17	Electricity, gas and water supply	0.774	0.766	0.495	0.671	0.732	0.732
18	Construction	1.032	0.956	0.660	0.847	0.916	0.917
19	Sale, maintenance and repair of motor vehicles and motorcycles; retail sale of fuel	1.184	1.073	0.757	0.953	1.029	1.029
20	Wholesale trade and commission trade, except of motor vehicles and motorcycles	0.948	0.806	0.606	0.740	0.783	0.783
21	Retail trade, except of motor vehicles and motorcycles; repair of household goods	1.023	0.876	0.654	0.801	0.850	0.850
22	Hotels and restaurants	0.972	0.909	0.622	0.803	0.870	0.870
23	Inland transport	1.079	1.051	0.690	0.922	1.005	1.006
24	Water transport	0.894	1.012	0.572	0.849	0.954	0.955
25	Air transport	1.157	1.189	0.740	1.028	1.132	1.133
26	Other supporting and auxiliary transport activities; activities of travel agencies	1.117	0.948	0.715	0.866	0.919	0.919
27	Post and telecommunications	1.277	1.266	0.817	1.112	1.211	1.212
28	Financial intermediation	0.838	0.810	0.536	0.721	0.779	0.781
29	Real estate activities	0.547	0.581	0.350	0.500	0.552	0.552
30	Renting of M & Eq. and other business activities	1.056	0.893	0.675	0.821	0.868	0.868
31	Public admin. and defence; compulsory social security	1.122	0.960	0.718	0.876	0.930	0.930
32	Education	1.527	1.267	0.977	1.164	1.230	1.230
33	Health and social work	0.982	0.850	0.628	0.773	0.822	0.822
34	Other community, social and personal services	0.932	0.841	0.596	0.760	0.813	0.813
	MAD	0.177	0.214	0.370	0.136	0.125	0.124

Steedman's (1999) benchmark level; so the properties of the circulating capital matrix **H** ensure a relatively fast convergence of DP to PP. As a consequence, DP and PP are not only too close to each other and to market prices but also the PP can be derived and are in fact the result of the DP times a markup matrix made up by a series of bracketed terms.

The analysis for the US economy for the input-output data covering the period 1995–2009 was restricted to the last year, 2009, for reasons of economy in space because the results for the other years are not expected to be too different. In similar fashion, we experimented with the Greek input-output data using a circulating capital model in current prices spanning the period 1987–1997, and for the same reasons with the USA, we report in Table 4.10 the results only for a single year, namely, 1997, the last year of the series.

The accuracy of the estimation depends on the number of terms included in the markup matrix and also on the level of the relative rate of profit, ρ. In the case of the USA of the year 2009 using a circulating capital model, the approximation is satisfactory enough, although not so much as in the case of countries with a much lower relative rate of profit, as in the case of Greece. In fact, the estimates for the Greek economy show closer approximation which we attribute to a much lower ρ than that of the US input-output data. The results displayed in Table 4.10 show that the proximity of PP through DP is extremely good, as the MAD is less than 5%,

Table 4.10   Direct prices, prices of production and their approximation, Greece, 1997

	Sectors	DP	PP	1st term	2nd term	3rd term	4th term
1	Agriculture	1.034	0.909	0.909	0.755	0.872	0.876
2	Fish and fishing	1.580	1.302	1.302	1.152	1.266	1.268
3	Coal mining and oil	0.858	0.786	0.786	0.626	0.746	0.747
4	Other mining	1.215	1.039	1.039	0.886	1.000	1.001
5	Food, beverage and tobacco	1.073	1.121	1.121	0.783	1.046	1.072
6	Textiles	1.129	1.079	1.079	0.824	1.018	1.026
7	Wood and wood products	1.299	1.200	1.200	0.947	1.140	1.146
8	Pulp, paper and printing	1.434	1.382	1.382	1.046	1.297	1.310
9	Petroleum refineries	0.845	0.924	0.924	0.617	0.853	0.878
10	Chemicals, rubber and plastic products	1.425	1.522	1.522	1.040	1.387	1.425
11	Other non-metallic minerals	1.023	0.985	0.985	0.746	0.929	0.932
12	Basic metals	1.185	1.369	1.369	0.864	1.222	1.247
13	Fabricated metals	1.338	1.385	1.385	0.976	1.263	1.280
14	Machinery radio, TV, etc.	2.134	2.086	2.086	1.557	1.944	1.968
15	Utilities	0.877	0.777	0.777	0.639	0.744	0.747
16	Construction	0.931	0.967	0.967	0.679	0.890	0.895
17	Wholesale and retail	0.784	0.687	0.687	0.572	0.660	0.662
18	Hotels and restaurants	0.721	0.687	0.687	0.526	0.649	0.652
19	Transport and communication	1.195	0.998	0.998	0.871	0.969	0.970
	MAD	0.266	0.251	0.234	0.059	0.050	0.049

indicating that the first two terms of the polynomial [Eq. (4.23)] are sufficient to reach quite accurately the prices of production. This is not surprising, as $\rho = r/R = 0.238/0.882 = 0.25$, which is half of the 50% borderline meaning that the convergence of PP towards DP is attained quite fast.

In evaluating Steedman's approximation as well as Krylov's idea, we conclude that the small number of terms utilized for a tolerably good approximation has to do with the elements of matrix $\mathbf{A}$. We do know that the sum of columns of the matrix $\mathbf{A}$ must be less than one, and given the empirical observation that the diagonal elements of the matrix $\mathbf{A}$ are usually the larger in the column, it follows that the remaining elements are far too small; thus given that all elements in matrix $\mathbf{A}$ are bordered by two upper limits (the sum of columns is not greater than one, and the diagonal elements of the matrix are usually the largest in their respective column), it follows that between the columns of the matrix $\mathbf{A}$ is very likely to appear linearities or very near linearities rendering, thus, redundant the collection of many terms for a better approximation. In addition, the technology, described by the matrix of technological coefficients $\mathbf{A}$ and the vector of labour (employment) coefficients, $\mathbf{l}$, changes only slowly, and whatever the change in an industry rapidly diffuses (although not necessarily in a uniform way) to all industries; significant structural changes are not expected but only after the passage of a sufficiently long period of time. Consequently, the structure of DP and PP is anticipated and in fact found to remain fairly constant over the examined periods. Therefore, the main interindustry relations remain mostly intact; however, if changes take place, since they are short range, they do not result in reordering between different prices, even over a relatively long span of time. In addition, the value compositions of capital remain approximately the same, meaning that any technological change takes place uniformly across industries.

4.4   Price Changes as an Effect of Income Redistribution

In both, the classical and neoclassical analysis, the centrality of the effects of income distribution on relative prices is the litmus test of the internal consistency of the theory. This is the reason why classical economists paid particular attention to this issue and neoclassical economists were engaged in the capital theory critique and the associated with it debates. Starting with the classical approach, we invoke Ricardo's 'fundamental theorem of distribution', that is, the inverse relationship between profits and wages. In particular, Ricardo argued that:

> [...] in proportion then as wages rose, would profits fall.

or

> Profits depend on high or low wages.

> (*Works* I, p. 119)

The effect of changes in distribution on relative prices depends mainly on the capital-intensity and the price elasticity with respect to the distributive variables. In

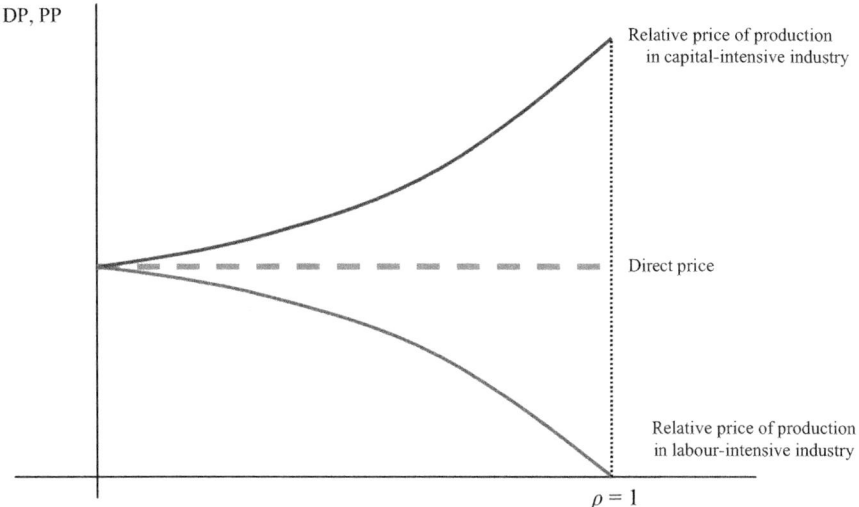

DP, PP

Relative price of production
in capital-intensive industry

Direct price

Relative price of production
in labour-intensive industry

$\rho = 1$

Fig. 4.7 Prices and relative rate of profit

Chap. 1, we have already shown that the elasticity of price in Eqs. (1.18) and (1.21) with respect to distributive variables (profits and wages) is highly inelastic (less than 0.1 in Ricardo's numerical examples) which is another way to say that the effect of changes in distribution on relative prices is not only very small but, also, theoretically predictable. In effect, the presence of capital and distribution variables does not lead to significant deviations of the resulting prices from their respective labour times. Marx's position was very similar in this respect as this can be judged by the numerical examples that he utilized in *Capital* III, Chap. 9. There is no doubt that both Ricardo and Marx argued that the effect on relative prices of the changes in income distribution is, in general, small and predictable.

Moreover, in classical analysis, as presented in Ricardo's (1819, pp. 30–43) and Marx's (*Capital* III, Chap. 11) writings, the sign and size of changes in relative prices as an effect of changes in income distribution depend decisively on the capital-labour ratio relative to the economy-wide average one. The argument usually starts by hypothesizing a falling wage across industries which leads to rising rates of profit; however, the increase in the rates of profit is not uniform but varies according to capital-intensities of industries. Profits increase by more in the labour-intensive industries, and, therefore, their rates of profit are higher than those of the capital-intensive industries. This inequality in profit rates implies disequilibrium, which can be only short run, since in the longer run relative prices must change to equalize the profit rates across industries. Consequently, prices in labour-intensive industries will decrease, while prices in the capital-intensive industries will increase, so that the rate of profit will be equalized across industries. These typical changes in prices are portrayed in Fig. 4.7.

Prices of production (PP) and direct prices (DP) are on the vertical axis, while on the horizontal axis is the relative rate of profit, $\rho = rR^{-1}$, which takes on values ranging between zero (minimum) and one (maximum). For $\rho = 0$, PP and DP become identical. As the wage rate falls, the capital-intensive industries' profits increase but by less than the labour-intensive ones. The relative price of the capital-intensive industries must increase in order to make up for their deficient profits resulting from the income redistribution relative to the labour-intensive industries. The converse will be true in the labour-intensive industries. If an industry displays the economy's average composition of capital, its direct price will be equal to its price of production; that is, the industry is neutral to income redistribution.

While Ricardo and Marx shared this idea of monotonicity in price changes to the upward or downward direction, Sraffa (1960, pp. 37–38) changed radically the way of thinking by arguing that prices are expected to show by far more complex trajectories than those hypothesized by the old classical economists in their usual and simple (2 × 2 or 3 × 3 industries) numerical examples. The idea is that in actual economies characterized by many interdependent industries, as prices change induced by changes in the distributive variables give rise to various complex feedback effects making exceedingly more difficult to anticipate their final configuration. The reason is that theoretically, at least, the development of complex feedback price effects leads to the revaluation of capital and an industry starting as labour-intensive (mathematically speaking) may end up as capital-intensive and vice versa. Therefore, according to Sraffa, we cannot a priori determine the direction of the movements in the new prices brought about by changes in income distribution; and, therefore, we cannot a priori characterize an industry as capital- or labour-intensive. Hence, for Sraffa, the relation between income distribution and relative prices is non-linear, and therefore the prediction of the particular direction of prices and the characterization of an industry as capital- or labour-intensive remains uncertain (Pasinetti 1977, Chap. 5).

In recent years, there has been made significant progress in both theoretical and empirical aspects of these issues (Tsoulfidis and Mariolis 2007; Mariolis and Tsoulfidis 2009, 2011, 2012, 2016 and 2018; Schefold 2011; Shaikh 2016). This more recent literature resorts to the Sraffian device of the standard commodity [Eq. (4.14)]. By postmultiplying Eq. (4.19) with the so derived standard commodity, **s**, we end up with the relation (4.20). Setting $\rho = rR^{-1}$ and solving for w, we get

$$w = \frac{1 - \rho}{1 + r} \tag{4.24}$$

and by replacing in Eq. (4.19), we get

$$\mathbf{p} = \mathbf{p}\mathbf{H}R\rho + \mathbf{v}(1-\rho) \tag{4.25}$$

We postmultiply Eq. (4.25) by the inverse of the diagonal matrix of DP, and we arrive at

$$\mathbf{p} < \mathbf{v}>^{-1} = \mathbf{p}\mathbf{H} < \mathbf{v}>^{-1}R\rho + \mathbf{e}(1-\rho) \qquad (4.26)$$

where $\mathbf{p}{<}\mathbf{v}{>}^{-1}$ denotes the ratio of PP to DP. Equation (4.26) can be restated as

$$\left(\frac{P}{v}\right)_j - 1 = R\rho\left[\left(\frac{\mathbf{p}\mathbf{H}}{v}\right)_j - R^{-1}\right] \qquad (4.27)$$

where $\mathbf{H}_j$ is the j-th column of $\mathbf{H}$, $\mathbf{p}\mathbf{H}_j/v_j$ is the so-called capital-intensity of the vertically integrated industry producing commodity j and R^{-1} is the capital-intensity of the standard system (which is independent of prices and distribution). Finally, the derivative of Eq. (4.27) with respect to ρ gives

$$\frac{d\left(\frac{P}{v}\right)_j}{d\rho} = \frac{d}{d\rho}\left\{R\rho\left[\left(\frac{\mathbf{p}\mathbf{H}}{v}\right)_j - R^{-1}\right] + 1\right\}$$

$$\frac{d\left(\frac{P}{v}\right)_j}{d\rho} = R\left[\frac{dk_j}{d\rho}\rho + \left(k_j - R^{-1}\right)\right]$$

where $k_j \equiv \mathbf{p}\mathbf{H}_j/v_j$. We factor out k_j from the bracketed term and we get

$$\frac{d\left(\frac{P}{v}\right)_j}{d\rho} = Rk_j\left[\underbrace{\frac{dk_j}{d\rho}\frac{\rho}{k_j}}_{\text{Sraffian Effect}} + \underbrace{\left(1 - \frac{R^{-1}}{k_j}\right)}_{\text{Ricardo-Marx Effect}}\right] \qquad (4.28)$$

The first bracketed term is the elasticity of industry's j capital-intensity w.r.t. the relative rate of profit and can be positive, negative or even zero; in our discussion of a similar elasticity in Ricardo's numerical examples, we hypothesized this elasticity to be equal to zero. The sign of change in prices of production relative to unchanged direct prices w.r.t. to redistribution depends exclusively on the second bracketed term which, for obvious reasons, we call Ricardo-Marx effect. Sraffa's great contribution is the introduction and the accounting of the complex price effects which may not let the Ricardo-Marx effect to play its dominant role. It is possible therefore the Sraffian effect to enhance, lessen or completely neutralize and even supersede the Ricardo-Marx effect. These possibilities become particularly important in the capital theory controversies whose theoretical dimensions are presented in Chap. 3, while their empirical dimensions are discussed in the next sections.

Equation (4.28) for the two extreme and hypothetical situations for relative rate of profit gives

when $\rho = 0$ then

$$\frac{\mathrm{d}\left(\frac{p}{v}\right)_j}{\mathrm{d}\rho} = R\left[k_j(0) - R^{-1}\right] \tag{4.29}$$

when $\rho = 1$ then

$$\left(\frac{p}{v}\right)_j = Rk_j(1) \tag{4.30}$$

From Eqs. (4.29) to (4.30), we conclude the following:

1. If the Ricardo-Marx effect is positive $\left(1 - \frac{R^{-1}}{k_j}\right) > 0$, this means that the capital-intensity of industry j is higher than the standard ratio. On the other hand, the Sraffian effect can be $e_j = \frac{\mathrm{d}k_j}{\mathrm{d}\rho}\frac{\rho}{k_j} \lessgtr 0$. If it is positive, it may strengthen the upward direction of the price movement; however, if the elasticity is negative, then the final outcome depends on the relative strength of these two effects. Usually the elasticity of capital-intensity w.r.t. ρ is very close to zero, and so the likelihood for the change in the direction of price movement depends on how close are the industry's capital-intensity, k_j, to the standard capital-intensity, R^{-1}. We distinguish two models to examine the trajectories of price movements as a consequence of changes in ρ, the fixed and circulating capital models. The capital-intensities of industries in the the fixed capital model are usually quite distant from the standard capital-intensity, and so of a weak Sraffian elasticity effect, which even though it may move to the opposite (to Ricardo-Marx's) direction; nevertheless, it does not change the movement in prices. The situation becomes less pronounced when we move to circulating capital models, where the elasticity of capital-intensity w.r.t. ρ (the Sraffian effect) remains low, but the differences in the capital-intensities of industries relative to the standard capital-intensity are much smaller than those in the fixed capital model. As a consequence, we cannot rule out the case that a change in ρ may give rise to an elasticity of capital-intensity with a sign opposite to that of the Ricardo-Marx effect; furthermore, the value of this elasticity may exceed that of the Ricardo-Marx effect and thus may even change the direction of the price trajectory displaying extremes and switching points. It goes without saying that one may not exclude results which are opposite to those expected from Ricardo and Marx.
2. A vertically integrated industry for low values of ρ may start as capital (labour)-intensive relative to the standard system, but as ρ increases, it may be transformed to a labour (capital)-intensive sector.

Hence, our focus is mainly empirical and is restricted to showing the results of relevant analyses of the US and Greek economies for the years 2010 and 1993, respectively. In the equation of prices of production, we allow the relative rate of profit ρ to take on values ranging from zero to one (maximum). The new vector of prices of production normalized by the standard commodity is divided, element by element, by the corresponding vector of direct prices which of course is not affected by changes in ρ.

In the case of US input-output data of 34 industry detail using constant (1995) prices and depreciation and capital stock matrices for the period 1995–2009 (WIOD 2013)[14], the result was absolute monotonicity in the movement of prices in either direction. A circulating capital model of the same 34 industry input-output structure also did not give quite different results from the fixed capital model with the exception of two non-monotonically moving PP (industries 25, air transportation, and 29, real estate activities) whose non-monotonicity appeared for a relative rate of profit in the vicinity of 80 and 90%, respectively. Thus, we decided to present in Fig. 4.8 only the results of our experiment using the circulating capital model and data available from WIOD (2016) whose input-output data are at the 54 industry detail and the base year is 2010.[15]

The results in Fig. 4.8 are absolutely consistent with the expectation of the old classical theory of Ricardo and Marx, that is, the Sraffian effect regardless of its sign is negligible to give rise to non-monotonic movement of relative prices let alone for the PP to cross over the line of PP-DP equality. The trajectories of estimated prices with respect to the changing relative rate of profit are nearly straight lines going either to the upward or to the downward directions drifting further and further away from the line of DP and PP equality. The particular directions are dependent mainly on the vertically integrated capital-intensity of the specific industry relative to the economy-wide average measured in any kind of prices; hence, the majority of the price trajectories display monotonic movement either in the upward or in the downward direction.

There are exceptions; some of the industries display maximum, others display minimum and others cross over the PP-DP equality line. In the second category of trajectories belong two rather identical industries: industry 24 (electricity, gas, steam and air conditioning supply) and industry 25 (water collection, treatment and supply) which attain their maximum for a relative rate of profit at $\rho = 30\%$ and cross over the PP-DP line of equality at an $\rho = 40\%$. Industries 33 (air transport) and 39 (telecommunications) reach their maximum at $\rho = 40\%$ and 50%, respectively, and their crossing over the horizontal line takes place at $\rho = 90\%$ and $\rho = 80\%$, respectively. Industry 36 (accommodation and food service activities) displays a minimum at $\rho = 90\%$ and remains above the line of PP-DP equality, while industry 44 (real estate activities) reaches a maximum at $\rho = 80\%$. Knowing that the equilibrium $\rho = 33.4\%$, it follows that only the first two (identical) industries are likely candidates for crossing over the PP-DP line of equality for realistic values of ρ, whereas the other two cases are simply remote theoretical possibilities, and the same is true with the industries displaying extremes. However for the case of the four industries that display reswitching, it is interesting to note that they take on prices which are very near one and they do not move far away from one. It is important to

---

[14]See Appendix 1 for the construction of capital and depreciation matrices.

[15]For the nomenclature of the industries, see Appendix 2.

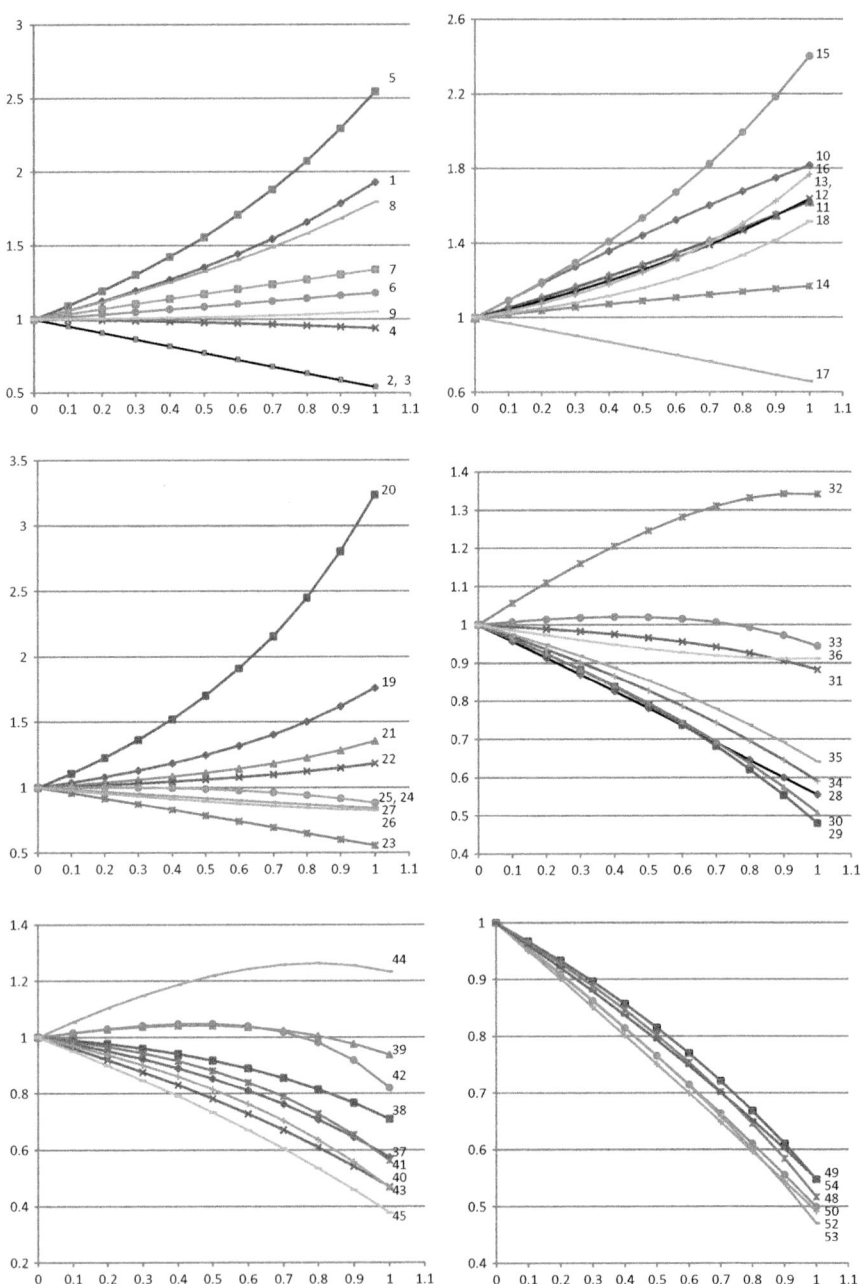

Fig. 4.8 Changes in prices of production and relative rate of profit, USA, 2010

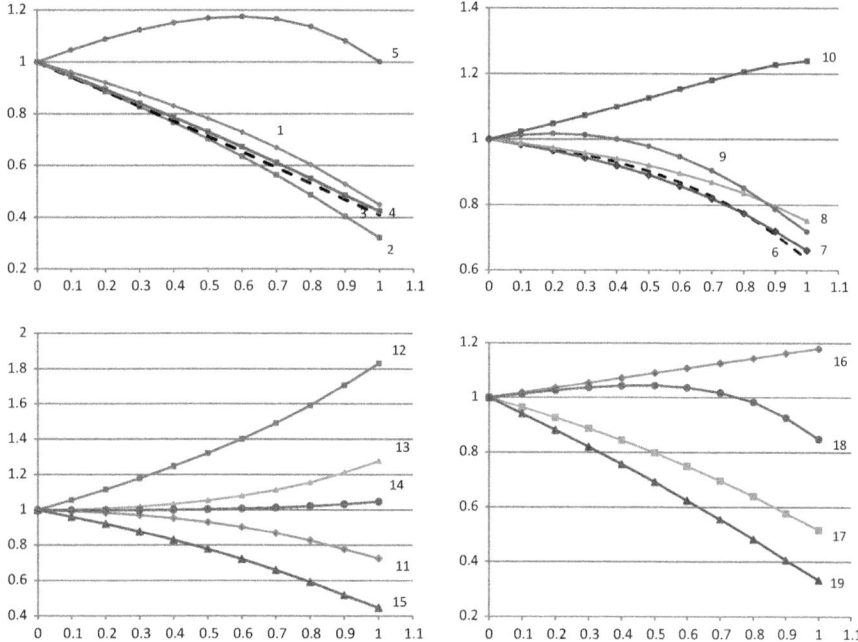

Fig. 4.9 Changes in prices of production and relative rate of profit, Greece, 1997

stress that the PP in the case of fixed capital stock model displayed absolutely monotonic paths to either direction depending on the start values of their capital-output ratios, whose monotonic and rigid paths did not lead to any different ranking of capital-intensities finding as the relative rate of profit takes on values ranging from zero and approaching to its maximum equal to one.[16]

These are quite interesting results on account of the Sraffian and Ricardo-Marx effects and related with these elasticities of capital-intensity with respect to the standard ratio; but before we examine these two effects, let us take a quick look of the results with circulating capital for the case of the Greek input-output data. In Fig. 4.9, we present the results with current prices circulating capital model of the Greek economy for the year 1997.[17]

Hence, once again, we find the expected monotonicity in prices caused by changes in ρ for each of the 19 industries of the input-output table used. From the panel of graphs, we observe that only industries 5 (food beverage and tobacco), 9 (petroleum refineries) and 18 (wholesale and retail trade) display curvatures with maximum, and from these industries, only 9 and 18 cross the line of price-value

---

[16]The results from other similar studies agree that the use of fixed capital stock model for the estimation of changes in prices of production as a consequence of changes in income distribution gives rise to monotonic trajectories of PP.

[17]See Table 4.10 for the nomenclature of industries.

equality; industry 9 for $\rho = 10\%$ reaches its maximum and crosses the line of equality at $\rho = 40\%$, whereas industry 18 is maximized at $\rho = 50\%$ and crosses over the PP-DP line of equality for a too high relative rate of profit, $\rho = 80\%$, while industry 5 attains its maximum point at a $\rho = 60\%$ and nearly touches but does not pass over the line of equality with its DP. From all trajectories of PP, only industry 14 (machinery, radio, TV, etc.) displays a minimum point at about $\rho = 10\%$ and passes from the other side of the line of its equality with DP at $\rho = 30\%$. It is interesting to note that the PP of industry 14 is near and remains in the vicinity of one as ρ tends to its maximum. These results are also consistent with those derived for Japan, China and of course the USA (Tsoulfidis 2008; Mariolis and Tsoulfidis 2016; Shaikh 2016).

A more complete picture for both sets of Figs. 4.8 and 4.9 is obtained by supplementing the above numerical findings of the movements of the prices of production with their corresponding changes in capital-output ratios of individual industries and their differences from the economy's average, as this is reflected in the inverse of the maximum profit rate R^{-1}, where $R = $ **Ps/PAs**. More specifically, the term **Ps** is the value of the standard commodity (standard output), and **PAs** is the value of the means of production in terms of the standard commodity indicated by the marked line in the panel of graphs in Fig. 4.10 for the US economy and the year 2010.

It is interesting to note that the trajectories of the capital-output ratios of the 54 industries of the US move monotonically usually above or below the standard ratio indicating that once an industry is characterized as capital- or labour-intensive, the characterization remains the same regardless of changes in distribution as they are reflected in the relative rate of profit. There is an exception in the leather and footwear (industry 5) which from labour becomes capital-intensive without, however, changing the characterization of the movement of PP which remains always monotonic and in the upward direction. The results in the case of a fixed capital stock model are by far stronger than those of circulating capital model, and we do not report for reasons of their lack of interest and brevity of presentation.

Similar are the results of circulating capital model in the case of the Greek economy that we present in a panel of graphs in Fig. 4.11.

Figure 4.11 shows that only industries 9 and 18, for a very high relative rate of profit, turn from capital- to labour-intensive industries crossing the line of the standard ratio, R^{-1}. By contrast industry 5's capital-output ratio approaches the standard ratio but remains a capital-intensive industry; at the end of our hypothetical exercise, it becomes a capital-intensive neutral industry. Finally the capital-intensity of industry 14 switches characterization according to the path of PP. The empirical findings are not different for each of the other years of the period 1988–1997, and in the interest of brevity, we display only the results for the year 1997.

In conclusion, the change in the characterization of an industry from capital- to labour-intensive and vice versa has to do, to a great extent, with the initial difference of the specific industry's capital-intensity relative to the economy's average; if the initial difference is relatively small, then the likelihood of change in the characterization of the industry is possible. In contrast, if the initial difference of capital-intensities is relatively large, the characterization of an industry is very unlikely to change in the

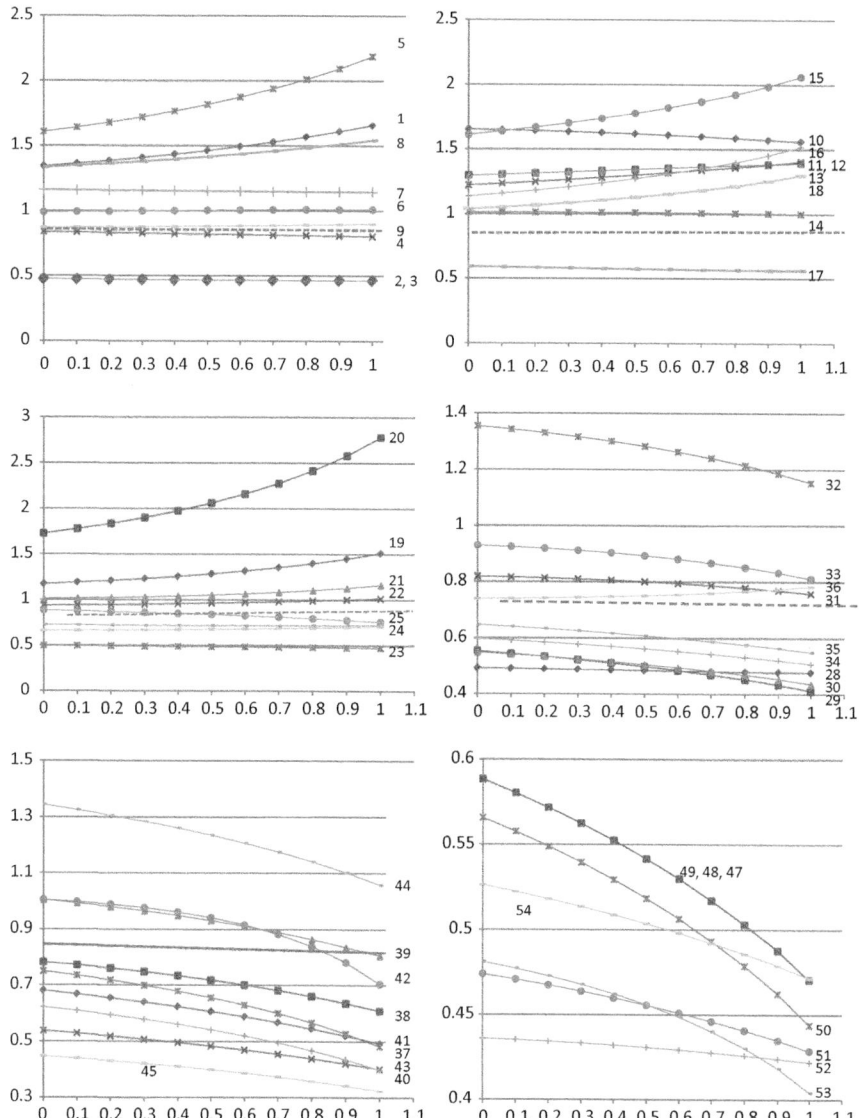

Fig. 4.10 Movement of capital-output ratios relative to the economy's average, USA, 2010

face of changes in the distributive variables. Thus, it comes as no surprise that the likelihood of switching or crossing the line of equality between PP and DP very rarely occurs in the case of a fixed capital stock model precisely because the difference in capital-intensities of industries from the average is by far larger than those in circulating capital models. Finally, the cases of reswitching in our two economies may increase slightly using more disaggregating data as is ascertained, for example, in highly disaggregated circulating capital models (see Torres and Yang 2018).

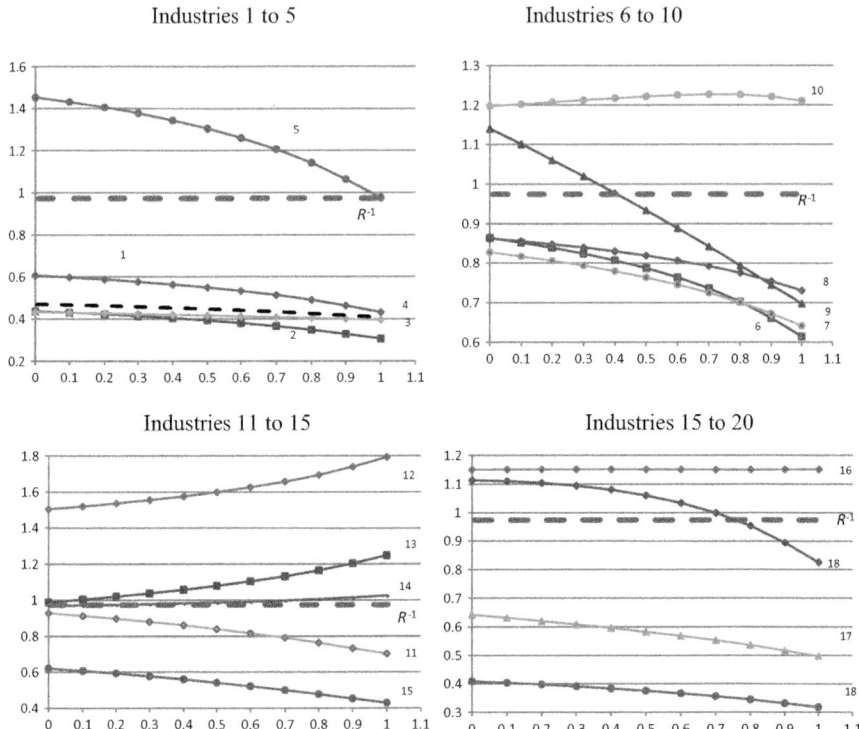

Fig. 4.11 Movement of capital-output ratios relative to the economy's average, Greece, 1997

4.4.1 *Empirical Estimates of the Wage Rate of Profit Frontiers*

The changes in the distribution and their effects on relative prices and capital-intensities are one of Sraffa's major contributions. According to Sraffa the paths of PP are expected to evolve in a non-linear way and to display curvatures which may cross each other once or, theoretically speaking, more than once. Similarly, the wage rate of profit curves (WRPC or *w-r* curves), which attracted most of the attention in the literature, are usually plotted with few curvatures crossing each other more than once (reswitching). The argument that was put forward was that one cannot define the capital-intensity of an industry in any indisputable way because it depended on income distribution and the subsequent changes in prices. Thus the discussions in the 1960s and 1970s were largely theoretical, and the participants in the debates had no clue as to how the WRPC looked like in the real world.

Sraffa, as the classical economists of the past, was interested mainly in the movement of prices of production and not so much in the shape of the wage rate of profit curves and frontiers. In fact, Sraffa's book and analysis are more about the price trajectories; nevertheless, the Sraffa-based literature paid by far more attention to the shape of the wage rate of profits curves and frontiers as the means to expose primarily the problems of logical consistency of the neoclassical theory of capital. The idea is that the *w-r* curves are the mirror image of the isoquant curves on the basis of which neoclassical theory derives the demand curves for the factors of production (see Chap. 3); hence, the reswitching of the *w-r* curves gives rise to inconsistent results with respect to the demand for factors of production rendering the idea of scarcity pricing untenable.

The hitherto empirical research, however, has shown that the prices of production, by and large, move monotonically; nevertheless, there are cases that the price paths display extremes or inflection points and there are even fewer cases that the PP cross over the line of their equality with DP. Under these circumstances, it has been argued that if the direct prices (values) are those on the basis of which entrepreneurs make their decisions, we may end up with inconsistent results in a way very similar to the neoclassical economists in their evaluation of capital goods.[18] In fact capital theory critique has been misinterpreted as if it argues that the value of capital cannot be measured. This is not exactly right; capital can be measured in terms of labour values and certainly in market prices. If the value of capital could not be measured then, very few things, we would be able to say about capitalism and its laws of motion. The problem of measuring capital lies exclusively with the neoclassical theory of value and its idea of scarcity prices. This problem does not appear in the classical theory of value, where one of the distributive variables, usually the real wage, is assumed constant, and with given technology, the other distributive variable along with the relative equilibrium prices can be estimated, thereby making possible the consistent estimation of the quantity of capital.

It is interesting to note that the theoretical analysis of the movement of prices and the WRPC was and even today often continues without being backed by the necessary empirical documentation. The empirical research on this issue starts with Krelle's (1977) article on the former West German economy, where he found the near linearity of the WRPC using national income account data and simple techniques. These findings passed nearly unnoticed by the participants on both sides of the debate. Probably because neoclassical economists admitting their weakness or even their defeat (see Samuelson 1962a) in the meantime lost interest in the questions at hand and were very much convinced that the argument is logical and not necessarily empirical. Sraffian economists, would also argue that if a theory is found logically inconsistent the empirical research is totally redundant. Krelle's (1977) estimates on the other hand were not so rigorously formulated and regrettably they were not in the search of the truth but rather in providing evidence to support the neoclassical theory. He himself, however, had no problem whatsoever to arrive at the verdict which was that 'some of the arguments of the reswitching debate are similar

---

[18]Sraffian economists claim that choices that are being made on the basis of values (direct prices) may differ from those made on the basis of prices of production or market prices. Economists that follow this line of thought (e.g. Steedman 1981) do not really distinguish between prices of production and market prices; the two types of prices are treated as if they were equal.

to the arguments of a physicist inventing the ether and 'proving' that Einstein's relativity theory is wrong' (Krelle 1977, p. 301). On further consideration, however, empirical findings such as those presented by Krelle and others should not be particularly surprising if one takes into account that even Leontief's (1986) important contribution designed to settle the debate on both camps passed almost unnoticed by those that not too many years ago were debating fiercely about the shape of the *w-r* curves. Only a few scholars cite Leontief's results that show quasilinearities in the WRPC in the case of the US economy for the year 1979 using input-output tables of 85 industries.

Till now, we have showed that labour value magnitudes are too close to prices of production as measured by the various non-parametric statistics that we utilized (Sect. 4.3). Consequently, choices that are being made in terms of values are not expected to differ from those made in terms of prices of production. Moreover, while true that the mathematical structure of the problem allows the theoretical possibility for many curvatures in the WRPC (and therefore the Sraffa's-inspired critique appears to be justified from a purely mathematical viewpoint), from a practical viewpoint such a possibility (of reswitching) seems to be minimal, if non-existent. The shape of the WRPC is quasilinear, a result which has been observed in the economies of West Germany (Krelle 1977), the USA (Leontief 1986; Mariolis and Tsoulfidis 2016), Brazil (da Silva 1991), Greece (Tsoulfidis and Maniatis 2002) and for a number of other countries (Mariolis and Tsoulfidis 2016). As a result, the reswitching of techniques while mathematically possible and naturally is expected, practically it becomes a remote possibility for reasons that we have explicated.

The estimation of WRPC in the case of the presence of the matrix of fixed capital stock coefficients, $\mathbf{K}$, the matrix of depreciation coefficients, $\mathbf{D}$, as well as the diagonal matrix of indirect tax coefficients $<\mathbf{t}>$, is carried out starting from the prices of production [Eq. (4.4)]. The fact that money wage is equal to $w = \mathbf{pb}$, after its substitution in the equation of prices of production and some manipulation, we get

$$\mathbf{p}[\mathbf{I} - \mathbf{A} - \mathbf{D} - <\mathbf{t}> -r\mathbf{K}] = w\mathbf{l} \quad \text{or} \quad \mathbf{p} = w\mathbf{l}[\mathbf{I} - \mathbf{A} - \mathbf{D} - <\mathbf{t}> -r\mathbf{K}]^{-1}$$

We postmultiply by $\mathbf{x}$ (the column vector of the gross output of each sector), and with the usual normalization $\mathbf{px} = \mathbf{ex}$, we arrive at the *w-r* relation

$$w = \frac{\mathbf{ex}}{\mathbf{l}[\mathbf{I} - \mathbf{A} - \mathbf{D} - <\mathbf{t}> -r\mathbf{K}]^{-1}\mathbf{x}} \tag{4.31}$$

If we consider one of the variables, for example, the rate of profit, as the independent variable and we assign to it different hypothetical prices starting from zero (which corresponds to the maximum wage) up until we reach the maximum rate of profit (which corresponds to zero wage), we can generate the WRPC. Such a curve of course refers to a multicommodity world and clearly has as many curvatures as the number of industries reduced by one. Figure 4.12 portrays the *w-r* curve derived

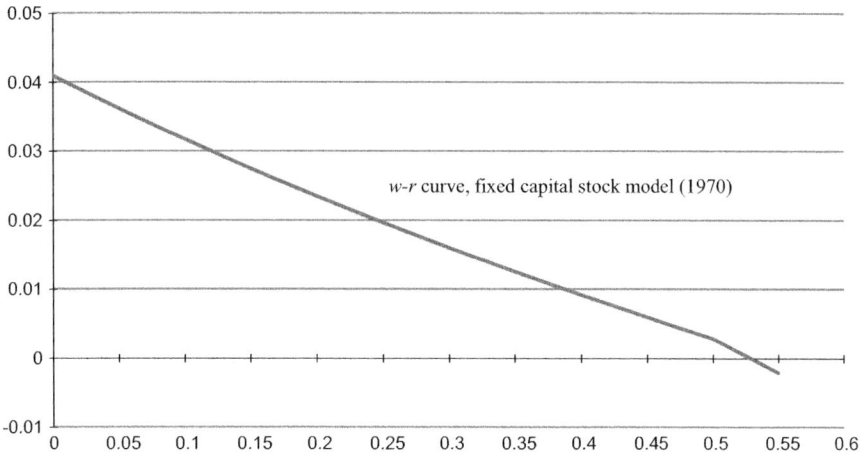

Fig. 4.12 The WRPC, Greece, 1970

from data of the Greek economy for the year 1970 using a fixed capital stock model (Tsoulfidis and Maniatis 2002); hence, gross output was used for normalization purposes, but the results would not be affected by the use of the net output and if we fix a numéraire to unity (**px** = **ex** = 1).

In similar fashion, we have estimated the wage-relative rate of profit for the Korean economy in a fixed capital stock model with the difference that we do not use the matrix of indirect tax coefficients (Tsoulfidis and Rieu 2006) as in the case of Greece above and in a circulating capital model in which we assumed that wages are paid ex ante and so profits are estimated on both circulating capital and real wages, as it is usually applied in the classical analysis. Furthermore, we use the relative rate of profit, $\rho = rR^{-1}$, as our distributive variable on the horizontal axis which increases by tenths starting from zero approaching its maximum which is equal to one. The panel of two graphs in Fig. 4.13 describes the w-ρ curves in the case of circulating and fixed capital stock model for the years 1995 and 2000, respectively.

We observe that the WRPC is quasilinear which means that alternative techniques either must be in the interior of the WRPC or they can cross the WRPC at most once; more importantly this outcome appears so frequently that we may treat it as a stylized fact. The WRPC display some curvature which precludes the case of two switch points, while a single switch point may occur for unrealistically high relative rates of profit (near the maximum rate of profit). Furthermore, the WRPC in the circulating capital model is concave while that of the fixed capital stock model is convex. In both cases, the difference from a straight line is minimal, and so we can characterize the shape of the WRPC as 'quasilinear'. The following Fig. 4.14 is from the input-output data of the UK for the year 1998. The estimations are carried out in a way similar to those of the Korean economy with the difference that we fixed the numerator or the maximum wage to be equal to one.

Very similar are the results in the case of the US economy obtained for the years 2000 and 2005 using 34 industries and for the year 2014 using 54 industries (see

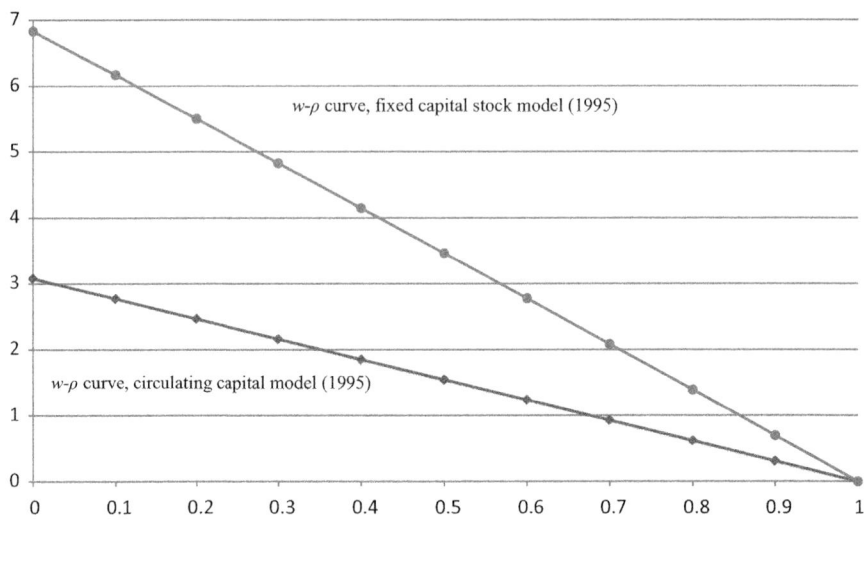

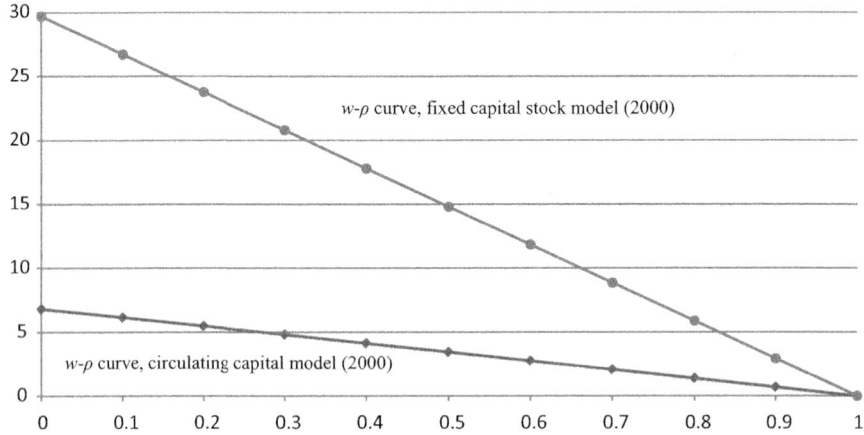

Fig. 4.13 The WRPC, Korea, 1995 and 2000

Fig. 4.15). The results, as expected, showed a convex WRPC for the fixed capital stock model, while for the circulating capital model, the WRPC was found slightly concave. Clearly, the results are in accordance with previous findings that rule out the case of reswitching for the total economy.[19]

---

[19]The sectoral analysis gives very similar results and for reasons of economizing space is not reported (see Zambeli 2017; Han and Schefold 2006; Chilcote 1997; Ochoa 1989).

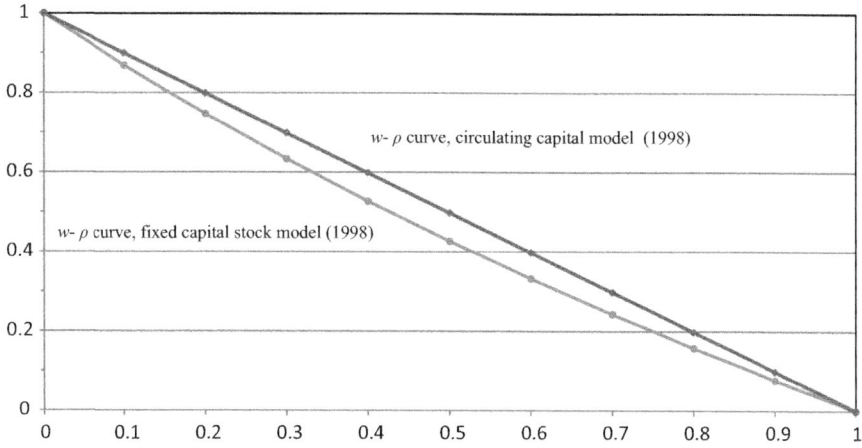

Fig. 4.14 The WRPCs; circulating and fixed capital stock models, UK 1998

Krelle (1977) based on the WRPC that he constructed for the economy of the West Germany for the years 1958, 1960, 1962, 1964 and 1966 arrived at the following conclusions which by now could be taken as stylized facts of capitalist economies:

- The WRPC are convex. More specifically, in the case of a fixed capital stock model, the empirical studies ascertain the convexity of the WRPC, while in circulating capital models, the concave shape is more representative. In both cases, we do not observe too much curvature to make this an issue.
- For low profit rates, the WRPC frontiers shift upwards in the course of technical progress.
- The wage-profit frontiers either do not cross or cross only once, in the relevant region.
- The realized points on the WRPC are situated in such a way that a rising wage rate results in reswitching to another technology.

These results are repeatedly found in many other studies such as Ochoa (1984), Leontief (1986) and Shaikh (1995).

The empirical results are fully consistent with the Marxian theory and raise serious questions on the validity of the Cambridge critique at least as it has been expressed by the first Cambridge economists in the UK side. Leontief (1986) using a methodology different from the one that we follow confirms the near linearity of w-r curves of the US economy for the year 1977 and concludes that his results

> should contribute to settlement of the switching and reswitching controversy that for many years pitted the sharpest minds of Cambridge, Massachusetts, against the brightest theoretical lights of Cambridge, England.
>
> (Leontief 1986, p. 410)

The results of the near linearity of w-r curves for the various economies, however, should not lead to the conclusion that the neoclassical theory escapes criticism. The

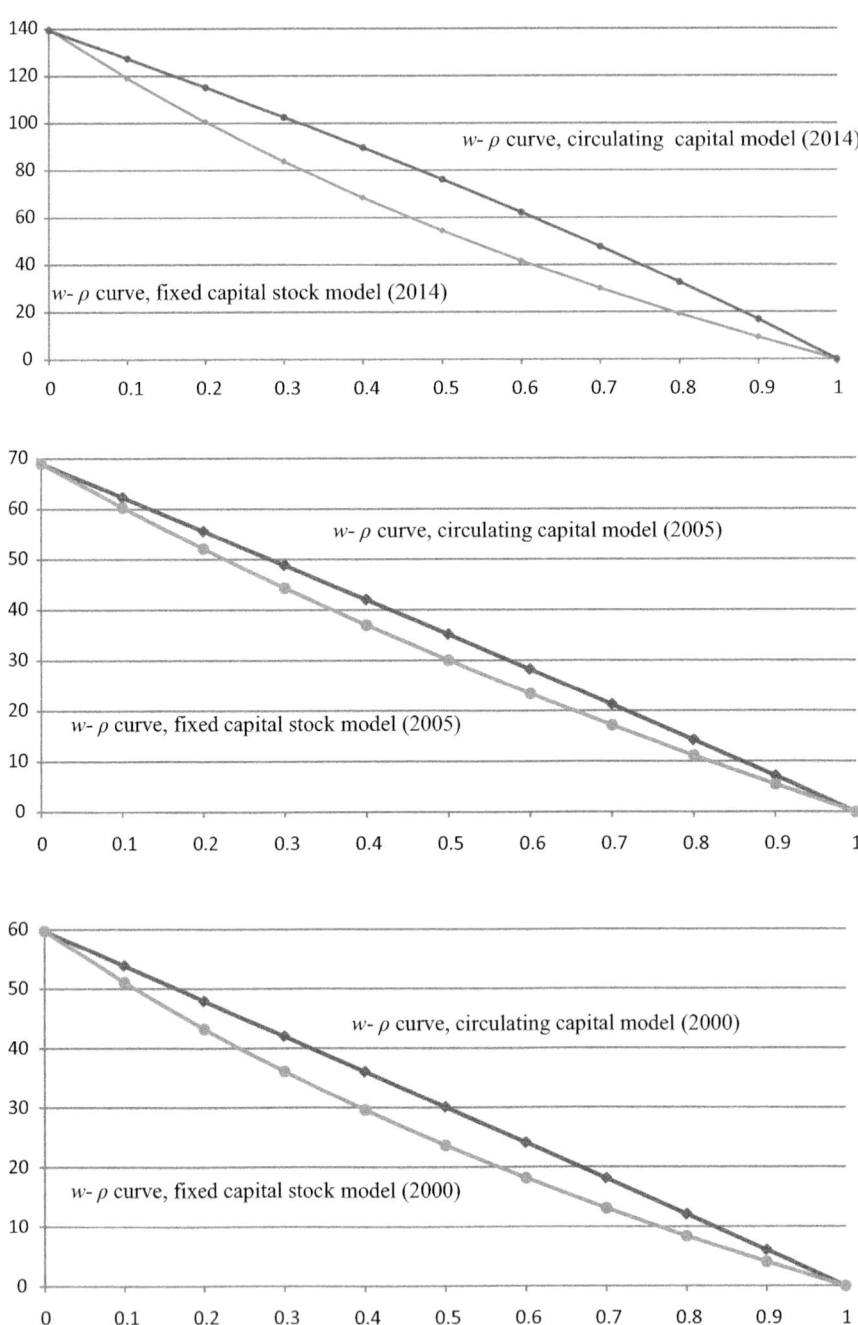

Fig. 4.15 WRPC for the USA, 2000, 2005 and 2014

marginal productivity theory of income distribution, the cornerstone of neoclassical economics, is based on the assumption of perfect competition in all markets which allows for the substitution of factors of production that leads to choice of technique vindicating the optimization behaviour of the firm. However, the idea that capitalists must choose between alternative techniques is without meaning in conditions of real (classical) competition since the 'choice' of technique is not realized in a smooth fashion as is usually claimed in the neoclassical approach, where an infinitesimal small change, for example, in wage leads to the immediate substitution of labour for other productive services. In reality techniques change after the passage of a relatively long time period (a few years); moreover, the substitution between factors of production is limited if not nearly prohibitive, since many of the factors are not sensitive to price changes. In fact, if we were to choose between the neoclassical notion of perfect substitution and the Leontief's conception of constant proportions (the famous 'cooking recipe' analogy), we would say that the latter is closer and represents better the reality.

4.5 Summary and Conclusions

In this chapter we showed that the classical theory of value, that is, the theory of value that we find in Ricardo and has been further advanced in Marx's *Capital*, when is cast in a linear model of production and utilize the latest advancements in linear algebra contains a lot of explanatory power which has not been appreciated as much as it deserves. We say that because not only the equilibrium prices estimated within this approach predict extremely well the actual market prices of the economy but also enable us to make theoretical statements about the state of technology and how much it changes over time.

In an overall evaluation of the circulating capital model with that of fixed capital stock for the US economy, we observe that in both the paths of prices of production relative to labour values display more often than not monotonicity while the position of the capital-output ratios relative to the standard ratio which is not very different from the economy-wide average is maintained in most cases. In such a comparison, we further observe that in the circulating capital model, the paths of PP in a relatively few cases display extrema and in fewer cases cross over the line of equalization with values, while in the fixed capital stock model, no switch point was observed in our data; of course there are such points in rare situations when the dimensions of input-output tables increase to more than 70 (see Ochoa 1989 and Shaikh 1998) or more that 500 as in the recent article by Torres and Yang (2018). Analogous are the movements of the vertically integrated capital-output ratios which in a relatively few cases display switch positions between themselves and the standard ratio giving rise to the appearance of curvatures and the likelihood of switching of the PP with the line of DP. The repeated occurrence of these interesting empirical findings, virtually in every country and year that has been tested, renders them the characterization of 'law-like regularities'.

Starting with the case of circulating capital, the vertically integrated capital-output ratios are not very far from each other, and their difference from the standard ratio is not that large. Because the industries are more connected to each other, as this is reflected in the elements of matrix $\mathbf{A}$ where the zero elements are by far less than those of matrix $\mathbf{K}$, a change in the relative rate of profit (ρ) may exert in some cases a significant effect on relative prices and capital-output ratios. As a result, the revaluation of capital-output ratio of an industry with respect to the new set of prices may be strong enough and even change the capital-intensity of an industry with respect to that of other industries as well as the standard ratio and in so doing to give rise to curvatures and shapes with extrema and also switch points.

As for the case of fixed capital stock model, the interindustry capital-output ratios are far more distant from each other and also from the standard ratio. Furthermore, the elements of the matrix $\mathbf{K}$ are less connected with each other; that is, there are many zero elements and particularly small or large capital stock coefficients. Therefore the changes in the relative rate of profit lead to revaluations of fixed capital stock which are weaker than those in the case of circulating capital, and so it must come as no surprise that there are no switch of orderings of capital-intensities, between industries and changes in the characterizations of industries from capital- to labour-intensive and vice versa. As a matter of fact, the capital-output ratios in the circulating capital model of the year 2010 and 54 industries estimated from $\mathbf{vA}$ $[\mathbf{I} - \mathbf{A}]^{-1}$ gave an average capital-output ratio equals to 0.831 and a standard deviation of 0.298 with a coefficient of variation of 0.358 for the US economy. The capital-output ratios in the fixed capital stock model estimated from $\mathbf{vK}$ $[\mathbf{I} - \mathbf{A}]^{-1}$ gave an average capital-output ratio equal to 2.543 and a standard deviation of 1.398 which amount to a coefficient of variation of 0.549, which is much higher than that of the circulating capital model. These results make on an average much (perhaps at least twice as) harder to find switch points in the fixed capital stock model.

Clearly, there are many near linearities in the two important matrices: the matrix of technological coefficients, $\mathbf{A}$, and the capital stock matrix, $\mathbf{K}$. As for the matrix $\mathbf{A}$, since the sum of its columns cannot exceed one and the diagonal elements of the matrix usually exceed by far the other elements of the column many of which may be zero, it follows that near linearities are very natural to be formed as this becomes evident from the distribution of eigenvalues of matrix $\mathbf{A}$ or $\mathbf{A}[\mathbf{I} - \mathbf{A}]^{-1}$ which is in effect a matrix $\mathbf{A}[\mathbf{I} - \mathbf{A}]^{-1} = \mathbf{A} + \mathbf{A}^2 + \mathbf{A}^3 + \ldots$ whose terms become progressively smaller and smaller since we multiply figures smaller than one. The near linearities of matrix $\mathbf{A}$ are enhanced because the effect of the diagonal elements is strengthened relative to the elements off the main diagonal which become much smaller. Regarding the matrix of fixed capital stock coefficients, we know from a number of studies that it has many zero elements, whereas some of its elements are particularly high relative to the others. In particular, as the fixed capital stock coefficients are derived from the investment matrices, only the investment producing goods industries have positive elements, whereas the remaining by definition have most, if not all, of their elements equal to zero. Thus linearities and near linearities are more frequent to be present in matrix $\mathbf{K}$. The multiplication of the latter by the Leontief's inverse matrix enhances these linearities as this becomes evident from the distribution of eigen-values of the respective matrices and from the eigenvalue gap, that is, the ratio of the maximum eigenvalue over the second eigenvalue and by extent the subdominant eigenvalues.

Appendices

Appendix 1: Estimation of Matrices of Capital Stock and Depreciation Coefficients

The vector of capital stock for the 34 industries in constant 1995 prices for the period 1995–2011 is provided in the world input-output database (WIOD) http://www.wiod.org along with the necessary documentation. The vector of capital stock of the year 2009 was dot divided by the respective investment deflator (1995), and the capital stock in current prices that we obtained was subsequently divided by the current output. The matrix of fixed capital stock coefficients was derived from the product of the column vector of investment shares of each industry times the row vector of capital stock per unit of output (see also Montibeler and Sánchez 2014). The resulting new matrix of capital stock coefficients **K** possess the properties of the usual capital stock matrices derived and employed in the hitherto empirical studies (see Mariolis and Tsoulfidis 2016 and the literature cited there). The idea is that the investment matrices contain many rows with zero elements (consumer goods and service industries do not produce investment goods) and so the subdominant eigen-values will be substantially lower (indistinguishable from zero) than the dominant which is another way to say that the equilibrium prices are determined almost exclusively by the dominant eigenvalue. The same is true with our case whose maximal eigenvalue will not be different from that we would obtain had we used a matrix of investment shares, while the difference between the dominant and the subdominant ones (which are nearly zero) is at maximum.

In similar fashion, the matrix of depreciation, **D**, was estimated as the product of the column vector of investment shares of each industry times the row vector of depreciation per unit of output. Data for depreciation by industry is not available in the world input-output database, so we use data from other sources, namely, from the database of structural analysis of the OECD (STAN) https://stats.oecd.org/Index.aspx?DataSetCode=STAN08BIS. In order to minimize the effects of any possible methodological differences between databases, we estimated the ratio of deprecia-tion to gross value-added by industry for each country from the OECD and RIETI data sets, and then we multiplied it by the corresponding gross value-added data that is available in the world input-output database.

Appendix 2: Nomenclature of Industries WIOD, 2016

1	A01	Crop and animal production, hunting and related service activities
2	A02	Forestry and logging
3	A03	Fishing and aquaculture
4	B	Mining and quarrying
5	C10–C12	Manufacture of food products, beverages and tobacco products
6	C13–C15	Manufacture of textiles, wearing apparel and leather products
7	C16	Manufacture of wood and of products of wood and cork, except furniture; manufacture of articles of straw and plaiting materials
8	C17	Manufacture of paper and paper products
9	C18	Printing and reproduction of recorded media
10	C19	Manufacture of coke and refined petroleum products
11	C20	Manufacture of chemicals and chemical products
12	C21	Manufacture of basic pharmaceutical products and pharmaceutical preparations
13	C22	Manufacture of rubber and plastic products
14	C23	Manufacture of other non-metallic mineral products
15	C24	Manufacture of basic metals
16	C25	Manufacture of fabricated metal products, except machinery and equipment
17	C26	Manufacture of computer, electronic and optical products
18	C27	Manufacture of electrical equipment
19	C28	Manufacture of machinery and equipment n.e.c.
20	C29	Manufacture of motor vehicles, trailers and semitrailers
21	C30	Manufacture of other transport equipment
22	C31–C32	Manufacture of furniture; other manufacturing
23	C33	Repair and installation of machinery and equipment
24	D35	Electricity, gas, steam and air conditioning supply
25	E36	Water collection, treatment and supply
26	E37–E39	Sewerage; waste collection, treatment and disposal activities; remediation activities and other waste management services
27	F	Construction
28	G45	Wholesale and retail trade and repair of motor vehicles and motorcycles
29	G46	Wholesale trade, except of motor vehicles and motorcycles
30	G47	Retail trade, except of motor vehicles and motorcycles
31	H49	Land transport and transport via pipelines
32	H50	Water transport
33	H51	Air transport
34	H52	Warehousing and support activities for transportation
35	H53	Postal and courier activities
36	I	Accommodation and food service activities
37	J58	Publishing activities

(continued)

38	J59–J60	Motion picture, video and television programme production, sound recording and music publishing activities
39	J61	Telecommunications
40	J62–J63	Computer programming, consultancy and related activities; information service activities
41	K64	Financial service activities, except insurance and pension funding
42	K65	Insurance, reinsurance and pension funding, except compulsory social security
43	K66	Activities auxiliary to financial services and insurance activities
44	L68	Real estate activities
45	M69–M70	Legal and accounting activities; activities of head offices; management consultancy activities
46	M71	Architectural and engineering activities; technical testing and analysis
47	M72	Scientific research and development
48	M73	Advertising and market research
49	M74–M75	Other professional, scientific and technical activities; veterinary activities
50	N	Administrative and support service activities
51	O84	Public administration and defence; compulsory social security
52	P85	Education
53	Q	Human health and social work activities
54	R–S	Other service activities

Chapter 5
Competition: Classical and Neoclassical

Marshall's crime is to pretend to handle imperfect
competition with tools only applicable to perfect competition.
Paul Samuelson (1974, Vol. 3)

Abstract The classical theory of competition is analysed as a dynamic process of rivalry in the struggle of units of capital (or firms) to gain the largest possible market share for themselves at the expense of their rivals. We argue that the classical dynamic theory of competition is characteristically different from the neoclassical static conception of competition as an end-state, where actual prices and quantities produced are compared to those that would have been established had perfect competition prevailed. In fact, the neoclassical analysis of competition is quantitative in nature for its focus is on the number (manyness or fewness) and also the size of contestants. After a comparison of the two characteristically different conceptualizations of competition, the analysis continues with deriving the laws of classical or real competition between and within industries and their integration with the mediation of regulating capital.

Keywords Classical competition · Neoclassical competition · Inter-industry competition · Intra-industry competition · Regulating capital

5.1 Introduction

The classical theory of competition was initially developed by Adam Smith, David Ricardo and John S. Mill in the main, and it was extended and further elaborated by Marx in *Capital* III, among his other writings. In the classical theory, competition is conceived as a rivalrous process, where firms compete with each other for their

---

This chapter draws freely on materials and information included in articles by Tsoulfidis and Tsaliki (2005, 2013), Tsoulfidis (2009, 2015).

survival. Despite of the realistic nature of the classical conceptualization of competition, the advent of neoclassical theory, in the late nineteenth century, gradually marginalized it and led to its replacement by the concept of competition as an end-state. Notwithstanding most of the phenomena commonly associated with actual competition, such as predatory pricing, increasing concentration of firms in industries and their centralization under the direction of a dominant firm, widespread uncertainty and the like, are viewed in neoclassical economics as deviations from the model of perfect competition. In contrast, the classical approach to competition theorizes these allegedly 'deviations' as the expected outcomes of the operation of actual competition which is regarded as a dynamic process of rivalry whereby each and every one of the contestants seeks out ways to expand its market share at the expense of the others. The usual method of eliminating firms in the market is the aggressive and predatory pricing which becomes possible through large and expensive investment in new technologies embodied in fixed capital. The latter lowers the unit cost of production and prices making nearly impossible the survival of the less efficient firms. The same objective may become even more effective *through* mergers or acquisitions, reorganization of the labour process, higher advertising expenditures and other promotional efforts and the like.

The analysis in this chapter begins with the discussion of the salient features of the classical competition and continues with the neoclassical approach and the associated with it model of perfect competition. We argue that the model of perfect competition is more of a theoretical device dictated by the needs for consistency of the neoclassical theory rather than a historical observation of the way in which firms are actually organize and compete with each other in reality. This discussion paves the way for the internal critique expounded by Piero Sraffa in the mid-1920s concerning the Marshallian theory of firm and its logical consistency with the assumptions of partial equilibrium and the various returns to scale reflected in the usual U-shaped cost curves. This critique, whose stated objective was the neoclassical theory of the perfectly competitive firm, in the early 1930s turned the attention of economists and found fertile ground to the theorization of imperfect or monopolistic competition situations, in so doing led to the so-called monopolistic competition revolution (Blaug 1997; Tsoulfidis 2009, 2010). The unplanned result of all these developments was not only the restoration but rather the strengthening and finally the dominance of the model of perfect competition and the associated with it perfectly competitive firm whose price and optimum quantity selections constitute the 'yardstick' to measuring the deviation of actual economic life from the ideal identified with the perfectly competitive one.

The chapter concludes with a detailed discussion of competition as a dynamic and rivalrous process; in this presentation, central role plays the analysis of the first classical economists (mainly Smith, Ricardo and J.S. Mill), Marx and Schumpeter, along with the Austrian economists. Particular attention is paid to Marx's analysis of competition, where we present and critically evaluate the two moments of intra-industry and inter-industry competition and their integration through the notion of regulating capital. Finally, the chapter concludes with the presentation of the idea of dominant technique whose details are in Appendix 1.

5.2 Classical Competition

Classical economists viewed competition as the mechanism that coordinates the conflicting self-interests of independently acting individuals upon each other and directs them to the attainment of equilibrium in a dynamic sense of the term, that is, a never-ending process of elimination of any excess profits or losses and the tendential establishment of normal (natural, production, long-run equilibrium) prices as the centres of gravitation of market prices. This is the reason why Smith notes that although each individual is pursuing the satisfaction of his own self-interest, nevertheless each

> is led by an invisible hand to promote an end which was no part of his intention.
>
> (*Wealth*, p. 456)

J.S. Mill is more explicit about the role of competition as the coordinating mechanism, which enables the study of economic phenomena in a rigorous and therefore scientific way. In his own words:

> only through the principle of competition has political economy any pretension to the character of a science. So far as rents, profits, wages, prices, are determined by competition, laws may be assigned for them. Assume competition to be their exclusive regulator, and principles of broad generality and scientific precision may be laid down, according to which they will be regulated.
>
> (*Principles*, p. 147)

Although from the above quotation it is not exactly clear how Mill defines competition, nevertheless one cannot but agree with Mill's view that only through competition both natural prices and the associated with them distributive categories of wages, profits and rents can be determined in a credible and analytically rigorous way and what is more important 'independently of people's will'. Thus, Mill explicitly recognizes that in the economy there are objective mechanisms (or 'laws') in operation that can be subjected to abstract theorization (modelling).

Classical economists described competition as a rivalrous dynamic equilibrating process and not as a static state portrayed in neoclassical economics. For instance, Smith (*Wealth*, p. 706) describes this rivalrous price-cutting process through which capitals (firms) are under constant pressure to innovate 'in order to undersell one another', and such an undertaking can only be possible through the further divisions of labour and new technologies whose introduction has been necessitated by competition. Furthermore, in this competitive process, actual prices are attracted to their natural ones, and by doing so the rate of profit together with wages and rents (in the case of agricultural products) gravitates towards their normal analogues. The condition sine qua non for the attainment of these normal positions of the economy is the free mobility of capitals, or what Smith calls 'perfect liberty'. The latter is described as the situation arising when someone, without violating the laws of society, is free to pursue her own self-interests and in so doing to confront with other similarly motivated individuals (*Wealth*, p. 687). Hence, Smith reiterates, this time implicitly, the importance of the 'invisible hand', when he points out that competition in effect directs the actions of each individual pursuing her own self-interest to promote society's welfare, even though this is not part of her intentions (*Wealth*, p. 338).

However, classical economists, in general, were not particularly clear as to the requirements of competitive behaviour and how it was affected by the number of participants. Thus, although competition was conceived as a rivalrous and tumultuous process, nevertheless we can often find statements that could be interpreted to imply a quantitative and therefore neoclassical perspective of competition. The following quotation from Smith has attracted attention over the years and gave rise to controversial interpretations as to its true meaning. Smith notes:

> The quantity of grocery goods, for example, which can be sold in a particular town, is limited by the demand of that town and its neighbourhood. The capital, therefore, which can be employed in the grocery trade, cannot exceed what is sufficient to purchase that quantity. If this capital is divided between two different grocers, their competition will tend to make both of them sell cheaper than if it were in the hands of one only; and if it were divided among twenty, their competition would be just so much the greater, and the chance of their combining together, in order to raise the price, just so much the less. Their competition might, perhaps, ruin some of themselves; but to take care of this, is the business of the parties concerned, and it may safely be trusted to their discretion. It can never hurt either the consumer or the producer; on the contrary, it must tend to make the retailers both sell cheaper and buy dearer, than if the whole trade was monopolized by one or two persons.
>
> (*Wealth*, p. 272)

Hence, one might interpret the rising number of grocers literally in a quantitative sense of competition, the 'manyness' of competitors. In effect, Stigler (1957, 1987) interpreted the above quotation as the preliminaries for the definition of the basic requirements of perfect competition, according to which the number of participants is the defining characteristic of the kind of competition. Krugman and Wells (2009) return to Smith's grocers example and in that they view competition in its quantitative sense in line with Stigler's interpretation. More specifically, Krugman and Wells note:

> It's important to realize that an oligopoly isn't necessarily made up of large firms. What matters isn't size *per se*; the question is how many competitors there are. When a small town has only two grocery stores, grocery service there is just as much an oligopoly as air shuttle service between New York and Washington.
>
> (Krugman and Wells 2009, p. 387)

On closer examination of Smith's often-cited passage, one reveals that competition is conceived through the lowering of prices regardless of the industry's structure, that is, the number of combatants (McNulty 1967; Moudud 2010). Nevertheless, major neoclassical authors interpret statements such as the above to mean that in Smith there was an early development of the notion of perfect competition, which he could not define with the adequate precision, because economic theory was still in its makings and its full development ought to wait until (or even long after) the marginal revolution, as we will discuss in the next section. But, if only one thinks of Smith's 'trifling example' of the pin factory where there is an ever-present pressure to undercut unit costs by increasing productivity through the division of labour, then by attributing to Smith, the neoclassical notion of (perfect) competition is a (neoclassical) perspective-imposed concept. In fact, the above-cited quotation is more in the context of a mercantile economy dominated by trade guilds monopolizing both production (producers) and consumption (shop-keepers) rather than to capitalist enterprises properly operating in towns or cities in accordance with the mobility of capital and labour. In similar fashion, one can interpret Marx's often-cited quotation:

> competition rages in direct proportion to the number, and in inverse proportion to the magnitudes, of the antagonistic capitals.
>
> (*Capital* I, p. 626)

Which in effect refers to competition in the context of a pre-capitalist society. The trouble with Smith, Ricardo and Mill was that they did not distinguish in any sufficiently clear and, therefore, theoretically adequate way between inter-industry and intra-industry competition; thereby, they subsumed the differences of these two distinctive categories of competitive behaviour and associated with them phenomena to various time spans. In a nutshell, Smith, Ricardo and Mill conceived competition as a dynamic process, whose short-run expression was the establishment of an equal price ('law of one price') and unequal profit rates between firms within industries, and its long-run expression was the equalization of prices to their natural ones as a consequence of the inflow and outflow of capital ('law of equal profitability').

However, 'the law of one price' (LOOP) is accepted by both classical and neoclassical theories despite their differences in the conceptualization of competi-tion. For instance, Smith's *claim that* 'the prices of bread and butchers' meat are generally the same, or very roughly the same throughout the greater part of the United Kingdom' (*Wealth*, p. 177); Jevons's 'law of indifference' (cf., Schumpeter 1954, p. 973) and Walras's (1874, p. 255) idea 'that each service and each product have only one price in the market' are different expressions of the LOOP. In similar fashion, Marshall (1890, p. 325) notes that 'the more nearly perfect a market is, the stronger the tendency for the same price to be paid for the same thing at the same time in all parts of the market'. Hence, Marshall clearly discerns the LOOP as a tendency of prices to crowd near an average price following a distribution akin to normal. In this sense, Marshall remains within the spirit of the classical economists, and the LOOP is supposed to operate in a rather short time span.

By contrast, the attainment of natural prices requires longer time spans, as capital flows in and out of industries, and by so doing tendentially equalizes the rates of profit across industries. This idea of inflows and outflows of capital—and not necessarily of firms—becomes particularly pronounced in Ricardo when he expli-cates the adjustment mechanism of establishing equilibrium (natural) prices between industries. He argues that in the face of differential profitability, the expected outcome is not the inflow or outflow of firms but rather the inflow or outflow of investment regardless of the industry that it comes from. If, for instance, in an industry there is excess profitability, one expects the expansion of investment expenditures in this particular industry from internal funds—if they are suffi-cient—or the inflow of funds from other less profitable industries, mainly through the credit system. The converse process is expected in the case of falling profitability in an industry, that is, the contraction of investment activity which subsequently will lead to the contraction of supply and to price increase in order to restore profitability towards the economy-wide rate of profit. The credit system facilitates this long-run equilibrating process in both directions (*Works* I, p. 90).

Classical economists, despite the realism of their approach to competition and their deep understanding of its importance in the advancement of the scientific status of economic theory, left many key issues unsettled, and thus their analysis remained vague about various important aspects of competition and the phenomena associated with it. These aspects of competition, we argue in the next section, cannot be effectively addressed within the neoclassical theory whose conceptualization of competition arises not from direct observation of the way in which firms actually organize and compete with one another but rather as a way to satisfy the requirements of a theory oriented in the attainment of equilibrium as an end-state. In so doing, the neoclassical competition does not let the internal mechanisms of the market system to work themselves out rendering visible these mechanism through the surface phenomena of prices and profits. The dynamic approach of the classical competition was further advanced by Marx and the recent modern classical approach to competition which also draws on Austrian and Schumpeterian inspirations as well as from developments in the empirical and econometric literature. We grapple with these advancements in the fifth section of the current chapter and in Chap. 6.

5.3   The Neoclassical Conception of Competition

The analysis of competition in the neoclassical theory is contained in the model of perfect competition, which describes the ideal conditions that must hold in the market to ensure the existence of perfectly competitive behaviour from the typical firm and, by extension, the characterization of the industry as competitive or not. The model of perfect competition describes a market form consisting of a large number of small—relative to the size of the market—firms selling a homogeneous commodity to many consumers. All market participants have perfect information about the prices and the costs of each good, consumer preferences are given and, finally, there are no impediments whatsoever in the mobility of the factors of production. The results of the above conditions are that both producers and consumers—because of their large number and small size—are incapable of affecting the price of the product, which becomes a *datum* for all firms and consumers in the market. Under these circumstances, firms behave completely passively with respect to the price of the product ('price taking behaviour'), and as for the production, firms simply select the level of output consistent with the condition of profit maximization attained at the point where the price (or marginal revenue) is equal to the marginal cost of the product. Similarly, consumers are endowed with optimum behaviour in the sense that they select the quantity which maximizes their benefit (utility), and such a point is attained where the given price equals the marginal utility derived from the consumption of a specific combination of goods and services.

In perfect competition, firms are 'price takers' in the sense that each faces a horizontal demand curve for its perfectly substitute product. Hence the question is how can every market participant be a price taker? And if every participant is a price taker, then how do prices change? The usual answer to this paradox is that prices change exogenously, e.g. changes in consumer preferences; the latter lead to an increase (or decrease) in demand creating a deficit (or surplus) of the good in the market. The exogenous price change leads to the assumption that all firms collectively face a negatively sloped demand curve, which is another way to say that all firms operate under conditions of monopolistic competition, and if one of them deviates, for instance, by increasing its price, the demand for its product becomes zero. On the other hand, there is no reason for any single firm to reduce the price because at the current price sells all it produces and with a lower price will not accomplish anything different.

If an industry makes profits over and above normal, the entry of firms from other industries will lead to an oversupply, and the subsequent price reduction will ensure in the long run just normal profits. If, however, sectoral profits are lower than normal, the exit of firms will lead to supply reductions and price increases which eventually will bring about, once again, normal profits. The above mechanism, when it works without impediments of any sort, establishes a price for the firm equal to its marginal cost of production, which in turn equals to firm's minimum average cost of production. Hence, long-term equilibrium is attained because in the neoclassical model of perfect competition the firm is assumed infinitesimally small compared to the size of the market, there are no entry or exit barriers and any movement takes place in no time and cost. The long-run equilibrium may change in the face of external shocks such as sudden changes in demand, technological changes and the like. But the economy sooner than later returns to its equilibrium position, due to the assumption of free entry and exit of firms in an industry resulting in the convergence of industries' profit rates towards the economy-wide rate of profit.

Figuratively speaking, in neoclassical theory, the equalization of industries' rates of profit r_i and r_j is usually described as converging to economy's average rate of profit, r, after an initial 'disturbance' or a shock at time t_1 (Fig. 5.1). If for some reason, an industry's profit rate, r_i, remains higher than the average and their difference persists over time, then this behaviour is interpreted to mean as the presence of monopoly power in the particular industry.

In neoclassical theory, the comparison of prices and quantities in successive equilibria becomes the usual method of characterizing different market forms and their economic effects with respect to efficiency. However, on a closer examination, we find that the attainment of equilibrium is based on a series of 'unrealistic' assumptions, namely:

- The disturbance of equilibrium—due to a shock—and the transition to new equilibrium position are assumed to take place in a short time.
- In perfect competition, the participants are passive price takers; therefore, the new equilibrium position is essentially predetermined.

Hence, neoclassical analysis does not address what takes place in between equilibrium positions, but it is limited to compare them in a comparative static exercise. In fact, the strict assumptions serve this purpose, since the hypotheses of:

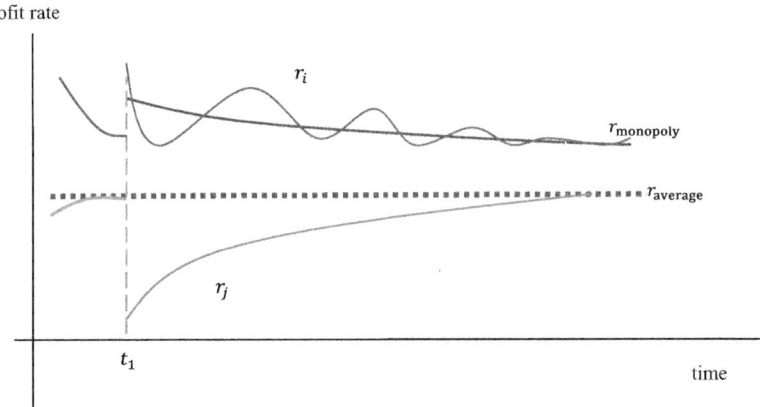

Fig. 5.1 The convergence of the rate of profit in neoclassical analysis

- Large number and small size of economic units
- Homogeneous goods
- Perfect mobility of production factors (together with the assumption of homoge-neous cost structure and firm's size)

All of the above establish the firms' behaviour as 'price takers', rendering impossible any effort for product diversification, impose the assumption of same technology in the production process and imply uniform profit margins within and between industries, at least in the long run.

The above brief presentation of the neoclassical theoretical framework of com-petition reveals that usual features of real business world conduct, such as aggressive price policy, product differentiation through advertising and generally every effort to increase market share, are perceived as deviations from standard competitive behav-iour and as evidence of oligopolistic or monopolistic market structure. Similarly, if the size and scale of production of one or more firms in an industry is relatively large, the differentiation in intra-industry profit margins is attributed to the lack of perfect capital mobility caused by the minimum capital optimum size requirements.

Moreover, the intensity of competition is conceived as being directly proportional to the number of producers and, in general, to the structure of an industry. In this 'quantitative notion of competition', the firm is conceived as the legal entity which by hiring and organizing the services of the factors of production supplies goods and services to the market. It is important to note that within the neoclassical framework, the firm does not own any of the factors of production; it merely hires their services offered by their owners, that is, the individuals. The larger the number of firms operating in an industry, the more vigorous is their competitive behaviour and so is the establishment of a uniform rate of profit across firms and industries. By contrast, the smaller the number of firms in an industry, the more monopolistic or oligopolistic is the form of competition and, therefore, the higher the inter-industry profit rate differentials. In this non-competitive state of equilibrium, some prices are above the marginal cost, so society suffers welfare losses from the underproduction and the underutilisation of the disposable productive resources. In the neoclassical microeconomic theory, if profits above normal are displayed by a firm or industry for a fairly long period of time, they are attributed to imperfections in the operation of the market and thus to the presence of some degree of monopoly.

The concept of perfect competition appears, for the first time and in embryonic form, in Cournot (1838), whose analysis was premised on the optimizing behaviour of the participating firms at the point where their marginal revenue equates marginal cost. Cournot's analysis also relates to the number of producers with the market price arguing that the greater the number of firms, the lower the price of the product, whereas in the case of 'unrestricted competition' (the number of firms increases to infinity), the equilibrium prices become equal to their respective marginal costs. These concepts are also present in the writings of other French engineers in the early nineteenth century, who, although did not know anything about perfect competition, nevertheless, knew well the efficiency gains or losses of the marginal cost pricing and the difficulties in its applications. The often-cited didactic example of such inconsistencies has been advanced by Dupuit (1844) and is related to the imposition of the correct price of crossing a bridge.[1]

The 'innovative' ideas of Cournot and other French engineers in the early- to mid-nineteenth century could not attract sufficient attention at that time due to the absolute domination of the classical economic theory and its conceptualization of competition as a rivalrous dynamic process and not as usually described independently operating firms in a static analytical framework. Although there have been systematic efforts by the first neoclassical economists (in the late nineteenth and the early twentieth century) to promote the static notion of competition as an essential component in the formation of the neoclassical economic theory, mainly two reasons made difficult its acceptance:

- The first is the unrealistic nature of its assumptions that deterred economists to adopt it.
- The second and perhaps more important is the dominance of the classical notion of competition not only during the nineteenth century but also during the first decades of the twentieth century.

One question that might be raised is that if each agent in the perfectly competitive model is supposed to be a 'price taker' and incapable of setting the price, how do market participants know the equilibrium price in the first place, and how does equilibrium price change? Here is where the Walrasian auctioneer enters the picture, and as the deus ex machina fixes the equilibrium prices after experimenting with

---

[1]We know that the marginal cost of person crossing a bridge, other things equal, is zero, and so it must be the optimal price (toll) of crossing it. But for a price equal to zero, there is no private incentive to build bridges while a positive price (toll) leads to resource misallocation and society's net welfare loss.

various vectors of possible equilibrium prices. More specifically, for each announced vector of prices the economic agents reveal their plans about the quantities that are willing and able to buy, and the auctioneer, by continually correcting the price vectors so as to eliminate deviations between supplies and demands, enables the economic agents to grope towards the equilibrium. This hypothetical experiment reveals the necessity of the concept of perfect competition for the proper operation of the Walrasian auctioneer, because in this hypotetical auction no single independently acting participant knows anything more than anybody else and in this sense, there is perfect information in the economy. These conditions are met in a hypothetical market with an infinitely large number of infinitesimally small, with respect to the size of the market, participants. Under these circumstances and as the actual exchange takes place only and exclusively at equilibrium prices, the auctioneer really obliterates any possibility of understanding the way in which actual markets attain their equilibrium positions. One consequence of the above is that the classical notion of competition that deals with the attainment of equilibrium, as a tendency in real (calendar) time, is eventually sidestepped for it does not fit with the analytical framework of neoclassical economics oriented towards equilibrium as a state (see also Clifton 1977; Eatwell 1982; Eatwell et al. 1987; Blaug 1997, inter alia).

From the above, it becomes clear that the givens (data) of the neoclassical theory, that is, the preferences of individuals, their endowments and technological alternatives, when combined, impose a type of competition which cannot be different from that of perfect competition. As a consequence, perfect competition is a sine qua non require-ment in the Walrasian model for the determination of equilibrium prices. In similar fashion, Jevon's (1871) consumer's equilibrium position requires the passivity of consumers who simply react to given prices; the same is true in welfare economics and the attainment of Pareto optimality condition. Wicksteed's product exhaustion theorem of income distribution, according to which when factors of production are paid their marginal contribution to production exhaust the total product, constitutes another example which holds only under conditions of perfect competition.

The formal requirements of the perfect competition were laid out by Edgeworth (1877) in his model of exchange, where the attainment of optimality requires the absolute submissiveness of the behaviour of economic agents to given prices. Naturally, Edgeworth promoted the concept of perfect competition albeit without much success not only because of its patently unrealistic nature but mainly because of the dominance of the ideas of classical economists. Marshall sought to circumvent the problems of acceptance of the new theory by assimilating the classical tradition with neoclassical economics and by embracing a more dynamic and less static theory of competition. Marshall frequently parallels economy's operation with that of biological world; hence expressions such as 'perfect' or 'full' competition are entirely absent from his writings (Stigler 1957). Moreover, even in Marshall's time, perfect competition was not fully formulated into an operational model, and this job was accomplished, to a great extent, by Knight $(1921)^2$ who described, in a comprehensive and meticulous way, the requirements of perfect competition that could be used in a real economy.

In the late 1920s onwards, the classical dynamical process of competition gradually was cast into static terms, and it was replaced by the neoclassical description of competition as a state rather than as a process of rivalry between firms in their struggle for survival through technological change and expansion.[3] In fact, the notion of perfect competition fits perfectly to the core data of the neoclassical theory and suitably corroborates with the way in which technology is integrated into the theory. More specifically, perfect competition secures that firms, from the blueprint of available technologies, choose the lowest cost one. In this sense, the firms in actual economies by no means bear features suitable to the neoclassical competitive model, simply because they are in an inescapable pressure to innovate in the effort to introduce cost-minimizing techniques aiming at lower unit costs and eventually prices in order to increase their market share at the expense of their competitors. Consequently, the requirements of perfect competition are not applicable to real economies, and this, according to Stigler (1949, 1956), paved the way for the development and wide acceptance of the notion of monopolistic competition in the 1930s.

5.4 Sraffa's Critique of the Marshallian Competitive Firm

Sraffa's critique refers to the internal consistency of the notion of perfectly competitive firm with the assumptions of partial equilibrium and the usual U-shaped average and marginal cost curves of such firms.[4] In perfect competition with U-shaped curves of average and marginal costs (AC and MC, respectively), the supply curve of a firm up until Q_c is zero and for output greater than Q_c is in effect

---

[2]Knight's book was, in fact, his Ph.D. dissertation written under Allyn Young's from what we know diligent supervision. It is interesting to note that Allyn Young was the supervisor of another famous dissertation written by Edwin Chamberlin that we discuss in the next pages (Marchionatti 2003).

[3]We may argue that the gradual replacement was affected, to some extent, by the so-called long depression of 1873–1896 during which competition intensified and price-cutting behaviour led to the elimination of a large number of weaker firms, massive unemployment and concentration and centralization of capital. It has been observed, time and again, that in dismal situations such as those of depressions, people, often, distant themselves from the harsh reality of the present and start fantasizing idealized situations. Clearly, an idealized situation is where firms are pictured small, powerless, independent of one another and impotent with respect to the omnipresent powerful market forces that dictate prices.

[4]Sraffa's critique took place in two articles. The first published in Italian in 1925, and a version (more concise) of it was published a year later (1926) in *Economic Journal* after Edgeworth's suggestion and consent of J. M. Keynes, the editor of the journal at that time.

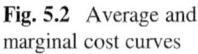 **Fig. 5.2** Average and marginal cost curves

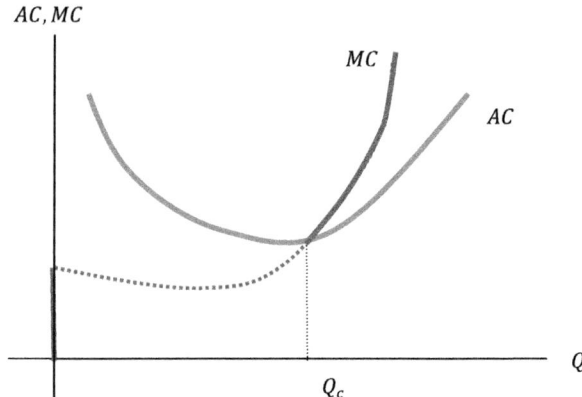

the part of the marginal costs over and above the minimum average (variable) costs (Fig. 5.2).[5]

Sraffa took issue with Marshall's hypothesis of returns to scale in production and the assumptions of the competitive firm in a partial equilibrium framework of analysis. In particular, Sraffa argued that in the case of increasing returns to scale, which are internal to the firm, there would be continuous pressure on the firm to expand its output until it can supply the whole market. Obviously, the hypothesis of increasing returns to scale prima facie contradicts the notion of perfect competition for it leads to monopoly. Marshall (1890, p. 666, n. 3) also had noticed this inconsistency and acknowledged Cournot as the precursor of this idea (Marshall 1890, p. 380, n. 1), that is, the incompatibility of increasing returns and perfect competition. Marshall was keen to downplay the importance of this inconsistency to the theory by characterizing it as 'Cournot's dilemma'. This is the reason why Sraffa pointed out that the case of increasing returns to scale 'was entirely abandoned, as it was seen to be incompatible with competitive conditions' (Sraffa 1926, pp. 537–538).[6] Economies of scale, however, Sraffa (ibid, p. 540) argued, can be external to the firm and internal to the industry, a case however which is rarely met in real economies. Furthermore, this type of returns to scale cannot be limited to a single industry, and sooner or later its effects are diffused throughout the economy, and in so doing the Marshallian partial equilibrium framework is rendered inadequate to deal with the complexities emanating from the subsequent development of strong interactions among industries (ibid, pp. 538–539). The same is true a fortiori with the economies of scale which are external to the firm and to the industry, since

[5]The U-shape of the curves is due to the presence of increasing, constant and decreasing returns to scale.

[6]It is interesting to note that the discussion, about the economies of scale and the perfectly competitive firm, was totally dismissed by Stigler (1937, p. 708) on the basis that he found it 'too vague to be meaningful at present'.

the interactions across industries are expected to be much stronger and, therefore, the case for abandoning the analysis of partial equilibrium is strengthened.

Turning to the case of diminishing returns to scale and perfect competition, it follows that since firms buy their inputs in competitive markets, they face no restrictions whatsoever in the quantities that they buy and, therefore, there is no reason for the increasing part of the usual U-shaped average cost curves. Hence, the structure of the theory of perfect competition does not allow for the case of increasing cost as the scale of production increases, simply because there is no reason whatsoever for firms to abandon their minimum average cost and move to a higher point on their U-shaped average cost curves. On further consideration, however, in neoclassical theory, decreasing returns to scale in production arise if and only if we assume that one factor of production, let us say land, is constant, whereas the other factor, let us say labour, is variable. The increase of the variable factor of production past the point of optimization of production gives rise to decreasing returns to scale.[7] However, the obvious question is why would someone leave the perfect combination of factors of production (e.g. land and labour) and would produce at a level beyond that optimal level of production?

Consequently, the only assumption that seems to pass the test of logical consistency is that of constant returns to scale which is described by constant average cost curves whose shape is straight line parallel to the horizontal line representing output produced (Sraffa 1926, p. 540). Thus, Sraffa through a critique of the Marshallian theory of the firm was led to a realistic configuration of the average cost characterized by constant returns to scale very similar to that of classical economists (ibid, p. 544). Figure 5.3 below displays a straight line infinitely elastic with respect to the output produced average cost curve, which is equivalent to saying that there is no difference between the marginal and the average cost curves of the firm.

If we suppose that the demand for this particular firm is higher than its average cost, the excessive profits will attract new firms in the industry, and the demand curve d_2 will decrease moving to the downward direction. If again firm's demand curve is below the average cost, then, once again, there is disequilibrium, and firms will exit the industry causing demand curve d_1 to increase for the remaining firms, that is, to move in the upward direction. The 'equilibrium' is attained if, and only if, the demand curve (and by extent marginal revenue, MR, and price, P) coincides with the marginal and average cost curves. But in this limiting case and while we are in the quest of a single equilibrium point, we arrive at a situation of infinite equilibrium points, a result which leads to the conclusion that we simply cannot define the supply decisions of the perfectly competitive firm in the presence of constant returns to scale and, therefore, we cannot determine the size of the perfectly competitive firm. Consequently, the assumption of returns (increasing, decreasing or even constant) to

---

[7]The usual example employed in such analysis is that of the cultivation of a parcel of land, whereby as the number of workers increases, the output produced initially increases at an increasing rate, but past a point (inflection point) the rate of increase slows down until the attainment of the optimum combination of land and labour, that is, the point that maximizes the output produced. Beyond this optimal point, the returns to land become diminishing.

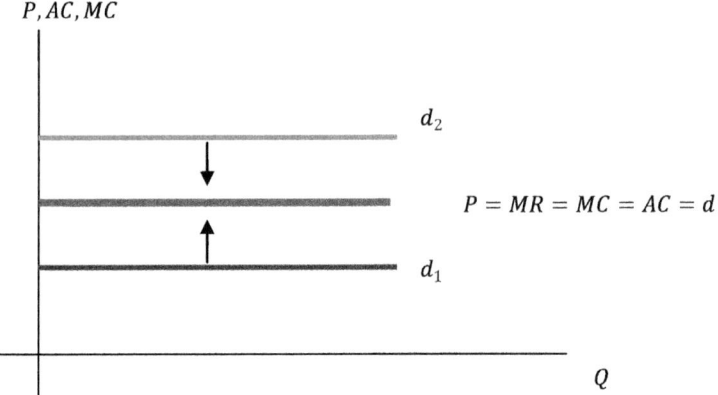

Fig. 5.3 Average and marginal cost with constant returns to scale

scale, which are internal to the perfectly competitive firm, are inconsistent with the requirements of the theory of the perfect competition. If, on the other hand, we suppose that the returns to scale are external to the firm and internal to the industry, then we have shown that the notion of partial equilibrium is no longer applicable, and therefore it must be abandoned.

Sraffa concluded that a simple and, at the same time, viable solution to the internal inconsistencies of the perfectly competitive model might be its replacement by the imperfect (or monopolistic) competition model which remains in the context of partial equilibrium analysis. The imperfect competition model maintains the hypothesis of a sufficiently large number of firms with the difference that their product is differentiated, at least, in the eyes of consumers (Sraffa 1926, p. 545); also consumers' preferences do not easily change, because they are determined by factors, such as the marketing of the product, the personal acquaintance and the loyalty of customers to a specific firm that last for long. Thus, he proposed the replacement of the model of perfect competition by that of monopolistic competition. Notes Sraffa

> It is necessary, therefore, to abandon the path of free competition and turn in the opposite direction, namely, towards monopoly.
>
> (Sraffa 1926, p. 542)

In short, the theory of firm cannot be built on the assumption of perfect competition, because in actual competition it is unrealistic to say that firms sell any quantity they produce at a given price. The production is not limited by cost, but rather by the downward-sloping demand curve.

The consequence of Sraffa's critique of perfect competition was the development of the model of imperfect competition by Robinson (1933) in Cambridge, England, and in the same year of the model of monopolistic competition by Chamberlin (1933) in Cambridge, Massachusetts. Between the two, Robinson openly admitted that her work was directly influenced from Sraffa's articles; nevertheless, her analysis was based on the tools of the Marshallian tradition and not to the classical approach. It is important to note that Robinson, soon after the publication of her book, essentially abandoned the further development of 'imperfect competition' and the associated with it 'revolution'.[8] Chamberlin, on the other hand, was not at all willing to admit any external influences to his work other than his supervisor's Allyn Young. He vehemently denied any influence especially coming from Sraffa's articles and the theoretical developments in Cambridge, England. In spite of all these, Chamberlin produced a body of work which was much more faithful to Sraffa's suggestion, and he managed to develop new analytical tools promoting the concept of 'monopolistic competition' until the very end of his life.

One of the surprising results of the analysis of monopolistic competition lies in the triumphal comeback of perfect competition. We already mentioned that the idea of perfect competition was a very old one and can be traced back to Cournot (1838) whose duopoly exercise was based on profit maximizing choice of output by equating the marginal revenue to marginal cost. Cournot's ideas, however, could not attract attention in the early nineteenth century because of the absolute domination of classical approach. The long depression of 1873–1896 created the necessary conditions for the advent and acceptance of new ideas. In fact, Edgeworth (1877) developed further the notion of perfect competition by detailing its requirements; however, his analysis did not receive broad acceptance because of the dominance of the ideas of classical economists.

Marshall with respect to the classical notion of competition, as in many others, sought to assimilate it into the neoclassical theory and through its mathematization and the use of marginal analysis to give it the status of positive science. He was fully aware that such an assimilation is not easy to carry out and in short time but rather gradually and above all silently over the passage of long time. The reason for the gradual and silent abandonment of classical competition was that its replacement, that is, perfect competition, a patently unrealistic model was extremely hard to be accepted. Classical competition is not the only concept characterized by realism and at odds with the neoclassical theory but one from many that Marshall sought to assimilate for the exact same reason and the same strategy. Starting with Smith's notion of increasing returns to scale which take place over the passage of real and long time, Marshall by eliminating the time factor reduced Smith's and the classical notion of returns to scale to simply what happens to output in the face of a given change in the amount of a factor of production holding all the others constant. In similar fashion, Ricardo's decreasing returns to scale (law of diminishing returns, see Chap. 8) that are supposed to take place in agriculture or mines after the passage of long actual time was cast, once again, by Marshall in the neoclassical static

---

[8]In fact, she had written very little (after the publication of her book) about imperfect competition, apparently because she had lost faith in the concept and she did not like the developments around it. Her few brief articles on competition (perfect or imperfect) that she published after 1933 did not have anything really new, but rather they summarized and further elaborated previously advanced positions (Robinson 1934, 1953). Her interests were diverted to the neoclassical theory of capital and economic growth that were to become fiercely debated topics in economics.

framework of analysis. Ricardo's labour theory of value (see Chap. 1), is another example of Marshallian assimilation strategy, according to which Ricardo's theory is interpreted as a cost of production theory with the difference that rent was not included as a constituent component of cost and demand was unaccounted for. Thus, Ricardo's incomplete or rather less developed theory of price determination, was supposed to become more precise once the cost of all the factors of production along with the demand side of the market were fully integrated into a cost of production theory. The classical notion of productive and unproductive labour (see Chap. 9) is another example of this assimilation strategy. In all cases, Marshall made systematic efforts to fit the classical analysis into neoclassical 'garment'. He argued that classical economists simply did not know supply and demand theory and partial equilibrium analysis, and this is essentially the reason why they presented their theories in an incomplete and imprecise manner; hence, the classical theories ought to be reformulated and integrated gradually and silently into the neoclassical theory. Returning to the concept of perfect competition, it was not until the interwar period that perfect competition was fully formulated, mainly because of Knight's (1921) book (for details see Stigler 1957; McNulty 1967; Marchionatti 2003). However, it took many years before the explicit incorporation of perfect competition into neoclassical economics was fully accomplished.

A salient feature of perfect competition is that there is no reason for price competition, the quintessence of competition in classical economics. Hayek pointed out the gap that exists between actual competition and perfect competition as follows:

> what the theory of perfect competition discusses has little claim to be called 'competition' at all and that its conclusions are of little use as guides to policy.
>
> (Hayek 1948, p. 92)

In effect, whenever competition is manifested in price-cutting behaviour, neoclassical economics takes it as indication of imperfection in competition! By contrast, in the classical analysis, competition is expected to elicit price changes which tendentially conform to cost of production. The requirement for the operation of competition, as a dynamic process of rivalry according to Smith, was the situation of 'perfect liberty', that is to say, an institutional environment supportive to the free mobility of capital and labour. By contrast, the notion of perfect competition does not refer to a process but rather to a specific industrial structure in which each individual firm is so small relative to the size of the market that cannot exert any influence on price.

5.4.1   The Rise and Fall of the 'Imperfect Competition Revolution'

The theory of imperfect competition that was developed in the interwar period is also based on a static analysis, and it can be viewed as a situation that arises when each individual firm is large enough relative to the size of market. Consequently, a firm with these characteristics can practice some control over prices and output produced. During 'the years of high theory'—as Shackle (1967) characterized the period that begins in 1926 and continues up to World War II—the theory of monopolistic competition in combination on the one hand with the theory of general equilibrium of Hicks and Samuelson and on the other hand with the advent of the new welfare economics achieved almost the total replacement of the classical idea of competition, as a process of rivalry between firms, with the idea of competition as a final situation.

As we pointed out in the previous section, the neoclassical notion of competition up until the first two decades of the twentieth century was closer to that of classical economists (Stigler 1957) rather than to that of Cournot and Edgeworth. Marshall envisioned competition more like as a dynamic process as this can be judged by the use of metaphors from the natural world to describe competition in the economic world. Marshall's theorization of competition is not independent of the fact that he studied in Germany (1868 and 1871–1872) and he was influenced by the German Historical School known for its search for realism and theories that pass successfully the historical test (Hodgson 2005). With such a theoretical background, it comes as no surprise that Marshall does not acknowledge the hypothesis of perfect information in his notion of competition (Hart 2003); in fact, there is only a single reference in Marshall's (1890, p. 314) book to the notion of 'perfect competition'. Stigler (1957) mentions that in the first edition of Marshall's book, competition is taken to mean the exact same thing as in Adam Smith, and only in the later versions of his book does Marshall refer to competition to mean a perfectly elastic demand curve for the individual firm. And while this situation continued in the 1930s, the books of Chamberlin and Robinson sparked a renewed interest in the static analysis of market forms. Keywords such as monopoly, oligopoly, price stickiness, market power, price discrimination, labour exploitation, excess capacity and the like activated the interest of economists and policymakers in order to eliminate these undesired features of markets.

The intellectual atmosphere in the 1890s up until the 1920s was that of liberalism that was conducive to the development of a merger wave that led to the creation of big business in the years before the collapse of the stock market and the outbreak of economic crisis in the 1930s. In particular, after 1932 government intervention was deemed necessary for the limitation of market power of big businesses. In fact, the usual argument (e.g. Berle and Means 1932) was that prices in the US economy became increasingly stickier in the consumer goods' industries due to the concentrated and, therefore, monopolistic structure. Berle and Means (1932) further argued that these 'sticky prices' undermined the already constrained purchasing power of consumers. The same phenomenon was observed in the capital goods' sectors, meaning producers were less willing to invest in new plant and equipment. Price stickiness thus inhibited the recovery of both the demand for consumer goods and the demand for intermediate or investment goods thereby precipitating the depression. Naturally, such views offered the necessary economic rationale for government intervention in the markets. In fact, governments became increasingly more interested in correcting the operation of actual markets in the effort to bring them closer to the hypothetical perfectly competitive market structures (Bishop 1963; Dilorenzo and High 1988). This is equivalent to saying that the actual markets were characterized by some degree of imperfection in their operation, and hence they were found in divergence from an ideal operation which was identified in the notion of perfect competition.

The preparatory work already had begun with Cournot, continued with Edgeworth and its details became more specific in Knight's (1921) book. The change in the intellectual atmosphere can be better understood by comparing the US economy in the 1930s with that of 1890s. More specifically, in the 1890s, the Sherman antitrust legislation found more opposition than support for reasons that have to do with the widespread acceptance of the classical notion of competition among economists and policymakers. Phenomena such as price competition, product differentiation, innovation and dominant position of a firm in a market were perceived as natural and therefore expected phenomena; thus, government intervention in the markets, as argued, could only be against free competition (Stigler 1982; Dilorenzo and High 1988).

In the interwar period, however, because of Sraffa's critique, the focus of attention had shifted on the development of the theory of imperfect (or monopolistic) competition and the suppression of the unrealistic and logically inconsistent theory of perfect competition. The theorization of competition in its imperfect form during the 1930s led to the development of the field of industrial organization (particularly in the USA), which on the one hand encompassed the new theoretical refinements of the theory of the firm and forms of competition and on the other hand made an effort to give quantitative content to these forms. Policy interventions required the collection of detailed industry data on prices, costs, output and concentration ratios whose systematic collection begins approximately the same time with similar efforts towards a system of national income accounts for the aggregate economy and macroeconomic policy purposes. These parallel developments lend support to the view of outbreak of two revolutions (one in microeconomics or monopolistic competition and the other in macroeconomics or Keynesian revolution) in economic theory that took place at approximately the same time. However, these developments in monopolistic competition theory were not to last for long, and gradually economists rediscovered the notion of perfect competition. As Stigler notes:

> The theory of imperfect competition has raised questions which it cannot answer satisfactorily until the theory of perfect competition has been much more fully developed. [...] the chief work of economic theorists should for the present still be in the theory of perfect competition.
>
> (Stigler 1937, p. 707)

Consequently, from the early 1930s onwards, the notion of perfect competition comes back stronger, thus disappointing Sraffa, who apparently realized that the direction of research on monopolistic competition had created its own momentum and inescapably was drifting further away from the dynamic classical theory of competition going towards the neoclassical static notion of perfect competition.

5.4.2 Salt and Sweet Waters Economic Perspectives

Meanwhile many neoclassical economists in the USA (this time in Chicago) perceived the 'monopolistic competition revolution' as a departure from scientific analysis that economics ought to follow in a way similar to physics and the other 'hard' sciences; worse of all, it was perceived as a critique of the actual market system which in turn created the need for government's corrective role in the economy. Stigler was very specific about the implications of monopolistic competition to the neoclassical theory of the firm. He described monopolistic competition and its implications in the following terms:

> The new theory, in other words, has become something of a destructing fad. It seems often to be an escape from the very hard thinking necessary to secure a satisfactory and useful theory of perfect competition. Sound theories of price and production are indispensable to the solution of even the simplest practical problems. Yet the majority of the writers on imperfect competition seem not to realise that almost all the important concepts they have taken from perfect competition are suspect.
>
> (Stigler 1937, p. 708)

Furthermore, Stigler (1937) claimed that the 'newer literature of imperfect competition' is so complex that it is incomprehensible for the legislator and the lawman, and so it is extremely difficult to find useful applications. In fact, both Stigler and Friedman opposed vehemently to all efforts for further elaboration and possible improvement of the theory of monopolistic competition. An example of how much Stigler objected to the theory of monopolistic competition is that in his microeconomics textbook (published in 1942), there is not even a single reference to Chamberlin's work, while Robinson is only mentioned en passant in the discussion of price discrimination. Stigler's opposition was based on the idea that such a direction of research in monopolistic competition would render economic analysis more case-oriented and, therefore, the lack of generalizations would deprive economic theory from its scientific content. It is interesting to note in this connection that Hicks (1946) also recognized that the abandonment of perfect competition and its replacement by monopolistic competition would undermine the scientific status of economic theory:

> A general abandonment of the assumption of perfect competition, a universal assumption of monopoly, must have very destructive consequences for economic theory. Under monopoly the stability conditions become indeterminate; and the basis on which economic laws can be constructed is therefore shorn away [...].
>
> (Hicks 1946, p. 83)

Friedman (1953) argued also against monopolistic competition mainly on methodological grounds, i.e. a model is judged according to its predictive content and not the realism of its assumptions. On further consideration, however, we discover that the methodological rejection of imperfect competition was, in fact, first launched by Stigler (1949); nevertheless, Friedman (1953) popularized this methodological principle so much that at the end it came to be associated with his name. In this context, he used the example of the price changes of an indirect tax imposed on cigarettes whose results could be predicted with sufficient accuracy using partial equilibrium analysis in the context of perfect competition.

Similarly aggressive was the stance of both Stigler and Friedman with regard to the concept of 'workable competition' that was introduced and promoted by Clark (1940). According to workable competition, the efficiency results of perfect competition can be obtained, while its unrealistic assumptions could be relaxed and perhaps abandoned. The idea is that the existing imperfections in real markets may neutralize each other and the end result might be similar to this obtained in perfect competition. Stigler (1968) argued that the trouble with the workable competition approach was the same with that of monopolistic competition, that is, he found it vague enough to be translated into a practical model, and since such a model (i.e. perfect competition) already exists and it has been used successfully as a standard for purpose of comparisons, there is no reason to replace it by another one. A characteristically different effort was that of Triffin (1941) who sought to reorient the theory of monopolistic competition away from partial equilibrium towards general equilibrium analysis. Friedman's response was immediate and directed against such a general equilibrium approach for the practical problems since economists want to apply their theories at the level of industries, not at the level of firms or of the economy as a whole. Consequently, since industries are so important and are not accounted for in the analysis of monopolistic competition, it follows that monopolistic competition must go. Stigler (1949) was also dismissive of Triffin's version of monopolistic competition characterizing it as 'ad hoc empiricism'.

These developments led to the idea of testing empirically the alleged imperfections of the actual market system claimed by the monopolistic competition economists. Stigler (1949), for example, argued that the predictions of the monopolistic competition model are not far from those of perfect competition. The ensuing research gave rise to several studies in the University of Chicago and elsewhere about the limited empirical significance of monopoly and monopolistic competition. Meanwhile, at the macroeconomic level, the welfare implications of monopoly for the economy as a whole were estimated to exert a negligible effect that did not exceed 1% (approximately, one-seventh of 1%) of the GDP in the US economy (Harberger 1954; Schwartzman 1960). These results were in favour of the perfectionists, at the University of Chicago, who claimed that the actual economies do not differ in any empirically significant way from the ideal of perfect competition and thus there is no need for the corrective role of government intervention in the markets.

Stigler and economists in the University of Chicago tradition were more interested in downplaying the importance of actually observed features of real competition such as the degree of concentration, high capital requirements, advertising expenditures and the like which are strictly connected to monopolistic competition and give rise to power over market forces. They argued that, if the time period is long enough, industry profit rates tend to equate to the economy's normal that is the competitive (average) rate of profit. It is interesting to note that the above arguments were developed in the context of a dynamic analysis completely distant from the static analytical framework utilized in the paradigm of perfect competition. Hence, the empirical dimension of this approach has only nominal similarities to neoclassical theory of perfect competition and surprisingly enough displays startling similarities to the classical theory of competition as a dynamic process that evolves over long stretches of time.

By contrast, the research at Harvard University sought to expose the imperfections of the actual market system and to stress the need for government intervention; nevertheless, since the model of perfect competition was always present in the background of the analysis, naturally, it became the unambiguous standard for comparisons and the objective of economic policy measures.[9] The economic crisis of the 1930s and the intellectual atmosphere of that time were against big firms which were considered responsible for the depressive economy; as a consequence, interventionist policies were in the agenda. The government was supposed to have the power to 'correct' the functioning of real markets, which apparently were far from being perfect; hence, government's role in this neoclassical economic perspective was to correct market imperfections in a way such that the actual economic life to come as close as it gets to the perfectly competitive one. In this spirit antitrust laws were introduced, mainly in the 1930s, in order to deter and ultimately prevent monopolies and enhance, if not establish, perfect competition conditions. The idea was that if the economy is left to its own devices, it is driven either to monopolistic competition, or it takes much longer to return to its ideal state of perfect competition. In Harvard University, Mason (1939) promoted the so-called structure-conduct-performance paradigm of industrial organization, according to which the structure (i.e. the number and the size distribution of firms) of an industry determines the conduct and performance of firms in the industry (Caves 1964).[10]

Clearly, the monopolistic competition revolution did not last for long, and its initial outbreak and brief ascent only had, as an unintentional effect, the restoration and upgrading of the perfect competition model as the ideal standard that actual economies with the help of government intervention may approximate. In other words, the economists in Chicago were promoting the idea of perfect competition in a direct way and in direct opposition to monopolistic competition. The economists at Harvard, on the other hand, were promoting the idea that monopolies and oligopolies dominate the markets and the result of their dominance is higher prices and under-utilization of capacity. Nevertheless, they also promoted the perfectly competitive model as the ideal standard that markets ought to emulate.

Meanwhile in macroeconomics, the emergence of Monetarism in the 1970s and 1980s together with its successor, the New Classical Economics and the associated with it 'rational expectations hypothesis', questioned some of the fundamental

[9]For a comprehensive survey of the empirical research in industrial organization, see Semmler (1983) and Scherer and Ross (1990).

[10]These efforts were continued by Mason's student, Joe Bain, who introduced the concept of limit pricing according to which the price setting of firms does not necessarily relate to current but rather to future profit targets (Bain 1949). He also discussed pricing schemes according to which firms could charge a price higher than average cost for a long period of time because of entry barriers (Bain 1956).

premises of Keynesian economics. In so doing, once again the issue of the ineffectiveness of economic policies and, in general, government intervention in the markets was brought to the attention of economists and in a sense 'policymakers'. The new analytical framework was based on the idea that economic agents on an average act on the basis of rational expectations and in so doing they are capable of predicting the long-run results of government intervention in the very short run, thereby negating the effectiveness of economic policies with respect to the level of output and employment. Consequently, according to the New Classical approach, economic policies, in the long run, are purely inflationary with negligible effects on output and employment; thus government's role in the economy, once again, should be kept to a minimum, and its focus must be on deregulation issues in enhancing (perfect) competition in the effort to promote economic growth and employment. However, the continuing slowdown in the 1980s discredited even the New Classical approach along with their rational expectations hypothesis paving the way for the development of new macroeconomic approaches based on market imperfections and the guiding role that a government may have in the economy. Thus, in the late 1980s and 1990s, the advent of New Keynesian and more recently the New Consensus Macroeconomics (Arestis 2009) are associated with what we may call as the 'second monopolistic competition revolution' (Tsoulfidis 2010).

Monopolistic competition modelling in its comeback was by far more realistic as it theorized the salient features of competitive behaviour utilizing game theory and in so doing gained popularity once again. However, in retrospect, and up until now, although there has been a whole host of game models, none of them are generally accepted as representative of the behaviour of an actual competitive industry. These imperfect competition models were further elaborated so as to become part of new theories of labour economics, international trade and economic growth. On further examination, one discovers that the currently popular imperfect competition models have *one* element in common with their counterparts of the 1930s, their fundamental faith in perfect competition. This faith in perfect competition featuring all these models is described pretty well in Krugman and Wells' (2009) popular microeconomic text, when they state that:

> much of what we learn from the study of perfectly competitive markets—about costs, entry and exit, and efficiency—remains valid despite the fact that many industries are not perfectly competitive.

(Krugman and Wells 2009, p. 388)

In the recent decades, there has been more and more reliance on game theory, but on further consideration we discover that the route through the game theory is an admission that the usual textbook analysis of competition is far from being satisfactory since there is no generally agreed-upon game to characterize the behaviour of a competitive industry.

5.4.3 Monopoly and Other Heterodox Approaches

The dominance of neoclassical analytical framework of competition is due, at least in part, to its uncritical acceptance by many heterodox economists. For reasons that are not entirely understood, many from the heterodox economists theorized, and not few even today still hypothesize, that the model of perfect competition was realistic for the analysis of capitalism in the nineteenth and perhaps in the early twentieth centuries, when the (absolute) size of firms was undoubtedly smaller than today's firms; therefore, at that time, firms were following price signals simply because they were weak to confront the power of market forces. Many, therefore, heterodox economists (Kalecki, Sweezy, Foster, among others) have argued, time and again, that the last decade of the nineteenth and early twentieth centuries marked a new era of capitalism, where a small number of giant corporations (megacorps) succeeded to acquire, because of their size, power over market forces thereby fixing their prices at levels which establish rates of profit higher than the economy's average one.

The problem with this particular heterodox perspective of competition, according to which firms have power over the market, is that it does not provide the required theoretical and empirical justification. There is no doubt that, with the passage of time, the absolute size of firms, on average, has increased, but in any case, this alone does not mean that their command on market forces has increased because the size of the market has increased as well. Only an empirical research that relates firms' size to market power could make sense, but such empirical analysis is extremely difficult to be contacted due to lack of data. Moreover, a greater relative size does not necessarily imply higher profitability, and this is certainly an empirical issue that gave rise to an extensive list of studies in the USA and elsewhere. The evidence, to the extent that we know the literature, does not lend support to the view of 'market power', especially when the time span of the analysis is sufficiently long (Mueller 1990; Tsoulfidis and Tsaliki 2013; Shaikh 2016).

In closing the brief presentation of the way which the model of perfect competition was perceived by economists, we should refer to Schumpeter's (1942) keen analysis of competition. Schumpeter and also other Austrian economists (e.g. Kirzner 1987) are critical of the state conception of competition, either in its perfect or in its monopoly form. Schumpeter has many interesting insights on the nature of competition as a rivalrous process of discovery in which entrepreneurs seek new profit opportunities in a world whose only constant is its continued change; he is also famous for his oxymoron description of the dynamic competitive process known as 'creative destruction', whereby excess profits are not a sign of lack of vigorous competition but rather manifestation of entrepreneurial response to ever-changing market conditions. In spite of the realism of their premises, Austrian and also evolutionary economists have not managed, so far at least, to present their views in an accepted and, at the same time, a workable and testable model of competition. Furthermore, Schumpeter was dismissive of the idea of the supposedly existence of a perfectly competitive stage of capitalism, which, from a point onwards, was 'metamorphosed' to its 'monopolistic stage' (ibid, p. 81) and characterized the existence of such a stage of capitalism 'wishful thinking' (ibid, p. 106). Nevertheless, it is important to point out that Schumpeter is not always consistent with his views on competition as he was influenced by the writings of Chamberlin and other economists at Harvard University; thus, one cannot pinpoint with certainty what exactly he thinks, and it seems that he did not completely break with the neoclassical view although he notes that '[p]erfect competition is not only impossible but inferior' (ibid, p. 106).[11]

5.5 Competition as a Process of Rivalry

As we have already discussed in Sect. 5.2, classical economists, Smith, Ricardo and J.S. Mill, define competition as a process characterized by the free flow of capital and labour leading to the tendential equalization of inter-industry rates of profit. It is important to emphasize that the elimination of differences in inter-industry rates of profit and their long-term tendential equalization towards the economy's general rate of profit rate is attained through the acceleration or deceleration of capital accumulation (investment) and not necessarily by the entry or exit of firms. Thus, for classical economists competition is a dynamic process, and the equalization of industries' rates of profit takes place on an average through a 'cycle of fat and lean years'. Unlike the neoclassical analysis, it is clear that the classical approach to competition attempts to theorize the real features of the way in which markets function; it does not envision a hypothetical ideal market model and then to compare it with the actual functioning of markets in order to identify possible discrepancies.

Marx's analysis of competition is based and, at the same time, extends the classical conception of competition. The salient feature in Marx's analysis is that competition is a derived concept and not the starting point of the analysis. In fact, the starting point of Marx's analysis is the expansion of profits as an end in itself, and therefore the analysis of competition among capitals follows the laws of capital accumulation (Rosdolsky 1977; Shaikh 1980a; Semmler 1983). For example, Ricardo begins his analysis of the determination of the value of commodities by assuming at the outset that the equalization of the inter-industry rates of profit to the economy-wide one is the final result of the whole process. In contrast, for Marx, such a determination of values of commodities requires a number of intermediate steps which are detailed in the first two volumes of *Capital* and eight chapters from *Capital* III. As the units of capital strive to expand their market share, production and profits, they must take actions to confront the efforts of other similarly engaged units of capital. This is the reason that Marx argues that the analysis of the laws of accumulation, what he calls the 'inner nature of capital' (*Capital* I, p. 316), precedes the analysis of competition. And, furthermore, the competition of capitals is the mechanism by which the laws of capital accumulation be:

> felt by each individual capitalist, as external coercive laws.

> (*Capital* III, p. 592)

---

[11] See also Michaelides and Milios (2005).

For Marx, competition is envisioned as a turbulent and inherently violent process that resembles, in many respects, actual 'war' (Marx 1847). The market share of firms, for example, is like the territory of countries engaged in war, while technical change is like the arms race, since it is through technical change that firms can lower their unit cost and prices, attack their competitors and expand their market share at the expense of their competitors (Shaikh 1980a, b). The warlike aspect of competition in Marx is discussed in his writings already prior to *Capital* (e.g. Marx 1847) and also can be found in the writings of Engels, who generalized the rivalrous competition to many aspects of economic life. For instance, he notes:

> Competition is the completest expression of the battle of all against all which rules in modern civil society. This battle, a battle for life, for existence, for everything, in case of need a battle of life and death, is fought not between the different classes of society only, but also between the individual members of these classes. Each is in the way of the other, and each seeks to crowd out all who are in his way, and to put himself in their place. The workers are in constant competition among themselves as are the members of the bourgeoisie among themselves. The power-loom weaver is in competition with the hand-loom weaver, the unemployed or ill-paid hand-loom weaver with him who has work or is better paid, each trying to supplant the other.
>
> (Engels 1845, pp. 75–76)

Hence, the notion of capitalist competition is beyond the relationship of individual capitals with one another; it includes workers and potentially it extends to include government agencies, such as antitrust authorities and the like.

Marx's analysis of competition is further elaboration, extension and advancement of the analysis at a level much higher than that developed by the old classical economists. Hence, competition is described as a process of rivalry between involved entities in their incessant struggle for survival which, in the conditions of capitalism, is manifested by the insatiable desire of capital to obtain the largest possible profit as a condition sine qua non for its own survival. Their repressible desire for profit leads each capital in rivalry with any thing standing as an obstacle to fulfilling its primary objective. This rivalry, leading to the extinction of some capitals (firms) and the strengthening of others, turns:

- Each individual capital against others in the battle for a larger market share and the reduction of the number if not the displacement of other capitals
- Capital against labour in order to cut wages, increase length and intensity of labour process
- Capital against the state in order to eliminate any legal obstacles standing as barriers and restrictions to its actions
- State against other states to safeguard or even to conquer markets or sources of raw materials for their firms
- Workers against other workers for employment positions

Of course, here we can distinguish other more specific competitions such as between genders, races, employed versus unemployed and the young versus the older known as intergenerational competition, among others. In other words, capitalism creates the conditions for generalized competition; boldly put, 'war of all against all' according to the famous Hobbesian phrase which is similar to the Heraclitus' *dictum* that 'the father of all is *war* [= competition]'.

But if competition in Marx was confined to these avowedly highly interesting aspects, then essentially, we would be limited to Marx's political, sociological or philosophical writings and not his mature work in *Capital*. In this second and more mature stage of analysis, Marx argued that competition gives rise to a number of consequences with more and of course far-fetching implications which are not restricted to generalized rivalry; in particular, competition allows the 'laws of motion' that govern the capitalist society to become visible. Marx systematically develops such a theory of realistic competition, which is mainly found in *Capital* III, whereby, competition is described as warfare between units of capital literally battling 'over prices and markets'. Some central features of this conceptualization of competition also exist in the writings of Schumpeter (1942, 1954) and other Austrian economists, but the *differentia specifica* is that Marx distinguishes between the two moments of competition, namely, competition between and within industries. It is important to stress at this point that the introduction of the notion of regulating capital not only integrates the two moments of competition, but what is more important is that it derives regularities specific to each moment. Such a crucial distinction is not made, at least with the same analytical rigor and the same content, neither by the old classical economists nor by Schumpeter and the Austrian economists. The neoclassical economists, on the other hand while they distinguish between inter-industry and intra-industry competition, nevertheless their analysis is conducted mostly on formal and not on substantive grounds. For example, the equalization of profit rate must take place not only between but also within industries.

The salient feature of competition within industries is the prevalence of a single market price out of 'individual values of commodities', whereas the salient feature of competition between industries is the tendential equalization of the industrial rates of profit and the formation of the prices of production (*Capital* III, p. 180). In short, competition leads (tendentially) to the establishment of a common rate of profit and the formation of equilibrium prices across industries and a uniform price with differential rates of profit between firms in the same industry. In what follows, we analyse these two moments of competition and their synthesis through the concept of regulating capital and its relation to dominant technique.

5.5.1 *Competition Within Industries*

Starting with the aspect of competition between firms within an industry (*Capital* III, pp. 138–139, 178–186, 197–198 and 641–645), firms are viewed as large units of capital engaged in a fierce price-*war* with one another in their continuous struggle to secure and, if possible, to expand their *share* at the expense of their competitors. Capitals in this warlike competition are successful only by slashing unit costs through new innovations usually associated with the introduction of fixed capital enabling the further division of labour and increase in productivity, thereby making possible the undercutting of price, the elimination of competitors and competition itself at the end.

> The battle of competition is fought by cheapening of commodities. The cheapness of commodities depends, ceteris paribus, on the productiveness of labour and this again on the scale of production. Therefore, the larger capitals beat the smaller.
>
> *(Capital* I, p. 626)

Although Marx was writing in the nineteenth century, his analysis, contrary with the expectations of the monopoly school and other heterodox approaches, begins with large units of capital, which are already in the battle to reduce unit production costs through increasing mechanization. Thus, the units of capital that manage to innovate are in a position to undercut their selling price and increase their market share. Imitators cannot follow immediately for they are stuck with their fixed capital, which must be kept in operation for a certain period of time in order for their owners to be compensated for their investment at least up to a certain point. The innovators as they increase their capital per unit of output produced will temporarily decrease their profit rates. However, by decreasing the selling price of their commodity and expanding their market share, they raise their profit margin on sales (or cost), and gradually their rate of profit becomes from the highest, if not the top, in the industry. Eventually, all producers sell the same commodity for approximately the same price; thus, the first consequence of intra-industry competition is the establishment of the same price, or what is known as the 'law of one price' (LOOP) *(Capital* III, p. 865).

It is important to emphasize that the equalization of prices between firms (capitals) operating within an industry is only tendential, that is, all firms in an industry are likely to sell at approximately the same price. This does not mean that there is no dispersion in prices inside the industry, on the contrary; however, the expectation is that the standard deviation of this dispersion to vary from product to product and to depend on the different conditions of its provision, such as the proximity to the market, the lack of adequate information, the consumer habits and the like. Figure 5.4a exemplifies the price dispersion in accordance with the classical analysis of competition, while Fig. 5.4b illustrates the uniform pricing within the neoclassical analysis of perfect competition.

It follows, therefore, that firms with lower unit costs will end up making rates of profit in excess of those operating with higher unit costs since in the market all face approximately the same price. Hence, the LOOP imposes differential profitability between firms within the same industry, and this is the second consequence of intra-industry competition. The differential rates of profit within industries are expected to persist because some of the elements of production, such as location, climate, natural resources, management and the like, are not easily reproducible and because the innovative business activity and expectations are not the same (Shaikh 1980a; Semmler 1983). As a consequence, although both classical and neoclassical conception of competition have in common the LOOP, nevertheless the implications of this law are entirely different in the two approaches. In neoclassical economics, the LOOP is the consequence of firms' homogeneity, whereas in Marx and more generally in the classical approach, the same law reveals and underscores firm heterogeneity. In short, in Marx, firm heterogeneity is the corollary of the tendential

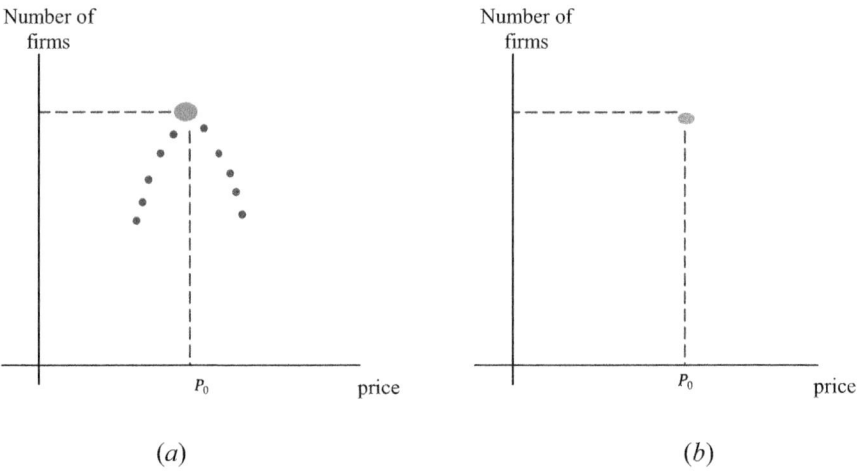

Fig. 5.4 Tendential equalization versus uniform price

establishment of the LOOP which gives rise to a stratification of both profit margins and rates of profit.[12] However, the ranking of the firms comprising the industry by no means remains the same and with the passage of time changes.

The numerical example of Table 5.1 below shows the effects of intra-industry competition on the profitability diversification within an industry. In this example, we hypothesize three firms (or units of capital) with different capital stocks (K) signifying differences in their production technique and therefore in their unit costs of production (k); the expectation is that the profit margin on sales to be proportional to capital stock.

The unit costs of the three firms in Table 5.1 are inversely related to their capital-output ratios (C/x). The idea is that the more mechanized the production process of a firm, the higher the productivity and therefore the lower the unit cost (see Chap. 4, Tables 4.1 and 4.2 and Fig. 4.3). The LOOP imposed by intra-industry competition leads to a hierarchy of profit margins on sales (m) and rates of profit (r); more specifically, the profit margins on sales together with the rates of profit will be higher for the firms with the higher capital-output ratio. As firms change their production process and efficiency over time, their position in industry's profitability scale may change. Moreover, at any given time, the presence of unequal rates of profit between firms within an industry does not necessarily signify monopoly or more generally power of firms over the market forces; contrary, differential profitability is the direct consequence of the process of real competition. One wonders whether the LOOP is established in international exchanges, and our answer is in the affirmative as we argue in Chap. 7.

---

[12]The intra-industry profit rates maybe in general the same only if there is perfect correlation between the capital-output ratios and profit margin on sales or costs. For instance, firms with capital-output ratio twice higher than that of others are expected to experience profit margins twice higher.

Table 5.1 Inter-industry competition and profit rate diversification

Capitals (firms)	Capital stock C	Per unit cost k	Per unit profit π	Output x	Price $P = k + \pi$	Profit margin $m = \pi/x$	Capital-output ratio C/x	Profit rate $r = m/(C/x)$
A	480	10	30	40	40	$30/40 = 0.75$	12	$0.75/12 = 6.25\%$
B	400	20	20	40	40	$20/40 = 0.50$	10	$0.50/10 = 5.00\%$
C	320	30	10	40	40	$10/40 = 0.25$	8	$0.25/8 = 3.12\%$

5.5.2 Competition Between Industries

The first consequence of competition between industries is the activation of such economic forces that ensure the tendential equalization of the rates of profit across industries towards an average one. These forces arise from the fact that capitals in every industry are compelled by competition to sell their commodities at prices that incorporate the economy-wide average rate of profit. The rationale behind the formation of the inter-industry average rate of profit is based on the following sequential stepwise process:

- If the rate of profit of an industry is above the economy-wide average, then the capital accumulation in the particular industry accelerates, as new capitals (inside or outside the industry) are attracted and engaged in investment.
- If the rate of profit of an industry is below the average, capital accumulation decelerates in the specific industry, and capital flows out to other more profitable industries.

We note that the tendential equalization of profit rates across industries is a long-run process and it does not exclude the entry or exit of new capitals. In general, industries with the highest rates of profit are expected to experience acceleration of investment, which increase their supply faster than their demand; as a consequence, the price of their product and their rate of profit are driven to lower levels, approaching the long-term average profit rate. The converse is true if the industry's rate of profit is lower than the economy's average; accumulation of capital, i.e. new investment and supply, will grow at a slower pace than industry's demand, causing prices to rise to a level that will incorporate the average rate of profit. According to Marx:

> Competition levels the rates of profit of the different spheres of production into an average rate of profit through the continual transfer of capital from one sphere to another. The fluctuations of profits caused by the cycle of fat and lean years succeeding one another in any given industry within given periods must, however, receive due consideration [...]. Experience shows, moreover, that if a branch of industry such as say, the cotton industry, yields unusually high profits at one period, it makes very little profit, or even suffers losses, at another, so that in a certain cycle of years the average profit is much the same as in other branches. And capital soon learns to take this experience into account.
>
> (*Capital* III, p. 208)

This turbulent process of equalization in the rates of profit means that the variation in industry's profitability does not follow any specific course; that is, the ranking of industries' rates of profit alternates over time. The mechanism that generates the tendential equalization of industry profitability is the acceleration or deceleration of capital accumulation and not necessarily the entry or exit of firms; that is, the continuous flows of capital in and out of industries in the incessant quest of profit opportunities. This process of continuous flow of capital does not imply that the rates of profit among industries converge to the economy's average rate of profit, $\bar{r}$, but rather it implies that this equalization is only attained on average and after the passage of long enough time. At any particular time, there are differences in the rates

profit rates

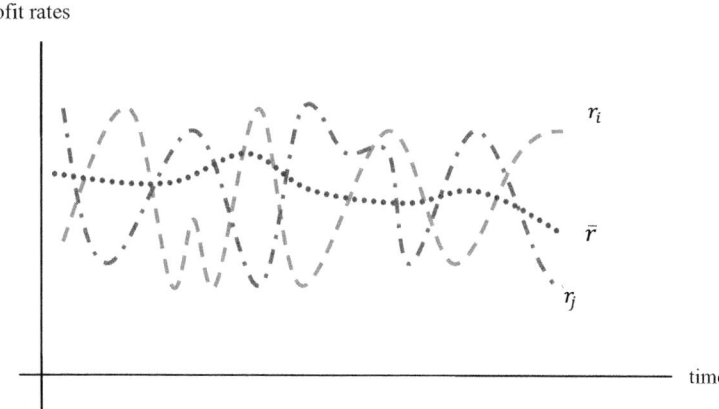

Fig. 5.5 Long-run tendential equalization of inter-industry profit rates

of profit between industries. Figure 5.5 shows such a long-run equalization process of industries i and j rates of profit to economy's average rate of profit, $\bar{r}$.

In Fig. 5.5, we observe that industries' rates of profit orbit around the economy's average one; and only over long stretches of time, the positive and negative deviations cancel each other out, establishing thus equalization towards an ideal average. That is to say, the average rate of profit is more of a conceptual device rather than an actual figure known a priori to any individual industry. The process of equalization of the rates of profit implies that each industry's rate of profit should repetitively cross over with the economy's average one. In econometric terms, the time series data of the deviation of an industry's rate of profit from the economy's average one should be stationary. In other words, the dispersion of the rates of profit around their average takes place quite regularly and never comes down to zero. This is equivalent to saying that the two rates of profit (r_i and r_j) do not converge to each other; in effect, they are unequal and only after long stretches of time adding up their positive and negative differences, we end up with a nearly zero outcome. Put it in statistical terms, the variance of the deviations of sectoral rates of profit from the economy's average is not expected to display any particular pattern over time.[13]

The second consequence of the tendential equalization of the rates of profit across industries is that the profit margins on sales (or on cost) are directly related to capital-output ratios. This result is derived in a straightforward manner from the definition of an industry's rate of profit. Thus, we can write

---

[13]For a formal presentation of the long-run equalization of the rates of profit as a gravitational process, see Duménil and Lévy (1987), Flaschel and Semmler (1987) and Tsaliki and Tsoulfidis (1998).

$$r_j = \left(\frac{s}{C}\right)_j = \frac{(s/x)_j}{(C/x)_j} = \frac{m_j}{(C/x)_j} \quad \text{or} \quad m_j = r_j(C/x)_j \qquad (5.1)$$

where r_j is industry's j rate of profit, s is total profits, C is fixed capital stock, x is gross output or total sales, m_j is its profit margin on sales and $(C/x)_j$ is its capital-output ratio. The above formulation shows the direct relationship between the profit margin on sales, m_j, of an industry j with its capital-output ratio $(C/x)_j$. Since inter-industry competition establishes the tendential equalization of the rates of profit across industries $(r_j \approx \bar{r})$, we have

$$m_j = \bar{r}(C/x)_j, \qquad (5.2)$$

which indicates that the profit margins on sales tend to be proportional to relative capital-output ratios.[14] Thus, the high profit margin on sales (or cost) of capital-intensive industries do not necessarily reflect a kind of monopoly power over the market forces ascertaining the operation of capitalist competition and the inter-industry equalization of profit rates to the economy-wide average.

For further elaboration, let us suppose industries i and j whose profit margins on sales are m_i and m_j, respectively; we may write

$$\frac{m_i}{m_j} = \frac{(C/x)_i}{(C/x)_j} \quad \text{and} \quad m_i \overset{<}{\underset{>}{-}} m_j \quad \text{in so far as} \quad \left(\frac{C}{x}\right)_i \overset{<}{\underset{>}{=}} \left(\frac{C}{x}\right)_j. \qquad (5.3)$$

Hence, the necessary condition for the tendential equalization of inter-industry profit rates to the economy's average is that the industries' profit margins on sales to be proportional to their respective capital-output ratios. In neoclassical economics, by comparison, inter-industry differences in profit margins are taken as prima facie evidence of imperfection of competition. The reason is that in perfect competition and in the long run, the profit margins on sales (or costs) are expected to equate to zero, because prices should be equal to average cost; otherwise they reflect some degree of power of firms or industries over the market forces. In contrast, in the classical theory of competition, this phenomenon is viewed not only as normal but also expected and manifested through the tendential equalization of the rates of profit.

The capital-output ratio indicates the degree of mechanization of an industry and simultaneously captures the size of the investment required per unit of sales. In the neoclassical theory of industrial organization, a high capital-output ratio is taken more often than not as a barrier to entry (minimum efficient plant) in the particular industry and, at the same time, as a deviation from the small (relative to the overall market) size of the firm required axiomatically for the fulfilment of the conditions of

---

[14]For the empirical investigation of this proposition along with others, see Shaikh (1980a and 2016), Semmler (1983), Ochoa and Glick (1992) and Tsaliki and Tsoulfidis (1998).

perfect competition. Therefore, in neoclassical, post-Keynesian and monopoly capital theories, the high positive correlation between the profit margins and capital-output ratios is viewed as evidence of the presence of oligopolistic conditions in the industry. By contrast, in the theory of real competition, this high positive correlation is an anticipated result of the competitive process itself. Furthermore, higher capital requirements just specify the form and input (or output) features in an industry, and they do not necessarily entail insurmountable obstacles to the flow of capital. In other words, the level of capital requirements determines the form of capital mobility, whether it will be less flexible in case of high capital requirements and more flexible where the investment requirements are small. The justification of this view is that the credit system is almost always ready to grant access to the necessary funding, provided that new investment promises profits even despite the high capital requirements. Moreover, as pointed out by Ricardo, the acceleration or deceleration of the new investments can be made by entities that are already active in the industry by just varying their equity and not necessarily by the entry or exit of new capitals.

Another 'equally interesting consequence' of inter-industry competition is that for industries with high capital-output ratio and thus high entry (and also exit) costs, variations in demand will be reflected more in variations in their capacity utilization and less in price variations caused by the acceleration or deceleration of capital accumulation. In other words, when demand changes, industries with a high capital-output ratio tend to absorb the changes in demand more through changes in the rate of capital utilization and employment and by far less in prices. As a consequence, these industries are characterized by a smaller percentage change in profit margin for each percentage change in sales, that is to say, with lower elasticity of profit margin with respect to sales. Hence, the stylized fact of price rigidities in industries with heavy capital requirements per unit of output is not necessarily a reflection of monopoly power but rather the expected result of the actual operation of competition.

In similar fashion, the rates of profit in these heavy capital requirements industries are also expected to display smaller variability than those industries characterized by light capital requirements per unit of output. The intuitive idea is that if more of the variability in demand is absorbed in output than in price changes, it follows that the rate of profit will be less variable in high capital-output ratio industries than in the low ones. Practically, this means that the heavy capital requirements industries will display rates of profit that will remain above (or below) the average for longer periods of time than the industries with light capital requirements (Botwinick 1993, pp.143–150). These consequences of inter-industry competition can be shown starting from the definition of the profit margin on sales $m = r(C/x)$ whose total differential (in discrete time) gives

$$\Delta m = r\Delta\left(\frac{C}{x}\right) + \Delta r\left(\frac{C}{x}\right) + \underbrace{\Delta r \cdot \Delta\left(\frac{C}{x}\right)}_{\approx 0}.$$

We divide through by m and we convert the above relationship in terms of percentages

$$\frac{\Delta m}{m} = r\frac{\Delta\left(\frac{C}{x}\right)}{r\left(\frac{C}{x}\right)} + \frac{\Delta r}{r} = \left[\frac{\frac{\Delta Cx - \Delta xC}{x^2}}{\frac{C}{x}}\right] + \frac{\Delta r}{r},$$

or

$$\frac{\Delta m}{m} = \frac{\Delta C}{C} - \frac{\Delta x}{Qx} + \frac{\Delta r}{r}$$

and

$$\frac{\Delta r}{r} = \frac{\Delta m}{m} + \frac{\Delta x}{x} - \frac{\Delta C}{C}.$$

By expressing the above relation in terms of elasticities with respect to sales (output), we may write

$$\frac{\Delta r\, x}{\Delta x\, r} = \frac{\Delta m\, x}{\Delta x\, m} + 1 - \underbrace{\frac{\Delta C\, x}{\Delta x\, C}}_{\approx 0}. \tag{5.4}$$

We stipulate that a percentage change in sales ($\Delta x/x$) or growth in demand leads to infinitesimally small changes in capital stock[15]; hence, for all practical purposes, we can set $\Delta C/C = 0$. In so doing, the elasticity of the rate of profit with respect to sales becomes proportional to the elasticity of the profit margin on sales. By invoking the second consequence of inter-industry competition according to which the profit margins on sales (cost) are directly related to industry's capital-intensity, it follows that an industry with higher capital-intensity relative to the economy-wide average will be characterized by relatively rigid profit margins on sales and hence low elasticity of profit margins with respect to the growth rate of demand. Moreover, the elasticity of the rate of profit with respect to demand will be proportional to the elasticity of the profit margin on sales.

Summing up, the observed relatively large amounts of reserve capacity and price rigidity in the capital-intensive industries have been interpreted by neoclassical, but also some heterodox, economists as indexes of monopoly power. However, on closer examination, these same phenomena are precisely those expected from the operation of actual competition between capitals. The firms in the heavy capital requirements industries tend to maintain relatively large amounts of reserve capacity; but this is quite normal for the size of these firms because it costs them less to accommodate variations in demand by fluctuations in their reserve capacity rather than by changes in prices. Only in the longer run are these large-size firms expected

---

[15]As explained above, industries with high capital requirements respond to changes in demand with changes in their degree of capacity utilization and not by changes in their invested capital.

to respond to persistent changes in demand by changing prices, profit margins on sales and rates of profit. Thus, if demand increases, the heavy capital requirements industries will experience high profits, as they increase their capacity utilization rate; at the same time, new investment and entry of firms in the industry are not easy because of high capital requirements. The converse will be true if demand falls; the increase in excess capacity and low profitability act in a way like disinvestment, while the exit of firms from these industries become costly in the short run (see also Shaikh 1980a; Semmler 1983, Chap. 3; Botwinick 1993, Chap. 4; Moudud 2010, Chap. 2).

5.5.3   The Regulating Capital

In the analysis of competition in *Capital*, we are confronted with the following seemingly contradictory situation where the tendential equalization of inter-industry rates of profit must come to terms with profit rate differentials between firms within the same industry. As we presented in the previous sections, the competition between industries establishes the tendential equalization of inter-industry rates of profit to the economy-wide average, whereas the competition within an industry brings about on the one hand the LOOP and on the other hand differential profitability among firms.[16] The answer to this seemingly paradoxical result is that the equalization of the rates of profit across industries takes place not for all but only for a specific type of capitals (firms) activated within industries known as the regulating capitals.

Classical economists were well aware of the limitations in the flows of capital[17] and considered that the relevant rate of profit which participates in the inter-industry equalization process is the one corresponding to the type of capital whose production conditions make possible the expansion or contraction of industry's capital accumulation and in this sense of 'marginal capital'.[18] In Ricardo (*Works* I, pp. 73, 86–87), for example, this kind of marginal capital is associated with the worst or, in Ricardo's wording, 'the most unfavourable' conditions of production, whereas on the other side of the spectrum with the best according to Mill (1848, p. 131). Smith's pin factory lies somewhere between these two extreme situations as he notes that this 'very trifling manufacturing' is the type of capital that changes take place and shape the rhythm of capital accumulation in the industry. Hence, new capitals are expected to enter into an

---

[16]The reason is that an industry consists of a number of firms of different efficiencies resulting from differences in management and other non-reproducible factors (location, climate, etc.); hence, some firms use the latest technology and ideal location, and some others are stocked with outdated technology and less privileged and therefore higher cost location.

[17]This is a reason for firms' heterogeneity within an industry.

[18]In a sense, classical economists had a view of marginal capital not in the neoclassical (or strictly mathematical) sense of infinitesimally small change but rather as the type of capital on which changes through investment flows take place.

industry with the method of production or technology of the marginal or regulating capital, which can be easily emulated, and, at the same time, the anticipated rate of profit is high enough. In fact, the regulating capital of each industry is a concept similar to what business people and also input-output economists call 'the best-practice method of production', which is not necessarily the top method or the worst but rather the one that makes the returns on investment worth taking.

More specifically, new competitors, by and large, aim at the most up-to-date available production conditions (or plants) in the industry and not the outdated or those of top efficiency. The outdated production methods, other things equal, display profitability lower than the average, whereas the most profitable methods of production may not be easily duplicated, or their reproduction may entail a certain degree of risk, thereby discouraging potential new entrants. According to Shaikh (2008, p. 167), the regulating conditions will differ in general from the industry's average, and they will be determined by the type of capital or technology in use associated with 'the lowest cost methods operating under generally reproducible conditions' defining the socially necessary labour time needed for the production of the commodity and by extent its value. Hence, investment flows are attracted, neither to the outmoded capitals simply because of their low profitability nor to the ultra-modern technologies because of their high risk. Consequently, during 'a cycle of fat and lean years', that is, over a long period of time, there is tendential equalization of inter-industry profit rates for the regulating capitals.

The regulating capital is the concept that integrates the intra-industry and inter-industry moments of competition. The profit rate of regulating capital determines the return on new investments and also guides the industry's growth rate. When two regulating capitals display differential profitability, new investment flows differently between the two industries; however, even an industry with low profitability will experience some new investments because of the presence of different expectations and uncertainty. Also, the regulating conditions do not necessarily determine a single profit rate but rather one with a relatively small dispersion range. This is true even in the case of a single regulating production method since there will always be differences in administrative capacities, demand, location and the like giving rise to differential profit rates. As a consequence, in a rather short span of time, the profit rates in regulating capitals of various industries may differ even significantly from each other and from the average and only after the passage of long time and on average there will be equalization of the rates of profit.[19]

The problem with the concept of regulating capital is its identification and quantification in actual economies. In principle, this appears theoretically, at least, possible by observing the evolution of an industry over time and collecting data for a group of firms with certain persistent characteristics. Practically, however, such observations are extremely difficult to obtain for all industries in a single year, let alone over many years. These difficulties lead to indirect methods of quantifying

---

[19]The discussion of the regulating conditions of production is intrinsically connected to the notion of dominant technique which is presented in Appendix 1.

the concept of regulating capital, and one of these is through the measurement of profit flows resulting from recent investment activity and the assessment of the corresponding rate of profit. Shaikh (1995, 2008) calls the particular rate of profit taking part in the equalization process incremental rate of return (IROR) on capital, and it can be approximated starting from the definition of the rate of profit

$$r_t = \frac{\pi_t}{C_{t-1}} \qquad \text{or} \qquad \pi_t = r_t C_{t-1}, \tag{5.5}$$

where r_t is the rate of profit, π_t is profits, C is fixed capital stock and t stands for time. Hence, the capital stock is lagged by one time period simply because profits come after and not simultaneously with investment. If we differentiate Eq. (5.5) with respect to C_{t-1}, we get

$$\frac{\mathrm{d}\pi_t}{\mathrm{d}C_{t-1}} = r_t + C_{t-1}\frac{\mathrm{d}r_t}{\mathrm{d}C_{t-1}} = r_t\left(1 + \frac{\mathrm{d}r_t}{\mathrm{d}C_{t-1}}\frac{C_{t-1}}{r_t}\right).$$

The term $\mathrm{d}\pi_t/\mathrm{d}C_{t-1}$ indicates the change in profits caused by a change in capital stock of the past period, which is equivalent to saying caused by investment flows of the past period, I_{Nt-1},[20] since $\mathrm{d}C_t = \Delta C_t = I_t - \delta C_{t-1} = I_{Nt} = $ net investment. Thus, we have

$$\mathrm{d}\pi_t/\mathrm{d}C_{t-1} \approx \Delta\pi_t/I_{Nt-1} = \rho_t, \tag{5.6}$$

which is the IROR, a concept introduced by Shaikh (1995) as a proxy for the rate of profit of regulating capitals.

If information about the best method of production used by enterprises in a sector is limited, the above relationship provides a practical way to determine ρ_t which is based on the reasonable assumption that investment flows are determined by short-term returns and not by the rate of profit throughout the length of time of the investment good in question. Hence, data on current firm's profits (π_t) can be partitioned into profits from recent investments, e.g. of previous year (ρI_{Nt-1}), and profits from earlier investments (π^*), which is current profits in the absence of new investments. That is, total firm's profits are defined as

$$\pi_t = \rho I_{Nt-1} + \pi^*.$$

Subtracting profits of previous periods from both sides of the above equation we get

---

[20]This is derived from the usual definition of the capital stock, $C_t = (1 - \delta)C_{t-1} + I_t$, where δ is the depreciation rate and I_t is gross investment.

$$\pi_t - \pi_{t-1} = \rho I_{Nt-1} + (\pi^* - \pi_{t-1})$$

or

$$\Delta\pi_t = \rho I_{Nt-1} + (\pi^* - \pi_{t-1}).$$

The term in parenthesis $(\pi^* - \pi_{t-1})$ is expected to be smaller, much smaller than the term ρI_{Nt-1}, and for all practical purposes, it can be ignored, since the shorter the time horizon of estimation, the current total profits will refer to profits derived from the recent investment (I_{Nt-1}) and less from profits from the already existing capital (or accumulated investment).[21] Therefore, the current rate of return of new investment is

$$\rho_t = \Delta\pi_t / I_{Nt-1}, \tag{5.7}$$

that is, the change in industry profits over investment in previous period.[22] In other words

$$\frac{\Delta\pi_t}{\Delta C_{t-1}} = \rho_t = r_t\left(1 + \frac{\Delta r_t}{\Delta C_{t-1}} \frac{C_{t-1}}{r_t}\right). \tag{5.8}$$

The term $(\Delta r_t/\Delta C_{t-1})(C_{t-1}/r_t)$ above stands for the elasticity of the rate of profit with respect to capital stock for which the following hold

$$\left(\frac{dr_t}{dC_{t-1}} \frac{C_{t-1}}{r_t}\right)\overset{>}{\underset{<}{=}}0 \qquad \text{then} \qquad \rho_t\overset{>}{\underset{<}{=}}r_t. \tag{5.9}$$

Clearly, the volatility of ρ_t is determined by the elasticity of the rate of profit with respect to capital stock, and the variability of this elasticity is what distinguishes the IROR from the usual average rate of profit.

In effect, ρ_t is a key variable whose variability reflects the effects of a number of key factors, such as the wage share, labour productivity, capacity utilization and capital capacity-output ratio, which are important in business decisions. We can show these relations starting from the definition of value of current output (or income), x, as

---

[21]Moreover, as uncertainty and risk with respect to profitability increase with the passage of time, it is reasonable to assume that short term (1 year, or fraction of a year in case we have quarterly data) is the relevant time horizon of entrepreneurs. Furthermore, current profits are influenced by many ephemeral factors, and particularly high or low profits affect investment decisions accordingly which in turn raise new uncertainty, etc. Keeping this in mind, it is reasonable to assume that expectations about returns on investments are near-sighted and are determined by the short-term performance of the firm.

[22]It is worth pointing out that the IROR is closely related to another profitability index, the marginal efficiency of capital, (d), which is widely used in industrial economics and investment decisions of the firms (see Appendix 2).

$$x_t = r_t C_{t-1} + w_t l_t,$$

where w_t is the wage rate and l_t is the employment at time t. Taking the first differences and dividing by ΔC, we get

$$\frac{\Delta x_t}{\Delta C_{t-1}} = r_t + C_{t-1}\frac{\Delta r_t}{\Delta C_{t-1}} + w\frac{\Delta l_t}{\Delta C_{t-1}} + \frac{\Delta w_t}{\Delta C_{t-1}}l_t = \rho_t + w_t\left[\frac{\Delta l_t}{\Delta C_{t-1}} + \frac{\Delta w_t}{\Delta C_{t-1}}\frac{l_t}{w_t}\right].$$

Solving for ρ_t

$$\rho_t = \frac{\Delta x_t}{\Delta C_{t-1}}\frac{C_{t-1}}{x_t}\left[1 - w\frac{l_t}{x_t}\left(\frac{\Delta l_t}{\Delta x_t}\frac{x_t}{l_t} + \frac{\Delta w_t}{\Delta x_t}\frac{x_t}{w_t}\right)\right]u_t\left(\frac{x_t}{C_{t-1}}\right)^*. \qquad (5.10)$$

From the last expression, we observe that the incremental rate of return on capital is positively related to:

- Income (output) elasticity with respect to capital[23]

$$\frac{\Delta x_t}{\Delta C_{t-1}}\frac{C_{t-1}}{x_t}$$

- Capacity utilization ratio of capital

$$u_t = \left(\frac{x_t}{C_{t-1}}\right)$$

- Growth rate of labour productivity

$$\frac{\Delta l_t}{\Delta x_t}\frac{x_t}{L_t}$$

- Normal output-capital ratio

$$\left(\frac{x_t}{C_{t-1}}\right)^*$$

Moreover, the IROR is negatively related to the

- The wage share

---

[23]It goes without saying that this elasticity, in the case of one good world or with same sectoral capital-labour ratios, equals to profit share.

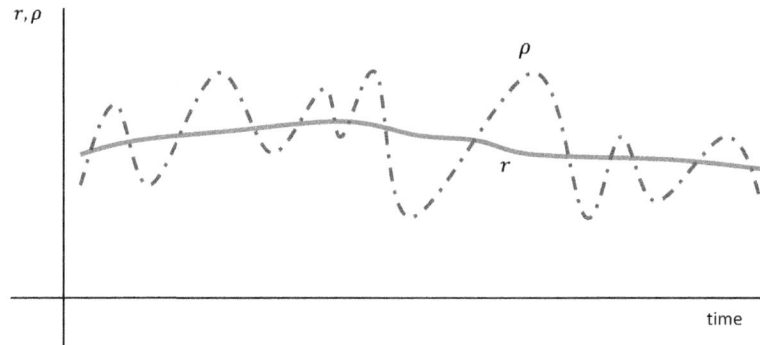

Fig. 5.6 Industry's average rate of profit vs. IROR

$$w\frac{l_t}{x_t}$$

- The wage elasticity with respect to income

$$\frac{\Delta w_t}{\Delta x_t}\frac{x_t}{w_t}$$

Figure 5.6 below depicts the expected trajectories of the usual average rate of profit of an industry and the IROR of the same industry. The IROR is designed and therefore is expected to reflect the uncertainty and all the noise and short-run behaviour in the economy. Thus, the IROR is depicted as orbiting around the industry-wide average rate of profit which displays much less variability.

Figuratively speaking, the two measures of profitability share approximately the same mean, although the variability of the IROR is much higher than that of the average rate of profit. The justification is that the average rate of profit is the profits of all firms comprising the industry divided by the total capital of the industry; as a result, in the so-estimated average are included firms with excessively high profitability and firms with the lowest one. As a consequence, such extreme rates of profits will most likely tend to cancel each other out giving rise to an average rate of profit with relatively low variability. By contrast, the group of firms forming the regulating conditions of production pretty much depicts the same type of production methods and consists of those firms, where the bulk of inflow and outflow of investment takes place; thus, their mean profitability is expected to display considerably more variability than that of the industry-wide average one. Hence, the standard deviation of the regulating firms' rate of profit will be higher than that of the rate of profit of all firms comprising the industry.

The notion and operation of the regulating capital and regulating production methods give rise to phenomena that easily can be interpreted as evidence of monopolistic or oligopolistic behaviour. Because the price of production of regulating capital forms the ground on which industry's market price is formed, the regulating capital (or firm) can be seen as industry's dominant firm that imposes its price policy. But in reality, what happens is that the production conditions and the rate of profit of the regulating capital are those prevailing through inter-industry competitive process as the industry representative (not necessarily average) conditions participate in the process of the tendential equalization of inter-industry profit rates.

It is interesting to note that the ratio of the IROR to the industry's average rate of profit, which we may call the profit-flatness ratio (PFR),[24] reflects the extent to which the constituent firms in an industry perform the same way with the leading firms or the most efficient ones. In real life, the PFR shows the extent to which the average-practice technologies keep up with the best-practice technologies within the same industry. If, for example, $\rho/r > 1$, it means that the leading or rather the regulating firms are doing better than the average, which might be the usual case in manufacturing industries. We may also have the case where $\rho/r < 1$, an outcome which is expected in agriculture or mining industries, where the regulating firms are the least efficient ones, since the expansion or contraction of economic activity takes place in the least productive parcels of land or mines.

5.6 Summary and Conclusions

In this chapter we argued that the concept of competition as a rivalry process of economic units, developed by classical economists and Marx, and to some extent by Austrian economists, is a realist approach to the way in which firms operate and compete with each other in real economies. In contrast, the popular nowadays neoclassical theory of perfect competition did not arise from the observation of the real competition, but it was rather the necessary mathematical add-on to the neoclassical paradigm in order to reach a number of conclusions that result by the optimal behaviour of economic agents (producers and consumers). We have also shown, through the logical critique of Sraffa, that the theory of the perfectly competitive firm leads to absurd conclusions and led to the development of the models of imperfectly competitive market structures (monopoly, oligopoly among others). The end result of this was the promotion and ultimately establishment of the perfect competition as a reference model which could evaluate the deviation of actual from its ideal form. A basic reason for this domination is linked to the idea that imperfect market forms are analysed with the use of tools found within the perfect competition framework.

Subsequently, we examined the theory of classical competition, as developed in Marx's texts, and other economists who accept the process concept of cut-throat

---

[24]The PFR is a concept that has not been tested so far, and it would be interesting to see its use in real economies.

competition. We introduced the concepts of inter-industry and intra-industry competition and their synthesis which is the regulating capital. We argued that this alternative theory of competition presents unexplored, until now, properties that should become the focus of future research efforts. By a way of an example, it has been shown that the incremental rate of profit is one of the fundamental variables in determining the stock profitability index in the US economy and Japan (Shaikh 1995; Tsoulfidis et al. 2015). Still, there are similar findings for a number of other countries lending further support to the explanatory power 'contained' in the evolution of the IROR.

Appendices

Appendix 1: Dominant Technique and Regulating Production Conditions

The discussion on regulating capital and conditions of production makes us to take a closer look at the regulating capital which in one way or another is associated with the dominant technique in relative and not necessarily in the absolute sense of the term. The dominant technique is important in its own right for it is inextricably connected to the theories of value and distribution. Starting with the old classical approach, the dominant technique is identified, at least as a first approximation, with the commonly used technique in operation. In the neoclassical approach, Marshall's concept of the 'representative firm' may be different from the average or the best kind of business in an industry, but it is broad enough to encompass those firms using the technique that dominates in the sense that it determines the equilibrium price and defines the rate of capital accumulation in a given industry.

The most comprehensive analysis of the concept of dominant (regulating) technique is found at a very abstract level of analysis in *Capital* I where the average technique determines the value or direct price of a commodity. At a lower (and therefore much more concrete) level of abstraction, the dominant technique is related to regulating or threshold (marginal) method, which could be linked to either higher production costs or lower production cost technique in an industry as long as this technique is accessible to new investors. Thus, the dominant technique is identified with the lower cost production technique generally accessible to new entrants in the industry and defines the regulating capitals where the acceleration or deceleration of investment activity takes place (Tsaliki and Tsoulfidis 2010, 2015). The dominant technique could match the best type of capitals (firms), if they were accessible to newcomers, or even the worst kind of capitals if they happen to be the only ones available for prospective investors (such as usually happens in agriculture and mining). The so-defined dominant technique in effect describes the production conditions of the regulating capitals in an industry which determine the socially necessary labour time required for the production of a commodity. Thus, at the very high level of abstraction in *Capital* I, the dominant technique is associated with the average capital, and the value (or direct price) is determined by using this average technique.[25] According to Marx:

> The labour-time socially necessary is that required to produce an article under the normal conditions of production, and with the average degree of skill and intensity prevalent at the time. The introduction of power-looms into England probably reduced by one-half the labour required to weave a given quantity of yarn into cloth. The hand-loom weavers, as a matter of fact, continued to require the same time as before; but for all that, the product of one hour of their labour represented after the change only half an hour's social labour, and consequently fell to one-half its former value.
>
> (*Capital* I, p. 39)

From the above it follows that a whole spectrum of techniques is in use within the same industry producing commodities of different unit values; if every of the produced commodities were sold at its unit value, that is, according to its labour embodied, then we would arrive at the absurd result that the least efficient producers would produce the most valuable commodities. This paradoxical result is resolved in *Capital* I, by hypothesizing the average technique as the dominant (regulating) one, in the relative sense of the term, namely, the production conditions associated with the production of commodities that embody the socially necessary labour time; the latter, in turn, determines the value or direct price that acts as a centre of gravity for market value. In fact, the market is indifferent to the deviations in the embodied labour time in each particular unit of commodity produced by individual capitals and treats all participants indiscriminately with the same market value. Thus, within the same industry, the individual values of backward producers are higher than the average, whereas the individual values of the more efficient producers are lower than the average. Finally, in *Capital* III where the inter-industry and intra-industry competition as well as the formation of the average rate of profit are introduced, Marx inserts into the analysis the concept of regulating capital as the more concrete expression of dominant technique and arrives at the conclusion that producers, with a unit value below the average or market value, extract surplus profits, whereas the converse is true for the less efficient producers (*Capital* III, p. 178).

Let us now further illustrate the above by hypothesizing three producers (or groups of firms) activated in an industry, the better (A), the average (B) and the worse (C). The characterizations have to do with the type of technology employed by each type of producer and the associated productivities and unit values. Clearly, the better conditions correspond to a more leading-edge technology relative to the average, to higher than average productivity and therefore to lower than average unit value; whereas the worse conditions correspond to an outmoded technology, lower than average productivity and higher than average unit value. A graphical representation of the above three conditions is illustrated in Fig. 5.7, where we depict the three types of capital, A, B and C whose output x is shown on the

---

[25]More specifically, the value of a commodity (and its monetary expression, the direct price) equals to the ratio of total abstract labour time expended in the production over the total number of goods produced.

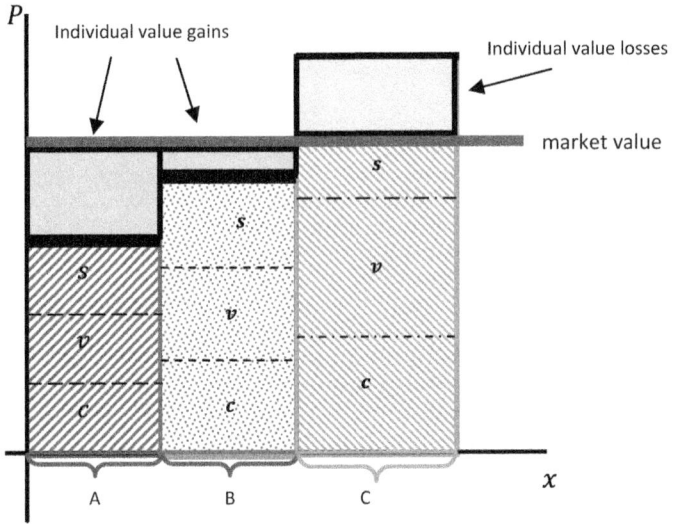

Fig. 5.7 Social value as an average (market) value

horizontal axis; capital B's individual value, P, measured on the vertical axis is closer, but it does not necessarily coincide with the market value, that is, the one associated with the socially necessary labour time. From this simple presentation, we can see that intra-industry transfers of value take place from the least efficient producer type C to the more efficient producers of types A and B in inverse proportion to their unit values, estimated for each particular industry as the sum of constant capital, c, variable capital, v, and surplus-value, s. It is important to bear in mind that the market value may coincide with the individual value produced by the average type of capital only by a fluke.

The difference between the individual from the market value and the associated possibility of gains in values of the more efficient at the expense of the less efficient producers is what really motivates technological change. Every unit of capital strives to undercut its unit cost by keeping wages low, extending the length of the working day and intensifying the labour process. But such methods have only limited impact on unit costs and, therefore, are by far inferior to those derived from the advancement in new technologies, which undercut the unit values below the average market value and bring about extra surplus-value for the innovators.[26]

The second notion of market value is introduced in Chap. X of *Capital* III (p. 178), and it is associated with the type of capitals producing 'the great mass' of

---

[26]The non-uniform individual values (or unit costs) of firms comprising the industry leads neoclassical economists to perceive them as forming a step industry supply schedule and in turn to hypothesize infinitesimally small differences and to arrive at the usual supply schedule while the market value forms a horizontal demand curve.

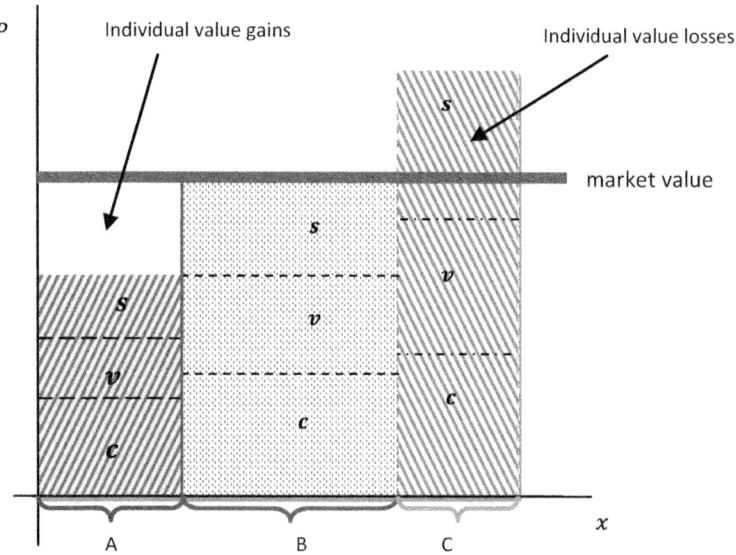

Fig. 5.8 Market value determined by the bulk of commodities

commodities in an industry. Figuratively speaking, this case of the bulk of commodities might be depicted in Fig. 5.8 below.

As the greater bulk of commodities is produced by type B capitals (or firms), it follows that these are going to determine the weighted average value and, therefore, the market value of commodities. As a result, a transfer of values takes place only from type C firms (or capitals) to those of type A, whereas type B capitals realize fully in the market the value they produce. Clearly, the two notions of market value which are determined either by the simple average or 'the great mass average' are expected to be close to each other.

The dominant technique associated with the average value is not, therefore, an engineering or purely statistical concept, but an economic one. State-of-the-art or outmoded techniques may coexist with the so to speak regulating or price-determining technique of production, which at this stage is an average (simple or weighted) of all possible techniques that are activated in a particular industry. It is important to emphasize at the outset that the use of the so-defined average technique is not necessarily a bad approximation to reality. That is to say, the average technique and the associated average value, in most cases, is a good first good approximation of the centre of gravity around which market prices fluctuate. However, when the analysis becomes more concrete, as is in *Capital* III where the competition of capitals is introduced, the notion of socially necessary labour time expands to account for the particular conditions characterizing each individual industry.

The determination of the value of commodities which is the basis for the formation of the regulating price (equilibrium price or price of production) of a commodity is specified in the sphere of production and is modified in the sphere of circulation, according to the difference between the expected and the realized demand. Thus, if the production of commodities in an industry exceeds the amount actually demanded, then two outcomes may occur:

- Less product will be sold at the current market price which coincides with the social value that encompasses the social necessary labour value.
- If all production is to be sold, the market price of the product should be less than its social value, in order for the supply to meet demand.

In both cases, the realized socially necessary labour time in the sphere of circulation deviates from that realized in the sphere of production. The same takes place for the total value of commodities produced which, however, does not disappear; in the first case, the value is just stored in the form of unsold commodities for future needs, whereas in the second, as we will discuss next, is transferred to other industries.

Until now the discussion was limited to the intra-industry competition and the LOOP; the inter-industry competition establishes a uniform rate of profit which allows the formation of prices of production or equilibrium prices (*Capital* III, p. 180). Together, inter-industry and intra-industry competition set up the regulating conditions (techniques) of production that determine the pace of expansion or contraction of accumulation in the industry. Figuratively speaking, we may distinguish three cases in inter-industry competition (Fig. 5.9). The different outcomes arise from the fact that each industry is characterized by different regulating production conditions and by extent dominant technique. Hence, in industry C the regulating capital coincides with that of group C, in industry B with group B and in industry A with group A.

Let us now assume that we deal with an industry in which the expansion or contraction of accumulation takes place in group C, that is, the least efficient firms set the market value of the commodity; hence, the dominant technique and by extent the regulating production conditions are defined by the capital with the higher per unit labour value. With a price of production determined by the least efficient producers, the more efficient ones sell at market value that secures profits in excess of their produced surplus-value; the additional surplus-value is transferred to them from other industries. This is a case usually identified with Ricardo's analysis of agricultural and mineral production, where capital accumulation, usually, takes place in the least productive parcels of land or mines and the more efficient parcels of land give rise to differential rents. The size of differential rents equals the value transfers into the more efficient firms activated in the more fertile parcels of land.

Let us now hypothesize the other extreme situation which coincides with Mill's argument, where the dominant technique is associated with the most efficient producers (industry A), who set the market value (lowest market value in Fig. 5.9). Under these circumstances, there is no transfer of surplus-value into the industry, and the less efficient producers for such a low market value are either eliminated, or a portion of their surplus-value is transferred to other industries, since in the market they manage to realize less value than that brought. In these conditions, the dominant

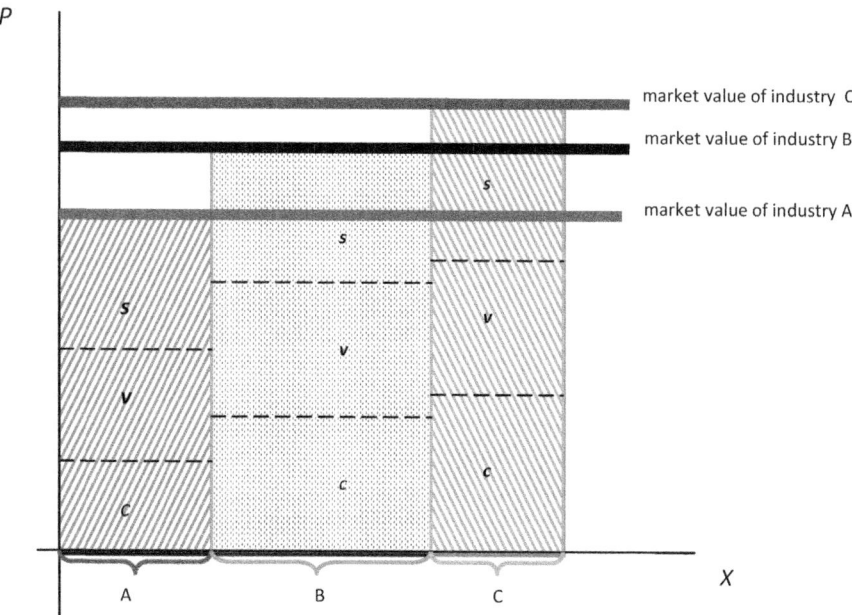

Fig. 5.9 Market value determined by the marginal technique

technique is also the one dominating absolutely because of its association with the most efficient producers. Finally, industry B in Fig. 5.9 presents the case where the average conditions of production are the regulating (dominant) ones in the industry. In this case, due to competition between and within industries and the formation of the corresponding laws, LOOP and tendential equalization of profitability, we may have both inter-industry and intra-industry transfers of surplus-value.

An increase (or decrease) in demand raises the market price higher (lower) than the market value, and so there is excess (deficient) profitability that accelerates (decelerates) capital accumulation; this change in profitability determines the type of regulating capital and the associated with it dominant or price-determining technique. In general, if demand keeps rising for a particular industry, because of capacity constraints, surplus profits will be transferred towards this industry, and a larger number of less efficient firms will manage to survive. The converse is true for a contracting demand which makes more and more difficult the survival of the less efficient firms by squeezing the excessive profits transferred to the more efficient ones.[27]

---

[27]It is important to note that capital accumulation takes place in all types of capital. The *differentia specifica* between the regulating from the other types of capital is that the former becomes the locus, where the acceleration or deceleration of capital accumulation takes place. This does not mean that there is no investment activity in the other types of capital; on the contrary, even in the case of the worst type of capitals, entrepreneurs are forced to stay active because of the maintenance of their fixed capital which locks them in for long periods of time.

The departure from the notion of average to that of the marginal conditions and techniques of production is a great advancement of classical economists and Marx, which has not received the attention that it deserves. Despite the differences, the idea of marginal analysis is indispensable in both classical and neoclassical approaches. In neoclassical theory, the marginal analysis is explicitly incorporated through the use of calculus. In effect, the notion of substitutability, absolutely necessary for neoclassical theory, makes the infinitesimal changes decisive both in consumers' choice of demand for goods and the producers' choice of cost-minimizing technique. By contrast, in the classical analysis, the term 'marginal' is used to signify the changing conditions which may be associated with pretty substantial changes, e.g. in agriculture or mining, new parcels of land are brought into cultivation, and in manufacturing new quantities of capital may be invested. These changes are by no means infinitesimal, because in the classical thinking, consumption patterns and technology are rigid and, therefore, insensitive to infinitesimal small changes in prices. Furthermore, in the classical analysis, the concept of the marginal is being used in order to establish limits which in turn determine the range of possible variations in variables, such as normal price and output produced.

However, when it comes to practical matters, most of the empirical literature, neoclassical or classical in the absence of data on marginal variables, often resorts to the (weighted) average of variables, in the statistical sense. The notion of 'best practice technology' (Salter 1966) in business and input-output literature (Miller and Blair 2009) is essentially an effort to differentiate between average and dominant technique. In the same spirit is the concept of the 'survivor technique' which avoids both the problems of valuation of resources and the hypothetical nature of the technological studies (Stigler 1969).

The implications of the analysis regarding the dominant technique along the classical lines can be found in the discussions on the choice of technique which usually refers to the most efficient (minimum cost) technique. As we discussed, this assumption is not necessarily realistic, in as much as the minimum cost technique, for a number of reasons, may differ from the dominant technique. Moreover, it is important to stress at this point once more that by restricting to the average instead of the more appropriate dominant technique does not necessarily introduce substantial biases, for example, in the estimation of direct or prices of production; but, at the same time, one should not abandon the idea of further concretisation of the notion of dominant technique. The discussion on dominant technique and domestic competition extends to international competition in Chap. 7.

Appendix 2: The IROR and Marginal Efficiency of Capital

There is a close relationship between the IROR and the marginal efficiency of capital or rather marginal efficiency of capital (MEC) or investment. In effect, starting with the well-known definition of the MEC, d

$$I_{t-1} = \frac{\pi_t}{1+d} + \frac{\pi_{t+1}}{(1+d)^2} + \ldots$$

where I is the investment expenditures on the supply price of capital according to Keynes (1936, Chap. 11), S is the expected profits and t is time. The first derivative of investment with respect to d is

$$\frac{dI_{t-1}}{dd} = -\frac{\pi_t}{(1+d)^2} - \frac{2\pi_{t+1}}{(1+d)^3} - \ldots$$

In turn, if we assume that $\pi_t = \pi_{t+1} = \ldots = \pi$, a usual and realistic assumption, then investment will be less attractive as the time horizon of the entrepreneur extends. In other words, the marginal return on capital systematically encourages short-run investment. If now, based on the myopic expectations of investors, we define the analysis to 1 year, we get

$$d = \frac{\pi_t}{I_{t-1}} - 1.$$

Once investment is financed from profits, then both profitability indicators, the incremental rate of return on capital (ρ) and the marginal efficiency of capital (d), are very closely related to each other, and one does not expect to find huge differences in their evolution over time.[28]

---

[28]In the recent years, the MEC is one of the major variables reported in AMECO's database (http://ec.europa.eu/economy_finance/ameco/user/serie/SelectSerie.cfm) estimated as the current change in real GDP over the midyear real investment.

Part II
Competition, Trade and Long Cycles:
Theory and Empirical Evidence

Chapter 6
Real Competition and Empirical Evidence

Abstract The empirical aspects of the classical theory of competition are examined as well as the extent to which a central proposition or economic law of the classical theory of competition, that is, the inter-industry equalization of profit rates, is confirmed. The discussion extends to include important issues of classical competition, such as the presence of monopoly in actual economies and whether or not phenomena usually attributed to monopoly and its power over market forces may have an explanation based on the classical theory of competition. The empirical research refers to the Greek economy, continues with the Japanese and ends with the US economy. Empirical results corroborate the classical theory of competition and the tendential equalization of inter-industry profit rates and rule out the case of monopoly and its power over market forces.

Keywords Interindustry equalization of profit rates · Monopoly power · Concentration · Profit margins · Regulating capital · Actual economies

6.1 Introduction

The purpose of this chapter is to examine if and to what extent the classical theory of competition is consistent with the empirical facts and may shed further light on some phenomena usually attributed to monopoly power. The discussion and empirical investigation are based on the dialectical separation of competition within and between industries and their integration in the concept of regulating capital.

The analysis begins with intraindustry competition in the Greek economy by examining whether and to what extent the profit margins on sales of industries depend on their degree of concentration or monopolization. We deal with this issue using cross-sectional data from 91 industries (three-digit SIC) from the industrial censuses of the years 1978, 1984 and 1988. The availability of data on the Greek manufacturing industries and the fact that most empirical studies on monopoly refer to the US economy shifted our focus to a less well-known economy. In this effort, we present and critically review the findings of similar empirical studies for the USA and other economies.

The second major issue that we attempt to shed light on is to what extent, if any, there is a tendential equalization of rates of profit across industries. For this purpose, we utilize data from 20 Greek manufacturing industries spanning the period 1959–1991, 52 Japanese manufacturing industries spanning the period 1974–2008 and 24 US industries spanning the period 1980–2016. It goes without saying that our investigation requires long-run time series data on profit rates for a sufficiently detailed industry classification. Such data are available for a number of countries, and from these, we opted to use the available from domestic sources for Greece and Japan. We also report results for the US economy using time series data available from the KLEMS (www.euklems.net) database, providing that the analysis for other major economies is not expected to give very different results.

6.2 Competition or Monopoly in Greek Manufacturing Industries?

As we have pointed out in Chap. 5, the concept of monopoly pops out once one accepts the notion of perfect competition; hence monopoly is defined as the direct other side of perfect competition, both reflecting the quantitative aspect of the neoclassical conceptualization of competition. Characteristically, the intensity of competition in neoclassical economics depends upon the number of participants in the market; the analysis may begin with a single producer, that is, a monopoly, and may continue by expanding to include the duopoly, triopoly and oligopoly up to the 'attainment' of the upper limit, that is, the infinite number of infinitesimal, relative to the size of the market, producers. The scene is set, then; *with such a theoretical background*, it comes as no surprise that in neoclassical economics, the 'manyness' and its quantification through an index, such as the degree of concentration, become a key feature defining a whole new field of economics, that is, industrial organization. As a consequence, most studies subject to empirical testing the presence of monopoly power in an industry by examining various measures of profitability (profit rate, profit share, profit margin on sales or costs) against the degree of concentration of the industry under study. A positive and statistically significant relationship between the degree of concentration and profitability is considered prima facie evidence of monopoly power lending support to the view that firms possess power over the market forces and through that extract excessive profits.

All economic approaches agree that profits are the difference between sales (or value of shipments) minus the cost of production. The trouble begins with the definition and, therefore, the proper estimation of cost in that whether one should include or not the opportunity cost. In the classical approach, the definitions of cost are not different than that in the accounting identified with the sum of prime (materials and wage) cost plus depreciation of fixed capital. By contrast, neoclassical economics on top of these explicit costs adds opportunity or implicit costs usually identified with the product of interest rate (the least questionable available alternative) times the invested capital. It is important to stress at this point that the opportunity cost only augments the total cost, but not the marginal cost on the basis of which the entrepreneurial decisions are made.

The proper measurement of profit is a challenging issue to neoclassical economics for which there is no consistency to the theory solution (Tsaliki 2006). In the empirical studies of industrial organization, however, neoclassical economics resorts also to accounting profits and disregards the basis on which profitability is estimated. In effect, any base (sales, cost or capital stock) could be used, and what matters is only the extent to which the estimated profitability exceeds the economy-wide average reflecting the lack of adequate competition. In the classical analysis, by contrast, is of extreme importance the base upon which profitability is estimated. In particular, the meaningful estimate of profitability is on the invested capital; the latter is motivated by profits, not profits in general but rather as a (rate of) reward or compensation for the invested capital. The rationale is that the current and past profitability is crucial in the determination of the future expected profitability which actually shapes the entrepreneurial decisions with regard to the expansion or contraction of investment in the current or in alternative activities. Moreover, the equalization of inter-industry profit rates on invested capital to an average gives rise to differential profit margins on sales or costs as we discussed in Chap. 5, that is, the profit margins on sales or costs are expected to be higher in industries with higher capital-intensity, as measured by the capital to sales ratio. Such a relationship described by Eq. (5.3) is absolutely consistent with the long-run tendential equalization of profit rates to the economy-wide one, as the only way that firms, activated in capital-intensive industries, be compensated for their high capital requirements.

In what follows, using data from the Greek economy, we put under empirical investigation the claim that profit margins on sales depend on industries' degree of concentration. It is worth pointing out that in the 1980s, there have been several studies examining the competitive conditions in Greek manufacturing industries reflecting the antimonopoly atmosphere of the period and the desire for policy intervention of the socialist government in order to reduce the alleged excessive profits enjoyed by the 'greedy and voracious' monopolies (Droucopoulos 1979, 1991; Dragasakis 1981; Pakos 1982; Doxiadis 1984; Chasid 1987; Bourlakis 1988).[1] It is ironic that notwithstanding all of the above, studies were inspired by socialist ideals and nevertheless shared a common feature; they were entrenched in the neoclassical conceptualization of competition and implicitly recognized that

---

[1]For instance, Droucopoulos (1991, p. 117), although he noted that between the years 1978 and 1984 the degree of concentration in most industries declined, nevertheless he concluded that the oligopolistic nature of the Greek manufacturing continued; such a conclusion shows that he was influenced by the antimonopoly stance of the socialist-oriented economists of that period. Returning on the same issue, Droucopoulos and Papadogonas (2000) using detailed data sets argued that the degree of concentration of Greek large-scale (that is, establishments operating with at least ten workers) industry for the years 1989 to 1992 has not changed substantially.

perfect competition is a desirable market structure because of lower prices and higher output compared monopoly or monopolistic competition and also in the long run earns normal profits as opposed to monopoly featuring supernormal profits.

For the purpose of the analysis, we employ data at the 3-digit industry detail giving a classification of 91 large-scale (establishments employing at least 10 workers) industries for 3 manufacturing censuses (of the years 1978, 1984 and 1988) conducted by the National Statistical Service of Greece. The employed concentration ratios of the industries refer to the percentage employment of the top 4 firms over the total employment in the industry of each of the 91 large-scale industries; unfortunately, there are no data on firms' sales to estimate the respective concentration ratios, the usual index in many studies of the field; it is recognized though that both bases (employment or sales) are highly correlated (Scherer and Ross 1990; Sawyer 1981) and therefore they are likely to give rise to qualitatively similar results.

The employed proxy for profitability is the share of gross profits estimated in producer prices (prices received by producers) to total sales of large-scale industry. Note that for the year 1978, while census data on employment are available, we lack the necessary information on sales per establishment, as well as the detailed components of value-added of each of the 91 industries. Thus, the analysis necessarily is limited to industrial censuses for the years 1984 and 1988.[2] The reason we chose the profit margin on sales as an index of profitability is that the neoclassical analysis is interested in profits per se irrespective of the base on which these profits are being estimated. And in the absence of detailed data on capital stock, which is available only at the two-digit industry level, we restricted the presentation to the share of profits in total sales. Furthermore, such empirical testing is quite usual and expected in neoclassical studies of industrial organization, making, at the same time, our findings comparable to those of other economies. Table 6.1 reports some metrics and measures of association between the profit margins on sales (PMS) and the employment concentration ratio of the top four firms in the industry (CR4) as well as the Herfindahl index (HI).

An inspection of Table 6.1 shows that over a decade (from 1978 to 1988), there has not been any fundamental change in the structure of the Greek large-scale manufacturing. The employment concentration index of the top four firms for the 3 census years does not reveal anything quite different, as this can be judged from the summary statistics presented in Table 6.1. The results are similar for the HI. In pooling together the data on CR4 and HI along with the PMS, we present in pairs the one variable against all the others in Fig. 6.1.

---

[2]Since then, there are no relevant industry censuses either because the Statistical Services are reluctant to provide estimates for the politically sensitive ratio (the Greek Statistical Service is no exception) or because of the constantly decreasing importance of the share of manufacturing in GDP and total employment. Consequently, it is not possible to continue a cross-section analysis based on data from the Greek Statistical Service. We report, however, the concentration index of the year 1978 in order to show that the changes in the degree of concentration of the large-scale Greek industries are rather slow. Unfortunately, there are no more recent censuses.

Table 6.1 Summary statistics of concentration ratios in Greek manufacturing

	CR4-78	CR4-84	CR4-88	HI-78	HI-84	HI-88
Average	0.451	0.435	0.423	0.101	0.096	0.089
Median	0.452	0.404	0.398	0.075	0.065	0.069
Maximum concentration	1.000	0.965	0.972	0.530	0.508	0.540
Minimum concentration	0.040	0.049	0.045	0.002	0.002	0.002
Standard deviation	0.242	0.230	0.229	0.101	0.098	0.088
Coefficient of variation	0.536	0.528	0.542	0.998	1.015	0.981
Number of observations	91	91	91	91	91	91

Note: The numbers 78, 84 and 88 denote census years

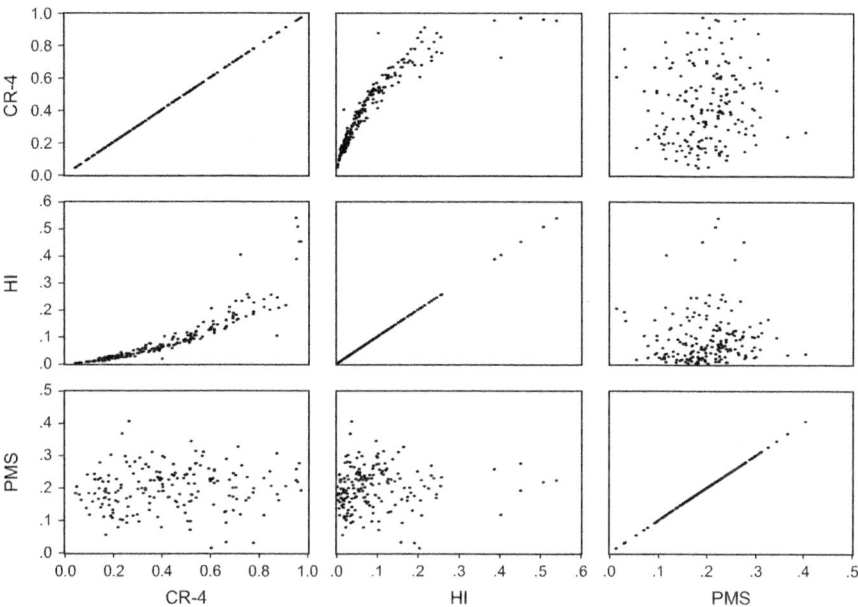

Fig. 6.1 Concentration ratios vs. profit margins on sales

From the above scatter graphs, we see that the CR4 and HI are too closely related. It is of great interest the hornlike pattern of the CR4 and HI which is quite usual in this type of studies, and it is theoretically and empirically investigated by Kwoka (1979) and Sleuwaegen and Dehandschutter (1986). The implication of the horn-shaped relationship is that the HI is a superior measure of the degree of concentration relative to the CR of the top (usually) four firms. The CR4 tends to overestimate the concentration of the top firms, whereas the HI, as it takes into account the size distribution of all firms and squares and the shares of each of these firms, gives more weight to the top firms. At this point it is enough to note that the two measures of concentration are not out of touch with each other and this result is also derived in our study.

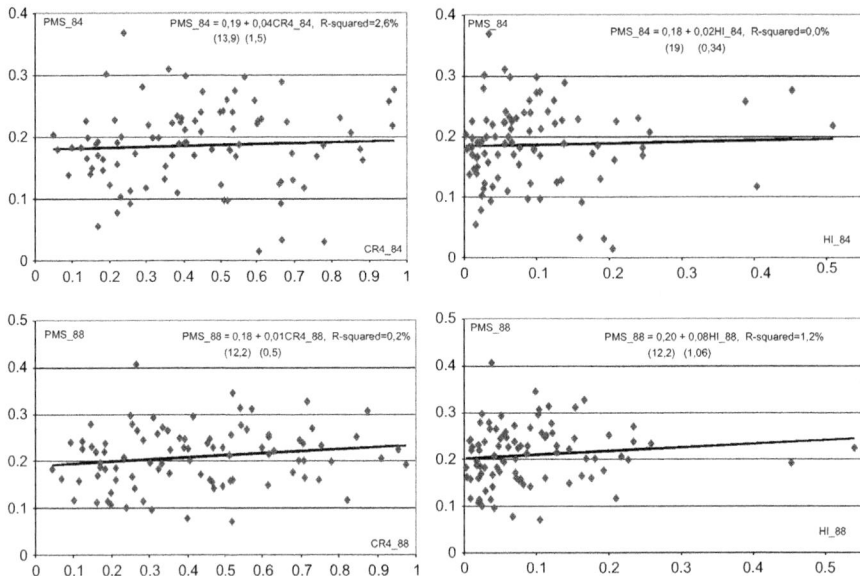

Fig. 6.2 Regressions between profit margin and concentration indexes

More importantly, each of these two concentration indexes (CR4 and HI) is not connected in any systematic way with the PMS; the visual inspection reveals no relationship of the variables involved something that is confirmed by the statistical analysis that follows. In Fig. 6.2 and for the years 1984 and 1988, we present scatter plots of data on the relation between PMS and concentration indices for the 91 large-scale Greek manufacturing industries.

In the various regressions displayed in Fig. 6.2, PMS is the dependent variable, and the concentration ratios, namely, the CR4 or HI, are the independent variables. The estimated regression lines are not found statistically significant. This comes as no surprise, because even the famous study by Bain (1956), on which much of the literature on monopoly in the USA is based on, the R^2 is not mentioned and only its squared root is reported which anyway was very small. In our case, we also tested for non-linear relations having as explanatory variables the concentration indices raised in square or cube powers with the same negative results for the hypothesis that monopoly power is concentrated in the top firms of the industries. Hence, the correlation of profitability with concentration indicators is found weak, lending no support to the view that large-size firms, usually identified with monopolies, enjoy higher profitability as a result of their market power. It is, therefore, safe to argue that for the Greek large manufacturing industries, the empirical evidence overwhelmingly supports the view that there is no systematic relationship between profit margins on sales and concentration indicators.

The lack of a statistically significant relationship between concentration ratios and profit margins on sales is further conferred by the information provided in Table 6.2, where the lower triangle presents the Pearson correlation coefficients of the variables at

Table 6.2 Matrix of correlation coefficients

	CR4-84	CR4-88	HI-84	HI-88	PMS-84	PMS-88
CR4-84	–	0.932 (0.00)	0.978 (0.00)	0.900 (0.00)	0.108 (0.30)	0.147 (0.16)
CR4-88	0.928 (0.00)	–	0.915 (0.00)	0.978 (0.00)	0.180 (0.08)	0.190 (0.07)
HI-84	0.886 (0.00)	0.792 (0.00)	–	0.894 (0.00)	0.105 (0.32)	0.144 (0.17)
HI-88	0.796 (0.00)	0.871 (0.00)	0.801 (0.00)	–	0.207 (0.04)	0.204 (0.05)
PMS-84	0.052 (0.62)	0.132 (0.21)	0.037 (0.73)	0.188 (0.07)	–	−0.004 (0.99)
PMS-88	0.142 (0.17)	0.163 (0.12)	0.145 (0.17)	0.112 (0.29)	−0.041 (0.70)	–

hand along with their statistical significance as this can be judged by their probability values shown in parenthesis, for the years 1984 and 1988. The upper triangle of the same table displays estimates of the Spearman's rank correlation coefficients, whose advantage over the Pearson's one is that they account for possible non-linear relations.

The probabilities, shown in the parentheses, indicate that the correlations between profit margin on sales and concentration ratios are not statistically significant, with possible exception of the Spearman's rank correlation coefficient between the pairs of variables PMS (1988) and HI (1988) as well as PMS (1988) and CR (1988) which are found marginally statistically significant at the 5% and the 10% level of significance (p-values: 0.05 and 0.07, respectively).

The analysis so far has been static because we examined whether and to what extent profit margins on sales are positively correlated with concentration ratios. The results of the statistical analysis for the Greek large manufacturing industries are definitely negative giving no support to the neoclassical and, in general, the quantitative hypothesis of competition, in which the number of firms (degree of concentration) in an industry delineates the intensity of competition and by extension the level of profitability measured by the profit margin on sales. More importantly, the conducted cross-sectional empirical studies for various economies have not provided overwhelming evidence to support the neoclassical hypothesis according to which there is a statistically significant positive relationship between an industry's profit margin on sales and its concentration ratio measured by an index, such as Herfindahl index (Sawyer 1981, Chap. 6; Schmalensee 1989: 975; Polasky and Mason 1998).

6.3 Tendential Equalization of Profit Rates Across Industries

In this section, the analysis attempts to give answer to the second issue posed at the beginning of this chapter, that is, to examine the extent to which there is a long-term equalization of the rate of profit in an economy under conditions of free competition.

In other words, the empirical analysis now becomes dynamic and examines the extent to which the competition between industries establishes tendentially the equalization of profitability across industries. Nevertheless, as we have discussed in Sect. 5.5.2, the tendential equalization of the rates of profit across industries is a long-run and turbulent process caused by the continuous flows of capital in and out of industries in the incessant quest of profit opportunities. This process of continuous flows of capital does not imply that the rates of profit among industries converge to the economy's average rate of profit, but rather it implies that this equalization is only attained on average and after the passage of long enough time. At any particular time, there are differences in the rates of profit between industries.

The analysis is carried out for the Greek two-digit manufacturing industries over the period of 1959 to 1991, for the Japanese three-digit manufacturing industries for the years 1974–2008 and for the USA three-digit industries spanning the years 1987–2015. It is worth noting here that:

- The rate of profit is usually calculated as a ratio of profits to fixed capital stock of the same period. In order to be consistent with the classical analysis, however, earnings should be calculated on the invested capital in the beginning of the production period, while profits are made at the end of the period, after the sale of goods. For this reason, for the estimation of the rate of profit, the capital stock is lagged by 1 year.
- Capital invested includes circulating capital (i.e. raw materials and wages) together with fixed capital (i.e. plant and equipment). From the available data, it is not possible to estimate the stock of circulating capital in any reliable way and for all the years; thus, our estimations of the rate of profit are based on the fixed capital stock provided that we do not expect qualitatively different results from the presence or not of the invested circulating capital because of its relative small quantitative significance in manufacturing.

In what follows, we describe the autoregression model that we employ to test the hypothesis of the inter-industry tendential equalization of profit rates. A similar formulation has been used for the empirical studies for various economies, such as the USA (Glick 1985), Canada (Webber and Tonkin 1990), Turkish manufacturing (Bahçe and Eres 2010) and Greek manufacturing (Tsoulfidis and Tsaliki 2005). Mueller (1990) and Vaona (2012) refer to most empirical studies derived based on autoregression models for various countries. However, Mueller (1986) suggested regressions of the profit rate deviations against the reciprocal of time trend raised to various powers.[3] In the more recent studies, the same questions are being pursued with the use of various tests of stationarity and cointegration techniques (Zacharias 2001) and panel data (Tsoulfidis et al. 2015). However, we opted for the suggested autoregressive schemes, which have been traditionally used in similar studies for they are simple and also economically meaningful.

---

[3]Lianos and Droucopoulos (1993) and Droucopoulos and Lianos (1993) pursue the question of equalization of profit rates in Greek manufacturing with somewhat different methodology.

We start off with the analysis of the autocorrelation (AR) model in order to examine the hypothesis of the inter-industry tendential equalization of the rates of profit. We consider that the AR model holds useful properties that can capture the inter-industry behaviour of profitability. Let us suppose that the rate of profit (r_t^i) is defined as

$$r_t^i = \frac{\pi_t^i}{C_{t-1}^i},$$

where π_t^i is the net profits and C_{t-1}^i is the capital stock of industry i in period $t = 1, 2, \ldots, n$. If $\bar{r}_t$ is weighted by the output produced economy-wide rate of profit, then we have

$$z_t^i = r_t^i - \bar{r}_t.$$

which is the deviation of industry's i rate of profit from the weighted average one at period t. In turn, we hypothesize that the following AR model can describe the deviation series[4]:

$$z_{t+1} = a + bz_t + u_{t+1},$$

where the disturbance term u_t is white noise. The AR model in the second period is

$$z_{t+2} = a + bz_{t+1} + u_{t+2} = a + ab + b^2 z_t + bu_{t+1} + u_{t+2}$$

and the nth period will be

$$z_{t+n} = a\left(1 + b + b^2 + \ldots b^{n-1}\right) + b^n z_t + u_{t+n} + bu_{t+n-1} + \ldots + b^n u_t. \quad (6.1)$$

Here, we distinguish the following three cases which are related to the three terms that are included in the last equation:

1. If $b > 1$, the term in the parenthesis will increase with n. If, however, $b < -1$, the term in the parenthesis will increase in absolute terms as n increases but with alternating sign. In both cases, the deviation series is not stationary; the variance of the series grows exponentially over time displaying explosive behaviour. Obviously, this case should be excluded from our analysis as economically implausible. In the extreme case that $b = 1$, the model is still not stationary, and its long-run variance increases over time as it is not bounded; hence, the model does not have a steady equilibrium solution, and the values of x_t wander without any systematic pattern. This behaviour is not expected in the classical analysis that supports the long-term attraction of inter-industry rates of profit to the economy-wide one.

---

[4]For simplicity reasons, we do not include in the presentation the superscripts i defining the industry under study.

2. If $-1 < b < 1$, the term in the parenthesis will approximate the limit $1/(1 - b)$, while the second term $b^n z_t$ approaches zero. If, in this case, $a = 0$ the above limit equals zero indicating that the series of the deviations of rates of profit approaches the mean rate of profit of all industries. If $a > 0$, the rate of profit of the industry approaches a limit which is above the economy-wide one. Finally, if $a < 0$, the rate of profit of the industry approaches a limit which is below the average one.
3. Finally, the third term is the sum of error terms of the above equation. Since each term has a conditional mean equal to zero, it follows that the mean of the sum of the stochastic terms will be also equal to zero. In addition, each stochastic term is independent of the others (by assumption), and it is characterized by constant variance, which we symbolize by σ^2. Consequently, the sum of errors has a bounded variance equal to $(1 + b + b^2 + \ldots b^{n-1})\sigma^2$. If $-1 < b < 1$ and n increases, the above expression tends to the limit $(1 - b)^{-1}\sigma^2$. If $b > 1$ or $b < -1$, the variance of the stochastic term increases as n increases.[5]

The empirical investigation about the long-run tendential equalization of profitability in the various economies of our analysis has been guided by the above considerations. For each industry's deviation series, an estimate of a and b is obtained from the above autoregressive equation using the ordinary least squares method. The value of the term $a/(1 - b)$ is calculated as the best estimate of the long-run projected rate of profit. The significance of the difference of this limit from zero is the significance of the difference of a and b from zero as well as their covariance.[6] A closer examination of the issue, however, reveals that since both the numerator and denominator of the fraction $a_i/(1 - b_i)$ are estimated parameters, it follows that the standard error of the above term should be estimated from the matrix of estimated covariances of the coefficients (Kmenta 1991, pp. 485–491 and Green 1990, pp. 230–234). More specifically, the estimated variance of the projected returns will be

$$Var\left(\frac{\hat{a}_i}{1 - \hat{b}_i}\right) \approx \left(\frac{1}{1 - \hat{b}_i}\right)^2 Var(\hat{a}_i) + \left(\frac{\hat{a}_i}{1 - \hat{b}_i^2}\right)^2 Var(\hat{b}_i)$$

$$+ 2\left[\frac{1}{1 - \hat{b}_i}\right]\left[\frac{\hat{a}_i}{1 - \hat{b}_i^2}\right] Cov(\hat{a}_i, \hat{b}_i).$$

In a nutshell, we define convergence as the movement of the actual rate of profit of an industry towards the long-run economy-wide profitability. The mechanism through which this convergence takes place is the inflow or outflow of capital or, what amounts to be the same thing, the acceleration or deceleration of capital accumulation. It is worth pointing out that in neoclassical economics, this mechanism refers to the assumption of free entry and exit of new firms. But a much more

---

[5] About the exact statistical properties, see Tsoulfidis and Tsaliki (2013).
[6] For more see Tsaliki and Tsoulfidis (2016).

realistic mechanism is based on the assumption that the increase or decrease in industry's supply depends on the increase or decrease of industry's investment which is facilitated by the credit system regardless of whether it originates from the already existing firms or from the new ones. In other words, starting with disequilibrium rates of profit with the passage of time and in absence of stochastic disturbances, the deviations tend to approach asymptotically a common value which we expect to be zero, that is, the case with no excess profits or losses (see Fig. 5.5). If convergence takes place at a positive value, this may be taken as evidence of some degree of monopoly, and if it takes place at negative values, this might be attributed to some sort of government regulation of the industry. On the other hand, the term gravitation is used to indicate the random oscillation of actual profit magnitudes around their projected equilibrium values.[7]

In terms of our autoregressive scheme, convergence needs the slope coefficient, b, to have an absolute value less than one. In addition, gravitation requires bounded fluctuations around this trend line which is ensured by the value of b being less than one in absolute value. In this context, convergence refers to the deterministic part of the model, and gravitation refers to the bounded fluctuations around the trajectory of the deterministic part of a stochastic model. In this case, the model is in statistical equilibrium in the sense that the standard deviation of each series does not display any known systematic functional form[8] and approaches an upper limit.

The empirical analysis of the hypothesis of equalization of the rates of profit is extended to include the incremental rate of return (IROR), that is, the rate of profit on regulating capitals is the relevant variable to the hypothesis of the tendential equalization of rates of profit between industries. Botwinick, for instance, notes:

> empirical investigations attempting to utilize Marx's analysis of competition between and within industries must be careful to distinguish which profit rates are being observed-individual, regional, industry average or regulating [...].
>
> (Botwinick 1993, p. 154)

In this sense, an industry's average profitability that has been used in a number of studies is not necessarily the appropriate index of profitability that attracts the investment flows. The idea is that the average rate of profit measures the profitability of all the firms comprising the industry and in this average are included both firms using advanced technology or have privileged location and firms with outdated technology or other kinds of 'deficiencies'. By taking the industry's average, we may not select the type of capital which is representative of the vitality of the industry and targeted by prospective investors. However, this does not necessarily mean that the average is a bad approximation to reality; on the contrary, the average rate of profit may not be always the best regulator of acceleration or deceleration of

---

[7]Convergence and gravitation are intertwined, and the former is a prerequisite for the latter (see also Duménil and Lévy 1987; Vaona 2011, 2012).

[8]In econometric terms, the time series data does not display any known systematic functional form such as ARCH or GARCH.

accumulation, but it is not too far from the best to ignore its significance, especially in manufacturing.

6.4 Inter-Industry Competition and the Rate of Profit

In what follows, we apply the above-described autoregressive model for the Greek, Japanese and the US manufacturing industries in order to investigate the extent to which there is tendential equalization of profitability across industries in these countries.

6.4.1 Twenty, 2-Digit Manufacturing Industries, Greece, 1959–1991

The empirical analysis utilizes data for the two-digit large-scale manufacturing industries, that is, establishments that employ more than ten workers for the period 1959–1991. Data on gross capital stock for the large-scale manufacturing industries come from Handrinos and Altinoglou (1993). Profits are estimated as the difference between the value-added net of indirect business taxes and wages. Both capital stock and profits are expressed in current prices. For the years of the analysis in general and in manufacturing in particular, the capital invested in wages represents a small percentage of the total invested capital, and it can be excluded without exerting any significant impact on the analysis. The idea is that businesses, through the credit line that they have in their disposal, can relatively easily obtain the necessary funding they need in order to carry out their production process for the time before the sale of their output produced. Therefore, the variable capital advanced can be excluded from the estimation of the total capital advanced without affecting in any significant way the reliability of the estimation of the rate of profit. Also, the capital invested in raw materials can be safely omitted because, on the one hand, it is not a significant part of the total capital invested in manufacturing industries, and, on the other hand, like wages, it is relatively easy to secure through the credit system, and therefore there is no any urgent need to advance these sums of money as circulating capital. The above holds true in manufacturing; we cannot, however, argue for the same thing in the trade sector of the economy, where the stock of circulating capital (raw materials and wages) may constitute a significant proportion of the total capital advanced and by omitting this part of capital to overestimate the rate of profit.[9] In Fig. 6.3, we present the deviations of the rate of profit from the economy's average for each of the 20 industries of our study.

---

[9]In addition, for the calculation of the stock of the circulating capital, we need to obtain data on the turnover time of production, data which are hard to get.

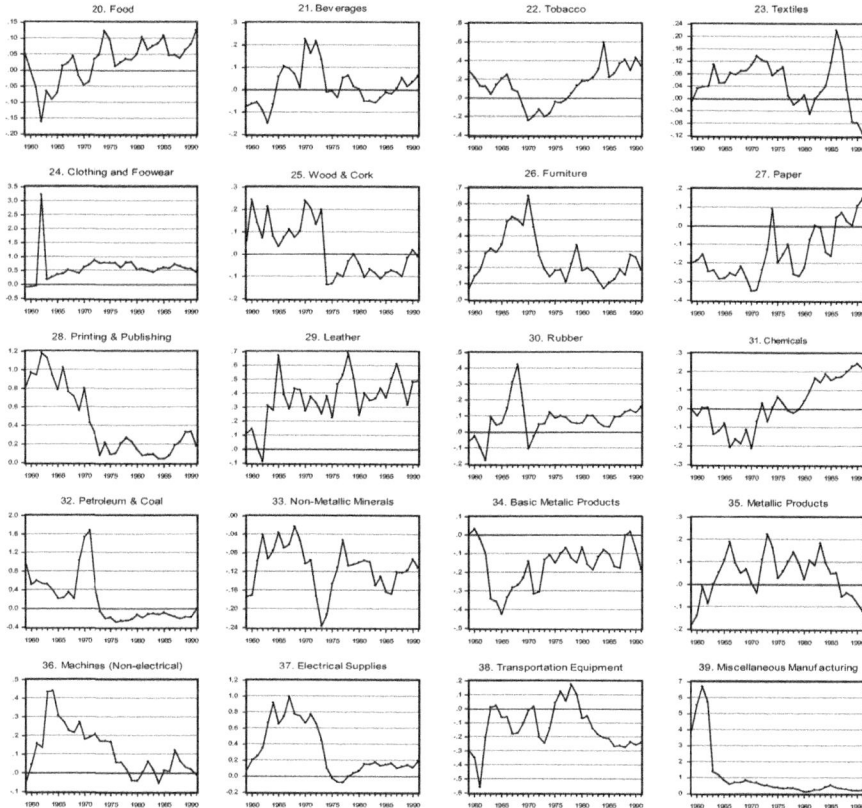

Fig. 6.3 Deviations from average rate of profit, Greek manufacturing industries, 1959–1991 (Source: Tsoulfidis and Tsaliki 2013)

The visual inspection of the 20 graphs does not lend overwhelming support to the classical gravitational process, and the trajectories of the profit rate deviations are far from displaying a convergent or strongly gravitational behaviour towards zero. In order to use the proposed autoregressive scheme [Eq. (6.1)], we need to test for the stationarity properties of each of our 20 industries. We know that in cases such as the deviation series of rates of profit from the economy-wide one, many non-linearities are present which are not captured by the usual linear unit root tests.[10] However, in the turbulent kind of dynamics characterizing the tendential equalization of inter-industry profit rates, it is not unrealistic to hypothesize that the deviation series exhibit strong non-linearities. These nonlinearities may be attributed to a host of factors ranging from uncertainty, difference in expectations, credit restrictions, patents, indivisibilities, government regulations and the like.

---

[10]In fact, the obtained results from the usual Augmented Dickey-Fuller (ADF) tests (not shown) are mixed and more likely are contaminated by the presence of nonlinearities not captured by the test. In fact the ADF test assumes that the deviation series of profit rates exhibit linear movements.

Under the linearity framework, whenever there is deviation in industry's profit rate from its long-run weighted average, this gives rise to a risk-free profit opportunity through the forces of arbitrage, which in our case is reflected in the inflow or outflow of capital. However, the presence of such 'impediments' as those described above gives rise to a threshold or band of 'no arbitrage' on both sides of the rate of profit. If the observed rate of profit deviation from the economy-wide average one crosses the threshold (in our case is zero), only then arbitrage is likely to occur; otherwise, the deviation series is likely that it will not tend to correct itself. More specifically, the visual inspection of the paths of deviation series shows that in most cases, the rates of profit deviation series cross the zero line at least once with only a few exceptions. These are the industries 26 (furniture), 28 (printing and publishing), 33 (non-metallic minerals) and 39 (miscellaneous manufacturing) where there is no crossing of the zero line. However, in no single case, we observe explosive behaviour in the upward or downward direction, and the paths of deviation series remain in the vicinity of the zero line.

The above results encourage us to employ non-linear stationarity tests. A simple and, at the same time, powerful non-linear stationarity test was developed by Kapetanios et al. (2003, p. 364) according to which the test statistic does not have an asymptotic standard normal distribution and, therefore, provides the critical values which we use to evaluate the results of these tests. The results are displayed in Table 6.3.

Table 6.3 The non-linear KSS unit root test (Source: Tsoulfidis and Tsaliki 2013)

Industries	t_{KSS_1}	t_{KSS_2}	t_{KSS_3}
20. Food	−2.84***	−2.55	−3.28*
21. Beverages	−1.97*	−2.10	−2.06
22. Tobacco	−3.17***	−3.37**	−3.42**
23. Textiles	−2.94***	−2.63	−2.82
24. Clothing and footwear	−9.86***	−1.80	−1.79
25. Wood and cork	−3.05***	−3.06**	3.23*
26. Furniture	−1.98*	−2.33	−2.66
27. Paper	−1.05	−1.69	−4.16***
28. Printing and publishing	−3.82***	−3.85***	−2.18
29. Leather	−1.94*	−2.86*	−3.51**
30. Rubber	−1.44	−1.41	−2.29
31. Chemical	−1.13	−1.68	−3.14*
32. Petroleum and coal	−4.13***	−4.33***	−4.52***
33. Non-metallic minerals	−1.92*	−2.16	−2.11
34. Basic metallic products	−1.73	−1.48	−1.49
35. Metallic products	−2.67**	−2.54	−2.53
36. Machines (non-electrical)	−2.14*	−2.63	−0.36
37. Electrical supplies	−1.61	−1.79	−3.93***
38. Transportation equipment	−4.72***	−5.27***	−5.27***
39. Miscellaneous manufacturing	−3.01***	−4.95***	−1.40

Notes: *, ** and *** denote rejection of the unit root null hypothesis at the 0.10, 0.05 and 0.01 significance level, respectively. The symbols t_{KSS_1}, t_{KSS_2} and t_{KSS_3} indicate the *t*-statistic that results from the implementation of the test to the raw data, the demeaned data and the detrended data, respectively. The critical values have been recovered from Kapetanios et al. (2003)

Table 6.4 Profit rate deviations from the average, Greek manufacturing industries, 1959–1991 (Since stationarity is a requirement for the application of our AR(1) scheme for industries 27 (paper) and 31 (chemicals), we detrended them first, and then we proceeded with the estimation of coefficients which we display along with their t-ratios.)

Industry	a	b	$a/(1-b)$	R-squared
20. Food	0.01 (0.9)	0.76 (5.9)	0.03 (1.0)	0.54
21. Beverages	0.01 (0.9)	0.69 (5.4)	0.03 (0.3)	0.49
22. Tobacco	0.02 (0.9)	0.84 (8.1)	0.14 (1.1)	0.69
23. Textiles	0.01 (0.7)	0.80 (6.0)	0.04 (0.9)	0.54
24. Clothing and footwear	0.10 (2.0)	0.84 (10.5)	0.61 (4.9)	0.80
25. Wood and cork	0.01 (0.3)	0.70 (5.3)	0.02 (0.3)	0.49
26. Furniture	0.06 (1.9)	0.79 (7.5)	0.27 (3.8)	0.65
27. Paper	−0.02 (0.8)	0.79 (5.9)	−0.10 (1.1)	0.54
27*. Paper	−0.00 (0.1)	0.48 (2.94)	−0.00 (0.1)	0.22
28. Printing and publishing	0.02 (0.5)	0.91 (13.1)	0.21 (0.6)	0.85
29. Leather	0.20 (3.2)	0.49 (3.2)	0.38 (7.5)	0.26
30. Rubber	0.04 (2.0)	0.58 (4.0)	0.09 (2.3)	0.35
31. Chemicals	0.01 (0.7)	0.92 (10.6)	0.10 (0.6)	0.79
31* Chemicals	−0.00 (0.4)	0.61 (4.71)	−0.01 (0.4)	0.43
32. Petroleum and coal	0.01 (0.2)	0.78 (7.6)	0.05 (0.2)	0.66
33. Non-metallic minerals	−0.04 (2.2)	0.66 (5.1)	−0.11 (5.5)	0.46
34. Basic metallic products	−0.05 (2.2)	0.70 (5.6)	−0.18 (3.7)	0.51
35. Metallic products	0.02 (1.3)	0.65 (5.1)	0.05 (1.4)	0.47
36. Machines (non-electrical)	0.02 (1.3)	0.81 (7.6)	0.13 (1.8)	0.66
37. Electrical supplies	0.04 (1.1)	0.90 (11.5)	0.36 (1.5)	0.81
38. Transportation equipment	−0.04 (1.4)	0.71 (5.7)	−0.12 (1.8)	0.52
39. Miscell. manufacturing	0.07 (0.4)	0.831 (9.6)	0.43 (0.5)	0.75

Note: Industries with an asterisk have been detrended prior to the application of AR1

The results of Table 6.3 suggest that in almost all industries, the profit rate deviation series display stationarity properties for the standard confidence levels and, therefore, the AR(1) scheme can be applied. In case where there is no stationarity in the raw data, the AR(1) model can be applied in the detrended data, and this is the case with industries 27 (paper) and 31 (chemicals). There is an uncertainty with regard to industries 30 (rubber) and 34 (basic metallic products), where perhaps the AR(1) model could be used in the differences of the series. However, the visual inspection of the graphs in Fig. 6.3 suggests that, as these two industries cross the zero line a few times, they are almost stationary and in fact the ADF test lends support to this hypothesis as we found that industry 30 (rubber) is stationary at the 5% probability value and industry 34 (basic metallic products) was found weakly stationary with probability value somewhat higher than 10%.[11]

Table 6.4 shows the estimates of the parameters of our autoregressive scheme for the deviation series of profitability for each of the 20 manufacturing industries. The

---

[11]When we ran regressions of differences of these two series, we found that the intercept and the slope coefficients of the regressions are not statistically different from zero, whereas the R-squared is near zero.

results show that the autoregressive equation used in the analysis is statistically significant in all industries and that the value of R^2 is high enough indicating that in most industries the autoregressive scheme explains a pretty high proportion of the variance of industries' profit rate deviations.

From Table 6.4, we observe that the estimates on b are significantly different from zero at $p = 1\%$ in all industries. The absolute values of t-ratios (shown in parenthesis) are pretty high which means that the confidence interval of the estimated parameters is in the vicinity of the estimated coefficient which is always much less than one in absolute value; only in three industries, 28 (printing and publishing), 31 (chemicals) and 37 (electrical supplies), are in the vicinity of 0.90 which is another way to say that there is increased probability for explosive behaviour to the extent that the b coefficients may exceed one. Thus, we have an attraction (usually weak) for the deviation series of all 20 industries towards their long-term (equilibrium) value determined by the ratio $a/(1 - b)$.

However, as was mentioned above, since the limit $a/(1 - b)$ is a ratio of two estimated parameters, we must compute its standard error from the covariance matrix of the coefficients. From the results displayed in Table 6.4, we observe that 6 industries—clothing and footwear (24), furniture (26), leather (29), rubber (30), non-metallic mineral products (33) and basic metallic products (34)—out of the 20 industries display a value of $a/(1 - b)$ statistically significant at $p = 5\%$. From these six industries, the profit rate deviation series of the non-metallic mineral products (33) together with the basic metallic product (34) industries are attracted to a projected rate of profit $a/(1 - b)$ lower than zero, whereas in the other four industries, the difference series is attracted to a rate of profit higher than the economy's average. From these four industries, only in three —clothing and footwear (24), furniture (26) and leather (29)—the projected rate of profit differs from zero in an empirically significant way, whereas in the rubber industry (30), the difference of the projected rate of profit from zero is statistically significant at $p < 10\%$.[12]

From the above we may argue that our empirical finding with respect to the rate of profit does not lend overwhelming support to the classical idea of gravitation of industry profit rates to the economy-wide average rate of profit, since in 6 out of 20 industries, the results show gravitation towards profit rates different from the average. These results may lend support to the view that various impediments to free mobility of capital and also risk associated with some activities related to market power, government intervention and regulation of industries may give rise to profit rate (positive or negative) differences from the long-run average rate of profit.[13]

---

[12]If industries 30 and 34 are nonstationary, it follows that the AR(1) scheme cannot be applied; on the other hand, by differencing the data of these two industries, they become stationary but, at the same time, with no economic meaning.

[13]See Mueller (1990) for relevant studies about time series data from many countries and results suggesting that the deviations of profit rates from the economy-wide average persist lending support to the idea of the presence of monopolistic characteristics.

The hypothesis of equalization of profit rates has been tested so far in terms of the average profitability of each industry against the economy's average, and the statistical results were mixed with respect to the hypothesis of tendential equalization of the rates of profit. We now apply the same method using data for the IROR which, as we have already explained, is a more appropriate profitability index to test the tendential equalization of the inter-industry rates of profit. In Fig. 6.4, we portray both the weighted average rate of profit (AROP) and the IROR for the Greek manufacturing industries. Because the time periods are defined by the data availability in investment and capital stock, the average rate of profit begins from the year 1959 and extends until the year 1991, while the availability of investment data allows the estimation of the IROR from the year 1962 to 1992. Past the year 1992, it is extremely difficult to extend the data set because of the change in the definitions of industries. Nevertheless, the time period is long enough to test the proposition of the long-run tendential equalization of profit rates.

An inspection of Fig. 6.4 shows that the IROR and AROP are not out of touch with each other and their difference, as expected, is the volatility of the IROR which reflects all the noise and short-run behaviour in the economy. Thus, the IROR orbits around or, rather, on the vicinity of the AROP, and both share a nearly common long-term average. In effect, the mean value of the average rate of profit is 0.47 with a standard deviation 0.10, while for the IROR, the average value is somewhat higher at 51%, and the standard deviation is much higher at 0.27. In short, the two rates of profit share almost the same mean value although the variability of the IROR is estimated to be about three times higher than that of the AROP.

In estimating the IROR, both numerator and denominator in the case of Greece and Japan are expressed in current prices. The use of current prices might make some difference especially when we refer to an inflationary period like the 1970s and 1980s; the idea is that inflation not only increases profit expectations but also actual

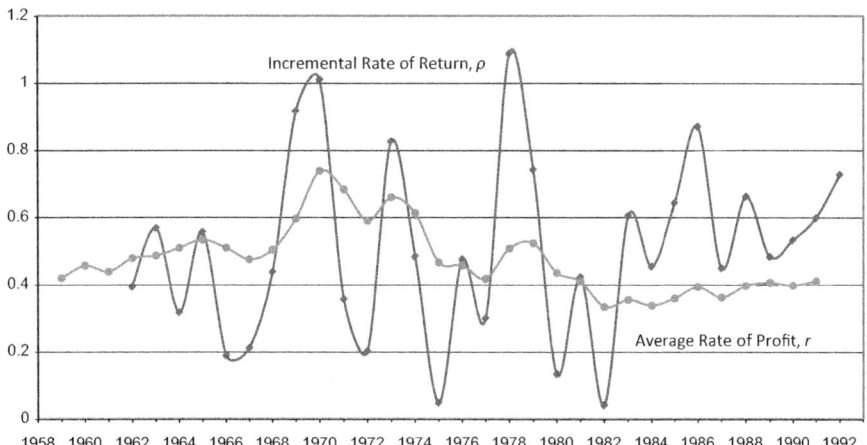

Fig. 6.4 Average rate of profit vs. average IROR in Greece, 1959–1992

profits, which in turn affect capital accumulation. In an earlier work (Tsoulfidis and Tsaliki 2005), we deflated both profits and investment by their respective price deflators, and the results were supportive of the idea of tendential equalization of the rates of profit; however, on closer examination one might argue that the results were derived because of the removal of the effects of inflation though the deflators. More specifically the denominator of the IROR, that is, investment in constant prices, is usually an I(1) variable, and real profits are also an I(1) variable; by taking the change in profits, we transform the numerator to an I(0) variable, and this might impose stationarity in the whole fraction. In the current study, we take the nominal values of variables, and so even though we take the first difference of profits in the numerator of IROR, still we have a nonstationary numerator. In Fig. 6.5, we plot industries' deviations from the average IROR.

An inspection of the graphs reveals that the deviation series gravitate towards zero indicating that over time the deviation of each industry's IROR from the economy's average dissipates. The time series data of the differences of industry

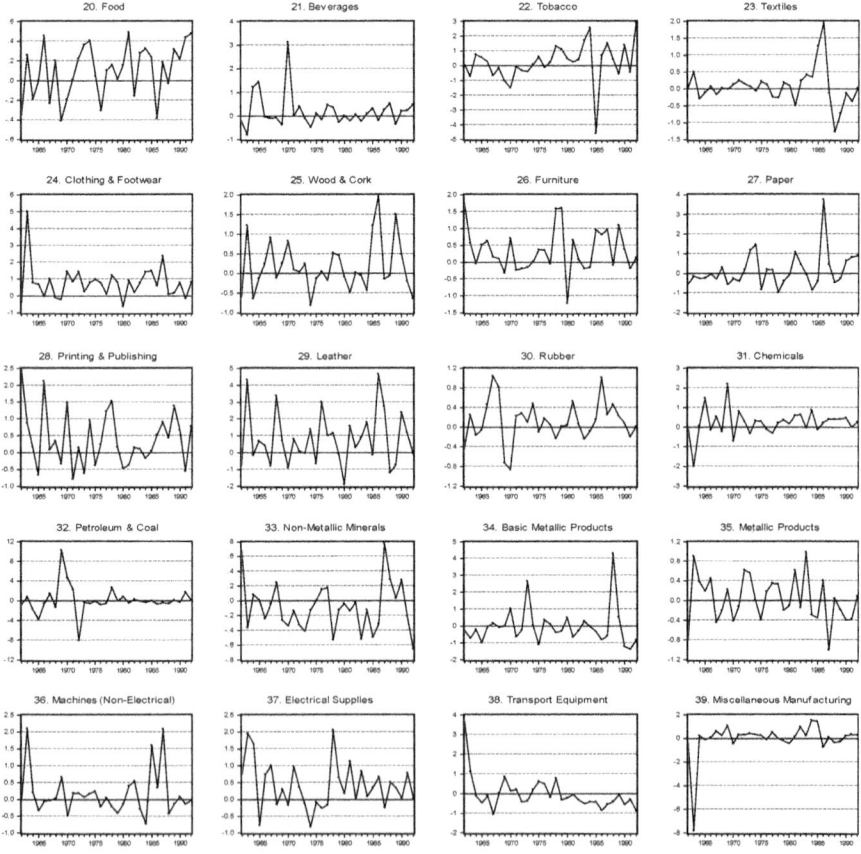

Fig. 6.5 Deviations from the average IROR, Greek manufacturing industries, 1962–1992

profit rates from their average is obviously stationary, and therefore we need not run any particular statistical test. Unlike the average rates of profit (Fig. 6.3), we observe that the trajectories of IROR deviations cross the zero line much more frequently. The visual inspection of the graphs leaves no doubt that the IRORs of all of our 20 industries are mean-reverting variables; however, it is not clear whether this mean is always zero or some other centre of attraction which may be different from zero and statistically significant (positive or negative) number.

In order to ascertain the mean value of each series, we employ the autoregressive scheme of first order to each of these 20 industry deviation series [Eq. (6.1)], whose additional characteristic is their high volatility. From this volatility, we would like to drop the exceptionally high or low frequencies of the data; the reason is that the noise embedded in the data may fail to give the required information of the actual behaviour of the series. The task of isolating the frequencies that are of economic interest from those that are not is carried out through the use of band-pass filter, and in our case, we employed a Baxter-King filter with one lag and frequencies 2 and 8. In Table 6.5, we display our estimates of the intercept, a, and slope coefficients, b, as well as the projected rate of profit $a/(1 - b)$ along with their t-statistics of the filtered times series data. The R-squared is displayed in the last column. In the regressions that we ran, we tried autoregressive schemes of various lags; however, in the interest of brevity and of clarity of presentation, we restricted to the first-order

Table 6.5 Tendential equalization of IRORs, Greek manufacturing industries, 1962–1992

Industry	a	b	$a/1 - b$	R-squared
20. Food	−0.003 (0.09)	−0.680 (5.18)	−0.002 (0.09)	0.508
21. Beverages	0.016 (0.19)	−0.654 (4.72)	0.010 (0.19)	0.462
22. Tobacco	−0.014 (−0.09)	−0.632 (3.92)	−0.009 (0.09)	0.372
23. Textiles	−0.012 (0.24)	−0.213 (1.15)	−0.010 (0.24)	0.049
24. Clothing and footwear	−0.022 (0.26)	−0.518 (5.18)	−0.015 (0.26)	0.508
25. Wood and cork	−0.005 (0.07)	−0.397 (2.56)	−0.004 (0.07)	0.202
26. Furniture	−0.015 (0.19)	−0.595 (3.76)	−0.009 (0.19)	0.352
27. Paper	−0.001 (0.01)	−0.496 (2.92)	0.000 (0.01)	0.247
28. Printing and publishing	−0.027 (0.31)	−0.754 (5.53)	−0.015 (0.08)	0.540
29. Leather	0.003 (0.01)	−0.553 (3.94)	0.002 (0.01)	0.374
30. Rubber	−0.003 (0.07)	−0.364 (2.06)	−0.002 (0.07)	0.140
31. Chemicals	0.009 (0.11)	−0.678 (5.51)	0.005 (0.11)	0.539
32. Petroleum and coal	−0.015 (0.05)	−0.677 (4.71)	−0.009 (0.05)	0.460
33. Non-metallic minerals	0.007 (0.22)	−0.461 (3.03)	0.005 (0.22)	0.261
34. Basic metallic products	−0.002 (0.01)	−0.468 (2.71)	−0.001 (0.01)	0.220
35. Metallic products	0.000 (0.00)	−0.595 (4.18)	0.000 (0.00)	0.402
36. Machines (non-electrical)	−0.005 (0.08)	−0.657 (5.44)	−0.003 (0.08)	0.532
37. Electrical supplies	0.008 (0.10)	−0.583 (3.66)	0.005 (0.10)	0.340
38. Transportation equipment	−0.024 (0.47)	−0.500 (3.00)	−0.016 (0.47)	0.257
39. Miscell. manufacturing	−0.024 (0.47)	−0.500 (7.16)	0.037 (0.74)	0.663

autoregressive scheme, provided that the autoregressive scheme with two or more lags did not change the results of the econometric analysis qualitatively.

We observe that in all industries, the constant term of the regressions (i.e. coefficient a) is not statistically significant, so we cannot reject the null hypothesis that it is zero. The slope coefficient, b, is always negative and much less than one and that the projected rate of profit, that is, the term $a/(1 - b)$ is not statistically significant and different from zero. The results with respect to the intercept and the slope coefficients are therefore consistent with the hypothesis of gravitation of our deviation series of IRORs to the economy-wide average IROR. For industry 23 (textiles), the estimated slope coefficient displays relatively smaller than the other industries t-ratio; however, when we add a second lag term, the overall fit improved without affecting the projected rate of profit whose statistical significance remained not different from zero.

6.4.2 Fifty-two, 3-Digit Manufacturing Industries, Japan, 1974–2008

Our analysis continues by testing the hypothesis of inter-industry profit rate equalization using time series annual data of 52 manufacturing industries of Japan spanning the period 1974–2008. Given the level of detail of the Japanese data, we define the average rate of profit as the ratio of net operating surplus to net capital stock both estimated in current prices.[14] In a like manner, we estimate the IROR as the current difference of gross operating surplus to gross investment lagged by one year. We removed from our analysis the government enterprises because they are not profit motivated. The agriculture and financial services sectors were also removed, either because of extensive self-employment (agriculture) or because they are not production proper and their treatment would be too complicated and beyond the scope of the analysis (financial services and wholesale-retail trade).

The results of the Augmented Dickey-Fuller (ADF) test for each of the 52 industries that we derive are based on the autoregressive scheme of the first order described in Sect. 6.3 and they are displayed in Table 6.6.

From Table 6.6, we observe that the ADF statistics for 10 out of 52 industries reject the null hypothesis of unit root. The constant coefficient α is found to be statistically significant in 13 out of 52 industries, whereas the slope coefficient b is statistically significant in 49 out of 52 industries. The mean of the slope coefficient of all industries is 0.688, and 35 of 52 industries are above this mean slope coefficient. It is interesting to note that this estimate of the mean of b's is somewhat higher than those estimated of the already developed economies (see Glen et al. 2001). The pharmaceutical products (22) industry displays the highest slope coefficient (0.983),

---

[14]For data details see Industrial Productivity Database http://www.rieti.go.jp/en/database/JIP2011/.

Table 6.6 Summary statistics for the AR(1) and the average rate of profit deviations in Japanese manufacturing industries, 1974–2008

	Industry	ADF	a	b	$a/(1-b)$	R^2
1	Livestock products	-1.90^{***b}	0.008 (0.62)	0.777 (6.95)*	0.035 (0.61)	0.60
2	Seafood products	-3.33^{**a}	0.073 (2.49)*	0.667 (5.23)*	0.219 (7.53)*	0.46
3	Flour and grain mill products	-3.76^{*b}	-0.100 (-0.49)	0.935 (31.97)*	-1.530 (-0.15)	0.96
4	Miscel. foods, etc. products	-1.95^{**b}	0.014 (0.88)	0.876 (10.60)*	0.112 (0.99)	0.77
5	Animal foods and organ fertil.	-2.80^{***a}	0.031 (0.67)	0.764 (8.20)*	0.131 (0.77)	0.67
6	Beverages	-1.31^b	0.033 (0.79)	0.875 (10.33)*	0.264 (1.11)	0.76
7	Tobacco	-4.25^{**}	0.027 (0.89)	0.819 (8.18)*	0.149 (1.39)	0.67
8	Textile products	-2.66^{***a}	-0.050 (-2.63)*	0.666 (5.31)*	-0.149 (-13.1)*	0.46
9	Lumber and wood products	-3.78^{**}	-0.019 (-1.57)	0.807 (8.06)*	-0.098 (-2.43)**	0.67
10	Furniture and fixtures	-2.15	-0.003 (-0.23)	0.779 (7.70)*	-0.013 (-0.17)	0.64
11	Pulp, paper, etc.	-7.07^{***}	0.009 (1.11)	0.615 (10.07)*	0.023 (1.13)	0.76
12	Paper products	-2.71^{***a}	0.016 (1.38)	0.627 (4.55)*	0.042 (1.60)	0.39
13	Printing and book binding	-16.89^*	0.014 (0.47)	0.780 (8.47)*	0.063 (0.43)	0.69
14	Leather and leather products	-3.45^{***}	-0.010 (-0.20)	0.483 (3.21)*	-0.019 (-0.19)	0.24
15	Rubber products	-7.69^*	-0.006 (-0.49)	0.772 (8.62)*	-0.026 (-0.42)	0.69
16	Chemical fertilizers	-0.89^b	-0.004 (-0.83)	0.886 (9.43)*	-0.035 (-0.85)	0.73
17	Basic inorganic chemicals	-1.65^{***b}	0.001 (0.27)	0.717 (3.98)*	0.003 (0.14)	0.33
18	Basic organic chemicals	-1.56^b	0.006 (0.52)	0.846 (9.01)*	0.038 (0.49)	0.71
19	Organic chemicals	-1.36^b	0.0002 (0.01)	0.864 (8.29)*	0.001 (0.01)	0.68
20	Chemical fibres	-1.42^b	-0.011 (-1.52)	0.838 (10.13)*	-0.067 (-0.96)	0.76
21	Miscel. chemical products	-2.32	0.021 (1.06)	0.904 (11.77)*	0.218 (2.10)**	0.81
22	Pharmaceutical products	-2.08	-0.020 (1.79)***	0.983 (23.77)*	-1.176 (-0.23)	0.94
23	Petroleum products	-2.27^a	0.062 (1.79)***	0.777 (7.95)*	0.278 (1.95)***	0.66
24	Coal products	-6.96^*	0.099 (4.06)*	0.274 (2.00)**	0.136 (5.74)*	0.11
25	Glass and its products	-2.19^{**b}	0.018 (1.46)	0.696 (5.97)*	0.059 (1.94)***	0.52

(continued)

Table 6.6 (continued)

	Industry	ADF	a	b	$a/(1-b)$	R^2
26	Cement and its products	-5.50^*	$-0.005\ (-0.70)$	$0.176\ (1.18)$	$-0.006\ (-0.68)$	0.04
27	Pottery	-2.32^a	$-0.021\ (-2.00)^{**}$	$0.723\ (5.94)^*$	$-0.075\ (-4.47)^*$	0.52
28	Miscel. ceramic, etc.	-3.42^{***}	$-0.005\ (-1.11)$	$0.694\ (5.98)^*$	$-0.016\ (-1.09)$	0.52
29	Pig iron and crude steel	-2.92	$-0.009\ (-1.22)$	$0.827\ (8.69)^*$	$-0.052\ (-1.60)$	0.70
30	Miscel. iron and steel	-25.91^*	$0.014\ (1.21)$	$0.453\ (24.20)^*$	$0.025\ (1.22)$	0.94
31	Smelting and refin. of non-fer.	-3.77^{**}	$-0.018\ (-1.42)$	$0.459\ (3.37)^*$	$-0.033\ (-1.39)$	0.26
32	Non-ferrous metal products	-1.95^{**b}	$0.012\ (0.67)$	$0.817\ (8.70)^*$	$0.065\ (0.83)$	0.70
33	Fabric, etc. metal products	-2.76^{***a}	$-0.037\ (-2.70)^*$	$0.555\ (3.95)^*$	$-0.083\ (-5.76)^*$	0.32
34	Miscel. fabricated metal	-3.08^{**a}	$-0.041\ (-2.43)^{**}$	$0.713\ (6.43)^*$	$-0.142\ (-4.07)^*$	0.56
35	General industry machin.	-4.02^{*b}	$-0.007\ (-0.51)$	$0.778\ (7.24)^*$	$-0.031\ (-0.54)$	0.62
36	Special industry machin.	-3.73^{***}	$0.002\ (0.19)$	$0.792\ (7.58)^*$	$0.009\ (0.18)$	0.64
37	Miscellaneous machinery	-9.13^*	$-0.018\ (-1.21)$	$0.744\ (6.34)^*$	$-0.070\ (-1.59)$	0.55
38	Office, etc. machines	-3.92^{**}	$0.015\ (0.89)$	$0.921\ (15.38)^*$	$0.189\ (0.98)$	0.88
39	Electrical machinery	-3.52^{***}	$-0.040\ (-1.66)^{***}$	$0.431\ (2.84)^*$	$-0.07\ (-1.75)^{***}$	0.20
40	Household electric applian.	-3.90^{*a}	$0.068\ (1.36)$	$0.608\ (4.52)^*$	$0.173\ (1.50)$	0.38
41	Elec. data processing machin.	-3.46^{***}	$0.014\ (0.33)$	$0.894\ (10.92)^*$	$0.132\ (0.36)$	0.78
42	Communication equipment	-3.04	$-0.018\ (-1.75)^{***}$	$0.742\ (6.56)^*$	$-0.069\ (-3.17)^*$	0.57
43	Electr. eqp. and electr. instrum.	-2.85^{*b}	$0.088\ (1.75)^{***}$	$0.352\ (2.92)^*$	$0.135\ (1.965)^{**}$	0.21
44	Semic. devices, etc. circuits	-4.02^{*a}	$0.147\ (0.89)$	$0.375\ (2.49)^{**}$	$0.235\ (0.93)$	0.16
45	Electronic parts	-3.29^{***}	$0.111\ (0.68)$	$0.899\ (11.57)^*$	$1.099\ (0.81)$	0.80
46	Miscel. electr. machin. eqp.	-4.80^*	$0.034\ (0.87)$	$0.666\ (6.44)^*$	$0.101\ (0.95)$	0.56
47	Motor vehicles	-1.75^{***b}	$0.018\ (1.61)$	$0.693\ (5.46)^*$	$0.058\ (2.03)^{**}$	0.48
48	Motor vehicle parts and access	-2.20^{**b}	$0.031\ (1.26)$	$0.759\ (6.59)^*$	$0.128\ (1.58)$	0.57
49	Other transportation eqp.	-3.66^{*b}	$-0.053\ (-2.10)^{**}$	$0.709\ (6.42)^*$	$-0.182\ (-5.39)^*$	0.56
50	Precision machinery and eqp.	-7.63^{*a}	$0.009\ (0.44)$	$0.151\ (1.36)$	$0.010\ (0.44)$	0.05

| 51 | Plastic products | -1.20^b | $-0.011 (-1.30)$ | $0.730 (8.10)^*$ | $-0.040 (-1.12)$ | 0.67 |
| 52 | Miscel. manuf. industries | -2.70^{***a} | $-0.067 (-4.61)^*$ | $0.102 (0.58)$ | $-0.074 (-10.71)^*$ | 0.02 |

Note: The numbers in parentheses are t-ratios

Superscript a, no trend; superscript b, no constant and no trend

*, **, *** indicate significance at 1%, 5% and 10%, respectively

whereas the miscellaneous manufacturing industries (52) have the lowest price of the coefficient (0.102).

The sixth column of Table 6.6 gives the projected (or long-run) profit rate, $a/(1 - b)$. Most of these long-run values are not statistically significant except for 16 industries: Seafood products (2), textile products (8), lumber and wood products (9), miscellaneous chemical products (21), petroleum products (23), coal products (24), glass and its products (25), pottery (27), fabricated constructional and architectural metal products (33), miscellaneous fabricated metal products (34), electrical machinery (39), communication equipment (42), electronic equipment and electric measuring instruments (43), motor vehicles (47), other transportation equipment (49) and miscellaneous manufacturing industries (52). These results may lend support to the argument that in the Japanese economy, there is not enough competition, and there are monopolistic and oligopolistic markets. Such results are in agreement with those derived by Odagiri and Yamawaki (1990), Komoto (2001) and Maruyama and Odagiri (2002), who on the one hand ascertain a tendential equalization of profit rates, and, on the other hand, identify groups of (surviving over the years of their study) firms that maintain profit rates above the average, attributing this deviation to their oligopolistic character.

On closer examination of the results presented in Table 6.6, we derive that from these 16 industries with rates of profit different from the average, only seven display positive projected rates of profit, and they possess potentially market power and therefore display persistently rates of profit much higher than the norm. However, we discover that from these seven industries, there are two industries (25 and 47) characterized by very low projected rates of profit, nearly 6%, whereas from the remaining five, the maximum deviation from the economy-wide AROP is 27.8%, and this is in the petroleum products (23) and next the seafood products (2) and miscellaneous products (21) with a deviation approximately 22%. The remaining 2 industries (24 and 43) are with a projected rate of profit of approximately 13%, which is moderately higher than the economy-wide AROP. Consequently, if we are looking for statistically significant monopoly or oligopoly situations, these would amount to 3 out of 52 industries that is something less than 6% of the cases. Turning now to the negative deviations, which are observed in 9 out of 16 industries, in most cases these deviations are around 10% and might be explained by government intervention or regulation of these industries or other institutional characteristics specific to Japan (Komoto 2001).

The next step is to focus on the regulating capital and the associated with it IROR. In this effort, we use the exact same autoregressive scheme of the first order presented in Eq. (6.1). The results of the econometric analysis are displayed in Table 6.7.

We observe from Table 6.7 that the IRORs gravitate towards the economy's average IROR, with only three exceptions which on further examination show that for them the equalization is rather a matter of time. More specifically, the pharmaceutical products (22) and the electronic parts (45) display exceptionally high profit rates in the 1970s and early 1980s, which plummeted in the last years of our analysis. As for the chemical fibres (20), we observe large deviations in the first years of our

Table 6.7 Summary statistics for the AR1 and the IROR's deviations in Japanese manufacturing industries, 1974–2008

	Industry	ADF	a	b	$a/(1-b)$	R^2
1	Livestock products	-5.29^*	-0.002 (-0.3)	0.052 (0.29)	-0.002 (-0.02)	0.01
2	Seafood products	-6.05^*	0.048 (0.55)	0.013 (0.07)	0.048 (0.54)	0.01
3	Flour and grain mill products	-5.09^*	-0.056 (-0.08)	0.308 $(2.31)^*$	-0.080 (-0.08)	0.14
4	Miscel. foods, etc. products	-4.62^*	0.028 (0.44)	0.205 (1.19)	0.035 (0.44)	0.04
5	Animal foods and organ. fertil.	-4.39^{*a}	-0.231 (-1.5)	0.184 (0.99)	-0.283 (-1.49)	0.03
6	Beverages	-6.52^*	0.013 (0.14)	-0.123 (-0.73)	0.011 (0.14)	0.02
7	Tobacco	-7.63^*	0.105 (0.64)	-0.282 $(-1.69)^{***}$	0.081 (0.64)	0.08
8	Textile products	-4.53^*	-0.065 (-1.01)	0.186 (1.01)	-0.079 (-1.04)	0.03
9	Lumber and wood products	-6.83^*	-0.123 (-1.42)	-0.182 (-1.04)	-0.104 (-1.45)	0.03
10	Furniture and fixtures	-7.25^*	-0.074 (-0.73)	-0.258 (-1.51)	-0.058 (-0.73)	0.07
11	Pulp, paper, etc.	-9.97^*	-0.043 (-1.01)	-0.371 $(-2.69)^*$	-0.031 (-0.99)	0.19
12	Paper products	-7.74^{*a}	-0.052 (-0.54)	-0.188 (-1.23)	-0.043 (-0.53)	0.05
13	Printing and bookbinding	-4.06^{**}	0.056 (0.82)	-0.120 (-0.68)	0.050 (0.79)	0.02
14	Leather and leather products	-5.06^*	0.235 (0.70)	0.127 (0.73)	0.269 (0.71)	0.02
15	Rubber products	-5.82^*	-0.025 (-0.29)	-0.230 (-1.41)	-0.020 (-0.28)	0.06
16	Chemical fertilizers	-7.23^*	-0.115 (-1.48)	0.127 (0.95)	-0.131 (-1.45)	0.03
17	Basic inorganic chemicals	-7.24^*	-0.057 (-1.11)	-0.125 (-0.73)	-0.050 (-1.10)	0.02
18	Basic organic chemicals	-4.98^*	-0.051 (-0.37)	0.027 (0.16)	-0.052 (-0.37)	0.01
19	Organic chemicals	-5.77^*	-0.048 (-0.67)	0.033 (0.18)	-0.049 (-0.67)	0.01
20	Chemical fibres	-7.78^*	-0.083 $(-1.96)^{**}$	-0.100 (-0.72)	-0.075 $(-2.05)^{**}$	0.02
21	Miscel. chemical products	-6.03^*	0.095 (1.28)	0.115 (0.60)	0.107 (1.38)	0.01
22	Pharmaceutical products	-5.97^*	0.157 $(1.91)^{***}$	0.107 (0.63)	0.175 $(2.00)^{**}$	0.01
23	Petroleum products	-4.84^*	0.201 (0.68)	-0.194 (-1.12)	0.168 (0.68)	0.04
24	Coal products	-5.54^*	-0.164 (-0.43)	-0.268 $(-1.71)^{***}$	-0.129 (-0.44)	0.08
25	Glass and its products	-5.97^*	0.045 (0.68)	-0.072 (-0.41)	0.041 (0.69)	0.01

(continued)

Table 6.7 (continued)

	Industry	ADF	a	b	$a/(1-b)$	R^2
26	Cement and its products	−6.59[*]	−0.051 (−0.53)	−0.216 (−1.19)	−0.041 (−0.53)	0.04
27	Pottery	−6.11[*]	−0.051 (−0.47)	−0.103 (−0.58)	−0.046 (−0.47)	0.01
28	Miscel. ceramic, etc.	−7.26[*]	−0.034 (−0.60)	−0.048 (−0.32)	−0.032 (−0.59)	0.01
29	Pig iron and crude steel	−4.85[*]	0.047 (0.08)	0.140 (0.80)	0.054 (0.08)	0.02
30	Miscel. iron and steel	−6.79[*]	−0.070 (−0.81)	−0.099 (−0.57)	−0.063 (−0.80)	0.01
31	Smelting and refin. of non-fer.	−5.41[*a]	0.033 (0.23)	0.064 (0.37)	0.035 (0.23)	0.01
32	Non-ferrous metal products	−7.65[*]	0.093 (0.77)	−0.337 (−1.96)[**]	0.069 (0.78)	0.11
33	Fabric, etc. metal products	−6.88[*]	−0.039 (−0.49)	−0.141 (−0.85)	−0.034 (−0.49)	0.02
34	Miscel. fabricated metal	−4.51[*]	−0.045 (−0.47)	0.155 (0.89)	−0.053 (−0.46)	0.03
35	General industry machin.	−5.02[*]	0.022 (0.44)	0.276 (1.63)	0.030 (0.44)	0.08
36	Special industry machin.	−4.76[*]	0.038 (0.64)	0.400 (2.47)[*]	0.063 (0.64)	0.16
37	Miscellaneous machinery	−4.33[*]	0.003 (0.07)	0.268 (1.60)	0.004 (0.06)	0.07
38	Office, etc. machines	−3.44[***]	0.070 (0.90)	0.456 (2.70)[*]	0.128 (0.95)	0.19
39	Electrical machinery	−8.68[*]	−0.019 (−0.35)	−0.403 (−2.49)[*]	−0.013 (−0.34)	0.16
40	Household electric applian.	−6.35[*]	0.074 (0.98)	−0.014 (−0.08)	0.072 (0.97)	0.01
41	Elec. data processing machin.	−4.44[*]	0.060 (0.84)	0.317 (1.89)[***]	0.087 (0.85)	0.10
42	Communication equipment	−5.29[*]	0.034 (0.54)	0.047 (0.26)	0.035 (0.53)	0.01
43	Electr. eqp. and electr. instrum.	−6.00[*]	−0.002 (−0.02)	−0.071 (−0.40)	−0.001 (−0.01)	0.01
44	Semicon. devices, etc. circuits	−4.00[**]	0.054 (0.58)	0.157 (1.13)	0.064 (0.57)	0.04
45	Electronic parts	−1.98[**b]	0.424 (1.68)[***]	0.236 (1.45)	0.554 (1.77)[***]	0.06
46	Miscel. electr. machin. eqp.	−7.38[*]	0.087 (1.17)	−0.280 (−1.64)	0.067 (1.18)	0.08
47	Motor vehicles	−5.13[*]	0.068 (0.92)	−0.264 (−1.44)	0.053 (0.93)	0.06
48	Motor vehicle parts and access.	−7.07[*]	0.039 (0.89)	−0.216 (−1.24)	0.032 (0.87)	0.05
49	Other transportation eqp.	−7.20[*]	−0.052 (−0.62)	0.028 (0.15)	−0.053 (−0.62)	0.01
50	Precision machinery and eqp.	−7.80[*]	−0.021 (−0.34)	−0.261 (−1.59)	−0.016 (−0.32)	0.07

| 51 | Plastic products | -6.68^* | $-0.030\,(-0.82)$ | $-0.166\,(-0.95)$ | $-0.025\,(-0.80)$ | 0.03 |
| 52 | Miscel. manuf. industries | -4.20^{**} | $-0.047\,(-1.20)$ | $-0.373\,(-2.58)^*$ | $-0.034\,(-1.20)$ | 0.17 |

Note: The numbers in parentheses are *t*-ratios

Superscript *a*, no trend; superscript *b*, no constant and no trend

*, **, *** indicate significance at 1%, 5% and 10%, respectively

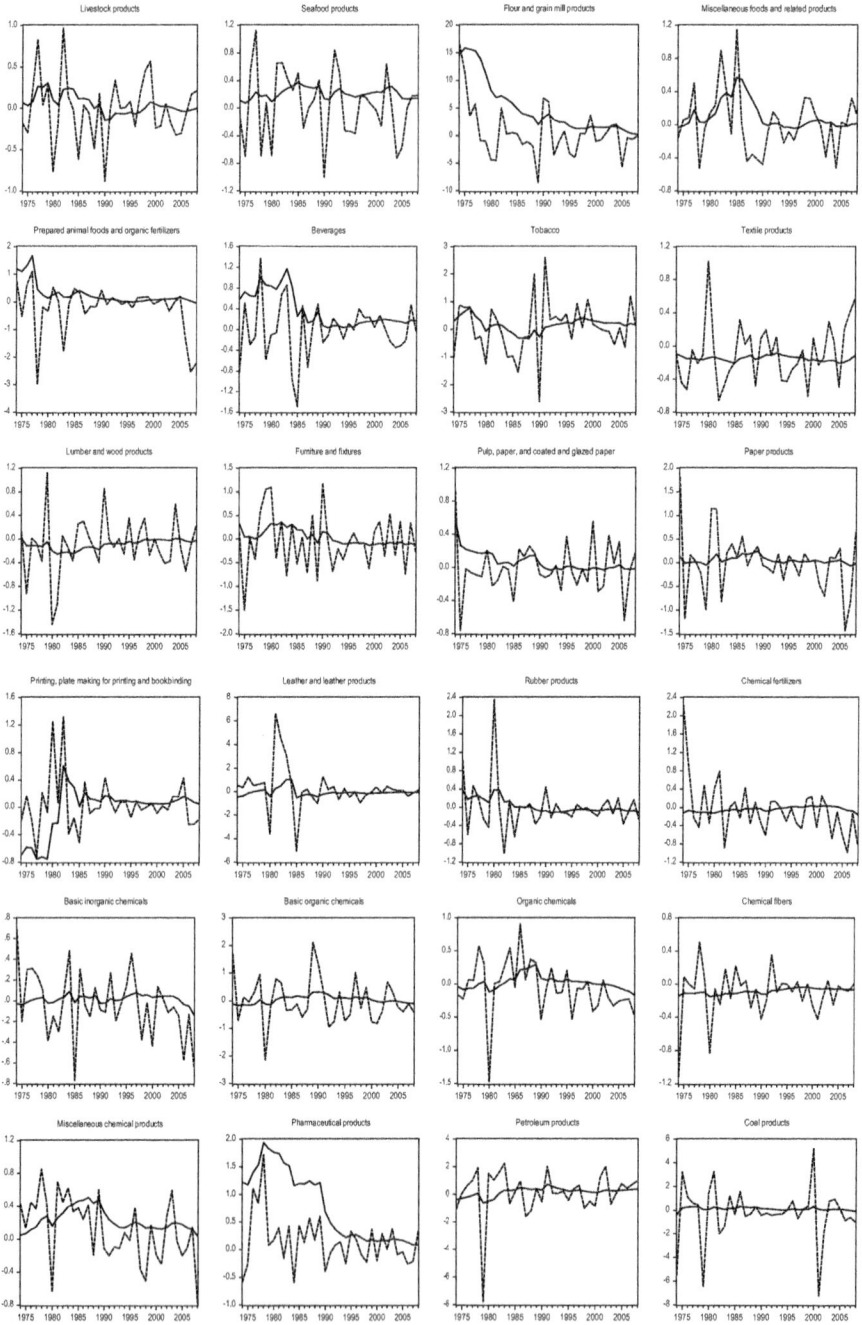

Fig. 6.6 Deviations of industries' AROPs and IRORs from their respective cross-sectional averages, Japanese manufacturing industries, 1974–2008

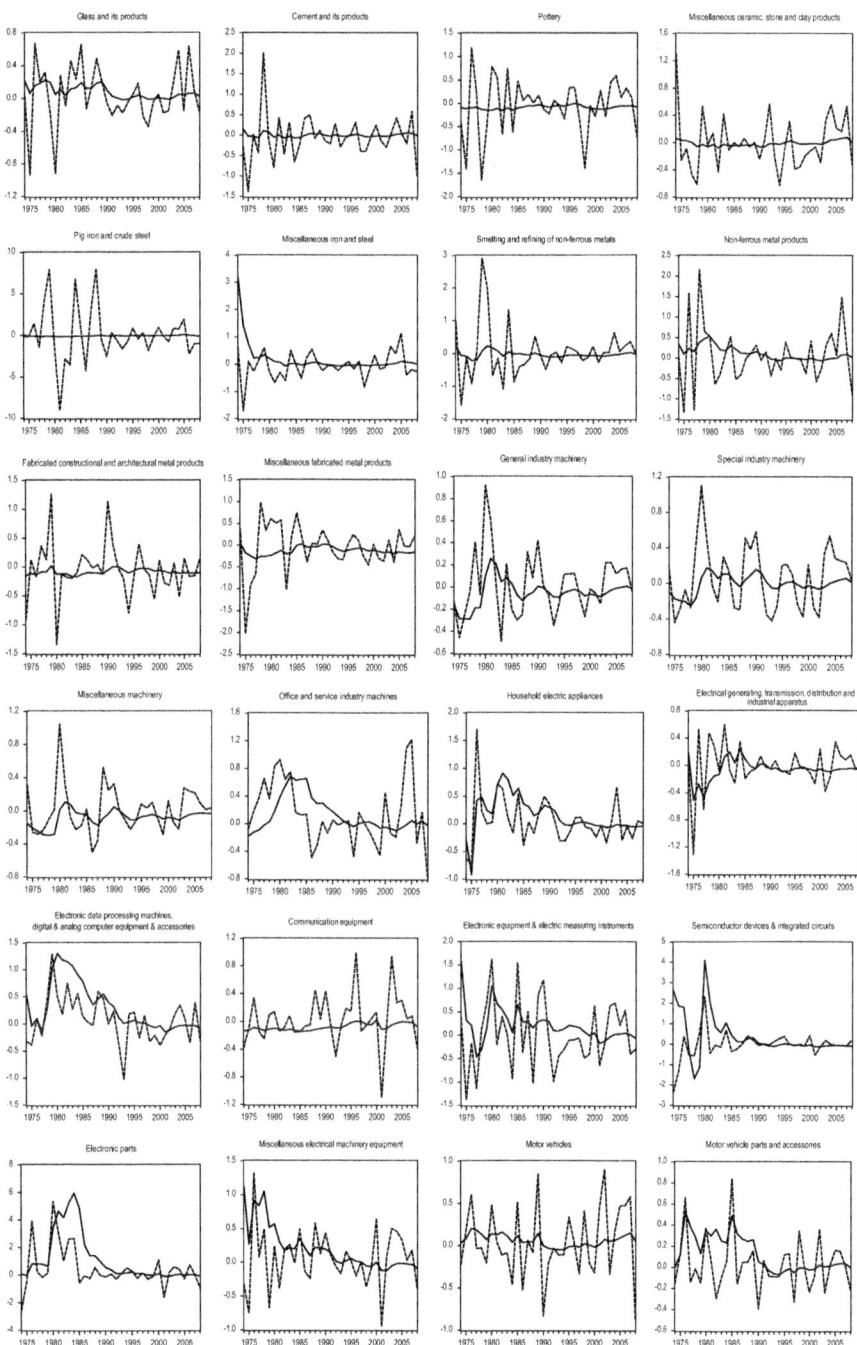

Fig. 6.6 (continued)

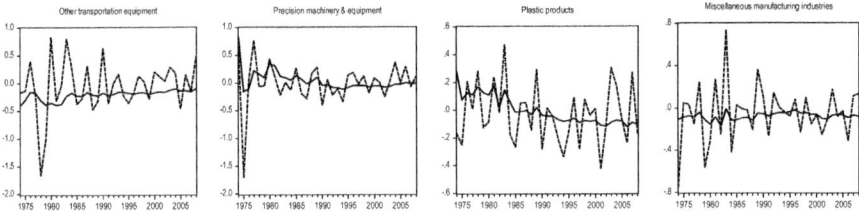

Fig. 6.6 (continued)

analysis and oscillatory behaviour thereafter winding up to a slightly negative projected rate of profit which is pretty close to the average rate of profit (see also Fig. 6.6). In most cases the b (slope) coefficient is near zero with a mean value at -0.0285. The minus sign indicates oscillatory behaviour around the zero-deviation line, and the low value of the parameter signifies that the attainment (on an average) of equilibrium rate of profit is rather speedy. In all cases, the IRORs' deviation series are characterized by stationarity, as this is indicated by the ADF test (displayed in the first column of Table 6.7), and also in very few cases, the projected IROR attains a level slightly above zero. In Table 6.7, we also display the coefficients of determination (R^2) which is very low in every industry; there is no industry with an R^2 above 20%. A low R^2 coefficient indicates a nearly perfect gravitational pattern of the deviation series, which is equivalent to saying that the movement of present deviations of IROR is not related to past deviations. These results are consistent with our hypothesis that the IROR is the right measure of industry's profitability that motivates and therefore directs entrepreneurial investment behaviour.

Figure 6.6 displays the deviation series of both the average rate of profit and the IROR and allows a visual inspection and cross-examination of their long-term patterns. The IROR indicated by the dotted line and as expected displays a much larger variability than the average deviation series (the solid line). The latter can be seen as a centre of attraction around which the IROR fluctuates indicating that the two indexes of profitability are moving together and they are connected to each other. In effect, our statistical analysis shows that the two deviation series despite wide differences in their variability nevertheless share nearly the same long-term (projected) mean.

The deviation series of the IROR of every industry exhibit oscillatory behaviour crossing over the zero line much more frequently than their respective average rates of profit; furthermore, there is no discernible trend in the path of the IRORs. This oscillatory behaviour confirms the thesis that the rate of return of new investment is equalized by competition between industries. The econometric tests for the IRORs reveal that only for 3 out of 52 industries, there is no gravitation of the industries' IRORs at the economy-wide average IROR. More specifically, the IROR of chemical fibres (20) industry is attracted to a level which is somewhat below the economy-wide average IROR, whereas the IROR of pharmaceutical products (22) and electronic parts (45) gravitates at a point which is slightly higher than the average IROR, behaviour that we also found when we examined the AROPs. Furthermore, the pharmaceutical products (22) industry has been found to display similar (persistent) behaviour also in other developed countries (Komoto 2001; Maruyama and Odagiri 2002). Nevertheless, the visual inspection of the pharmaceutical products (22) in Fig. 6.6 reveals that the persistence of IROR above norm might be illusionary and due almost exclusively to its extreme behaviour in the 1970s and 1980s. The exact same argument holds for the electronic parts (45) industry. The chemical fibres (20) industry with an IROR slightly below the norm might be explained by its institutional specificities of Japan.

6.4.3   Twenty-Four NAICS Industries, USA, 1987–2015

The hypothesis of convergence or divergence of the time series data in the rates of profit of the US economy has been studied extensively since the early 1980s when the theoretical questions of inter-industry equalization of the rates of profit and, in general, the dynamics of competition were under empirical investigation in a number of studies such as those by Flaschel and Semmler (1987) and Duménil and Lévy (1987), among others. The first econometric analyses within this spirit were contacted by Glick (1985), Cooney (1990) and Ochoa and Glick (1992), while summaries of their results and their updating up until the year 2005 for the USA and other countries can be found in Shaikh (2016). In our study, we present estimates of the deviations of the IROR and the average rate of profit for the US economy up until the year 2015, the last year that there are available reliable data. The data were recently made accessible from the EU KLEMS (www.euklems.net) database and refer to a number of variables and industries or sectors from which we have selected 24 that in our view give us a detailed enough picture and provide a satisfactory answer to the question of inter-industry equalization of profitability as they span 28 years, a long enough time period. Using this database we obtain the gross value-added (VA) from which we subtract the total employment compensation (LAB); the resulting gross profits are deflated by the sectoral value-added price index with 2010 as the base year. The respective sectoral current prices data on gross investment are also provided from which we subtract the gross investment of the residential structures. The so-derived industries' investment is deflated by the respective invest-ment price indexes (with the 2010 as the base year). The IROR is estimated as the ratio of real gross profits of the current period over real gross investment of the previous year (Eq. (5.7)). The AROP is obtained as the ratio of real profits over the real (in 2010 prices) gross capital stock from which we have subtracted the residen-tial capital stock. In the case of the US industries we used constant prices in the estimation of IROR since we refer to a non-inflationary period and in any case one does not expect any qualitatively different results. Figure 6.7 displays the evolution of the weighted average IROR and AROP of the total US economy during the 1987–2015 period.

A comparison of the US IROR against the IRORs of the Greek and Japanese economies that we studied, we observe that it displays a lot more variability than the economy-wide AROP. The difference in variability is possible to be connected with

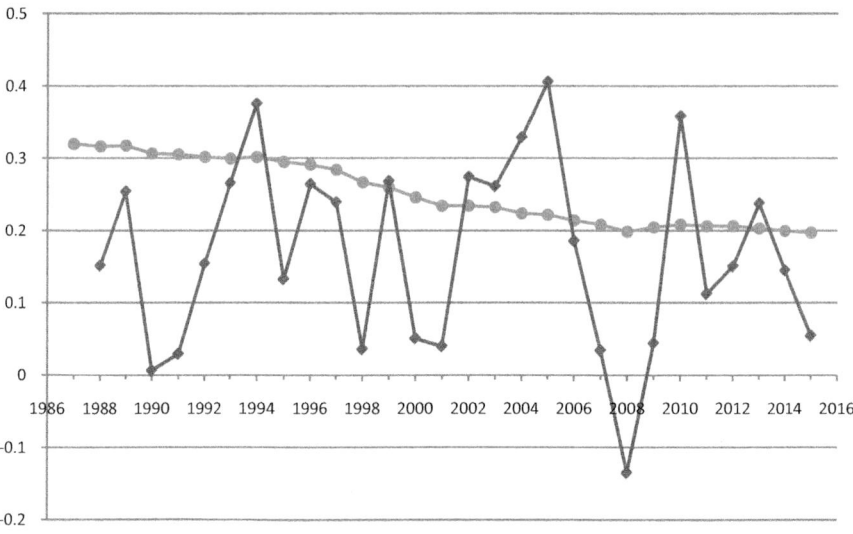

Fig. 6.7 Economy-wide average IROR and AROP, US industries, 1987–2015

the Great Recession (and in particular the years 2007–2008) that the USA seems to remain under its impact; this is reflected in the increasing variability of the IROR and the falling tendencies in the two profitability indexes. The two variables are closely related to each other, and the AROP is like an anchor for the IROR which wanders around it. The overall falling tendencies of the two rates of profit are quite evident, and this is an issue whose details are examined in Chaps. 8 and 10 of the book.

In Fig. 6.8 we display the graphs of each of the 24 industries where their IROR and AROP are subtracted from the economy-wide weighted respective average.

A visual inspection of the graphs in Fig. 6.8 shows that the IRORs of industries cross many times the zero line of equality with the economy-wide average IROR; so, it is certain that summing-up the positive and negative differences from the average over the 28 years of our investigation, we end up with a result no different than zero. The amplitude of its deviations over time in most industries is large enough precisely because of the by far higher volatility of investment relative to capital stock, since by its very nature, the IROR is designed to capture the fluctuations of profitability in a specific group of firms forming the regulating capital as opposed to the average rate of profit which, by capturing the effects of all firms activated in the entire industry, is expected to display lower volatility. In both variables, there is no evidence that the deviations neither increase nor they display any statistically significant pattern. In fact, in Fig. 6.9 in a panel of two graphs, we display the estimated standard deviation and coefficient of variations for both the IROR and AROP of all industries for the full 1987–2015 period.

We observe that the standard deviation of the economy-wide IROR displays large fluctuations without any discernible pattern. The linear trend is upward but not

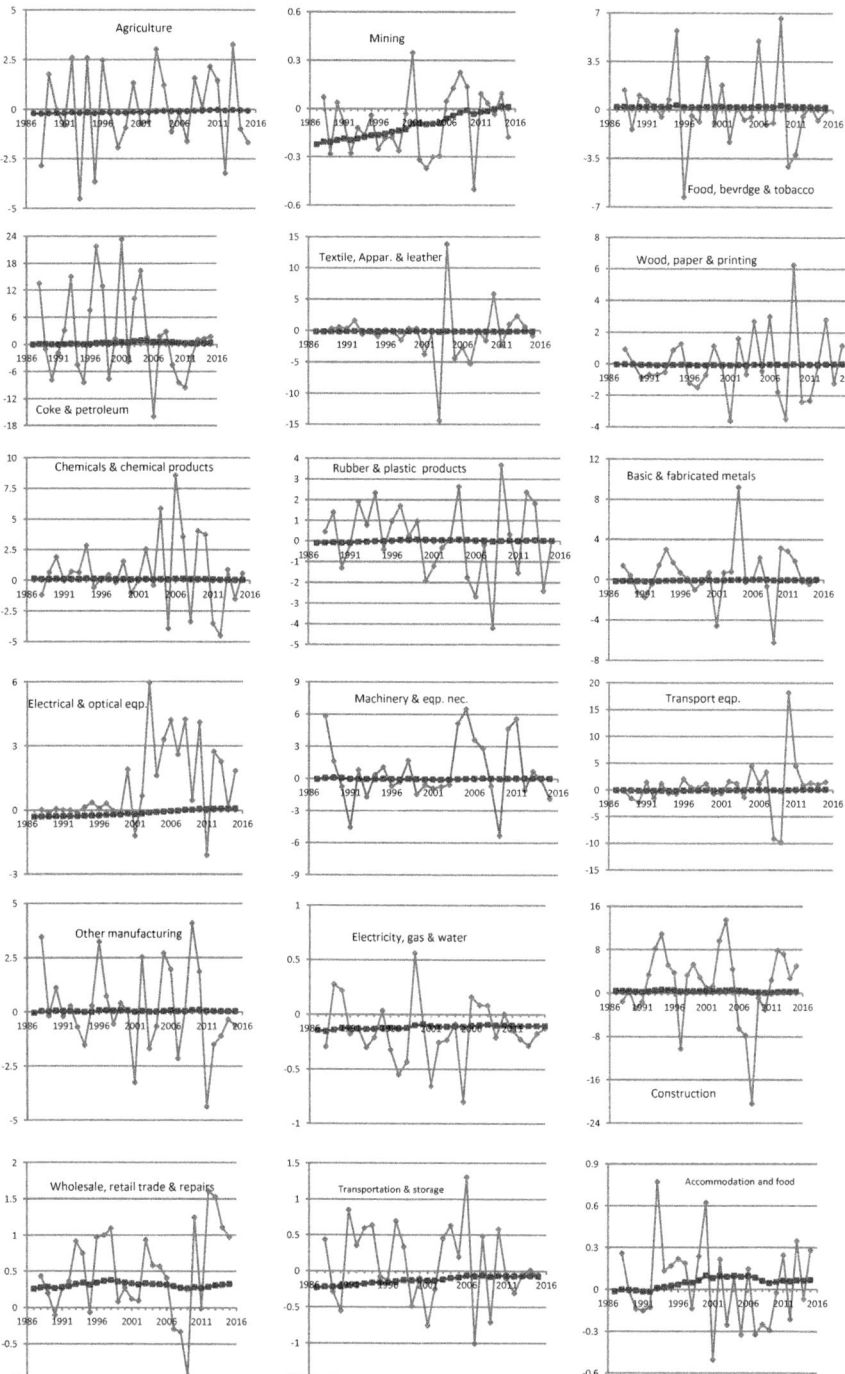

Fig. 6.8 Economy-wide average IROR and AROP, US industries 1987–2015

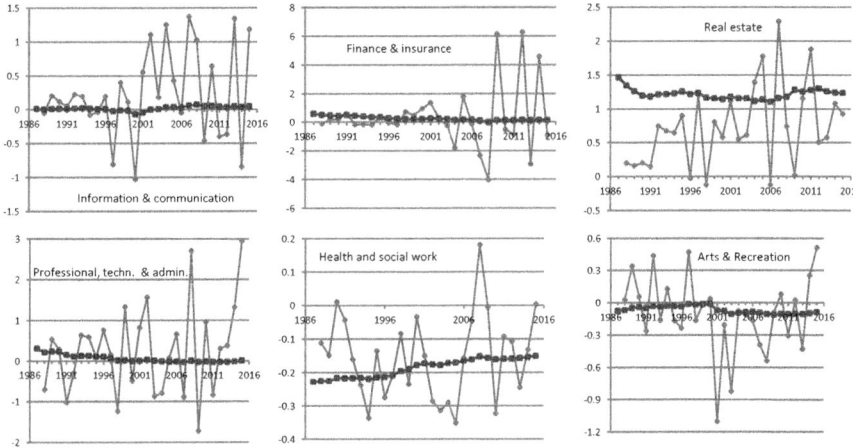

Fig. 6.8 (continued)

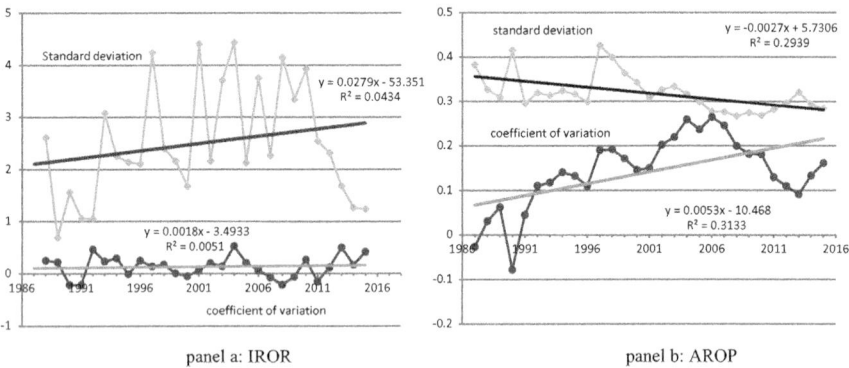

Fig. 6.9 Standard deviation and the coefficient of variations of the IROR and AROP, US industries, 1987–2015

statistically significant, and perhaps it is the result of the Great Recession of the post-2007 years. The coefficient of variation is also stationary, and its linear trend line has slope indistinguishable from zero. The statistical results are consistent and confirm the view of gravitation of individual estimates of profitability around the centre of gravity, that is, the economy-wide average IROR. As for the average rate of profit, we observe that the standard deviation displays a slightly downward trend meaning that the industry AROPs are attracted (and not repelled) towards the economy's weighted AROP. Such findings lend additional support to the classical political economy view of competition and the idea of inter-industry equalization of profit rates over the long run.

6.5 Summary and Conclusions

Our empirical investigation shows that the concept of competition as a process of rivalry of economic units developed by the old classical economists and Marx is a viable alternative approach to the neoclassical theory of competition rooted in the model of perfect competition. We have argued that this alternative to the neoclassical approach to competition, by theorizing the characteristics of real competition between and within industries, provides satisfactory explanations of the phenomena observed in real economies.

In our empirical analysis, we found that the profit margins on sales are not related to the degree of concentration in the case of the Greek manufacturing three-digit industries. This implies that it is not necessarily right the popular view that high profit margins per se indicate the presence of monopoly power in the market. In addition, we have shown that, when profitability is defined for the regulating capitals of the various industries, the hypothesis of the equalizing trend of the inter-industry (incremental or marginal) profit rates is established, based on the available data of 22-digit industries of Greek manufacturing in the period 1959–1992. Similar experiments were running for the economies of Japan and the USA, and the findings ascertained the classical view of competition at least with reference to the tendential equalization in the rates of profit. In the case of the USA, we invoked two additional measures of dispersion, namely, the standard deviation and the coefficient of variation, to capture this gravitational process.

In all cases, we showed that the two rates of profit, IROR and AROP, are strictly connected to each other. Moreover, the IROR, due to its short-term nature, might be one of the fundamental determinants in the movement of the stock market, as the analysis of Shaikh (1995) showed in the case of the USA and the analysis by Tsoulfidis et al. (2015) indicated in the case of the stock market in Japan. There is no doubt that both, the IROR and AROP, are two key variables that might be central in the explanation of economic phenomena of capitalism.

Chapter 7
Asymmetries in International Trade

When a rich man and a poor man deal with one another, both of them will increase their riches, if they deal prudently, but the rich man's stock will increase in a greater proportion than the poor man's. In like manner, when a rich and a poor nation engage in trade the rich nation will have the greatest advantage and therefore the prohibition of this commerce is most hurtful to it of the two.

Adam Smith (*Wealth of Nations,* p. 512)

Abstract The discussion of competition from the domestic extends to international markets and the formation of international prices. We raise the old discussion on unequal exchange and transfer of values. In our analysis, we use input-output data available from the WIOD base for the German, Greek, US and Chinese economies, and we attempt to estimate the transfer of value between three pairs of countries, Greece-Germany, China-USA and Germany-USA. We do not find significant transfers in the trade between the USA and Germany, apparently because of their similar technologies and productivities which do not present wide differences. However, when we compare the German with the Greek economy in terms of unit labour values, we find large differences in favour of Germany, and, when the exchange takes place, it follows that there are significant transfers from Greece to Germany. Similarly, in the USA-China bilateral trade, we find that productivity in the USA is several times higher than that of China and the wage rate in China much lower than that of the USA; however, both productivity and wage differentials in the last years of the analysis tend to get narrower. Hence, if we rely only on these, the USA appears to have an absolute advantage; however, on further examination, we find that, once we take the purchasing power parity into account, China appears to possess and maintain an absolute cost advantage.

Keywords Unequal exchange · International prices · Transfer of values · Absolute cost advantage · Purchasing power parity · Trade between the USA and China

© Springer Nature Switzerland AG 2019

L. Tsoulfidis, P. Tsaliki, *Classical Political Economics and Modern Capitalism,*
https://doi.org/10.1007/978-3-030-17967-0_7

7.1   Introduction

The prevailing idea in international trade textbooks is that international exchanges benefit all partners involved. The idea always is one and the same; 'free trade' should be the guiding principle in the contemplation of economic policies, despite the fact that policymakers of major economies (countries) occasionally complain about the negative for them consequences. However, the grievances are not directed against the principle of 'free trade', per se, but rather against applied practices that allegedly distort it. Nevertheless, economic history, repeatedly, teaches that all advanced economies at some time in the past had adopted protectionist trade policies in their incessant effort to acquire, one way or another, an absolute advantage over their current and even potential competitors. In addition, the historical evidence has repeatedly ascertained the view that trade liberalization policies for the relatively weak economies not only was not accompanied by economic growth but instead further deteriorated their economic and social problems (Chang 2002; Shaikh 2004, 2007, 2016).

The usual argument put forwards in support of 'free trade' is that a national economy benefits by specializing and exporting (importing) those commodities that produce relatively more (less) efficiently. The argument draws on Ricardo's famous four-number numerical example forming the principle of comparative cost advantage, which is acknowledged by neoclassical economics and also by many heterodox economists as:

> One of the few bits of statical logic that economists of all schools understand and agree with.
> (Samuelson 1976, p. 96)

According to this principle, trading countries are better off by specializing in the goods that they can produce relatively (and not absolutely) cheaper and if there are no impediments to international competition all trading partners manage not only to establish trade balance (exports to be equal to imports) but also economic growth to the benefit of their people.[1]

Neoclassical economists from the very beginning found the Ricardian principle of comparative advantage conformable with their theory and downplayed the Smithian, as we argue below, more pragmatic approach of the absolute advantage. In fact, the neoclassical theory, as it has been cast in the Heckscher-Ohlin model, argues that countries should specialize in the production of those goods that use more intensively the endowment of domestic factor(s) of production in relative abundance; hence, countries with abundant labour (capital) should specialize in the production of labour (capital) intensive goods. The idea is that the use of the factor of production in relative abundance will entail a more efficient production and therefore a lower cost and price for the good that uses this particular factor. As a result, countries specializing in goods which use intensively their factor of production in relative abundance and trade them against other goods that they use the factor of production which is domestically relatively scarce will gain from international trade. Such a

---

[1]It is important to emphasize that this principle has wider than international trade applications, and it is further elaborated to include aspects of economic and social life, such as marriage, childbearing and discrimination, among others (Becker 1971).

trading activity, therefore, cannot but lead to trade balance between trading countries and benefit them all, albeit not necessarily equally; hence, in traditional economics, trade is for the benefit of all involved and 'autarky' is not an option.

The alternative principle of absolute cost advantage in international trade, originating in the writings of Adam Smith and other classical economists, states that the individual capital that holds a cost advantages in production in the beginning of the international transactions will put forward every possible effort to maintain it over its international competitors, in the exact same way as in its struggle to prevail over domestic competitors. In fact, the historical record has repeatedly shown that in those countries whose capitals have, one way or another, established absolute cost advantage managed to maintain a favourable balance of trade to the detriment of their partners. In other words, international trade does not always work symmetrically for the countries involved, and more often than not asymmetries between the economies involved are increasing instead of decreasing due to (without accounting for other factors) the transfer of values from the less developed countries (LDC) to the already developed countries (DC).

In the present chapter, some of the fundamental tenets of mainstream trade theory are discussed, and, at the same time, the requirements for an alternative approach based on the principle of absolute cost advantage, the labour theory of value and distribution and classical competition are put together. Specifically, we focus on the international trade theory developed by Smith, then on the objections raised by Ricardo and the way he was led to the configuration of the principle of comparative cost advantage and the consequent country specialization. We continue with a brief summary of the theories of transfers of value by paying particular attention to Emmanuel's unequal exchange argument. Subsequently, we present how Marx's labour theory of value and theory of competition are combined together in the course of international trade and the way in which they account for the appearance of particular trade patterns. In so doing, we lay out the expected outcomes which are empirically tested using data from three pairs of quite diverse economies in the effort to derive useful theoretical and practical conclusions. The first pair of countries refers to Germany and Greece, the second pair to the USA and China and finally, the third pair to the USA and Germany.

It is important to note from the outset that in our analysis, we make use of the notion of domestic capital or firm instead of a country which is featuring in most discussions on international trade; the idea is that capitals and not countries (at least directly) compete with each other in both domestic and international markets. In addition, in order to analyse and comprehend the outcomes of international trade transactions, we focus on the developments brought about by the classical (real) competition in international markets.

7.2   Absolute vs. Comparative Cost Advantage

Smith (1776) argued that the division of labour increases productivity, reduces production costs and therefore lowers the prices of commodities. As demand rises, the necessary and sufficient conditions for greater division of labour are met through the technological change and the subsequent mechanization of the production process leading to further division of labour and therefore to improved efficiency in production lowers unit costs and prices. Hence, if we hypothesize two countries, e.g. Portugal and England, and two goods, e.g. wine and textile, and if we further suppose that Portugal produces wine more efficiently than England and England produces textile cheaper than Portugal, it is in the interest of both countries to specialize in the product in which they have the absolute cost advantage. The reason is that the economies of scale resulting from higher demand and the lower prices bring in more revenues from higher exports and so the consumption of both goods increases. The two countries will be placed in a better position after trading with each other since, at the end of the process, they will produce and consume more of the products (textile and wine) than before the opening of their markets (trade). According to Smith, if each of the two countries specializes in the products that they possess absolute cost advantage, then thanks to the opportunities offered by the free trade both countries are expected to improve their efficiency and possibly enhance their absolute cost advantage to the benefit of their people.

Here one might object to Smith's view, because the products in which each country specializes may determine the level of its future prosperity. For example, the wine production, a traditional good, by its very nature is not liable to any significant and perhaps meaningful division of labour; by contrast, the textile industry, a leading one in Smith's times, experienced epoch-making technological changes characterizing the era of industrial revolution of the late eighteenth century. A second objection that may one raise is that international trade (in the time of Smith, even more so today) is not conducted between states, but between capitals or firms. Smith's analysis, however, does not show the precise mechanisms through which specialization will potentially improve the overall well-being of the trading partners. Finally, a third objection, which is really Ricardo's critique and through that the advancement of his principle of comparative cost advantage, is what if a country possesses an absolute cost disadvantage in the production of both trading goods? In this case, according to Smith's analysis, there will be no grounds for meaningful international transactions.

This last description of the two trading partners enabled Ricardo to advance his theory of comparative advantage (costs), the cornerstone of the modern neoclassical theory of international trade. As is usual in Ricardo, he starts his analysis with Smith's views; in his attempt to find their weaknesses and in his effort to correct them, he advances his own important contributions. Smith was, in general, a fervent supporter of free trade for it enhances the prosperity of nations,[2] and Ricardo shared Smith's view that international trade is beneficial to countries when they export products for which have developed an absolute cost advantage in their production.

---

[2]Contrary to the popular view which portrays Smith as a champion of 'free trade', it is worth noting that he was not that doctrinaire in his approach as this can be judged by his position with regard to the British navigation laws (beginning in 1651) that prohibited 'free trade' of colonies to the benefit of England. This strengthens the view that the discussions about free trade are a pretext for the application of effective protection policies.

Table 7.1 Ricardo's principle of comparative cost advantage		Countries	
	Goods	England	Portugal
	Textile	100 labour hours	90 labour hours
	Wine	120 labour hours	100 labour hours

However, Ricardo posed the following question; what happens if one of the two countries possess an absolute cost advantage in the production of both goods? And his answer was that even in this case—which is not dealt within Smith's analysis—trade can still be beneficial to both trading countries.

Ricardo's international trade theory is presented through a 2×2 model (two countries which produce and trade two goods) using a numerical example of four numbers that we repeat in Table 7.1. It is interesting to note that this particular example, along with a host of others, is what Schumpeter (1954) characterizes as 'Ricardian vice', that is, the description of a complex operation of the economy with the use of super-simple numerical examples based on extreme assumptions. In Table 7.1 England is presented as having an absolute disadvantage in her trade with Portugal in the production of both goods. Ricardo, as is usual for him, tries to prove his thesis under the most unfavourable circumstances; in this particular example, Smith would argue that there is no basis for trade, while Ricardo argued that a more careful and thorough investigation shows that trade is both possible and to the benefit of the trading partners, provided of course that the absolute advantage or disadvantage in the production of the two goods is not the same.

In Table 7.1 we observe that Portugal produces both goods more efficiently than England. In particular, it takes 90 h of labour to produce a unit of textile in Portugal while in England 100 h of labour. Similarly, the production of wine in Portugal takes 100 h of labour while in England 120 h of labour.[3] Initially, the Portuguese companies possess an absolute advantage in the production of both goods, and according to Smith's view, there is no basis for international transactions, since each country pays for its imports through the revenues from the sale of its exports; consequently, if a country does not export (in this case England), it follows that it lacks the required revenues for its imports.

Ricardo, however, argued that initially Portugal exports to England both goods; as a result, England suffers from a trade deficit which is covered by exports of gold to Portugal. According to Ricardo, the gold exported from England will reduce the money supply in the country and decrease the price level, whereas the influx of gold in Portugal will have the converse results. Over time, the continuing rise in prices in Portugal and the falling prices in England will lead to a point that England will be producing one of the two goods at the same, if not, cheaper price. Ricardo notes that the product that England will be producing cheaper will be the textile and certainly not the wine because the initial cost difference in wine production is far too large to

---

[3]The original example assumes the presence of national currencies convertible into gold. The example can be extended to include exchange rates (Shaikh 1980b, 2016); nevertheless, such analysis is beyond the scope of this chapter.

be neutralized by price changes.[4] Thus, the textile is the good on which England may specialize and wine is that of Portugal; hence, specialization is the expected outcome from international transactions, which can be proven to the benefit of both countries according to Ricardo and the defenders of 'free trade'. The above statement highlights the essence of the principle of comparative cost advantage, which is adopted by the majority of economists and figures prominently in the opening chapters of every single textbook in international trade theory.

The salient mechanism which is not openly acknowledged and plays, however, a decisive role in the analysis of comparative cost advantage is the quantity theory of money developed by the so-called Bullionist economists and Ricardo and has been criticized by the so-called Banking School mainly for its unrealistic assumptions of the exogenous character of money and its lack of support by empirical facts. Marx shared the views of the Banking School and further developed them by utilizing his labour theory of value and by extending it to grapple with issues of money (see Appendix 1). In fact, by replacing the quantity theory of money used in Ricardo's analysis, we may arrive at radically different (and more realistic) conclusions. More specifically, other things equal the chain of events is expected to evolve not as Ricardo proposed but as follows:

- England, because of her cost disadvantage in the production of both goods, imports them from Portugal.
- Hence, England exports gold and therefore reduces its domestic quantity of money, and so the interest rate increases, and investment is discouraged leading to the reduction in domestic production.[5]
- The converse processes take place in Portugal, that is, the inflow of gold will increase the money supply, interest rates will fall, investment will rise and production and exports will further increase.
- As international trade continues, there comes a moment when the gold reserves of the Bank of England will be found at alarming low levels.
- England's persistent trade deficit will eventually be covered by short-term international borrowing. In effect, it will be in the interest of Portugal to lend (deposit), ceteris paribus, their surplus money to English rather than to Portuguese banks.
- The end result of this process for England will be a chronic trade deficit and spiralling up of her international debt, which is equivalent to saying that Portugal will become a net lender of England in this trading relationship.
- As this trend continues, the interest rates between the two countries will tend to equalize, and sometime in the future, the Portuguese will no longer be interested in depositing their capital in England, and thus the English economy, other things equal, will collapse and so will the trade between the two countries.

---

[4]In the hypothetical and very unlike situation, where the initial cost differences were the same, then, other things equal, there is no way to establish a comparative advantage, and trade would therefore discontinue. Perhaps, this is the case that Smith and Ricardo would agree with each other.

[5]The domestic production might not be zero, because there will always be some consumers who will continue to purchase the specific goods using, for instance, patriotic criteria.

The above-described sequence of events is not at all hypothetical, and there are many examples even from recent economic history attesting to that. In fact, there is no serious mechanism or currently effective policy to enforce trade surplus countries to spend and not save their surpluses, increase their aggregate demand and in so doing increase their own price level and their exchange rates, thereby undermining their cost advantages and competitiveness in general.

All of the above considerations seem to go unaccounted for in most modern international trade theories whose foundation remains the Ricardian principle of comparative cost advantage and its alleged properties. For instance, the Heckscher-Ohlin (H-O) trade model, which is the back bone of the neoclassical international trade theories, argues that differences in the endowment in the factors of production give rise to their relative abundance or scarcity and in so doing determine the comparative advantage of each country and the associated with it trade pattern.[6] The poor empirical performance of the H-O model as it has been repeatedly shown starting with Leontief's (1953) pioneering empirical study led to the idea of 'paradoxical results', that is, results in deviation of common sense, which have been put under the rubric of 'Leontief Paradox' (Wolff 1985, Paraskevopoulou et al. 2016). Similar to Leontief's, results were found in the trade data of many countries, and these led to the formation of new trade models which integrate into their analysis elements of imperfect competition such as economies of scale and scope, strategic business behaviour and innovation, among others (Dixit and Stiglitz 1977; Krugman 1981; Ethier 1982). There is no doubt that all these attempts inject elements of realism into international trade and, in a sense, improve the neoclassical H-O model. On further examination, however, we discover that underneath these contributions are the Ricardian principle of comparative advantage and the associated with it quantity theory of money casting doubt to the explanatory content of those efforts.

The neoclassical old and new trade models by their very equilibrating nature predict the long-run net trade balance. In effect, there are various mechanisms built into this type of models predicting that 'free trade' leads economies not only to balancing trade but moreover and in the long run to attaining similar levels of competitiveness and technological development. The problem is that almost never has this prediction been confirmed by adequate empirical evidence. Several surveys, examining the above adjustment mechanisms in relation to the comparative advantage and alleged benefits of 'free trade', result in outcomes quite different from those expected (see Kaldor 1978; Milberg 2001).

In a nutshell, the principle of comparative cost advantage, as developed by Ricardo, depends critically on the quantity theory of money according to which, the trade between two initially unevenly developed economies initiates changes in their price levels caused by respective changes in the money supply redressing their trade balance. However, an alternative theory of money may give rise to quite

---

[6]Other adjustment mechanisms that have emerged within the framework of the traditional neoclassical pattern of international trade refer to productivity differences, wages differentials and exchange rates to mention only a few.

different results (Shaikh 1980b, 2016; Tsoulfidis 2010, pp. 98–101; Weeks 2010, pp. 94–102), and the initial absolute cost advantage may persist, if not enhanced by international trade. Also, the real exchange rate regimes, in and of themselves, cannot shape trade patterns, since they are determined by real labour cost and, in a way, reflect the relative competitiveness of an economy. Empirical research, by Shaikh (1991) for the USA, Japan, Germany, UK and Canada; Ruiz-Napoles (1996) for Mexico; Antonopoulos (1999) for Greece; Ersoy (2010) for Turkey; Martinez-Hernandez (2010, 2017) for Mexico, the USA, Taiwan and 16 OECD countries; and Shaikh and Antonopoulos (2012) for the USA and Japan, has given results which lend support to the hypothesis that real exchange rates are determined by relative labour costs and in effect reflect the relative competitiveness of an economy.

7.3 Asymmetries in Trade

According to mainstream trade theory, any free exchange involves the transfer of equal value between the trading partners which are supposed to exchange goods of equal value. In fact, the sphere of exchange implies equality of the value of products that voluntarily change ownership and international exchanges appear as 'innocuous and fair acts' rendering benefits to all participants alike. By contrast, in the Marxian tradition it has been long-established that behind the seemingly equality in (domestic or international) exchange of commodities, a mechanism of transfer of labour values takes place underneath the surface economic category of market prices. Michael Grossmann and Otto Bauer were among the first who indicated the inequalities in international exchanges. For example, Grossmann (1929) argued that:

> In international trade there is not an exchange of equivalents, because, just as in the domestic market, there is a tendency toward equalization of profit rates. Therefore the commodities of the highly developed capitalist country, that is, of a country with a higher average organic composition of capital, are sold at prices of production which are always greater than their values. On the other hand, the commodities of countries with a lower organic composition of capital are sold under free competition at prices of production that as a general rule must be less than their values [...] In this manner, *transfers of the surplus value* produced in the less developed country take place within the sphere of circulation in the world market, since the distribution of the surplus value is not according to the number of workers employed but according to the magnitude of the capital involved.
>
> (Grossmann 1929, pp. 278–9)

while Otto Bauer noted:

> it is not true that peoples exchange commodities, the production of which requires equal quantities of labor. For prices conceal profits and losses from exchange. The countries with developed industry are the countries that gain profits in exchange at the expense of the agricultural countries.
>
> (cited by Rosdolsky 1977, p. 311)

In the post-war decades, the works of Baran (1957), Mandel (1970), Emmanuel (1972), Amin (1974) and Frank (1978), initiated by the question of whether there is convergence or divergence in the growth performance between countries, led to an important debate in the 1960s and 1970s for the sources and mechanisms of uneven development. Their work formed the theories of dependency and unequal exchange utilizing aspects of Marx's theory of value in their effort to explain uneven development as the outcome of transfers of value through international trade. The analysis of the above pioneering authors was thought-provoking and important in its own right; nevertheless, it was limited and remained mainly in the sphere of circulation, and therefore the emphasis was placed on the ways in which the surplus (wealth) produced is transferred from the less to the more developed countries through commodity trade.

Mandel (1970) argued that the economically advanced countries realize postcolonial excess profits because of their higher labour productivity and the lack of profit rate equalization in the world market. These transfers of supra-profits from the less developed to the already developed countries are realized through international trade. According to the dependency approach, the underdevelopment is a byproduct not of the malfunction of international capital accumulation but rather its normal and expected outcome. For instance, Baran (1957) argues that there are specific developmental characteristics (e.g. dual economy) in the underdeveloped countries which promote unequal development. Furthermore, Amin (1974) argues that the accumulation process takes place in a world scale, in which the centre or the already DC and the periphery or the LDC intertwined; the underdevelopment of the LDC is shaped in such a way so as to serve the growth of the economies in the already DC. This dependency relationship is reproduced and is strengthened with the passage of time perpetuating if not worsening the gap between the DC and LDC. Finally, Frank (1978), although supports the basic argument of the dependency approach that development and underdevelopment are two faces of the same coin, argues that both developed and underdeveloped economies are conditioned upon each other. The dependency approach presumes international trade as the basic mechanism of transfers of value by resorting to an underconsumption kind of argument according to which the need for external markets forces the capital in the centre to impose onto periphery economic structures and trade patterns that at the end benefit the countries in the centre at the expense of the countries in the periphery (Shaikh 1980b; Carchedi 1991; Weeks 1998, 1999). The common feature shared by the above theories is their valiant efforts to reconcile their views with the classical and in particular Marx's labour theory of value.

The theory of unequal exchange was initiated by the analysis of Singer (1950) and Prebisch (1959) who, by following the scheme of centre and peripheral countries, argued that trade relations between countries enhance unequal levels of development. Their argument is that peripheral countries export mainly primary products as opposed to the countries in the centre which export industrial ones. Furthermore, they argue that prices of primary products have a tendency to fall faster than the industrial ones; the rationale is that the rising incomes in the centre, on the one hand, lead to a reduction in demand for primary goods (inferior goods) and lower prices and, on the other hand, to higher demand for industrial products (normal goods) and higher prices (Singer 1950, 1975; Prebisch 1959). As a consequence, the terms of trade between the centre and periphery are worsening to the detriment of the peripheral, mainly agricultural and primary products, countries. The above is further supported by the so-called Balassa-Samuelson effect according to which an increase in the wages of the tradable goods sector of a peripheral economy soon leads to higher wages in the non-tradable sector of their economy. However, the resulting inflation is higher, and the exchange rate is lower in the lesser developed economies, because of their lower productivity relative to the centre countries.[7]

The 'unequal exchange' argument was particularly popular in the 1970s when various radical economists/sociologists in an effort to show that the growth of the more DC was to the detriment of the less DC argued that commodity trade entails transfers of value (or labour time) from the latter to the former. The term 'unequal exchange' was coined by Emmanuel (1972), who unlike other heterodox economists of his time sought to discover exploitative relations not in the flows of capital or imperialism in general, but rather in ordinary international exchanges. Emmanuel argued that the tendential equalization of the profit rates across trading countries leads to the formation of international prices of production, whose difference from the domestic labour values give rise to two types of international transfers of labour values and, in a sense, unequal exchange.

- First, transfers of value from differences of capital-intensities between industries; that is, excess value (or surplus-value) is transferred from the labour-intensive to capital-intensive industries and by extension to the countries in which the capital-intensive industries are located. Presumably, inter-industry capital-intensities are compared against a kind of relevant international average capital-intensity, and in this comparison, the more DC are those with the more capital-intensive industries by virtue of their advanced technologies. According to Emmanuel, this is the unequal exchange in the 'broad sense' whose presence is quite normal and its quantitative significance in international trade is supposed to be minimal.
- Second, transfers of value induced by lower wages in the LDC, which combined with the use of the up-to-date technology give rise to higher rates of surplus-value and create the potential for massive transfers of labour value from the less to the more DC. According to Emmanuel this type of transfers of labour values, whose size was thought to be substantial, characterize the unequal exchange 'in the strict sense' of the term.

The great merit in Emmanuel's theoretical work is his effort to demonstrate the possibility of unequal exchange and the resulting transfer of values not in the easy case, that is, in the presence of extra-economic forces such as monopoly power, dependency or imperialism of any sort, but rather, in the much harder case of the ordinary international trade of commodities. In so doing, the analysis of the transfers of value can be subjected to rigorous economic theorization and also assess the

---

[7]Balassa (1964) and Samuelson (1962b, 1964) independently and at the same time argued that the exchange rates but also wages of the developed countries are higher than those in the peripheral countries as a result of higher (growth rate in their) productivity.

quantitative importance of the possible effects on the development gap between the less and the more DC. This is the reason why Emmanuel's ideas attracted the critique of heterodox economists (for the various views, see Brown 1978) but also orthodox economists (see, e.g. Samuelson 1975, 1976, 1978).

Emmanuel (1972) argued that the transfer of (surplus) value takes place because the LDC happen to have wages much lower than those of their trading partners, while at the same time, the flow of capital and commodities makes both more and less DC to share roughly the same technology. Emmanuel notes:

> [T]he inequality of wages as such, all other things being equal, is alone the cause of the inequality in exchange.
>
> (Emmanuel 1972, p. 61)

In particular, Emmanuel (1972, p. 64) argued that the wage is institutionally given, which is equivalent to saying that the wage is exogenous to the system and a country is classified as core or peripheral according to the level of wage. Assuming away differences in preferences, transportation costs and the like, which are also assumed away in the currently dominating variants of the H-O model of international trade, it follows that the much lower wage in the LDC and the establishment of an international price of production leads to a transfer of surplus-value to the more DC. Emmanuel further argued that there is enough mobility in the flows of capital to bring about tendential equalization of profit rates internationally; while, the relative immobility of labour is what may preserve sizable wage differences across countries and thus large international differences in the rates of surplus-value, which become the primary source of transfer of surplus-value from the less to the more DC.[8]

Samuelson (1975, 1976, 1978) criticized Emmanuel's view on the grounds that as capital will flow from the more to the less DC in order to take advantage of the lower real wages, the demand for labour in LDC will raise the real wages by more than the fall in the more DC; consequently, the limit of this process will be reached with the international equalization of both profit rates and real wages. In other words, the tendential equalization of rates of profit is an indication that inefficiencies and inequalities tend to be eliminated, a result which is quite the opposite of what the unequal exchange theory claims.[9] Emmanuel (1978) in his rather lukewarm response to Samuelson states that the money, not the real wage, is the key variable in his system and, therefore, Samuelson's critique is misplaced and misdirected. Emmanuel, however, neither in his book nor in his answer to Samuelson explains in any straightforward way the relationship between money and real wage. In his analysis, it seems that the money wage is given exogenously and more importantly it is not related in any strict sense to the real wage, that is, the bundle of use values normally consumed by workers.

---

[8]For example, Emmanuel (1972, p. 48) claimed that the wage in the peripheral countries is 1/30 of the core countries while labour productivity is at most 1/2; thus competitiveness in the peripheral countries is about 1/15 of the centre countries.

[9]It may be noticed in passing that Samuelson (1976, p. 96) praises Emmanuel as a serious scholar whose research is 'one of the few attempts to put Marxian analytics to work on a genuine real-world problem'.

It is important to stress at this juncture that the bundle of use values forming the workers' real wage may not be the same between centre and peripheral countries for a number of historical, physical and socioeconomic reasons, and in the more DC, the real wage may contain more use values than that in the peripheral countries. So, money wage may be higher in a DC and lower in a LDC, but in both it is barely adequate to purchase the necessary bundle of use values required for the reproduction of the labour power. As a consequence, the real wage across countries is, in a sense, tendentially equalized, whereas the money wage might be quite different. The implication of this analysis is that real wages in effect tend to be equalized from the point of view of workers as they manage to reproduce their ability to work and reproduce continuously their labour services. At the same time, money wages (cost of labour) in effect are different from the point of view of businesses as they pay differently for the same amount of labour services. It seems that such issues either were not taken into account or, what is more likely, were downplayed by an economist of the lucks of Samuelson, while Emmanuel was puzzled with such issues, although there are hints in his work; nevertheless, he did not manage to explicate his position in any straightforward way.

Emmanuel's response to Samuelson's critique was really a retreat from what appeared to be a promising alternative to the standard neoclassical international trade theory. It seems that Emmanuel was trapped in the neoclassical H-O and, in a sense, Samuelson's model of international trade and this is the reason why he did not bring his unequal exchange argument down to its logical conclusion; that is, the outright rejection of the Ricardian principle of comparative cost advantage shared by neoclassical and many heterodox economists. The logical path for Emmanuel would have been the replacement of the principle of comparative cost advantage with the theory of absolute cost advantage, which as Shaikh (1980b, 2016, ch. 11) has argued in effect rules international trade and bears responsibility for transfers of value between industries and countries leading to unequal exchange in the broad sense, at least.

In particular, Shaikh (1980b) argued that the competitive position of any capital (firm) depends on its ability to produce commodities of a given quality with less direct and indirect labour requirement than its competitors. The less efficient capitals may stay in business for some time to the extent that they enjoy certain other benefits, such as lower wages, lower taxation, subsidies, proximity to resources or markets and the like. However, such benefits do not protect forever; with the progress of time as the gap in direct and indirect labour requirements per unit of output widens, other things equal, the less efficient firms will suffer losses and eventually will be compelled away from the industry. What takes place in the domestic market also takes place in the international arena, where competition between capitals expels the weak ones from the markets, regardless of the nature of the markets, that is, national or international.

The debates among heterodox economists during the 1960s and 1970s were more about conceptual issues which were rarely supported by actual data and estimations. Not surprisingly, Emmanuel did not derive any reliable quantitative estimates of the extent and magnitude of the unequal exchange. And in fact, there are only scant efforts to operationalize the unequal exchange hypothesis by estimating the actual transfers of value from peripheral to centre regions or countries. Among the first efforts is Marelli's (1980, 1983) who, by using regional input-output tables, estimated the transfers of values between different Italian regions. Marelli's results showed that transfers of value actually take place from the less developed to the more developed regions of Italy, thereby enhancing the regional inequalities in economic development, as a consequence of unequal exchange.[10] There have been two other attempts to estimate the extent of unequal exchange in the trade between two countries; the first by Gibson (1980) who, by using input-output data of the year 1969 for Peru and the USA, showed that Peru suffered a loss of value of about 38% of its exports to the USA. The second study by Webber and Foot (1984) in their interesting paper on the trade between the Philippines and Canada in the year 1961 arrived at very striking results as they found that for Canada a given amount of money purchases nearly five times more labour time of Philippines's imports. In the recent years, there is renewed interest in the concept of unequal exchange. Ricci (2018) working with WIOD base and all possible countries and applying the new solution to the transformation problem finds significant transfers of value from the less to the more developed countries. Along the same line but with a focus on the rentier economy (unproductive in general activities) seen as a burden to the real economy is the work of Baiman (2014, 2017).

There is no doubt that the empirical estimates of unequal exchange were not easy to carry out for mainly two reasons: first, the necessary data for such calculations were hard to come by for a single year, let alone for a number of years and countries. Under these circumstances, naturally one could not derive any reliable estimates and conclusions. Second, the theoretical concepts were not well developed, and their empirical analogues for the theoretical variables had to wait for at least a decade (see, e.g. Shaikh 1984, 2016; Mariolis and Tsoulfidis 2016; and the literature cited there). Nowadays, input-output tables are compiled more or less with the same methodology, the same industry detail for a number of countries and years (WIOD) and expressed in the same monetary units (dollars); consequently, both comparisons across countries and intertemporal comparisons for the same country are much easier to carry out. Finally, many theoretical issues of the classical theory of value and distribution have been further clarified, and the empirical analysis is at a stage that can address the complex issue of unequal exchange in an effective and economically meaningful way.

7.4   Transfers of Value

As discussed in Chap. 1, the 'law of value' becomes the regulator of the capitalist economy since it shapes the social division of labour, determines the exchange relations and ensures the normal reproduction of the system. The coordination of the numerous actions of many independently acting individual capitals takes place in

---

[10]Marelli's study, although it is conducted in the framework of transfers of value literature, it is not concerned with the unequal exchange 'in the strict sense' of the term.

the sphere of circulation, where they come to terms with the result of their efforts which are rewarded generously, adequately or even penalized. In Chaps. 3, 4 and 5, we show that the shift from one form of value to another, that is, from direct prices to prices of production, gives rise to transfers of value leaving the amount of the total value produced (in the production sphere) and realized (in the circulation sphere) the same despite the presence of individual deviations (Shaikh 1984). In fact, the law of value makes producers realize that those with individual value higher than the socially necessary are placed into a harsh position for they are forced either to cut their cost (individual value) or to perish; in other words, through the law of value, producers realize the hard way that competition, by eliminating weak capitals, increases the market share and thus profits for the remaining more efficient capitals.

In effect, the 'law of value' becomes visible via the forces of real competition, that is, a dynamic process of rivalry between units of capital struggling for survival through profit making. The major feature of the units of capital is their need to expand profits, as a condition sine qua non for their very existence and reproduction. As we showed in Chap. 5, in Marx's analysis there is a clear distinction of competition between firms (units of capital) operating within the same industry (intra-industry competition) and competition among industries (inter-industry competition). These two moments of competition give rise to two distinct laws, the 'law of one price' (LOOP) within an industry and the 'law of the tendential equalization of rates of profit rate' across industries. In the same chapter, we argued that the price of production of an industry is formed by the regulating capital (production conditions) of the industry, that is, the capital that employs the dominant technique (Tsaliki and Tsoulfidis 2010, 2015). The regulating capital and its associated dominant technique encompass the socially necessary labour time which determines the price of production around which the market price gravitates. This regulating so to speak price of production determines both the domestic and international competitiveness. As a consequence, the capitals employing a state-of-the-art technique sell their output at approximately the same price with the other less efficient capitals and in so doing realize excess profits due to positive transfers of value, whereas capitals with outdated and less efficient techniques because of their higher unit cost of production realize a fraction of the value that they have produced. In that way, although the total value produced in the sphere of production is (fully) realized in circulation, its distribution among the various competing capitals rewards the more efficient capitals with excess profits and penalizes the less efficient capitals with significant losses. As Marx (*Capital* III, pp. 141–162) argues, the equalization of profit rates is compatible with the labour theory of value only in the case of unequal exchange and transfers of value, where we allow commodities to be exchanged in prices which do not directly relate to labour time directly or indirectly employed in their production (see Appendix 1 in Chap. 5).

Real competition renders absolute real costs and differences in productivity the critical determinants of trade patterns in the domestic as well as in international markets. In fact, all end results of trade may become traceable and not a mystery from the moment it is recognized that competition of capitals within and between industries operates in a way such that the end results favour the strong capitals (and eventually the economies in which they are located) to the detriment of the weak ones (Milberg 1994; Weeks 2001; Shaikh 2007; Seretis and Tsaliki 2012, 2016; Tsaliki et al. 2018).

It should be clear that uneven development on a world scale, although not necessarily caused, nevertheless is enhanced by international trade as a result of differential productivity across countries, rendering the exports of capital (due mainly to lower wages in less developed countries) or transfers of value as secondary phenomena and not the primary causes of underdevelopment (Shaikh 1980b, p. 57). The root causes of uneven development should be looked for in the sphere of production, where differences in productivity and unit costs in combination with the LOOP make possible the transfers of value in both the domestic and international transactions. In fact, differences in productivity and unit costs between capitals activated in the same industry give rise to transfers of values, as we move from one form of value, that is, the individual direct price, into another form of value, that is, the domestic or the international price of production.

The approach to international trade based on the notion of absolute cost advantage and classical competition makes possible the unfolding of a characteristically different mechanism with results quite other than those predicted by the principle of comparative cost advantage. Thus instead of deriving mutually beneficial trade, we may derive trade that benefits the one party at the expense of the other, which is another way to say that competition is levelled from the domestic to the international arena and in so doing strengthens rather than weakens the asymmetries caused by the differences in productivity. Within this absolute cost advantage approach phenomena usually attributed to monopoly or unequal exchange now become the immediate consequences of 'free trade' or what amounts to the same thing, international competition. The latter instead of negating the uneven development enhances it, and instead of closing the gap between rich and poor countries tightens the grip of the strong over the weak (Shaikh 1980b).[11]

7.5 Modelling the Transfers of Value

In general, the transfers of value can be defined as the difference, δ, between the prices of production, p, and labour values, λ[12]

---

[11]In fact, the proposed 'free trade' policies benefit the economies which possess an absolute cost advantage in the production of traded goods, whereas openness to international competition of the less advanced countries enhances their initial underdevelopment. More importantly, the standard neoclassical economic theory must come to terms with the well-known fact from the economic history of the already developed economies all of which, at some point in their past, applied protectionist and in general mercantilist policies in order to grow and become developed (Chang 2002).

[12]The analysis that follows is conducted in terms of labour values and the estimated prices of production are only first-step prices of production (see Chaps. 2 and 3), that is, modified labour values (Shaikh 1977).

$$\delta = p - \lambda$$

If we divide the world into less and more DC, then the transfer of value is defined as the difference, δ, between the internationally formed prices of production, p^*, and the country's average labour values, λ_i. Thus, we have

$$\delta_i = p^* - \lambda_i, i = A, B \qquad (7.1)$$

A positive (negative) difference indicates the gain (loss) in the transfer of value to country $A(B)$ from country $B(A)$.

For a country i the labour values, λ_i, are defined as the sum of constant capital, c_i, variable capital, v_i, and surplus-value, s_i

$$\lambda_i = c_i + v_i + s_i$$

Competition and the mobility of capital equalize the rates of profit across industries and economies and forms the prices of production, p^*, as

$$p^* = (1 + r^*)(c_i + v_i)$$

and an average rate of profit, r^*, as

$$r^* = \frac{s}{c + v} = \frac{s/v}{c/v + v/v} = \frac{e}{(1 + k)}$$

which can be expressed in terms of the international rate of surplus-value, e, and the average international value composition of capital, $k = c/v$.[13] Hence for the country, i, the size of the transfer of value will be

$$\delta_i = p^* - \lambda_i = (1 + r^*)(c_i + v_i) - (c_i + v_i + s_i)$$
$$= r^*(c_i + v_i) - s_i$$

Substituting for r^* and after rearrangement of the terms, we have[14]

$$\delta_i = \left(\frac{e}{(1 + k)}\right)(c_i + v_i) - s_i = v_i\left(e\frac{1 + k_i}{1 + k} - e_i\right) \qquad (7.2)$$

From the above relation, given the tendential equalization of the various domestic rates of profit to an international average, we derive that the necessary condition to rule out the case of unequal exchange is that the rates of surplus-value and value

---

[13]The circulating capital model is the basis of most theoretical and empirical studies in the unequal exchange discussions.

[14]For further discussions see Marelli (1980) and da Silva (1987).

compositions of capital of the trading partners to be equal to their respective international average ones. Hence, even in the case of equal rates of surplus-value by the trading countries, transfers of value may arise due to differences in their value composition of capital. This latter kind of unequal exchange, which Emmanuel calls unequal exchange 'in the broad sense', is quite regular and appears within every economy, and as such it is expected in both domestic and international trade and not much can be done about it. If, however, the value compositions of capital across trading countries are equal to the international average and the rates of surplus-value differ, then we have Emmanuel's case of unequal exchange in the 'strict sense' of the term. Of course, we cannot rule out possible intermediate cases, which may appear in an empirical analysis, and this is where we lay our focus.

7.6   Implementation of the Model

The ideas expressed so far are general enough, and in order to become meaningful, they need to be operationalized. In what follows, we make an effort to quantify the transfers of value and, at the same time, to test the realism of the assumptions usually made in the unequal exchange debates. For this purpose, we investigate the bilateral trade between three pairs of countries which are also major trading partners, namely, Germany and Greece, USA and China and finally USA and Germany. The empirical analysis that is applied uses input-output data for Germany and Greece spanning the period 1995–2007,[15] while the same set of data in the case of the USA and China is extended up to the year 2009. For all countries, we employ actual input-output data in order to represent the constant returns, single product and single primary input technology through the use of the matrix $\mathbf{A}$, the matrix of technological coefficients estimated in constant (1995) prices. The vector of employment coefficients $\mathbf{l}$ is derived as the ratio of the total wages of the employed and self-employed population to the product of the gross output of each industry times the economy's average deflated wage. Hence, unlike Emmanuel's claim and the usual neoclassical assumption that the trading economies employ the same technology, we actually estimate the technology matrix $\mathbf{A}$ and the employment coefficients $\mathbf{l}$ for each country using their respective actual input-output and employment data.[16] As expected, both the

---

[15]In some cases, because of data availability, the analysis is carried out up to the years 2009 and 2011.

[16]The assumption of dissimilar technologies which are in effect utilized in actual economies is in sharp contrast to Emmanuel's and H-O models of international trade that hypothesize uniform technology across trading partners. The realistic assumption of different technology has been used quite early by economists like Gomulka (1971) but also by Elmslie and Milberg (1992, 1996), among others. For instance, Elmslie and Milberg (1992, p. 466) note 'the results show that the assumption of identical technologies across OECD countries is not justified by the [input-output] data'.

technology (described by the matrix **A** and the vector **l**) and the real wage vector **b** turn out to be quite different in the four countries.

Subsequently, the labour values of each industry under examination are estimated from the well-known equation

$$\lambda = \mathbf{l}[\mathbf{I} - \mathbf{A}]^{-1} \qquad (7.3)$$

In this way, we estimate the vector of labour values, λ, that is, the direct and indirect labour-years required to produce output worth a million dollars in constant 1995 prices for each pair of countries in comparison in our empirical analysis. The next step is to estimate the constituent components of the rate of profit, that is, the rate of surplus-value and the value composition of capital. For the estimation of the rate of surplus-value, we stipulate that the real wage, **b**, is equal to the average annual deflated money wage allocated over the basket of goods and services normally purchased by workers. Hence, the rate of surplus-value is

$$e = \frac{1 - \lambda\mathbf{b}}{\lambda\mathbf{b}} = \frac{\lambda(\mathbf{I} - \mathbf{A} - \mathbf{bl})\mathbf{x}}{\lambda\mathbf{blx}} \qquad (7.4)$$

and the economy-wide average rate of profit, r, on circulating capital is

$$r = \frac{\lambda(\mathbf{I} - \mathbf{A} - \mathbf{bl})\mathbf{x}}{\lambda(\mathbf{A} + \mathbf{bl})\mathbf{x}} \qquad (7.5)$$

In the presence of fixed capital stock, **K**, the respective rate of profit, ρ, is

$$\rho = \frac{\lambda(\mathbf{I} - \mathbf{A} - \mathbf{bl})\mathbf{x}}{\lambda\mathbf{Kx}} \qquad (7.6)$$

The vertically integrated value compositions of (fixed) capital is

$$VIVCC = \frac{\lambda\mathbf{K}[\mathbf{I} - \mathbf{A}]^{-1}\mathbf{x}}{\lambda\mathbf{bl}[\mathbf{I} - \mathbf{A}]^{-1}\mathbf{x}} \qquad (7.7)$$

The international rate of profit is assumed to be equal to the average of the two countries' profit rates, while the international price of production is approximated by the average of the two domestic prices of production. This is a simplified assumption and runs against the hypothesis of transfers of value. The idea is that the international regulating rate of profit will be much closer to the more efficiently producing country, and so by taking the simple average rate of profit in effect, we reduce the extent of transfers. The prices of production are in accordance to Emmanuel's (and Samuelson's 1975, 1976) numerical examples which are literally Marx's first step prices of production of *Capital* III which, however, are pretty close to the fully transformed prices of production as Shaikh (1977) has shown, and we presented in Chap. 4.

The unequal exchange could be estimated as the difference between the international price of production of an industry $j = 1, \ldots n$ estimated in terms of labour values and the country's ($i = A, B$) domestic labour values. As a result, the deviation, δ, of the international price of production of industry j from the domestic labour value of the same industry for country i will be

$$\delta_i = p_j^* - \lambda_{i,j} \qquad (7.8)$$

In order to estimate the magnitude of transfers and their net result for each trading country, we need to estimate the transfer, positive or negative, for each exported and imported commodity. Let us now focus on one country, whose total transfers in exports, ue_z, is estimated from

$$ue_z = \frac{(\mathbf{p}^* - \lambda) \times \mathbf{z}}{\lambda \mathbf{z}} \qquad (7.9)$$

where the numerator in the above ratio is an element-by-element (or dot) multiplication of the differences between the row vectors of international prices of production and domestic labour values times the respective column vector of exports, $\mathbf{z}$; the denominator presents the value contained in the total exports. In similar fashion, the transfers of value through imports, ue_m, are estimated from

$$ue_m = \frac{(\mathbf{p}^* - \lambda) \times \mathbf{m}}{\lambda \mathbf{m}} \qquad (7.10)$$

where $\mathbf{m}$ stands for the column vector of imports. Furthermore, we can estimate the gain or loss in value as a share of the total economy's gross output by dividing the numerators of the above fractions (Eqs. 7.9 and 7.10) by the product of labour values times the real gross output, $\lambda \mathbf{x}$.

7.6.1   Transfer of Values Between Greece and Germany

We start off with the first pair of countries, Greece and Germany, two countries with levels of economic development quite apart from each other for which the hypothesis of unequal exchange is much easier and suitable to be tested. The reason is that as both countries are members of the EU and EMU, it is reasonable to assume that there is sufficient mobility of capital for the formation of a general rate of profit in the two countries, a testable hypothesis that is possible from the available data of the two economies.[17] We do not stipulate any particular assumption as to the direction of the

---

[17]This mobility of capital might take the form of direct foreign investment, through the purchase of plant and equipment, or indirect through the form of purchase of equity from the domestic stock market and other channels of financing of investment.

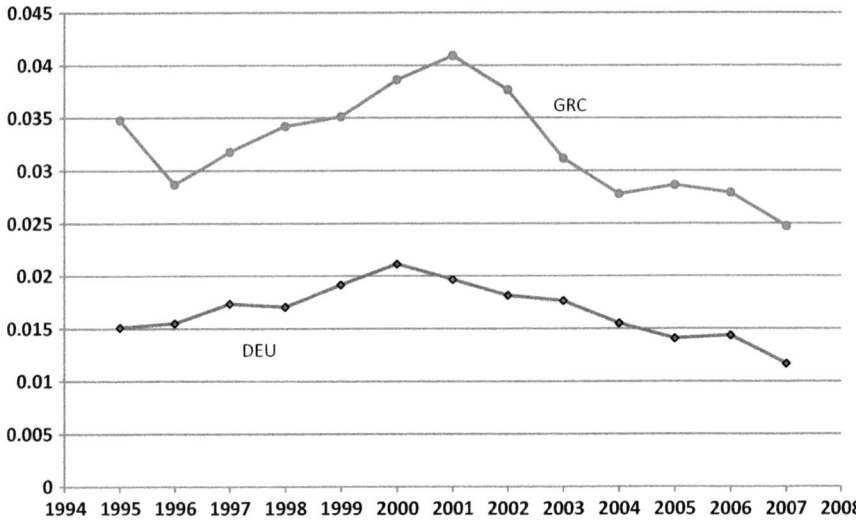

Fig. 7.1 Labour values, Greece and Germany, 1995–2007

flows of capital; we just assume that the mobility of capital will equalize tendentially the rates of profit in the two countries in the long run. Furthermore, the two countries, by no means, are at the same level of technological development and so their labour productivities will be different; thus, the much lower real wage in Greece will not necessarily lead to rates of surplus-value much higher than those in Germany.

We begin the analysis by estimating the labour values using Equation (7.3) in each country for the period 1995–2007. The average values of each country for the period 1995–2007 and for the 16 industries producing tradable goods that we have reliable time series data are displayed in Fig. 7.1.[18] The labour values, as we pointed out, are important in their own right especially because they are comprehensive indexes of efficiency of an economy; the lower the labour values the higher the vertically integrated productivity of an economy, which, in fact, is a major component of its overall competitiveness.

In Fig. 7.1, we observe that Germany's average labour values for the 16 tradable producing goods industries are always much lower than those of Greece, more than one-half, and this difference persists over the years. It is interesting to note that in both economies, the labour values display moderate fluctuations and overall display falling tendency reflecting the technological change and the rise in productivity; hence, the labour content of produced goods is reduced contributing to unit cost reduction of commodities. This is a result that has been well documented in the

---

[18]The interested reader may find the estimates of labour values for each country, individual industry and year in Appendix 2. Also, Table 7.2 lists the nomenclature of tradable goods common to each pair of countries.

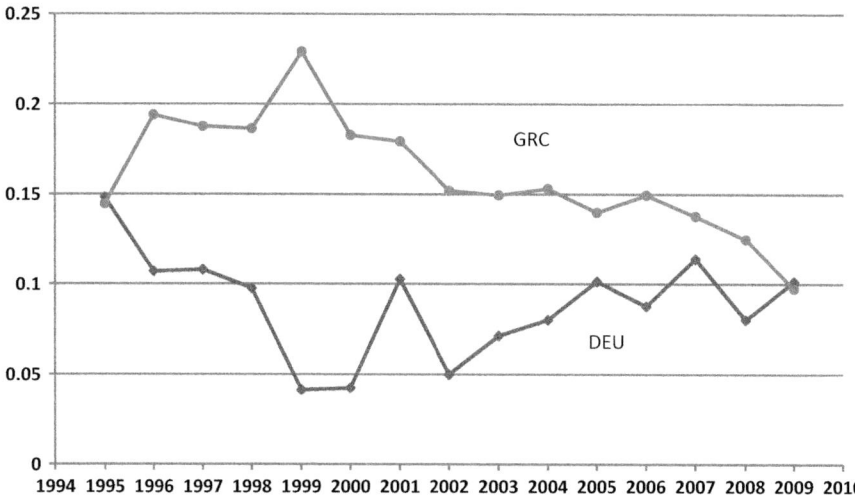

Fig. 7.2 Average rate of profit, Germany and Greece, 1995–2009

input-output literature starting with the work of Carter (1970) and continuing to more recent studies (see, e.g. Miller and Blair 2009; Seretis and Tsaliki 2016); in fact, our results for the four economies under investigation (USA, China, Germany and Greece) confirm the hypothesis of diminishing labour content with the progress of time (see Tables 7.6, 7.7, 7.8 and 7.9 in Appendix 2). The visual inspection of Fig. 7.1 furthermore shows that the higher efficiency of German over the Greek economy persists throughout the years of the analysis.

Figure 7.2 depicts the economy-wide rates of profit estimated on fixed capital of the two countries (Eq. 7.6). Furthermore, on the basis of this average rate of profit, we estimate the international prices of production, i.e. the average of the national prices of production for the 16 tradable commodities in our analysis.

A visual inspection of the graph shows that the two economy-wide rates of profit on fixed capital stock do not display statistically significant differences; they both tend to the same long-run average. It is important to stress, at this point, that in the classical political economy the equalization of the rates of profit does not mean that there is a single rate of profit which once attained it remains still throughout the investigated period (see Chap. 5 for details). In the classical approach to competition, the international average rate of profit is a kind of an ideal average obtained over long stretches of time during which positive and negative deviations of the relevant to this equalization rates of profit cancel each other out.

Figure 7.3 displays the rates of surplus-value, one of the key variables in the unequal exchange debates for the two countries for the period 1995–2009.

From Fig. 7.3 we observe that the rates of surplus-value of the two countries do not display that large differences; nevertheless, in most years of our study, the rate of surplus-value in Greece is higher than that of Germany (apart from the years 1995

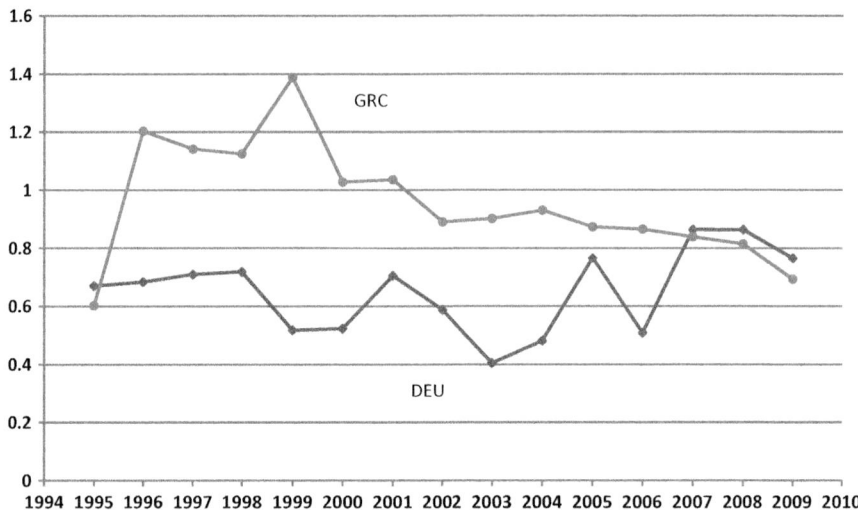

Fig. 7.3 Rates of surplus-value, Greece and Germany, 1995–2009

and 2007–2009).[19] Despite the fact that the real wage in Germany is on an average approximately twice higher than that of Greece, the wage gap between the two countries is more than fully compensated by the much higher German relative to Greek labour productivity. Hence, this may come as a surprise to those expecting that the lower real wages in a country would give rise to a much higher rate of surplus-value; implicit in such expectation is the assumption of uniform technology across countries established through commodity trade, which apparently is not true in the case of the two countries under study and is confirmed by the different value compositions of capital shown in Fig. 7.4.[20] More importantly, the relatively small differences in the rates of surplus-value between the two countries render the argument of unequal exchange in the 'strict sense' a not so vigorous testing hypothesis.

Figure 7.4 depicts the value compositions of fixed capital stock for Germany and Greece estimated from Equation (7.7). The figures on the compositions of fixed capital stock for the Greek economy refer to the period 1995–2009, whereas that for

---

[19]It is important to note that the estimated rate of surplus-value in this study is more like the gross operating surplus-wage ratio and not the rate of surplus-value proper, whose estimation would require the distinction between productive and unproductive labour. However, the available empirical studies have shown that neither the estimation of labour values nor of prices of production is affected by the lack of such distinction. This does not rule out the need for the estimation of the rate of surplus-value on the basis of productive and unproductive labour for other issues and questions (see Chaps. 8, 9 and 10). The gross operating surplus is a residually determined income that includes depreciation and various taxes, among others.

[20]This assumption is stipulated in both the neoclassical Heckscher-Ohlin international trade model and in Emmanuel's radical unequal exchange explanation of underdevelopment.

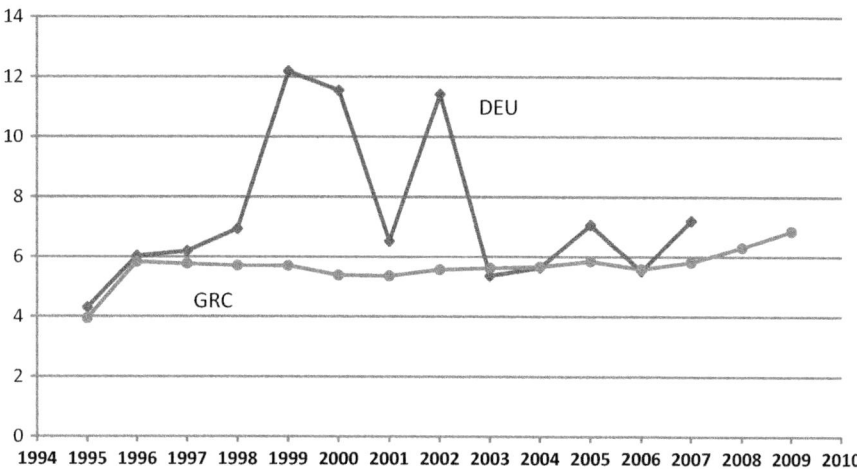

Fig. 7.4 Value composition of fixed capital, Greece and Germany, 1995–2007 and 2009

the German economy refer to the period 1995–2007. The reason for this, as we mentioned, is the availability in data on fixed capital.

We observe quite different trajectories in the value compositions of fixed capital in the two countries. In Germany, it is higher than that of Greece not only with respect to the overall average of the two countries but also in an industry-by-industry comparison that we calculated, but we do not report for the brevity of the presentation. This is an indication that the German economy invested more in fixed capital and, by doing so, significantly contributed to the reduction of its unit national labour values shown in Fig. 7.1. The higher value composition of fixed capital is what makes unit labour values in Germany in all tradable commodities lower than those of Greece over the period under examination and lays the ground for transfers of value from Greece to Germany rendering the argument of unequal exchange in the 'broad sense' a vigorous testing hypothesis. Furthermore, the different trajectories in the compositions of fixed capital rule out the assumption of uniform technology, a prerequisite of both the unequal exchange argument and the neoclassical theory of international trade; in effect, the value composition of fixed capital, measuring the capital-intensity in the two countries, is distinctly higher in Germany than in Greece.

Figure 7.5 displays rough estimates of the total gains from transfers of value in the trade between the two countries. The aggregate results are derived utilizing the indexes ue_x and ue_m (Eqs. 7.9 and 7.10, respectively) for each year of our study.

Figure 7.5 shows that the bilateral trade between Greece and Germany during the 13 years of our analysis implies significant transfers of labour values; specifically, the German economy gains in transfers in both exported and imported goods. For example, the amount of transfers from both imports and exports in the year 2007 was approximately 77.6% of the total traded goods. It is important to emphasize that these transfers of values, as a percentage in the value of the total output produced, are much higher for Greece than in Germany. In Fig. 7.6, we present the transfers of

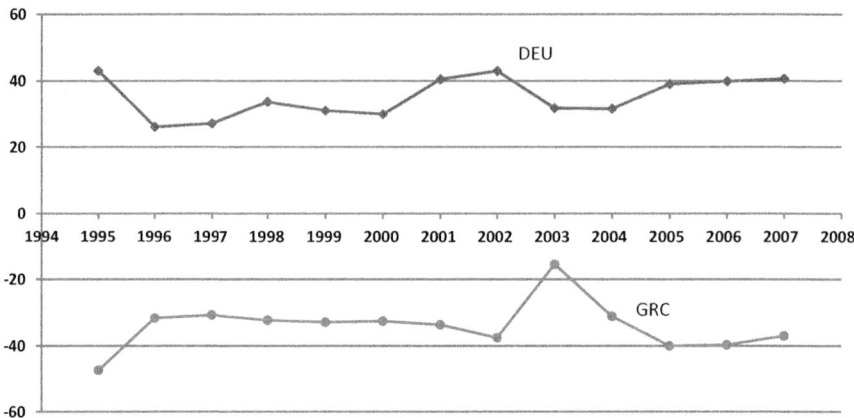

Fig. 7.5 Aggregate effect of unequal exchange as proportion of total bilateral trade, Germany and Greece, 1995–2007

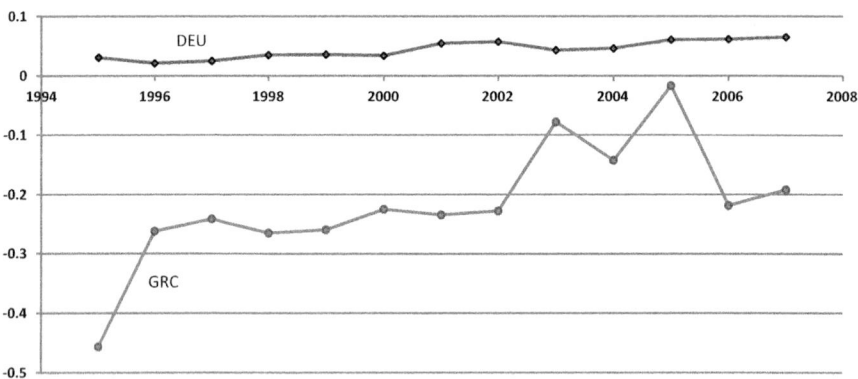

Fig. 7.6 Aggregate effect of bilateral unequal exchange as a proportion to total gross output, Greece and Germany, 1995–2007

value as a percentage to total gross output produced over the 13 years of our investigation. Germany's positive transfers from its exports to Greece amount to an average 0.044% of its total gross output produced, whereas the losses of Greece amount to an average 0.216% of its total gross output produced.

In our effort to show in an analytical and, at the same time, practical way the extent and the significance of these transfers for the German and Greek economies, we take a typical year, for example, the year 2007, on the basis of which we form Table 7.2, where we display the transfers of value for each of the 16 industries producing tradable commodities. Starting with Germany, the labour values for each of the 16 tradable goods of German industries are displayed in column 1, while the imported goods evaluated in thousand dollars are displayed in column 2; column 3 is

Table 7.2 German worker year vs. Greek worker year in 2007

2007	Germany			Greece		
	Labour values (worker years) (1)	Imports (thousand \$) (2)	$Vx = d*z$ Worker hours exported (3) = (1)*(2)	Labour values (worker years)	Exports (thousand \$)	$Vx = d*z$ Worker hours exported
Agriculture, hunting, forestry and fishing	0.014	272,437.0	3,931.755	0.040	39,818,502.7	1,599,244.7
Mining and quarrying	0.014	23,091.0	320.804	0.021	3501.4	72.0
Food, beverages and tobacco	0.012	448,665.0	5234.090	0.027	474,696.6	12,897.1
Textiles and textile products	0.012	258,590.1	3057.911	0.028	218,905.1	6147.0
Leather, leather and footwear	0.011	95,642.9	1084.851	0.026	110,637.2	2826.4
Wood and products of wood and cork	0.012	1870.0	22.068	0.025	114,050.3	2902.1
Pulp, paper, paper, printing and publishing	0.011	10,301.0	113.767	0.028	662,378.6	18,226.6
Coke, refined petroleum and nuclear fuel	0.006	31,720.0	202.949	0.010	41,280.5	404.2
Chemicals and chemical products	0.011	352,225.0	3710.641	0.027	5,954,476.5	161,282
Rubber and plastics	0.012	45,025.0	521.968	0.019	642,238.5	12,347.3
Other non-metallic mineral	0.012	6078.0	3931.755	0.021	507,885.0	10,605.4
Basic metals and fabricated metal	0.011	456,501.0	320.804	0.022	1,802,143.5	39,837.7
Machinery, Nec	0.012	77,729.0	5234.090	0.026	4,167,685.6	108,369.9

(continued)

Table 7.2 (continued)

2007	Germany			Greece		
	Labour values (worker years) (1)	Imports (thousand $) (2)	$Vx = d*z$ Worker hours exported (3) = (1)*(2)	Labour values (worker years)	Exports (thousand $)	$Vx = d*z$ Worker hours exported
Electrical and optical equipment	0.014	210,097.0	3057.911	0.021	22,670,764.7	483,937.7
Transport equipment	0.012	72,640.0	1084.851	0.029	12,613,504.3	361,241.4
Manufacturing, Nec; recycling	0.012	10,181.0	22.068	0.026	347,253.1	9185.0
Total		2,372,793.0	**28,031.1**		**90,149,903.7**	**2,829,526.5**
Labour commanded in 1000$			**84.6**			**31.9**

the product of columns 1 and 2, and it is the total labour content of imports. Dividing the total imports evaluated in thousand dollars (sum of column 2) by the total labour-years per million dollars (sum of column 3), we derive the labour commanded, that is to say, the average cost of a labour year in Germany which is estimated to be 84.6 thousand dollars. In a similar way, we estimated that a labour year in Greece is worth only 31.9 thousand dollars. Alternatively, each dollar spent on imported commodities from Germany fetches 0.0118 (1/84.6) German worker-years; for the same worker year, a dollar spent from Germany on imports from Greece fetches 0.0314 (1/31.9) worker-years. Clearly, a German worker year or hour is 2.661 times higher than the same Greek worker year or hour (assuming the same length of working day).

The process was repeated for each of the years 1995–2007 of our study, and the results are summarized in Table 7.3.

As it becomes evident from the estimates presented in Table 7.3, Germany with the same amount of money, i.e. one dollar, extracts through trade at least twice more labour-years than Greece. The ratio of purchasing power of Germany to Greece is displayed in the last column of Table 7.3. Moreover, in the last years of our analysis, the situation remains the same if not worse for Greece indicating the loss of international competitiveness of its economy and the harsh situation that it was entering in the following years.

The results of the bilateral trade between Germany and Greece show that the unequal exchange 'in the strict sense' of the term argument does not necessarily hold in any significant extent. Thus, although there is equalization of profit rates, we did not find any so significant and persistent differences in the rates of surplus-value between the two countries, as the unequal exchange 'in the strict sense' would require. Moreover, the lower wages in Greece do not necessarily give rise to higher rates of surplus-value because German productivity exceeds the Greek productivity

Table 7.3 Equivalence of one dollar to worker year between Germany and Greece, 1995–2007

Year	Germany (dollar-worker year equivalence)	Greece (dollar-worker year equivalence)	Greece/Germany
1995	0.0152	0.0430	2.829
1996	0.0152	0.0289	1.901
1997	0.0174	0.0310	1.782
1998	0.0173	0.0329	1.902
1999	0.0192	0.0355	1.849
2000	0.0215	0.0403	1.874
2001	0.0198	0.0435	2.197
2002	0.0182	0.0427	2.346
2003	0.0194	0.0357	1.840
2004	0.0168	0.0323	1.923
2005	0.0145	0.0332	2.290
2006	0.0152	0.0361	2.375
2007	0.0118	0.0314	2.661

and more than compensates for the wage differentials. This difference in productivity is due mainly of higher capital-intensity in Germany combined with a more 'disciplined' labour force and possibly from differences in the product mix.

Our analysis showed that once the LOOP holds in the international exchange, German and Greek industries expect to gain from trade; that is why they are trading partners, but the aggregate gains of Germany are much higher than those of Greece, and they are the result of transfer of labour values. Trade in other words is asymmetric in the sense that one of the partners benefits more than the other. In particular, the transfer of values from Greece to Germany certainly is of a relatively small magnitude given the large size of the German economy, but of great significance to the Greek economy given its relatively smaller size. It is worth pointing, however, that the transfers of labour values from Greece to Germany in and of themselves do not necessarily mean or imply exploitative relations between the two countries and respective class alliances, but rather indicate the difference in the level of development in the two countries, a difference that persisted, if not increased, over the years of our study.

7.6.2   Transfer of Values Between the USA and China, 1995–2011

We continue the analysis by investigating the trade relations between the USA and China, two major economies with a rising volume of trading goods between themselves over the last three decades. The effects of trade between these two countries often become the focus of attention of both economists and policymakers. The recent policy proposals about increasing tariffs and the grievances about manipulation of the exchange rate of Chinese Yuan Renminbi (CNY) relative to the US dollar (USD) reflect, in fact, the intensity of competition between the two countries.

We start off the analysis with the estimation of labour values that is the direct and indirect labour time (years in our case) per unit of output. As we have pointed out, labour values are important in their own right especially because they are comprehensive indexes of labour productivity, one of the major indexes of the competitiveness of an economy; the lower the labour values the higher the labour productivity and, other things equal, the lower the cost per unit of output and, thus, the higher competitiveness of an economy. Figure 7.7 displays the labour values for the two economies. It is interesting to note that the socioeconomic database of the WIOD ends for these two countries in the year 2009 although the input-output tables are available for 2 more years.[21] The trouble is that we could not extend our analysis of transfer of values beyond the year 2011 for the lack of data on international trade of these two countries. Thus, we present the results for the period 1995–2009 based on

---

[21] A more detailed socioeconomic database along with corresponding input-output data of 58 dimensions has been recently made available spanning the period 2000–2014.

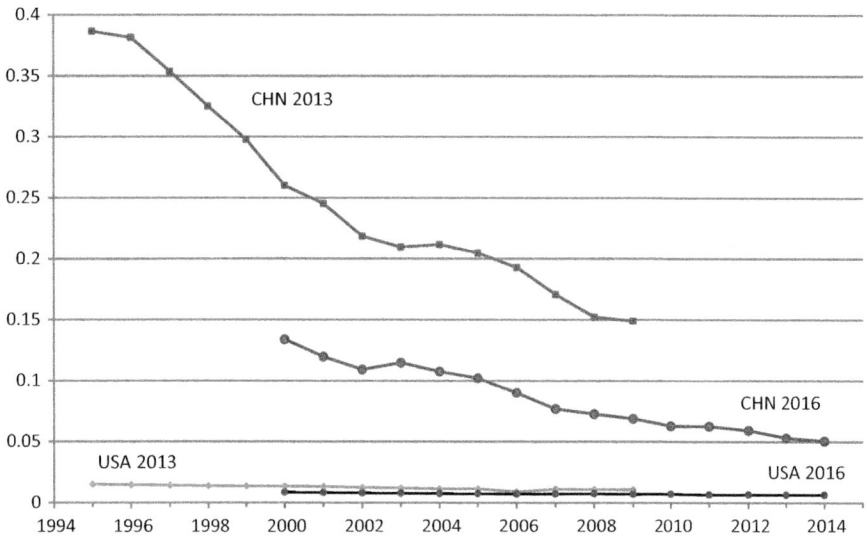

Fig. 7.7 Average unit labour values, USA and China, 1995–2009 and 2010–2014

WIOD (2013) and extended the findings using the WIOD (2016) for the estimation of unit labour values for the full period to get a more precise idea of the trends underway and make educated guesses about their future paths.

From Fig. 7.7 we observe that the average unit labour values in both economies maintain their falling tendency regardless of the database used as a result of the technological change which is labour-saving and capital-using. The USA's average unit labour values for the 34 industries of WIOD (2013) are always much lower than those of the Chinese economy, and this difference persists over the years; similar are the results when we use the data of 58 industries from WIOD (2016). It is worth noting, however, that the labour values of China display a drastic fall over the years although they remain far enough from those of the US economy.[22] This drastic fall of the labour values in the Chinese economy reflects its initial backwardness and the subsequent rapid technological change which slashed the labour content and, therefore, contributed the most to the lowering of the unit cost of the commodities produced. Hence, the falling labour values gradually enhanced China's position in its trade with the US economy and also with the rest of the world. However, two issues emerge from this discussion; first, the labour values per se do not suggest absolute cost advantage of one country over another, but rather that if exchange takes

---

[22]The labour values for the individual industries are displayed in Appendix 2. The parallel movement for the common years in the two databases (1995–2009 and 2000–2014) of the two countries has to do with the different base years (1995 and 2010, respectively) that were used as deflators. We felt that constant prices would be a better choice of intertemporal and intercountry comparisons provided that the inflation rates (during the investigation period) in both countries are moderate.

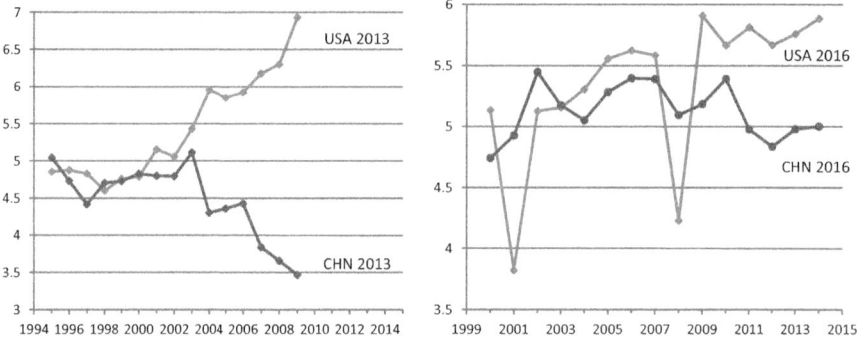

Fig. 7.8 Value composition of fixed capital, USA and China, 1995–2009 and 2000–2014

place and the LOOP holds, then the country with the higher labour values transfers value to the other, and this is something that can be quantified.

In Fig. 7.8, we present the evolution of the value compositions of fixed capital stock for the two economies under investigation from both datasets, namely, WIOD (2013) and WIOD, (2016) put side by side. According to the analysis of the absolute cost advantage, it is expected that the falling labour values over the years will be accompanied by an increasing VCC a result attributed to the form of technological change, that is, capital using-labour saving.

The data from WIOD (2013) show that only the US economy displays a rising VCC, whereas China's VCC after the year 2003 surprisingly enough is plummeting and never returns to the previous level. This path of China's VCC probably is due to country-specific assumptions in the construction of the capital stock data provided in WIOD. Moreover, the surprisingly falling VCC in China may be attributed to real wages which rise faster than the capital stock. On further consideration, the re-estimated VCC using the more recent data from the WIOD (2016) shows that it is rising for both economies, albeit the VCC of the USA is higher than that of China's; nevertheless, they are both in their upward trends.

The lower unit labour values in the USA imply that for the same price (i.e. the LOOP holds internationally), the profit margins of the US producers are expected to exceed by far those of China. This means that one party, and in this particular case, the USA, gains a lot more in its trade with China. Figure 7.9 displays the total gains of the USA and the total losses of China resulting from the transfers of value taking place in the trade between the two countries over the period 1995–2009. The aggregate results are derived utilizing the indexes ue_x and ue_m (Eqs. 7.9 and 7.10, respectively) for each year of our study.

On the vertical axis of Fig. 7.9, we display the percentage of transfers of value in the total trade of the two countries, and we find that the bilateral trade between the USA and China, during the years of our analysis, gives rise to significant transfers of labour values; specifically, the US economy gains in transfers at the expense of the Chinese economy. For example, in the year 2003 the USA gained 9% from its exports to China and gained another 10% from its imports from China. The transfers

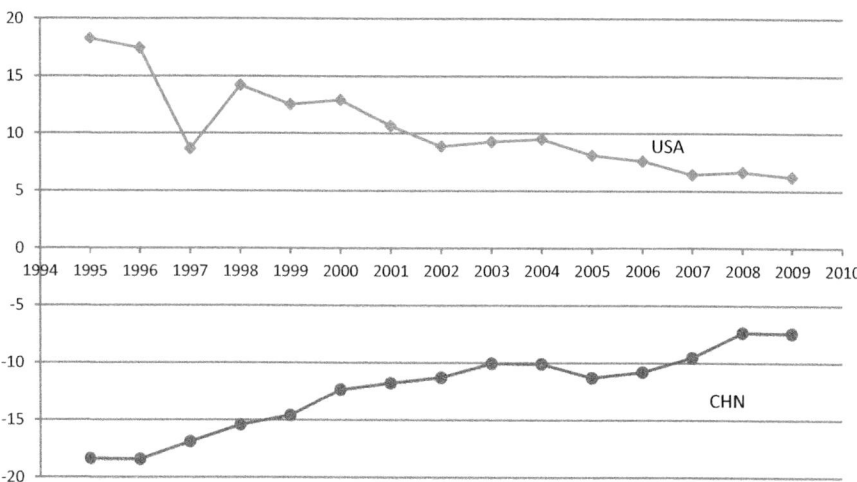

Fig. 7.9 Aggregate effect of unequal exchange as proportion of total bilateral trade, USA and China 1995–2009

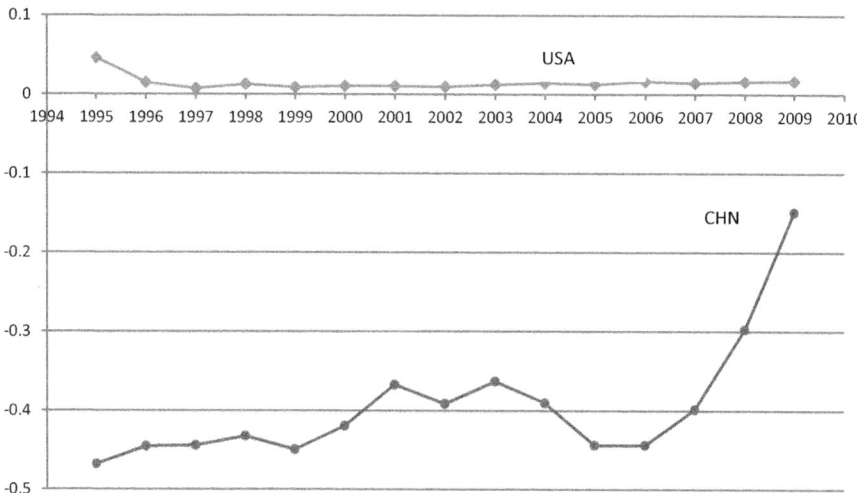

Fig. 7.10 Aggregate effect of bilateral unequal exchange as a proportion of the USA's and China's total gross output, 1995–2009

are much higher in the first years of our study and get smaller at the last years. The size of these transfers as a percentage to total gross output produced is presented in Fig. 7.10. As expected given the size of the two economies, the volume of transfers to the US economy is significantly less than 1% a year.

In our effort to show in an analytical and, at the same time, practical way the extent and the significance of these transfers for the US and Chinese economies, we

Table 7.4 Equivalence of one dollar to worker year between the USA and China, 1995–2009

Year	USA (dollar-worker year equivalence)	China (dollar-worker year equivalence)	China/USA
1995	0.015	0.411	27.07
1996	0.015	0.370	24.94
1997	0.015	0.341	22.93
1998	0.015	0.312	21.43
1999	0.015	0.286	19.27
2000	0.015	0.253	16.49
2001	0.016	0.240	15.06
2002	0.014	0.215	14.98
2003	0.014	0.206	14.79
2004	0.013	0.211	15.81
2005	0.014	0.207	15.19
2006	0.011	0.194	17.36
2007	0.013	0.172	12.84
2008	0.013	0.157	12.38
2009	0.012	0.155	12.88

form Table 7.4 where we display for the years of our study the results on how many labour-years the USA extracts through trade from China, following the same logic and method as in the previous case of the trade between Germany and Greece.

As it becomes evident from the estimates presented in Table 7.4, the USA with the same amount of money, by way of an example one dollar, extracts through trade 12.88 times more labour time (years) than the same dollar in China in the year 2009. In the USA, the gains were much higher in the first years of our study during which the unit values in the USA were much lower than those in China.

One may wonder whether the unit labour values of China are much higher than those of the USA; the answer to this is positive as this can be judged from our estimates of unit labour values from both databases (Fig. 7.7) for the two economies. Nevertheless, we bring additional evidence, and we estimate the evolution in productivity, a variable strictly related to the inverse of unit labour values, using data from the Penn World database. Hence, we measure productivity as the ratio of real GDP in constant prices of 2011 in dollars (denoted by rgdpna in Penn database) over the total employment (denoted by emp in Penn database). The estimates of productivity for both countries are measured on the left-hand side (l.h.s.), whereas their ratio is measured on the right-hand side (r.h.s.) of Fig. 7.11. The estimates of productivity are carried out in terms of constant dollars (base year 2011).[23]

Based on Fig. 7.11, we observe that the productivity in the USA is much higher than that of China, although the gap in productivities shrinks with the passage of

---

[23]If we express the dollars in terms of purchasing parity, the difference diminishes but still remains far too high even in the estimates up to the year 2015.

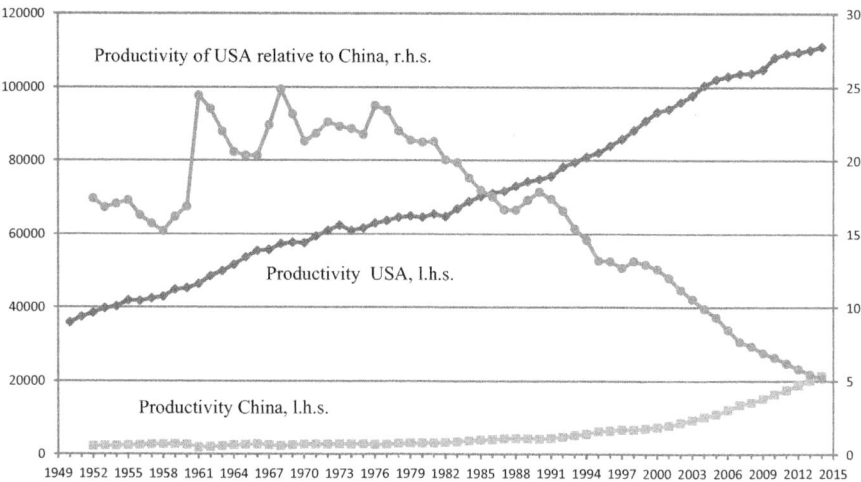

Fig. 7.11 The evolution of productivity in the USA and China, 1950–2014

time indicating that the technological progress undergoing in the Chinese economy is quite fast and accelerating during the last years of the analysis.

7.6.2.1   Absolute Cost Advantage in the Trade Between USA and China

The trade between the USA and China is a highly contested area and the arguments are usually around aspects that ostensibly prohibit 'free trade'. More specifically, the main charge of the USA against China is its exchange rate policy that keeps the value of Yuan relative to the US dollar at abnormally low levels. As a consequence, the Chinese products—because of the artificially low exchange rate of Yuan, other things equal, resulting from particular policies and not from the free market operation—may penetrate the US market and compete, in a sense, unfairly against US businesses leading to job losses. Little attention, however, is paid to the issue of transfers of values resulting from differences in the unit labour values and the operation of the LOOP in international exchanges. Apparently, and this is what our research and empirical results show, the US economy is more productive and therefore it is a lower cost economy selling at an international price much higher than its cost reaping profits more than the surplus-value produced domestically and in accordance to the value composition of capital. The size of these transfers is substantial and is directly related to the volume of trade between the two countries.

The Chinese exports, although penetrate in the US economy, sell at international prices that are below its labour values, and, therefore, surplus-value is lost to the benefit of competing capitals. However, the value of exports of the Chinese economy exceeds the value of imports giving rise to a trade surplus which increases over time because, on the one hand, the trade between the two countries increases and, on the other hand, the productivity gap and, therefore, the difference in unit labour values have decreased impressively as our findings indicate which are also ascertained by independent estimates as those depicted in Fig. 7.11. These findings suggest that competition in domestic and international markets give rise to the same phenomena, although they are much more difficult to explain in international markets. Also, classical competition indicates that the relative position of a region or a country may change over time.

Because of these highly debated issues that arise in the analysis of the trade between the USA and China, in what follows we make an effort to estimate the competitiveness of the two countries through the absolute cost advantage reflected in their real unit labour (vertically integrated) cost in constant domestic prices, which are in fact indexes of productivity expressed in USD through the nominal exchange rate. The results of these estimations for both countries over the years are shown in Fig. 7.12.

Clearly, the unit vertically integrated labour cost of China is below that of the USA up until the year 2009 for both (WIOD 2013 and 2016) databases; however, from the year 2010 onwards, China appears to be losing its competitive absolute cost advantage. Clearly, the rising (vertically integrated) productivity in China was more than fully offset by the rising real wages, and so the unit cost of production started its upward path. Instead, in the USA the slowly falling unit values were accompanied by stagnant or even falling real wages driving down the unit labour cost.

Hence, we look at the foreign sector from the point of view of the US economy, which means that the US exports to China incorporate US labour and cost of production and the US imports incorporate Chinese labour inputs and cost of production. It is important to stress that if exports and imports are looked from the point of view of China, we have deviations in the amounts as these are reported by the OECD structural analysis tables of international exchanges. Although the Chinese products incorporate more labour time than the respective US product, we end up with different costs having to do with the huge differences in wages which are

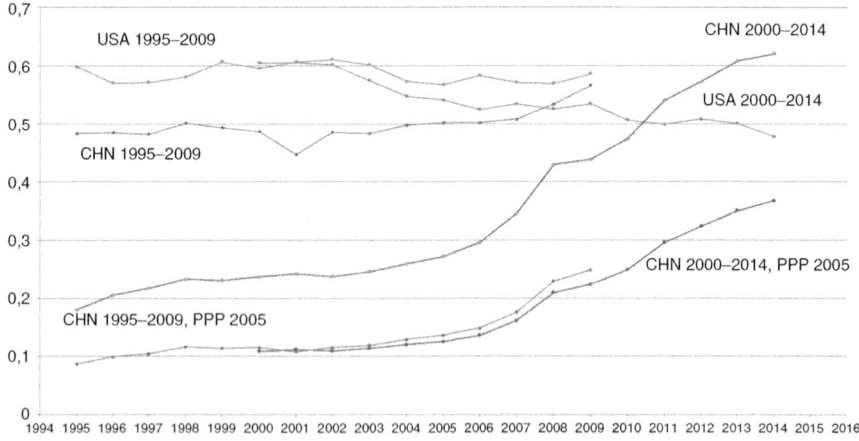

Fig. 7.12 Average absolute cost of tradables, USA vs. China

evaluated in USD. Of course, we take into account the domestic price level in each country, but, nevertheless, one may argue that the purchasing power of dollar in China might be even higher than that reported in the official exchange rate, and so one should use the available data on purchasing power parity of dollar evaluations. The purchasing power parity argument is questionable for a number of reasons which go beyond the scope of the chapter and the reported data are for the total economy and not on an industry basis. However, it is not difficult to use the available data by deflating the Chinese wage data by the PPP data available at Penn database www.rug.nl/ggdc/productivity/pwt. In Fig. 7.12, it is shown that the PPP evaluation of Chinese exports to the USA becomes even cheaper. In fact, the average absolute competitive advantage is persistent during all the years of the analysis. We should stress at this point that our analysis has dealt with an old, subtle and not resolved yet issue of transfers of value. We hope that our theoretical discussion and empirical findings may shed additional light and contribute to the resolution of a crucial importance and highly debated issue.

7.6.3   Transfer of Values Between the USA and Germany, 1995–2009

The last stage of our analysis refers to the trade relations between the USA and Germany, two economically advanced major trading partners. As in the previous cases, our analysis begins with a comparison of the unit labour values of the two countries displayed in Fig. 7.13

We observe that the USA's average unit labour values for the 34 industries of WIOD (2013), with the exception of the year 1996, are lower than those of the German economy, and this difference persists over the years. We observe that the unit values in both countries fall on average with the progress of time and at the end

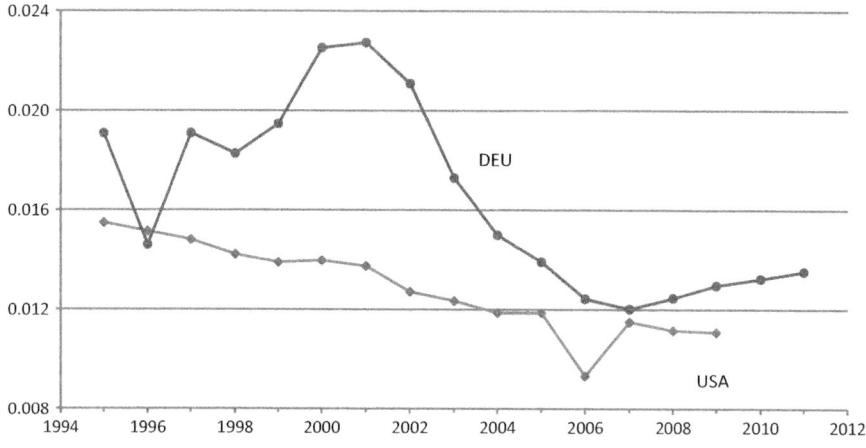

Fig. 7.13 Average unit labour values, USA and Germany, 1995–2009 and 2010–2012

become indistinguishable from each other. Although the unit values of the US economy on average are somewhat lower, nevertheless, there are German industries which are more efficient, and so the net transfer of values switches sign between the two economies.

We know (see Figs. 7.4 and 7.8) that both economies display a rising vertically integrated value composition of fixed capital indicating increasing mechanization of their production process which is another way to say that technological change is of the Marxian kind, that is, capital-using and labour-saving. In effect, this is a rough estimate of the Marxian value composition of capital provided that we cannot become more detailed at this stage of analysis because the construction of the time series data of the capital stock differs in each country depending on the available information from local sources of data and differences in estimating methods (Erumban et al. 2012).

Figure 7.14 displays the total gains and losses occurring in the trade between the USA and Germany resulting from the transfers of value taking place in the trade between the two countries over the period 1995–2009. The aggregate results are derived utilizing the indexes ue_x and ue_m from Equations (7.9 and 7.10), respectively, for each year of our study.

Figure 7.14 shows that the bilateral trade between the USA and Germany during the years of our analysis implies significant transfers of labour values; specifically, the USA economy gains in transfers at the expense of the German economy. The size of these transfers as a percentage to total gross output produced is presented in Fig. 7.15.

In our effort to show in an analytical and, at the same time, practical way the extent and the significance of these transfers for the US and German economies, we form Table 7.5 as in the previous cases, where we display for the years of our study the results on how many labour-years the USA extracts through trade from Germany.

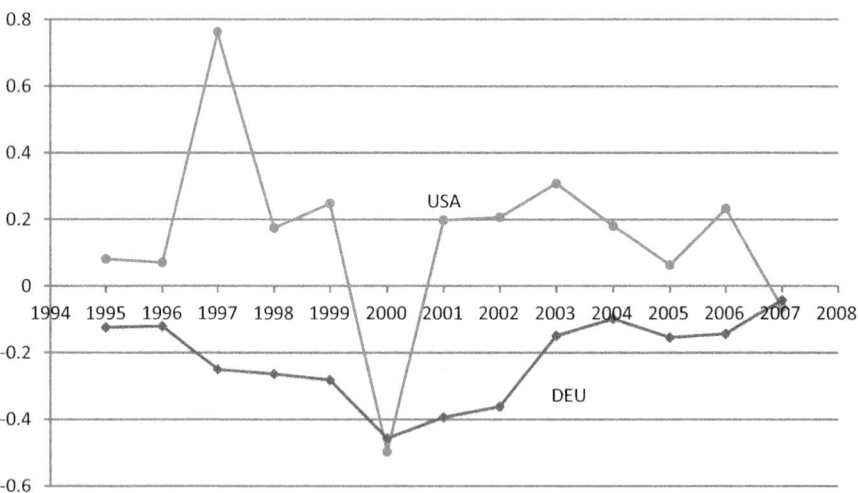

Fig. 7.14 Aggregate effect of unequal exchange as proportion of total bilateral trade, USA and Germany, 1995–2009

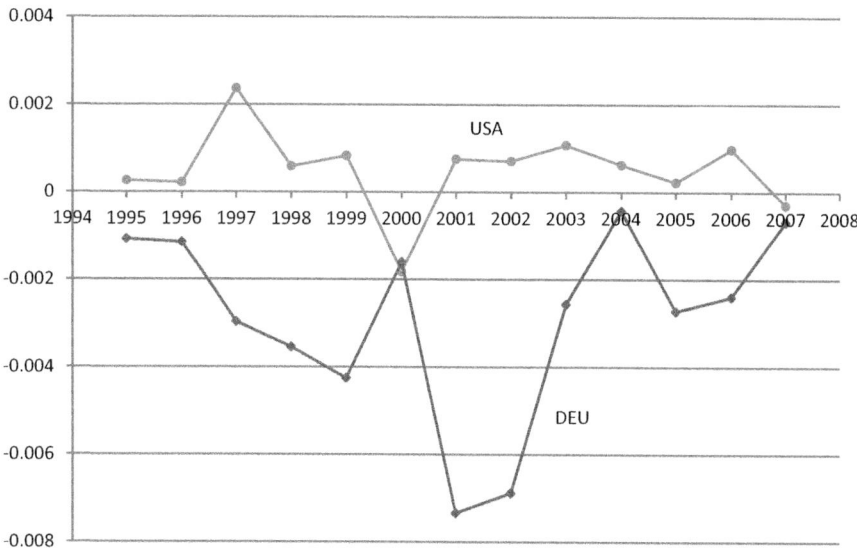

Fig. 7.15 Aggregate effect of bilateral unequal exchange as a proportion of USA's and Germany's total gross output, 1995–2009

Table 7.5 Equivalence of one dollar to worker year between the USA and Germany, 1995–2009

Year	USA (dollar-worker year equivalence)	Germany (dollar-worker year equivalence)	Germany/USA
1995	0.0142	0.0154	1.0799
1996	0.0130	0.0157	1.2066
1997	0.0134	0.0179	1.3326
1998	0.0134	0.0173	1.2891
1999	0.0140	0.0183	1.3098
2000	0.0144	0.0211	1.4659
2001	0.0144	0.0215	1.4878
2002	0.0135	0.0200	1.4863
2003	0.0126	0.0169	1.3396
2004	0.0117	0.0143	1.2195
2005	0.0124	0.0138	1.1133
2006	0.0101	0.0128	1.2695
2007	0.0117	0.0119	1.0139
2008	0.0111	0.0118	1.0645
2009	0.0111	0.0142	1.2763

The results show that the lower average unit values of the US economy relative to Germany's lead to positive net transfers from Germany to the USA. The size of these transfers however is by far lower than those observed in the trade of the USA relative to China or of the Germany relative to Greece.

7.7 Summary and Conclusions

In this chapter, we started off with a brief review of the key concepts of absolute and comparative cost advantage presented by Smith and Ricardo, respectively. We argued that despite the fact that Smith's absolute cost advantage is realistic and, therefore, relevant to modern economies, nevertheless, it was sidestepped for some of its negative and disturbing for the 'free trade' argument of the neoclassical economics. By contrast, the Ricardian principle of comparative advantage was conveniently assimilated in the neoclassical theory of international trade based on the availability of endowments and the idea that prices reflect their relative scarcity. A hypothesis fraught with problems of internal logical consistency as it has been shown already in the famous Cambridge Capital controversies in the 1960s and later in the 'Leontief's Paradox' literature for the USA initially and subsequently for a number of other economies (see Paraskevopoulou et al. 2016). Moreover, the same hypothesis is not representative of the actual trade flows in the sense that one would expect international trade to be intense between countries at quite different levels of development; in contrast, the evidence shows that the trade is more intense between countries at the same level of development and also endowments (see Krugman and Obsefeld 2012, Ch. 4). Our estimates of labour values (or direct and indirect labour requirements per unit of output) showed that the US and German economies share approximately the same technology whereas Greece and China lay behind. Greece's trade gap persists over the examined period, whereas China's gap lessens with the passage of time. If the trends continue, China pretty soon will approach even closer and perhaps surpass the unit values of both the US and German economies, a result consistent with the classical theory of competition according to which the relative position of a region or a country may change over time.

In addition, the trouble with Ricardo's original principle of comparative cost advantage is that it is derived on the basis of the quantity theory of money according to which the trade surplus (or deficit) in one of the trading partners increases (or decrease) its quantity of money resulting in higher (or lower) prices and eventually in lower (higher) competitiveness. At the end, the disadvantaged country manages to produce cheaper one of the two commodities, specialization follows, the balance in trade is redressed and the countries continue to trade with each other. Hence, the key hypothesis for all of the above sequence of events is the implementation of the premises of the quantity theory of money. However, an alternative theory of money as was developed by economists of the currency and banking schools and later by Marx (see Appendix 1) gives rise to quite different and more pragmatic results. In effect, this alternative theory of money endorses the proposition that the trade relations between unequal partners give rise to asymmetric results in the sense that one of the partners benefits at the expense of the other. For example, Smith recognized the unequal distribution of benefits from trade, by noting that:

> Trade which, without force or constraint, is naturally and regularly carried on between any two places is always advantageous, though not always equally so, to both.
>
> (*Wealth*, IV. iii, c. 2)

We showed that the classical theory of value and distribution is applicable to international trade and the transfers of value give rise to asymmetries in the trade partners involved. The analysis was carried with the use of input-output and bilateral trade data for three pairs of countries with quite different levels of development, namely, Greece and Germany, USA and China and USA and Germany. Hence, the acknowledgement of the transfers of labour values (as a generalized phenomenon) dictates economic policies that have to do mainly with the direction of investment in the effort to equalize technologies and productivities across countries and less with the depression of wages in the LDC in such a way so that to increase their competitiveness. Marx had anticipated these arguments long time ago and had a very good grasp of the gains and losses resulting from international trade. The following quotation is particularly revealing of his deep understanding of what was underneath the surface of seemingly equal international exchanges:

> Loss and gain within a *single* country cancel each other out. But not so with trade between different countries three days of labour of one country can be exchanged against one of another country [...]. Here the law of value undergoes essential modification [...]. The relationship between labour days of different countries may be similar to that existing between skilled, complex labour and unskilled simple labour within a country. In this case, the richer country exploits the poorer one, even where the latter gains by the exchange.
> (*TSV* III, pp. 105-6)

The transfers of value is the mechanism through which acceleration or deceleration of capital accumulation takes place at international level aggravating trading countries inequalities in their composition of capital and thus in technology. These inequalities are responsible for the lower unit labour values and international prices which further enhance transfers of value and so forth. Thus, we come to a full cycle, a vicious cycle for the LDC and a virtuous cycle for the more DC feeding upon itself over time. However, past a point for the cycle to continue needs considerable borrowing from the part of the LDC which usually ending up with accumulated debt.

Summing up, we may, therefore, say that on the surface, the prevalence of the LOOP, the tendential equalization of the economy-wide rates of profit and possibly the rates of surplus-value give the impression of complete equality in exchange. We show that underneath these seemingly equal relations, there are significant and systematically arising inequalities consequent upon differences in the unit labour values of the tradable commodities which are fully consistent with differences in real wages and also unequal development. The recent example of China indicates that less developed countries may also climb in the ladder of competitiveness by the implementation of meaningful industrial policies. However, when they are noticed and become disturbing, especially in conditions of slowdown in economic activity like the current, give rise to international tensions.

Appendices

Appendix 1: Marx's Quantity Theory of Money

As we discussed in the first chapter of the book, a commodity has a dual character: it is at the same time a use value and an exchange value. The exchangeability of commodities presupposes the existence of a common element that makes them commensurable to each other. Classical economists argued that the common element contained in commodities is that they are products of labour. Hence, the quantity of labour time spent to produce any commodity becomes the measurement stick of its worthiness. Of course, as we show in Chap. 1, there are significant differences and qualifications within this broad classical approach. According to Marx the abstract socially necessary labour time, that is, the labour time without its specific characteristics, is what gives worthiness to commodities.

The term 'value' in Marx's analysis is of special significance, since Marx means that the circulation of commodities reflects the presence of the abstract labour time spent on their production, which is the regulator of commodity prices. In other words, the commodity price reflects the amount of abstract labour time that is socially necessary for its production whose form of value in the sphere of circulation is always in money. This is the essence of the discussion regarding the forms of value of the first volume of *Capital* which does not even require money to mediate. Money simply becomes the general equivalent (universal commodity) through which we have the manifestation of the above process of subtraction of the individual properties of each labour and its reduction to labour in general, that is, to abstract labour. When Marx refers to the price as a form of value, he means that the value is reflected by the commodity's monetary price and not by its relative price, as the neoclassical economics does, where only relative values are determined and the transition from relative values to absolute is devoid of substance.

At first sight, it is clear that there are so many ways to express the exchange value of a commodity as the number of commodities. Barter, which so often refers to orthodox economic analysis as a historical stage of production without money, must never have been in a systematic and generalized way, because there was always a universal commodity (money) that served as a means of facilitating transactions. Historically certain commodities, owing to certain useful attributes they possessed, became money commodities; that is, the means through which the other commodities can express their worthiness and in so doing become the medium for quoting prices. If gold, for example, is the money commodity, the other commodities express their worthiness in terms of a certain quantity of gold (e.g. 1 US dollar = 1/4 ounce of gold).[24] The value—the abstract socially necessary labour time—contained in a commodity relative to the value of gold, that is, the abstract socially necessary labour time contained in it, gives the direct price or a first approximation of the monetary expression of value and a centre of gravity for observed (market) prices (Shaikh 1990).

At the level of abstraction of the analysis in *Capital* I, the regulator of the market price is the direct price defined

---

[24]Commodity money in the form of gold coins appeared for the first time in the sixth century BC in Greece and Asia Minor and approximately in the same period in East Asia.

$$p_0 = \frac{\lambda}{\lambda_g} = \frac{\text{value of commodity}}{\text{value of gold}}$$

If we assume that the value of a commodity is equal to 10 h of abstract labour while the value of gold represents 40 h of abstract labour per ounce, then we have

$$p_0 = \frac{\lambda}{\lambda_g} = \frac{10\,\text{h}/\text{commodity}}{40\,\text{h}/\text{oz}} = \frac{1}{4}\,\text{oz}/\text{commodity}$$

In turn, let us hypothesize that the currency is the Euro and its exchange rate (R) is 1 oz of gold to 8€. Hence, the direct price of the commodity expressed in euro $(p^{€})$ is

$$p^{€} = p_0 R = (1/4) \times (8) = 2€/\text{commodity}$$

The function of money as a standard of price refers to the particular unit of gold that is used to measure value. As a result, the measure of value and standard of price functions are not the same. The measure of value is the abstract socially necessary labour time contained in a commodity. The standard of price is a unit of weight (pound, gram and so on). It is similar to the difference between distance and a metre. A metre is a unit of measurement and distance is the concept to be measured in metres. Historically, for instance, the British pound initially represented a quantity of silver weighing one pound (*Capital* I, p. 99), and the US dollar also represented a certain weight of silver. With the passage of time, however, debasement separated the money names of these units from their actual precious metal content and gradually led to the determination of the standard by law.

The measure-of-value property of the money commodity may also make it the medium of exchange and thereby enable the generalization of commodity production, thus making possible the increasing specialization of labour and the associated increase in productivity and reduction in unit production costs and prices. History is replete with examples of commodities that played the role of money commodity. For example, in ancient times cattle, salt and copper, among other goods, served as mediums of exchange, and in more recent times even commodities such as cigarettes, under certain circumstances (such as in prisoners-of-war camps), have also played that role. However, the money commodity in an economy of generalized market relations must possess the universal function of the general equivalent—that is, it must be the commodity through which the other commodities express their value—and so it must be characterized by a number of useful properties (it must be easily recognizable, divisible, transferable, durable and so forth). Precious metals, more than other commodities, possess these required properties and for these reasons have become the means that can effectively perform the functions of the universal or general equivalent commodity.

We observe that the price level can change due to many reasons. That is if the price $p^{€}$ increase that might be, for instance, due to decrease in λ_g holding everything else constant (λ, R) or to decrease in λ_g but λ and R decrease by less and so on. Hence, the quantity of money required for the circulation of commodities is

$$M_c = \frac{PQ}{k} = \left[\frac{\lambda}{\lambda_g}\right](R)\left[\frac{1}{k}\right]Q$$

where k is the velocity of money in circulation and PQ the product of the price level (P) times the total output produced (Q).

As we argued in Chap. 2, the quantity of money in circulation is a quite flexible magnitude, and its volume depends on the needs for the circulation of commodities. The quantity of money that circulates in an economy should not be confused with the total quantity of money that exists in an economy. The latter is equal to

$$M = M_c + M_h$$

where M_c is the money in circulation and M_h is the money which is actively hoarded. For Marx, the quantity of money does not determine the general price level, but the general price level, defined by the ratio λ/λ_g, is the one that determines the quantity of money in use. Hence, with given the Q, the price level determines the quantity of money in circulation and not the other way around as the quantity theory of money postulates.[25]

It does not take a lot of imagination to see that the above version of a quantity theory of money may be of help in the determination of exchange rates by simply replacing the unit values with prices in domestic currency P and foreign in terms of the USD P in the place of λg, and then we may write

$$R = (M - M_h)\left(\frac{k}{Q}\right)\left(\frac{P^\$}{P^¥}\right)$$

Clearly the exchange rate of a domestic currency expressed in USD depends on the M_h that is the hoarding money which includes among other things foreign currencies which can pump in and out of circulation and maintain, for example, a planned exchange rate. It goes without saying that respective price levels, productivities and incomes play a significant role and place a limit to how long and by how much such a government intervention in the exchange rate market can be effective.

Appendix 2: Estimates of Unit Labour Values for Each Country, Individual Industry and Year[26]

The last row in each table presents the average unit value of the 34 industries.

---

[25]It is worth noting that in Marx, the assumption of given output is based on the assumption of normal utilization of capital; hence, normal output may be accompanied by significant unemployment of labour (Tsaliki 2008, 2009). In contrast, in neoclassical analysis the hypothesis of given output is derived from the assumption of full employment of the factors of production.

[26]The last row in each table of Appendix 2 presents the average labour unit values.

Table 7.6 Unit labour values, Germany, 1995–2011

1995	1996	1997	1998	1999	2000	2001	2002	2003	2004	2005	2006	2007	2008	2009	2010	2011
0.017	0.013	0.023	0.024	0.024	0.027	0.026	0.025	0.022	0.019	0.020	0.014	0.016	0.013	0.019	0.017	0.017
0.020	0.020	0.026	0.024	0.025	0.027	0.028	0.025	0.022	0.019	0.018	0.015	0.014	0.012	0.016	0.014	0.014
0.017	0.014	0.018	0.018	0.019	0.022	0.022	0.020	0.017	0.014	0.014	0.012	0.012	0.011	0.012	0.014	0.012
0.020	0.015	0.018	0.017	0.018	0.021	0.021	0.020	0.016	0.014	0.014	0.013	0.012	0.012	0.013	0.011	0.011
0.019	0.015	0.018	0.017	0.018	0.021	0.021	0.018	0.015	0.013	0.013	0.013	0.012	0.012	0.012	0.012	0.011
0.022	0.016	0.020	0.018	0.020	0.023	0.024	0.022	0.018	0.016	0.016	0.012	0.012	0.011	0.012	0.012	0.012
0.017	0.014	0.017	0.017	0.016	0.018	0.019	0.018	0.015	0.013	0.013	0.010	0.011	0.011	0.011	0.011	0.011
0.018	0.012	0.015	0.014	0.016	0.013	0.013	0.014	0.010	0.009	0.008	0.011	0.006	0.006	0.007	0.008	0.007
0.017	0.014	0.016	0.016	0.017	0.019	0.020	0.018	0.015	0.013	0.012	0.011	0.011	0.010	0.012	0.011	0.011
0.019	0.014	0.017	0.017	0.017	0.021	0.021	0.019	0.016	0.014	0.013	0.012	0.012	0.011	0.013	0.012	0.012
0.018	0.015	0.018	0.018	0.018	0.022	0.023	0.021	0.017	0.015	0.015	0.013	0.012	0.012	0.013	0.013	0.012
0.019	0.017	0.019	0.018	0.020	0.022	0.023	0.021	0.017	0.014	0.013	0.012	0.011	0.010	0.013	0.014	0.014
0.020	0.016	0.018	0.018	0.019	0.021	0.022	0.020	0.016	0.015	0.014	0.013	0.012	0.012	0.013	0.013	0.014
0.020	0.016	0.019	0.018	0.019	0.021	0.023	0.022	0.018	0.016	0.016	0.015	0.014	0.015	0.015	0.013	0.016
0.021	0.016	0.018	0.017	0.018	0.022	0.021	0.020	0.016	0.014	0.014	0.013	0.012	0.012	0.017	0.016	0.012
0.020	0.017	0.019	0.018	0.019	0.022	0.022	0.021	0.017	0.015	0.015	0.015	0.013	0.012	0.015	0.012	0.011
0.014	0.011	0.014	0.014	0.015	0.019	0.019	0.017	0.014	0.011	0.010	0.009	0.008	0.008	0.012	0.008	0.009
0.021	0.015	0.057	0.054	0.060	0.072	0.067	0.059	0.050	0.040	0.016	0.013	0.013	0.034	0.013	0.034	0.035
0.019	0.016	0.018	0.017	0.019	0.023	0.023	0.021	0.018	0.016	0.015	0.015	0.015	0.016	0.015	0.015	0.015
0.017	0.014	0.017	0.015	0.017	0.022	0.022	0.022	0.018	0.016	0.015	0.012	0.013	0.013	0.014	0.012	0.013
0.017	0.016	0.021	0.019	0.021	0.024	0.024	0.023	0.019	0.017	0.017	0.014	0.015	0.016	0.015	0.015	0.015
0.019	0.015	0.022	0.018	0.021	0.024	0.025	0.023	0.019	0.017	0.016	0.014	0.014	0.014	0.015	0.015	0.016
0.021	0.019	0.021	0.021	0.021	0.024	0.023	0.022	0.018	0.016	0.015	0.014	0.013	0.014	0.016	0.015	0.016
0.021	0.012	0.014	0.013	0.015	0.014	0.014	0.016	0.013	0.011	0.010	0.008	0.010	0.010	0.011	0.009	0.012
0.021	0.012	0.013	0.013	0.014	0.016	0.018	0.017	0.014	0.012	0.012	0.010	0.010	0.009	0.011	0.012	0.011

(continued)

Table 7.6 (continued)

1995	1996	1997	1998	1999	2000	2001	2002	2003	2004	2005	2006	2007	2008	2009	2010	2011
0.021	0.015	0.019	0.017	0.019	0.022	0.022	0.020	0.016	0.014	0.013	0.014	0.012	0.012	0.013	0.013	0.014
0.022	0.012	0.014	0.014	0.015	0.017	0.018	0.016	0.012	0.010	0.011	0.009	0.010	0.011	0.011	0.010	0.013
0.015	0.013	0.016	0.016	0.016	0.022	0.023	0.021	0.016	0.013	0.013	0.012	0.013	0.013	0.013	0.014	0.014
0.010	0.004	0.008	0.008	0.008	0.009	0.009	0.007	0.006	0.005	0.004	0.003	0.003	0.004	0.003	0.004	0.005
0.020	0.011	0.014	0.013	0.015	0.018	0.018	0.017	0.014	0.013	0.013	0.012	0.011	0.011	0.013	0.014	0.017
0.022	0.018	0.020	0.021	0.020	0.024	0.025	0.023	0.018	0.016	0.016	0.016	0.014	0.014	0.015	0.015	0.014
0.029	0.021	0.023	0.024	0.024	0.028	0.028	0.026	0.022	0.019	0.019	0.019	0.017	0.016	0.018	0.018	0.017
0.020	0.016	0.020	0.019	0.020	0.024	0.024	0.022	0.018	0.016	0.016	0.014	0.014	0.013	0.014	0.013	0.015
0.019	0.013	0.019	0.016	0.019	0.022	0.022	0.021	0.016	0.015	0.014	0.011	0.012	0.013	0.011	0.011	0.012
0.019	**0.015**	**0.019**	**0.018**	**0.019**	**0.023**	**0.023**	**0.021**	**0.017**	**0.015**	**0.014**	**0.012**	**0.012**	**0.012**	**0.013**	**0.013**	**0.014**

Table 7.7 Unit labour values, Greece 1995–2011

1995	1996	1997	1998	1999	2000	2001	2002	2003	2004	2005	2006	2007	2008	2009	2010	2011
0.039	0.041	0.041	0.042	0.015	0.059	0.064	0.065	0.06	0.048	0.055	0.065	0.058	0.055	0.081	0.062	0.057
0.025	0.024	0.026	0.029	0.034	0.032	0.034	0.03	0.026	0.021	0.023	0.022	0.019	0.016	0.025	0.025	0.028
0.034	0.033	0.036	0.038	0.026	0.05	0.051	0.047	0.041	0.033	0.038	0.029	0.031	0.029	0.027	0.028	0.029
0.031	0.032	0.037	0.04	0.034	0.047	0.043	0.042	0.034	0.029	0.03	0.027	0.03	0.03	0.034	0.035	0.038
0.032	0.033	0.036	0.041	0.036	0.046	0.044	0.04	0.032	0.032	0.037	0.033	0.027	0.023	0.023	0.026	0.029
0.034	0.036	0.041	0.044	0.038	0.052	0.054	0.048	0.037	0.039	0.037	0.034	0.028	0.024	0.025	0.025	0.022
0.031	0.03	0.036	0.038	0.036	0.045	0.041	0.036	0.031	0.027	0.031	0.025	0.029	0.033	0.024	0.028	0.026
0.027	0.025	0.026	0.033	0.023	0.018	0.023	0.023	0.019	0.013	0.012	0.029	0.01	0.008	0.016	0.016	0.017
0.026	0.026	0.031	0.034	0.033	0.039	0.038	0.036	0.029	0.024	0.03	0.023	0.027	0.029	0.034	0.031	0.035
0.025	0.026	0.03	0.033	0.032	0.033	0.036	0.031	0.025	0.022	0.021	0.019	0.019	0.019	0.03	0.055	0.042
0.027	0.027	0.028	0.03	0.032	0.033	0.033	0.032	0.025	0.022	0.024	0.024	0.021	0.019	0.021	0.021	0.026
0.026	0.028	0.031	0.033	0.035	0.036	0.043	0.042	0.035	0.028	0.028	0.025	0.023	0.026	0.039	0.034	0.036
0.03	0.029	0.034	0.037	0.042	0.044	0.048	0.042	0.037	0.03	0.033	0.032	0.028	0.035	0.04	0.042	0.064
0.025	0.027	0.031	0.032	0.034	0.033	0.04	0.035	0.029	0.026	0.028	0.027	0.022	0.023	0.026	0.023	0.023
0.04	0.041	0.045	0.046	0.045	0.049	0.048	0.044	0.036	0.029	0.033	0.027	0.028	0.04	0.035	0.045	0.061
0.03	0.031	0.036	0.039	0.035	0.045	0.052	0.047	0.043	0.037	0.035	0.031	0.029	0.031	0.026	0.04	0.043
0.013	0.016	0.018	0.02	0.024	0.024	0.03	0.024	0.02	0.017	0.016	0.014	0.014	0.012	0.015	0.016	0.015
0.025	0.026	0.027	0.03	0.027	0.036	0.034	0.036	0.029	0.022	0.026	0.023	0.023	0.021	0.029	0.04	0.046
0.02	0.022	0.025	0.03	0.023	0.033	0.036	0.03	0.026	0.024	0.025	0.023	0.024	0.021	0.022	0.022	0.024
0.026	0.024	0.027	0.032	0.031	0.048	0.035	0.034	0.027	0.02	0.026	0.032	0.021	0.021	0.026	0.033	0.037
0.04	0.039	0.044	0.049	0.034	0.071	0.076	0.058	0.036	0.039	0.04	0.04	0.038	0.037	0.052	0.059	0.05
0.026	0.025	0.025	0.027	0.02	0.037	0.034	0.031	0.026	0.023	0.024	0.022	0.02	0.019	0.015	0.016	0.016
0.059	0.062	0.076	0.081	0.063	0.118	0.106	0.101	0.078	0.059	0.055	0.056	0.048	0.041	0.051	0.087	0.099
0.045	0.044	0.04	0.04	0.024	0.03	0.028	0.029	0.021	0.016	0.015	0.01	0.012	0.014	0.015	0.015	0.014
0.026	0.029	0.041	0.038	0.049	0.05	0.052	0.033	0.024	0.024	0.016	0.017	0.015	0.021	0.019	0.021	0.021

(continued)

Table 7.7 (continued)

1995	1996	1997	1998	1999	2000	2001	2002	2003	2004	2005	2006	2007	2008	2009	2010	2011
0.047	0.048	0.047	0.051	0.042	0.048	0.05	0.044	0.036	0.025	0.031	0.036	0.026	0.037	0.052	0.053	0.042
0.022	0.022	0.022	0.024	0.023	0.024	0.027	0.019	0.017	0.016	0.013	0.012	0.012	0.011	0.01	0.011	0.012
0.027	0.028	0.03	0.03	0.033	0.033	0.037	0.032	0.027	0.019	0.024	0.021	0.02	0.019	0.021	0.023	0.024
0.003	0.003	0.004	0.004	0.004	0.006	0.004	0.004	0.002	0.002	0.002	0.002	0.002	0.002	0.002	0.003	0.003
0.032	0.034	0.036	0.042	0.033	0.053	0.059	0.056	0.056	0.041	0.055	0.057	0.046	0.045	0.039	0.054	0.071
0.03	0.031	0.033	0.035	0.045	0.04	0.043	0.037	0.03	0.024	0.028	0.027	0.024	0.022	0.022	0.024	0.025
0.034	0.034	0.038	0.041	0.05	0.051	0.059	0.048	0.036	0.032	0.034	0.038	0.03	0.024	0.026	0.028	0.028
0.029	0.029	0.033	0.036	0.038	0.043	0.042	0.04	0.03	0.023	0.028	0.028	0.022	0.018	0.017	0.021	0.023
0.024	0.024	0.026	0.029	0.03	0.034	0.042	0.036	0.03	0.026	0.028	0.025	0.025	0.033	0.027	0.03	0.028
0.029	**0.030**	**0.033**	**0.036**	**0.033**	**0.042**	**0.044**	**0.039**	**0.032**	**0.027**	**0.029**	**0.0281**	**0.025**	**0.025**	**0.028**	**0.032**	**0.034**

Table 7.8 Unit labour values, China, 1995–2009

1995	1996	1997	1998	1999	2000	2001	2002	2003	2004	2005	2006	2007	2008	2009
0.611	0.586	0.537	0.482	0.439	0.383	0.353	0.308	0.305	0.307	0.305	0.294	0.260	0.221	0.217
0.363	0.352	0.319	0.292	0.266	0.222	0.206	0.179	0.162	0.150	0.131	0.115	0.096	0.079	0.082
0.440	0.440	0.401	0.359	0.325	0.288	0.267	0.234	0.236	0.258	0.254	0.247	0.233	0.204	0.201
0.401	0.406	0.370	0.344	0.319	0.278	0.265	0.242	0.232	0.244	0.238	0.224	0.207	0.189	0.184
0.423	0.401	0.374	0.336	0.307	0.266	0.247	0.218	0.213	0.229	0.221	0.209	0.192	0.175	0.173
0.406	0.418	0.385	0.352	0.315	0.277	0.261	0.232	0.229	0.245	0.238	0.223	0.203	0.182	0.179
0.406	0.377	0.357	0.324	0.293	0.253	0.232	0.201	0.195	0.200	0.196	0.187	0.169	0.151	0.150
0.310	0.309	0.295	0.285	0.262	0.215	0.207	0.190	0.178	0.165	0.154	0.150	0.126	0.110	0.106
0.343	0.341	0.319	0.300	0.268	0.212	0.200	0.179	0.167	0.157	0.143	0.136	0.118	0.100	0.102
0.362	0.358	0.340	0.321	0.296	0.262	0.251	0.223	0.210	0.207	0.198	0.185	0.162	0.148	0.143
0.366	0.360	0.333	0.307	0.285	0.258	0.245	0.221	0.208	0.202	0.198	0.184	0.157	0.139	0.129
0.360	0.364	0.343	0.319	0.298	0.266	0.252	0.226	0.206	0.190	0.180	0.164	0.131	0.116	0.120
0.353	0.349	0.325	0.300	0.281	0.256	0.247	0.225	0.215	0.217	0.210	0.195	0.168	0.152	0.144
0.346	0.345	0.322	0.293	0.269	0.241	0.230	0.206	0.200	0.205	0.206	0.193	0.171	0.161	0.158
0.345	0.342	0.319	0.292	0.271	0.245	0.235	0.212	0.206	0.212	0.212	0.201	0.177	0.163	0.155
0.352	0.354	0.322	0.298	0.273	0.242	0.229	0.204	0.196	0.203	0.194	0.181	0.162	0.148	0.142
0.290	0.273	0.236	0.203	0.182	0.160	0.146	0.126	0.121	0.121	0.120	0.115	0.100	0.092	0.084
0.420	0.399	0.362	0.325	0.294	0.257	0.239	0.209	0.191	0.183	0.172	0.156	0.129	0.110	0.103
0.375	0.361	0.329	0.290	0.262	0.228	0.209	0.181	0.166	0.155	0.141	0.123	0.098	0.085	0.084
0.375	0.361	0.329	0.290	0.262	0.228	0.209	0.181	0.166	0.155	0.141	0.123	0.098	0.085	0.084
0.418	0.413	0.364	0.314	0.276	0.234	0.212	0.183	0.175	0.182	0.173	0.162	0.145	0.125	0.121
0.375	0.365	0.337	0.300	0.275	0.235	0.217	0.190	0.174	0.165	0.151	0.134	0.109	0.096	0.092
0.350	0.342	0.316	0.280	0.255	0.217	0.199	0.172	0.159	0.152	0.141	0.125	0.102	0.091	0.086
0.281	0.276	0.256	0.230	0.213	0.181	0.170	0.150	0.146	0.148	0.145	0.135	0.115	0.104	0.098
0.351	0.346	0.323	0.290	0.265	0.222	0.205	0.178	0.166	0.163	0.150	0.134	0.112	0.101	0.097

(continued)

Table 7.8 (continued)

1995	1996	1997	1998	1999	2000	2001	2002	2003	2004	2005	2006	2007	2008	2009
0.238	0.236	0.221	0.200	0.186	0.159	0.150	0.133	0.126	0.123	0.115	0.104	0.088	0.077	0.075
0.267	0.258	0.236	0.218	0.202	0.179	0.168	0.150	0.143	0.139	0.132	0.119	0.096	0.082	0.080
0.179	0.172	0.154	0.139	0.133	0.119	0.116	0.105	0.093	0.083	0.072	0.060	0.045	0.038	0.036
0.394	0.379	0.335	0.285	0.251	0.214	0.193	0.168	0.156	0.152	0.144	0.133	0.113	0.099	0.095
0.497	0.478	0.428	0.374	0.339	0.297	0.276	0.245	0.240	0.243	0.240	0.231	0.206	0.177	0.174
0.602	0.571	0.507	0.443	0.399	0.344	0.314	0.274	0.259	0.252	0.240	0.223	0.192	0.165	0.162
0.478	0.456	0.402	0.347	0.313	0.275	0.254	0.225	0.206	0.197	0.184	0.168	0.141	0.124	0.118
0.436	0.421	0.376	0.324	0.288	0.247	0.224	0.194	0.174	0.162	0.147	0.128	0.103	0.090	0.087
0.379	**0.370**	**0.338**	**0.305**	**0.278**	**0.241**	**0.225**	**0.199**	**0.188**	**0.187**	**0.178**	**0.165**	**0.143**	**0.127**	**0.123**

Table 7.9 Unit labour values, USA, 1995–2009

1995	1996	1997	1998	1999	2000	2001	2002	2003	2004	2005	2006	2007	2008	2009
0.013	0.010	0.011	0.012	0.013	0.013	0.013	0.012	0.011	0.009	0.011	0.009	0.010	0.009	0.010
0.013	0.011	0.011	0.012	0.011	0.009	0.009	0.008	0.007	0.006	0.005	0.004	0.005	0.005	0.006
0.014	0.013	0.013	0.013	0.012	0.012	0.011	0.011	0.010	0.010	0.010	0.008	0.010	0.010	0.009
0.017	0.017	0.016	0.015	0.015	0.016	0.015	0.014	0.014	0.013	0.013	0.011	0.013	0.013	0.013
0.017	0.017	0.016	0.015	0.015	0.015	0.014	0.015	0.014	0.015	0.016	0.013	0.017	0.016	0.018
0.016	0.016	0.015	0.015	0.014	0.015	0.015	0.014	0.014	0.012	0.013	0.011	0.014	0.014	0.014
0.015	0.015	0.015	0.014	0.013	0.014	0.013	0.012	0.012	0.012	0.011	0.009	0.011	0.011	0.010
0.012	0.011	0.010	0.011	0.011	0.008	0.008	0.008	0.006	0.005	0.004	0.003	0.004	0.004	0.004
0.013	0.013	0.013	0.012	0.012	0.013	0.012	0.011	0.011	0.010	0.010	0.007	0.009	0.009	0.008
0.015	0.015	0.015	0.014	0.014	0.014	0.014	0.013	0.013	0.012	0.012	0.009	0.011	0.012	0.011
0.015	0.015	0.013	0.013	0.012	0.013	0.013	0.011	0.011	0.011	0.011	0.008	0.010	0.010	0.010
0.017	0.016	0.016	0.015	0.015	0.015	0.016	0.014	0.014	0.013	0.012	0.009	0.011	0.011	0.011
0.017	0.016	0.016	0.014	0.014	0.014	0.014	0.013	0.013	0.013	0.012	0.010	0.012	0.011	0.010
0.016	0.017	0.017	0.016	0.017	0.019	0.021	0.019	0.019	0.019	0.019	0.016	0.020	0.019	0.019
0.017	0.017	0.016	0.015	0.015	0.015	0.015	0.013	0.014	0.013	0.013	0.011	0.013	0.013	0.012
0.017	0.017	0.017	0.014	0.015	0.014	0.014	0.014	0.013	0.012	0.011	0.009	0.011	0.011	0.010
0.009	0.009	0.009	0.009	0.010	0.010	0.010	0.009	0.008	0.007	0.008	0.005	0.007	0.006	0.006
0.019	0.018	0.017	0.016	0.016	0.016	0.015	0.014	0.014	0.013	0.013	0.010	0.012	0.012	0.012
0.018	0.016	0.017	0.016	0.016	0.016	0.016	0.016	0.016	0.016	0.016	0.013	0.016	0.015	0.015
0.015	0.015	0.014	0.014	0.014	0.014	0.014	0.013	0.013	0.012	0.012	0.010	0.012	0.012	0.011
0.016	0.016	0.015	0.015	0.014	0.014	0.014	0.013	0.013	0.013	0.013	0.010	0.012	0.012	0.012
0.017	0.016	0.017	0.016	0.015	0.015	0.014	0.013	0.013	0.013	0.012	0.010	0.012	0.012	0.012
0.017	0.017	0.017	0.016	0.015	0.015	0.014	0.013	0.013	0.013	0.012	0.010	0.012	0.012	0.012
0.015	0.015	0.015	0.013	0.012	0.011	0.011	0.010	0.009	0.009	0.009	0.007	0.009	0.008	0.009
0.016	0.016	0.015	0.015	0.016	0.016	0.018	0.017	0.015	0.014	0.014	0.010	0.013	0.012	0.012

(continued)

Table 7.9 (continued)

1995	1996	1997	1998	1999	2000	2001	2002	2003	2004	2005	2006	2007	2008	2009
0.018	0.018	0.018	0.017	0.016	0.016	0.016	0.014	0.014	0.014	0.014	0.010	0.012	0.012	0.013
0.014	0.014	0.014	0.014	0.014	0.014	0.013	0.012	0.012	0.012	0.012	0.010	0.012	0.012	0.011
0.014	0.013	0.013	0.012	0.012	0.012	0.012	0.011	0.011	0.011	0.011	0.008	0.011	0.010	0.010
0.004	0.005	0.004	0.004	0.004	0.004	0.004	0.004	0.004	0.004	0.004	0.003	0.004	0.003	0.003
0.018	0.017	0.017	0.016	0.016	0.017	0.016	0.014	0.014	0.014	0.013	0.011	0.013	0.012	0.013
0.020	0.020	0.019	0.018	0.017	0.017	0.017	0.015	0.015	0.015	0.015	0.012	0.014	0.014	0.014
0.021	0.020	0.020	0.019	0.018	0.018	0.017	0.016	0.016	0.016	0.016	0.012	0.015	0.014	0.015
0.018	0.017	0.017	0.016	0.015	0.016	0.015	0.013	0.013	0.013	0.013	0.010	0.013	0.012	0.012
0.017	0.016	0.016	0.015	0.013	0.014	0.013	0.012	0.012	0.012	0.012	0.010	0.012	0.011	0.011
0.015	**0.015**	**0.015**	**0.014**	**0.014**	**0.014**	**0.014**	**0.013**	**0.012**	**0.012**	**0.012**	**0.009**	**0.012**	**0.011**	**0.011**

Chapter 8
The Rate of Profit, Economic Growth and Crises

It is often assumed that an economy of private enterprise has an automatic bias towards innovation, but this is not so. It has a bias only towards profit.

Eric Hobsbawm (1969, p. 40).

Profit is the life blood of capitalism. [...] Profits are for capitalism the functional equivalent of the acquisition of territory of plunder for military regimes, or an increase in the number of believers for religious ones, or the legitimation of recognized authority for states in which a change of rulership has taken place.

Robert Heilbroner (1985, p. 76).

Abstract The argument in this chapter is that besides the more or less expected short-term (inventory and investment) cycles, there are other longer-term economic cycles. For this purpose, we present data on a number of variables that lend support to the view of long cycles lasting around 50 years. Five such long cycles are ascertained starting from the industrial revolution to our times. A number of phenomena appear regularly with the long cycles, and we try to go beyond the surface and identify the causes of the phenomena. To conclude, we argue that the evolution of profitability is responsible for the 'ebbs and flows' of economic activity and the phenomena associated with it. The discussion continues with the views of major economists of the past on the tendential fall in the rate of profit and the attainment of the 'stationary economy' of the old classical economists associated with this, expressed in Marx as the 'point of absolute overaccumulation'.

Keywords Long cycles · Innovations · Law of the falling rate of profit · Stationary economy · Absolute overaccumulation

© Springer Nature Switzerland AG 2019
L. Tsoulfidis, P. Tsaliki, *Classical Political Economics and Modern Capitalism*,
https://doi.org/10.1007/978-3-030-17967-0_8

335

8.1   Introduction

The normal operation of a capitalist economy is the growth and expansion of its output produced which is estimated by the evolution and usually is measured by the gross domestic product (GDP) over long stretches of time. The deviations of the real GDP from its long-term trend stem from the acceleration or the deceleration in the accumulation of capital resulting in economic booms or recessions, respectively. There are several theories that seek to explain the trend of the observed real GDP as well as the causes of the acceleration or deceleration of its long-term growth rate.

For instance, neoclassical economists usually do not accept the presence of patterns in the observed deviations of the real GDP from its trend, and they attribute such deviations to purely exogenous socks and not to internally generated dynamics of the system. Capitalism is viewed as a virtually healthy system and, in the absence of any serious external shocks, is expected to remain in equilibrium having both capital and labour at their full employment equilibrium levels. Keynesian economists, in contrast, argue that the deviations from the equilibrium may be persistent and significant; as a consequence, if the system is left to its own devices, it may not generate the required aggregate demand to fully employ its capital and labour. Therefore, the management of effective demand, through a combination of fiscal and monetary policy, is absolutely necessary for the utilization of capital at levels that give rise to the maximum possible employment of labour or what amounts to tolerable unemployment rates. Monetarists, on the other hand, opine that the observed fluctuations in the level of economic activity are only ephemeral and if there are no further external shocks or government intervention, the economy soon will find itself on its normal equilibrium path of steady growth provided that the central bank allows the money supply to grow pari passu with the growth rate of the real GDP. In the early 1980s, there were other neoclassical economic approaches arguing that cyclical fluctuations in the level of economic activity are inherent in the capitalist system and they are an integral part of its normal functioning. As the root cause of the historically observed serious fluctuations in the level of economic activity, they put forward arguments based on variables that are related to the introduction of major new innovations and institutions which in the beginning promote growth but after some long-time are worn out and past a point are no longer suitable to the emerging new challenges.

In what follows, we briefly review the extant literature on long-term economic growth and fluctuations. The discussion continues about the causes of this long-run behaviour of the economic systems characterized by long-lasting periods of economic growth and prosperity, which are succeeded by nearly of equal duration periods of slowdown in economic activity and social misery. In such discussion, inescapably comes to the fore the evolution of the rate of profit, whose long-term falling tendency shapes the actual state of the economy. It is important to emphasize that in analysing the expansion or contraction of economic activity, we are not referring to business cycles of short or medium duration, i.e. those with an average length of 3 to 5 years (inventory or Kitchin cycles) or to those with a longer duration around 10 years (investment or Juglar cycles). Our discussion focuses on much longer cycles lasting from 40 to 50 years which are known as long cycles or waves whose discovery is attributed mainly to the Russian statistician-economist Nikolai Kondratiev (1892–1938).

8.2 Economic Fluctuations

Orthodox economists, by and large, do not accept the idea of cycles let alone of long cycles, in spite of the fact that they recognize some coincidences in the movement of some variables; they argue that these coincidences took place in the past and there is no reason whatsoever to believe that they will be repeated in the future. However, a few major economists in the orthodox camp, for example, Joseph A. Schumpeter (1883–1950), Walt W. Rostow (1916–2003), Angus Maddison (1926–2019) and Jay Forrester (1918–2011), not only accept the long-cycle or long-wave hypothesis, but they have developed their own theoretical explanations. In this short list of economists having in high regard the long-wave hypothesis, the name of Paul A. Samuelson (1915–2009) could not be missing as this can be judged by his following description of the post-1970s slowdown in economic activity:

> It is my considered guess that the final quarter of the 20th century will fall far short of the third quarter in its achieved rate of economic progress. The dark horoscope of my old teacher Joseph Schumpeter may have particular relevance here.
>
> (Samuelson 1981)

Hence, Samuelson, inspired by Schumpeter, sides with the idea of long-term outlook and also of the long cyclical fluctuations. The trouble here is that he did not notice or rather downplayed the slowdown in economic activity that started already in the late 1960s and that his publication appeared near the end of this slowdown and not far from the beginning of the upward phase of the long cycle. Perhaps the relatively low unemployment rates in the USA and in general the moderate manifestation of the downturn in the 1970s, compared to the 1930s, made economists think that the worse may come later.

The long-wave hypothesis did not have a much better reception among heterodox economists. For example, when Kondratiev, as the director of the Institute of Conjecture in Moscow in the early 1920s, presented his statistical results, consisting of data for 36 time series variables, he discovered that 25 of them displayed long-cycles. More specifically, the long cycles were discovered in time series data on the production of various goods through a double decomposition procedure, whereby the trend in the data was eliminated by running a regression of the variable under investigation against a polynomial function of time. Kondratiev's colleagues in the Institute instead of expressing their admiration for the collection of detailed time series data for a number of variables and countries, as well as the application of advanced (for their times) statistical techniques and more importantly for the results that were absolutely consistent with the view that the long cycles and the phenomena associated with these which are in effect built-in mechanisms of the normal operation of capitalism, they launched a polemic against Kondratiev and his findings. In particular, Kondratiev's critiques argued (and, in a sense, they were right) that the

Table 8.1 Idealized long cycles

First long cycle	1790–1845	(55 years)
Recovery (industrial revolution)	1790–1815	(25 years)
Recession (the hungry 1840s)	1815–1845	(30 years)
Second long cycle	1845–1896	(51 years)
Recovery (Victorian boom)	1845–1873	(28 years)
Recession (the Great Depression)	1873–1896	(23 years)
Third long cycle	1896–1940	(44 years)
Recovery (Bélle époque)	1896–1920	(24 years)
Recession (depression of 1930s)	1920–1940	(20 years)
Fourth long cycle	1945–1982	(37 years)
Recovery (golden age of accumulation)	1945–1966	(21 years)
Recession (silent depression)	1966–1982	(16 years)
Fifth long cycle	1982–?	(? years)
Recovery (information revolution)	1982–2007	(25 years)
Recession (Great Recession)	2007–202(?)	202(?)

results were sensitive to the degree of the utilized polynomial function of time and there was no a priori reason to select one degree of a polynomial function over another. Moreover, they expressed the view that trend and cycles are two entwined aspects of the same phenomenon and they cannot be separated unless one uses artificial statistical techniques. His critiques, however, did not notice that in the price data (either normalized by the price of gold or not) there was no need for any further detrending procedure for the extraction of long cycles which were visible by the 'naked eye'. Also, Kondratiev's use of a 9-year moving average to eliminate the short-term cycles simply enhanced the visibility (transparency) of the cyclical behaviour of mainly price data and by no means generated their cyclical pattern (Kondratiev 1926, 1998).

In Table 8.1, we list the long cycles based on Kondratiev's work (1935) until the year 1920, and for the years after, we expand the periods of recovery-recession phases following Kondratiev's spirit and having the USA as the representative economy. We call these various periods idealized long cycles, since we put precise dates for the years of turning point. Nevertheless, in Kondratiev's analysis, the turning years range from ±5 years and vary from country to country (Kondratiev 1935, p. 32). In the same table, we also give the most established, in our opinion, names of the ascending or descending phases of each separate long cycle.

Kondratiev claimed that the long cycles were generated by internally operating dynamics. His critiques argued that purely exogenous shocks such as wars, opening of new markets, introduction of new technologies and the like give rise to long waves, and only the decennial investment cycles were supposed to be endogenously generated whose duration was attributed to the average life of fixed capital. Kondratiev defended his position by arguing that large-scale application of new methods of production (i.e. innovations) are by no means stochastic phenomena but, rather, the symptoms of the early stage of economic expansion. During this stage, savings in the absence of investment are accumulated exerting a downward pressure on the interest rate; meanwhile, the rate of profit during the depression phase increases due to both: the fall in wages and the devaluation of capital stock. As a consequence, the rate of profit of enterprise, that is, the difference between the rate of profit and interest rate, increases, and the gap between the two variables stimulates and, in effect, activates investment expenditures. More specifically, businesses have strong incentives to adopt innovations as fast as they can, so as to obtain an advantage over their competitors. Innovations, in turn, lead to the increased demand for money, which enhances the profitability of the gold industry and leads to the expansion of the supply of money through the discovery of (more productive) gold mines, or the application of further innovations in the old gold mines,[1] the creation of new credit institutions, and the like. In short, it is not the discoveries of gold and the expansion of money supply in general that propel economic growth but rather the other way around, that is, the growth of output increases the monetary requirements of the economy and leads to the expansion of the supply of money.

The expansionary phase of the long cycle—not necessarily in the beginning—is accompanied by wars and revolutions. The idea is that as soon as economies enlarge their capacity to produce domestically, an internally generated imperative drives them to expand to even larger markets in order to dispose of their products and, at the same time, to secure an adequate supply of raw materials. Hence, competition intensifies not only in the domestic but also in international markets resulting in international conflicts and increases the likelihood of warm conflicts or even wars. As for the social unrests and revolutions, the idea is that in the phase of recovery the new institutional and structural forms have to bring about 'a new order', which intensifies social struggles and may lead to periods of social turbulence.

In short, the economic mechanism that brings about the Kondratiev cycles is based on the investment in innovative products and hence high-cost investments (I) that increase employment, income, demand, prices and expected profits which set the stage for an economic boom. The economic growth continues to the extent that the expected return (profit rate) on investment, r, exceeds the interest rate, i, thus encouraging investment and, therefore, the rate of capital accumulation which is a function of the expected profit rate-interest rate gap, $I = f(r^e - i)$. With the passage of time (approximately two to three decades), the interest rate is expected to increase more than the rate of profit resulting in zero or even negative (in as much as depreciation exceeds gross) net investment. The stock of capital (buildings, plant and mainly machinery) is not renewed and the existing capital stock is underutilized. As a result, unemployment of labour rises, and demand and prices decrease, discouraging business activity and leading the economy to a depressionary state. However, in capitalism 'there are no permanent crises'; the slowdown in investment activity leads to an increase in savings, and the interest rate starts to fall while the rate of profit increases for the remaining capitals (enterprises), the rising profit-interest rate gap is expected to be filled by investment activity. The idea is that the elimination or absorption of the inefficient capitals, in other words the concentration and centralization of capital, is accompanied by an increase in the average rate of profit. The shaken confidence is restored, and an atmosphere of optimism about the future characterizes society.

---

[1]This is the case of differential rent II (*Capital* III, Part VI).

The data displayed in Table 8.2 summarize some of the major phenomena associated with the long cycles; for each of the five long cycles that we managed to collect data, we form the relevant percentage in the upswing and downswing stages. Thus, besides the percentage of the basic innovations introduced in each phase of the long cycle, we also display the growth rate of the volume of international trade, the growth rate of the real GDP of US economy as well as the percentages of wars and of sovereign debt defaults taking place during the upswing and downswing phases of each long cycle.

In Table 8.2, we observe the timing of the introduction of basic innovations which in the downswing of the long cycle outnumber those in the upswing. The reason for this timing might be that during the upward phase of the long cycle, when profitability is rising, businesses have no compelling reasons whatsoever to risk their good performance by introducing radical innovations. By contrast, in the downturn of the long cycle when profitability is stagnant or falling and the prospects are bleak, challenging the survival of the enterprise, the pressure to innovate is at its highest. Capitalists facing, on the one hand, the abyss of default and, on the other hand, their possible survival through their innovative activity are more prone to 'choose' the innovation path. Nevertheless, this is only a quantitative comparison without taking into account the significance of each of the basic innovations and the extent to which they characterize a whole era.

The growth rates of the volume of world trade tend to be by far larger during the upswing phase of the long cycle than during the downswing phase. Thus, the upswing of the long cycle tends to be related to an intensified globalizing evolution of the capitalist system. It is important to note that unlike GDP and other national income account data, the volume of world trade data are available from the mid-nineteenth century. In similar fashion, trade openness measured by the amount of exports over GDP for the world economy also displays a long-wave pattern.

Kondratiev further argued that the long upswings are characterized by more warfare and social unrest than the long downswings, and he explained this through the creation of new markets during the upswing that intensify geopolitical competitions between the major economies. In Table 8.2, we observe that the percentage of wars during the upswing of the long cycles is by far higher than those during the downswings.

The last two variables of Table 8.2 were not in the list of phenomena described by Kondratiev probably for the following reasons. The national income accounts were constructed mostly in the post-WWII period, and the prewar estimates were assembled retroactively (see Chap. 9). Sovereign defaults were many before WWI; however, they were not interesting from an economic analysis perspective for they were attributed mainly to irresponsible government borrowing and spending and not to the operation of systematic economic dynamics which may be subjected to theoretical analysis. Besides, there were no national income account data that would enable such theorization. Only in the recent decades, did public debt and its size relative to GDP along with other related variables became subject to intensive

Table 8.2 Major phenomena of long cycles

Variables	Long cycles									
	First long cycle 1790–1845		Second long cycle 1845–1896		Third long cycle 1896–1940		Fourth long cycle 1940–1982		Fifth long cycle 1982–	
	1790–1815	1815–1845	1845–1873	1873–1896	1896–1920	1920–1940	1940–1966	1966–1982	1982–2007	2007–2014
Basic innovations (% share)[a]	27	73	36	64	30	70	–	–	–	–
Volume of world trade (growth rate)[b]			4.62	3.00	3.75	2.55	8.49	5.49	6.55	2.78
Wars %[c]	59	41	58	42	68	32	63	37	–	–
Sovereign[d] defaults %	14	86	44	56	36	64	31	69	–	–
GDP USA[e] (growth rate, %)	4.78	3.80	4.67	4.02	3.21	2.94	4.53	2.73	3.45	1.22

[a]Source: Tsoulfidis and Papageorgiou (2017)

[b]Sources: World Trade (1850–2014)—Bank of England (2015), Table 18: 'Trade Volumes and Prices'. There is no data about the growth rates of world trade for the periods 1914–1920 and 1939–1949, that is, for the time periods related to the two World Wars

[c] Source of data: https://en.wikipedia.org/wiki/List_of_wars_1945%E2%80%9389#cite_note-2

[d] Source: https://en.wikipedia.org/wiki/List_of_sovereign_debt_crises

[e]Johnston and Williamson (2018), https://www.measuringworth.com/usgdp/

studies. And in these studies, based on the accumulation of a lot of historical and descriptive factual material, it becomes increasingly evident that sovereign defaults, although they may occur at any phase of the long cycle, have a much greater likelihood, and therefore frequency, of occurrence during periods of stagnation rather than during periods of prosperity. As we will argue in the following section, a falling rate of profit, past a point, leads to a stagnating mass of real net profits which discourages investment. Financial institutions then, in order to recover the money, they have lent out, are interested in increasing the level of the economy's output, something which can be achieved through higher investment spending. As a consequence, financial institutions are prone in reducing their interest rates to make borrowing even more attractive and thus initiate investment spending. However, the lower interest rates force financial institutions to lend out much higher amounts of money in order to acquire the same amount of interest revenues and thus pay much less consideration to the fundamentals of both, their own and their borrowers'. Under these circumstances, the lower interest rate encourages governments to increase borrowing, not necessarily for meaningful long-term investment projects but mainly for immediate consumption purposes and thus build a debt bubble along with other related bubbles developed in other markets, such as the real estate and financial markets. The burst of one of these bubbles is capable of triggering the burst of all the other ones especially in those economies with weak fundamentals and also with governments eager to give in to populist demands.

The last of our reported important economic variables is the growth rate of the real GDP of the US economy which pretty much follows the rhythm of long cycle; this is especially true for the years after WWII. It is important to point out that although we have data for the pre-WWII years, these estimates were constructed retroactively and, therefore, are less reliable than those of post-WWII years, when data began to be collected systematically. We should also point out that, for the post-WWII years, the growth rate of the world real GDP follows the rhythm of the growth of the US economy. It is important to stress at this point that the per capita real GDP gives a very similar, although more emphatic, picture of the same trend. We opted not to use it precisely because we wished to make our argument under the least favourable circumstances.

An illustration of long cycles is presented in the following figures which since the year 1951 depict the rate of change in real (2012 base year) GDP of the world economy (Fig. 8.1), of the US economy (Fig. 8.2) and of the Greek economy (Fig. 8.3). The trend of the real GDP (the dotted line) for each economy is extracted using the Hodrick-Prescott filter that essentially replaces Kondratiev's 9-year moving average.

From Fig. 8.1, we observe that the trend of the rate of change of world GDP reveals the post-war boom that lasted until about the mid to late 1960s, the recession of the 1970s till the mid-1980s, the booming phase with slow growth rates during the so-called neoliberal period and the collapse of the growth rates and the onset of the Great Recession in the post-2007 years. It is interesting to note that the fluctuations in the world's growth rates of GDP are not as wide as might be expected from the mere fact that it is made up of the real GDPs of all the countries, and so wild

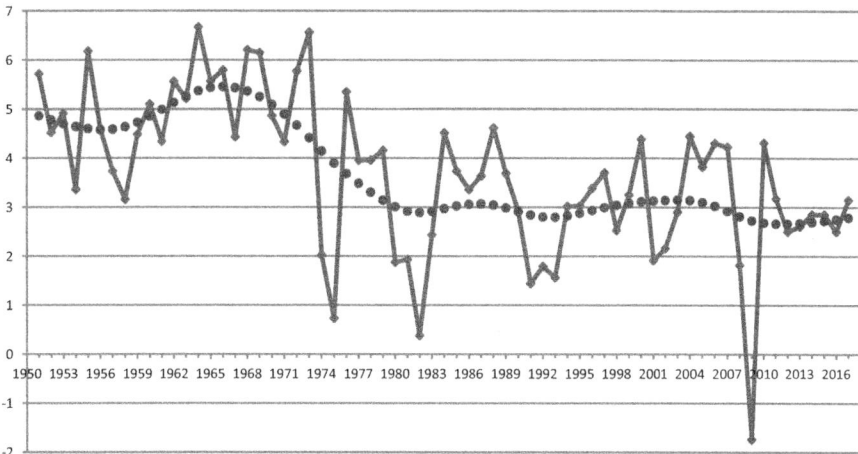

Fig. 8.1   Growth rates and trend of world real GDP, 1951–2017 (base year 2012)

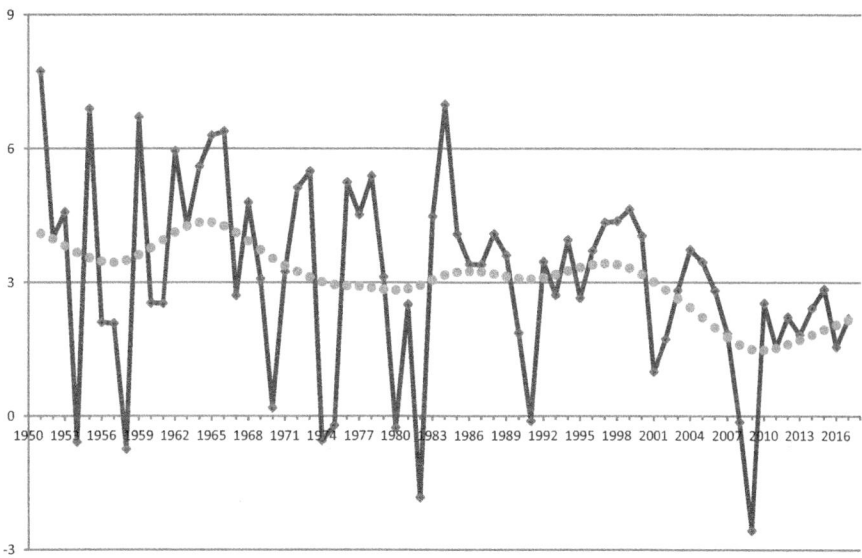

Fig. 8.2   Growth rates and trend of real GDP of US economy, 1951–2017 (base year 2012)

fluctuations tend to cancel each other out and give rise to a rather smoother evolution. Given that the US real GDP weights a lot in the world GDP, one expects to find very similar trends and in effect.

Fig. 8.2 depicts clearly enough the three phases of the post-war growth rates in GDP with the difference that the fluctuations are wider. Similar, although not quite so, are the results with respect to the growth rate of real GDP of the Greek economy

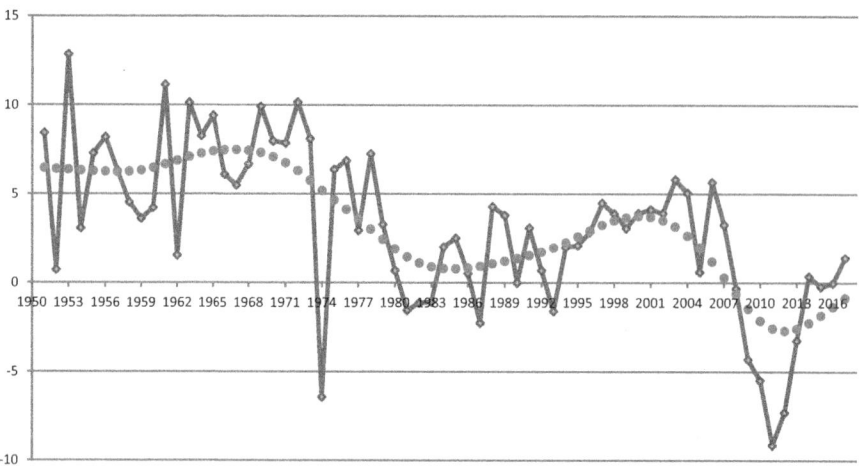

Fig. 8.3 Growth rates and trend of real GDP of Greek economy, 1951–2017 (base year 2012)

(Fig. 8.3) which in the last decade has attracted a lot of attention for its high public debt, its negative growth rates and the depth of the recession, the longest among the major advanced economies since the 1930s.[2]

A visual inspection of Fig. 8.3 indicates that the trends that we identified in the world and US economies appear in a much more emphatic way in the case of Greece.[3] To give a quantitative sense of our discussion, we have estimated the following coefficients of variations, namely, 0.43, 0.73 and 1.40 for the world, US and Greek economies, respectively. The much higher coefficient of variation of the Greek economy indicates the dramatic fall in its real GDP during the post-2007 years and the loss of more than one-quarter of its total GDP. Similar phenomena are observed also in other OECD countries, rendering this noteworthy 'dreadful' performance of the Greek economy a case that requires particular attention and further investigation. The other important common feature that stands out from the visual inspection of the data in Figs. 8.1, 8.2 and 8.3 is that the trend of the growth rate of real GDP is downward lending support to a number of views, starting from a Schumpeterian which is promoted by Gordon (2015, 2016) who argued the case of the diminishing returns to new innovations and continuing to the resurrection of the 'secular stagnation' thesis by Keynesian persuasion economists like Summers

[2]It is interesting to note that during the depression of 1930s, Greece, experienced a mild fall in real GDP during the years 1929–1932; however, for the entire period 1929–1939 displayed an average annual growth rate of 9% which was the second only to Japan's for the same time period (Tsoulfidis 2012, Chap. 10).

[3]For the years before 1961, data is taken from http://www.economics.gr. For the following years data is taken from AMECO http://ec.europa.eu/economy_finance/ameco/.

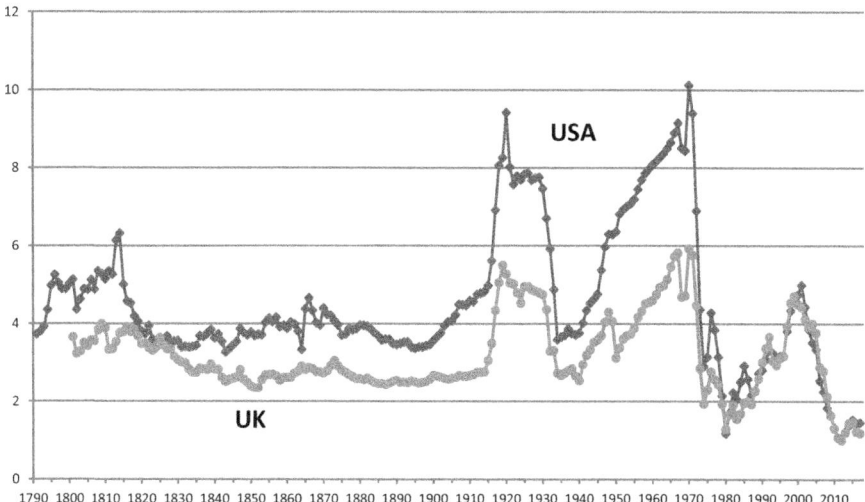

Fig. 8.4 The GDP deflator (base year 2012) over the gold price in the USA and the UK

(2014) and Krugman (2014) among others.[4] Finally, the observed downward trend in the real GDP may be consistent with the falling rate of profit view, whose theory we discuss in the next sections and its empirics in Chap. 10.

We continue the analysis of long cycles by utilizing, perhaps, the longest time series data available, namely, the price data used by Kondratiev to support his long-wave hypothesis. It is important to note that the system of national accounts had not yet been developed during the Kondratiev's period and the existed data did not always follow the same rules, whereas their collection was not regular. These data usually referred to variables such as international trade, interest rates, production of strategic importance inputs such as wheat, various precious metals (gold, silver) or basic metals (iron, steel). From the available data, Kondratiev used the wholesale prices divided by the price of gold comprising a composite index, a barometer we would daresay, that describes the evolution of the economy and its changing phases. The rise in the price index (inflation) indicates a booming period, whereas a fall (deflation) denoted a recessionary one. Indeed, the major long downturns of the past 1815–1840, 1873–1896 and in the 1930s were characterized by a fall in the general price level (deflation). It is worth noting that falling prices were considered as the worst that could happen to an economy, as the downward trend in the price index may paralyze the economic activity since the selling price of output may fall short of what is required to pay for the cost of inputs!

Figure 8.4 displays the ratio of wholesale price index over the price of gold for the period 1790–2017 for the USA and 1800–2017 for the UK. The wholesale price index, approximated by the GDP deflator, shows the purchasing power from the

---

[4]For other views, see Teulings and Baldwin (2014) and for a critique see Mejorado and Roman (2017).

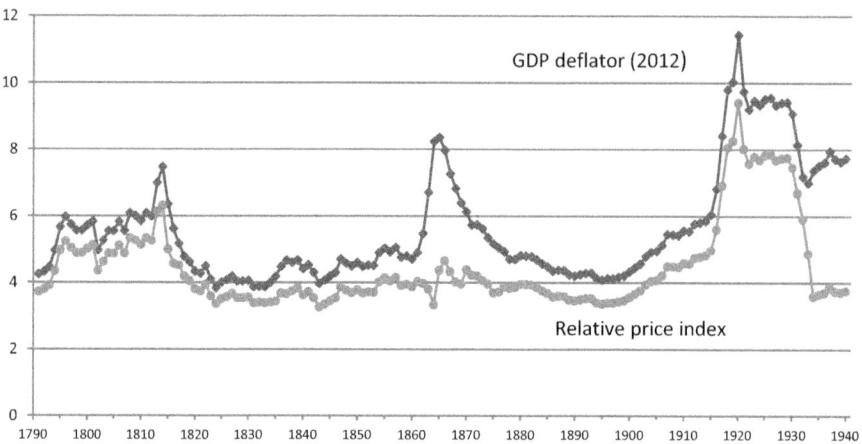

Fig. 8.5 Price indexes, USA, 1790–1941

point of view of the entrepreneur, that is, it shows the amount of inputs that a monetary unit possessed by the entrepreneur can buy. The ratio of the wholesale price index over the price of gold is essentially the direct gold price rule and denotes the amount of gold commanded by a unit of output.[5] Both prices are in terms of indexes with 2012 being the base year.

The following Fig. 8.5 shows that the evolution of the US GDP deflator, which is not very different from the wholesale price, coincides with the established in economic literature cyclical fluctuations for the period 1790–1941. The same result is obtained with the relative price index, i.e. GDP deflator over the price of gold.[6] The deviations that appear, e.g. during the period of the American Civil War 1861–1865 and the 1930s crisis, are associated with the suspension of the gold standard during those particular periods. However, despite the nominal suspension of its standard, gold never ceased to play its role; in fact, we found that the normalized prices, that is, the prices that would have been formed had the golden rule been applied, reflect the phases of the US economy during this long period of time.

In the post-WWII period (Fig. 8.6), when the golden rule ceased to be followed, at least, with its prewar rigour, the phenomenon of inflation appears during recessionary periods. The inflation in the 1960s and 1970s was the result of the relative looseness of the application of the golden rule and, of course, the implementation of expansionary policies that stimulated international aggregate demand, as was the case of the US government expenditures during the war in Vietnam.

As shown in Fig. 8.6, during the period 1945–2017, we observe the steady increase in the GDP deflator (and the other price indices follow a pretty similar

---

[5]The data are from Johnston and Williamson (2018).
[6]Data is taken from Officer and Williamson (2014).

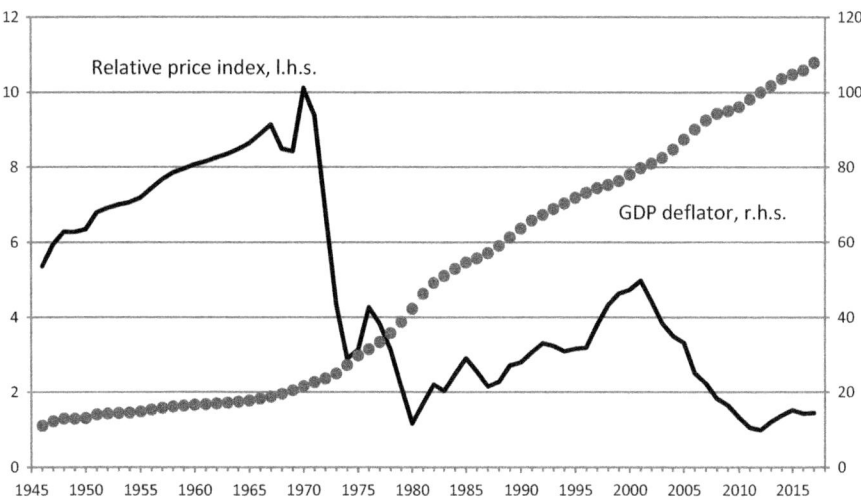

Fig. 8.6 GDP deflator and relative price index, USA, 1945–2017

path with small time lags) measured on the left-hand-side axis, while the price index, i.e. GDP deflator over the price of gold, is depicted on the right-hand-side axis for the US economy. The cyclicality of the US economy is obvious, which of course gives the tone to the international economy due to the interconnections that have been strengthened during the last decades.

8.2.1   Long Cycles in Economic Literature

For the interpretation of long cycles (waves), in the relevant literature, we come across with three main approaches: the Schumpeterian, the Social Structures of Accumulation and the classical based on the law of the falling profitability. Each of these approaches focuses on a key factor that is considered to be systemic and, by extension, the root cause of a long economic cycle; other factors are viewed as secondary or the side effects of the operation of the root cause.

In the theoretical scheme of Schumpeter (1942, 1954), innovation is the key factor to economic growth. Here there is a need to distinguish among the following three concepts, namely, invention, innovation and diffusion. Inventions are a prerequisite for innovations and may exist for many years without being used; innovation refers to the application of inventions into the production processes, that is, their commercialization. The diffusion of innovations across industries follows along with a period of economic growth. It is important to note that within the Schumpeterian framework innovations are viewed as 'swarms' in that they are introduced in a massive manner (in 'clusters' according to Schumpeter's wording) and then diffused throughout the economy. The introduction of innovations is carried out by the entrepreneurs who are considered exceptionally talented people whose activities include the introduction of new business schemes, new products, discovery of new markets and sources of raw materials and so on. In this sense, not all business leaders, executives or owners (capitalists) are necessarily innovative entrepreneurs, as they can maintain a temporary relationship with businesses by providing the necessary financing or managing and directing the business in the attainment of certain goals. In other words, entrepreneurs are considered individuals gifted with special talents (e.g. inventiveness and imagination and, of course, leadership) that enable them to exploit available or create new opportunities.

According to Schumpeter, the macroeconomic cycles represent the ways in which the economic system adapts to disturbances or shocks arising from large-scale innovations (steam engine, railroads, electricity, automobiles, computers, etc.). In Schumpeter's analysis, the economic system tends to equilibrium, but innovator entrepreneurs interrupt this equilibrium process as they introduce major (epoch-making) innovations that create the conditions for a new long-lasting stage of economic growth. This dynamic process generates cyclical variations, but at the same time growth, where each booming period is seen as repulsion from equilibrium (identified with the recessionary stage of the economy) and each downward period as a return to equilibrium at which the system can come close to or pass through but certainly cannot remain. In other words, equilibrium is only notional and not actual which can be attained in any lasting way; the idea is that so long as the economy is near such a situation, the disturbing activity of innovating entrepreneurs is brought about. It is obvious that in the booming phase a number of variables, such as prices, profit and interest rates are on their upward trend, which is reversed during the recession phase. In the recovery phase, the various institutions also contribute to creating economic growth-enhancing conditions. It is worth noting that the phase of the long-term recession is considered the most appropriate to nurture the conditions necessary to increase the likelihood for the introduction of innovations.

Similar is the theory of Social Structures of Accumulation (SSA) introduced by David Gordon (1978, 1980; Gordon et al. 1982; Kotz 2017). According to SSA, the new institutions that define the relations between capitalists and workers, the organization of the labour process and the like are massively introduced (in national and international level) during the downturn of the long cycle and in so doing contribute to its expansionary state. The central idea of SSA is that the existing relationships defined by a given institutional setup are not flexible but at the same time are not permanent. Over time and with the capital entering into the new phase of accumulation, the existing institutional framework instead of contributing and enhancing the operation of the capitalist system puts obstacles rendering inevitable the need for the introduction of altogether new institutions. This period marks the onset of the crisis, which lasts for the time required to form this new institutional framework and to attain new agreements that will lead again to a period of long-term economic growth and so on.

It is important to note that in the depression of the 1930s and the first post-WWII years, we had the launching of new national and international institutions which, if not contributed, certainly were more or less consistent with the intellectual climate of that period. However, we cannot say the same thing for the stagflation crisis during which the prevailing idea was that the past institutions and the state, in other words the whole apparatus of the so-called mixed economy, were responsible for the depressing state of the economy. The neoliberal growth that followed the post-1982 years was accompanied by the weakening or dismantling of the old institutional setup and certainly not with the creation of any major (epoch-making) ones. This is not to say that the current institutions are not important, but just to indicate that the arguments of the proponents of SSA are difficult to come to terms with the current facts. The counter-argument, however, might be that precisely because of the lack of new major institutions, the growth rates in the post-1982 years were lower than those of the post-war years.

The SSAs and Schumpeter's approaches to long cycles assign an important role to the institutions and innovations, respectively, by arguing that they initially contribute to increasing the rate of profit leading to economic boom and then (due to the exhaustion of innovations or the outdated of institutions) lead to the economic downturn and, of course, to the fall in the rate of profit. In other words, the rate of profit is a dependent variable of either innovation (in the Schumpeterian approach) or institutional framework (in the SSA approach). By contrast, in Marx and, in general, in the classical approach of interpreting the long cycles, the central role is held by the trajectory of the rate of profit, which is viewed as an independent variable and, in combination with the evolution in the mass of net profits, determines the growth and stagnation phases of an economy. In fact, the Marxian analysis of long cycles and, by extension, of economic crisis theory is a proposal where both the Schumpeterian idea about innovations and the new institutional framework of the SSA approach become essential components of a single and unified theory in which the 'cause of the causes' is the evolution of the rate of profit and its underlying factors that give rise to its long-term falling tendency that we discuss next.

8.3 The Law of the Falling Rate Profit

The evolution of the rate of profit is an important issue in economic theory, classical and neoclassical. We could say that (almost all) the major economists of the past opined, one way or another, the long-term downward trend in the rate of profit and the attainment of the economy's stationary state. Smith among the first argued, according to the most popular interpretations, that the fall in the rate of profit is the result of the intensity of competition (in labour, capital and product markets), which leads to higher costs, decreases the total profits and finally lowers the rate of profit. An alternative interpretation of Smith (Eltis 1985) attributes the falling path of the rate of profit to the rising capital-intensity which appears first in agriculture where the division of labour is limited and, given the more or less constant shares of incomes, the rate of profit falls. The higher rate of profit in the nonagricultural sectors leads to the intensification of competition in all markets and eventually the economy's average rate of profit falls. The end result is a rising capital-intensity and a fall in the rate of profit in the total economy. A third interpretation of Smith's argument is that as the capitalization of the production increases, the higher depreciation expenses reduce the share of net profits to income and eventually decreases the rate of profit (Tsoulfidis and Paitaridis 2009; Tsoulfidis 2010).

The lack of data led Smith to study the evolution of the interest rate as a proxy indicating the movement in the rate of profit.

> [...] as the usual market rate of interest varies in any country, we may be assured that the ordinary profits of stock must vary with it, must sink as it sinks, and rise as it rises. The progress of interest, therefore, may lead us to form some notion of the progress of profit.
>
> (*Wealth*, pp. 105–6)

In fact, the interest rate was from the very few variables for which there was sufficient information in his era. Smith then hypothesized that the rate of profit is about double the interest rate:

> The proportion which the usual market rate of interest ought to bear to the ordinary rate of clear profit necessarily varies as profit rises or falls. Double interest is in Great Britain reckoned what the merchants call a good, moderate, reasonable profit; terms which I apprehend mean no more than a common and usual profit.
>
> (*Wealth*, pp. 98–99)

The idea is that the interest payment being part of the surplus (or gross profits) reflects to a great extent the evolution of profits; therefore, according to Smith, the downward trend in the interest rates can be used as a proxy of the evolution of the rate of profit. However, he argued that the fall in both the rate of interest and the rate of profit is very slow and the stationary state of the economy characterized by zero net investment would be attained in the very distant future. Therefore, the long-run fall in the rate of profit should not be a cause of current concerns because the emerging from feudalism capitalist society is characterized by a far higher productivity and wealth creation capacity from which all social classes may benefit. Thus, according to Smith, the focus should be on the elimination of whatever feudalistic, institutional and other obstacles that prevent the emerging capitalist society to attain its full wealth creating potential.

Ricardo considered that an economy is inevitably led to its stationary state as a consequence of the downward trend in the rate of profit, whose evolution is shaped by the law of diminishing returns in the agricultural (broadly defined) sector in the economy. In particular, Ricardo argues that the investment of the entrepreneurs leads to an increase in wages above their subsistence level which is defined as the basket of goods required for the reproduction of the working class. Hence, the standard of living of the working class improves, infant mortality rates fall, while people marry in younger ages, and so the birth rate and population increase. The growing demand for agricultural products forces the cultivation of less and less fertile parcels of lands and results in increased cost of food production. Given the real wage (=subsistence level), this implies payments of higher wages and reduction in profits leading to lower rate of profit, decrease in net investment and finally attainment of the stationary state.

It is important to stress a similar view about the long-run evolution of the rate of profit held by the first neoclassical economists who argued that this fall in the rate of profit was an issue that needed further investigation. For example, Jevons pointed out:

> Our formula for the rate of interest shows that unless there be constant progress in the arts, the rate must tend to sink towards zero, supposing accumulation of capital to go on. There are sufficient statistical facts, too, to confirm this conclusion historically. The only question that can arise is as to the actual cause of this tendency.
>
> (Jevons 1871, p. 254)

The idea is that in neoclassical theory, and Jevons as one of its founders, the price of a productive factor expresses its relative scarcity; if there is a shortage (abundance) of a factor of production, its remuneration will be high (low). Hence, we have the operation of the law of the diminishing marginal product of factors of production, and on this point, Jevons observed that:

> In many ill-governed countries, where the land is wretchedly tilled, the average produce is small, and yet the rate of interest is high, simply because the want of security prevents the clue supply of capital: hence more capital is urgently needed, and its price is high. In America and the British Colonies the produce is often high, and yet interest is high, because there is not sufficient capital accumulated to meet all the demands. In England and other old countries the rate of interest is generally lower because there is an abundance of capital, and the urgent need of more is not actually felt.
>
> (Jevons 1871, p. 254)

In the same pattern, another major neoclassical economist, Walras (1874), draws the reader's attention to two laws. The first law states that:

> In a progressive economy, the price of labour (wages) remaining substantially unchanged, the price of land-services (rent) will rise appreciably and the price of capital-services (the interest charge) will fall appreciably.
>
> (*Elements*, pp. 390–1)

In the second law, Walras asserts that the price of capital services decreases, while, at the same time, the price of capital goods equals to their production cost that remains almost constant, hence:

> In a progressive economy, the price of capital goods proper remaining constant, the price of personal faculties will rise in proportion to the fall in the rate of net income, and the price of land will rise both by reason of the fall in the rate of net income and by reason of the rise in rent.
>
> (*Elements*, p. 391)

Other neoclassical economists generalized the Ricardian analysis and claimed the falling tendency in the rate of profit as a result of the rising capital-intensity and the diminishing marginal productivity of capital. For example, John B. Clark argues that increasing capital-labour and capital-output ratios practically diminish the rate of return. He notes:

> Capital is the element that is outgrowing labor. [...] As the accumulation of capital actually goes on, it shows itself more and more in qualitative changes of existing instruments [...] they thus represent a greater outlay incurred for a smaller gain. [...] Tools are, of course, employed in the order of their productivity [...] it soon ceases to be possible to add to a working equipment anything that produces a multiple of its own cost in a year, and the interest on the final increment of capital becomes a fraction of the total capital itself. This

fraction steadily diminishes as the productive fund grows larger [...] as accumulation proceeds, there are always made costlier machines, representing more capital; and the product that comes from using them is a smaller fraction of their cost [...] we are utilizing the opportunities for investment that stand late in the series, and are low in the scale of productivity.

(J.B. Clark 1902, pp. 183–186)

It is important to note that J.B. Clark does not refer to static situations where technology is given, but rather to dynamic ones, and in this sense, his analytical framework is similar to that of classical economists. In the neoclassical analysis, the rise in the price of one factor of production would mean its substitution with a relatively cheaper factor of production and so forth. Thus, in neoclassical economics technological change is expected neutral in the long run, which amounts to an approximately constant capital-output ratio in the long run.

Keynes (1936) and Schumpeter (1934, 1939) also argued that the rate of profit, in the long run, is falling. For example, Keynes is convinced that falling profitability— as this is manifested in his concept of the marginal efficiency of capital (MEC)—is a stylized fact of capitalism. He claims:

Today and presumably for the future the schedule of the marginal efficiency of capital is, for a variety of reasons, much lower than it was in the nineteenth century.

(*General Theory*, p. 308)

Keynes's idea of the 'euthanasia of the rentier' is precisely a way to slow down the falling tendency in profitability and to encourage investment spending. The causes for the expected falling tendency in MEC according to Keynes are:

- Firstly, the forces in the supply side of the market (short-term argument) and the intensification of competition in the labour and capital markets, which, given the average cost curves and prices, entail an increase in production costs leading to a decrease in the mass of profits and profitability.
- Secondly, the forces in the demand side of the market (long-term argument) which compel enterprises to invest and thus produce a larger volume of output. However, in order to sell this larger volume of output, i.e. to increase its demand, the firm has to reduce the price of its product which inevitably leads to a lower mass of profits and rate of profit.

Then generalizing the result across firms, Keynes concludes that the rate of profit (or MEC) decreases for the economy as a whole. The two arguments (short run and long run) are not mutually exclusive but rather combined together may contribute to an even greater fall in the MEC.

From the discussion, it is clear that, although Keynes uses the term MEC, nevertheless his analysis and conclusions, like of the classical economists, are not based on the idea of scarcity or abundance, and thus on the marginal product of inputs. Thus, the law of decreasing returns to scale cannot be applied to Keynes's analysis, because that law presupposes that at least one factor of production remains constant, which cannot be either land, whose relative importance is far too small to justify decreasing returns for the total economy, nor labour due to the presence of unemployment which is a persistent rather than a temporary phenomenon of the capitalist economy; and of course we cannot take capital as fixed, since we are interested in studying the returns to this factor of production.

In addition, Schumpeter (1934) points out that the path to the stationary state is not reversible and that the rate of profit along with the long-term interest rate tends to zero; this is the reason why the motive for 'creative destruction' through the introduction of innovations fades away over time. In this sense, Schumpeter's conclusion is similar to that of Keynes's and classical economists'.

From the above, we find surprisingly enough that there is consensus among the great economists of the past that the long-run tendency of the rate of profit is falling. Moreover, the views of neoclassical economists and Keynes are, in most cases, further elaborations of Smith's and Ricardo's views about the intensification of competition as a cause of the falling rate of profit. In contrast, Marx argues that the intensity of competition—that many economists considered as principally responsible for the falling rate of profit—simply makes visible the internal laws of capitalist production and allows their realization. Competition, in other words, does not impose laws externally on capital and that the intensity of competition is the result of the falling rate of profit, not its cause. Marx explains:

> the fall in the rate of profit calls forth the competitive struggle among capitalists, not vice versa. To be sure, the competitive struggle is accompanied by a transient rise in wages and a resultant further temporary fall of the rate of profit.
>
> (*Capital* III, p. 301)

The most fundamental difference, however, between the Marxian and neoclassical approach is that in the latter the fall in the rate of profit is caused by the diminishing marginal physical productivity of capital. Marx does not base his argument of the falling rate of profit on the marginal productivity of capital and on the yields of capital for its contribution to production. Instead, Marx's theory is based on the explicit relationship between the stock of capital and the output produced. Historically, there is an increase in the capital-output ratio (Mejorado and Roman 2014), a result that we grapple with in the next section where we also show the relationship between the falling rate of profit and the stagnation phase of the economy.

8.4   Mechanics of the Law of the Falling Rate of Profit and the Crisis

In the third volume of the *Capital*, Marx sets forth the law of the falling tendency in the rate of profit (FROP) which he considers:

> in every respect the most important law of modern political economy, and the most essential for understanding the most difficult relations. It is the most important law from the historical standpoint. It is a law which, despite its simplicity, has never before been grasped and, even less, consciously articulated.
>
> (*Grundrisse*, pp. 748–9)

However, the argument for the falling rate of profit (FROP) has often been the source of confusion, not only because of its objective difficulty but also because the analysis in the third volume of *Capital*, which usually attracts the attention of most scholars, presupposes a knowledge and the applications of concepts and mechanisms whose details have been discussed earlier in particular in the first volume of *Capital*. In fact, the argument of the FROP is based on the dual nature of the commodity as use value and exchange value which is discussed in *Capital* I. Between the two, under capitalist conditions, the priority of production is placed on the exchange value of the commodity. Every capitalist produces in order to sell (exchange value) and make profit, and not just make any profit, but as much as possible; only then will he be able to successfully pursue his business. Without profits, and even with positive profits but not satisfactorily high, the capitalist is doomed, sooner or later, to be eliminated from the market.

The extraction of the greatest possible profit, however, is not an easy and by no means a certain task, because the capitalist is not alone in the market but also his rivals who share the same goal. Therefore, the entrepreneur faces fierce competition, and his survival in such a market-rivalrous environment dictates a continuous accumulation of capital, that is, the reinvestment of profits into improvements in technology and the reorganization of the labour process so as to remain competitive. By doing so, capitals increase their productivity and reduce the unit value of their commodities even below the industry's average and more specifically the industry's regulating value or price of production, making thus possible the extraction of excess profits. Hence, the very nature of the capitalist production oriented towards the extraction of the greatest possible profit leads capitalists into two major competitions.[7]

In the first (and most discussed especially in the sociological literature) competition, the capitalist fights against labour to keep wages at the lowest possible level, to increase the length of the working day and to intensify the work effort in order to extract the maximum out of workers' labour. However, in this effort the capitalist faces physical, legal and even moral limits. Soon the capitalist realizes that the most effective method to increasing profits is to reorganize the labour process through the further subdivision and routinization of the labour activity. The division of labour, which is a sine qua non condition for increasing productivity, however, is more effective through the introduction of new technologies which are made possible mainly by investment in fixed capital. The great advantage of fixed capital is that on the one hand it replaces labour and on the other hand it simplifies the labour activity, reducing it to simple repetitive tasks and making thus possible the effective reduction in real wages.[8] A side effect of the mechanization of the production process is that it leads to the subordination of labour to capital inasmuch as the worker becomes, more and more, part of the operation of machines and works following their rhythm. From the entrepreneur's point of view, Marx notes that 'a machine is a perfect worker

---

[7]The analysis is based on Shaikh (1978 and 1987).

[8]The routinazation of labour activity enhances the scope of mechanization.

while a worker is an imperfect machine'. Thus, the mechanization of the production process through the introduction of fixed capital makes the workers much more disciplined and by deskilling them keeps their wages as low as possible. Meanwhile, the entrepreneur through the rising productivity manages to reduce the per unit cost of production and so even for the same price earns more profits whereas by decreasing the price expands the market share at the expense of competitors.[9]

In the second (and from the economic perspective most important) competition, the capital fights for prices and markets against other capitalists; in other words there is a 'civil war'. The most effective 'weapon' in this competition is the reduction in cost and prices; capitals that manage to undercut their price undersell their competitors and expand their market share. As in the first competitive front against labour, the introduction of fixed capital is the means that provides a better position to the capitalists and defines the outcome in the confrontation with the other capitalists. The reduction in the average cost of production is attained through the introduction of more fixed capital (buildings, machinery, raw materials) in place of variable capital (labour).

8.4.1 The Cost Curves

In the first and third volumes of *Capital*, it is made clear that investment in capital goods is taking place in order to rationalize the production process, increase labour productivity and thus reduce the unit costs even below the industry's average in the effort to extract excess profits and in so doing to secure a rate of profit above the economy's average. For reasons of clarity and simplicity of presentation, the analysis is carried out only with fixed capital stock; hence the definition of the rate of profit is simplified as follows:

$$r = \frac{s}{C} = \frac{s/v}{C/v} \qquad (8.1)$$

where r is the rate of profit, s is total gross profits (surplus-value), C is the total capital invested in plant and equipment[10] and v is the variable capital. Capital letters

---

[9]For further discussion, see Tsaliki (2008) and the literature cited there.

[10]The rate of profit is usually expressed as $r = s/(c + v) = (s/v)/(c/v + 1)$ where all variables are in terms of flows. The proper presentation, however, requires capital to be expressed in terms of stocks, namely, the stock of fixed capital, C^f, of circulating capital, C^c, (mainly raw materials) and of variable capital, V. The idea is that the entrepreneur advances both the raw materials and wages before the completion of the production process and the sale of output produced. As a consequence, the capitalist must have a certain amount of money put aside for the purchase of materials and the payment of wages. The latter is the famous *wage fund* of the classical economists and also of Jevons (1871) and Walras (1874). In the effort to estimate the stocks of circulating and variable capital, we need to know the number of turnovers for circulating capital (n_c) and variable capital (n_v) during a

Table 8.3 Average fixed, constant, variable and total costs

Output	FC	AFC = FC/q	AVC = VC/q	AC = TC/q	AFC'	AVC'	AC'
100	10,000	100.0	60	160.0	140.0	15	155.0
150	10,000	66.7	60	126.7	93.3	15	108.3
200	10,000	50.0	60	110.0	70.0	15	85.0
250	10,000	40.0	60	100.0	56.0	15	71.0
300	10,000	33.3	60	93.3	46.7	15	61.7
350	10,000	28.6	60	88.6	40.0	15	55.0
400	10,000	25.0	60	85.0	35.0	15	50.0
450	10,000	22.2	60	82.2	31.1	15	46.1
500	10,000	20.0	60	80.0	28.0	15	43.0

stand for the stock variables and lowercase letters for the flow variables. The increase in the ratio of fixed capital to variable capital (C^f/v) generally requires the introduction of new, more efficient techniques that change radically the whole labour process and increase productivity. It is important to note that the increase in productivity and the consequent decrease in the unit value of the product are the results of the mechanization of the production process, which implies more and more fixed capital per unit of output.

In Table 8.3 we provide a fairly simple numerical example bearing similarities with the usual cost examples in microeconomic textbooks. The major characteristic of our numerical example is that we do not assume static economies or diseconomies of scale and also the shape of the resulting curves is in line with the empirical findings (Hall and Hitch 1939; Moudud 2010, Chap. 2).

Let us now hypothesize a firm, whose various costs per unit of output are displayed in Table 8.3. The firm starts off with an investment in fixed capital equal to 10,000 monetary units (mu). For the first 100 units of output, q, the average fixed cost is $AFC = FC/q = 10,000/100 = 100$ mu. Let us further hypothesize that production increases by 50 units, and so the AFC is decreasing following the shape of a rectangular hyperbola curve approaching asymptotically the horizontal axis. Following the typical empirical finding of many studies of industrial corporations (e.g. Hall and Hitch 1939; Moudud 2010, Chap. 2), constant returns to scale prevail for fairly large amounts of output; hence, so the cost per unit of output (average cost) which is no different than the marginal cost which are assumed equal to 60 mu (in terms of standard microanalysis, we have $AVC = VC/q$).[11]

---

year. If we hypothesize that the final product is produced four times a year, then C and V should be divided by the respective turnover time, which, in this case, is 4. That is, the capitalist advances one-fourth of his capital in materials and wages in order to initiate the production process. Therefore, the rate of profit in its complete form will be $r = \frac{s}{C^f + C^c/_{n_c} + V/_{n_v}} = \frac{s}{C^f + C^c/_4 + V/_4}$.

[11]Hence, for the shake of simplicity, we assume that the total variable cost (wages and materials), VC, is 6000 mu which divided by the 100 units of output produced, we obtain $AVC = VC/q = 60$ mu. When production increases to 150 units, it means that the AVC remains 60 mu and

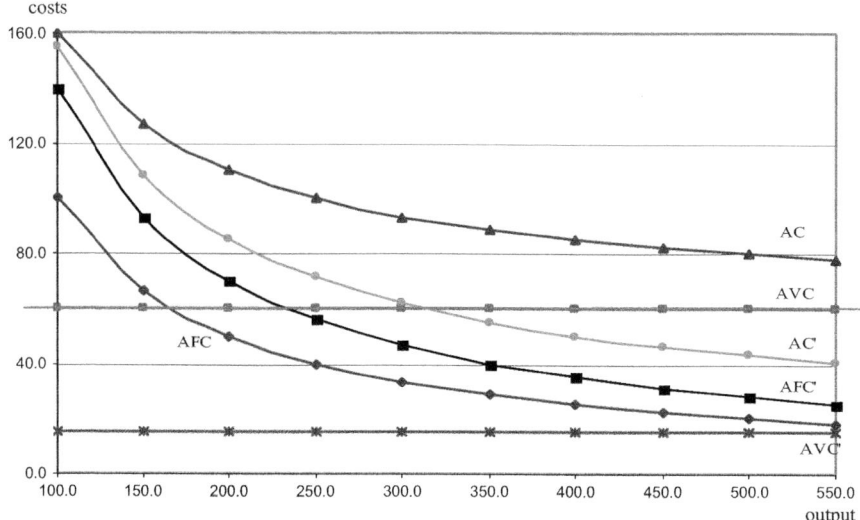

Fig. 8.7 Fixed capital and average cost curves

Adding the two costs together, we get the average total cost, $AC = AFC + AVC$. It is important to point out that the AFC imposes its form on the AC which decreases with the increases in output produced. If we now assume a larger fixed capital due to investment in plant and equipment, i.e. $FC' = 14{,}000 > FC = 10{,}000$, then $AFC' > AFC$ for each production level. We cannot say the same thing for the variable costs $AVC' < AVC$ and by extension for the $AC' < AC$ for every level of output produced. The idea is that by investing in plant and equipment (fixed capital), the entrepreneur is bound to reorganize the labour process and also to improve the division of labour and by doing so to increase productivity and reduce the cost per unit of output, AC. As a consequence for the same price, the entrepreneur earns more profits per unit of output and, moreover, by reducing the price may increase his market share at the expense of his competitors.

Figure 8.7 illustrates the above discussion of the shifts of the various cost curves that resemble, to some extent, the cost curves that we find in the usual microeconomics textbooks. For example, we have a fall in the average cost, which figuratively speaking is shown by moving the average cost curve from the AC position down to the new AC' position. This shift is due to the sacrifice made by the capitalist to install the new machinery (=fixed capital), which results to the shift of the average fixed cost from the AFC to the new AFC'.

The inherent need of capital for rationalization, mechanization and in general increasing capitalization of the production process leads to a reduction in the unit values and thereby cost of commodities caused by the rising productivity. The same

---

so forth. In other words, AVC and marginal cost (MC) are the same, since we assume constant returns to scale.

logic, which dictates the mechanization of the labour process and the increase in productivity, in effect, determines the distribution of benefits resulting from the increase in productivity and the resulting cost reductions. Obviously, the increase in productivity is not to the benefit of workers because the purpose of introducing innovations is not to increase the real wages but rather to increase profits as an end in itself. At the same time, the permanent presence of the industrial reserve army (i.e. the unemployed seeking for employment) does not allow the real wage to grow systematically at a rate higher than the growth in productivity.

The evolution of the distribution of new output between labour and capital, as expressed through the rate of surplus-value, depends on the relative rates of change in labour productivity and real wages, as shown by the breakdown of the surplus-value to its components:

$$\frac{s}{v} = \frac{y - v}{v} = \frac{(y/l - v/l)}{(v/l)} = \frac{y/l - w}{w} \tag{8.2}$$

where $y = v + s$ is the total new value produced, that is, the sum of variable capital, v, and surplus-value, s, l is the number of workers or better the labour hours, y/l is the productivity of labour and w is the average real wage. From the above analysis, it follows that the rate of surplus-value in a typical capitalist economy is expected to display a rising trend.

8.4.2   *Capital and Its Compositions*

The various expressions of capital-intensity or composition of capital become a key issue in the discussions of the falling rate of profit (FROP). The configurations of Rosdolsky (1977), Steedman (1977), Weeks (1981) and Fine (1982) are of particular interest; however, Shaikh (1987) gives a comprehensive and detailed analysis of the various compositions of capital which we follow and subsequently try to operationalize in actual economies.

We start off with the technical composition (TC), the so-called internal measure of composition of capital, which refers to the ratio of heterogeneous capital goods per worker. This is a purely theoretical measure and refers to the ratio of a set of heterogeneous use values over workers or labour hours and as such cannot be used practically. The TC, we could say, expresses the mechanization of the production process, that is, the confrontation of a given worker with more and more fixed capital (machines). If the production was characterized by a single capital good and uniform labour, the discussion would have been simple and easy. However, the reality is far too complex; hence, a vector of heterogeneous capital goods is to be compared against another vector of labour inputs, and both vectors must be homogenized in order to have meaningful comparisons. This is another way to say that the vectors, in order to be homogenized, must be converted to scalars through appropriate multiplications; for this purpose, we utilize prices, which make possible the expression of both numerator and denominator of the TC ratio in terms of comparable units, in our case money units (mu) per worker or mu per hour of simple labour. Therefore, the numerator of the TC which consists of many heterogeneous elements is converted into a scalar, which is the product of two vectors (the row vector of direct prices of a base year times the column vector of use values). The resulting scalar makes possible the construction of an index that is called technical composition of capital (TCC). The TCC, as expected, tends to grow in the long run due to technological progress which is capital-using and labour-saving.

In order to facilitate the analysis, we introduce the concept of materialized composition of (fixed) capital (MCC), a term that, to the extent that we know the relevant literature, was devised by Shaikh (1987), as it is not explicitly found in Marx's texts except for some hints for a possible characterization. Such a hint is in the following quotation:

> Since the mass of the employed living labour is continually on the decline as compared to the mass of materialized labour set in motion by it, *i.e.*, to the productively consumed means of production.
>
> (*Capital* III, p. 213)

The MCC, that is, the ratio of invested capital to value-added, is an intermediate step between the value composition of capital (VCC) and the TCC. The MCC is defined as the ratio of the value of dead labour (C) to the creative powers of the living labour (l) to produce new (added) value; therefore, MCC = C/l.

Another key variable in our discussion for the falling tendency of the rate of profit is that of the VCC, i.e. the ratio of the value of invested capital (C) to the value of variable capital (v), both expressed in current prices. The VCC is a complex variable that encompasses all of the above already discussed compositions of capital (TCC and MCC). Furthermore, and under particular circumstances, the VCC may give rise to the organic composition of capital (OCC) which Marx defines as follows:

> The value composition of capital, inasmuch as it is determined by, and reflects, its technical composition of capital, is called the organic composition of capital.
>
> (*Capital* III, pp. 145–6)

But let us disentangle the relations between the various compositions with other variables that are important in their own right and, as we will see, shape the long-run movement of the rate of profit. Starting with the VCC and MCC, which are both depended on the TCC, but also on the relative direct prices of capital to consumer goods, as well as on redistributive factors, i.e. the rate of surplus-value. From all these factors, the TCC is the critical determining factor. The idea is that relative direct prices are expected to fluctuate very close to each other; therefore, their ratio is not very different from one, and thus their net effect is expected to be negligible over the long run. The link between the VCC and the MCC is the rate of surplus-value as shown below:

$$\frac{C}{v} = \frac{C}{l}\frac{l}{v} = \frac{C}{l}\left(\frac{v+s}{v}\right) = \frac{C}{l}\left(1 + \frac{s}{v}\right) \tag{8.3}$$

If the MCC or in neoclassical terms the capital-output ratio in current prices is increasing, then the VCC is also increasing, and if the rate of surplus-value increases, then the VCC is increasing even more. In this case, it follows that a growing VCC reflects the changes in both, the MCC, i.e. the ratio C/l, but also the changes in income distribution. As a consequence, it is likely (theoretically at least) for the MCC to remain constant and a rising VCC to be attributed exclusively to the rising income distribution factor or what amount to the same thing to a rising rate of surplus-value. Therefore, by assuming that the market prices of capital and consumer goods will not differ from their respective direct prices, it follows that all variables can be expressed in terms of market prices. Therefore, for the VCC adjusted for the capacity utilization (i.e. AVCC), we may write

$$\underbrace{\frac{C}{v}}_{\text{AVCC}} = \underbrace{\left[\frac{\lambda_k}{\lambda_y} \frac{K \cdot u}{l}\right]}_{\text{MCC}} \underbrace{\left(\frac{\lambda_y l}{v}\right)}_{1+e} \tag{8.4}$$

where K is the value of the capital invested (fixed capital stock in constant prices), v denotes the variable capital, λ_k and λ_y denote the direct prices of capital and output produced, respectively, C is the invested capital in current prices and $l = y$ is the value-added expressed in constant prices. Finally, u represents the degree of capacity utilization of capital, which for classical economists and Marx is assumed to be fully utilized. In other words, aggregate demand and aggregate supply are assumed to be equal to each other, and, therefore, there is no underutilization of capacity.[12]

The bracketed term in relation (8.4) includes the components of the MCC, while the term in the parenthesis is the value-added which divided by the workers' wages (variable capital) gives us the term $1 + e$. Then, taking the growth rates of the relationship (8.4), we break down the growth rate of the AVCC in its four major components, and so we can evaluate the contribution of each and every one of them to its overall rate of change. So, we may write

$$AVCC = \underbrace{\left(\frac{\widehat{C}}{v}\right)}_{\substack{\text{total} \\ \text{effect}}} = \underbrace{\left(\frac{\widehat{\lambda_k}}{\lambda_y}\right)}_{\substack{\text{price} \\ \text{effect}}} + \underbrace{\left(\frac{\widehat{K}}{l}\right)}_{\substack{\text{technology} \\ \text{effect}}} + \underbrace{\widehat{u}}_{\substack{\text{demand} \\ \text{effect}}} + \underbrace{\left(\frac{\widehat{\lambda_y l}}{v}\right)}_{\substack{\text{distribution} \\ \text{effect}}} \tag{8.5}$$

where the hat over a variable or a term implies its average annual rate of change. The first term on the right-hand side of the above equation gives us the contribution of relative prices to the evolution of the AVCC; the second term of the same equation 'captures' the influence of the evolution of technology effect or the capital-output

---

[12]However, in our discussion and estimates, we will relax this assumption. For the old classical economists, the so-called Say's law assumed away any problem of discrepancy between supply and demand, whereas in Marx and in the level of abstraction of *Capital* even in volume III, capital is assumed fully utilized.

ratio in constant prices. The third term reflects the rate of change in the degree of capacity utilization of the economy and thus captures the impact of the aggregate demand relative to aggregate supply The last term of the above relationship estimates the effect of the distribution factor over time, that is, the effect of the ratio of value-added to variable capital which is equal to $1 + e$. As a consequence, the AVCC encapsulates not only the changes in the material characteristics of the production process but also the changes in the price structure (relative prices), the strength of demand relative to supply as well as the changes in income distribution. It is important to stress at this point that the distribution effect can be rewritten as $\left[\widehat{(y/l)}\widehat{(1/v)}\right]$, which is equal to the growth rate of productivity, $\widehat{(y/l)}$, minus the growth rate of the variable capital, $(\hat{v})$.

Therefore, technological change which is inherent in the operation of the capitalist system leads to an increasing TCC which sooner or later is expected to exert its impact on both the VCC and OCC. The idea is that the unit values of capital and consumer goods will be very close to each other, and for this reason, their ratio will be close to 1, that is, $\lambda_k/\lambda_y \approx 1$. We do know from a number of studies (whose details are discussed in Chap. 4) that the labour values deviate only slightly (on average) from market prices; therefore, the proximity between the two types of prices is surprisingly small. In addition, we know that when the number of sectors is aggregated to just a few (e.g. three), the differences between the relative values become even smaller (see, e.g. Tsoulfidis 2010, ch. 5). Therefore, the impact of relative unit values is expected to be neutral or negligible in the long run. The reason is that capital and consumer goods sectors are aggregations of a large number of industries and there is overlap between them. In other words, the product of an industry may be partly capital and partly consumer goods depending on their use.[13] In fact, this equalizing trend in the unit values of the two departments of production results from the aggregation of a large number of industries and their classification in the two department of social reproduction (see Chaps. 2 and 4). Meanwhile, the technological change cannot be contained within an industry and quite rapidly diffuses into the totality of the economy as Marx notes:

> If it is further assumed that this gradual change in the composition of capital is not confined only to individual spheres of production, but it occurs more or less in all, or at least in the key spheres of production, so that it involves changes in the average organic composition of the total capital of a certain society [...].
>
> (*Capital* III, p. 212)

It is, therefore, useful to highlight the necessary conditions under which Marx's argument for his law of the FROP holds true. In this context, Marx does not really need to rely on a Ricardian-type argument to support his view of the FROP, as argued by Schefold (1976), Hollander (1991) and Kurz (1998, 2010). We recall that the Ricardian argument for the downward trend in the rate of profit is based on the given real wage, the capitalist passion for profits as a purpose in itself and the law of

---

[13]A vehicle can be a capital good as long as is used in production. The same vehicle can be regarded as a consumer good as long as is purchased by households.

diminishing returns to land. The sequence of the relationship is: profits→ investment → wage increase → population growth → increase in demand for agricultural products → increase in wage → decrease in profits →stationary state. We do know that Marx was critical to the views of Ricardo and of J.S. Mill because they opined that the rate of profit displays a falling tendency as a consequence of the 'niggardliness' of nature. On the contrary, Marx argued that the limits of profitability come not from 'nature' but from the 'inner nature' of capital; he criticized Ricardo for escaping from political economy to organic chemistry and all those economists:

> who like Ricardo, regard the capitalist mode of production as absolute, feel at this point that it creates a barrier itself, and for this reason attribute the barrier to nature (in the theory of rent) not to production.
>
> (*Capital* III, p. 242)

Marx's argument is that the inherent tendency for mechanization, automation and capitalization of the production process is initially reflected in the upward trend in the TCC, resulting in an increase in the VCC and ultimately in an increase in the OCC. This is despite the drop in the unit value of the fixed (and variable) capital or the savings that can be made in the use of fixed capital.

> If it is further assumed that this gradual change in the composition of capital is not confined only to individual spheres of production, but that it occurs more or less in all, or at least in the key spheres of production, so that it involves changes in the average organic composition of the total capital of a certain society, then the gradual growth of constant capital in relation to variable capital must necessarily lead to *a gradual fall of the general rate of profit*, so long as the rate of surplus-value, or the intensity of exploitation of labour by capital, remain the same.
>
> (*Capital* III, p. 212)

The increase in the OCC, i.e. the increase in the C/V ratio, contributes to the fall in the rate of profit, despite the increasing trend of the rate of surplus-value and its upward pressure on the rate of profit.

8.4.3   Views and Criticisms of the Law of the Falling Trend in the Rate of Profit

The simultaneous examination of the changes in all these factors creates some confusion, and thus some argue that the impact of these factors on the rate of profit is either indeterminate or may work in a direction opposite to that of Marx. For example, Fine and Harris (1979) make the distinction between empirical (or visible) and theoretical or, more precisely, abstract trend of the rate of profit. The visible trend, they argue, is the result of a regression of the variable under consideration, in this case the rate of profit and time; if the time factor receives a negative sign, then we say there is a downward trend. However, Fine and Harris claim that this is not exactly correct, because the law of the FROP only works as an abstract trend, and that at the same time the counter-factors are in action whose effect has now been removed. Therefore, they argue that limiting the analysis to the simple observable empirical tendency, without taking into account the counteracting factors, is not exactly correct, because the law only exists by subtracting them. In Marx, the counteracting factors are described in Chap. 15 of *Capital* III and include the prolongation of the working day, the increase of productivity in Department I resulting in a reduction in the value of *C*, the increase of the reserve army of labour force (unemployment) and thus the wage reduction, the expansion of international trade (or globalization in modern terms) and the increase in the turnover time of capital, all in full operation in the recent years. However, we note that these counteracting factors may slow down or weaken, but certainly do not reverse, the long-term downward trend in the rate of profit.

Moreover, when we place the same importance on the trend (or law) and the potentially counter-factors, it is normal to arrive at agnostic conclusions such as 'everything is possible, and nothing can be said a priori'. The objection we raise against Fine and Harris' view is that the purpose of the process of abstraction is to extract the essential elements of a phenomenon and to reveal the unterlying mechanisms that go beyond the possible impediments that obscure its operation and make it less visible. By way of an example, the law of gravity is given in its pure form, but this does not mean that its function is not modified as a consequence of atmospheric frictions. If the law of gravity cannot reasonably be proven, then it is not abstract but simply non-existent. At the same time, we do not have to try several times an experiment or observe a phenomenon in order to collect a sufficient number of observations and proceed to an empirical analysis in order to give reliable estimates and ascertain the extent to which the law is in operation. The law should in principle be derived logically even without the experiment and the collection of observations; empirical research simply shows whether and to what extent the available data are consistent with the law. Similar should be the argument with the law of the FROP. The rate of profit is subject to persistent fluctuations, but in the long run, one expects to be able to observe the downward trend in the rate of profit, because if it is not observed, then simply the law does not exist.

8.4.4 The Mathematics of the Falling Profitability

We start off with by pointing out that Marx's analysis is based on the increasing mechanization of the production process and hence on the increase in the C/l ratio, that is, the MCC whose rate of increase in the long run offsets any increase in the rate of surplus-value and leads to a downward trend in the rate of profit. If we limited the analysis to include only the capital stock and therefore do not include the stocks of variable and circulating capital as part of the total invested (or advanced) capital, then the rate of profit is written as:

$$r = \frac{s}{C} = \frac{s}{l}\frac{l}{C} = \frac{s}{s+v}\frac{l}{C} = \frac{s/v}{1+s/v}\frac{l}{C} = \frac{e}{1+e}\frac{1}{Q}$$

where C stands for the total capital stock and $e = s/v$ stands for the rate of surplus-value. Independently of how fast the rate of surplus-value increases, the term of the above expression $s/(v + s) = e/(1 + e)$ increases by a decreasing rate, since its upper limit for $v \to 0$ is equal to 1; the latter, past a certain point, inevitably leads the rate of profit to start its falling path provided that the ratio $Q = C/l = MCC$ increases due to capital-using and labour-saving technological change.

The above formula of the rate of profit often is written without the implicit presence of the limiting conditions of the total labour time or value-added. Thus, we usually find the following rate of profit expressed in terms of flows:

$$r = \frac{s/v}{c/v + 1} \tag{8.6}$$

As $v \to 0$, the limit of relation (8.6) is

$$\lim_{v \to 0} \frac{s/v}{c/v + 1} = \frac{\infty}{\infty}$$

which is a seemingly indeterminate form. In this case, it has been argued that all depend on the rate of change of the two terms of the fraction. If the c/v increases faster than the s/v, the limit is zero, and thus we have a FROP, and if the s/v rises faster than the c/v, we do not have a FROP. As a consequence, anything is possible between zero, the lower limit, and infinity, the upper limit (Meek 1973; Sweezy 1942).[14]

A thorough examination of Equation (8.6), reveals that the speed with which the numerator and the denominator tend to infinity is of great importance for the seemingly indeterminate final result. Misconceptions of this type are removed by applying the L'Hôpital's rule, according to which we differentiate numerator and the denominator of Eq. 8.6 separately, and in doing so, in effect, we determine the different rates of change of the numerator and the denominator. Thus, the application of L'Hôpital's rule gives

---

[14]Sweezy (1942), for instance, based on the definition of the rate of profit in terms of flows, $r = s/(c + v) = e(1 - \kappa)$ where $e = s/v$ and $\kappa = c/(c + v)$, argues that the end result is an indeterminate form and everything depends on the speed of change in e and c/v. Nevertheless, if we take the total differential of the rate of profit and cast it in terms of differences, we get $\Delta r = \Delta e - (e\Delta\kappa + \kappa\Delta e)$ and $\Delta r = -e\Delta\kappa + \Delta e(1 - \kappa)$ as $v \to 0$ and $\kappa \to 1$. Hence, we end up with the following relationship $\Delta r = -e\Delta\kappa < 1$.

$$\lim_{v \to 0} \frac{\left(\frac{s}{v}\right)'}{\left(\frac{s}{v}+1\right)'} = \lim_{v \to 0} \left[\frac{-s/v^2}{-c/v^2}\right] = \frac{s_{\max}}{c}$$

and because as $v \to 0$ it follows that the surplus-value that we end up with cannot be other than the maximum surplus-value, $s_{\max}$. We derive the exact same answer if we take into account that $l = s + v$ and for $v \to 0$, then $s = s_{\max} = l.$[15] The above result surfaces in due time, but if we like to know better for the intermediate periods, then we examine explicitly the limitations for the rising rate of surplus-value $e = s/v$ and by taking into account the total labour time $l = s + v$, we express v in terms of s through the rate of surplus-value, e. Thus, we may write $l = s + se^{-1}$, and by factoring out the surplus-value, we get

$$l = s\left(1 + e^{-1}\right)$$

The derivative of the above relation with respect to time gives

$$\frac{dl}{dt} = \frac{ds}{dt}\left(1 + \frac{1}{e}\right) - \frac{s}{e^2}\frac{de}{dt}$$

And by solving for ds/dt, we get

$$\frac{ds}{dt}\left(\frac{1+e}{e}\right) = \frac{dl}{dt} + \frac{s}{e^2}\frac{de}{dt}$$

By dividing through by s, we express the above relation in terms of growth rates

$$\frac{ds}{dt}\frac{1}{s}\left(\frac{1}{e}+1\right) = \frac{dl}{dt}\frac{1}{s} + \frac{s}{e^2}\frac{de}{dt}\frac{1}{s} = \frac{dl}{dt}\frac{1}{s} + \frac{1}{e^2}\frac{de}{dt}$$

We then solve for the rate of change in surplus-value

$$\underbrace{\frac{ds}{dt}\frac{1}{s}}_{\hat{s}} = \frac{dl}{dt}\left(\frac{e}{1+e}\right)\frac{1}{s} + \underbrace{\left(\frac{1}{1+e}\right)\left(\frac{de}{dt}\right)\frac{1}{e}}_{\approx 0}$$

Consequently, as the rate of surplus-value s increases over time, the term

---

[15]There is no doubt that the total working time (l) is the variable that should be used to get a more accurate picture of the change in the profit rate and the possible limits of this change.

$$\frac{dl}{dt}\left(\frac{e}{1+e}\right)\frac{1}{s} \longrightarrow 0$$

tends to zero, since the surplus-value produced, s, is already a very large number with a tendency to increase furthermore leading, inevitably, the above relation towards zero. If, in addition, we consider that the growth rate of working population is negligible relative to other variables, then we safely arrive at the following relation:

$$\underbrace{\frac{ds}{dt}\frac{1}{s}}_{\hat{s}} \approx \left(\frac{1}{1+e}\right)\underbrace{\frac{de}{dt}\frac{1}{e}}_{\hat{e}} \tag{8.7}$$

according to which the growth rate of surplus-value, $\hat{s}$, requires a multiple increase in the growth rate of the rate of surplus-value, $\hat{e}$, to keep the equality going. If the rate of surplus-value increases (as is the usual case), then the term $(1+e)^{-1} < 1$ and with the progress of time gets smaller; therefore, it requires a much higher growth rate in $\hat{e}$ in order to match the growth rate in $\hat{s}$.

The relationships among the three variables involved in our analysis (Eq. (8.7)), that is, the wage share in value-added $v(v+s)^{-1} = (1+e)^{-1}$, the growth rate of surplus-value, $\hat{s}$, and the growth rate of rate of surplus-value, $\hat{e}$, are displayed in Fig. 8.8. On the horizontal axis we display the rate surplus-value e, which takes on values varying from 0 to 4 (0% to 400%), while on the vertical axis, we place the growth rate of surplus-value ($\hat{s}$), the required rate of increase in the rate of surplus-value ($\hat{e}$) in order to establish the equality between $\hat{s}$ and the wage share in value-added $(1+e)^{-1}$ whose fall implies an increase of the share of surplus-value in value-added. We assume that the average annual growth rate of surplus-value, $\hat{s}$, is constant and equal to 0.05 (=5%). We find that if, for example, the rate of surplus-value $e = 100\%$, the required growth rate in $\hat{e}$ will be 10%, that is, the growth in the rate of surplus-value must increase by a rate twice higher than that of the surplus-value. If the rate of surplus-value $e = 200\%$, then in order to attain the equality with 5% growth rate of surplus-value, the growth of the rate of surplus-value must quadruple, that is, $\hat{e} = 20\%$. The higher required rate of increase in $\hat{e}$ in order to attain a given growth rate of $\hat{s}$ is accompanied by a respective fall in the wage share depicted by its exponential fall.

Alternatively, if we set on the horizontal axis the growth of surplus-value, $\hat{s}$, and on the vertical axis the rate of increase in the rate of surplus-value, $\hat{e}$, as is shown on Fig. 8.9, then we identify the rate of surplus-value corresponding to a given growth rate in $\hat{s}$. From Fig. 8.9, we can see that the higher the rate of surplus-value, the higher the rate of increase in the rate of surplus-value, $\hat{e}$, which is required to obtain a given growth rate of surplus-value. Consequently, the higher the rate of surplus-value, e, or equivalently, the lower the labour time needed to produce the value of the labour power, the greater should be the growth in the rate of surplus-value, $\hat{e}$, so as to

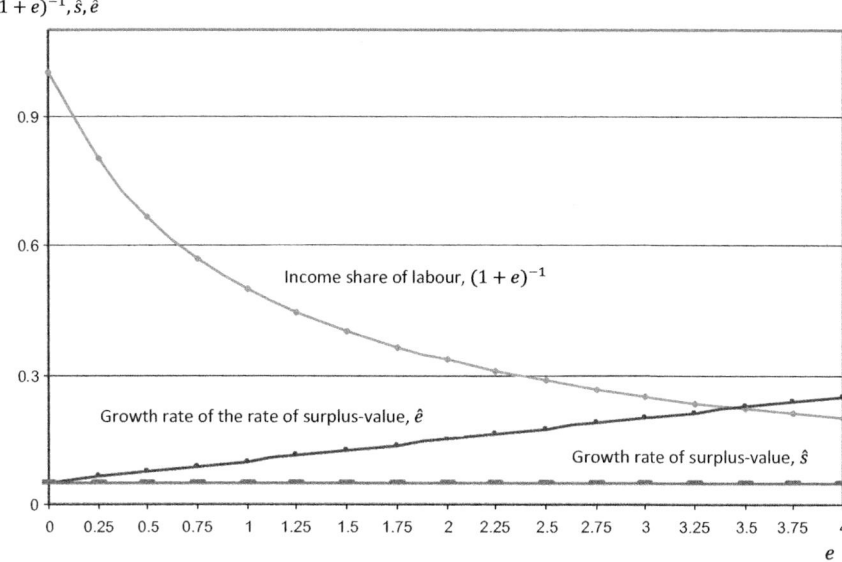

Fig. 8.8 The evolution of the income share of labour and growth rates of surplus-value and rate of surplus-value

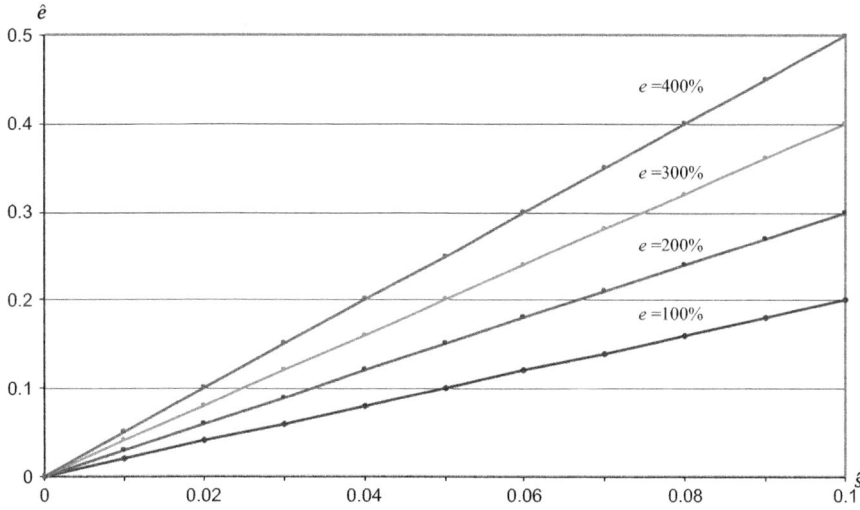

Fig. 8.9 Growth rate of the surplus-value ($\hat{s}$) and the rate of surplus-value ($\hat{e}$)

increase the total surplus-value produced and reverse the fall in the profit rate caused by the rising value composition of capital. The downward trend in profitability is a long-term consequence of the growing difficulty in increasing the surplus-value as capitalism evolves. This is precisely what Marx points out:

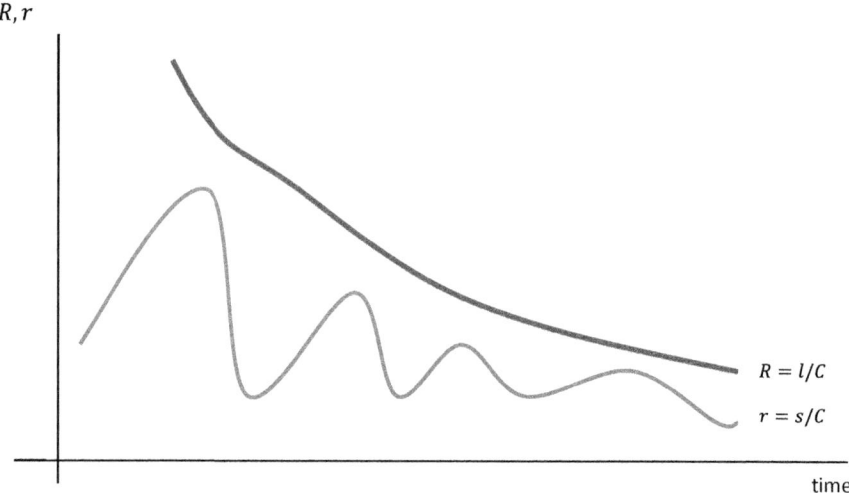

Fig. 8.10   The falling tendency in the maximum and average rate of profit

> In this respect, then, the compensation of the reduction in the number of labourers by means
> of an intensification of exploitation has certain impassible limits. It may, for this reason,
> check the fall of the rate of profit, but cannot prevent it entirely.
>
> *(Capital* III, p. 247)

A necessary and sufficient condition for the fall in the rate of profit is the increase in the capital cost per unit of output, i.e. the capitalization of output. The ratio l/C or $y/C = R$ is the maximum rate of profit (achieved when $v \to 0$), and its downward trend implies that the economy-wide rate of profit (whose magnitude depends on the size of v) displays fluctuating behaviour depending on a number of factors, but it is depressed from above by a decreasing ceiling, as shown in Fig. 8.10.[16] That is, the average rate of profit (r) in the long run will necessarily start its falling path, as it is depressed from above by the downward trajectory of the maximum rate of profit, R.

Marx's argument may be summarized as follows:

- In the process of capitalist accumulation, the results of the mechanization of the production process increase both the TCC and MCC leading to an increase in the VCC and the OCC.
- The real wage generally increases at rates below the growth of labour productivity; thus the surplus-value and the rate of surplus-value are expected to increase over time.
- The increase in the ratio C/y counterbalances the increase in the ratio s/y and inevitably causes the falling tendency in the evolution of the rate of profit. In effect, from the formula of the rate of profit, we have

---

[16]The reason is that $y = l$ since l refers to creative powers of living labour to produce new value-added.

$$r = \frac{s/y}{C/y} = \frac{s/(v+s)}{C/y}$$

Gross value-added, y, equals to the sum of wages (or variable capital) plus (gross) profits (or surplus-value), that is, $y = s + v$. Independently of how fast the numerator of the rate of profit increases as v decreases (i.e. $v \rightarrow 0$), the numerator of the above fraction cannot exceed one, which is its upper limit. At the same time, the denominator of the ratio has no such limit for it increases indefinitely; thus, the rate of profit in the long run cannot but display a falling trajectory.

- The limit of the above relation for $v \rightarrow 0$ is the inverse capital-output ratio, y/C or MCC, and in fact is another expression of the maximum rate of profit, whose falling tendency implies that the average rate of profit (whose magnitude depends on v) also fluctuates within a range with a falling upper bound.
- Thus, the falling trajectory of the maximum rate of profit in the long-run imposes its trend on the average rate of profit.

The rise in the rate of surplus-value cannot reverse the falling tendency in the rate of profit. The latter can be shown by taking the derivative of the above formula of the rate of profit with respect to the rate of surplus-value. For this purpose, we restate the rate of profit in terms of the rate of surplus-value and the MCC, which for convenience we symbolize by Q. Thus, we have

$$r = \frac{s/(v+s)}{C/y} = \frac{e}{(1+e)}\frac{1}{Q}$$

The partial derivative of r with respect to e gives

$$\frac{\partial r}{\partial e} = \frac{Q(1+e) - eQ}{[Q(1+e)]^2} = \frac{1}{Q(1+e)^2}$$

Because the denominator of the above equation is squared and the whole fraction is smaller than one, then the impact of the rising rate of surplus-value is diminishing over time. In fact, the second partial derivative is negative:

$$\frac{\partial^2 r}{\partial e^2} = -\frac{2Q(1+e)}{Q(1+e)^4} = -\frac{2}{Q(1+e)^3} < 0$$

Having established the diminishing effect of the rate of surplus-value on the rate of profit, our interest is the elasticity of the rate of profit w.r.t. the rate of surplus-value:

$$\frac{\partial r}{\partial e}\frac{e}{r} = \frac{1}{Q(1+e)^2}\frac{e}{r} = \frac{1}{1+e} < 1 \qquad (8.8)$$

which, not surprisingly, is smaller than one.

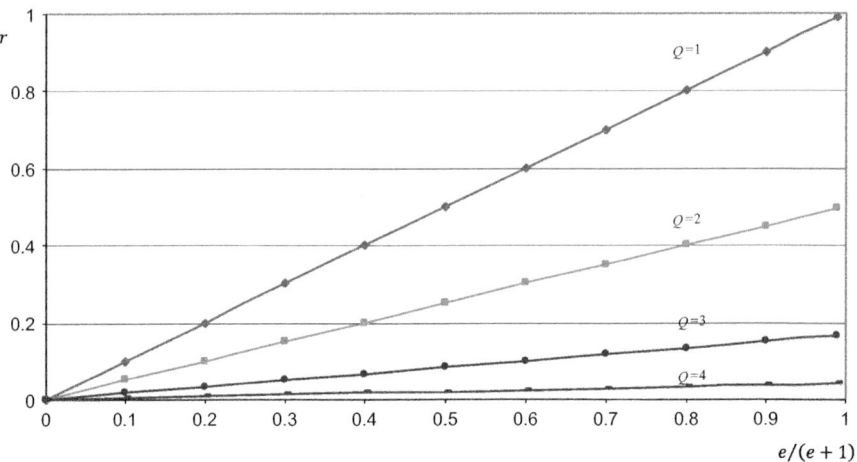

Fig. 8.11 Rate of profit, capital-output ratio (MCC) and share of surplus-value

Diagrammatically (see Fig. 8.11) we can derive the relation between the MCC or the capital-output ratio, Q, and the ratio $e/(e + 1)$, that is, the share of surplus-value in value-added (horizontal axis) and the rate of profit, r (vertical axis).

In Fig. 8.11, we observe that as the share of surplus-value increases and approaches its maximum equal to 1, then for a given Q, the rate of profit increases. However, as Q increases, the impact of the share of the surplus-value $e/(e + 1)$ in value-added (and by extension that of the rate of surplus-value) on the rate of profit diminishes and the rate of profit is bound to follow a downward path.

This relation can be shown with the use of calculus. The partial derivative of the rate of profit with respect to Q gives

$$\frac{\partial r}{\partial Q} = -\frac{e(1+e)}{(1+e)^2 Q^2} = -\frac{e}{(1+e)Q^2}$$

and the second partial derivative gives

$$\frac{\partial^2 r}{\partial Q^2} = \frac{2e(1+e)Q}{((1+e)Q^2)^2} = \frac{2e}{(1+e)Q^3} > 0$$

which is positive and indicates that the effect of Q on r increases with the progress of time. The elasticity of the rate of profit with respect to Q is given from

$$\frac{\partial r}{\partial Q}\frac{Q}{r} = -\frac{e(1+e)}{(1+e)^2 Q^2}\frac{Q}{\frac{e}{(1+e)}\frac{1}{Q}} = -1 \qquad (8.9)$$

which is unitary elastic and negative indicating the inverse relationship between the rate of profit and the MCC; as we showed in Fig. 8.11, the effect of the change in Q is by far stronger than that of e. Given the unitary and negative elasticity of the average rate of profit with respect to Q, it follows that in the long-run the rate of profit cannot escape from its falling tendency. This, however, is not a sufficient proof of the downward trend in the rate of profit, as it needs to be shown that the downward limit of the rate of profit is zero (Kurz 1998, p. 133).

The proof of the proposition is derived by explicitly using growth rates of the variables involved in the formula of the rate of profit and their limits. Under these circumstances there is no better limiting condition other than the total working time l. For this reason, we express all the variables involved in terms of l, that is, $C' = C/l$, $s' = s/l$, $v' = v/l$ or $v' = 1 - s'$. Therefore, the rate of profit can be rewritten as:

$$r = \frac{s'}{C'}$$

Subsequently, let us assume that C' increases at a constant rate equal to $\alpha < 1$, while the variable capital decreases at a constant rate equal to $\beta < 1$. Hence, we assume that the rate of surplus-value increases not only as the stylized fact of the dynamics of the capitalist economies but because an assumption of a steady or decreasing rate of surplus-value would make it easier to show a FROP. If we date the variables, we can show the evolution[17] of each one of them by stipulating the following relations:

$$C'_t = C'_0(1 + a)^t, \, v'_t = v'_0(1 + \beta)^t \text{ and } s'_t = 1 - v'_0(1 - \beta)^{t\cdot}$$

Hence, the evolution of the rate of profit is given by the following:

$$r_t = \frac{1 - v'_0(1 - \beta)^t}{C'_0(1 + a)^t}$$

From the above, it follows that

$$\lim_{t \to \infty} v'_0(1 - \beta)^t = 0$$

and thus, the numerator of the above relation tends to 1, while the denominator increases without limits. As a consequence, the overall limit of the rate of profit as $t \to \infty$ cannot be other that zero.

Hence, it is important to refer to Okishio's work (1961, 1963, 1990) who argued that the fall in the maximum rate of profit also shapes the fall of the economy-wide average rate of profit, but this is only a theoretical result, because in reality, as he claimed, the rational capitalists would not choose techniques that would reduce their maximum profit. On further examination, however, we discover a typical example of

---

[17]For a different presentation based on exponential function, see Shaikh (1992a, b).

behaviour that can be described in terms of game theory and the famous prisoners'
dilemma (Shaikh 1980a), where individual rationality leads to collective irrational-
ity. Individual rationality forces a capitalist to introduce fixed capital in order to
reduce the unit value and cost of production and therefore lower the price to expand
the market share and to increase profits. Other capitalists follow suit or are eliminated from the market. The end result is a rising OCC, rising productivity and rate of
surplus-value and finally falling rate of profit for the economy as a whole. The
trouble with Okishio's work is that is based on a circulating capital model and on
perfect competition, two assumptions that are utterly distant from reality.[18]

8.5   Rate of Profit, Mass of Profits and Economic Crisis

The interpretation of long waves, which we have already presented, should be
sought in the movement of the fundamental variables that govern the evolution of
economies and among these variables, a prominent position holds the rate of profit.
As we have pointed out, all major economists of the past (Smith, Ricardo, Marx,
Walras, J.B. Clark, Keynes, Schumpeter) have argued that the rate of profit is what
determines the pace of capital accumulation in an economy and its long-run falling
tendency leads to stagnation. Ricardo notes:

> Long indeed before this period, the very low rate of profits will have arrested all accumu-
> lation, and almost the whole produce of the country, after paying the labourers, will be the
> property of the owners of land and the receivers of tithes and taxes [...] The farmer and
> manufacturer can no more live without profit, than the labourer without wages. Their motive
> for accumulation will diminish with every diminution of profit, and will cease altogether
> when their profits are so low as not to afford them an adequate compensation for their
> trouble, and the risk which they must necessarily encounter in employing their capital
> productively.
>
> (*Works* I, pp. 121–122 and 123)

However, from all the above economists, only Marx theorized the detailed
relationship between the long-term downward trend in the rate of profit and the
onset of the economic crisis. The fall in the rate of profit alone does not necessarily
imply an economic recession, or even more an economic crisis, as the profit rate may
exceed the long-term interest rate. Therefore, the level of the rate of profit, in and of
itself, does not necessarily affect the investment behaviour of entrepreneurs.

> the expansion of the actual process of accumulation is promoted by the fact that the low
> interest [...] increases that portion of profit which is transformed into profit of enterprise.
>
> (*Capital* III, p. 495)

Still, a fall in the profit rate is perfectly compatible, even with an increase in the
mass of profits, as Marx explains in *Capital* III, Chap. 13. A declining rate of profit

---

[18]For more on Okishio's theorem, see Shaikh (1978, 1980a, 1998), Nakatani (1980), Semmler
(1983), inter alia.

for some time may be consistent with rising investment and a growing economy; in fact, the downward trend in the rate of profit may go on for some time even under conditions of rapid economic growth.

> A fall in the rate of profit and accelerated accumulation are different expressions of the same process only in so far as both reflect the development of productiveness.
>
> (*Capital* III, p. 241)

Furthermore, in Chap. 15 of *Capital* III, Marx argues that the level of the rate of profit does not lead to recession; what is important is the cumulative long-run effect of its falling tendency on investment and mass of the real net profits, which past a point generates the conditions for the manifestation of economic crisis:

> There would be absolute over-production of capital as soon as additional capital for purposes of overproduction $=0$. The purpose of capitalist production, however, is self-expansion of capital, *i.e.*, appropriation of surplus-labour, production of surplus value, of profit. As soon as capital would, therefore, have grown in such a ratio to the labouring population that neither the absolute working-time supplied by the population, nor the relative surplus working-time, could be expanded any further (this last would not be feasible at any rate in the case when the demand for labour were so strong that there were a tendency for wages to rise); at a point therefore, when the increased capital produced just as much, or even less, surplus-value than it did before its increase, there would be absolute over-production of capital; i.e., the increased capital $C + \Delta C$ would produce no more, or even less, profit than capital C before its expansion by ΔC.
>
> (*Capital* III, p. 251)

The above causal relationship between the rate of profit and the mass of net profits and the manifestation of economic crisis is usually lost in the writings of many modern Marxist economists. For example, Duncan Foley notes:

> If the rate of profit were indeed falling consistently, why would the capitalist system not adapt to this fall although a gradual reduction in the rate of accumulation? Such a gradual reduction might not be welcome to capitalists, but it is not obvious that it must lead to the characteristic phenomena of capitalist crisis that we examined earlier. In other words, this explanation for capitalist crisis has to produce some systematic reason why a fall in the rate of profit leads at certain moments to sharp and discontinuous adjustments in economic activity.
>
> (Foley 1986, p. 163)

In what follows we show Marx's argument using a numerical example. We know that profits are estimated on both old and newly invested capital. As the sum of total profits increases in the years that follow, investment activity will continue to the point where profits from the new investment do not add to the existing mass of real net profits. At this point, the incentive for investment weakens or completely disappears on an average. To understand this mechanism, let us look at the example presented in Table 8.4.

If in the first period (a period might be, for instance, the average of a decade) the rate of profit is $r=30\%$ and the invested capital is $C=250{,}000$ monetary units (mu), the profits will be $\pi=75{,}000$ mu ($30\% \times 250{,}000$). If in the following period, the rate of profit drops to 25%, profits on the already invested capital are reduced to 62,500. If, however, the capital increases by the amount of all the profits of the previous

Table 8.4 An example of the mechanism of absolute accumulation

Periods	r (%)	C	$\Delta C = I$	$\pi = r * C$	$\pi' = r * I$	$\Pi = \pi + \pi'$	$\Delta\Pi$	$\Delta\Pi / I_{t-1}$
First	30	250,000	–	75,000	–	75,000	–	–
Second	25	250,000	75,000	62,500	18,750	81,250	↑	6250/7500 = 8.33%
Third	20	325,000	81,250	65,000	16,250	81,250	0	0
Fourth	15	406,250	81,250	69,973	12,160.5	73,500	↓	−7750/ 81,250 = − 7.75%

period, that is, by 75,000 mu ($\Delta C = I = 75{,}000$ mu), then the gains in the new investment, 18,750 mu, are added, and the total profits in the second period increase (62,500 + 18,750) to 81,250 mu resulting in improved profits (81,250 mu vs. 75,000 mu of the previous period). In the third period, if the rate of profit is supposed to fall to 20%, then the profits from the old investments will be 0.20 (250,000 + 75,000) = 65,000 mu, while the new investments equal 81,250 mu will yield profits of 16,250 mu assuming that all profits of the second period are invested. Therefore, total profits will be 81,250 mu, which means that the new investment does not generate additional profits; that is, the change in total profits is zero, and the additional investment does not improve the profit picture which remains the same as in the second period. Profits in other words are stationary. Put it in the usual microeconomic language, the marginal profits are evaporated and the incentive for new investments is weakened to the point that it makes them redundant. If, for example, in the fourth period old and new profits are invested meanwhile the rate of profit drops further down, say to 15%, the current change in profits over investment of the last period, that is, the incremental rate of return (IROR), will be −7,750/ 81,250 = − 7.75%. The lack of new investment means that the old capital is not renewed and also is underutilized, people are laid off, no new jobs are created and, therefore, unemployment is rising. When these phenomena are prolonged, the recession is converted into an economic crisis.

Marx's view can be shown in a rigorous way starting with the simple formula of the rate of profit where π denotes real net profits

$$r = \pi/C \text{ or } \pi = rC$$

Taking the first differences we have

$$\Delta\pi = r\Delta C + C\Delta r$$

We divide both parts of the above equality by ΔC and factor out the rate of profit. So we get

$$\frac{\Delta\pi}{\Delta C} = r\left(1 + \frac{\Delta r}{\Delta C}\frac{C}{r}\right) \tag{8.10}$$

The term $\Delta\pi/\Delta C$ denotes the change in profits resulting from a change in the invested capital which is not different from the IROR or alternatively the change in profits per unit of capital invested ($I = \Delta C$), while the term $(\Delta r/\Delta C)(C/r)$ is the elasticity of the rate of profit with respect to the change in capital stock, i.e. the percentage change in the rate of profit caused by a percentage change in invested capital. It is clear that the change in profits over the change in capital is equal to zero, if the elasticity of the rate of profit is unitary and negative; this occurs when the mass of real net profits attains its maximum level. Only at this point (or vicinity) of the total real net profits, a percentage change in the capital stock (or real investment) leads to an equal change in real net profits but to the opposite direction. Under these circumstances, the motivation of entrepreneurs for new investment dissipates because the change in the net real profits brought about by an additional investment, past a critical point, is offset more than fully by the negative growth in the rate of profit; the end result is the discouragement (on an average) of any new investments on account of no change in their profit situation, and thus we are led to a stagnating mass of real net profits.

This situation characterizes the stationary economy which, however, unlike Smith or Ricardo and in general of the old classical economists is a transitionary and by no means permanent stage of the economy. In this stationary state, the economy is ripe for the introduction of innovations and legislation for new institutions. The introduction of both is not independent of the prevailing balance of political power and may work to the benefit of the few or to the vast majority of the people. What is absolutely certain is that capitalism is subjected to structural changes while it remains in its stationary state and, at the same time, sets the requirements for a new phase change of economic growth until the attainment of a new stationary state. This has been repeated five times in the history of capitalism (see Table 8.1). A history begins with the industrial revolution of the last quarter of the eighteenth century and continues to our days. One interesting question is will the system start the sixth and the nth cycle in the future? Our answer is that what is certain is that the system is with endemic capacity to innovate, to introduce new institutions and to expand; in this expantion process assimilates new markets and sources of raw materials. And in this respect, we observe that in the fifth long cycle, the expansion included the former Soviet Republic and China; in the near future, Africa might be the continent to see this scenario to be played once again.

Meanwhile, we can become more specific of the process of attaining the stationary state of the economy by assuming that the pace of capital accumulation ($\Delta C/C$) is directly determined by the rate of profit whose falling path is described by a function of the following realistic form:

$$r_t = r_0(1 + a)^{-t} \tag{8.11}$$

where $r_o > 0$ is an initial level of the rate of profit, a is the annual average rate of change in the rate of profit and t refers to time (years in our case). The pace of capital accumulation ($\Delta C/C$) depends on the rate of profit through the average propensity to save. Hence, we assume the well-known Cambridge equation according to which the rate of economic growth or capital accumulation depends on the rate of profit. In particular, we have

$$\Delta C / C = s_c \cdot r_0 (1 + a)^{-t}$$

where $0 < s_c < 1$ denotes the constant average propensity to save (=invest) out of profits π. The growth in the rate of profit in discrete time, $\Delta t = 1$, will be $\Delta r / r = -\ln(1 + a)$. Hence, the turning point of the behaviour of the real mass of real net profits is approximated when

$$\frac{\Delta r}{\Delta C} \frac{C}{r} = \frac{-\ln(1 + a)}{s_c \cdot r_0 (1 + a)^{-t}} = -1 \tag{8.12}$$

which means that real net profits stagnate since at that time t^* the economy reaches the point where $\Delta C / C = \Delta r / r = s_c \cdot r_0 (1 + a)^{-t} = -\ln(1 + a)$ and therefore the incentive for new investments vanishes. The idea is that the profits for each new investment are fully offset by the fall in the rate of profit; the latter allows only for small new additions to profits which past a point become negative, as we have showed in our numerical example (Table 8.4). Thus, the total mass of real profits attains its maximum and ironically this is the point of the beginning of a downturn in economic activity or the gradual gathering of requirements for another long cycle. This critical point is that moment in time during which the system changes its behaviour, and it can be defined by solving the above equation with respect to t. Hence, we get

$$t^* = -\frac{\ln \left[\frac{\ln(1+a)}{s_c \cdot r_0} \right]}{\ln(1 + a)} \tag{8.13}$$

Obviously, the time required to attain the phase change point is inversely proportional to the rate of change in real net profit, $a \leq e^{s_c \cdot r_0} - 1$, which (given the constancy of s_c and the initial value of the rate of profit r_0) is very much dependent on the growth of non-productive sectors of the economy. From the above it becomes clear the importance of distinguishing between productive activities and labour in relation to non-productive ones. The larger the share of non-productive activities in the overall surplus produced, the smaller the amount of remaining profits and potential surplus to be invested. In the case of a downward trend in the rate of profit, the trend is exacerbated by the expansion of non-productive activities, and this is reflected in the value of the parameter a in Equation (8.11). Consequently, the rise in non-productive expenditures, which mean higher value for the parameter a, make the economy to reach its critical point sooner rather than later and, therefore, the fall in the rate of profit accelerates. In fact, and around the critical point, some very interesting dynamics are being developed depending on the value of parameter a. More specifically, the partial derivative of t^* with respect to parameter a gives

$$\frac{\partial t^*}{\partial a} = \frac{\ln\left[\frac{\ln(1+a)}{s_c \cdot r_0}\right] - 1}{\ln(1+a)^2(1+a)} < 0 \tag{8.14}$$

which is negative suggesting that the time required for the attainment of the turning point is inversely proportional to the size of the parameter a. We note that the analysis refers to the case of a rate of profit whose fall is characterized by duration and persistence, and so its rate of decline, $\ln(1+a)$, will be negative, and furthermore the process is relatively slow and, therefore, meaningful only in the long run. The fall in the rate of profit for a few years is not enough to cause economic activity to stagnate. Ultimately, only a long-lasting downward rate of profit causes stagnation in the mass of actual (deflated) net profits, which is the same as the idea that the economy is entering its crisis phase. This situation can be described in terms of Fig. 8.12.

At the lower panel of the graph, we display both the percentage change in the rate of profit ($\Delta r/r$) which is hypothesized steadily negative and the percentage change in the capital invested ($\Delta C/C$), which of course is equal to the growth rate of the economy. From Fig. 8.12, we find that as long as the marginal profits $\Delta\pi$ increase, total profits increase and even at an increasing rate, until the marginal profits reach their maximum which, from the mathematical point of view, corresponds to the turning point of the mass of real total net profits. Beyond that point, marginal profits follow a downward trend, while the mass of profits increases at a decreasing rate until marginal profits cross the zero line as shown in Fig. 8.12. Then we reach the point of "absolute overaccumulation", that is the point where the mass of real net profits is maximized and the additional investment, on average, does not imply higher profits.[19]

Similarly, the presentation by Mariolis (2014) explicitly sets the above analysis in terms of differential equations and shows that the downward trend in the rate of profit may initially accelerate the increase in total profits till the turning point, and then it slows it down until we get to the stagnation (maximization) point of profits and eventually to their fall. In other words, total real net profits are evolving according to the well-known logistic curve whose S-shaped pattern resembles the movement of a long cycle. His analysis, however, continues with a few unrealistic counterexamples featuring a slowly falling rate of profit approaching asymptotically a limit sufficiently higher than zero; not surprisingly, he does not get stagnating profits. His last counterexample, however, with the inclusion of foreign trade is worth further study (see also Malikane 2017).

---

[19]Foley (1986) and Duménil and Lévy (1993) have argued that the fall in the rate of profit may be accompanied by a continuous accumulation of capital, without necessarily leading to stagnation. In addition, in the writings of modern leading economists (Summers, Krugman and R.J. Gordon, among others), we are witnessing a remake of the late 1930s concept of the 'secular stagnation' introduced by Hansen (1939).

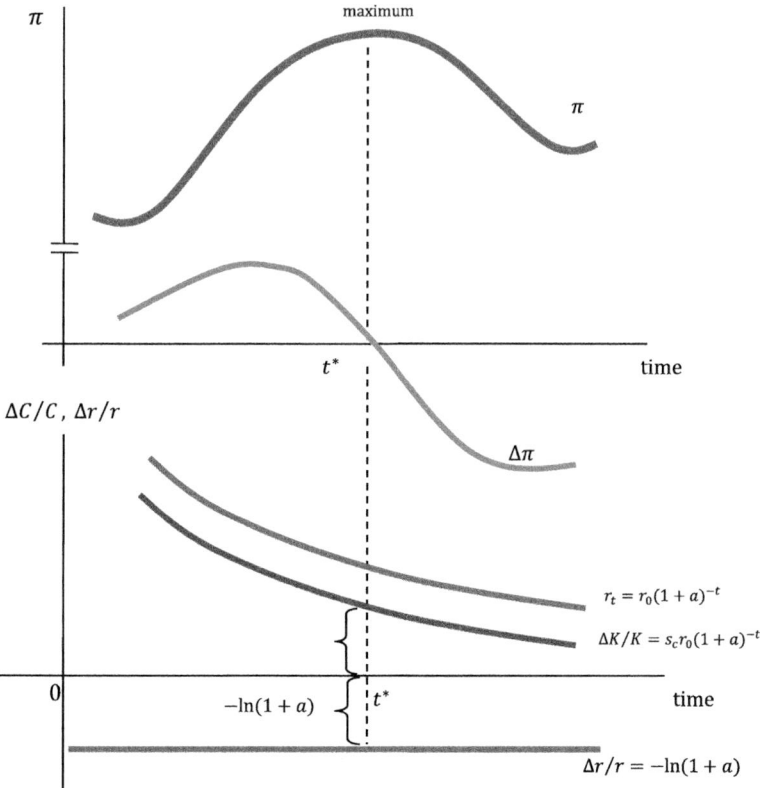

Fig. 8.12 Mass of net profits, rate of change in the rate of profit and capital accumulation

In conclusion, for Marx the crises in capitalism have intrinsic causes and therefore are not conjectural and in this sense are inevitable. This does not mean that we cannot apply social policies which may ameliorate its consequences. In Chap. 10, we attempt an empirical verification of Marx's crisis theory using data from the US economy to show its explanatory content. We will see that Ricardo's analysis that the crisis is the result of the very low profit rate is not far from being a reality. It is certain that the profit rate has fallen to such a low level that, even when it starts its upward course, it might be extremely difficult to restore to the level of the period up until the late 1960s. Therefore, any recovery is expected to be weak and short lived whereas the economy would be drifting more frequently in recessionary situations.

8.6   Summary and Conclusions

In this chapter, we outlined the basic arguments for the long-term falling tendency in the rate of profit, 'the most important law of classical political economy'. In our analysis, we have shown that this law reflects the very essence of the capitalist system, which is the production of commodities, that is, the production for the profit-making as a purpose in itself. The pursuit of the maximum possible rate of profit brings the capitalist to come to terms with a number of competitions from which two are warlike competitions and of utmost importance for the FROP argument. The first competition is of capital against workers in the labour process over the extraction of the maximum possible surplus-value. The second is against other similarly motivated capitals, a 'civil war' kind of competition over reduction of unit cost and attainment of higher share in the market.

We have argued that the competition between capitals forces every individual capitalist to introduce fixed capital to reduce the unit cost as a condition sine qua non for his survival in the market and the only way to succeed in this competition. In this 'civil war' between capitals, competition takes place within industries, and in the end, the 'winner' either takes it all by absorbing the defeated (other capitals) or by marginalizing if not eliminating them from the 'face of the market'. In all cases, the 'weapon of mass destruction' of competing firms is the introduction of innovations involving large-scale investments in fixed capital. The further mechanization of the production process simplifies the labour process and increases the productivity of labour, while at the same time decreases workers' skills by degrading the labour process and thus making possible a substantial reduction in wages. The mechanization of the production process is manifested in the rising capital-intensity leading to the falling maximum rate of profit, which sooner or later shapes the downward movement of the economy's average rate of profit.

However, the fall in the average rate of profit does not necessarily mean a slowdown in capital accumulation. The fall in the profit rate may be absolutely consistent with any (accelerating or decelerating) phase of capital accumulation. Simply, if the downward trend in the rate of profit is a long-term condition, then it starts to gradually negatively affect the accumulation of capital. Thus, as the capital-intensity of the economy increases and the rate of profit decreases, the total mass of profits (i.e. the product of these two variables) may increase if the accumulation of capital (new investments) outweighs the loss of profits as a result of the fall in the profit rate. If the positive effect of capital accumulation on total profits is eliminated or even falls short to profit losses caused by the decrease in the rate of profit, then investment activity is discouraged, unemployment is rising and, if these developments continue, the economy slides into its crisis phase.

Chapter 9
Productive-Non-productive Labour and National Accounts

The worker, therefore, justifiably regards the development of the productive power of his own labour as hostile to himself; the capitalist, on the other hand, always treats him as an element to be eliminated from production. These are the contradictions with which Ricardo struggles in this chapter (XXXII). What he forgets to emphasize is the constantly growing number of the middle classes, those who stand between the workman on the one hand and the capitalist and landlord on the other. The middle classes maintain themselves to an ever-increasing extent directly out of revenue, they are a burden weighing heavily on the working base and increase the social security and power of the upper ten thousand.

Karl Marx (*TSV* II, p. 573).

Mr. Bastiat could have found convincing testimony that a mass of parasitic bodies come to cluster around capital, and, under one or another title, they lay hands on so much of the total production as to leave little danger of the workers being overwhelmed by abundance.

Karl Marx (*Grundrisse*, p. 757).

Abstract The main focus of this chapter is on official national income accounts (NIA) and their differences from those of the classical political economy (CPE). The differences are the result of the distinction of economic activities in production and non-production, which exists in the classical analysis and not in the neoclassical one, on which the official NIA are based. We further argue that the CPE distinction is similar to that followed in good business practices and accounting of production businesses. Thus, by applying the CPE distinction of production and non-production activities, we may derive entirely different results from those of the neoclassical NIA.

Keywords National income accounts · Production and non-production labour · CPE · Good accounting practices

© Springer Nature Switzerland AG 2019   381
L. Tsoulfidis, P. Tsaliki, *Classical Political Economics and Modern Capitalism*,
https://doi.org/10.1007/978-3-030-17967-0_9

9.1 Introduction

The evolution of unproductive activities and their effects on the growth potential of an economy is central to economic thought dating back to the Physiocrats continuing in the old classical economists and Marx. The fundamental unified idea in all of these approaches is the concept of surplus, a residually determined income available for either consumption or investment purposes. In the discussion of the reproduction schemes in Chap. 2, starting with the Physiocrats, the emphasis of the analysis was placed on the way in which the surplus is allocated to different activities and its implications onto the scale (increasing, decreasing or stationary) of social reproduction. In the discussion of the 'transformation problem' in Chap. 3, we showed that, when capitalists' personal consumption decreases towards zero, the economy attains its maximum expanded reproduction, that is, the case where the total surplus (value) is invested productively. Hence, within the classical approach, the higher the share of the surplus going to the investment, the higher the growth potential of the economy, or in Marxian terms the economy is reproduced on an expanding scale.

The analysis of the social surplus necessitates the distinction between productive and non-productive labour, that is, the distinction between surplus-producing labour and surplus-consuming labour, respectively. Notwithstanding, all schools of economic thought make the distinction between productive and unproductive labour (PUPL); however, there are substantial differences in the theorizing of what is and what is not productive labour.[1] These differences are manifested in the national accounting systems and are materialized in the estimates of the national income and its distribution as well as the accumulated wealth in the economy. For instance, the Physiocrats argued that agriculture (defined in the broad sense) is the only surplus-generating sector of the economy and moreover the creation of surplus was not the result of the labour activity but rather a kind of a 'gift of nature'. Smith and Ricardo challenged and at the same time expanded the physiocratic view in the sense that the labour activity is in effect surplus-generating and that surplus is created in both agricultural and industrial production. Marx argued that productive is the wage labour employed by capital in the sphere of production to produce new output. Marshall, by contrast, considered productive the labour producing any use value (good) for which there is a buyer in the market.

It is clear, therefore, that the distinction between PUPL encapsulates the underlying theoretical underpinnings of each school of economic thought. Hence, in the classical political perspective and Marx, in particular, the distinction relates to whether there is production of surplus (value) and by extent new wealth, whereas in Marshal, following and promoting the utilitarian perception of the neoclassical approach in every aspect of economic life, the distinction is related to whether or not

---

[1] We use the term 'unproductive' labour because this is how it has been established in the literature. The more appropriate classification with the negative connotation term would be 'non-production' or with the positive connotation, as we will explain below, 'distribution' and 'social maintenance' labour activity.

the labour activity produces objects of utility to consumers, who may be willing and able to pay for them. It is interesting to note that the way in which the different schools of economic thought conceive the distinction of labour into productive and unproductive is not a matter of choice for it affects the estimation of the surplus produced in the economy and, by extent, the other related key economic variables such as the rate of profit, labour productivity and output produced, among others, which define the actual state of the economy and the possible effects of various economic policies.

In fact, this difference in the conceptualization of what is and what is not productive labour may give rise to a completely different assessment of the true state of the economy. For example, the official measurement of productivity based on neoclassical economics by including all labour as productive may give rise to a downward sloping trend in productivity; by contrast, in the classical accounts, by including only the productive labour, the estimated productivity, for the same time period, may give rise to an upward trend. It is important to point out that the two (orthodox and classical) accounting systems give markedly different estimates of the total output produced or the total value-added in the economy. It, therefore, becomes increasingly important to keep the classical distinction of labour activity separate by mapping the existing official national accounts into classical ones. Nevertheless, it is one thing to state the desire to map the orthodox national accounts into classical ones and an altogether different thing to carry out such a mapping. The reason is that not only the construction of the variables but also the collection of data is not independent of the prevailing economic theory and view point of the researchers; and for this reason, a series of assumptions and rearrangements of the official accounts need to be made prior to get approximate estimates and mappings according to the perception of PUPL.

9.2 Productive and Unproductive Labour

It is important to emphasize at the outset that the classification of PUPL is a matter of fundamental importance in the history of economic analysis, in general, and in the classical political economy, in particular. In its general terms, the distinction between PUPL refers to whether a kind of labour, in the context of dominant relations of production, produces new value and wealth and a kind of labour which, not only, does not create new value but consumes a portion of the already produced wealth. Hence, economic theories clarify the labour activity as productive or unproductive according to whether it is surplus-creating or surplus-consuming.

For instance, Mercantilists thought that the surplus is generated exclusively in the activities within the sphere of circulation and, more specifically, in international trade. Consequently, in their approach, productive labour was defined only that employed in domestic or international trade. Therefore, the mercantilist economic policies aimed at facilitating and enhancing the activities and employments which were directly related to international trade which was considered the major surplus and therefore wealth-generating activity of the economy.

By contrast, Physiocrats transferred the inquiry from the sphere of circulation (trade) to the sphere of production and not to production in general but very specifically to agricultural production. Agriculture was thought to be the only economic activity capable of generating surplus, as the outcome of nature's capacity to create output greater than that of the utilized inputs. Nonagricultural sectors, and in particular manufacturing, were considered 'sterile' in that they were not endowed with a surplus-generating capacity but were merely restricted to a formal change of the agricultural inputs, and therefore nothing really new was created.

Smith, who spent two years in France, came to know first-hand the key physiocratic concepts of surplus creation and the economy's scale of reproduction: two concepts that were absent in his writings prior to his trip and discussions with the French Physiocrats. For example, in the *Theory of Moral Sentiments*, Smith in the employment of servants by landlords, he sees another manifestation of the operation of an 'invisible hand' through which the poor people participate in the social wealth through the provision of their services to landlords. Hence, there is no reference to the scale of reproduction of society and the detrimental effects of the expansion of unproductive activities on economic growth, concepts that Smith studied much later, apparently, under the influence of the Physiocrats. However, upon his return to Scotland and in writing his major work, *The Wealth of Nations*, at the eve of the Industrial Revolution and for the rapidly growing capitalist society, Smith had no problem in his evaluation of the physiocratic system by arguing that:

> the capital error of this system, however, seems to lie in its representing the class of artificers, manufacturers, and merchants as altogether barren and unproductive.
>
> (*Wealth of Nations*, p. 176)

Furthermore, Smith argued that the creation of a surplus by no means was the result of '$\varphi\acute{\upsilon}\sigma\eta\varsigma$' (physis $=$ nature) as in Physiocrats but of labour activity, not of all labour activity but only that particular one engaged in production (be it agricultural or industrial) which is paid a wage out of the invested capital. Hence, productive labour is defined in accordance to social relations. Thus, a worker employed in industrial or even agriculture production and paid a wage which is part of total invested capital and therefore part of the cost of production is viewed as productive. By contrast, the labourer employed in the provision of services and paid out of revenues for his services rendered, he is categorized as unproductive. As a consequence, unproductive is the labour which is paid out of revenues regardless of the sphere of social reproduction in which is engaged. Smith further explicates:

> There is one sort of labour which adds to the value of the subject upon which it is bestowed; there is another which has no such effect. The former, as it produces a value, may be called productive; the latter, unproductive labour. Thus the labour of a manufacturer *adds*, generally, to the value of the materials which he works upon, that of his own maintenance and of his master's profit. The labour of a menial servant, on the contrary, adds to the value of nothing. Though the manufacturer has his wages advanced to him by his master, he, in reality, costs him no expense, the value of those wages being generally restored, together with a profit, in the improved value of the subject upon which his labour is bestowed. But the *maintenance* of a menial servant never is restored. A man grows rich by employing a multitude of manufacturers; he grows poor by maintaining a multitude of menial servants.
>
> (*Wealth of Nations*, pp. 429-430, emphasis added)

However, right after his definition of productive labour and the negative effects of unproductive labour, Smith hastened to note that:

The labour of the latter [unproductive labourer], however, has its value, and *deserves* its reward as well.

(*Wealth of Nations*, p. 430)

And by doing so, Smith stressed that ethical connotations are placed onto the productive labour and that unproductive workers should be paid for their services regardless of their necessity and their surplus-consuming effects.

However, as with his theory of value, Smith conflated his first and in the right direction definition by a second according to which the wage labour employed in the provision of services and whose work does not concretize into a 'vendible product' is unproductive. Hence, the character of use value decides upon the productive or unproductive nature of labour. Apparently, Smith thought that the two definitions cannot give quite different answers, and he was perhaps right from a practical point of view and for the time that he was writing. In fact, the service sector was limited generally to the government activities and expenditures, whose size relative to the whole output produced in the economy, to the extent we know from the available statistics, was minimal, and also private services very rarely were provided through wage labour. Surprisingly enough, the use-value properties of a commodity became the basis of the national accounting system in the former centrally planned economies giving, thus, additional credence to Smith's distinction of productive-unproductive labour on the basis of use values as a very rough approximation of a character of an economy and its scale of reproduction.

Ricardo also accepts the distinction of PUPL and states his position in the following straightforward way:

It must be understood that all the productions of a country are consumed; but it makes the greatest difference imaginable whether they are consumed by those who reproduced, or by those who do not reproduce another value. When we say that revenue is saved, and added to capital, what we mean is, that the portion of revenue, so said to be added to the capital, is consumed by productive instead of unproductive labourers.

(*Works* I, p. 151)

Marx criticized Smith who, although improved the concept of productive labour in comparison to that of the Physiocrats, ended up with a definition limited to the material properties of a product. In fact, Marx criticized both, Smith and Ricardo, for failing to extend an originally correct definition the basis of which is the social relations of production, by focusing instead on the properties of use values. According to Marx, the respective analysis should consider that, on the one hand, the distinction of labour activity into productive and unproductive is determined by the sphere of the social activity in which it is employed, and on the other hand, the theoretical content of the distinction must be different in capitalism from the previous modes of production. Notes Marx:

> Only the narrow-minded bourgeois, who regards the capitalist form of production as its absolute form, hence as the sole natural form of production, can confuse the question of what are *productive labour* and *productive workers* from the standpoint of capital with the question of what *productive* labour is in general, and can therefore be satisfied with the tautological answer that all that labour is productive which produces, which results in a product, or any kind of use value, which has any result at all.
>
> (Results, p. 1039)

The distinction between PUPL was part of the economic orthodoxy throughout the nineteenth century, and what is more important the distinction was deeply rooted in the business treatment of production expenses. In the business accounting system, it is quite clear who produces directly and who merely assists in the production process and also what happens when non-productive labour and the associated with it indirect costs grow at the expense of production labour and directly related costs. The distinction is crucial for the survival of the firm, and any different treatment may have severe consequences for the evaluation of its economic status.

Important as the PUPL distinction may be for the classical economists and the business people alike; nevertheless, the distinction was gradually abandoned with the emergence and dominance of the neoclassical school of economic thought in the last quarter of the nineteenth century. In the new approach, the issue of production and non-production labour activities is thought of as redundant or simply wrong. All the factors of production (labour, land and capital) contribute, according to their marginal productivities, to the creation of new output, and in this sense, they are all productive. Thus, in neoclassical economics to the extent that a factor of production contributes, one way or another, to the creation of output for which there is demand for is considered productive. In this sense, labour activity to the extent that is paid for, it follows that it produces utility and therefore is regarded as productive. Thus, in neoclassical economics, all paid (not household) labour is treated as productive and so the distinction so central in the CPE becomes trivial and uninteresting in neoclassical economics.

Marshall, who was no doctrinaire and always ready to make compromises, predicted, and he was right in a sense, that the distinction of PUPL will fade away and will eventually disappear in the not so distant future; he further thought that this should not be done immediately, presumably because the economists of the early twentieth century were not prepared to abandon a concept whose function was so crucial to the estimation of profits or losses of business people. Marshall, in an attempt to reconcile and not necessarily to break altogether with the CPE tradition sought to assimilate the concept of PUPL, so well established in economic and business world, into the emerging neoclassical theory. The following quotation encapsulates his spirit:

> we may define labour as any exertion of mind or body undergone partly or wholly with a view to some good other than pleasure derived directly from the work. And if we had to make a fresh start it would be best to regard all labour as productive except that which failed to promote the aim towards which it was directed, and so produced no utility.
>
> (Marshall 1890, p. 54)

Therefore, according to neoclassical theory, any form of labour whose product or outcome can secure remuneration in the labour market is considered to create new value and thus increases the value of the total produced output. Schumpeter (1954) has exemplified the view held by neoclassical economists by criticising the dichotomy of PUPL in the following harsh way:

> The only reason why this dusty museum piece interests us at all is that it affords an excellent example of the manner in which the discussion of meaningful ideas may lose sight of their meanings and slip off into futility [...] And so meaningless discussion became a standard item of nineteenth-century textbooks in spite of the increasing awareness of its futility, which eventually killed it.
>
> (Schumpeter 1954, p. 631)

It goes without saying that the fundamental distinction of PULP and related activities, so crucial in the CPE perspective, comes to the fore when the economies are in lasting recessionary situations. The reason is that the distinction becomes particularly useful for it helps in the determination of the potentially available capital for investment and, by extent, the long-run productive potential of an economy. This is the reason that during periods of economic slowdowns, such as the one underway since 2007, the interest of neoclassical economists in the old distinction of PUPL is revived, and in this revival, urgent becomes the need to reinvent the concept although dressed, when possible, in a different garment. There is no doubt that the 'spectre' of PUPL hunts neoclassical economists who are bound to reinvent it under different names instead of directly invoking and admitting its relevance and usefulness by addressing new challenging issues and by concretizing it with the available data. However, as we will argue below, by reinventing the concept of PUPL, neoclassical economists leave many issues open to criticisms. In what follows, we briefly discuss three main efforts to sidestep the concept of PUPL and its replacement by a kind of surrogate or proxy-concept to explain the post-WWII economic performance.

Famous is Baumol's (1967) 'cost disease of the service sector' explanation of the stagflation crisis of the late 1960s to early 1980s which reappeared in some recent publications; nevertheless, its reappearance followed by too many challenging issues. According to this view, the stagflation in the USA and in other advanced economies was attributed to the expansion of the services, that is, the 'less progressive' sectors of the economy at the expense of the industrial or 'progressive' ones. The service sectors are characterized by slow growth in productivity mainly because of their rigid labour-intensive character which makes them innovation-averse sectors. By contrast, the industrial sector is characterized by high productivity, because of its capital-intensive and therefore innovation-prone character. As a consequence, wages in the industrial sector were expected and in fact were increasing (in the 1960s and early 1970s) to keep pace with the rising productivity, but because of a number of institutional reasons, the wages in the growing service sector followed fairly close the increase in wages of the 'progressive sector', thereby increasing the cost of production and prices, depressing profits and discouraging investment resulting in rising unemployment and therefore stagflation.

In similar vein, Bacon and Eltis (1976), in their effort to explain the decline in the productivity of the UK economy, distinguished between the 'marketed' sector identified with private along with the segments of the public sector that produce, sell and earn profits and the 'non-marketed sector' identified with the part of the public sector that does not exactly sell its product. According to their analysis, the hypertrophy of the non-market sector, created by the Keynesian post-war policies, was the cause of the stagnation observed in the British economy in the 1970s and other advanced economies. Such a diagnosis of the causes of stagflation crisis was in the spirit of the times and the neoliberal policies of late-1970s onwards targeted to the growth of the market sectors and the shrinkage of the non-marketed sectors of the economy.

The expansion of 'rent-seeking', that is, activities aiming at increasing one's share of produced wealth without creating any new wealth (Tullock 1967), is another effort to reinvent the old and tested over the last two centuries, at least, concept of PUPL within the neoclassical approach. In the recent years, the rent-seeking explanation may gain more attention due to the expansion of financialization, that is, excess profit-seeking activities without production. However, more and more is recognized that profits and rents (excessive profits) without production sooner or later end up to a 'zero sum game', a result known very well in the classical political economy.

From the above history of economic thought excursion, we discover that suppressed meaningful ideas for some time are bound to re-emerge at some later time, however, in distorted forms. The timing for the 'puffing out' of these distorted ideas is during harsh economic conditions, as the ones under way, when people are more eager to discuss and perhaps accept new and especially convenient explanations. However, time and again, we discover that once a theoretical explanation is built on unrealistic (neoclassical) foundations soon will come to face facts that contradict its basic assumptions. For example, in the case of Baumol's 'cost disease' explanation, nowadays, we find that the service industries of finance and trade have completely changed their mode of operation by introducing innovations which mechanize the provision of their "output". It is important to note that in the past these particular industries were thought as labour-intensive and relative immune to any significant technological changes. As a consequence, employment positions are lost in these industries, and their once thought stagnant "productivity" or rather efficiency has been improved substantially. With respect to the popular Bacon and Eltis's explanation which was on the rise in the 1980s, currently there is no similar follow-up. Of course, the unproductive character of the services of public sector and their detrimental to economic growth effects were well known already from times even before Smith. The 'rent-seeking' view of classifying economic activities as productive and non is still in search of a rigorous and all-inclusive theorization of economic activities. Such a search is without success, although some of its supporters would deny that they are interested in an all-inclusive explanation and they would argue that their focus is on particular explanations (for more see Medema 1991 and Tullock 2008).

9.2.1 Productive and Unproductive Labour in Marx

Marx's view of the distinction between PUPL can be found in a series of works, written in different time periods and also analytical rigour. This fact explains, at least in part, the confusion that exists in the extant literature regarding the definition, meaning and use of this distinction. Marx in his analysis successively concretizes his theory of PUPL starting from a very general standpoint trying to identify the common elements characterizing all historical modes of production and then proceeds by arguing that his analysis is meaningful when applied to the capitalist mode of production whose salient feature is production for exchange value at a profit as a purpose in itself. Thus, it is important to emphasize that the distinction of PUPL *does not* refer to the following misconceptions:

- Whether the labour is necessary or important for society.[2]
- Whether the labour is considered to be good or bad with some ethical or ideological connotations (defence vs. peace goods).
- Whether the labour is engaged in the production of a particular type of goods (basic vs. non-basic); hence, the use of the output produced does not characterize the labour.[3]
- Whether we are dealing with the material or non-material nature of the commodity in question.
- Whether an employee can be classified as a member of the working class.[4]

For Marx, productive labour is the wage labour that produces surplus-value. All other forms of labour, not included in this definition, are considered as non-productive. In addition, labour that produces either use values for the producer's own consumption or commodities for sale by independent producers is not productive.

The distinction is better understood if placed in the broader classification of activities of social reproduction, common to any mode of production, and in this

---

[2]On the basis of the same logic, this categorization does not refer to whether an activity will continue or disappear into a socialist economy. Baran and Sweezy (1966) argued that many activities such as advertising, marketing and the like which are indispensable to capitalism will vanish in a rationally organized, that is, socialist economy as unnecessary and therefore as a pure waste of resources.

[3]For example, Bullock (1973) defined as productive the labour employed in the production of 'basic or reproductive goods', that is, commodities that are used as means of production (investment goods) and consumption goods, and as unproductive the labour producing commodities that are not used as inputs in the production process, that is, luxury and military goods.

[4]This view was mainly put forward by Marxist sociologists, such as Poulantzas (1975, p. 213), who argued that the working class consists mainly of productive workers, while all other workers, since they are supported by the surplus-value produced, are in a way more in alliance with the capitalist rather than the working class. This view has neither the theoretical nor historical backing since workers in the circulation and social maintenance activities may be super-exploited.

Table 9.1 Spheres of social reproduction

	Characteristics				
Spheres	Use values (1)	Sell for profit (2)	Wage labour (3)	Production of new value (4)	Ownership rights (new or maintenance of old) (5)
1. Production	✓	✓	✓	✓	X
2. Circulation	✓	✓	✓	X	✓
3. Reproduction of social order	✓	X	✓	X	✓
4. Consumption	✓	X	X	X	X

respect there are four spheres of social activity (Shaikh and Tonak 1994) which contribute, one way or another, to the reproduction of a society:

- Production: within which the various inputs are employed in order to create through the employment of labour new use values or to transform the already existing ones.
- Circulation or distribution: within which the different inputs are utilized together with human activity (labour), in order the various use values that have already been produced to change procession or ownership.
- Maintenance and reproduction of social order: within which the various inputs (use values) combined with human activity are engaged in preserving and reproducing the existing social order. This activity includes, inter alia, the public administration, the legal system, the army, the private and public security and the like.
- Social consumption: within which use values are consumed for the purpose of the reproduction of society at large. Hence, there is no labour activity, and its neoclassical analogy would be the sphere of non-labour or leisure time.

In Table 9.1 we present the four spheres of social reproduction which characterize all modes of production. The columns of the table depict the various ways in which labour participates in the production of use values.

The first row of Table 9.1 presents the sphere of production in which use values are created, a common feature to all modes of production. However, the line of reasoning with regard to the specific mode of production (capitalism or not) differs if we consider the following:

- The first cell (row 1 and column 1) of the matrix of social reproduction presents the production of use values, featuring in all societies. In capitalism, we can think of someone producing for his own use (e.g. cooking or gardening).
- The cell of the first row and second column describes the production of use values which are sold by the producer in the market; hence, there is production of use values and, at the same time, production of value but without the employment of wage labour and thus we do not exactly deal with capitalism proper yet (the vegetables from gardening are brought to the market by individual).

- The cell formed by the first row and third column refers to the production of use values that take place with the employment of wage labour by capital for the purpose of extracting surplus-value and making profit. Hence, we deal with the capitalist mode of production proper.

In similar fashion, we can proceed in the sphere of circulation (distribution) where:

- The already produced use values (the cell formed by the second row and first column) are distributed among consumers (e.g. the vegetables are distributed to neighbours).
- The cell of the second row and second column refers to the sale of the use values (goods) for the purpose of obtaining income, such as in the case of a wholesaler or a vendor.
- While the cell of the second row and third column includes the circulation and sale of commodities from commercial capital, which hires labour for the purpose of profit as is the case with of supermarkets and department stores.
- The cell of the second row and fourth column indicates that nothing new is created; we just have a change of ownership.

Similar is the explanation with the other cells and their discussion is left to the interested reader.

Summing up the discussion of Table 9.1, we observe that the third column in both production and circulation activities refers to wage labour which is employed and in a sense is exploited by capital; nevertheless, new value and surplus-value are produced only in the sphere of production (cell of row 1 and column 4). In the sphere of circulation, the ownership of the already produced use values is simply transferred to its new owners, and the distribution of part of the surplus (already produced in the production sphere) in the form of commercial profits takes place. Thus, productive labour is defined only as the wage labour employed in the production (cell of row 1 and column 4) organized according to capitalist conditions, and it generates surplus-value. Rubin sums up the distinction as follows:

> Thus, according to Marx, every type of labor organized in *forms of the capitalist process of production,* or more precisely, labor hired by "productive" capital, i.e., capital in the *phase of production,* is *productive labor.* The labor of salesmen is not productive, not because it does not produce changes in material goods, but only because it is hired by capital in the phase of circulation. The labor of the clown in the service of the circus entrepreneur is productive[...] because it is employed by capital in the phase of production. On the other hand, the labor of a cashier in a circus, who sells tickets for the clown's performances, is unproductive, because he is hired by capital in the phase of circulation: he only assists in transferring the 'right to watch the show', the right to enjoy the jests of the clown, from one person (the entrepreneur) to another (the public).
>
> (Rubin 1928, p. 269, emphasis in the text)

The first three social activities necessarily involve human activity (labour), unlike the fourth one, which, however, is a prerequisite for the reproduction of the labouring class and to maintain its ability to supply its labour services. Moreover, only the first sphere of social reproduction is production, within which new use values are created through the planned and purposeful human activity (labour) and the use of other socially useful objects. In the remaining three spheres, there is consumption of the existing use values for the attainment of some socially desirable results (various forms of social and personal consumption).

Formally, the above definition can be expressed by the circuit of the industrial capital presented already in relation (1.30) to Chap. 1:

$$M - C <^{LP}_{MP} \ldots P \ldots C' - M' \tag{9.1}$$

where capitalists with their initial money capital (M) buy commodities of equivalent value (C), namely, means of production (MP) and labour power (LP), which in the production process (P) are transformed into new commodities (C') of higher value and, in turn, are sold making a corresponding amount of money (M'). Therefore, the purpose in the production process is to create surplus-value, that is, the difference between the revenues from the sale of commodities minus the value of the initially invested money:

$$M' - M = \Delta M = s$$

In contrast, the labour that is employed in the other spheres of the social reproduction, namely, the circulation and the maintenance and reproduction of social order, are not productive, because, although they may contribute to the extraction of surplus-value in the form of profits, their activities do not result in the production of new value and surplus-value. This is how Marx put it:

> The general law is that *all costs of circulation, which arise only from changes in the forms of commodities do not add to their value.* They are merely expenses incurred in the realisation of the value or in its conversion from one form into another. The capital spent to meet those costs (including the labour done under its control) belongs among the *faux frais* of capitalist production. They must be replaced from the surplus-product and constitute, as far as the entire capitalist class is concerned, a deduction from the surplus-value or surplus-product, just as the time a labourer needs for the purchase of his means of subsistence is lost time.
>
> (*Capital* II, pp. 149, emphasis in the original)

The activities are in the sphere of circulation, and they are described through the circuit of commercial capital as follows:

$$M - C <^{LP}_{MP} \ldots \ldots C' - M' \tag{9.2}$$

Hence, labour power is also exchanged against capital and performs activities that contribute to the realization of money capital higher than that of the originally money invested ($M' > M$). However, the gains in money capital in the sphere of circulation are not the result of the creation or transformation of new commodities and therefore the production of new value. The commodities are created in the sphere of production, and they are sold or realized in the sphere of circulation; hence, the value embodied in the commodities during the production process is realized in the process of exchange. The only real change that takes place in the sphere of circulation is the transfer of commodities' ownership for which there is a payment called commercial profit which is part of the surplus-value produced. The costs for the circulation of commodities were characterized by classical economists as *faux frais* which is another way to say that in effect these costs are incidental or secondary and as such deduct rather than add value to the produced commodities.

Similarly, in the circuit of the financial capital, there is no production of new value but only the circulation of money which is the form of appearance of the value contained in commodities. Owners of money (capital) employ labour power and other inputs to activate a money-lending process in order to extract part of the total surplus-value already produced in the form of interest. Formally, the circuit of financial capital can be described as follows:

$$M - C <_{MP}^{LP} \dots \dots M'$$ (9.3)

At this point, it is important to emphasize that the profits of commercial and financial capital are portions and distinct forms of appearance of the total surplus-value created by the productive labour employed in the sphere of production.

It is important to point out that the spheres of social reproduction are not tightly isolated from one another. Unproductive labour can be found in the sphere of production, if, for example, the labour is employed either in the supervision of the production process or in sales or other similarly related activities. By contrast, productive is the labour employed by businesses in transportation industry whose function is, in effect, to complete the useful properties of a commodity, that is, the use-value must be transferred from one place to another so as to become available to buyers. In this sense the transportation industry differs from the circulation industry whose function is to transfer the possession or ownership of already produced commodities.

> The distinguishing feature of [transportation] is that it appears as a continuation of the process of production within the process of circulation and for the process of circulation.
>
> (*Capital* II, p. 158)

Furthermore, in the sphere of circulation proper, there may be found some productive labour especially in activities that have to do with the completion of the production process, such as packaging, cutting and in general activities that complete the use value characteristics of the product. As in accounting, there are always 'grey areas' in the treatment of some kinds of labour and business expenses whose classification may be difficult or controversial; however, the 'grey areas' are, on the one hand, limited and, on the other hand, ascertain the basic principle of the division of social activities according to the PUPL, and in no way they lead to an altogether different accounting system. Finally, the non-productive labour in the sphere of circulation or in the sphere of maintenance of social order may not be less exploited than that in the production sphere. In effect, independently of the sphere of social reproduction, a worker (in order for the hiring to be meaningful) is paid for his labour power in order to be able to purchase the socially determined buddle of subsistence commodities whose labour time to produce, however, is by far less than that actually made available to the employer during the working day.

9.3   The Distinction of PUPL and the Accumulation of Capital

According to Physiocrats and the classical approach in general, the distinction of PUPL activity is very crucial in studying the process of capital accumulation. The reason is that this distinction allows the understanding of the extent to which the labour involved in the sphere of production gives rise to surplus sufficient enough to maintain or expand the non-productive activities (circulation and maintenance and reproduction of the social order) in an economy. If the non-productive activities grow at a rate slower than that of productive activities, the reproduction of this economy can be carried on an expanding scale. In contrast, if the non-productive activities grow at a rate higher than that of productive ones and the surplus-value is reduced in relative terms, then the overall reproduction of the economy becomes increasingly more difficult. Clearly, there must be a limit to how far the growth of unproductive activities can go without putting the stability of the whole system at stake.

Classical economists predicted the detrimental effects that the expansion of non-productive activities may exert on the growth potential of the economy. Smith, for example, was particularly worried about such an expansion of non-productive activities, albeit they were relatively limited in his time; nevertheless, he described in dramatic tones the devastating consequences of their potential expansion:

> Great nations are never impoverished by private, though they sometimes are by public prodigality and misconduct. The whole, or almost the whole public revenue, is in most countries employed in maintaining unproductive hands. Such are the people who compose a numerous and splendid court, a great ecclesiastical establishment, great fleets and armies, who in time of peace produce nothing, and in time of war acquire nothing which can compensate the expense of maintaining them, even while the war lasts. Such people, as they themselves produce nothing, are all maintained by the produce of other men's labour. When multiplied, therefore, to an unnecessary number, they may in a particular year consume so great a share of this produce, as not to leave a sufficiency for maintaining the productive labourers, who should reproduce it next year. The next year's produce, therefore, will be less than that of the foregoing, and if the same disorder should continue, that of the third year will be still less than that of the second.
>
> (*Wealth*, p. 325)

Marx seems to argue that the non-productive activities tend to increase over time, and this may have effects on the accumulation of capital. He notes:

> The extraordinary productiveness of modern industry [...] allows of the unproductive employment of a larger and larger part of the working class, and consequent reproduction, on a constantly extending scale, of the ancient domestic slaves, under the name of a servant class, including men servants, lackeys, *etc.* [...]
>
> (*Capital* I, p. 487)

The increase in non-productive activities is caused by the intensification of competition which forces capitals to spend more and more on sales promotion, management and general supervision activities in their constant effort to maintain and, if possible, expand their market share at the expense of their competitors. Moreover, the social cohesion in modern societies requires the absorption of more and more surplus-value by the state in order to provide social benefits to the people in need. Finally, the international competition for sources of raw materials and for new markets is putting additional pressure on governments to increase their military spending and to be on a permanent footing in order to defend their economic and political interests. All of the above lead to an expansion of the government expenditures; of course, here we refer to the expansion of its non-productive activities (administration and defence) and not necessarily of the productive services (such as health, education, recreation, etc.) or productive sectors (such as utilities, electricity, transport, etc.) usually operating under state ownership and regulation.

9.4   The Evolution of the System of National Income Accounts

The evolution of the system of national income accounts (NIA) shares many features with the development of the concepts related to the distinction between PUPL. Until the time of the Great Depression in 1930s, only a few countries collected national accounts data in any systematic way. The collected data were mainly concerned with international trade (imports and exports for taxation purposes), prices, interest rates, production and employment among others. These NIA reflected the classical distinction of activities into PUPL not only because of the dominance of classical economics until the first decades of the twentieth century but also because of convenience since the business practice and accounting system keeps the production activities separate from the rest, not necessarily less important, administrative and other related activities.

Studenski (1958), for example, opines that for the statistical authorities it was much easier to collect data on wages, profits, taxes and the like from the available income statements of businesses and thus to construct what can be called business-oriented NIA. Furthermore, income figures by industrial origin could easily be obtained from manufacturing censuses which in the USA even today continue to make the distinction of workers in production from those that are not (corporate officers and administration employees in general). Moreover, the estimation of the GNP or GDP from the final use side was not only redundant according to the economic philosophy of the pre-Keynesian era of the laissez-faire capitalism, but their estimation was exceedingly more difficult to carry out than from the income side, where the data were readily available. The reason is that not only the separation of the intermediate from the final use of output is not an easy task to accomplish, but in addition, the trade and transportation margins had to be added on, if the price of final goods purchased by the consumer was to be estimated.

The major reason for the lack of systematic NIA in the USA and the other advanced economies before the Great Depression must be also attributed to the classical perception about the unproductive nature of government, whose possible expansion was detrimental to the growth capacity of the economy. As a consequence, the economic philosophy of the nineteenth and early twentieth century suggested that government's size should be kept to the absolute necessary minimum and so (absolutely minimal) was to be kept government's intervention in the economy. This view was further strengthened with the emergence and establishment of neoclassical economics (since the late nineteenth century) according to which capitalism is a self-regulating and virtually healthy and growing system of production with no significant and long-term deviations from its equilibrium path. Therefore, government's role in the economy was restricted to some minor corrective interventions (fill some of the gaps and failures of the market mechanism) and not to implement any grant scale economic policy directing the economy to the attainment of specific goals. Consequently, the regular and consistent collection of economic data of various economic variables was not in any demand.

With the emergence of the Keynesian economics during the Great Depression of the 1930s and their dominance in the first post-war decades, it became commonplace among economists (until at least the late 1960s) that if the economy is left to its own devices, it may be driven into periodic crises and widespread unemployment. This change in the perception of the operation of the economic system made imperative the design and implementation of government stabilization (fiscal and monetary) policies. The prerequisite for the effectiveness of such policies was the availability of relevant data on the expenditure side because according to the Keynesian theory of effective demand, expenditures determine the level of equilibrium output produced and the associated with it level of employment. The system of NIA resulted from the need to intervene in the economy in depressionary situations such as that of the 1930s, and the theoretical background for such an intervention was provided in Keynes' *General Theory* (1936). In fact, the introduction of concepts such as 'demand-driven economy', 'investment multiplier', 'marginal propensity to consume', 'marginal efficiency of capital' and the like necessitated the need for a system of NIA consistent with both the income and the expenditure sides. For example, Ruggles and Ruggles (1956) note:

> It was because of this need [economic policy] that national income accounting has been developed, and the history of the development of national income accounting is in fact inseparable from the history of economic problems posed by the depression of the thirties, by the industrial mobility of World War II, and by the postwar economic readjustments among nations.
>
> (Ruggles and Ruggles 1956, p. 5)

A prerequisite for an effective implementation of Keynesian economic policies is, therefore, the collection of consistent, reliable and objective data regarding taxes, government expenditures, wages and other types of income, as well as their distribution in consumption, investment and savings. Therefore, the ability of the state to pursue various economic policies is based on data which show the way in which income is consumed or saved and then spent on investment goods; in addition, the government is interested in the (multiplier) effects of investment on the income and employment.

Table 9.2 Sectors in NIA and PUPL in general

Sector (NIA)	Productive labour	Non-productive labour
1.Agriculture, forest, fishery	✓	X
2.Mines	✓	X
3.Manufacturing	✓	X
4.Public utilities(electricity, gas, water supply)	✓	X
5.Construction	✓	X
6.Transportation, communications	✓	X
7. Trade	X	✓
8. Finance, insurance, real estate	X	✓
9. Public administration, security	X	✓
10.Health, education	Private ✓	Public ✓
11. Services	✓	✓

9.5 National Accounts and Classical Political Economy Categories

We have already mentioned that, for the neoclassical theory, any labour whose outcome can secure remuneration in the market is considered productive and contributes to the creation of new value. Thus, not only activities in the sphere of commodity circulation but also those aimed at maintaining and reproducing the social order are considered to produce new values and increase the level of prosperity and wealth of an economy. According to the logic of neoclassical theory and current NIA methodology, from the four spheres of social reproduction (see Table 9.1) only in the sphere of personal consumption, we do not find production (of new value and product). This perception is reflected in the measurement of total economic activity, as is usually estimated by gross domestic product (GDP) from the NIA of each country.

Based on the classical framework of analysis, in Table 9.2 we display the NIA sectors which are classified to sectors in the sphere of production that employ productive labour and to sectors that belong to the sphere of circulation and social maintenance that employ mainly non-productive labour or even no labour at all.[5] It is worth noting that in these non-productive sectors, the new value reported by NIA has been produced by labour employed in productive activities and simply it is realized in industries (e.g. trade) or involves transactions and changes in ownership or borrowing (e.g. financial institutions, insurance, real estate) or it might be completely fictitious (e.g. real estate)[6] or, lastly, it is counted for the second time

---

[5]We assume that each sector is characterized entirely by capitalist production relations.

[6]Homeowners are considered to rent their dwelling to themselves by paying (imputed) rents that increase artificially the total income and output of the economy.

Table 9.3   Orthodox (official) and classical NIA: production sector

Production	Classical NIA	Orthodox (official) NIA
90 $\Pi_p = S$	Gross output (value) $C + V + S = 140$	Gross output (value) $C + W_p + \Pi = 140$
30 $W_p = V$	Net value-added $V + S = 120$	Net value-added $\Pi_p + W_p = 120$
20 $C = m_p + D_p$ Constant cost $(C) =$ raw materials (m_p) + depreciation (D_p)	Variable capital $V = 30$	Wages $W_p = 30$
	Rate of surplus-value $S/V = 90/$ $30 = 300\%$	Profit-wage ratio $\Pi_p/W_p = 90/$ $30 = 300\%$

(e.g. public administration and defence).[7] It is evident that at least in the last two cases, the size of the total value of NIA is increased, but in a fictitious way.

The different conceptions in classical and neoclassical economic theories are reflected in the way in which each approach measures the outcome of the total economic activity, as well as the net contribution of each sector. As a result, the proper measurement of the level and the evolution of basic classical variables cannot be carried out using the published NIA categories. The mapping of the classical categories of political economy into those of official NIA is irrefutably related to PUPL distinction, that is, to distinction between the activities that create new value and the activities that result in the absorption of part of the already produced value.

In Table 9.3, we present a first approximation of mapping the classical categories to those of NIA. We begin with by assuming an economy limited to the sphere of production in which the total output is produced and realized without the mediation of any other sphere of social reproduction.

In this simplified hypothetical economy, the classical categories of total gross output (value), net value-added, constant capital, variable capital, surplus-value and rate of surplus-value correspond one to one to those of the orthodox NIA: gross output, net value-added, depreciation (and raw materials), wages, profits and profit-wage ratio.[8]

In the case where output is produced in the sphere of production but carried out in the sphere of circulation, the categories begin to differ systematically between the two (classical and orthodox) NIA systems (see Table 9.4). First of all, we assume that the total output is sold to the final buyer at a price exactly equal to its value

---

[7]In NIA, the contribution of the public sector to GDP is equal to the wages of its employees. However, these wages are paid out of taxes (on output and private incomes) and therefore have been already recorded in the measurement GDP. Thus, caution should be applied in order to avoid double counting.

[8]For convenience purposes we use capital letters for the flow variables.

Table 9.4 Orthodox and classical NIA: production and trade sectors

Classical NIA		Orthodox NIA	
Production and trade		Production	Trade
$S = 90$	$\Pi_t = 30$		$\Pi_t = 30$
	$W_t = 20$		$W_t = 20$
	$m_t + D_t = 20$		$m_t + D_t = 20$
	$\Pi_p = 20$	$\Pi_p = 20$	
$V = 30$	$W_p = 30$	$W_p = 30$	
$C = 20$	$m_p + D_p = 20$	$m_p + D_p = 20$	
Gross output $S + V + C = 140$		Gross output $(m_p + D_p + W_p + \Pi_p + m_t + D_t + \Pi_t + W_t) = 140$	
Net value-added $S + V = 120$		Net value-added $(W_p + \Pi_p + W_t + \Pi_t) = 100$	
Variable capital $V = 30$		Wages $W_p + W_t = 50$	
Surplus-value $S = \Pi_p + \Pi_t + (m_t + D_t) + W_t = 90$		Profits $\Pi_p + \Pi_t = 50$	
Rate of surplus-value $S/V = 300\%$		Profit-wage ratio $(\Pi/W) = 50/50 = 100\%$	

(which was equal to 140). This means that the productive capital sells the product to the commercial capital at a price below its value (let us say, 70), but of course above the production cost of constant and variable capital ($C + V = 50$). The difference between the value of the output and its purchase price from the trading capital ($140 - 70 = 70$) is called the gross trading margin and indicates the maximum profit margin that the commercial capital may obtain. The latter, in order to perform its function, that is, to realize or sell the final output, buys raw materials (m_t), uses fixed capital stock which depreciates (D_t) and hires wage labour (W_t). The difference in the gross trading margin from total trade costs is the profit of commercial capital of the economy (Π_t). From the point of view of total social capital, it is clear that the movement of goods for the purpose of carrying them entails a cost of additional intermediate inputs for materials and wages. This cost is financed by the total mass of surplus-value that has been created in the sphere of production, thus reducing its remaining portion for the further accumulation of capital.

However, orthodox NIA measure as net value-added in each sector the sum of income paid in this sector (wages and gross profits); they do not take into account the total value of raw materials and depreciation in the trade sector ($m_t + D_t$). These categories although not personal incomes nevertheless represent a quantity of value generated in the production sector and consumed for the realization of the commodities. As we can see in Table 9.4, the measure of the total net value-added of orthodox NIA is systematically less than the equivalent measure of the classical NIA. In addition, it is clear that the classical category of variable capital (which includes only the wages of productive workers) differs in general from the category 'wages and salary' referred in orthodox NIA, which includes the remuneration of both productive and non-productive labour. Moreover, the overall surplus generated by the productive workers also differs in general from the total profits reported by NIA, as part of it is absorbed by the costs of the sphere of circulation and either does not appear at all in NIA (raw materials and depreciation) or takes the form of wages of non-productive labour. As a result, the profit-wage ratio underestimates twice the ratio of surplus-value because on the one hand it underestimates the overall surplus-value and on the other hand overestimates the variable capital.

In the even more concrete and therefore realistic case, where the financial sector is introduced (Table 9.5), we see that because capitals from the production and trade sectors borrow money from the banking sector, a part of their gross income takes on the form of interest in servicing their loans. This interest represents the total revenue of the financial sector, which in turn spent on raw materials and depreciation ($m_f + D_f$) while the remainder, after the subtraction of wages (W_f),is the profits of the financial sector (Π_f).

As a result, the classical net value-added deviates even further from the corresponding measure of orthodox NIA, as the materials and depreciation of the financial sector are not included in the newly created value that, according to the classical view, has been exclusively created in the production sector. In addition, the total surplus-value diverges furthermore from the orthodox measure of profits, since another portion of surplus-value is now absorbed in materials, depreciation and wages in the financial sector. Also, the profit-wage ratio deviates even more from the rate of surplus-value, as not only earnings are reduced in relation to surplus-value, but also total wages increase by the amount of W_f in relation to variable capital.

We note that total surplus-value takes on the form not only of profits but also the form of various expenses needed for the circuit of total capital, including even the wages of non-productive workers, and the variable capital constitutes only a part of the total wage bill of the economy. Thus, the profit-wage ratio in orthodox NIA is by no means an appropriate empirical approach to the level of the rate of surplus-value. Furthermore, if the expenditures on materials and wages in non-productive activities increase over time as a percentage to total surplus-value, it is likely they will impose a fall in the profit-wage ratio while at the same time period the surplus-value will display an upward trend.[9]

Economists of the classical political economy tradition pay particular attention to the fact that the non-production sectors of trade and finance as well as government in order to perform their socially useful functions employ labour and other inputs while at the same time their capital stock depreciates; such expenses are drawn out from the surplus generated by the productive sectors of the economy. Finally, the government sector's unproductive activities are also supported out of surplus-value and in particular by taxation. As a consequence, the expenses of these activities must not be included in the estimations for reasons of double counting (Shaikh and Tonak 1994, p. 61).

---

[9]For a more detailed presentation of the transformation of the orthodox NIA into classical ones, see Shaikh and Tonak (1994).

Table 9.5 Orthodox and classical NIA: production, trade and financial sectors

Classical NIA		Orthodox NIA		
Production	Trade and credit	Production	Trade	Credit
$S = 90$	$\Pi_f = 10$			$\Pi_f = 10$
	$W_f = 15$			$W_f = 15$
	$m_f + D_f = 5$			$m_f + D_f = 5$
	$\Pi_t = 10$		$\Pi_t = 10$	
	$W_t = 20$		$W_t = 20$	
	$m_t + D_t = 20$		$m_t + D_t = 20$	
	$\Pi_p = 10$	$\Pi_p = 10$		
	$W_p = 30$	$W_p = 30$		
	$m_p + D_p = 20$	$m_p + D_p = 20$		
$V = 30$				
$C = 20$				
Gross output		Gross output		
$C + V + S = 140$		$m_p + D_p + W_p + \Pi_p + m_t + D_t + W_t + \Pi_t + m_f + D_f + W_f + \Pi_f = 140$		
Net value-added		Net value-added		
$S + V = 120$		$W_p + W_t + W_f + \Pi_p + \Pi_t + \Pi_f = 95$		
Variable capital		Wages		
$V = W_p = 30$		$W_p + W_t + W_f = 65$		
Surplus-value		Profits		
$S = \Pi_p + \Pi_t + \Pi_f + (m_t + D_t) + (m_f + D_f) + W_t + W_f = 90$		$\Pi_p + \Pi_t + \Pi_f = 30$		
Rate of surplus-value		Profit-wage ratio		
$S/V = 300\%$		$\Pi/W = 30/65 = 46\%$		

The main problem with orthodox NIA is that they present many activities as 'production' while they should be portrayed as 'social consumption'. As the 'personal consumption' sphere contributes to the reproduction of individuals in a capitalist society, the non-productive activities, such as trade, financial services or private security, in turn contribute to the reproduction and development of the capitalist system; however, their necessity does not negate the fact that as the total consumption (personal and social) increases, the part of surplus destined for the accumulation of capital is reduced and by extent the social wealth diminishes.

9.5.1 A Digression to Business Accounting Practices

Surprisingly enough such issues of NIA of the classical political economy are well known in business management, finance and accounting, where the labour costs in business engaged in production activities (see Table 9.2) are partitioned into direct labour costs and indirect labour (or overhead) costs, depending on the way in which a particular worker contributes to the production of goods. More specifically, direct labour describes workers that are directly occupied in the actual production of goods and services. For example, workers at a factory who physically produce products perform direct labour. Similarly, workers at a beauty salon services who actually do haircuts, hair colouring and provide other similarly related services are engaged in direct labour.[10] However, the cashier that receives the payments of all these services, although performs an extremely useful activity, nevertheless is an unproductive one. The materials that these workers use and therefore enter directly into the final product are characterized direct materials. The cost of paying wages to workers involved in production is business's direct labour cost (or variable capital in a Marxian perspective) in the sense that the directly involved labourers actually produce the commodities whose sales bring revenues enough to cover the direct cost of production (the labour and materials that went into the production) and leave profits sufficient to justify the whole business enterprise. By contrast, indirect labour cost describes wages paid to workers that perform tasks assisting direct labourers and is treated as part of the overhead cost. Thus janitors, supervisors, guards and security personnel, managers, accountants, maintenance staff, etc. are all workers occupied in indirect labour, because they do not actually produce any goods or provide any final services. Simply put, indirect labour and materials are not part of the genuine cost of production and the selling price of the product.

It is important to stress at this point that the indirect labour cost is treated as part of the business gross income along with taxes and insurance costs. The gross income is residually determined if from total revenues from sales all costs directly related to

---

[10]The major difference between goods and services is the time of consumption. Services are 'consumed' at the same time that they are produced and goods at a time other than that of their production.

Table 9.6 Simple presentation of income statements of a typical industrial enterprise, December 31, 2018

Total sales		11,000,000
Cost of sales		8,000,000
–Depreciation	1,000,000	
–Cost of raw material	4,000,000	
–Wage and salaries	3,000,000	
Gross profits		3,000,000
Overhead costs[a]	1,300,000	
–Advertisement	400,000	
–Accounting office	500,000	
–Depreciation	50,000	
–Salaries of administration	350,000	
Profits before taxes	1,700,000	
–Profit taxes	510,000	
Net profits		1,190,000
–Retained earnings		1,071,000
–Dividends		119,000

[a]Overhead costs are considered 'burden' for an industrial enterprise

production (such as direct labour costs and cost of raw materials) are subtracted. This treatment of gross income, in general, is quite similar to the classical political treatment of surplus-value in which besides the net profits the indirect wages along with the indirect material costs and all other overheads are included. Production activities may also be found in the non-production distribution such as the trade sector. We know that good accounting practices acknowledge this difference by separating trade activities in those that merely transfer goods and titles of ownerships from those that maintain inventories. The people who are engaged in inventories are treated as direct labour, and similar is the treatment of the related wage cost. In addition, a business with high indirect labour costs and other overheads could potentially have high gross income, but a low or even negative net income or profit. If a business has a low net income, relative to its invested capital, it underperforms, and if net income is negative, the business suffered losses over the examined period.

For a better understanding of business practices, Table 9.6 describes the accounts of a typical enterprise operating in the sphere of production.

From the way in which income statements are reported by an (industrial) enterprise, that is to say a unit of capital operating in the sphere of production, it is clear that entrepreneurs value differently the work of those employed in the production process from those employed, for instance, in the promotion of the commodity. The question, however, is why do businesses insist in making this distinction? And the argument is that the logic of accountants (or better of entrepreneurs) is no different than that of the Physiocrats, the old classical economists and Marx. Thus, labour is classified in direct and indirect terms and the essential criterion of this distinction lies in its relation to the production process. Direct labour is the one that results in a proportionate increase in production. Examples of such labour include the work of machine operators in the main production units and any other one employed directly in the processing of raw materials and semi-finished products, until full production is completed. Indirect labour is one that is not employed in the processing of raw materials but indirectly contributes to the production process. In other words, it is the labour of supporting services, where their presence is deemed necessary, so that direct labour can perform its duties. Examples of such indirect labour include the work of supervisors, maintenance, factory cleaners, service technicians and others.

In analysing direct and indirect cost, relative to profits, the clear demarcation line between direct and indirect labour costs allows management to view changes in production and profits, compared to labour figures. For example, if sales decline, the management may lay off direct labour and reduce the expenses on direct materials; if, however, direct labour has not increased while production levels and revenue have increased, but net profits have fallen, management may re-evaluate the growth of indirect labour costs. Trimming some of its indirect labour costs and expenses, in other words 'keeping lean' to use the jargon of the 1980s, is one of the ways that businesses may attempt to increase net profits as a reward for *undertaking* the risks of *business enterprise*. Understanding and valuing the two types of labour activity and related costs provides management with knowledge of how business generate revenue and control the costs associated with generating revenue. Although the above distinctions are so meaningful for businesses, one wonders why they should not be generalized for the entire economy. Finally, in business accounting practices as well as in classical NIA, there are always 'grey areas' that pose challenges to NIA accounting, but by no means these challenges set the whole accounting philosophy in question.

9.6 Summary and Conclusions

In this chapter, we presented the theoretical and empirical concerns that arise in economic theory from the distinction between PUPL. In our discussion, we placed particular emphasis in the distinction of the spheres of social reproduction and their effects on the creation of surplus and accumulation of capital. We argued that in the old classical economists and Marx, these distinctions and their exact role are very well specified. The same is not true in neoclassical economics which in effort to avoid this disturbing categorization of labour activity reintroduces it in various forms which, however, do not come to terms with the realities of actual economies.

On the basis of the above, the official (orthodox) NIA need to enter into a process of transformation and processing and to adopt the classical distinction of PUPL, a distinction that is already established in good business and accounting practices. In so doing, we can construct and measure the appropriate classical economic categories in contrast to the respective orthodox ones, a process particularly important in the empirical research of the classical political economy. Nevertheless, for the assessment of the level and the long-run behaviour of basic classical and Marxian variables, such as surplus-value, profit rate, etc., more detailed work in the mapping of the official NIA in classical categories is required on the basis of the distinction of PUPL.

Chapter 10
Classical Political Economy and the Evolution of Post-War Capitalism

> *In reality, the very opposite happens. It is the theory which decides what we can observe.*
> Albert Einstein (The quotation is from Heisenberg (1971, p. 63)).

Abstract In this chapter, the movement of the rate of profit is documented on the basis of data of the USA in the post-war period. We find a downward trend in the rate of profit as a result of the rising capital-output ratio measured in both nominal and real terms, and of the rising value composition of capital. The falling rate of profit is intrinsically connected to the economy's growth rate which also follows a downward trend. The econometric analysis we applied confirms this interconnection and bidirectional causality. We also test the extent to which unproductive expenditures are subject to limitations that restrict their 'ratchet expansion'. The chapter concludes with the idea that the falling rate of profit past a point should lead to a stagnating mass of real net profits. The testing terrain for this hypothesis is, once again, the US economy: the hypothesis is to what extent and in which time period the evolution of real net profits follows an S-shaped pattern. The empirical analysis uses quarterly data on corporate profits of the US economy in the post-war period. We distinguish two long cycles, one during the period 1947:1–1982:4 and the second in 1983:1–2018:2. The characteristics of these two long cycles are discussed, and an attempt is made to predict the end of the current recessionary period and the beginning of the expansion phase of a new, long cycle.

Keywords Rate of profit · USA economy · Unproductive expenditures · Real profits · S-shaped pattern · Secular stagnation · Long cycles

---

This chapter is based on materials and information included in articles by Tsoulfidis and Tsaliki (2014), Tsoulfidis and Papageorgiou (2017), Tsoulfidis and Paitaridis (2018) and Tsoulfidis et al. (2019).

© Springer Nature Switzerland AG 2019
L. Tsoulfidis, P. Tsaliki, *Classical Political Economics and Modern Capitalism*,
https://doi.org/10.1007/978-3-030-17967-0_10

10.1   Introduction

In this chapter, we document the evolution of the main macroeconomic variables of the classical political economy based on empirical data of the US economy. These estimates are part of an effort to prove the usefulness and interpretative value of classical national accounts (CNA) and to explain the recent phase change of the US economy, which is very similar to that of other OECD countries and essentially shapes the stage of the world economy. The estimates suggest that the evolution of profitability, as measured by the rate of profit, is linked to the increasing capitalization of the production process, which contributes to the increase in the rate of surplus-value but not enough to reverse the downward trend in both the maximum rate of profit and the average rate of profit. In addition, we find that the expansion of the non-productive sectors and related activities has also contributed and worsened the recession in the US economy, a result that prompts us to test the extent to which the rate of profit of the economy is responsible for the evolution of the unproductive activities as well.

The trajectories of all these classical political economy variables show that in the post-war period, the US and the world economy experienced two long periods of expansion and contraction (identified with the fourth and fifth long cycles as we discussed in Table 8.1), and they are heading towards the end of the fifth and the beginning of the sixth long cycle.[1] In these last two cycles, the growth rate of the real GDP displays a falling pattern for the world economy and also for the USA, as we show in Figs. 8.1 and 8.2, respectively. Hence, one may wonder if the same falling tendency is also found in profitability and the two variables are related to each other; the expectation is that this relation holds for other economies. Consequently, it is interesting to explore to what extent, if any, the long cycles depend on the evolution of profitability, that is, if there is an interplay between the average rate of profit, the mass of net real profit, and the economy's growth rate. Our main focus is the US economy, and the analysis is carried out by using the economic categories of the CNA as opposed to the official (orthodox) national income accounts (ONA).

The current situation of the US economy is characterized by a continuation of the recessionary phase although it seems to have recovered somewhat since the deep downturn of 2008–2009; however, the data and our estimates show that this recovery is still far from being a vigorous enough to set the stage for a new expansion wave. The phenomena observed in the two tipping points (middle to late 1960s and late 2000s) are quite similar to each other, and these are the falling rate of profit and the associated with it stagnating mass of real net profits which slows down new investment spending leading to the devaluation of capital and to quite severe

---

[1]It goes without saying that each long cycle and particular phase has, on the one hand, its own unique characteristics and, on the other, the very same common determinants.

unemployment.[2] As we have already discussed in Chap. 8, in classical political economy approach, the fall in the rate of profit is consistent with the hypothesis of a rising rate of surplus-value and a simultaneously increasing value composition of capital reflecting changes in the technical composition of capital. Furthermore, the fall in the rate of profit affecting, and being affected by, the expansion of unproductive expenditures may engender new developments in the area of technical change.

Hence, interesting questions arise as to what extent the following observations are stylized facts of the capitalist mode of production:

- A rising value composition engendered by the immanent tendency of capitalism for increasing mechanization of the production process in the effort to expand profits by reducing unit production cost.
- A rising rate of surplus-value as a consequence of mechanization and increase in productivity by more than the possible increase in the real wage.
- A rate of surplus-value growing at a rate lower than that of the value composition of capital giving rise, in the long run, to a falling rate of profit.
- A falling rate of profit, in the long run, gives rise to a stagnating mass of real net profits leading the economy to the point of 'absolute over-accumulation' or 'stationary state' of the classical political economy.
- A host of variables among which the unproductive expenditures and the growth rates affect and being affected by the economy-wide rate of profit.

The testing ground for all the above hypotheses will be the post-war US economy, and we begin the analysis by placing the North American Industry Classification System (NAICS) of industries and activities of the US economy in the context of productive and unproductive activities that we discussed in Chap. 9. By using the growth accounting framework of Chap. 9, we examine the relationship between the value composition of capital, the evolution of the so-called materialized composition of capital and the rate of surplus-value; in addition, we examine the effects that relative prices and the demand may exert on the value composition of capital and through that on the rate of profit. We continue the analysis by showing that the fall in the rate of profit affects—and is being affected—by the unproductive expenditures which subdue the investible product and, therefore, weaken the growth potential of the economy leading to recessionary situations such as the one underway. Furthermore, we subject to empirical testing the hypothesis of long cycles in profits and its relation with the level of economic activity; our results and the extremely good fit of our logistic curves lend support to our educated forecasts for the phases of the long-cycle underway and also the beginnings of the new the sixth long cycle. The details of the utilized logistic curves and their applications are also discussed.

---

[2]Especially, when the statistics of unemployment include the discouraged workers together with involuntary part-time employment while the rising number of the long-run unemployed population carries more weight.

10.2   Productive: Unproductive Labour and Activities

The question of productive-unproductive labour is of utmost importance in the classical and Marxian analyses of capital accumulation and economic crises; nevertheless, there is no consensus among followers of this tradition (Foley 1986; Shaikh and Tonak 1994; Duménil and Lévy 2004; Mohun 2014). Hence, we will treat as productive the wage labour which is activated in the sphere of production, where capital hires labour and purchases non-labour inputs in order to produce more value than the value of all the utilized inputs that go into the final product (commodity). By contrast, non-productive labour is activated in the spheres of distribution and social maintenance, and as such it does not change the total output produced (see Chap. 9 for details). Despite disagreements and differences in interpretations among economists in the old classical and Marxian traditions, the prevailing view is that the expansion of non-productive activities interferes with the system's ability to create and accumulate wealth; the larger the share of non-productive activities in the economy, the lower is the remaining investible product and, therefore, the lessening of the growth potential of the economy. Furthermore, the classification of economic activities into productive and unproductive is an absolutely necessary requirement for the meaningful estimation of the classical and Marxian categories of surplus-value, variable capital and the various compositions of capital.[3]

The estimations of the classical variables were based on data provided according to the *Standard Industrial Classification* (SIC) System of 1987.[4] However, the revision of the US industrial classification system from the SIC into the North American Industry Classification System (NAICS) in 1997 has necessitated the reconsideration of the productive and unproductive activities in a manner that suits better to the new and more detailed classification system as is displayed in Table 10.1 below.

The purpose of the revision of the accounting system was to capture the changing structure of the US economy of the recent decades with the emergence of the new (mainly information based) technology and the expansion of the service sector and especially its production activities. This revision resulted in the availability of more detailed data on productive and unproductive activities with respect to the service sector that made possible the more refined classification of industries than those in

---

[3]The reason is that the distinction between production and non-production activities may give rise to substantial differences in the two, classical and official, accounting systems. By way of an example, productivity measured in terms of ONA might be falling, while in classical and Marxian terms it might be rising. The reason is that in the ONA all paid employment is treated as if it were productive; by contrast, in the classical accounts, only the employment in production counts as output-creating and therefore is included in the definition of productivity.

[4]For a detailed presentation of the transformation of the official categories of national accounts into classical and Marxian categories, see the pioneering studies of Gillman (1957) and Mage (1963) and of course the classical by now work of Shaikh and Tonak (1994). For updated estimates of these variables for the US economy, see Paitaridis and Tsoulfidis (2012a), while for the Greek economy, see Tsoulfidis and Tsaliki (2014).

Table 10.1 Classification of sectors

Production activities	Non-production activities	
Farms	Trade	Wholesale trade
Forestry, fishing, and related activities		Retail trade
Mining		Real estate
Utilities		Rental and leasing services and lessors of intangible assets
Construction	Royalties	Federal reserve banks, credit intermediation and related activities
Manufacturing		Securities, commodity contracts and investments
Transportation and warehousing		Insurance carriers and related activities
Information		Funds, trusts and other financial vehicles
Computer systems design and related services		Legal services
Educational services		Miscellaneous professional, scientific and technical services
Healthcare and social assistance		Management of companies and enterprises
Arts, entertainment and recreation		Administrative and support services
Accommodation and food services		Waste management and remediation services
Other services, except government		Federal general government (defence)
Government enterprises (federal)		Federal general government (nondefense)
Government enterprises (state and local)		State and local general government

Source: Tsoulfidis and Paitaridis (2018)

the previous system.[5] With the NAICS industry detail, there is no doubt that the estimations of the categories of surplus-value, compositions of capital, net profits, wages and employment of workers in production and finally of gross capital stock are more accurate and therefore more reliable than those of the past studies.[6] At this point, it is important to emphasize that, in the context of empirical research, there will always be slippery issues that cloud the a priori and uncontroversial definition of the character of labour activity as to what extent is involved in production or not. But the challenges in empirical research should not discourage the efforts to using and analysing this fundamental category of the classical political economy approach (Foley 1986; Shaikh and Tonak 1994).

---

[5]For instance, Moseley (1991) assumed that one-half of the nonsupervisory employment in the trade sector is productive; of course, since more detailed data are now available, we need not recourse to such heroic assumptions.

[6]In our estimations, we follow the method suggested by Shaikh (2016) who applied it to the US corporate sector and also Malikane (2017) for the South African economy; hence, our estimates refer to the total US economy.

10.3   Compositions of Capital and the US Economy

As we discussed in Chap. 8, the various compositions of capital became the focus of analysis and debate during the 1970s and 1980s (e.g. Rosdolsky 1977; Shaikh 1987 and the literature cited there). The reason is that the definitions of these variables are complex as they are cast in terms of labour values and then one needs to hypothesize monetary expressions of labour values and subsequently compare these figures with their national income counterparts. In what follows, we define the technical, value, organic and the materialized compositions of capital[7] in terms of market prices and the ONA, holding though the concepts of production and non-production activities and related distinctions of employment. Starting with the value composition of capital (VCC), this can be written as follows:

$$\text{VCC} = \frac{p_k}{p_y} \frac{K}{wl_p} \tag{10.1}$$

where $p_k K$ is the (gross) capital stock in constant prices; hence we have a product of the price index, p_k, multiplied by the quantity of capital, K, expressed in constant prices. Similarly, $p_y wl_p$ is the nominal wage, that is, the product of the business value-added deflator, p_y, times the real product wage, w, times the number of employees in the production activities, l_p. We use the real product wage, that is, the money wage divided by the business value-added deflator in order to estimate the cost of labour from the point of view of businesses; by contrast, the use of the consumers price index would give us the workers' standard of living, which is not what businesses are really interested in.

The next variable of interest which is contained in the VCC is the so-called materialized composition of capital, MCC, which Shaikh (1987) defined as the ratio of nominal capital stock over CNA value-added in terms of current prices, $p_y y$, where y is the real value-added; that is, the MCC is the capital-output ratio and is estimated from

$$\text{MCC} = \frac{p_k}{p_y} \frac{K}{y} \tag{10.2}$$

Hence, an old empirical issue comes to the fore; that is, whether and too what extent the MCC (or the capital-output ratio) is rising as a result of capital-using and labour-saving technological progress. As shown in Fig. 10.1, the nominal capital-

---

[7]Ideally, these variables must be in terms of labour values; however, such time series estimates are extremely difficult to carry out for a single year, let alone for a long period of time such as in the study at hand. However, a stylized fact of the hitherto research has shown that the labour values and market prices are startlingly close to each other (see Chap. 4), and, therefore, our estimates of variables of interest in terms of market prices are not expected to differ in any empirically significant way from their labour value counterparts (Shaikh 1998; Tsoulfidis 2008, 2010, inter alia).

Fig. 10.1 Gross capital-net value-added ratio or MCC, USA, 1948–2016 (For the period 1948–1963, we utilize data of the CNA value-added (ISIC) which come from Shaikh and Tonak (1994), while our estimates on gross capital stock are for the period 1948–2017. The CNA value-added is from the NAICS revised and extended data in Tsoulfidis and Paitaridis (2018))

output ratio displays long fluctuations around a rising trend; from the early 1980s and the full decade of the 1990s, the nominal capital-output ratio is nearly trendless indicating that the growth in output is approximately equal to the growth in capital stock; and from the late 1990s onwards, the nominal capital-output ratio displays a rising trend up until the year 2009.[8]

As the capital-output ratio becomes ever more important in the movement of the rate of profit, we discover that the official estimates of this ratio become less and less reliable probably because of the built-in neoclassical conceptualization of the movement of this ratio. More specifically, in the neoclassical theory, the capital-output ratio is expected to be a mean-reverting variable. The reason is that if this ratio increases, it follows that capital is cheap (abundant) and labour is expensive (scarce); the extensive use of capital and the saving of labour will make capital scarcer than labour; and the capital-output ratio will start its falling pattern. Thus, the neoclassical theory expects a mildly cyclical and an approximately trendless capital-output ratio. The estimates of the capital stock by the Bureau of Economic Analysis (BEA) seem to bear this out to a certain extent. In fact, our estimates of the net capital-output ratio of the USA, based on data from the BEA for the year 1964, gave a net capital-output ratio of 2.70, while for the year 2016, this ratio increases to 3.03. Very similar are the estimates that one derives from the measurement of the real capital-output ratio by

---

[8]The estimates of the period 1948–1989 are from Shaikh and Tonak (1994), whereas those of 1964–2017 are revised and updated estimates from Tsoulfidis and Paitaridis (2018).

the EU's AMECO database.[9] Clearly, there is something mysterious in the estimates of the real capital-output data, and we daresay that the measurement of this ratio is ideologically ridden.[10] This is the reason why we opted for an alternative estimation of the capital-output ratio based on gross capital stock (Fig. 10.1) whose rationale and details of its construction are discussed in Tsoulfidis and Paitaridis (2018).

Clearly, both the VCC and MCC depend on the technical composition, TC, that is, the real capital-productive labour ratio, K/l_p, but also on the relative prices, p_k/p_y, along with the distributional factors of wages and profits. The crucial determinant of both is expected to be the TC since the two prices are not expected to be too far from each other and in the long run, their ratio is expected to be near to 1.[11] The idea is that a rising TC induces similar changes in the unit prices of the means of production and the means of consumption, because the two prices refer to general categories of commodities, which on the one hand may overlap, while on the other, it is in the nature of technological change not to be confined to any single industry or collection of industries but rather to rapidly diffuse throughout the economy.[12] The connecting link between the VCC and the MCC is the rate of surplus-value, $e = \frac{s}{p_y w l_p}$, where $s = p_y y - p_y w l_p$. Hence, equation (10.1) can be written as

$$\text{VCC} = \frac{p_k}{p_y} \frac{K}{y} \frac{p_y y}{p_y w l_p} = \frac{p_k K}{p_y y} \left(\frac{p_y w l_p + s}{p_y w l_p} \right) = \frac{p_k K}{p_y y} (1 + e) \qquad (10.3)$$

If the MCC or, what is the same thing, the capital-output ratio in current prices, as shown in Fig. 10.1, is rising, then the VCC will be higher than the MCC.[13] Furthermore, the VCC in the long run is expected to converge to the organic composition of capital, OCC, in so far as the relative price of capital, p_k/p_y, tends to one. By combining equations (10.1), (10.2) and (10.3), we derive the following relations between the various compositions of capital

---

[9]In EU's AMECO database (http://ec.europa.eu/economy_finance/ameco/user/serie/SelectSerie. cfm.), we observe, in most cases, trendless capital-output ratios. In the AMECO database, all countries are assumed to start off with the same real capital-output ratio which is equal to 3 in 1960. However, a few countries among which Greece and also Spain, two Great Recession-ridden countries, display in 2016 a real capital-output ratio substantially higher than its starting value, namely, 4.24 and 3.55, respectively.

[10]For further discussions on capital-output ratio of the US economy and its evolution since the nineteenth century, see Mejorado and Roman (2014, Chap. 7).

[11]The theoretical expectation but also the empirical findings on price-value deviations suggest that the more aggregated the input-output tables, the closer the labour values to market prices. This is an empirical regularity ascertained in a number of studies (Tsoulfidis 2010, and the literature cited there).

[12]See also Mage (1963, pp. 82–83).

[13]The equality between the two holds only in the hypothetical case that the total wages are equal to total net value-added.

$$\underbrace{\frac{p_k\,K}{p_y\,y}}_{\text{MCC}} \le \underbrace{\frac{p_k}{p_y}\frac{K}{wl_p}}_{\substack{\text{VCC} \approx \text{OCC} \\ \text{iff}\;\frac{p_k}{p_y} \approx 1}} \le \frac{K}{l_p} \qquad (10.4)$$

The availability of data allows us to estimate the VCC for a long enough time period of 53 years, 1964–2017 starting from 1964, a year near the end of a rising phase known as the 'golden age of accumulation'. The time period under scrutiny includes the 'stagflation crisis' of the 1970s and early mid-1980s which was followed by the period of neoliberalism of steady but moderate high growth rate, known as the 'new economy'. The latter was interrupted by the end of year 2007 which is the starting year of what has been characterized by orthodox and heterodox economists alike as the onset of the Great Recession whose impact extends up to the year 2017, the last year that we managed to collate reliable data (Fig. 10.2).[14]

The average annual growth rate of the VCC during the period 1964–2017 is estimated at 1.53%. Meanwhile, the MCC grows, albeit with long fluctuations, over

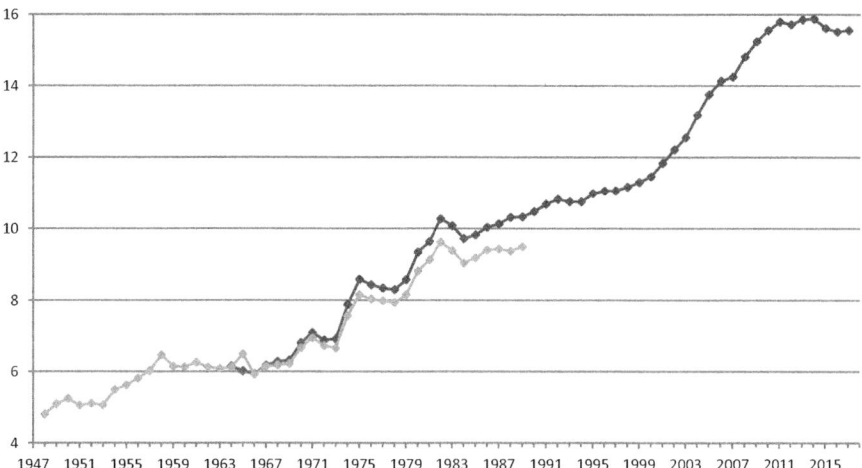

Fig. 10.2 Value composition of capital, USA, 1948–2017

---

[14]Our estimates are on gross capital stock data for the total US economy for the 1948–2017.The rationale of the utilization of gross (instead of the available from the BEA net) capital stock data as well as of the estimating method is discussed in Tsoulfidis and Paitaridis (2018). The estimates of gross capital stock are based on updated estimates from the same source, while the estimates of variable capital are from Shaikh and Tonak (1994) which start from the year 1948 and extend until 1989, the last year of their analysis. We observe that in the two data series, there are no significant differences in the estimates for the common time period, something that encourages us to link the two time series to a hypothetical single one spanning the whole post-war period.

the years at an average annual rate of 0.99%. From Figs. 10.1 and 10.2, we observe that during the period 1999–2009, the growth rates of both MCC and VCC accelerate and become negative the year after. Hence, the Marxian hypothesis of increasing composition of capital is confirmed in the case of the US economy.

10.3.1   A Growth Accounting Framework for the VCC

To what extent, if any, the rising trend in the nominal capital-output ratio (or MCC) is responsible for the rising VCC is a question that can be dealt with by breaking down the growth rate of the VCC into its four constituent components or factors, namely, the price, technological, demand and distributional effects (see also Equation (8.5) and the discussion there). The results of the growth accounting exercise conducted by Tsoulfidis (2017) on the basis of net capital stock showed that both the distributional and the technical factors are major determinants of the evolution of the VCC, and between the two, the technical factor, that is, the capital-output ratio in constant prices, was somewhat more influential. We repeat the growth accounting exercise using a longer time span and data for the gross capital stock of the total economy and also adjust them by the degree of capacity utilization.[15]

The breakdown of the VCC evaluated in market prices can be shown starting with the definition of the adjusted for capacity utilization, u, value composition of capital, AVCC, which will be

$$\text{AVCC} = \underbrace{\left[\frac{p_k K}{p_y y}\right]}_{\text{MCC}} u \underbrace{\left(\frac{p_y y}{p_y w l_p}\right)}_{1+e} \tag{10.5}$$

The bracketed term in relation (10.5) includes the components of the MCC, whereas the term in the parenthesis is the ratio of value-added to the variable capital or the term $1 + e$, with e the rate of surplus-value. By taking growth rates in equation (10.5), we can attribute the growth rate of the AVCC into its constituent components

---

[15]For the estimation of the gross capital stock of the total US economy, we extend the method employed by Shaikh (2016, Appendix 6.5) for the US corporate sector and apply it to the total economy. The capacity utilization estimates for the period 1967–2017 are derived by the annual averages of monthly data of the total industrial sector that are reported by Federal Reserve Bank (https://www.federalreserve.gov/releases/g17/ipdisk/utl_sa.txt). For the years 1964–1966 and due to the lack of data for the total industry, we used the annual average capacity utilization rates of the total manufacturing sector whose changes overtime are similar to those of total industry (Mattey 1996). Finally, we used data on nonresidential investment and net business value-added price indices from the BEA (https://www.bea.gov/) with 2012 as the base year.

(as in equation (8.5)) and assess their relative contribution to the overall growth of the AVCC. Thus, we have

$$
\underbrace{\widehat{\left(\frac{K}{w}\right)}} = \underbrace{\widehat{\left(\frac{p_k}{p_y}\right)}}_{\text{Price Effect}} + \underbrace{\widehat{\left(\frac{K}{y}\right)}}_{\substack{\text{Technology} \\ \text{Effect}}} + \underbrace{\hat{u}}_{\substack{\text{Demand} \\ \text{Effect}}} + \underbrace{\widehat{\left(\frac{p_y y}{p_y w l_p}\right)}}_{\substack{\text{Distribution} \\ \text{Effect}}} \tag{10.6}
$$

where a hat over a variable or a term indicates its annual average growth rate. It is important to stress at this point that the distribution effect can be further broken down into

$$
\widehat{\left(\frac{y}{l_p}\frac{1}{w}\right)} = \widehat{\left(\frac{y}{l_p}\right)} - \hat{w}
$$

that is, the growth rate of productivity minus the growth rate of the real wage rate. The growth of the AVCC, therefore, reflects not only the changes in the material features of the production process but also the induced changes in the structure of prices (relative prices) and income distribution as well as the strength of demand relative to supply as this is reflected in the degree of capacity utilization. The effects of each and every one of the terms in equation (10.6) along with the components of the distributional factor, for meaningfully selected periods of time, for the US economy are displayed in Table 10.2 below.

We start off with the two long periods 1964–1982 and 1983–2007: the first, a recessionary one at least from 1966 onwards during which the US economy experienced the so-called stagflation crisis and the second (moderately) expansionary one during which the US economy experienced steady growth rates; this particular phase came to be known as 'the new economy' or 'neoliberal growth'. The underlying idea here is to examine to what extent, if any, these two long periods of different phases of economic activity work in a way that their net effect leads to an overall rising AVCC. In examining each of these two successive phases, we observe that:

- In the 'stagflation crisis' of 1964–1982, the growth rate of the AVCC is 2.01%, a result attributed mainly to the technical change effect amounting to 2.24%, an all periods high. The effect of the distributional factor was positive but minimal amounting to the anaemic 0.33%, which is another way to say that during a recessionary period, real wages were growing at the rate of 0.88% and in so doing kept up with the growth rate in productivity, equal to 1.21%. The price effect was 0.29% reflecting the lack of devaluation of the gross fixed capital stock, as this can be estimated by the difference in the growth rates of the investment deflator minus the value-added deflator. Not surprisingly, in a recessionary period, the demand effect was negative, and its impact is estimated at −0.84%.
- By contrast, in the 1983–2007 period of the so-called new economy or sometimes called 'dot-com economy', the annual growth rate of AVCC of 1.76% continues

Table 10.2 Growth accounting of the AVCC, US economy (annual rates)

Periods	Growth rates						
	Adjusted value Composition of capital $(1) = (2) + (3) + (4) + (5)$	Relative price factor effect (2)	Technical change factor effect (3)	Demand factor effect (4)	Total distributional factor effect $(5) = (6)–(7)$	Productivity effect (6)	Real wage effect (7)
1964–1982	2.01	0.29	2.24	−0.84	0.33	1.21	0.88
1983–2007	1.76	−1.14	1.30	0.31	1.28	1.66	0.38
2008–2017	0.31	−1.04	0.93	−0.24	0.66	0.98	0.32
1964–2017	1.53	−0.69	1.65	−0.22	0.80	1.36	0.57

to be attributed, in large part, to the growth of the technical change factor of 1.30% while the demand factor (0.31%), although positive, nevertheless not strong enough as one would have expected for a growing economy. The price effect, however, is found negative and equal to -1.14% indicating that the information technologies that were massively introduced during these years impacted more on the devaluation of capital rather than to the output produced. It is worth pointing out the growth of the distributional factor, amounting to 1.28%, which is an all periods high; however, on further examination, we conclude that the growth of the distributional factor is due to the application of neoliberal austerity policies that kept the growth rate in real wages far too low (0.38%) for an economy in its expansion phase which in combination with the rapidly growing productivity equal to 1.66%, an all periods high, led to a sharply increased rate of surplus-value and the distributive factor. The contribution of the latter to the growth of the AVCC, although extremely high, nevertheless remains lower than that of the technical change factor, whose impact is always the highest.

For the period of the great recession which starts for the US economy from the year 2008 and continues as of this writing, we observe that the AVCC displays the all periods low growth rate of 0.31% which is attributed to the sluggish growth of the technical change factor (0.93%) the lowest of all periods. There is a negative relative price effect of -1.04%, while the demand effect is also negative and equal to -0.24%; the positive but weak distributional effect, the result of low growth rates in productivity of 0.98% and in real wages of 0.32%, the lowest in all periods, shaped the observed stationarity in the growth of the AVCC. These results strengthen the view that the Great Recession is not yet over and it is reasonable to expect that will continue as long as there has not been any significant devaluation of the capital stock such that to restore profitability at a sufficiently high level and rising trend. The examination of the whole 1964–2017 period completes the picture in which what stands out is the rising AVCC at the annual growth rate of 1.53% which is attributed mainly to the technical change effect of 1.65% with the distributional factor contributing only by 0.80%, while the effects of the other factors are negative and by far smaller.

It is interesting to note that our results do not change qualitatively in case we use the data on net capital stock provided by the BEA as the figures in Table 10.3 below show.

From Table 10.3, we observe that the technical change factor effect gets weaker, and although the distributional effect becomes more influential, by no means, its overall influence exceeds that of the technical change factor effect. The latter remains dominant in all periods with the exception of the 'neoliberal growth' (1983–2007) during which the rising rate of surplus-value was the result of a rising productivity of labour and depression of real wages. In general, the growth in the technical change factor during the examined 1964–1982 period as well as the Great Recession of the post-2007 years together with the negative growth in the rate of capacity utilization. Furthermore, the growth rate of the prices of capital goods was lower than that of the value-added deflator to a relatively slow growth in the VCC and MCC during the 'stagflation crisis' and the Great Recession periods. The

Table 10.3 Growth accounting of the AVCC, US economy (net capital stock)

Periods	Growth rates						
	Adjusted value Composition of capital (1) = (2) + (3) + (4) + (5)	Relative price factor effect (2)	Technical change factor effect (3)	Demand factor effect (4)	Total distributional factor effect (5) = (6)–(7)	Productivity effect (6)	Real wage effect (7)
1964–1982	1.63	0.29	1.86	−0.84	0.33	1.21	0.88
1983–2007	1.30	−1.14	0.84	0.31	1.28	1.66	0.38
2008–2016	−0.15	−1.04	0.47	−0.24	0.66	0.98	0.32
1964–2017	1.10	−0.69	1.21	−0.22	0.80	1.36	0.57

devaluation of capital was manifested in that the growth rates of the price index of capital goods was lagging behind the value-added deflator.

Hence, the Marxian hypothesis of the effect of technical change on the value composition of capital is confirmed in the case of the US economy. There has been discussion that the MCC is rather constant over the long run (Zarembka 2015, 2019) and that the rising value composition of capital is due exclusively to the rising rate of surplus-value. The logical conclusion of this view is that there is no falling rate of profit, or if there is this is due entirely to the movement in the rate of surplus-value. Our detailed growth accounting exercise, however, suggests that the technical factor effect measured by the capital-output ratio in constant prices exerts most of the influence on the value composition of capital.

10.4   The Rate of Profit and Its Elasticities

The next step in our analysis is to examine the impact of the technological and distributional variables on the movement of gross or general rate of profit. For this purpose, we express the gross rate of profit $r = s/C$ in terms of the nominal capital-output ratio or what is the same thing in Marxian terms of the MCC. In addition, we place limits to the variation of the rate of surplus-value, $e = s/(p_y w l_p)$, according to the total labour time l, with $l = p_y y = s + w_p$. Thus, we may write

$$r = \frac{p_y y - p_y w l_p}{p_k K} = \left(\frac{s}{s + p_y w l_p}\right)\left(\frac{p_y y}{p_k K}\right) = \left(\frac{e}{1+e}\right)\left(\frac{1}{\text{MCC}}\right) \qquad (10.7)$$

The expectation is that in the long run, both e and MCC will be rising, but the increase in e, although it may be higher than that of MCC, will have a positive but progressively diminishing effect on the rate of profit. The reason is that the potential increase in the profit share, $e/(1 + e)$, will be, at most, equal to 1 (Tsoulfidis 2017 inter alia), while the MCC increases without limits and supersedes, in general, the increase in e.

We can show the limited effect of the rate of surplus-value on the rate of profit by taking the partial derivative of the rate of profit of relation (10.7) with respect to (w.r. t.) e, and then by multiplying the resulting outcome by e/r, we arrive at the following elasticity formula:

$$\frac{\partial r}{\partial e}\frac{e}{r} = \frac{1}{(1+e)^2 \text{MCC}}\frac{e}{r} = \frac{1}{(1+e)^2 \text{MCC}}\frac{e}{\frac{e}{(1+e)}\frac{1}{\text{MCC}}} = \frac{1}{1+e} \qquad (10.8)$$

Hence, the elasticity of the rate of profit w.r.t. the rate of surplus-value, e, equals to $1/(1 + e)$, which is in fact the wage share. Clearly, the higher the rate of surplus-value, other things equal, the lower the wage share; or what amounts to the same, the lower the elasticity of the rate of profit w.r.t. the rate of surplus-value. As a consequence, in the hypothetical case that wages tend to zero, the elasticity of the rate of profit w.r.t. the rate of surplus-value becomes absolutely inelastic.

Alternatively, we could rewrite the relation (10.8) in Keynesian terms; that is, instead of the share of surplus-value in value-added, we estimate the gross rate of profit using the wage share, ω. We have

$$r = (1 - \omega)\left(\frac{p_y}{p_k}\right)\left(\frac{y}{K}\right) \qquad (10.9)$$

with a very similar interpretation. The elasticity of the rate of profit w.r.t. the wage share will be

$$\frac{\partial r}{\partial \omega}\frac{\omega}{r} = -\left(\frac{p_y}{p_k}\right)\left(\frac{y}{K}\right)\left(\frac{\omega}{(1-\omega)\left(\frac{p_y}{p_k}\right)\left(\frac{y}{K}\right)}\right) = -\frac{\omega}{1-\omega} = -e^{-1} \qquad (10.10)$$

The relation (10.10) signifies, on the one hand, the expected inverse relationship and, on the other hand, that a rising rate of surplus-value above 100% gives rise to an elasticity of the rate of profit w.r.t. the wage share less than 1 in absolute value. Theoretically speaking this particular elasticity decreases without bound, that is, it becomes absolutely elastic (minus infinite) in the hypothetical case that wages are at maximum and profits (or surplus-value in Marxian terms) tend to zero. Hence, the elasticity of the rate of profit w.r.t. the wage share takes on the value of zero, that is, it becomes absolutely inelastic in the hypothetical case when profits are at maximum and wages tend to zero.

In similar fashion with the relation (10.8), the zero or upper bound of the relation (10.10) shows that the wage (share) reductions in the effort to increase the profit rate, a promising measure taken by austerity policy programmes, become less and less efficient as this particular elasticity approaches its upper inelastic bound. By way of a realistic example, in year 2017 the rate of surplus-value is equal to 385.6%, and the elasticity of the rate of profit w.r.t. the wage share is equal to $-1/3.856 = -0.259$ indicating the limiting effect of wage reductions on the rate of profit.

As for the other important variable in the evolution of the rate of profit, that is, the capital deepening or technological factor, K/y, Marx argues that it tends to push the gross rate of profit down in the long run. Consequently, the whole discussion about the movement of the rate of the gross rate of profit boils down about the movement of K/y. Taking the elasticity of the rate of profit w.r.t. the technological factor, K/y, we may write

$$\frac{\partial r}{\partial (K/y)}\frac{(K/y)}{r} = -(1-\omega)\left(\frac{p_y}{p_k}\right)\frac{1}{\left(\frac{K}{y}\right)^2}\frac{\frac{K}{y}}{(1-\omega)\left(\frac{p_y}{p_k}\right)\left(\frac{1}{\frac{K}{y}}\right)} = -1, \qquad (10.11)$$

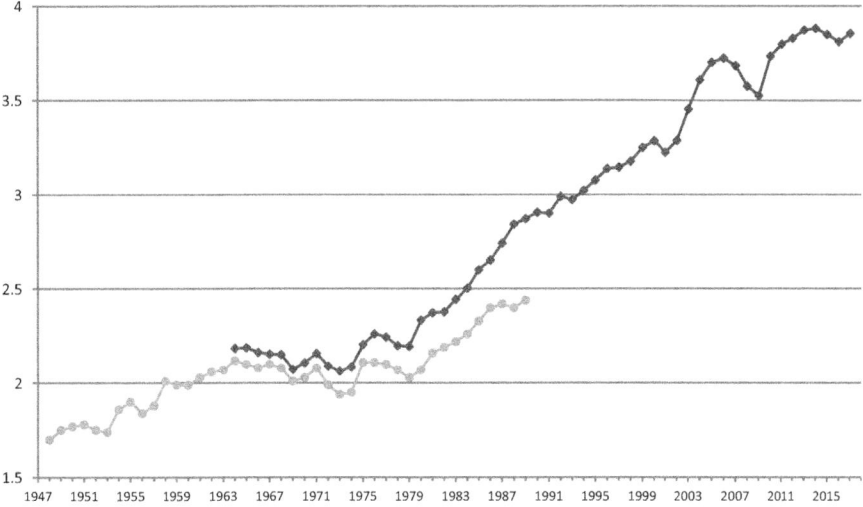

Fig. 10.3 The rate of surplus-values in the US economy, 1948–2017

that is, the elasticity of the rate of profit w.r.t. the technological factor, K/y, is unitary negative meaning that if the capital-intensity changes, say by 1%, all else constant, the rate of profit will also change by 1%, but in the opposite direction. In similar fashion, as the prices p_y and p_k are expected in the long run, at least, to give a ratio equal to one, it follows that the two elasticities of the rate of profit w.r.t. p_y and p_k will be equal to plus and minus one, respectively. As a consequence, the net effect of relative prices on the rate of profit either will tend to cancel each other out and so their joint effect will be negligible.

Figure 10.3 shows the evolution of the rate of surplus-value in the US economy. We place together two rates of surplus-value, one is based on revised and updated estimates from Tsoulfidis and Paitaridis (2018) and the second for the period 1948–1989 from Shaikh and Tonak (1994).

We observe that the rate of surplus-value in the US economy displays a rising trend; the average rate of surplus-value in the period 1948–1964 is 191%, while for the stagflation period 1965–1982, it increased to 207% (Shaikh and Tonak 1994). The estimates by Tsoulfidis and Paitaridis (2018) find the average rate of surplus-value in the 1965–1982 period at 219% which during the neoliberal period (1983–2007) increased to 309% while in the years of the Great Recession rose to the level of 377%.

Figure 10.4 shows the evolution of the rate of profit in the US economy. We place together the net average rate of profit (right-hand side) and the maximum rate of profit (left-hand side) both based on revised and updated estimates of profits and gross capital stock based on Tsoulfidis and Paitaridis (2018) spanning the period 1948–2017.

In Fig. 10.4, we observe that the rate of profit displays an overall falling trend. Based on the relations and elasticities discussed above, it follows that an increase in

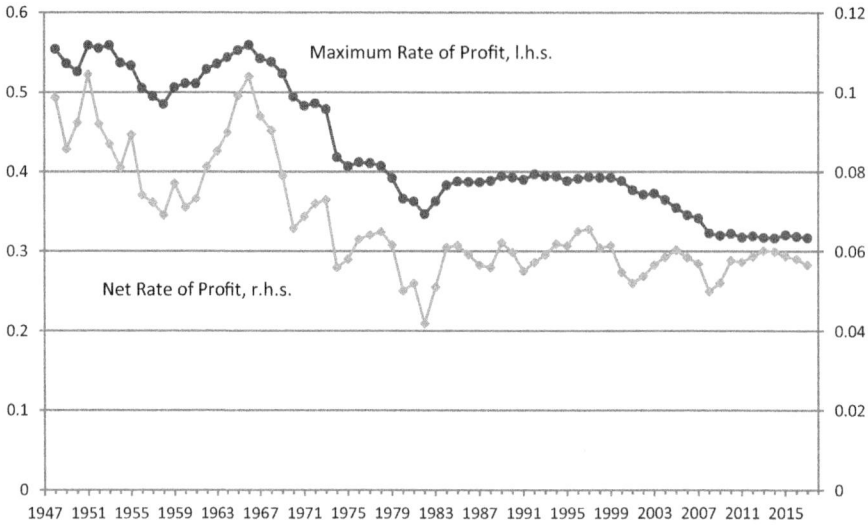

Fig. 10.4 The rate of profit in the US Economy 1946–2017

the capital-intensity by 1% requires, other things constant, a nearly fivefold increase in the rate of surplus-value to maintain the rate of profit at the same level. In other words, the movement of the capital-intensity is decisive in the actual movement of the rate of profit and that the effect of the rate of surplus-value weakens with the passage of time making even more inelastic the rate of profit with respect to changes in the rate of surplus-value. A corollary of this discussion has important policy implications since it shows that the wage reductions through austerity economic policy efforts in order to increase the rate of surplus-value are not so effective in restoring profitability in the long run. In contrast, the policy agenda in restoring profitability might include, for instance, the devaluation of capital through innovations and, in general, technological change.

10.5   Is the Falling Rate of Profit Indeed Falling?

In what follows, we connect the present analysis with the discussion in Chap. 8 by examining to what extent, if any, the falling rate of profit may lead to a stagnant mass of profits and then to a crisis. As we can see in Fig. 10.4, the net average rate of profit up to the year 1965 moves at high levels and upwards affirming the golden age of accumulation and reaches its trough in the year 1982 in the 'stagflation crisis', and from that year onwards, it displays an upward trend demarcating the period of neoliberalism whose vitality was maintained up until the year 2007 with the onset of the Great Recession. The above described evolution is true for both the net rate of profit measured on the left-hand side (l.h.s.) axis and the maximum rate of profit shown on the r.h.s. axis with the latter attaining its global minimum in 2009. In general, we may argue that the relatively low level of the rate of profit during the neoliberal period renders the USA a crisis-prone economy as this can also be judged by the relatively low GDP growth rates (see Fig. 8.2 and 10.5, below) which display a falling long-term tendency over the whole trajectory of US capitalism becoming much more pronounced during the post-WWII period.

10.5.1   Secular Stagnation or Secularly Falling Rate of Profit?

For the downward trend in the growth rate of the US GDP, over the years, various explanations have been put forward. Starting from the very simple according to which the growth rate during the Great Depression was low but accelerated because of the war preparations, the WWII and the Keynesian policies that followed the first decades of the post-war era which increased demand and stimulated the propensity to innovate; the combination of all these was translated into exceptionally high growth rates of the real GDP during the upward part of the fourth long cycle. The same pattern has been identified in the world GDP growth rates as well as in particular countries (Japan, Germany, Italy and Greece among others), all of which experienced their own country-specific economic miracle. There are other views such as that of R.J. Gordon (2012) arguing that during that particular period and even in the earlier ones, the new innovations had a particularly high productivity effect which, however, declined over the years. And so the growth rates of the fifth long cycle fall short of those of the fourth, and also the observed growth rates were stimulated by both low interest rates and depressed real wages.

In the recent years, we are witnessing a resurrection of an old explanation of the sluggish growth rates of the 1930s known as 'secular stagnation'. Authors like Summers (2014 and 2015) and Krugman (2014) claim that the declining population growth rate and the ageing of population in combination with the rising income and wealth inequalities give rise to high saving rates and low consumption expenditures and therefore lower aggregate demand. The rising savings because of the aged population keep interest rates low, and the economy falls into the so-called liquidity trap in that the interest rates are low enough to become amenable to further reductions in the effort to stimulate economic expansion.[16] Our findings confirm the claims made by the new secular stagnation approach, but our characteristic difference is that we place the secular stagnation in a long cycle perspective where the movement of the rate of profit is essentially behind the long-lasting periods of growth and stagnation. Furthermore, our findings of a far lower rate of profit during the so-called neoliberal period as compared to the past are absolutely consistent with

---

[16]For a critical evaluation of the old and new secular stagnation theses, see Mejorado and Roman (2014, 2017).

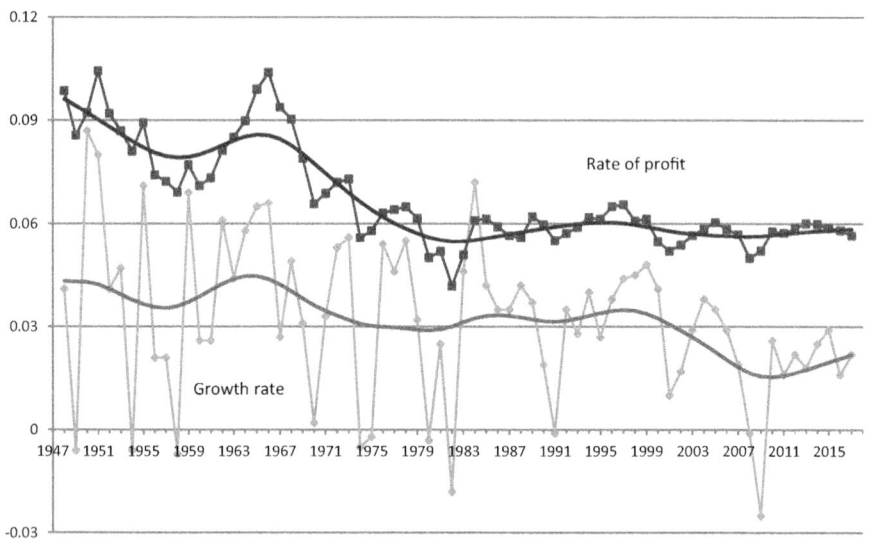

Fig. 10.5   Growth rate of GDP vs. the net rate of profit, USA, 1964–2016

the low level of the interest rate as well as with the withholding of investment and the widespread uncertainty characterizing the current period.

Within the classical political economy approach, the secular fall in the rate of profit may explicate that the long-lasting stagnation is only a (transitory) phase of the economy along its long wave-like expansions and contractions. In Fig. 10.5, we display our estimates of the rate of profit, r, from the year 1964 onwards and the growth rate of GDP in constant 2012 prices, g, along with their respective trends derived through the application of Hodrick-Prescott filtering process.

Clearly, the trends display pretty much similar patterns indicating on the one hand their strong interconnection as one could expect from our discussion in Chap. 8; on the other hand, one could identify the two long cycles of the post-war US economy and the associated with each cycle phase changes. We could further argue that the ratio of these two variables forms an indicator of the particular phase of the economy. In fact, as the ratio of the two variables, r/g, increases, the economy contracts, and when the profit growth rate ratio decreases, the economy finds itself on its expansionary path. In effect, the rate of profit over the growth rate of the real GDP over the period 1948–1965 is equal to 2.06[17]; the ratio increases to 2.22 during the stagflation crisis of 1966–1982, and for the neoliberal period of expansion (1983–2007), the ratio dropped to 1.72. Finally, during the Great Recession, that is, the 2008–2017 period, the ratio increased to 3.85, the highest ever in the post-war period. These results lend additional support to the view that the evolution of the rate

---

[17]We speculate that the ratio would be much lower had unproductive expenditures not increased to slow down the growth rate. This, in our view, is a very interesting hypothesis worth pursuing further.

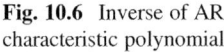

Fig. 10.6 Inverse of AR characteristic polynomial

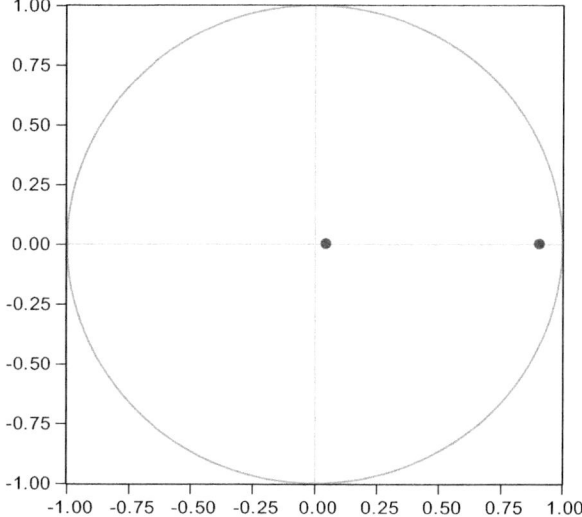

of profit is what stands behind the long-run movement of the economy's growth rate of the real GDP. Moreover, the current Great Recession seems that it did not run its full course, an issue whose details we examine in the next section.

10.5.2   The Econometrics of the Profit: Growth Rate Relationship

These preliminary findings encourage the specification of a VAR model with the rate of profit and the growth rate of the US economy.[18] Judging by the distribution of eigenvalues of our bivariate VAR model, we observe in Fig. 10.6 that both lie inside the unit circle indicating the stability of our simple bivariate model.

Since our VAR model is well specified (as justified by the distribution of eigenvalues) and the variables at hand are integrated of order one (the rate of profit after the application of a battery of tests was found nonstationary with a unit root) and zero (the growth rate in cross-checking unit root tests was found stationary), the appropriate method to test the presence of a possible causal relationship among them is the Toda-Yamamoto (TY) causality test. In addition, the TY test will help us to spot where the causality comes from and, in so doing, to test empirically the usual

---

[18]In the study by Tsoulfidis et al. (2019), the rate of profit is definitely an I(1) variable; the same is not true for the growth rate of output which does not pass all the tests to be considered an I (1) variable.

Table 10.4 Pairwise Granger causality tests, with two lags, USA, 1948–2017

VAR Granger causality/block exogeneity Wald tests			
Excluded	Chi-sq	Df	Prob.
Dependent variable: r			
g	8.21	1	0.004
All	8.21	1	0.004
Dependent variable: g			
r	6.57	1	0.01
All	6.57	1	0.01

post-Keynesian hypothesis, whether the growth rate is responsible for the movement of the rate of profit and not the other way around. The results of the TY causality test are reported in Table 10.4 and suggest that the null hypothesis according to which the growth rate does not Granger cause the rate of profit is rejected; and the same is true for the rate of profit. Thus, we conclude the bidirectional causality between the two variables.

The simple TY Granger causality results encourage the use of an autoregressive distributed lag (ARDL) model in which we include only the two variables precisely because we want to test in a pure and straightforward way the strength of the dependence of the growth rate on the rate of profit. For the application of the ARDL model, we need to ensure that at least one of the two variables is I(1). As we pointed out, the rate of profit after a battery of all possible unit root tests passed them as an I(1). However, we cannot say the same thing with the growth rate of real GDP which was found in most stationarity tests an I(0) variable, a result corroborating, to a certain extent, with the secular stagnation hypothesis. The econometric analysis suggested the ARDL model with one lag in both the growth rate and the rate of profit as the optimal ARDL model whose results along with those of the bound tests are presented in Table 10.5 below.

The bound test results indicate cointegration of the two variables at the 1% level of significance, and furthermore the two variables are directly related. The results with the error correction are presented in Table 10.6 where we observe that the error correction term is statistically significant and equal to -0.767 indicating that any deviations from the equilibrium are restored pretty soon back to the long-run relationship.

The ARDL results displayed in Tables 10.5 and 10.6 further suggest that the short-run effects of the rate of profit are stronger than the long-run effects as this is derived by the short-run coefficient $\Delta r = 3.00 > r = 0.748$. Finally, the ARDL results are robust as this can be judged by the CUSUM and CUSUMSQ tests, displayed on the l.h.s. panel and on the r.h.s. panel of Fig. 10.7, respectively.

In Fig. 10.7, we observe that the plot of the CUSUM test is within the criteria bands, while the CUSUMQ approaches to the lower band in the years of the onset of crisis but soon after returns within the 5% bounds indicating that our model is stable. Hence, once again the classical political economy hypothesis and argument for the

Table 10.5 ARDL(1,1) long run form and bounds test

Variable	Coefficient	Std. Error	t-Statistic	Prob.
Conditional error correction regression				
c	−0.012569	0.008787	−1.430383	0.1574
$g(-1)^*$	−0.767180	0.092121	−8.328005	0.0000
$r(-1)$	0.574090	0.143162	4.010075	0.0002
$\Delta(r)$	3.004309	0.304723	9.859159	0.0000
Levels equation				
Case 2: Restricted constant and no trend				
r	0.748312	0.155983	4.797399	0.0000
c	−0.016383	0.011138	−1.470834	0.1462
EC $= g - (0.8231 \times r - 0.0202)$				
F-bounds test		Null hypothesis: No levels relationship		
Test statistic	Value	Signif.	I(0)	I(1)
F-statistic	23.51461	10%	3.02	3.51
k	1	5%	3.62	4.16
		2.5%	4.18	4.79
		1%	4.94	5.58

*p-value incompatible with t-Bounds distribution

Table 10.6 ARDL error correction model

ECM regression				
Case 2: Restricted constant and no trend				
Variable	Coefficient	Std. Error	t-Statistic	Probability
Δr	3.004309	0.286292	10.49387	0.0000
Coint Eq(−1)	−0.767180	0.089968	−8.527275	0.0000
R-squared	0.780717	Mean dependent var		−0.000275
Adjusted R-squared	0.777444	S.D. dependent var		0.030577
S.E. of regression	0.014425	Akaike info criterion		−5.611174
Sum squared residuals	0.013941	Schwarz criterion		−5.546417
Loglikelihood	195.5855	Hannan-Quinn criterion		−5.585483
Durbin-Watson statistic	2.124655			

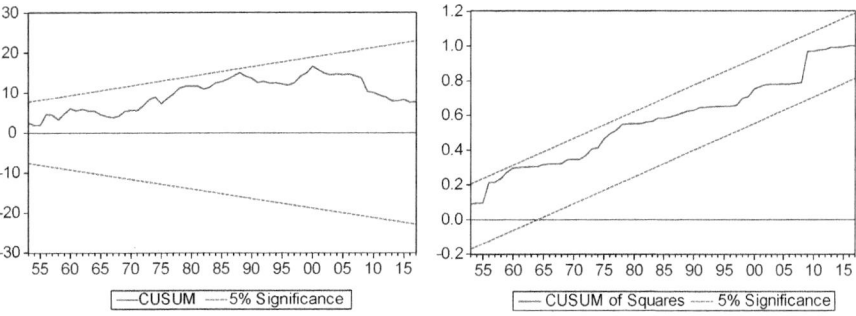

Fig. 10.7 CUSUM and CUSUMSQ tests

centrality of the rate of profit in determining the economy's growth rate finds strong statistical support.

10.5.3   Unproductive Expenditures and Their Underlying Factors

In Chap. 2, where we dealt with issues related to social reproduction and also in Chaps. 8 and 9, we argued that the unproductive expenditures and their expansion or contraction may exert an influence on the rate of growth as they affect the investible product. Although most studies theorize the growth of unproductive expenditures as being detrimental to capital accumulation because they reduce the investible product, and there are discussions about a kind of a 'ratchet effect' of this kind of activities-expenditures, we find that their growth is not without its limits, while the technological change may have an effect on them by 'sending' a large part of the working population in the ranks of unemployed. In Tsoulfidis et al. (2019), it was argued that the growth of unproductive expenditures, u_t, is controlled by a set of variables among which the principal ones are the economy-wide average rate of profit, r_t, the real interest rate, ir_t, and the degree of capacity utilization, cu_t. Hence, in revising and extending the data base by 2 years and restricting ourselves to the absolutely essential variables, we form a VAR model in order to investigate the way in which the growth of unproductive expenditures is influenced by the evolution of the above-mentioned variables.

The employed VAR model displayed the expected well-behaving properties as this can be judged by the associated with it eigenvalues all of which lie inside the unit circle suggesting the stability property of the utilized VAR model (Fig. 10.8).

Fig. 10.8 Inverse of AR characteristic polynomial

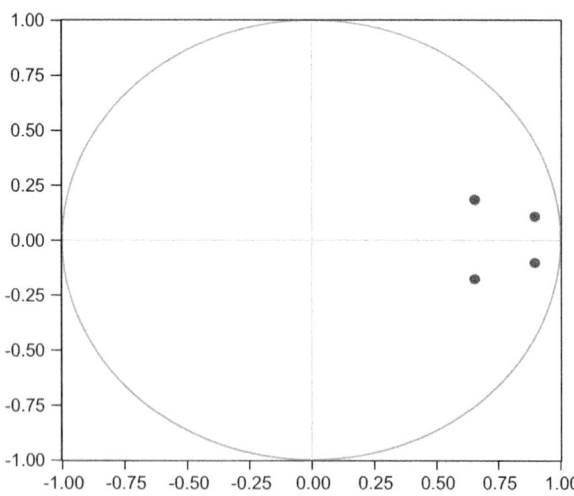

Table 10.7 Results of Toda-Yamamoto Granger non-causality

Excluded	Chi-sq	df	Prob.
Dependent variable: *u*			
r	7.987852	1	0.0047
rir	15.68743	1	0.0001
cu	17.36768	1	0.0000
All	31.16757	3	0.0000
Dependent variable: *r*			
u	2.026643	1	0.1546
rir	0.909684	1	0.3402
cu	11.41717	1	0.0007
All	12.38830	3	0.0062
Dependent variable: *rir*			
u	1.053501	1	0.3047
r	0.038186	1	0.8451
cu	0.053243	1	0.8175
All	4.911833	3	0.1784
Dependent variable: *cu*			
u	0.066830	1	0.7960
r	7.248872	1	0.0071
rir	3.351364	1	0.0671
All	17.06637	3	0.0007

The results prompt the use of the Toda-Yamamoto (TY) Granger causality test with these four variables and relevant data for the US economy spanning the period 1964–2017. The results are displayed in Table 10.7.

The results of Table 10.7 suggest that the rate of profit and real interest rate are statistically significant variables in predicting the movements of unproductive expenditures, as suggested by the estimated through the Wald-test p-value which is lower than the 1% level of significance. When the rate of profit, r, is the dependent variable, the results show that the arrow of causality runs from the capacity utilization to the rate of profit, while unproductive expenditures and the real rate of interest do not seem to play any role. In the third panel, we see that the real rate of interest is not caused by any of the three variables, and in the final panel, we observe that the capacity utilization rate is caused only by the rate of profit and the real interest rate is hardly statistically significant. It is important to stress at this point that our results are based on aggregate unproductive activities and one would wonder what happens to particular unproductive activities and expenditures, such as finance, real estate and trade. In our view this more detailed analysis would be particularly useful.

10.6 Real Net Profits and Long Cycles

Having established the connection between the economy's growth rate to the economy-wide average rate of profit, we now look at the hypothesis that the mass of real net profits of the post-war US economy may follow an S-shaped pattern. To confirm this, we use quarterly data on corporate real profits after taxes, capital consumption allowances and inventory valuation adjustments of the total economy.[19] The use of quarterly data, by offering a sufficiently large number of detailed observations, enables the derivation of more reliable and accurate results for the estimated coefficients and their stability. Moreover, the quarterly data allow us, on the one hand, to evaluate the current predicament and, on the other hand, to provide a reliable basis to make educated speculations about the future stage of the economy. We begin the discussion by splitting the post-war period into two subperiods or rather two long cycles: the first refers to the fourth long cycle for which the data coverage extends from 1947:1 until 1982:4; the second refers to the fifth long cycle starting in 1983:1 and continues till the present (2018:2), the last quarter that the data were available.

From the many forms of logistic curves that we experimented with, we found the following as more suitable to our case:

$$\Pi(t) = A + \frac{K - A}{1 + e^{-(a \cdot t + b)}} \tag{10.12}$$

where $\Pi(t)$ stands for the dependent variable, that is, real net (of taxes and depreciation expenses) corporate profits, t is the time variable, A is the lower asymptote of the non-linear regression, K is the upper asymptote of the logistic curve, a is the growth rate and b is the parameter indicating the precise location of the curve. By differentiating Equation (10.12) with respect to time, we get

$$\Pi(t)' = 0 + \frac{a e^{-(a \cdot t + b)} (K - A)}{\left(1 + e^{-(a \cdot t + b)}\right)^2} \tag{10.13}$$

By definition, a logistic curve has upper and lower asymptotes and no maximum or minimum points; however, it has an inflection point which can be found by setting its second derivative equal to zero. Hence, by taking the second derivative of relation (10.13) and setting it equal to zero, we get

---

[19]The quarterly data of corporate profits are from the Fred (https://fred.stlouisfed.org/) and were accessed on December 21, 2018. These data are deflated by the gross private domestic fixed nonresidential investment deflator index (2012 = 100) also available from the same source.

$$\Pi(t)'' = \frac{a^2 e^{-2(a \cdot t + b)} \left(-e^{a \cdot t + b} + 1\right)(K - A)}{\left(1 + e^{-a \cdot t - b}\right)^3} = 0 \qquad (10.14)$$

we solve for the inflection point of the logistic curve, which occurs at

$$t_m = -b/a$$

Substituting the so-derived t value in relation (10.12), which gives

$$\Pi(t) = A + \frac{K - A}{1 + e^{-\left[a\left(-\frac{b}{a}\right) + b\right]}} = A + \frac{K - A}{1 + e^0} = \frac{K + A}{2} \qquad (10.15)$$

Hence, the midpoint of the path of the logistic fit and the inflection point coincide in the relation (10.15). Elaborating that further, we note that the first derivative $\Pi(t)'$ is the time rate of change or velocity of the logistic function; if the velocity increases, there is a phase of acceleration in the variable, and if the velocity slows down, there is deceleration phase in the variable. The second derivative of the same function, $\Pi(t)''$, refers to the change in the time rate of change, and by setting equal to zero, we find the point of inflection of the mass of net real profit described by the estimated logistic function. Clearly, Equation (10.14) displays a maximum, and at that inflection point, the acceleration phase turns into deceleration one. The coordinates of the inflection point of the logistic curve are the following

$$\left(-\frac{b}{a}, \frac{K + A}{2}\right) \qquad (10.16)$$

Until the attainment of the inflection point, the logistic curve is convex, that is, it is 'looking upward' or in economic terms, its growth rate is accelerating; past this point, the logistic curve becomes concave, that is, it is 'looking downward' meaning that its growth rate is decelerating.

In what follows, using the above analysis, we attempt to define the 'details' of the two long waves in the post-war period for the US economy. Focusing firstly on the period 1947:1–1982:4, we display in Table 10.8 the estimated parameters of the non-linear regression.

Table 10.8 White heteroscedasticity-consistent standard errors and covariance using outer product of gradients

Long cycles	A Lower asymptote	K Upper asymptote	a	b	$t_m = \left(-\frac{b}{a}, \frac{K+A}{2}\right)$ Inflection point	R^2 (%)
1947:1–1982:4	67.2 (12.3)	227.9 (32.4)	0.0506 (6.73)	−3.384 (6.97)	1963:4	87.5
1983:1–2018:2	234.1 (10.19)	2004.1 (19.5)	0.0414 (9.57)	−9.812 (10.2)	2006:4	96.8

We observe that the estimated parameters are all economically meaningful, as this can be judged by their sign and also magnitude, and they are statistically significant (the t-statistic in parenthesis). In other words, all of the above features of our estimations paint very accurate descriptions of a well-behaved S-shaped pattern in the movement of real net corporate profits of the US economy. The R-square is pretty high given the statistically strict requirements of the S-shaped curves.

In Fig. 10.9, we show the estimated logistic (fitted) curve together with the actual curve formed by the actual quarterly data of real corporate profits spanning the period 1947:1 until 1982:4 shown in the upper panel along with the curves corresponding to the first and second derivatives of the fitted function shown in the lower panel. The inflection point is derived visually (lower panel) through the time rate of change of the logistic curve (or estimated trend); mathematically speaking, the first derivative of the function describing the dynamics of the logistic curve displays the upper and lower asymptotes as well as the maximum point, while the second derivative displays the turning point of the logistic curve, and this is when the logistic curve has ran 1/2 of its S-shaped trajectory.

The mathematical analysis but also the visual inspection of Fig. 10.9 shows that the inflection point occurs at $t_m = \frac{3.384}{0.0506} = \frac{66.9}{4} = 16.7$ years, which when added to the start year 1947, we get approximately the year 1964 or more precisely 1963:4. At this point, the first derivative of the logistic curve is equal to zero, while the second derivative from positive becomes negative. By taking the average of the two asymptotes (K and A), we get the profits corresponding to the year 1963:4, that is, $\frac{K+A}{2} = 147.5$ billion USD in constant 2012 prices. In the lower panel of Fig. 10.9, we plot both the first derivative of the logistic curve together with its second derivative. At the point that the second derivative becomes equal to zero, the first derivative is maximized, while the logistic curve attains its inflection point.

The applied mathematical presentation depicts pretty well the way in which the US economy was growing during the postwar years. From Figs. 8.2 and 10.4, we see that the US economy in the mid-1960s enters into the fourth long wave which lasted up until the mid-1980s.[20] Judging from the shapes of the moves of the first and second derivatives, we can say that the cycle was completed already in 1982:4. More specifically, the bell shaped curve of the first derivative (Fig. 10.9) indicates that the logistic growth has completed its full trajectory signifying the end of the fourth cycle and the beginning of the fifth on which turns now our attention.

The available quarterly data from the Fred span the period 1983:1–2018:2 which covers a great deal of the trajectory of the profits in the fifth long cycle which is, however, underway. As a consequence, the non-linear regression results for the fifth long cycle, presented in Table 10.8, are not definitive as those of the fourth long cycle. Figure 10.10 presents a logistic fit of the quarterly time series data of net corporate profits for the period 1983:1–2018:2. In similar with the fourth long cycle

---

[20]The year at which a logistic curve reaches from 10% to 90% of its asymptote conventionally is thought as a reasonable time threshold after which the end of the long cycle is approaching. In other words, we reach the point of saturation.

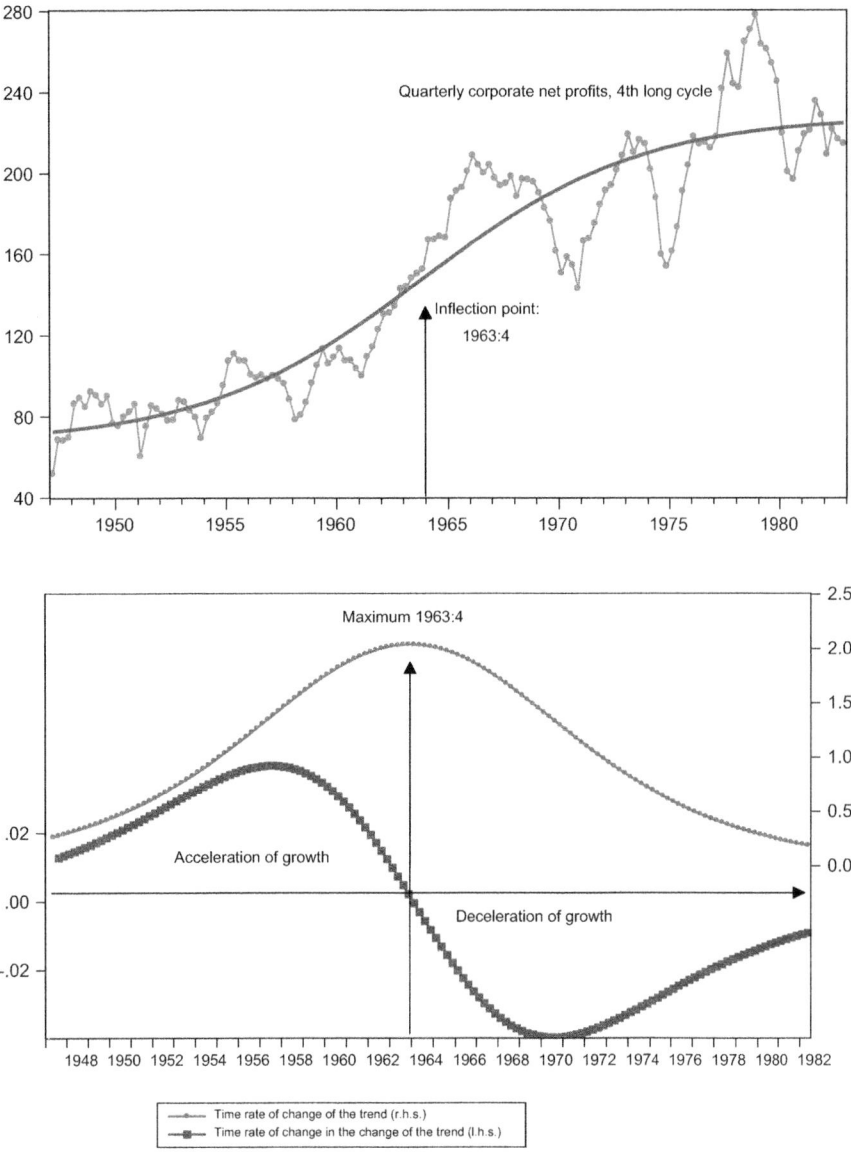

Fig. 10.9 Mass of real net corporate profits, USA, 1947:1–1982:4. Upper panel, estimated logistic (fitted) curve together with the actual curve; lower panel, first and second derivatives of the fitted function

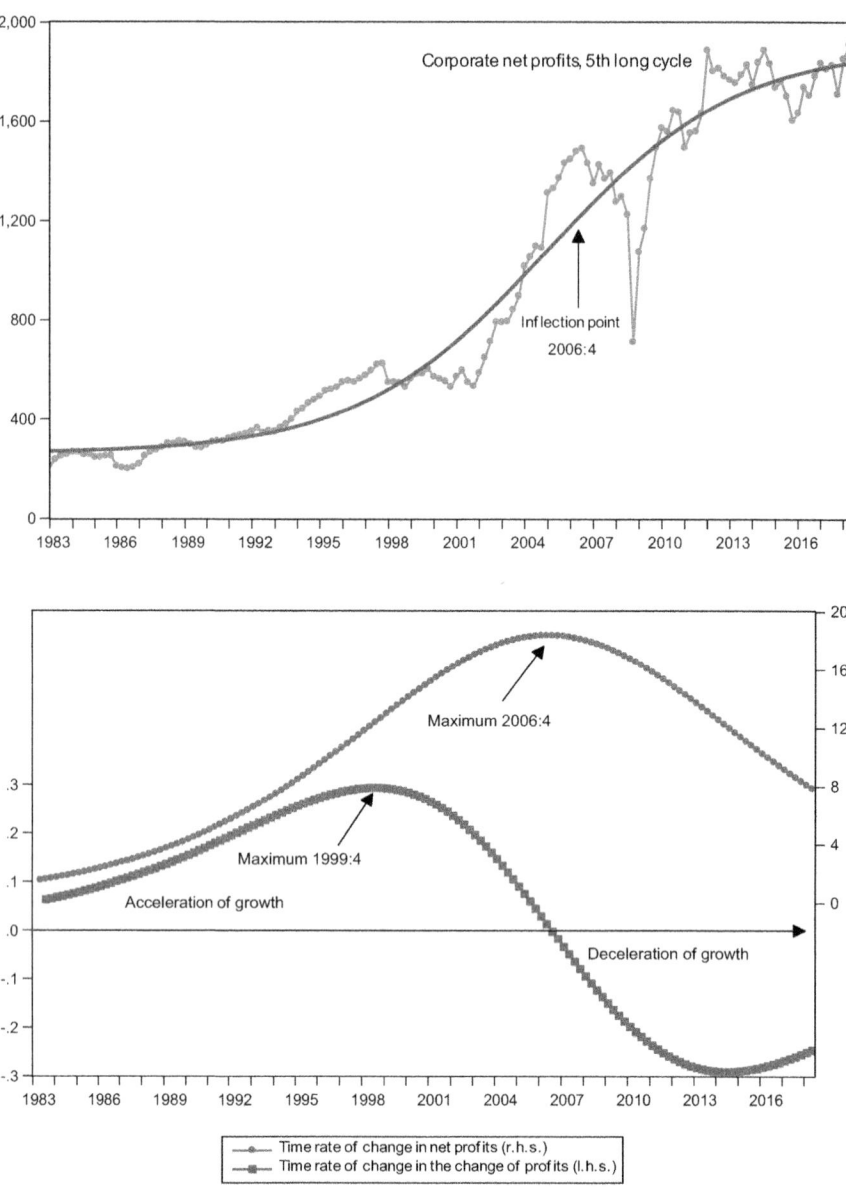

Fig. 10.10 Mass of real net corporate profits, USA, 1983:1–2018:2. Upper panel, estimated logistic (fitted) curve together with the actual curve; lower panel, first and second derivatives of the fitted function

fashion, we display in the same figure the two panels. The top panel refers to the observations and the fitted curve which is certainly of an S-shaped form.

Unlike the fourth long cycle which was completed by the year 1982, the fifth long cycle is still under way. Although, we can estimate its inflection point with relative accuracy, we cannot do the same with the point of saturation. The reason is that all parameters are time dependent, and so we can only make educated guesses or simply reasonable speculations; hence, judging by the lower panel, we expect the stagnation in profits to continue in the coming quarters and years. Although the estimated parameters show the year 2006:4 as the year of the inflection point, judging from the lower panel of Fig. 10.10, we find that the first derivative is maximized in the year 2006:4, while the saturation point needs not too many years to be attained. The first derivative is not exactly bell-shaped indicating that the cycle is not completed. And judging from the shape of the curves and the growth rate, we estimate to attain the saturation point sometime between 2023 and 2028 (see also Tsoulfidis and Papageorgiou 2017 where the annual time series data of net profits are much more refined).

The empirical evidence corroborates the idea that despite their differences, the Great Recession of the late 2000s shares the same salient features and bears startling similarities with the 'stagflation crises' of the 1970s. In fact, the falling rate of profit is responsible for this new phase change, and this fall in the rate of profit is attributed mainly to the rising value composition of capital (Fig. 10.2), further exacerbated by the rise in unproductive activities and the associated with these expenditures which reached a plateau somewhat earlier than 2007. Nevertheless, there are remarkable differences; unlike the 'stagflation crisis', in the current Great Recession period, the new technologies associated with computerization and automation seem to have expanded the scale of their application by including the service industries and the unproductive activities in general. Hence, the growth in employment in these industries slowed down, and the share of employment in unproductive activities in the total employment remained constant or slightly falling. However, this is not true for the share of unproductive wages which kept rising, lending support to the view that the managerial and supervisory labour has been rewarded by much higher salaries which explain, at least in part, the currently acknowledged increasing income and wealth disparities (Tsoulfidis and Paitaridis 2018).

The fall in the rate of profit led to the stagnant mass of net profits around the late 2000s which reduced the net investment up until the recent years. For example, net investment of the private sector of the US economy as a percentage of GDP during the Great Recession of 2007–2016 was on an average equal to 2.01% as opposed to the 1964–2016 period when it was on an average equal to 4.08%. It is interesting to note that this particular share displays a falling tendency as this is shown in Fig. 10.11, a result which is absolutely consistent with the classical view of the FROP, and the associated with it, deterrence of investment spending.

The evolution of the share of net investment in GDP reveals that from the year 2007 onwards, there has been a dramatic fall in investment activity as a result of the absolute over-accumulation in the US economy and by extent a phase change.

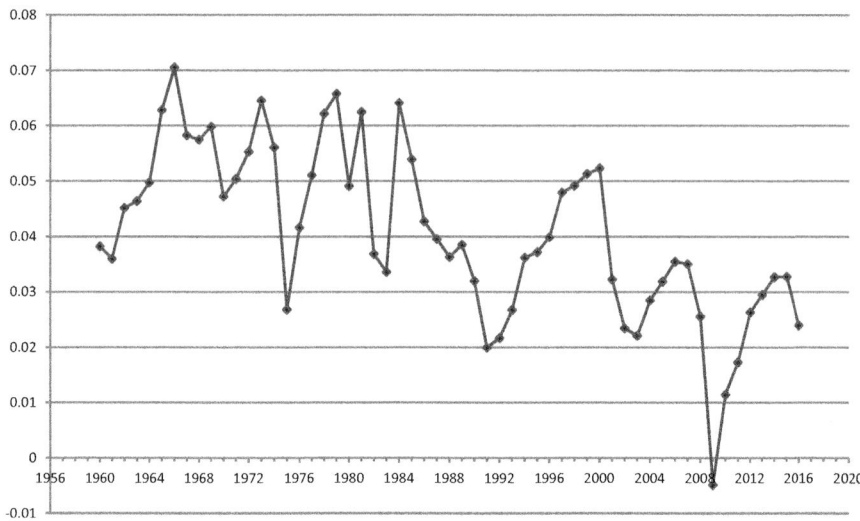

Fig. 10.11 The evolution of the share of net investment in GDP, USA 1960–2016. Source: Data from Fred https://fred.stlouisfed.org/series/W790RC1A027NBEA

10.7   Summary and Conclusion

The US and the world economy in the post-2007 years entered a new phase. The evolution of the profit rate and the mass of real net profits identify the year 2006:4 as the tipping point, that is, the year when profits reach their stagnating state or enter the famous Marx's absolute over-accumulation of capital phase or the classical economists' stationary state. Nevertheless, the old classical economists viewed the stationary state as the terminal state of the capitalist society, whereas Marx views this phase as a state of preparation for a new long period of capital accumulation. In fact, Marx's aphorism that in capitalism there is "no such thing as a permanent crisis" is confirmed repeatedly since our data and analysis shows that there are only recurrent crises.

From the analysis, one may argue that the vitality of the system seems to have been deteriorated over the years as this can be judged by the low rates of profit and the associated with it very low interest rates at the booming years of the fifth cycle. In fact, the low rates of profit discouraged investment spending which displayed a falling tendency (Fig. 10.11), and the financial institutions in order to promote their sales (that is loans) reduced interest rates even further without however exerting a positive effect in the economy; in fact, they accused the institutional framework of being very strict and asked (already from the early 1980s) for financial liberalization or deregulation. The outcome of all these acts was the buildup of various bubbles (real estate, stock market) whose burst revealed the bad shape of the economy's fundamentals (i.e. profitability). During these years it is not only the financial institutions that asked for lower interest rates but also the various pension funds that promise high returns to their customers whose number is on the rise (growing elderly population), the CEOs who want to offer better results to stock and bond-holders and also higher salaries-bonuses to themselves and finally governments who may prefer lower interest rates to finance their debt obligations. As a result, there has been over the period of the fifth long cycle a 'silent alliance' of many players in the field for higher savings, low interest rates and investment!

A superficial consideration of these relations would point the interest rate as the principal cause of the current stalemate in the economy and propose a reversal of the process by increasing interest rates. At the surface, one may think that interest rates went in the downward direction without difficulties, so the reversal would be equally possible. Furthermore, one may argue that higher interest rates will 'clear' the market from the less efficient capitals and the rate of profit will increase by the rising unemployment and the falling wages paving the way of a new phase of growth and investment. This is a possible scenario but, in and of itself, is not enough; what is absolutely necessary for a new long cycle is the devaluation of the capital stock which may take place mainly through large-scale innovations. In fact, the higher the devaluation of the capital stock, the higher the subsequent growth rate, as we can say from the economic history after the crisis of 1930 and the WWII through which there has been the most effective devaluation of capital ever. It seems that Marx's thesis (1857, p. 750) about major crises that '[...] these regularly recurring catastrophes lead to their repetition on a higher scale, and finally to its violent overthrow' might be fulfilled once again. At this point all we can say is that the mechanisms that regulate the operation of the capitalist system are still there and in operation set the stage for a new long cycle which will be necessarily accompanied also by major institutional changes. The sign and direction and whose favour (capital or labour) these changes will be depend on the way in which the political element will exert its influence or pressure.

Bibliography

Antonopoulos, R. (1999). A classical approach to real exchange rate determination with an application for the case of Greece. *Review of Radical Political Economics, 31*(3), 53–65.

Amin, S. (1974). *Accumulation on a world scale: A critique of the theory of underdevelopment* (Vol. I and II). New York: Monthly Review Press.

Arestis, P. (2009). *New consensus macroeconomics and Keynesian critique.* Mimeo, New York: Levy Institute.

Bacon, R., & Eltis, W. (1976). *Britain's economic problem: Too few producers.* London: Macmillan.

Bahçe, S., & Eres, B. (2010). *Testing for classical theory of competition: Evidence from Turkish manufacturing.* Paper presented at the annual conference of Eastern Economic Association, Philadelphia.

Baiman, R. (2014). Unequal exchange and the Rentier economy. *Review of Radical Political Economics, 46*, 4.

Baiman, R. (2017). *Global free trade error: The infeasibility of Ricardo's comparative advantage theory.* London: Routledge.

Bain, J. S. (1949). A note on pricing in monopoly and oligopoly. *American Economic Review, 39*(2), 448–464.

Bain, J. S. (1956). *Barriers to new competition.* Cambridge, MA: Harvard University Press.

Balassa, B. (1964). The purchasing power parity doctrine: A reappraisal. *Journal of Political Economy, 72*, 584–596.

Baran, P. A. (1957). *The political economy of growth.* New York: Monthly Review Press.

Baran, P., & Sweezy, P. (1966). *Monopoly capital.* New York: Monthly Review Press.

Bauer, O. (1907). *Die Nationalitaetenfrage und die Sozialdemocratie.* Wienna: Wiener Volksbuchhandlung.

Baumol, J. W. (1967). Macroeconomics of unbalanced growth: The anatomy of urban crisis. *The American Economy Review, 57*(3), 415–426.

Baumol, W. J. (2000). Leontief's great leap forward: Beyond Quesnay, Marx and Bortkiewicz. *Economic Systems Research, 12*(2), 141–152.

Becker, G. S. (1971). *The economics of discrimination.* Chicago: Chicago University Press.

Berle, A., & Means, G. (1932). *The modern corporation and private property.* New York: Harcour, Brace and World. [1967].

Bishop, R. (1963). Monopolistic competition after thirty years: The impact on the general theory. *American Economic Review, Papers and Proceedings, 53*, 33–43.

Blaug, M. (1997). *Economic theory in retrospect* (5th ed.). Cambridge: Cambridge University Press. [1984].

© Springer Nature Switzerland AG 2019

L. Tsoulfidis, P. Tsaliki, *Classical Political Economics and Modern Capitalism*,
https://doi.org/10.1007/978-3-030-17967-0

Böhm-Bawerk, E. V. (1898). *Karl Marx and the close of his system: A criticism*. London: T.F. Unwin.

Bortkiewicz, L. V. (1907). On the correction of Marx's fundamental theoretical construction in the third volume of capital. In P. Sweezy (Ed.), *Bohm-Bawerk's criticism of Marx*. New York: Augustus M. Kelley. [1975].

Botwinick, H. (1993). *Persistent inequalities: Wage differentials under capitalist competition*. Princeton: Princeton University Press.

Bourlakis, K. (1988). Are there monopoly profits in Greek manufacturing? *Economic Post*. 24.3.88. (in Greek).

Bródy, A. (1970). *Proportions, prices and planning: A mathematical restatement of the labor theory of value*. Amsterdam: North-Holland Publishing Company.

Brown, R. (1978). The theory of unequal exchange: The end of the debate? *Occasional Papers*. No. 65. Erasmus University Rotterdam.

Bullock, P. (1973). Categories of labour power for capital. *Bulletin of the Conference of Socialist Economists, 2*, 82–99.

Carchedi, G. (1991). *Frontiers of political economy*. New York: Verso.

Carter, A. P. (1970). *Structural change in the American economy*. Cambridge: Harvard University Press.

Carter, S. (2018). *The trinity 2.0 arrangement of Sraffa papers section D3/12 notes on production of commodities by means of commodities*. ResearchGate Profile.

Catephores, G. (1989). *An introduction to Marxist economics*. New York: New York University Press.

Caves, R. E. (1964). *American industry: Structure, conduct, performance*. New York: Prentice-Hall.

Chasid, I. (1987). The structure of the Greek manufacturing has not changed. *Economic Post*. 23.7.87. (in Greek).

Chamberlin, E. (1933). *The theory of monopolistic competition*. Cambridge: Harvard University Press. [1962].

Chang, H.-J. (2002). *Kicking away the ladder: Development strategy in historical perspective*. London: Anthem Press.

Chilcote, E. (1997). *Inter industry structure, relative prices, and productivity: An input-output study of the US and OECD countries*. Ph.D. Dissertation, New School for Social Research, New York.

Clark, J. B. (1902). *The distribution of wealth: A theory of wages, interest and profits*. London: Macmillan.

Clark, J. M. (1940). Toward a concept of workable competition. *American Economic Review, 30*(2), 241–256.

Clifton, J. (1977). Competition and the evolution of the capitalist mode of production. *Cambridge Journal of Economics, 1*, 137–151.

Cooney, P. (1990). *Competition vs. monopoly: An I-O analysis of profit rates and markups for the U.S. economy: 1958-1977*. Ph.D. Dissertation, Department of Economics, New School for Social Research, New York.

Cournot, A. (1838). *Researches into the mathematical principles of the theory of wealth*. New York: AM Kelley, Publishers. [1960].

da Silva, E. A. (1987). Unequal exchange. In J. Eatwell, M. Milgate, & P. Newman (Eds.), *The new Palgrave: A dictionary of economics* (pp. 1–4). New York: Palgrave Macmillan.

da Silva, E. A. (1991). The wage-profit curve in Brazil: An input-output model with fixed capital, 1975. *Review of Radical Political Economics, 23*(1–2), 104–110.

Desai, M. (1991). Methodological problems in quantitative Marxism. In P. Dunne (Ed.), *Quantitative Marxism*. Cambridge, UK: Polity Press.

Dilorenzo, T. H., & High, J. (1988). Antitrust and competition, historically considered. *Economic Inquiry, 6*, 423–435.

Dixit, A., & Stiglitz, J. (1977). Monopolistic competition and optimum product diversity. *American Economic Review, 67*(3), 297–308.

Dixit, A., & Norman, V. (1980). *Theory of international trade: A dual, general equilibrium approach.* Cambridge, UK: Cambridge University Press.

Dobb, M. (1973). *Theories of value and distribution since Adam Smith: Ideology and economic theory.* London: Cambridge University Press.

Domar, E. (1946). Capital expansion, rate of growth and employment. *Econometrica, 14,* 137–147.

Doxiadis, A. (1984). Is there monopoly capital in Greek industry. *Current Issues, 1,* 31–49. (in Greek).

Dragasakis, G. (1981). The capitalist monopoly. *Epstimoniki Skepsi, 2,* 10–22. (in Greek).

Droukopoulos, V. (1979). *The capital and production concentration in our Era.* Athens: Ollysous. (in Greek).

Droukopoulos, V. (1991). The degree of concentration of Greek manufacturing: Evolution and prospect. *Bulletin of Political Economy, 8,* 99–121. (in Greek).

Droucopoulos, V., & Lianos, T. (1993). The persistence of profits in the Greek manufacturing industry, 1963-88. *International Review of Applied Economics, 7,* 163–176.

Droucopoulos, V., & Papadogonas, T. (2000). Concentration indices: Back to the drawing board. *Ekonomia, 4,* 55–72.

Duménil, G. (1983). Beyond the transformation riddle: A labor theory of value. *Science and Society, 33*(4), 427–450.

Duménil, G. (1984). The so-called "transformation problem" revisited: A brief comment. *Journal of Economic Theory, 33,* 340–348.

Duménil, G., & Lévy, D. (1987). The dynamics of competition: A restoration of the classical analysis. *Cambridge Journal of Economics, 11*(2), 133–164.

Duménil, G., & Lévy, D. (1993). *The economics of the profit rate.* Aldershot: Edward Elgar.

Duménil, G., & Lévy, D. (2004). *Capital resurgent: Roots of the neoliberal revolution.* Cambridge, MA: Harvard University Press.

Dupuit, J. (1844). On the measurement of the utility of public works. In K. Arrow & T. Scitovsky (Eds.), *Readings in welfare economics.* Homewood, IL: Richard D. Irwin, Inc. [1969].

Eatwell, J. (1977). The irrelevance of returns to scale in Sraffa's analysis. *Journal of Economic Literature, 15,* 61–68.

Eatwell, J. (1980). A simple framework on the analysis of taxation, distribution and effective demand. In E. Nell (Ed.), *Growth, profits and property.* Cambridge, UK: Cambridge University Press.

Eatwell, J. (1982). Competition. In I. Bradkey & M. Howard (Eds.), *Classical and Marxian political economy.* New York: St Martin.

Eatwell, J. (1990). Walras's theory of capital. In J. Eatwell, M. Milgate, & P. K. Newman (Eds.), *The new Palgrave: Capital theory.* New York: Norton.

Eatwell, J., & Milgate, M. (1983). *Keynes's economics and the theory of value and distribution.* London: Duckworth.

Eatwell, J., Milgate, M., & Newman, P. K. (Eds.). (1987). *The new Palgrave dictionary of economics.* New York: Norton.

Eatwell, J., Milgate, M., & Newman, P. K. (Eds.). (1990). *The new Palgrave: Capital theory.* New York: Norton.

Eatwell, J., & Milgate, M. (2011). *The fall and rise of Keynesian economics.* Oxford, UK: Oxford University Press.

Edgeworth, F. Y. (1877). *New and old methods of ethics.* Oxford, UK: J. Parker. [2003].

Ekelund, R. B., & Hébert, R. F. (2007). *History of economic theory and method.* Long Grove, IL: Waveland Press.

Elmslie, B., & Milberg, W. (1992). International trade and the factor intensity uniformity hypothesis: An empirical assessment. *Weltwirtschaftliches Archiv.* September.

Elmslie, B., & Milberg, W. (1996). The productivity convergence debate: A theoretical and methodological reconsideration. *Cambridge Journal of Economics, 20*(2), 153–182.

Eltis, W. (1985). Ricardo on machinery and technological unemployment. In G. Caravale (Ed.), *The legacy of Ricardo.* Oxford: Basil Blackwell.

Emmanuel, A. (1972). *Unequal exchange: A study of the imperialism of trade.* New York: Monthly Review Press.

Emmanuel, A. (1978). A note on 'trade patterns reversals'. *Journal of International Economics, 8*(1), 143–145.

Engels, F. (1845). The condition of the working class in England. In *In the collected works of Karl Marx and Frederick Engels* (Vol. 4). New York: International Publishers. [1975].

Ersoy, E. (2010). Investigation of long-run real exchange rates: The case of Turkey. *Sosyal Bilimler Dergisi, 2*, 14–29.

Erumban, A., Gouma, R., & de Vries, G. (2012). *WIOD socio-economic accounts (SEEA): Sources and methods*. Groningen.

Ethier, W. J. (1982). National and international returns to scale in the modern theory of international trade. *The American Economic Review, 72*(3), 389–405.

Fine, B. (1982). *Theories of the capitalist economy*. London: Edward Arnold.

Fine, B., & Harris, L. (1979). *Rereading capital*. London: Macmillan.

Fisher, J., & Pry, R. (1971). A simple substitution model of technological change. *Technological Forecasting and Social Change, 3*(3), 75–88.

Foley, D. (1982). The value of money, the value of labor power and the transformation problem. *Review of Radical Political Economics, 14*(2), 37–47.

Foley, D. (1986). *Understanding capital, Marx's economic theory*. Cambridge, MA: Harvard University Press.

Flaschel, P. (2010). *Topics in classical micro- and macroeconomics: Elements of a critique of Neo Ricardian theory*. Heidelberg: Springer.

Flaschel, P. (2015). *A future for capitalism: Classical, neoclassical and Keynesian perspectives*. London: Edward Elgar Publishing.

Flaschel, P., & Semmler, W. (1987). Classical and neoclassical competitive adjustment processes. *The Manchester School, 55*(1), 13–37.

Frank, A. G. (1978). *Dependent accumulation and under-development*. London: Macmillan.

Freeman, C., & Louçã, F. (2002). *As time goes by: From the industrial revolution to the information revolution*. Oxford Scholarship Online.

Friedman, M. (1953). *Essays on positive economics*. Chicago: Chicago University Press.

Frohlich, N. (2012). Labour values, prices of production and the missing equalization tendency of the profit rates: Evidence from the German economy. *Cambridge Journal of Economics, 37*, 1107–1126.

Garegnani, P. (1983). Notes on consumption, investment and effective demand. In J. Eatwell & M. Milgate (Eds.), *Keynes's economics and the theory of value and distribution*. New York: Oxford University Press.

Gehrke, C., & Kurz, H. D. (1995). Karl Marx on the physiocrats. *European Journal of History of Economic Thought, 1*, 53–90.

Giacomin, A. (1995). *Il Mercato e il Potere*. Bologna: CLUEB.

Gibson, B. (1980). Unequal exchange: Theoretical issues and empirical findings. *Review of Radical Political Economics, 12*(3), 15–35.

Gillman, J. (1957). *The falling rate of profit: Marx's law and its significance to twentieth-century capitalism*. London: D. Dobson.

Glen, J., Lee, K., & Singh, A. (2001). Persistence of profitability and competition in emerging markets. *Economics Letters, 72*, 247–253.

Glick, M. (1985). Monopoly or competition in the US economy. *Review of Radical Political Economics, 17*, 121–127.

Gomulka, S. (1971). *Diffusion, and the stages of economic growth*. Institute of Economics, Aarhus, Denmark.

Gordon, D. M. (1978). Up and down the long roller coaster. In URPE (Ed.), *U.S. capitalism in crisis*. New York: URPE.

Gordon, D. M. (1980). Stages of accumulation and long economic cycles. In T. Hopkins & I. Wallerstein (Eds.), *Processes of the world system*. Beverley Hills: Sage.

Gordon, J. R. (2012). *Macroeconomics* (12th ed.). Boston, MA: Pearson.

Gordon, R. J. (2015). *Beyond the rainbow: The rise and fall of growth in the American standard of living*. Princeton, NJ: Princeton University Press.

Gordon, R. J. (2016). *The rise and fall of American growth: The U.S. standard of living since the civil war*. Princeton, NJ: Princeton University Press.

Gordon, D. M., Edwards, R., & Reich, M. (1982). *Segmented work, divided workers*. Cambridge: Cambridge University Press.

Green, W. (1990). *Econometric analysis*. London: Macmillan.

Green, R. (1992). *Classical theories of money, output and inflation: A study in historical economics*. London: Macmillan.

Grossmann, H. (1929). *The law of accumulation and breakdown of the capitalist system*. London: Pluto Press. [1992].

Grübler, A. (1990). *The rise and fall of infrastructures: Dynamics of evolution and technological change in transport*. Heidelberg and New York: Physica-Verlag.

Hall, R., & Hitch, C. (1939). Price theory and business behaviour. *Oxford Economic Papers, 2*, 12–45.

Han, Z., & Schefold, B. (2006). An empirical investigation of paradoxes: Reswitching and reverse capital deepening in capital theory. *Cambridge Journal of Economics, 30*(5), 737–765.

Handrinos, S., & Altinoglou, K. (1993). *Fixed capital sock in large scale industry of Greece, 1958-1990*. Mimeo, Athens: Center of Planning and Economic Research.

Hansen, A. (1939). Economic progress and declining population growth. *American Economic Review, 29*(1), 1–15.

Harberger, A. (1954). Monopoly and resource allocation. *American Economic Review, 44*, 77–87.

Harrod, R. (1948). *Towards a dynamic economics*. London and New York: Macmillan.

Hart, N. (2003). Marshall's dilemma: Equilibrium versus evolution. *Journal of Economic Issues, 37*, 1139–1160.

Hayek, F. A. (1948). *Individualism and economic order*. Chicago: University of Chicago Press. [1980].

Heilbroner, R. (1985). *Nature and logic of capitalism*. New York: Norton.

Heisenberg, W. (1971). *Physics and beyond*. New York: Harper.

Hicks, J. R. (1946). *Value and capital: An inquiry into some fundamental principles of economic theory*. Oxford: Clarendon Press.

Hilferding, P. (1910). *Finance capital*. London: Routledge & Kegan Paul. [1981].

Hobsbawm, E. J. (1969). *Industry and empire: From 1750 to the present day*. Harmonds-Worth: Penquin.

Hodgson, G. (2005). Alfred Marshall versus the historical school? *Journal of Economic Studies, 32* (4), 331–348. https://doi.org/10.1108/01443580510618563.

Hollander, S. (1991). Marx and the falling rate of profit. In G. A. Caravale (Ed.), *Marx and modern economic analysis* (Vol. 2). Aldershot: Edward Elgar.

Jevons, S. W. (1871). *The theory of political economy*. London: Macmillan. [2007].

Johnston, L., & Williamson, S. H. (2018). What was the U.S. GDP then? *Measuring worth*, http://www.measuringworth.org/usgdp/.

Kaldor, N. (1978). *Further essays on economic theory*. London: Holmes and Meier.

Kapetanios, G., Shin, Y., & Snell, A. (2003). Testing for a unit root in the nonlinear STAR framework. *Journal of Econometrics, 112*, 359–379.

Keynes, J. M. (1936). *The general theory of employment, interest and money*. Cambridge, UK: Cambridge University Press.

Kirzner, I. (1987). Competition: Austrian conceptions. In J. Eatwell, M. Milgate, & P. K. Newman (Eds.), *The new Palgrave*. London: Macmillan.

Kliman, A. (2007). *Reclaiming Marx's "capital": A refutation of the myth of inconsistency*. Lanham, MD: Lexington Books.

Kmenta, J. (1991). *Elements of econometrics*. New York: Macmillan.

Knight, F. (1921). *Risk uncertainty and profits*. Boston: Houghton Mifflin.

Komoto, K. (2001). *Do profit rate differentials diminish over time? A statistical analysis of long-term financial data*. NLI Research Institute.

Kondratiev, N. (1926). *The long wave cycle*. New York: Richardson & Snyder. [1984].

Kondratiev, N. D. (1935). The long waves in economic life. *Review of Economic Statistics, 17*(6), 105–115.

Kondratiev, N. D. (1998). Long cycles of economic conjuncture. In N. Makasheva & W. J. Samuels (Eds.), *The works of Nikolai D. Kondratiev* (Vol. I). London: Pickering and Chatto.

Kotz, D. M. (2017). Social structure of accumulation theory, Marxist theory, and system transformation. *Review of Radical Political Economics, 49*, 3.

Krelle, W. (1977). Basic facts in capital theory: Some lessons from the controversy in capital theory. *Revue d' Économie Politique, 87*, 282–329.

Krugman, P. (1981). Intra-industry specialization and the gains from trade. *Journal of Political Economy, 89*, 959–973.

Krugman, P. (2014). Four observations on secular stagnation. In C. Teulings & R. Baldwin (Eds.), *Secular stagnation: Facts, causes and cures*. A VoxEU.org eBook, London: Centre for Economic Policy Research.

Krugman, P., & Obsefeld, M. (2012). *International economics: Theory and policy*. New York: Pearson.

Krugman, P., & Wells, R. (2009). *Economics* (2nd ed.). New York: Worth Publishers.

Kurz, H. (1998). Marx on technological change: The Ricardian heritage. In R. Bellofiore (Ed.), *Marxian economics: A reappraisal* (Vol. 2, pp. 119–138). London: Macmillan.

Kurz, H. D. (2008). Innovations and profits: Schumpeter and the classical heritage. *Journal of Economic Behavior and Organization, 67*, 263–278.

Kurz, H. D. (2010). Technical progress, capital accumulation and income distribution in classical economics: Adam Smith, David Ricardo and Karl Marx. *European Journal of the History of Economic Thought, 17*(5), 1183–1222.

Kurz, H. D. (2018). Will the MEGA2 edition be a watershed in interpreting Marx? *The European Journal of the History of Economic Thought, 1*, 1–25. https://doi.org/10.1080/09672567.2018. 1523937.

Kurz, H. D., & Salvadori, N. (2000). 'Classical' roots of input-output analysis: A short account of its long prehistory. *Economic Systems Research, 12*, 2.

Kwoka, J. E. (1979). The effect of market share distribution on industry performance. *Review of Economics and Statistics, 61*, 101–109.

Leontief, W. (1939). *The structure of the American economy, 1919-1939*. New York: Oxford University Press.

Leontief, W. (1953). *Studies in the structure of the American economy: Theoretical and empirical explorations in input-output analysis*. London: Oxford University Press.

Leontief, W. (1986). Technological change, prices, wages, and rates of return in the U.S. economy. In W. Leontief (Ed.), *Input-output economics*. New York: Oxford University Press.

Lianos, T. P. (1979). Domar's growth model and Marx's reproduction scheme. *Journal of Macroeconomics, 1*(4), 405–412.

Lianos, T., & Droucopoulos, V. (1993). Convergence and hierarchy of industrial profit rates: The case of Greek manufacturing. *Review of Radical Political Economics, 25*, 67–80.

Lipietz, A. (1982). The so-called transformation problem revisited. *Journal of Economic Theory, 26*(1), 59–88.

Löwe, A. (1975). Adam Smith's system of economic growth. In A. S. Skinner & T. Wilson (Eds.), *Essays on Adam Smith*. Oxford, UK: Clarendon Press.

Luxembourg, R. (1913). *The accumulation of capital*. New York: Monthly Review Press. [1972].

Mage, S. H. (1963). *The law of the falling tendency of the rate of profit: It's place in the Marxian theoretical system and relevance to the United States*. Ph.D. Dissertation, Department of Economics, Columbia University.

Malikane, C. (2017). The labour share and the dynamics of output. *Applied Economics, 49*, 3741–3750.

Mandel, E. (1970). The laws of unequal development. *New Left Review, 59*, 19.

Mandel, E. (1991). *The fallacies of state capitalism: Ernest Mandel and Chris Harman debate the USSR*. London: Socialist Outlook.

Mantel, E. (1984). Gold, money and transformation problem. In A. Freeman & E. Mandel (Eds.), *Ricardo, Marx and Sraffa: The Langston memorial volume*. London: Verso.

Maniatis, T. (2012). Marxist theories of crisis and the current economic crisis. *Forum for Social Economics, 41*(1), 6–29.

Marchetti, C. (1991). Modeling innovation diffusion. In B. Henry (Ed.), *Forecasting technological innovation*. London: Springer.

Marchionatti, R. (2003). On the methodological foundation of modern microeconomics: Frank Knight and the "cost controversy" in the 1920s. *History of Political Economy, 35*(1), 49–75.

Marelli, E. (1980). An intersectoral analysis of regional disparities in terms of transfers of surplus value. *Rivista Internazionale di Scienze Economiche e Vommerciali, 27*(6), 507–526.

Marelli, E. (1983). Empirical estimation of intersectoral and interregional transfers of surplus value: The case of Italy. *Journal of Regional Science, 23*(1), 49–70.

Mariolis, T. (2014). Falling rate of profit and mass of profits: A note. *Review of Political Economy, 26*(4), 549–556.

Mariolis, T., & Tsoulfidis, L. (2009). Decomposing the changes in production prices into 'capital intensity' and 'price effects': Theory and evidence from the Chinese economy. *Contributions to Political Economy, 28*, 1–22.

Mariolis, T., & Tsoulfidis, L. (2010). Measures of production price-labour value deviation and income distribution in actual economies: A note. *Metroeconomica, 61*(4), 701–710.

Mariolis, T., & Tsoulfidis, L. (2011). Eigenvalue distribution and the production price – Profit rate relationship: Theory and empirical evidence. *Evolutionary and Institutional Economic Review, 8*, 1.

Mariolis, T., & Tsoulfidis, L. (2012). *On Brody's conjecture: Facts and figures from the US economy*. Discussion Paper Series 2012_06, Department of Economics, University of Macedonia.

Mariolis, T., & Tsoulfidis, L. (2016). *Modern classical economics and reality: A spectral analysis of the theory of value and distribution*. Tokyo: Springer.

Mariolis, T., & Tsoulfidis, L. (2018). Less is more: Capital theory and almost irregular-uncontrollable actual economies. *Contributions to Political Economy, 37*(1), 65–88.

Marshall, A. (1890). *Principles of economics*. London: Macmillan. [1920].

Maruyama, N., & Odagiri, H. (2002). Does the 'persistence of profits' persist?: A study of company profits in Japan, 1964–97. *International Journal of Industrial Organization, 20*(10), 1513–1533.

Marx, K. (1847). *Wage Labour and Capital*. Moscow: International Publishers Co. Inc.

Marx, K. (1857). *Grundrisse, foundations of the critique of political economy*. New York: Vintage Books. [1973].

Marx, K. (1859). *A contribution to critique of political economy*. New York: International Publishers. [1981].

Marx, K. (1867). *Capital* (Vol. I). New York: International Publishers. [1977].

Marx, K. (1885). *Capital* (Vol. II). New York: International Publishers. [1977].

Marx, K. (1894). *Capital* (Vol. III). New York: International Publishers. [1977].

Marx, K. (1969). *Theories of surplus value, parts I, II and III*. Moscow: Progress Publishers.

Marx, K. (1976). *Results of the immediate process of production. Appendix to capital I*. Harmondsworth: Penguin Books.

Martinez-Hernandez, F. A. (2010). An alternative theory of real exchange rate determination: Theory and empirical evidence for the Mexican economy, 1970-2004. *Investigación Económica, 69*(273), 55–84.

Martinez-Hernandez, F. A. (2017). The political economy of real exchange rate behavior: Theory and empirical evidence for developed and developing countries, 1960–2010. *Review of Political Economy, 29*(4), 566–596.

Mason, E. S. (1939). Price and production policies of large scale enterprises. *American Economic Review, 29*, 61–74.

Mattey, J. (1996). Capacity utilization and structural change. *FRBSF Economic Letter* (Nov15).

McNulty, P. (1967). Economic theory and the meaning of competition. *Quarterly Journal of Economics, 82*, 639–656.

Medema, S. G. (1991). Another look at the problem of rent seeking. *Journal of Economic Issues, 25*(4), 1049–1065.

Meek, R. (1973). *Studies in the labour theory of value.* London: Lawrence and Wishart.

Mejorado, A., & Roman, M. (2014). *Profitability and the great recession: The role of accumulation trends in the financial crisis.* New York: Routledge.

Mejorado, A., & Roman, M. (2017). Profitability and secular stagnation: The missing link. *International Journal of Political Economy, 46*(2–3), 150–166.

Meyer, C. D. (2001). *Matrix analysis and applied linear algebra.* Philadelphia: S.I.A.M.

Michaelides, P. G., & Milios, J. G. (2005). Did Hilferding influence Schumpeter? *History of Economics Review, 41*, 98–125.

Milgate, M. (1979). On the origin of the notion of 'intertemporal equilibrium'. *Economica, 46*(181), 1–10.

Milberg, W. (1994). Market competition and the failure of competitiveness enhancement policies in the United States. *Journal of Economic Issues, 28*(2), 587–596.

Milberg, W. (2001). Review of when economic crises endure by Jacques Mazier, Maurice Baslé, and Jean François Vidal. *Journal of Economic Literature, 39*, 171–173.

Mill, J. S. (1848). *Principles of political economy.* Fairfield New Jersey: Augustus M. Kelley.

Miller, R. E., & Blair, P. D. (2009). *Input-output analysis: Foundations and extensions.* New Jersey: Prentice-Hall.

Mohun, S. (1984). Abstract labour and its value form. *Science and Society, 48*, 388–406.

Mohun, S. (2004). The labour theory of value as foundation for empirical investigations. *Metroeconomica, 55*(1), 65–95.

Mohun, S. (2014). Unproductive labor in the U.S. Economy 1964-2010. *Review of Radical Political Economics, 46*(3), 355–379.

Montibeler, E., & Sánchez, C. (2014). *The labour theory of value and the prices in China: Methodology and analysis.* Working paper https://ideas.repec.org/p/anp/en2012/014.html.

Morishima, M. (1973). *Marx's economics: A dual theory of value and growth.* Cambridge, UK: Cambridge University Press.

Moseley, F. (1991). *The falling rate of profit in the Postwar United States economy.* London: Macmillan.

Moseley, F. (2000). The 'new solution' to the transformation problem: A sympathetic critique. *Review of Radical Political Economics, 32*(2), 282–316.

Moudud, J. K. (2010). *Strategic competition, dynamics and the role of the state: A new perspective.* New York: Edward Elgar Press.

Mueller, D. (1986). *Profits in the long run.* Cambridge, UK: Cambridge University Press.

Mueller, D. (1990). *The dynamics of company profits.* Cambridge, UK: Cambridge University Press.

Mueller, E., & Blair, P. (2009). *Input-output analysis: Foundation and extensions.* Cambridge, UK: Cambridge University Press.

Nikaido, H. (1996). *Prices, cycles and growth.* Cambridge, MA: MIT Press.

Nakatani, T. (1980). The law of falling rate of profit and the competitive battle: Comment on Shaikh. *Cambridge Journal of Economics, 4*(1), 65–68.

Ochoa, E. (1984). *Labor values and prices of production: An inderindustry study of the U.S Economy, 1947-1972.* Ph.D. Dissertation, New School for Social Research, New York.

Ochoa, E. (1989). Values, prices and wage-profit curves in the U.S. Economy. *Cambridge Journal of Economics, 13*, 413–430.

Ochoa, E., & Glick, M. (1992). Competing microeconomic theories of industrial profits: An empirical approach. In W. Milberg (Ed.), *The megacorp & macrodynamics: Essays in memory of Alfred Eichner.* New York: Sharpe.

Odagiri, H., & Yamawaki, H. (1990). The persistence of profits: International comparison. In D. C. Mueller (Ed.), *The dynamics of company profits.* Cambridge, UK: Cambridge University Press.

Officer, L. H., & Williamson, S. H. (2014). The price of gold, 1257-2011. *Measuring worth*, 18-09-2014, http://www.measuringworth.com/uscompare/.

Okishio, N. (1961). Technical change and the rate of profit. *Kobe University Economic Review, 7*, 86–99.

Okishio, N. (1963). A mathematical note on Marxian theory. *Weltwirtschaftliches Archiv, 91*, 2.

Okishio, N. (1974). Value and production price. *Kobe University Economic Review, 20*, 1–19.

Okishio, N. (1988). On Marx's reproduction scheme. *Kobe University Economic Review, 34*, 1–24.

Okishio, N. (1990). Constant and variable capital. In J. Eatwell, M. Milgate, P. K. Newman, & K. Peter (Eds.), *The new Palgrave: Marxian economics*. New York: W.W. Norton.

Paitaridis, D., & Tsoulfidis, L. (2012a). The growth of unproductive activities, the rate of profit, and the phase-change of the U.S. Economy. *Review of Radical Political Economics, 44*(2), 213–233.

Paitaridis, D., & Tsoulfidis, L. (2012b). Revisiting Adam Smith's theory of the falling rate of profit. *International Journal of Social Economics, 39*(5), 304–314.

Pakos, T. (1982). *Industrialization, structural change and policy: The case of Greece 1958-77*. Ph.D. Dissertation, The Victoria University of Manchester.

Paraskevopoulou, C., Tsaliki, P., & Tsoulfidis, L. (2016). Revisiting Leontief's paradox. *International Review of Applied Economics, 30*(6), 693–713.

Pasinetti, L. (1977). *Lectures on the theory of production*. New York: Columbia University Press.

Perez, C. (2002). *Technological revolutions and financial capital: The dynamics of bubbles and golden ages*. Cheltenham: Edward Elgar.

Phillips, A. (1975). The Tableau Économique as a Simple Leontief Model. *Quarterly Journal of Economics, 69*, 137–144.

Polasky, S., & Mason, C. F. (1998). On the welfare effects of mergers: Short run vs. long run. *Quarterly Review of Economics and Finance, 38*, 1.

Poulantzas, N. (1975). *Classes in contemporary capitalism*. London: New Left Books.

Prebisch, R. (1959). Commercial policy in the underdeveloped countries. *The American Economic Review, 49*(2), 251–273.

Quenay, F. (1758). *Le Tableau Économique*. London: British Economic Association. [1895].

Ricardo, D. (1819). In P. Sraffa (Ed.), *On the principles of political economy and taxation*. Cambridge, UK: Cambridge University Press. [1951].

Ricardo, D. (1951). In Sraffa P. with the collaboration of M. Dobb (Ed.), *The works and correspondence of David Ricardo*. Cambridge, UK: Cambridge University Press.

Ricci, A. (2018). Unequal exchange in the age of globalization. *Review of Radical Political Economics*. https://doi.org/10.1177/0486613418773753.

Rieu, D.-M. (2008). Estimating sectoral rates of surplus value: Methodological issues. *Metroeconomica, 59*(4), 557–573.

Robinson, J. (1933). *The economics of imperfect competition*. London: Macmillan.

Robinson, J. (1934). What is perfect competition? *Quarterly Journal of Economics, 48*(4), 104–120.

Robinson, J. (1953). 'Imperfect competition' revisited. *The Economic Journal, 63*, 579–593.

Rosdolsky, R. (1977). *The making of Marx's capital*. London: Pluto Press.

Rubin, I. (1928). *A history of economic thought*. London: Ink Links. [1979].

Rubin, I. (1972). *Essays on Marx's theory of value*. Detroit: Black and Red.

Ruggles, R., & Ruggles, N. D. (1956). *National income accounts and income analysis*. New York: MacGrow Hill.

Ruiz-Napoles, P. (1996). *Alternative theories of real exchange rate determination a case study: The Mexican Peso and the US Dollar*. Ph.D. Dissertation, New School for Social Research, New York.

Salter, W. E. G. (1966). *Productivity and technical change*. Cambridge, UK: Cambridge University Press.

Samuelson, P. A. (1962a). Parable and realism in capital theory: The surrogate production function. *Review of Economic Studies, 29*(3), 193–206.

Samuelson, P. A. (1962b). The gains from international trade once again. *The Economic Journal, 72*, 820–829.

Samuelson, P. A. (1964). Theoretical notes on trade problems. *Review of Economics and Statistics, 46*(2), 145–154.

Samuelson, P. A. (1966). A summing up. *The Quarterly Journal of Economics, 80*(4), 568–583.

Samuelson, P. A. (1974). Marx as a mathematical economist. *Collected Scientific Papers* (Vol. 3 and 4).

Samuelson, P. A. (1975). Trade pattern reversals in time-phased Ricardian systems and intertemporal efficiency. *Journal of International Economics, 5*(4), 309–363.

Samuelson, P. A. (1976). Is real-world price a tale told by the idiot of chance? *The Review of Economics and Statistics, 58*(1), 120–123.

Samuelson, P. A. (1978). Free trade's intertemporal pareto-optimality. *Journal of International Economics, 8*(1), 147–149.

Samuelson, P. A. (1981). Schumpeter's capitalism, socialism and democracy. In A. Heertje (Ed.), *Schumpeter's vision: Capitalism, socialism and democray after 40 years*. New York: Praeger.

Sawyer, M. (1981). *The economics of industries and firms: Theories evidence and policy*. New York: St. Martin's Press.

Schefold, B. (1976). Different forms of technical progress. *Economic Journal, 86*, 806–809.

Schefold, B. (2011). *Only a few techniques matter! On the number of curves on the Wage Frontier*. Paper presented in ESHET Conference in Instabul 2011.

Scherer, F. M., & Ross, D. (1990). *Industrial market structure and economic performance*. New York: Houghton Mifflin Company.

Schmalensee, R. (1989). Inter-industry studies of structure and performance. In R. Schmalensee & R. Willing (Eds.), *Handbook of industrial organization* (Vol. II). Amsterdam: North-Holland.

Schumpeter, J. A. (1934). *The theory of economic development: An inquiry into profits, capital, credit, interest and the business cycle*. London: Transaction Publishers. [2008].

Schumpeter, J. A. (1939). *Business cycles: A theoretical, historical, and statistical analysis of the capitalist process*. New York: McGraw-Hill.

Schumpeter, J. (1942). *Capitalism socialism and democracy*. New York: Harper and Row Publishers.

Schumpeter, J. (1954). *History of economic analysis*. New York: Oxford University Press.

Schwartz, W. (1961). The social worker in the group. In *New perspectives on services to groups: Theory, organization, and practice*. New York: National Association of Social Workers.

Schwartzman, D. (1960). The burden of monopoly. *The Journal of Political Economy, 68*, 627–630.

Semmler, W. (1983). *Competition monopoly and differential profit rates: On the relevance of the classical and Marxian theories of production prices for modern industrial and corporate pricing*. New York: Columbia University Press.

Seretis, S., & Tsaliki, P. (2012). Value transfers in trade: An explanation of the observed differences in development. *International Journal of Social Economics, 39*(12), 965–982.

Seretis, S., & Tsaliki, P. (2016). Absolute advantage and international trade: Evidence from four - Euro-zone economies. *Review of Radical Political Economics, 48*(3), 5–22.

Shackle, G. L. S. (1967). *The years of high theory: Invention and tradition in economic thought 1926–1939*. Cambridge: Cambridge University Press.

Shaikh, A. (1973). *Theories of value and theories of distribution*. Columbia University, Ph.D. (unpublished).

Shaikh, A. (1977). Marx's theory of value and the transformation problems. In J. Schwartz (Ed.), *The subtle anatomy of capitalism*. Santa Monica, CA: Goodyear.

Shaikh, A. (1978). Political economy and capitalism: Notes on Dobb's theory of crisis. *Cambridge Journal of Economics, 2*, 233–251.

Shaikh, A. (1980a). Marxian competition versus perfect competition: Further comments on the so-called choice of technique. *Cambridge Journal of Economics, 4*(1), 75–83.

Shaikh, A. (1980b). The laws of international exchange. In E. Nell (Ed.), *Growth, profits and property*. Cambridge, UK: Cambridge University Press.

Shaikh, A. (1981). The poverty of algebra. In I. Steedman (Ed.), *The value controversy*. London: New Left Books and Verso.

Shaikh, A. (1982). Neoricardian economics: A wealth of algebra a poverty of theory. *Review of Radical Political Economics, 14*, 67–83.

Shaikh, A. (1984). The transformation from Marx to Sraffa. In A. Freeman & E. Mandel (Eds.), *Ricardo, Marx and Sraffa: The Langston memorial volume*. London: Verso.

Shaikh, A. (1987). The falling rate of profit and the economic crisis in the U.S. In R. Cherry et al. (Eds.), *The imperiled economy*. New York: Monthly Review Press.

Shaikh, A. (1990). Abstract and concrete labour. In J. Eatwell, M. Milgate, & P. Newman (Eds.), *Marxian economics: The new Palgrave*. London: Palgrave Macmillan.

Shaikh, A. (1991). *Competition and exchange rates: Theory and empirical evidence*. Department of Economics, Graduate Faculty, New School for Social Research, Working Paper No. 25.

Shaikh, A. (1992a). The falling rate of profit as the cause of long waves: Theory and empirical evidence. In A. Kleinknecht, E. Mandel, & I. Wallerstein (Eds.), *New findings in long wave research*. London: Macmillan Press.

Shaikh, A. (1992b). Values and value transfers: A comment on Itoh. In B. Roberts & S. Feiner (Eds.), *Radical economics*. Norwell, MA: Kluwer Academic Publishers.

Shaikh, A. (1995). *The stock market and the corporate sector: A profit based approach*. Working Paper No 146. New York: Jerome Levy Institute.

Shaikh, A. (1998). The empirical strength of the labour theory of value. In R. Bellofiore (Ed.), *Marxian economics: A reappraisal* (Vol. 2, pp. 225–251). New York: St. Martin's Press.

Shaikh, A. (2004). The economic mythology of neoliberalism. In A. Saad-Filho (Ed.), *Neoliberalism: A critical reader*. London: Pluto Press.

Shaikh, A. (2007). Globalization and the myth of free trade. In A. Shaikh (Ed.), *Globalization and the myths of free trade: History, theory, and empirical evidence*. New York: Routledge.

Shaikh, A. (2008). Competition and industrial rates of return. In P. Arestis & J. Eatwell (Eds.), *Issues in finance and industry essays in honour of Ajit Singh*. Houndmills: Palgrave Macmillan.

Shaikh, A. (2016). *Capitalism: competition, conflict, crises*. New York: Oxford University Press.

Shaikh, A., & Antonopoulos, R. (2012). Explaining long term exchange rate behavior in the United States and Japan. In J. Moudud, C. Bina, & P. Mason (Eds.), *Alternative theories of competition: Challenges to orthodoxy* (pp. 201–228). London: Routledge.

Shaikh, A., & Tonak, E. A. (1994). *Measuring the wealth of nations: The political economy of national accounts*. New York: Cambridge University Press.

Singer, H. W. (1950). The distribution of gains between investing and borrowing countries. *American Economic Review, Papers and Proceedings, 11*(2), 473–485.

Singer, H. W. (1975). The strategy of international development: Essays in the economics of backwardness. In A. Cairncross & M. Puri (Eds.), *Economics of backwardness*. London: Macmillan.

Sleuwaegen, L., & Dehandschutter, W. (1986). The critical choice between the concentration ratio and the H-index in assessing industry performance. *Journal of Industrial Economy, 35*(2), 193–208.

Smith, A. (1776). In E. Cannan (Ed.), *The wealth of nations*. New York: Random House. [1937].

Sraffa, P. (1926). The laws of returns under competitive conditions. *Economic Journal, 36*, 535–550.

Sraffa, P., & Dobb, M. H. (Eds.). (1951–1973). *The works and correspondence of David Ricardo* (Vol. 11). Cambridge: Cambridge University Press.

Sraffa, P. (D3/12/7:161.1). Wren Library, Trinity College. https://janus.lib.cam.ac.uk/db/node.xsp?id=EAD%2FGBR%2F0016%2FSRAFFA. Also in Carter, S. (2018).

Sraffa, P. (1960). *Production of commodities by means of commodities: A prelude to economic theory*. Cambridge, UK: Cambridge University Press.

Steedman, I. (1977). *Marx after Sraffa*. London: New Left Books.

Steedman, I. (Ed.). (1981). *The value controversy*. London: New Left Books.

Steedman, I. (1999). Vertical integration and 'reduction to dated quantities of labour'. In G. Mongiovi & F. Petri (Eds.), *Value distribution and capital: Essaysin Honour of Pierangelo Garegnani*. London: Routledge.

Steedman, I., & Tomkins, J. (1998). On measuring the deviation of prices from values. *Cambridge Journal of Economics, 22*, 379–385.

Steenge, A. (2000). The rents problem in the tableau economique: Revisiting the Phillips model. *Economic Systems Research, 12*, 181–197.

Stigler, G. (1937). A generalization of the theory of imperfect competition. *Journal of Farm Economics, 19*, 707–717.

Stigler, G. (1942). *The theory of competitive price*. New York: Macmillan.

Stigler, G. (1949). *Monopolistic competition in retrospect*. Chicago: Chicago University Press. [1983].

Stigler, G. (1956). Factors in the trend of employment in the service industries. In *Chapter in NBER book trends in employment in the service industries*. New Jersey: Princeton University Press.

Stigler, G. (1957). Perfect competition historically contemplated. *Journal of Political Economy, 65*(1), 1–16.

Stigler, G. (1968). Competition. In *International encyclopedia of social science* (Vol. 3, pp. 181–182). New York: Macmillan.

Stigler, G. (1969). *The organization of industry*. Chicago: University of Chicago Press. [1983].

Stigler, G. (1982). Smith's travels on the ship of state. In *The economist as preacher and other essays*. Chicago: University of Chicago Press.

Stigler, G. (1987). Competition. In J. Eatwel, M. Milgate, & P. Newman (Eds.), *The New Palgrave. A dictionary of economics* (pp. 531–535). London: The MacMillan Press.

Stiglitz, J., & Walsh, K. (2006). *Economics*. New York: Norton.

Studenski, P. (1958). *The income of nations*. New York: New York University Press.

Summers, L. H. (2014). U.S. Economic prospects: Secular stagnation, hysteresis, and the zero lower bound. *Business Economics, 49*(2), 65–74.

Summers, H. L. (2015). *Rethinking secular stagnation after seventeen months*. IMF Rethinking Macro III Conference (April 16).

Sweezy, P. (1942). *The theory of capitalist development: Principles of Marxian political economy*. New York: Monthly Review Press.

Sweezy, P. (1975). *Bohm-Bawerk's criticism of Marx*. New York: Augustus M. Kelley.

Teulings, C., & Baldwin, R. (2014). *Secular stagnation: Facts, causes, and cures*. London: VoxEU Organisation Books.

Torres, G. L. D., & Yang, J. (2018). *The persistent statistical structure of the US input-output coefficient matrices: 1963-2007*. Working Paper 04/2018, Department of Economics, The New School for Social Research.

Triffin, R. (1941). Monopoly in particular-equilibrium and in general-equilibrium economics. *Econometrica, 9*(2), 121–127.

Trigg, A. B. (2006). *Marxian reproduction schemes: Money and aggregate demand in a capitalist economy*. London: Routledge.

Tsaliki, P. (2006). Marx on entrepreneurship: A note. *International Review of Economics, 53*(4), 592–602.

Tsaliki, P. (2008). Economic development, human capital and technical change: The question of machinery revisited. *International Review of Economics, 55*(3), 363–371.

Tsaliki, P. (2009). Economic development and unemployment: Do they connect? *International Journal of Social Economics, 36*, 773–781.

Tsaliki, P., Paraskevopoulou, C., & Tsoulfidis, L. (2018). Unequal exchange and absolute cost advantage: Evidence from the trade between Greece and Germany. *Cambridge Journal of Economics, 42*(4), 1043–1086.

Tsaliki, P., & Tsoulfidis, L. (1998). Alternative theories of competition: Evidence from the Greek manufacturing industries. *International Review of Applied Economics, 12*, 187–204.

Tsoulfidis, L., & Tsaliki, P. (2005). Marxian theory of competition and the concept of regulating capital: Evidence from Greek manufacturing. *Review of Radical Political Economics, 37*(1), 5–22. https://doi.org/10.1177/0486613404272324.

Tsaliki, P., & Tsoulfidis, L. (2010). Dominant technique and economic theory. *Paper presented in 14th conference of European society for the history of economic thought in Amsterdam*, The Netherlands.

Tsaliki, P., & Tsoulfidis, L. (2015). Classical economists, Marx and Marshall on dominant technique. *History of Economic Thought and Policy, 2*, 21–36.

Tsaliki, P., & Tsoulfidis, L. (2016). *Lectures in political economy* (3rd ed.). Thessaloniki: Tziolas Publications. (in Greek).

Tsoulfidis, L. (1989). The physiocratic theory of tax incidence. *Scottish Journal of Political Economy, 36*, 301–310.

Tsoulfidis, L. (2005). *Notes on Ricardo's theory of value and taxation*. MPRA Paper 35590, University Library of Munich, Germany.

Tsoulfidis, L. (2008). Price-value deviations: Further evidence from input-output data of Japan. *International Review of Applied Economics, 22*(6), 707–724.

Tsoulfidis, L. (2009). The rise and fall of monopolistic competition revolution. *International Review of Economics, 56*(1), 29–45.

Tsoulfidis, L. (2010). *Competing schools of economic thought*. Heidelberg: Springer.

Tsoulfidis, L. (2012). *Economic history of Greece*. Thessaloniki: Macedonia University Press. (in Greek).

Tsoulfidis, L. (2015). Contending conceptions of competition and the role of regulating capital. *Panoeconomicus, 62*(1), 15–31.

Tsoulfidis, L. (2017). Growth accounting of the value composition of capital and the rate of profit in the U.S. Economy: A note stimulated by Zarembka's findings. *Review of Radical Political Economics, 49*(2), 303–312.

Tsoulfidis, L. (2018). *Ricardo's theory of value is still alive and well in contemporary capitalism*. MPRA_paper_85822.pdf.

Tsoulfidis, L., Alexiou, C., & Parthenidis, T. (2015). Revisiting profit persistence and the stock market in Japan. *Structural Change and Economic Dynamics, 33*(2), 10–24.

Tsoulfidis, L., & Maniatis, T. (2002). Values, prices of production and market prices: Some more evidence from the Greek economy. *Cambridge Journal of Economics, 26*, 359–369.

Tsoulfidis, L., & Mariolis, T. (2007). Labour values, prices of production and the effects of income distribution. *Economic Systems Research, 19*, 425–437.

Tsoulfidis, L., & Paitaridis, D. (2009). On the labor theory of value: Statistical artefacts or regularities? *Research in Political Economy, 25*, 209–232.

Tsoulfidis, L., & Paitaridis, D. (2017). Monetary expressions of labor time and market prices: Theory and evidence from China, Japan and Korea. *Review of Political Economy, 29*(1), 111–132.

Tsoulfidis, L., & Paitaridis, D. (2018). Capital intensity, unproductive activities and the great recession in the US economy. *Cambridge Journal of Economics* (forthcoming). https://doi.org/10.1093/cje/bey051.

Tsoulfidis, L., & Papageorgiou, A. (2017). *The recurrence of long cycles: Theories, stylized facts and figures*. MPRA paper 82853. Forthcoming in World Review of Political Economy.

Tsoulfidis, L., & Rieu, D. M. (2006). Labour values, prices of production and wage-profit rate Frontiers of the Korean economy. *Seoul Journal of Economics, 19*, 275–295.

Tsoulfidis, L., & Tsaliki, P. (2005). Marxian theory of competition and the concept of regulating capital: Evidence from Greek manufacturing. *Review of Radical Political Economics, 37*(1), 5–22. https://doi.org/10.1177/0486613404272324.

Tsoulfidis, L., & Tsaliki, P. (2013). Classical competition and regulating capital: Theory and empirical evidence. In J. Moudud, C. Bina, & P. Mason (Eds.), *Alternative theories of competition: Challenges to orthodoxy* (pp. 267–297). London: Routledge.

Tsoulfidis, L., & Tsaliki, P. (2014). Unproductive labour, capital accumulation and profitability crisis in the Greek economy. *International Review of Applied Economics, 28*(5), 562–585.

Tsoulfidis, L., Tsimis, A., & Paitaridis, D. (2019). The rise and fall of unproductive activities in the US Economy 1964-2015: Facts, theory and empirical evidence. *Global Review of Political Economy* (forthcoming).

Tsuru, S. (1942). *Appendix in Sweezy's book the theory of capitalist development: Principles of Marxian political economy*. New York: Monthly Review Press.

Tullock, G. (1967). The welfare costs of tariffs, monopolies, and theft. *Western Economic Journal, 5*(3), 224–232.

Tullock, G. (2008). A note on redistribution. *Economic Affairs, 20*(3), 35–38.

Walras, L. (1874). *Elements of theoretical economics: The theory of social wealth*. Cambridge, UK: Cambridge University Press. [2014].

Webber, M., & Foot, S. (1984). The measurement of unequal exchange. *Environment and Planning, 16*(7), 927–947.

Webber, R., & Tonkin, T. (1990). Profitability and accumulation in Canadian manufacturing industries. *Presented in the conference: International perspectives on profitability and accumulation*, New York.

Weeks, J. (1981). *Capital and exploitation*. Princeton: Princeton University Press.

Weeks, J. (1998). *Orthodox and heterodox policies for growth in Africa south of The Sahara*. CDPR Discussion Paper 0298, Centre for Development Policy & Research (CDPR), SOAS.

Weeks, J. (1999). The essence and appearance of globalization: The rise of finance capital. In F. Adams, S. D. Gupta, & K. Mengisteab (Eds.), *Globalization and the dilemmas of the state in the south*. London: Macmillan.

Weeks, J. (2001). The expansion of capital and uneven development on a World scale. *Capital and Class, 74*, 9–30.

Weeks, J. (2010). *Capital, exploitation and economic crisis*. London: Routledge.

Wolff, E. N. (1985). Industrial composition, interindustry effects, and the U.S. productivity slowdown. *Review of Economics and Statistics, 67*, 268–277.

World Input-Output Database (WIOD). (2013). http://www.wiod.org/release13

World Input-Output Database (WIOD). (2016). http://www.wiod.org/wiots16

Vaona, A. (2011). An empirical investigation on the gravitation and convergence of industry return rates in OECD countries. *International Review of Applied Economics, 25*, 465–502.

Vaona, A. (2012). Further econometric evidence of the gravitation and convergence of industrial rates of return on regulating capital. *Journal of Post-Keynesian Economics, 35*(1), 113–136.

Von Neumann, J. (1945). A model of general economic equilibrium. *Review of Economic Studies, 13*, 1–9.

Zacharias, A. (2001). *Testing profit rate equalization in the U.S. manufacturing sector: 1947–1998*. Jerome Levy Economics Institute Working Paper No. 321.

Zambeli, S. (2017). The aggregate production function is NOT neoclassical. *Paper presented at the SIE conference*. 20–22 October, Milano.

Zarembka, P. (2015). Materialized composition of capital and its stability in the United States: Findings stimulated by Paitaridis and Tsoulfidis (2012). *Review of Radical Political Economy, 47*(1), 106–111.

Zarembka, P. (2019). *Anwar Shaikh's revised capital stock measurement and Marx's composition of capital*. Mimeo, New York: ResearchGate.net.

Index

Printed by Printforce, the Netherlands